SPANISH
ENGLISH

DICTIONARY • DICCIONARIO

INGLÉS
ESPAÑOL

Berlitz Dictionaries

Dansk	Engelsk, Fransk, Italiensk, Spansk, Tysk
Deutsch	Dänisch, Englisch, Finnisch, Französisch, Italienisch, Niederländisch, Norwegisch, Portugiesisch, Schwedish, Spanisch
English	Danish, Dutch, Finnish, French, German, Italian, Norwegian, Portuguese, Spanish, Swedish, Turkish
Español	Alemán, Danés, Finlandés, Francés, Holandés, Inglés, Noruego, Sueco
Français	Allemand, Anglais, Danois, Espagnol, Finnois, Italien, Néerlandais, Norvégien, Portugais, Suédois
Italiano	Danese, Finlandese, Francese, Inglese, Norvegese, Olandese, Svedese, Tedesco
Nederlands	Duits, Engels, Frans, Italiaans, Portugees, Spaans
Norsk	Engelsk, Fransk, Italiensk, Spansk, Tysk
Português	Alemão, Francês, Holandês, Inglês, Sueco
Suomi	Englanti, Espanja, Italia, Ranska, Ruotsi, Saksa
Svenska	Engelska, Finska, Franska, Italienska, Portugisiska, Spanska, Tyska

SPANISH ENGLISH

DICTIONARY • DICCIONARIO

INGLÉS ESPAÑOL

**with mini grammar section
con sección de mini-gramática**

Library of Congress Catalog Card Number 78-78079

2nd revised edition – 4th printing 1997
Printed in the Netherlands

Contents   Indice

Preface

In selecting the 12.500 word-concepts in each language for this dictionary, the editors have had the traveller's needs foremost in mind. This book will prove invaluable to all the millions of travellers, tourists and business people who appreciate the reassurance a small and practical dictionary can provide. It offers them—as it does beginners and students—all the basic vocabulary they are going to encounter and to have to use, giving the key words and expressions to allow them to cope in everyday situations.

Like our successful phrase books and travel guides, these dictionaries—created with the help of a computer data bank—are designed to slip into pocket or purse, and thus have a role as handy companions at all times.

Besides just about everything you normally find in dictionaries, there are these Berlitz bonuses:

- imitated pronunciation next to each foreign-word entry, making it easy to read and enunciate words whose spelling may look forbidding

- a unique, practical glossary to simplify reading a foreign restaurant menu and to take the mystery out of complicated dishes and indecipherable names on bills of fare

- useful information on how to tell the time and how to count, on conjugating irregular verbs, commonly seen abbreviations and converting to the metric system, in addition to basic phrases.

While no dictionary of this size can pretend to completeness, we expect the user of this book will feel well armed to tackle foreign travel with confidence. We should, however, be very pleased to receive comments, criticism and suggestions that you think may be of help in preparing future editions.

Prefacio

Al seleccionar las 12 500 palabras-conceptos en cada una de las lenguas de este diccionario, los redactores han tenido muy en cuenta las necesidades del viajero. Esta obra es indispensable para millones de viajeros, turistas y hombres de negocios, quienes apreciarán la seguridad que aporta un diccionario pequeño y práctico. Tanto a ellos como a los principiantes y estudiantes les ofrece todo el vocabulario básico que encontrarán o deberán emplear en el lenguaje de todos los días; les proporciona las palabras clave y las expresiones que les permitirán enfrentarse a las situaciones de la vida diaria.

Al igual que nuestros conocidos manuales de conversación y guías turísticas, estos diccionarios – realizados en computadora con la ayuda de un banco de datos – han sido ideados para llevarse en el bolsillo o en un bolso de mano, asumiendo de este modo su papel de compañeros disponibles en todo momento.

Además de las nociones que de ordinario ofrece un diccionario, encontrará:

- una transcripción fonética tan sencilla que facilita la lectura, aun cuando la palabra extranjera parezca impronunciable
- un léxico gastronómico inédito que le hará «descifrar» los menús en un restaurante extranjero, revelándole el secreto de los platos complicados y los misterios de la cuenta
- informaciones prácticas que le ayudarán a comunicar la hora y a contar, así como a utilizar los verbos irregulares, las abreviaturas más comunes y algunas expresiones útiles.

Ningún diccionario de este formato puede tener la pretensión de ser completo, pero el fin de este libro es permitir que quien lo emplee posea un arma para enfrentarse con confianza al viaje en el extranjero. Sin embargo, recibiremos con gusto los comentarios, críticas y sugestiones que con toda seguridad nos permitirán preparar las futuras ediciones.

spanish-english

español-inglés

Introduction

This dictionary has been designed to take account of your practical needs. Unnecessary linguistic information has been avoided. The entries are listed in alphabetical order regardless of whether the entry word is printed in a single word or in two or more separate words. As the only exception to this rule, a few idiomatic expressions are listed as main entries alphabetically according to the most significant word of the expression. When an entry is followed by sub-entries, such as expressions and locutions, these, too, have been listed in alphabetical order.[1]

Each main-entry word is followed by a phonetic transcription (see guide to pronunciation). Following the transcription is the part of speech of the entry word whenever applicable. When an entry may be used as more than one part of speech, the translations are grouped together after the respective part of speech.

Whenever an entry word is repeated in sub-entries a tilde ($\sim$) is used to represent the full entry word.

An asterisk (*) in front of a verb indicates that the verb is irregular. For details you may refer to the lists of irregular verbs.

The dictionary is based on Castilian Spanish. All words and meanings of words that are exclusively Mexican have been marked as such (see list of abbreviations used in the text).

Abbreviations

adj	adjective	*n*	noun
adv	adverb	*nAm*	noun (American)
Am	American	*num*	numeral
art	article	*p*	past tense
conj	conjunction	*pl*	plural
f	feminine	*plAm*	plural (American)
fMe	feminine (Mexican)	*pp*	past participle
fpl	feminine plural	*pr*	present tense
fplMe	feminine plural (Mexican)	*pref*	prefix
m	masculine	*prep*	preposition
Me	Mexican	*pron*	pronoun
mMe	masculine (Mexican)	*v*	verb
mpl	masculine plural	*vAm*	verb (American)
mplMe	masculine plural (Mexican)	*vMe*	verb (Mexican)

---

[1] Note that the alphabetical order in Spanish differs from our own in three cases: *ch*, *ll* and *ñ* are considered independent letters and come after *c*, *l* and n, respectively.

Guide to Pronunciation

Each main entry in this part of the dictionary is followed by a phonetic transcription which shows you how to pronounce the words. This transcription should be read as if it were English. It is based on Standard British pronunciation, though we have tried to take account of General American pronunciation also. Below, only those letters and symbols are explained which we consider likely to be ambiguous or not immediately understood.

The syllables are separated by hyphens, and stressed syllables are printed in *italics*.

Of course, the sounds of any two languages are never exactly the same, but if you follow carefully our indications, you should be able to pronounce the foreign words in such a way that you'll be understood. To make your task easier, our transcriptions occasionally simplify slightly the sound system of the language while still reflecting the essential sound differences.

Consonants

bh	a rather indecisive **b**, i.e. one verging on **v**
dh	like **th** in **th**is, often rather indecisive, possibly quite like **d**
g	always hard, as in **g**o
ġ	a g-sound where the tongue doesn't quite close the air passage between itself and the roof of the mouth, so that the escaping air produces audible friction; it is also on occasions pronounced as an indecisive **g**
kh	like **ġ**, but based on a **k**-sound; therefore hard and voiceless, like **ch** in Scottish lo**ch**
lʸ	like **lli** in mi**lli**on
ñ	as in the Spanish se**ñ**or, or like **ni** in o**ni**on
r	slightly rolled in the front of the mouth
rr	strongly rolled **r**
s	always hard, as in **s**o

Vowels and Diphthongs

ah	a short version of the **a** in c**a**r, i.e. a sound between **a** in c**a**t and **u** in c**u**t
igh	as in s**igh**
ou	as in lo**u**d

1) Raised letters (e.g. **ay^{oo}**, **^yah**) should be pronounced only fleetingly.

2) Spanish vowels (i.e. not diphthongs) are pure and fairly short. Therefore, you should try to read a transcription like **oa** without moving tongue or lips while pronouncing the sound.

Latin-American Pronunciation

Our transcriptions reflect the pronunciation of Castilian, the official language of Spain. In Latin America, two of the Castilian sounds are practically unknown:

1) **ll** as in the word ca**ll**e (which we represent by **l^y**) is usually pronounced like Spanish **y** (as in English **y**et); in the Río de la Plata region, though, both **ll** and **y** are pronounced like **s** in plea**s**ure.

2) The letters **c** (before **e** and **i**) and **z** are pronounced like **s** in **s**o instead of **th** as in **th**in.

A

a (ah) *prep* to, on; at; **a las ...** at ... o'clock

abacería (ah-bah-thay-*ree*-ah) *f* grocer's

abacero (ah-bah-*thay*-roa) *m* grocer

abadía (ah-bah-*dhee*-ah) *f* abbey

abajo (ah-*bah*-khoa) *adv* downstairs; down; **hacia ~** downwards

abandonar (ah-bhahn-doa-*nahr*) *v* abandon

abanico (ah-bhah-*nee*-koa) *m* fan

abarrotería (ah-bhah-rroa-tay-*ree*-ah) *fMe* grocer's

abarrotero (ah-bhah-rroa-*tay*-roa) *mMe* grocer

abastecimiento (ah-bhahss-tay-thee-*m^yayn*-toa) *m* supply

abatido (ah-bhah-*tee*-dhoa) *adj* down

abecedario (ah-bhay-thay-*dah*-r^yoa) *m* alphabet

abedul (ah-bhay-*dhool*) *m* birch

abeja (ah-*bhay*-khah) *f* bee

abertura (ah-bhayr-*too*-rah) *f* opening

abierto (ah-*bh^y*ayr-toa) *adj* open

abismo (ah-*bhee*-zmoa) *m* abyss

ablandador (ah-bhlahn-dah-*dhoar*) *m* water-softener

ablandar (ah-bhlahn-*dahr*) *v* soften

abogado (ah-bhoa-*gah*-dhoa) *m* barrister, lawyer, attorney; solicitor; ad-

vocate

abolir (ah-bhoa-*leer*) *v* abolish

abolladura (ah-bhoa-l^yah-*dhoo*-rah) *f* dent

abonado (ah-bhoa-*nah*-dhoa) *m* subscriber

abono (ah-*bhoa*-noa) *m* manure, dung

aborto (ah-*bhoar*-toa) *m* miscarriage; abortion

abrazar (ah-bhrah-*thahr*) *v* embrace; hug

abrazo (ah-*bhrah*-thoa) *m* hug; embrace

abrecartas (ah-bhray-*kahr*-tahss) *m* paper-knife

abrelatas (ah-bhray-*lah*-tahss) *m* can opener, tin-opener

abreviatura (ah-bhray-bh^yah-*too*-rah) *f* abbreviation

abrigar (ah-bhree-*gahr*) *v* shelter

abrigo (ah-*bhree*-goa) *m* coat, overcoat; **~ de pieles** fur coat

abril (ah-*bhreel*) April

abrir (ah-*bhreer*) *v* open; unlock; turn on

abrochar (ah-bhroa-*chahr*) *v* button

abrupto (ah-*bhroop*-toa) *adj* steep

absceso (ahbhs-*thay*-soa) *m* abscess

absolución (ahbh-soa-loo-*th^yoan*) *f* acquittal

absolutamente (ahbh-soa-loo-tah-*mayn*-tay) *adv* absolutely

absoluto (ahbh-soa-*loo*-toa) *adj* sheer; total

abstemio (ahbhs-*tay*-mᵞoa) *m* teetotaller

*****abstenerse de** (ahbhs-tay-*nayr*-say) abstain from

abstracto (ahbhs-*trahk*-toa) *adj* abstract

absurdo (ahbh-*soor*-dhoa) *adj* absurd; foolish

abuela (ah-*bhway*-lah) *f* grandmother

abuelo (ah-*bhway*-loa) *m* grandfather, granddad; **abuelos** *mpl* grandparents *pl*

abundancia (ah-bhoon-*dahn*-thᵞah) *f* abundance, plenty

abundante (ah-bhoon-*dahn*-tay) *adj* abundant, plentiful

abundar (ah-bhoon-*dahr*) *v* abound

aburrido (ah-bhoo-*rree*-dhoa) *adj* boring, dull

aburrimiento (ah-bhoo-rree-*mᵞayn*-toa) *m* annoyance

aburrir (ah-bhoo-*rreer*) *v* bore, annoy

abusar de (ah-bhoo-*sahr*) exploit

abuso (ah-*bhoo*-soa) *m* misuse, abuse

acá (ah-*kah*) *adv* here

acabar (ah-kah-*bhahr*) *v* end; **acabado** finished; over

academia (ah-kah-*dhay*-mᵞah) *f* academy; **~ de bellas artes** art school

acallar (ah-kah-*lᵞahr*) *v* silence

acampador (ah-kahm-pah-*dhoar*) *m* camper

acampar (ah-kahm-*pahr*) *v* camp

acantilado (ah-kahn-tee-*lah*-dhoa) *m* cliff

acariciar (ah-kah-ree-*thᵞahr*) *v* cuddle

acaso (ah-*kah*-soa) *adv* perhaps

accesible (ahk-thay-*see*-bhlay) *adj* accessible

acceso (ahk-*thay*-soa) *m* entrance, access; approach

accesorio (ahk-thay-*soa*-rᵞoa) *adj* additional; **accesorios** *mpl* accessories *pl*

accidental (ahk-thee-dhayn-*tahl*) *adj* accidental

accidente (ahk-thee-*dhayn*-tay) *m* accident; **~ aéreo** plane crash

acción (ahk-*thᵞoan*) *f* share; action; deed; **acciones** *fpl* stocks and shares

acechar (ah-thay-*chahr*) *v* watch for

aceite (ah-*thay*-tay) *m* oil; **~ bronceador** suntan oil; **~ de mesa** salad-oil; **~ de oliva** olive oil; **~ lubricante** lubrication oil; **~ para el pelo** hair-oil

aceitoso (ah-thay-*toa*-soa) *adj* oily

aceituna (ah-thay-*too*-nah) *f* olive

acelerador (ah-thay-lay-rah-*dhoar*) *m* accelerator

acelerar (ah-thay-lay-*rahr*) *v* accelerate

acento (ah-*thayn*-toa) *m* accent

acentuar (ah-thayn-*twahr*) *v* emphasize, stress

aceptar (ah-thayp-*tahr*) *v* accept

acera (ah-*thay*-rah) *f* pavement; sidewalk *nAm*

acerca de (ah-*thayr*-kah day) about

acercarse (ah-thayr-*kahr*-say) *v* approach

acero (ah-*thay*-roa) *m* steel; **~ inoxidable** stainless steel

*****acertar** (ah-thayr-*tahr*) *v* *hit; guess right

acidez (ah-thee-*dhayth*) *f* heartburn

ácido (*ah*-thee-dhoa) *m* acid

aclamar (ah-klah-*mahr*) *v* cheer

aclaración (ah-klah-rah-*thᵞoan*) *f* explanation

aclarar (ah-klah-*rahr*) *v* clarify

acné (ahk-*nay*) *m* acne

acogida (ah-koa-*khee*-dhah) *f* reception

acomodación (ah-koa-moa-dhah-*thᵞoan*) *f* accommodation

acomodado (ah-koa-moa-*dhah*-dhoa)
adj well-to-do

acomodador (ah-koa-moa-dhah-*dhoar*)
m usher

acomodadora (ah-koa-moa-dhah-*dhoa*-rah) *f* usherette

acomodar (ah-koa-moa-*dhahr*) *v* accommodate

acompañar (ah-koam-pah-*ñahr*) *v* accompany; conduct

aconsejar (ah-koan-say-*khahr*) *v* recommend, advise

*****acontecer** (ah-koan-tay-*thayr*) *v* occur

acontecimiento (ah-koan-tay-thee-m*Y*ayn-toa) *m* event; happening, occurrence

*****acordar** (ah-koar-*dhahr*) *v* agree;
*****acordarse** *v* remember, recollect, recall

acortar (ah-koar-*tahr*) *v* shorten

*****acostar** (ah-koass-*tahr*) *v* *lay down;
*****acostarse** *v* *go to bed

acostumbrado (ah-koass-toom-*brah*-dhoa) *adj* accustomed; customary;
*****estar ~ a** *be used to

acostumbrar (ah-koass-toom-*brahr*) *v* accustom

*****acrecentarse** (ah-kray-thayn-*tahr*-say) *v* increase

acreditar (ah-kray-dhee-*tahr*) *v* credit

acreedor (ah-kray-ay-*dhoar*) *m* creditor

acta (*ahk*-tah) *f* certificate; **actas** minutes

actitud (ahk-tee-*toodh*) *f* attitude; position

actividad (ahk-tee-bhee-*dhahdh*) *f* activity

activo (ahk-*tee*-bhoa) *adj* active

acto (*ahk*-toa) *m* act, deed

actor (ahk-*toar*) *m* actor

actriz (ahk-*treeth*) *f* actress

actual (ahk-*twahl*) *adj* present; topical

actualmente (ahk-twahl-*mayn*-tay) *adv* now

actuar (ahk-*twahr*) *v* act

acuarela (ah-kwah-*ray*-lah) *f* watercolour

acuerdo (ah-*kwayr*-dhoa) *m* approval; agreement, settlement; **¡de acuerdo!** all right!, okay!; *****estar de ~ con** approve of

acumulador (ah-koo-moo-lah-*dhoar*) *m* battery

acusación (ah-koo-sah-*th*Y*oan*) *f* charge

acusado (ah-koo-*sah*-dhoa) *m* accused

acusar (ah-koo-*sahr*) *v* accuse; charge

adaptador (ah-dhahp-tah-*dhoar*) *m* adaptor

adaptar (ah-dhahp-*tahr*) *v* adapt; suit

adecuado (ah-dhay-*kwah*-dhoa) *adj* adequate; convenient, appropriate

adelantar (ah-dhay-lahn-*tahr*) *v* *get on; **por adelantado** in advance; **prohibido ~** no overtaking

adelante (ah-dhay-*lahn*-tay) *adv* ahead, onwards, forward

adelanto (ah-dhay-*lahn*-toa) *m* advance

adelgazar (ah-dhayl-gah-*thahr*) *v* slim

además (ah-dhay-*mahss*) *adv* moreover, furthermore, besides; **~ de** beyond, besides

adentro (ah-*dhayn*-troa) *adv* inside, in; **hacia ~** inwards

adeudado (ah-dhay°°-*dhah*-dhoa) *adj* due

adición (ah-dhee-*th*Y*oan*) *f* addition

adicional (ah-dhee-th*Y*oa-*nahl*) *adj* additional

adicionar (ah-dhee-th*Y*oa-*nahr*) *v* add; count

¡adiós! (ah-*dh*Y*oass*) good-bye!

adivinar (ah-dhee-bhee-*nahr*) *v* guess

adjetivo (ahdh-khay-*tee*-bhoa) *m* adjective

administración (ahdh-mee-neess-trah-

th^yoan) _f_ administration; direction

administrar (ahdh-mee-neess-_trahr_) _v_ manage; direct; administer

administrativo (ahdh-mee-neess-trah-_tee_-bhoa) _adj_ administrative

admirable (ahdh-mee-_rah_-bhlay) _adj_ admirable

admiración (ahdh-mee-rah-_th^yoan_) _f_ admiration

admirador (ahdh-mee-rah-_dhoar_) _m_ fan

admirar (ahdh-mee-_rahr_) _v_ admire

admisión (ahdh-mee-_s^yoan_) _f_ admission; admittance

admitir (ahdh-mee-_teer_) _v_ admit; acknowledge

adonde (ah-_dhoan_-day) _adv_ where

adoptar (ah-dhoap-_tahr_) _v_ adopt

adorable (ah-dhoa-_rah_-bhlay) _adj_ adorable

adorar (ah-dhoa-_rahr_) _v_ worship

adormidera (ah-dhoar-mee-_dhay_-rah) _f_ poppy

adorno (ah-_dhoar_-noa) _m_ ornament

adquirible (ahdh-kee-_ree_-bhlay) _adj_ obtainable, available

*__adquirir__ (ahdh-kee-_reer_) _v_ acquire; *buy

adquisición (ahdh-kee-see-_th^yoan_) _f_ acquisition

aduana (ah-_dwah_-nah) _f_ Customs _pl_

adulto (ah-_dhool_-toa) _adj_ grown-up, adult; _m_ grown-up, adult

adverbio (ahdh-_bhayr_-bh^yoa) _m_ adverb

advertencia (ahdh-bhayr-_tayn_-th^yah) _f_ warning

*__advertir__ (ahdh-bhayr-_teer_) _v_ caution, warn; notice

aerolínea (ah-ay-roa-_lee_-nay-ah) _f_ airline

aeropuerto (ah-ay-roa-_pwayr_-toa) _m_ airport

aerosol (ah-ay-roa-_soal_) _m_ atomizer

afamado (ah-fah-_mah_-dhoa) _adj_ noted

afección (ah-fayk-_th^yoan_) _f_ affection

afectado (ah-fayk-_tah_-dhoa) _adj_ affected

afectar (ah-fayk-_tahr_) _v_ affect; feign

afeitadora eléctrica (ah-fay-tah-_dhoa_-rah ay-_layk_-tree-kah) electric razor

afeitarse (ah-fay-_tahr_-say) _v_ shave; **máquina de afeitar** safety-razor; shaver

afición (ah-fee-_th^yoan_) _f_ hobby

aficionado (ah-fee-th^yoa-_nah_-dhoa) _m_ supporter

afilar (ah-fee-_lahr_) _v_ sharpen; **afilado** sharp

afiliación (ah-fee-l^yah-_th^yoan_) _f_ membership

afiliado (ah-fee-_l^yah_-dhoa) _adj_ affiliated

afirmación (ah-feer-mah-_th^yoan_) _f_ statement

afirmar (ah-feer-_mahr_) _v_ claim

afirmativo (ah-feer-mah-_tee_-bhoa) _adj_ affirmative

aflicción (ah-fleek-_th^yoan_) _f_ grief

afligido (ah-flee-_khee_-dhoa) _adj_ sad; *__estar__ ~ grieve

afluente (ah-_flwayn_-tay) _m_ tributary

afortunado (ah-foar-too-_nah_-dhoa) _adj_ fortunate, lucky

África (_ah_-free-kah) _f_ Africa

África del Sur (_ah_-free-kah dayl soor) South Africa

africano (ah-free-_kah_-noa) _adj_ African; _m_ African

afuera (ah-_fway_-rah) _adv_ outside, outdoors; **hacia** ~ outwards

afueras (ah-_fway_-rahss) _fpl_ outskirts _pl_

agarradero (ah-gah-rrah-_dhay_-roa) _m_ grip

agarrar (ah-gah-_rrahr_) _v_ grasp, seize; **agarrarse** _v_ *hold on

agarre (ah-_gah_-rray) _m_ grip, grasp

agencia (ah-_khayn_-th^yah) _f_ agency; ~

de viajes travel agency
agenda (ah-*khayn*-dah) *f* diary
agente (ah-*khayn*-tay) *m* agent; ~ **de policía** policeman; ~ **de viajes** travel agent
ágil (*ah*-kheel) *adj* supple
agitación (ah-khee-tah-*th*^y*oan*) *f* excitement; bustle
agitar (ah-khee-*tahr*) *v* stir up
agosto (ah-*goass*-toa) August
agotado (ah-goa-*tah*-dhoa) *adj* sold out
agotar (ah-goa-*tahr*) *v* use up
agradable (ah-grah-*dhah*-bhlay) *adj* agreeable; enjoyable, pleasing, pleasant; nice
* **agradecer** (ah-grah-dhay-*thayr*) *v* thank
agradecido (ah-grah-dhay-*thee*-dhoa) *adj* grateful, thankful
agrario (ah-*grah*-r^yoa) *adj* agrarian
agraviar (ah-grah-*bh*^y*ahr*) *v* wrong
agregar (ah-gray-*gahr*) *v* add
agresivo (ah-gray-*see*-bhoa) *adj* aggressive
agrícola (ah-*gree*-koa-lah) *adj* agrarian
agricultura (ah-gree-kool-*too*-rah) *f* agriculture
agrio (*ah*-gr^yoa) *adj* sour
agua (*ah*-gwah) *f* water; ~ **corriente** running water; ~ **de mar** seawater; ~ **de soda** soda-water; ~ **dulce** fresh water; ~ **helada** iced water; ~ **mineral** mineral water; ~ **potable** drinking-water
aguacero (ah-gwah-*thay*-roa) *m* shower; downpour
aguafuerte (ah-gwah-*fwayr*-tay) *f* etching
aguanieve (ah-gwah-*n*^y*ay*-bhay) *f* slush
aguantar (ah-gwahn-*tahr*) *v* *bear
aguardado (ah-gwahr-*dhah*-dhoa) due
aguardar (ah-gwahr-*dahr*) *v* expect

agudo (ah-*goo*-dhoa) *adj* keen; acute
águila (*ah*-gee-lah) *m* eagle
aguja (ah-*goo*-khah) *f* needle; spire; **labor de** ~ needlework
agujero (ah-goo-*khay*-roa) *m* hole
ahí (ah-*ee*) *adv* there
ahogar (ah-oa-*gahr*) *v* drown; **ahogarse** *v* *be drowned
ahora (ah-*oa*-rah) *adv* now; **de** ~ **en adelante** henceforth; **hasta** ~ so far
ahorrar (ah-oa-*rrahr*) *v* save
ahorros (ah-*oa*-rrooss) *mpl* savings *pl*; **caja de** ~ savings bank
ahuyentar (ou-^y*ayn*-*tahr*) *v* chase
aire (*igh*-ray) *m* air; sky; breath; ~ **acondicionado** air-conditioning; **cámara de** ~ inner tube; ***tener aires de** look
airear (igh-ray-*ahr*) *v* air, ventilate
aireo (igh-*ray*-oa) *m* ventilation
airoso (igh-*roa*-soa) *adj* airy
aislado (ighz-*lah*-dhoo) *adj* isolated
aislador (ighz-lah-*dhoar*) *m* insulator
aislamiento (ighz-lah-*m*^y*ayn*-toa) *m* isolation; insulation
aislar (ighz-*lahr*) *v* isolate; insulate
ajedrez (ah-khay-*dhrayth*) *m* chess
ajeno (ah-*khay*-noa) *adj* foreign
ajetrearse (ah-khay-tray-*ahr*-say) *v* labour
ajo (*ah*-khoa) *m* garlic
ajustar (ah-khooss-*tahr*) *v* adjust
ala (*ah*-lah) *f* wing
alabar (ah-lah-*bhahr*) *v* praise
alambre (ah-*lahm*-bray) *m* wire
alargar (ah-lahr-*gahr*) *v* lengthen; renew; hand
alarma (ah-*lahr*-mah) *f* alarm; ~ **de incendio** fire-alarm
alarmante (ah-lahr-*mahn*-tay) *adj* scary
alarmar (ah-lahr-*mahr*) *v* alarm
alba (*ahl*-bhah) *f* dawn

albañil (ahl-bhah-*ñeel*) *m* bricklayer

albaricoque (ahl-bhah-ree-*koa*-kay) *m* apricot

albergue para jóvenes (ahl-*bhayr*-gay pah-rah *khoa*-bhay-nayss) youth hostel

alborotador (ahl-bhoa-roa-tah-*dhoar*) *adj* rowdy

alboroto (ahl-bhoa-*roa*-toa) *m* noise, racket

álbum (*ahl*-bhoom) *m* album

alcachofa (ahl-kah-*choa*-fah) *f* artichoke

alcalde (ahl-*kahl*-dhay) *m* mayor

alcance (ahl-*kahn*-thay) *m* reach, range

alcanzable (ahl-kahn-*thah*-bhlay) *adj* attainable

alcanzar (ahl-kahn-*thahr*) *v* achieve, reach

alce (*ahl*-thay) *m* moose

alcohol (ahl-*koal*) *m* alcohol; ~ **de quemar** methylated spirits

alcohólico (ahl-*koa*-lee-koa) *adj* alcoholic

aldea (ahl-*day*-ah) *f* hamlet

alegrar (ah-lay-*grahr*) *v* cheer up

alegre (ah-*lay*-gray) *adj* cheerful, merry, joyful; glad, gay

alegría (ah-lay-*gree*-ah) *f* gaiety; gladness

alejar (ah-lay-*khahr*) *v* move away

alemán (ah-lay-*mahn*) *adj* German; *m* German

Alemania (ah-lay-*mah*-nᵞah) *f* Germany

*alentar (ah-layn-*tahr*) *v* encourage

alergia (ah-*layr*-khᵞah) *f* allergy

alfiler (ahl-fee-*layr*) *m* pin

alfombra (ahl-*foam*-brah) *f* carpet

alfombrilla (ahl-foam-*bree*-lᵞah) *f* rug

álgebra (*ahl*-gay-bhrah) *f* algebra

algo (*ahl*-goa) *pron* something; *adv* somewhat

algodón (ahl-goa-*dhoan*) *m* cotton;

cotton-wool; **de** ~ cotton

alguien (*ahl*-gᵞayn) *pron* someone, somebody

alguno (ahl-*goo*-noa) *adj* any; **algunos** *adj* some; *pron* some

alhaja (ah-*lah*-khah) *f* gem

alharaca (ah-lah-*rah*-kah) *f* fuss

aliado (ah-*lᵞah*-dhoa) *m* associate

alianza (ah-*lᵞahn*-thah) *f* alliance

alicates (ah-lee-*kah*-tayss) *mpl* pliers *pl*

alienado (ah-lᵞay-*nah*-dhoa) *m* lunatic

aliento (ah-*lᵞayn*-toa) *m* breath

alimentar (ah-lee-mayn-*tahr*) *v* *feed

alimento (ah-lee-*mayn*-toa) *m* fare; food; **alimentos naturales** health food

alivio (ah-*lee*-bhᵞoa) *m* relief

alma (*ahl*-mah) *f* soul

almacén (ahl-mah-*thayn*) *m* depot, warehouse, depository, store-house; store; ~ **de licores** off-licence; **grandes almacenes** department store

almacenaje (ahl-mah-thay-*nah*-khay) *m* storage

almacenar (ahl-mah-thay-*nahr*) *v* store

almanaque (ahl-mah-*nah*-kay) *m* almanac

almendra (ahl-*mayn*-drah) *f* almond

almidón (ahl-mee-*dhoan*) *m* starch

almidonar (ahl-mee-dhoa-*nahr*) *v* starch

almirante (ahl-mee-*rahn*-tay) *m* admiral

almohada (ahl-moa-ah-*dhah*) *f* pillow; ~ **eléctrica** heating pad

almohadilla (ahl-moa-ah-*dhee*-lᵞah) *f* pad

almohadón (ahl-moa-ah-*dhoan*) *m* cushion; pillow

almuerzo (ahl-*mwayr*-thoa) *m* lunch, luncheon

alojamiento (ah-loa-khah-*mᵞayn*-toa)

m accommodation, lodgings *pl*

alojar (ah-loa-*khahr*) *v* lodge

alondra (ah-*loan*-drah) *f* lark

alquilar (ahl-kee-*lahr*) *v* hire; rent, lease, *let

alquiler (ahl-kee-*layr*) *m* rent; ~ de coches car hire; de ~ for hire

alrededor de (ahl-ray-dhay-*dhoar* day) around, round; about

alrededores (ahl-ray-dhay-*dhoa*-rayss) *mpl* environment, surroundings *pl*

altar (ahl-*tahr*) *m* altar

altavoz (ahl-tah-*bhoath*) *m* loudspeaker

alteración (ahl-tay-rah-*th*ʸ*oan*) *f* alteration

alterar (ahl-tay-*rahr*) *v* alter

alternar con (ahl-tayr-*nahr*) mix with

alternativa (ahl-tayr-nah-*tee*-bhah) *f* alternative

alternativo (ahl-tayr-nah-*tee*-bhoa) *adj* alternate

altiplano (ahl-tee-*plah*-noa) *m* uplands *pl*

altitud (ahl-tee-*toodh*) *f* altitude

altivo (ahl-*tee*-bhoa) *adj* haughty

alto (*ahl*-toa) *adj* high, tall; en ~ overhead

¡alto! (*ahl*-toa) stop!

altura (ahl-*too*-rah) *f* height

aludir a (ah-loo-*dheer*) allude to

alumbrado (ah-loom-*brah*-dhoa) *m* lighting

alumna (ah-*loom*-nah) *f* schoolgirl

alumno (ah-*loom*-noa) *m* scholar, pupil; schoolboy

alzar (ahl-*thahr*) *v* raise

allá (ah-*l*ʸ*ah*) *adv* over there; más ~ beyond; más ~ de past, beyond

allí (ah-*l*ʸ*ee*) *adv* there

amable (ah-*mah*-bhlay) *adj* kind, friendly

amado (ah-*mah*-dhoa) *adj* dear

amaestrar (ah-mah-ayss-*trahr*) *v* train

amamantar (ah-mah-mahn-*tahr*) *v* nurse

amanecer (ah-mah-nay-*thayr*) *m* sunrise, daybreak

amante (ah-*mahn*-tay) *m* lover

amapola (ah-mah-*poa*-lah) *f* poppy

amar (ah-*mahr*) *v* love

amargo (ah-*mahr*-goa) *adj* bitter

amarillo (ah-mah-*ree*-lʸoa) *adj* yellow

amatista (ah-mah-*teess*-tah) *f* amethyst

ámbar (*ahm*-bahr) *m* amber

ambicioso (ahm-bee-*th*ʸ*oa*-soa) *adj* ambitious

ambiente (ahm-*b*ʸ*ayn*-tay) *m* atmosphere

ambiguo (ahm-*bee*-gwoa) *adj* ambiguous

ambos (*ahm*-boass) *adj* both; either

ambulancia (ahm-boo-*lahn*-thʸah) *f* ambulance

ambulante (ahm-boo-*lahn*-tay) *adj* itinerant

amenaza (ah-may-*nah*-thah) *f* threat

amenazador (ah-may-nah-thah-*dhoar*) *adj* threatening

amenazar (ah-may-nah-*thahr*) *v* threaten

ameno (ah-*may*-noa) *adj* nice

América (ah-*may*-ree-kah) *f* America; ~ Latina Latin America

americana (ah-may-ree-*kah*-nah) *f* jacket

americano (ah-may-ree-*kah*-noa) *adj* American; *m* American

amiga (ah-*mee*-gah) *f* friend

amígdalas (ah-*meeg*-dhah-lahss) *fpl* tonsils *pl*

amigdalitis (ah-meeg-dhah-*lee*-teess) *f* tonsilitis

amigo (ah-*mee*-goa) *m* friend

amistad (ah-meess-*tahdh*) *f* friendship

amistoso (ah-meess-*toa*-soa) *adj* friendly

amnistía (ahm-neess-*tee*-ah) *f* amnesty

amo (*ah*-moa) *m* master

amoníaco (ah-moa-*nee*-ah-koa) *m* ammonia

amontonar (ah-moan-toa-*nahr*) *v* pile

amor (ah-*moar*) *m* love; darling, sweetheart

amorío (ah-moa-*ree*-oa) *m* affair, romance

amortiguador (ah-moar-tee-gwah-*dhoar*) *m* shock absorber

amortizar (ah-moar-tee-*thahr*) *v* *pay off

amotinamiento (ah-moa-tee-nah-*mᵞayn*-toa) *m* mutiny

ampliación (ahm-plᵞah-*thᵞoan*) *f* enlargement; extension

ampliar (ahm-*plᵞahr*) *v* enlarge; extend

amplio (*ahm*-plᵞoa) *adj* broad

ampolla (ahm-*poa*-lᵞah) *f* blister

amueblar (ah-mway-*bhlahr*) *v* furnish

amuleto (ah-moo-*lay*-toa) *m* charm

analfabeto (ah-nahl-fah-*bhay*-toa) *m* illiterate

análisis (ah-*nah*-lee-seess) *f* analysis

analista (ah-nah-*leess*-tah) *m* analyst

analizar (ah-nah-lee-*thahr*) *v* analyse; *break down

análogo (ah-*nah*-loa-goa) *adj* similar

anarquía (ah-nahr-*kee*-ah) *f* anarchy

anatomía (ah-nah-toa-*mee*-ah) *f* anatomy

anciano (ahn-*thᵞah*-noa) *adj* aged; elderly

ancla (*ahng*-klah) *f* anchor

ancho (*ahn*-choa) *adj* broad; wide; *m* breadth

anchoa (ahn-*choa*-ah) *f* anchovy

anchura (ahn-*choo*-rah) *f* width

andadura (ahn-dah-*dhoo*-rah) *f* walk

andamio (ahn-*dah*-mᵞoa) *m* scaffolding

*andar (ahn-*dahr*) *v* walk

andares (ahn-*dah*-rayss) *mpl* pace

andén (ahn-*dayn*) *m* platform

anemia (ah-*nay*-mᵞah) *f* anaemia

anestesia (ah-nayss-*tay*-sᵞah) *f* anaesthesia

anestésico (ah-ayss-*tay*-see-koa) *m* anaesthetic

anexar (ah-nayk-*sahr*) *v* annex

anexo (ah-*nayk*-soa) *m* annex, enclosure

anfitrión (ahn-fee-*trᵞoan*) *m* host

ángel (*ahng*-khayl) *m* angel

angosto (ahng-*goass*-toa) *adj* narrow, tight

anguila (ahng-*gee*-lah) *f* eel

ángulo (*ahng*-goo-loa) *m* angle

angustioso (ahng-gooss-*tᵞoa*-soa) *adj* afraid

anhelar (ah-nay-*lahr*) *v* desire, long for

anhelo (ah-*nay*-loa) *m* longing

anillo (ah-*nee*-lᵞoa) *m* ring; ~ **de boda** wedding-ring; ~ **de esponsales** engagement ring

animado (ah-nee-*mah*-dhoa) *adj* crowded

animal (ah-nee-*mahl*) *m* beast, animal; ~ **de presa** beast of prey; ~ **doméstico** pet

animar (ah-nee-*mahr*) *v* encourage, inspire; animate

ánimo (*ah*-nee-moa) *m* mind; courage

aniversario (ah-nee-bhayr-*sah*-rᵞoa) *m* anniversary; jubilee

anoche (ah-*noa*-chay) *adv* last night

anomalía (ah-noa-mah-*lee*-ah) *f* aberration

anónimo (ah-*noa*-nee-moa) *adj* anonymous

anormal (ah-noar-*mahl*) *adj* abnormal

anotación (ah-noa-tah-*thᵞoan*) *f* entry

anotar (ah-noa-*tahr*) *v* *write down

ansia (*ahn*-sᵞah) *f* anxiety

ansioso (ahn-*sᵞoa*-soa) *adj* anxious, eager

ante (*ahn*-tay) *prep* in front of

anteayer (ahn-tay-ah-ᵞayr) *adv* the day before yesterday

antecedentes (ahn-tay-thay-*dhayn*-tayss) *mpl* background

antena (ahn-*tay*-nah) *f* aerial

anteojos (ahn-tay-*oa*-khoass) *mpl* spectacles, glasses

antepasado (ahn-tay-pah-*sah*-dhoa) *m* ancestor

antepecho (ahn-tay-*pay*-choa) *m* window-sill

anterior (ahn-tay-*rᵞoar*) *adj* former, prior, previous

antes (*ahn*-tayss) *adv* before; formerly; at first; ~ **de** before; ~ **de que** before

antibiótico (ahn-tee-*bhᵞoa*-tee-koa) *m* antibiotic

anticipar (ahn-tee-thee-*pahr*) *v* advance

anticipo (ahn-tee-*thee*-poa) *m* advance

anticonceptivo (ahn-tee-koan-thayp-tee-bhoa) *m* contraceptive

anticongelante (ahn-tee-koang-khay-*lahn*-tay) *m* antifreeze

anticuado (ahn-tee-*kwah*-dhoa) *adj* old-fashioned; ancient, out of date, quaint

anticuario (ahn-tee-*kwah*-rᵞoa) *m* antique dealer

antigualla (ahn-tee-*gwah*-lᵞah) *f* antique

Antigüedad (ahn-tee-gway-*dhahdh*) *f* antiquity

antigüedades (ahn-tee-gway-*dhah*-dhayss) *fpl* antiquities *pl*

antiguo (ahn-*tee*-gwoa) *adj* ancient, antique; former

antipatía (ahn-tee-pah-*tee*-ah) *f* antipathy, dislike

antipático (ahn-tee-*pah*-tee-koa) *adj* nasty, unpleasant

antiséptico (ahn-tee-*sayp*-tee-koa) *m* antiseptic

antojarse (ahn-toa-*khahr*-say) *v* fancy, *feel like

antojo (ahn-*toa*-khoa) *m* fad, whim

antología (ahn-toa-loa-*khee*-ah) *f* anthology

antorcha (ahn-*toar*-chah) *f* torch

anual (ah-*nwahl*) *adj* annual, yearly

anuario (ah-*nwah*-ree-oa) *m* annual

anudar (ah-noo-*dhahr*) *v* tie; knot

anular (ah-noo-*lahr*) *v* cancel

anunciar (ah-noon-*thᵞahr*) *v* announce

anuncio (ah-*noon*-thᵞoa) *m* announcement; advertisement

anzuelo (ahn-*thway*-loa) *m* fishing hook

añadir (ah-ñah-*dheer*) *v* add

año (ah-*ñoa*) *m* year; **al** ~ per annum; ~ **bisiesto** leap-year; ~ **nuevo** New Year

apagado (ah-pah-*gah*-dhoa) *adj* mat

apagar (ah-pah-*gahr*) *v* extinguish; *put out, switch off

aparato (ah-pah-*rah*-toa) *m* appliance, apparatus; machine

aparcamiento (ah-pahr-kah-*mᵞayn*-toa) *m* parking; **zona de** ~ parking zone

*aparecer (ah-pah-ray-*thayr*) *v* appear

aparejo (ah-pah-*ray*-khoa) *m* gear; ~ **de pesca** fishing tackle

aparente (ah-pah-*rayn*-tay) *adj* apparent

aparición (ah-pah-ree-*thᵞoan*) *f* apparition

apariencia (ah-pah-*rᵞayn*-thᵞah) *f* appearance, semblance

apartado (ah-pahr-*tah*-dhoa) *adj* out of the way

apartamento (ah-pahr-tah-*mayn*-toa) *m* suite; apartment *nAm*

apartar (ah-pahr-*tahr*) *v* separate

aparte (ah-*pahr*-tay) *adv* aside; *adj* individual

apasionado (ah-pah-sᵞoa-*nah*-dhoa)

adj passionate

apearse (ah-pay-*ahr*-say) *v* *get off

apelación (ah-pay-lah-*th^yoan*) *f* appeal

apelmazado (ah-payl-mah-*thah*-dhoa) *adj* lumpy

apellido (ah-pay-*l^yee*-dhoa) *m* family name, surname; ~ **de soltera** maiden name

apenado (ah-pay-*nah*-dhoa) *adj* sorry

apenas (ah-*pay*-nahss) *adv* hardly, barely, scarcely; just

apéndice (ah-*payn*-dee-thay) *m* appendix

apendicitis (ah-payn-dee-*thee*-teess) *f* appendicitis

aperitivo (ah-pay-ree-*tee*-bhoa) *m* aperitif, drink

apertura (ah-payr-*too*-rah) *f* opening

apestar (ah-payss-*tahr*) *v* *stink

apetito (ah-pay-*tee*-toa) *m* appetite

apetitoso (ah-pay-tee-*toa*-soa) *adj* appetizing

apio (*ah*-p^yoa) *m* celery

aplaudir (ah-plou-*dheer*) *v* clap

aplauso (ah-*plou*-soa) *m* applause

aplazar (ah-plah-*thahr*) *v* postpone, adjourn, *put off

aplicación (ah-plee-kah-*s^yoan*) *f* application

aplicar (ah-plee-*kahr*) *v* apply; **aplicarse** a apply, *be valid for

apogeo (ah-poa-*khayoa*) *m* height; zenith; ~ **de la temporada** peak season

*apostar (ah-poass-*tahr*) *v* *bet

apoyar (ah-poa-*^yahr*) *v* support; **apoyarse** *v* *lean

apoyo (ah-*poa*-^yoa) *m* support; assistance

apreciar (ah-pray-*th^yahr*) *v* appreciate

aprecio (ah-*pray*-th^yoa) *m* appreciation

aprender (ah-prayn-*dayr*) *v* *learn; **aprenderse de memoria** memorize

apresar (ah-pray-*sahr*) *v* hijack

apresurado (ah-pray-soo-*rah*-dhoa) *adj* hasty

apresurarse (ah-pray-soo-*rahr*-say) *v* hasten, hurry

apretado (ah-pray-*tah*-dhoa) *adj* tight

*apretar (ah-pray-*tahr*) *v* press; tighten

apretón (ah-pray-*toan*) *m* clutch; ~ **de manos** handshake

aprobación (ah-proa-bhah-*th^yoan*) *f* approval

*aprobar (ah-proa-*bhahr*) *v* approve; pass

apropiado (ah-proa-*p^yah*-dhoa) *adj* appropriate, suitable, proper; fit

aprovechar (ah-proa-bhay-*chahr*) *v* profit, benefit

aproximadamente (ah-proak-see-mah-dhah-*mayn*-tay) *adv* about, approximately

aproximado (ah-proak-see-*mah*-dhoa) *adj* approximate

aptitud (ahp-tee-*toodh*) *f* qualification; faculty

apto (*ahp*-toa) *adj* suitable; ***ser** ~ **para** qualify

apuesta (ah-*pwayss*-tah) *f* bet

apuntar (ah-poon-*tahr*) *v* aim at; point out

apunte (ah-*poon*-tay) *m* note; memo; **libreta de apuntes** notebook

aquel (ah-*kayl*) *adj* that; **aquellos** *adj* those

aquél (ah-*kayl*) *pron* that; **aquéllos** *pron* those

aquí (ah-*kee*) *adv* here

árabe (*ah*-rah-bhay) *adj* Arab; *m* Arab

Arabia Saudí (ah-*rah*-bh^yah sou-*dhee*) Saudi Arabia

arado (ah-*rah*-dhoa) *m* plough

arancel (ah-rahn-*thayl*) *m* tariff; duty

araña (ah-*rah*-ñah) *f* spider; **tela de** ~

cobweb

arar (ah-*rahr*) *v* plough

arbitrario (ahr-bhee-*trah*-r^yoa) *adj* arbitrary

árbitro (*ahr*-bhee-troa) *m* umpire

árbol (*ahr*-bhoal) *m* tree; ~ **de levas** camshaft

arbolado (ahr-bhoa-*lah*-dhoa) *m* woodland

arbusto (ahr-*bhooss*-toa) *m* shrub

arca (*ahr*-kah) *f* chest

arcada (ahr-*kah*-dhah) *f* arcade

arce (*ahr*-thay) *m* maple

arcilla (ahr-*thee*-l^yah) *f* clay

arco (*ahr*-koa) *m* arch, bow; ~ **iris** rainbow

archivo (ahr-*chee*-bhoa) *m* archives *pl*

arder (ahr-*dhayr*) *v* *burn

ardilla (ahr-*dhee*-l^yah) *f* squirrel

área (*ah*-ray-ah) *f* area; are

arena (ah-*ray*-nah) *f* sand

arenoso (ah-ray-*noa*-soa) *adj* sandy

arenque (ah-*rayng*-kay) *m* herring

Argelia (ahr-*khay*-l^yah) *f* Algeria

argelino (ahr-khay-*lee*-noa) *adj* Algerian; *m* Algerian

Argentina (ahr-khayn-*tee*-nah) *f* Argentina

argentino (ahr-khayn-*tee*-noa) *adj* Argentinian; *m* Argentinian

argumentar (ahr-goo-mayn-*tahr*) *v* argue

argumento (ahr-goo-*mayn*-toa) *m* argument

árido (*ah*-ree-dhoa) *adj* arid

arisco (ah-*reess*-koa) *adj* unkind

aritmética (ah-reet-*may*-tee-kah) *f* arithmetic

arma (*ahr*-mah) *f* weapon, arm

armador (ahr-mah-*dhoar*) *m* shipowner

armadura (ahr-mah-*dhoo*-rah) *f* frame; armour

armar (ahr-*mahr*) *v* arm

armario (ahr-*mah*-r^yoa) *m* cupboard; closet

armonía (ahr-moa-*nee*-ah) *f* harmony

aroma (ah-*roa*-mah) *m* aroma

arpa (*ahr*-pah) *f* harp

arqueado (ahr-kay-*ah*-dhoa) *adj* arched

arqueología (ahr-kay-oa-loa-*khee*-ah) *f* archaeology

arqueólogo (ahr-kay-*oa*-loa-goa) *m* archaeologist

arquitecto (ahr-kee-*tayk*-toa) *m* architect

arquitectura (ahr-kee-tayk-*too*-rah) *f* architecture

arraigarse (ah-rrigh-*gahr*-say) *v* settle down

arrancar (ah-rrahng-*kahr*) *v* uproot, pull out; start off

arranque (ah-*rrahng*-kay) *m* starter motor

arrastrar (ah-rrahss-*trahr*) *v* haul, drag; *draw; **arrastrarse** *v* crawl

arrecife (ah-rray-*thee*-fay) *m* reef

arreglar (ah-rray-*glahr*) *v* settle; tidy up; repair, fix; **arreglarse con** *make do with

arreglo (ah-*rray*-gloa) *m* arrangement; settlement; **con** ~ **a** in accordance with

arrendamiento (ah-rrayn-dah-m^yayn-toa) *m* lease; **contrato de** ~ lease

*** arrendar** (ah-rrayn-*dahr*) *v* lease

arrepentimiento (ah-rray-payn-tee-m^yayn-toa) *m* regret, repentance

arrestar (ah-rrayss-*tahr*) *v* arrest

arresto (ah-*rrayss*-toa) *m* arrest

arriar (ah-r^yahr) *v* *strike, lower

arriate (ah-r^yah-tay) *m* flowerbed

arriba (ah-*rree*-bhah) *adv* upstairs; up

arriesgado (ah-rryayz-*gah*-dhoa) *adj* risky

arriesgar (ah-rr^yayz-*gahr*) *v* venture, risk

arrodillarse (ah-rroa-dhee-*lʸahr*-say) v *kneel

arrogante (ah-rroa-*gahn*-tay) adj snooty

arrojar (ah-rroa-*khahr*) v *throw

arroyo (ah-*rroa*-ʸoa) m stream, brook

arroz (ah-*rroath*) m rice

arruga (ah-*rroo*-gah) f wrinkle

arrugar (ah-rroo-*gahr*) v wrinkle

arruinar (ah-rrwee-*nahr*) v ruin; **arruinado** broke

arte (*ahr*-tay) m/f art; **artes industriales** arts and crafts; **bellas artes** fine arts

arteria (ahr-*tay*-rʸah) f artery; ~ **principal** thoroughfare

artesanía (ahr-tay-sah-*nee*-ah) f handicraft

articulación (ahr-tee-koo-lah-*thʸoan*) f joint

artículo (ahr-*tee*-koo-loa) m article

artificial (ahr-tee-fee-*thʸahl*) adj artificial

artificio (ahr-tee-*fee*-thʸoa) m artifice

artista (ahr-*teess*-tah) m/f artist

artístico (ahr-*teess*-tee-koa) adj artistic

arzobispo (ahr-thoa-*bheess*-poa) m archbishop

asamblea (ah-sahm-*blay*-ah) f assembly, meeting

asar (ah-*sahr*) v roast; ~ **en parrilla** roast

asbesto (ahdh-*bhayss*-toa) m asbestos

ascensor (ah-thayn-*soar*) m lift; elevator nAm

aseado (ah-say-*ah*-dhoa) adj tidy

asegurar (ah-say-goo-*rahr*) v assure, insure; **asegurarse de** ascertain

asemejarse (ah-say-may-*khahr*-say) v resemble

asesinar (ah-say-see-*nahr*) v murder

asesinato (ah-say-see-*nah*-toa) m murder, assassination

asesino (ah-say-*see*-noa) m murderer

asfalto (ahss-*fahl*-toa) m asphalt

así (ah-*see*) adv thus, so; ~ **que** so that

Asia (*ah*-sʸah) f Asia

asiático (ah-sʸah-tee-koa) adj Asian; m Asian

asiento (ah-*sʸayn*-toa) m seat

asignación (ah-seeg-nah-*thʸoan*) f allowance

asignar (ah-seeg-*nahr*) v allot; ~ **a** assign to

asilo (ah-*see*-loa) m asylum

asimismo (ah-see-*meez*-moa) adv also, likewise

***asir** (ah-*seer*) v grip

asistencia (ah-seess-*tayn*-thʸah) f attendance; assistance

asistente (ah-seess-*tayn*-tay) m assistant

asistir (ah-seess-*teer*) v assist, aid; ~ **a** assist at, attend

asma (*ahz*-mah) f asthma

asociación (ah-soa-thʸah-*thʸoan*) f association; club, society

asociado (ah-soa-*thʸah*-dhoa) m associate

asociar (ah-soa-*thʸahr*) v associate; **asociarse a** join

asombrar (ah-soam-*brahr*) v amaze, astonish

asombro (ah-*soam*-broa) m amazement; wonder

asombroso (ah-soam-*broa*-soa) adj astonishing

aspecto (ahss-*payk*-toa) m aspect; appearance, look; sight

áspero (*ahss*-pay-roa) adj harsh; rough

aspiración (ahss-pee-rah-*thʸoan*) f inhalation; aspiration

aspirador (ahss-pee-rah-*dhoar*) m vacuum cleaner; **pasar el** ~ hoover

aspirar (ahss-pee-*rahr*) v aspire; ~ **a** aim at

aspirina (ahss-pee-*ree*-nah) f aspirin

asqueroso (ahss-kay-*roa*-soa) adj disgusting

astilla (ahss-*tee*-lʸah) f splinter; chip

astillar (ahss-tee-*lʸahr*) v chip

astillero (ahss-tee-*lʸay*-roa) m shipyard

astronomía (ahss-troa-noa-*mee*-ah) f astronomy

astucia (ahss-*too*-thʸah) f ruse

astuto (ahss-*too*-toa) adj cunning; clever, sly

asunto (ah-*soon*-toa) m affair, matter; concern, business; topic

asustado (ah-sooss-*tah*-dhoa) adj afraid

asustar (ah-sooss-*tahr*) v scare; **asustarse** v *be frightened

atacar (ah-tah-*kahr*) v attack, assault; *strike

atadura (ah-tah-*dhoo*-rah) f binding

atañer (ah-tah-*ñayr*) v concern

ataque (ah-*tah*-kay) m attack, fit; stroke; ~ **cardiaco** heart attack

atar (ah-*tahr*) v tie, *bind; fasten; bundle

atareado (ah-tah-ray-*ah*-dhoa) adj busy

atención (ah-tayn-*thʸoan*) f attention; consideration, notice; **prestar** ~ *pay attention, look out

*atender a** (ah-tayn-*dayr*) attend to, see to; nurse

atento (ah-*tayn*-toa) adj attentive; thoughtful

ateo (ah-*tay*-oa) m atheist

aterido (ah-tay-*ree*-dhoa) adj numb

aterrador (ah-tay-rrah-*dhoar*) adj terrifying

aterrizar (ah-tay-rree-*thahr*) v land

aterrorizar (ah-tay-rroa-ree-*thahr*) v terrify

Atlántico (aht-*lahn*-tee-koa) m Atlantic

atleta (aht-*lay*-tah) m athlete

atletismo (aht-lay-*teez*-moa) m athletics pl

atmósfera (aht-*moass*-fay-rah) f atmosphere

atómico (ah-*toa*-mee-koa) adj atomic

átomo (*ah*-toa-moa) m atom

atónito (ah-*toa*-nee-toa) adj speechless

atontado (ah-toan-*tah*-dhoa) adj dumb

atormentar (ah-toar-mayn-*tahr*) v torment

atornillar (ah-toar-nee-*lʸahr*) v screw

atracar (ah-trah-*kahr*) v dock

atracción (ah-trahk-*thʸoan*) f attraction

atraco (ah-*trah*-koa) m hold-up

atractivo (ah-trahk-*tee*-bhoa) adj attractive

*atraer** (ah-trah-*ayr*) v attract

atrapar (ah-trah-*pahr*) v contract

atrás (ah-*trahss*) adv back

atrasado (ah-trah-*sah*-dhoa) adj overdue

*atravesar** (ah-trah-bhay-*sahr*) v cross, pass through

atreverse (ah-tray-*bhayr*-say) v dare

atrevido (ah-tray-*bhee*-dhoa) adj daring

*atribuir a** (ah-tree-*bhweer*) assign to

atroz (ah-*troath*) adj horrible

atún (ah-*toon*) m tuna

audacia (ou-dhah-*thʸah*) f nerve

audaz (ou-*dhahth*) adj bold

audible (ou-*dhee*-bhlay) adj audible

auditorio (ou-dhee-*toa*-rʸoa) m audience

aula (*ou*-lah) f auditorium

aumentar (ou-mayn-*tahr*) v increase, raise

aumento (ou-*mayn*-toa) m increase; rise; raise nAm

aun (ah-*oon*) adv (aún) yet; even

aunque (*oung*-kay) conj although, though

aurora (ou-*roa*-rah) f dawn
ausencia (ou-*sayn*-th^yah) f absence
ausente (ou-*sayn*-tay) adj absent
Australia (ouss-*trah*-l^yah) f Australia
australiano (ouss-trah-l^yah-noa) adj Australian; m Australian
Austria (*ouss*-tr^yah) f Austria
austríaco (ouss-*tree*-ah-koa) adj Austrian; m Austrian
auténtico (ou-*tayn*-tee-koa) adj authentic; true, original
auto (*ou*-toa) m car
autobús (ou-toa-*bhooss*) m coach, bus
autoestopista (ou-toa-ayss-toa-*peess*-tah) m hitchhiker
automático (ou-toa-*mah*-tee-koa) adj automatic
automatización (ou-toa-mah-tee-thah-th^yoan) f automation
automóvil (ou-toa-*moa*-bheel) m motor-car, automobile; ~ **club** automobile club
automovilismo (ou-toa-moa-bhee-*leez*-moa) m motoring
automovilista (ou-toa-moa-bhee-*leess*-tah) m motorist
autonomía (ou-toa-noa-*mee*-ah) f self-government
autónomo (ou-*toa*-noa-moa) adj independent, autonomous
autopista (ou-toa-*peess*-tah) f motorway; highway nAm; ~ **de peaje** turnpike nAm
autopsia (ou-*toap*-s^yah) f autopsy
autor (ou-*toar*) m author
autoridad (ou-toa-ree-*dhahdh*) f authority
autoritario (ou-toa-ree-*tah*-r^yoa) adj authoritarian
autorización (ou-toa-ree-thah-th^yoan) f authorization; permission
autorizar (ou-toa-ree-*thahr*) v allow; license
autoservicio (ou-toa-sayr-*bhee*-th^yoa)

m self-service
***hacer autostop** (ah-*thayr* ou-toa-*stoap*) hitchhike
auxilio (ouk-*see*-l^yoa) m assistance; **primeros auxilios** first-aid
avalancha (ah-bhah-*lahn*-chah) f avalanche
avanzar (ah-bhahn-*thahr*) v advance
avaro (ah-*bhah*-roa) adj avaricious
avefría (ah-bhay-*free*-ah) f pewit
avellana (ah-bhay-l^yah-nah) f hazelnut
avena (ah-*bhay*-nah) f oats pl
avenida (ah-bhay-*nee*-dhah) f avenue
aventura (ah-bhayn-*too*-rah) f adventure
***avergonzarse** (ah-bhayr-goan-*thahr*-say) v *be ashamed
avería (ah-bhay-*ree*-ah) f breakdown
averiarse (ah-bhay-r^y*ahr*-say) v *break down; **averiado** adj out of order
aversión (ah-bhayr-s^y*oan*) f aversion, dislike
avestruz (ah-bhayss-*trooth*) m ostrich
avión (ah-*bh^yoan*) m aeroplane; aircraft, plane; airplane nAm; ~ **a reacción** jet; ~ **turborreactor** turbojet
avíos (ah-*bhee*-oass) mpl kit; ~ **de pesca** fishing gear
avisar (ah-bhee-*sahr*) v inform
aviso (ah-*bhee*-soa) m notice
avispa (ah-*bheess*-pah) f wasp
aya (*ah*-^yah) f governess
ayer (ah-^y*ayr*) adv yesterday
ayuda (ah-^y*oo*-dhah) f help; relief; ~ **de cámara** valet
ayudante (ah-^yoo-*dhahn*-tay) m helper
ayudar (ah-^yoo-*dhahr*) v aid, help
ayuntamiento (ah-^yoon-tah-m^y*ayn*-toa) m town hall
azada (ah-*thah*-dhah) f spade
azafata (ah-thah-*fah*-tah) f hostess; stewardess
azar (ah-*thahr*) m chance, luck

azor (ah-*thoar*) m hawk

azote (ah-*thoa*-tay) m whip

azúcar (ah-*thoo*-kahr) m/f sugar; **terrón de ~** lump of sugar

azucena (ah-thoo-*thay*-nah) f lily

azul (ah-*thool*) adj blue

azulejo (ah-thoo-*lay*-khoa) m tile

B

babor (bah-*bhoar*) m port

bacalao (bah-kah-*lah*-oa) m cod; haddock

bacteria (bahk-*tay*-rʸah) f bacterium

bache (*bah*-chay) m hole

bahía (bah-*ee*-ah) f bay

bailar (bigh-*lahr*) v dance

baile (*bigh*-lay) m ball; dance

baja (*bah*-khah) f slump

bajada (bah-*khah*-dhah) f descent

bajamar (bah-khah-*mahr*) f low tide

bajar (bah-*khahr*) v lower; **bajarse** v *bend down

bajo (*bah*-khoa) adj low; short; *prep* under, below; m bass

bala (*bah*-lah) f bullet

baladí (bah-lah-*dhee*) adj insignificant

balance (bah-*lahn*-thay) m balance

balanza (bah-*lahn*-thah) f scales pl

balbucear (bahl-bhoo-thay-*ahr*) v falter

balcón (bahl-*koan*) m balcony; circle

balde (*bahl*-day) m pail, bucket

baldío (bahl-*dee*-oa) adj waste

balneario (bahl-nay-*ah*-rʸoa) m spa

ballena (bah-*lʸay*-nah) f whale

ballet (bah-*lay*) m ballet

bambú (bahm-*boo*) m bamboo

banco (*bahng*-koa) m bank; bench

banda (*bahn*-dah) f band; gang

bandeja (bahn-*day*-khah) f tray

bandera (bahn-*day*-rah) f flag; banner

bandido (bahn-*dee*-dhoa) m bandit

banquete (bahng-*kay*-tay) m banquet

bañador (bah-ñah-*dhoar*) m bathing-trunks

bañarse (bah-*ñahr*-say) v bathe

baño (*bah*-ñoa) m bath; **mMe** bathroom; **~ turco** Turkish bath; **calzón de ~** swimming-trunks; **traje de ~** swim-suit

bar (bahr) m bar; saloon, café

barajar (bah-rah-*khahr*) v shuffle

baranda (bah-*rahn*-dah) f banisters pl

barandilla (bah-rahn-*dee*-lʸah) f rail; railing

barato (bah-*rah*-toa) adj inexpensive, cheap

barba (*bahr*-bhah) f beard

barbero (bahr-*bhay*-roa) m barber

barbilla (bahr-*bhee*-lʸah) f chin

barca (*bahr*-kah) f boat

barco (*bahr*-koa) m boat

barítono (bah-*ree*-toa-noa) m baritone

barman (*bahr*-mahn) m bartender, barman

barniz (bahr-*neeth*) m varnish; **~ para las uñas** nail-polish

barnizar (bahr-nee-*thahr*) v varnish

barómetro (bah-*roa*-may-troa) m barometer

barquillo (bahr-*kee*-lʸoa) m waffle

barra (*bah*-rrah) f bar, rod; counter

barrer (bah-*rrayr*) v *sweep

barrera (bah-*rray*-rah) f barrier, rail; **~ de protección** crash barrier

barril (bah-*rreel*) m barrel, cask

barrilete (bah-rree-*lay*-tay) m keg

barrio (*bah*-rrʸoa) m quarter, district; **~ bajo** slum

barroco (bah-*rroa*-koa) adj baroque

barrote (bah-*rroa*-tay) m bar

basar (bah-*sahr*) v base

báscula (*bahss*-koo-lah) f weighing-machine

base (*bah*-say) f basis, base

basílica (bah-*see*-lee-kah) f basilica

bastante (bahss-*tahn*-tay) *adv* enough, sufficient; fairly, pretty, rather, quite

bastar (bahss-*tahr*) *v* suffice

bastardo (bahss-*tahr*-dhoa) *m* bastard

bastón (bahss-*toan*) *m* cane; walking-stick; **bastones de esquí** ski sticks

basura (bah-*soo*-rah) *f* trash, rubbish, garbage; **cubo de la** ~ rubbish-bin

bata (*bah*-tah) *f* dressing-gown; ~ **de baño** bathrobe; ~ **suelta** negligee

batalla (bah-*tah*-lᵞah) *f* battle

batería (bah-tay-*ree*-ah) *f* battery

batidora (bah-tee-*dhoa*-rah) *f* mixer

batir (bah-*teer*) *v* *beat, whip

baúl (bah-*ool*) *m* trunk

bautismo (bou-*teez*-moa) *m* baptism

bautizar (bou-tee-*thahr*) *v* christen, baptize

bautizo (bou-*tee*-thoa) *m* christening, baptism

baya (*bah*-ᵞah) *f* berry

bebé (bay-*bhay*) *m* baby

beber (bay-*bhayr*) *v* *drink

bebida (bay-*bhee*-dhah) *f* drink, beverage; ~ **no alcohólica** soft drink; **bebidas espirituosas** spirits

beca (*bay*-kah) *f* grant, scholarship

becerro (bay-*thay*-rroa) *m* calf skin

beige (*bay*-khay) *adj* beige

béisbol (*bayz*-bhoal) *m* baseball

belga (*bayl*-gah) *adj* Belgian; *m* Belgian

Bélgica (*bayl*-khee-kah) *f* Belgium

belleza (bay-*lᵞay*-thah) *f* beauty; **salón de** ~ beauty salon

bello (*bay*-lᵞoa) *adj* fine

bellota (bay-*lᵞoa*-tah) *f* acorn

***bendecir** (bayn-day-*theer*) *v* bless

bendición (bayn-dee-*thᵞoan*) *f* blessing

beneficio (bay-nay-*fee*-thᵞoa) *m* profit, benefit

berenjena (bay-rayng-*khay*-nah) *f* eggplant

berro (*bay*-rroa) *m* watercress

besar (bay-*sahr*) *v* kiss

beso (*bay*-soa) *m* kiss

betún (bay-*toon*) *m* shoe polish

biblia (*bee*-bhlᵞah) *f* bible

biblioteca (bee-bhlᵞoa-*tay*-kah) *f* library

bicicleta (bee-thee-*klay*-tah) *f* cycle, bicycle

biciclo (bee-*thee*-kloa) *m* cycle, bicycle

bicimotor (bee-thee-moa-*toar*) *m* moped

biela (*bᵞay*-lah) *f* piston-rod

bien (*bᵞayn*) *adv* well; **¡bien!** all right!; **bien ... bien** either ... or

bienes (*bᵞay*-nayss) *mpl* goods *pl*; possessions

bienestar (bᵞay-nayss-*tahr*) *m* ease; welfare

bienvenida (bᵞayn-bhay-*nee*-dhah) *f* welcome; *dar la ~ welcome

bienvenido (bᵞayn-bhay-*nee*-dhoa) *adj* welcome

biftec (beef-*tayk*) *m* steak

bifurcación (bee-foor-kah-*thᵞoan*) *f* road fork, fork

bifurcarse (bee-foor-*kahr*-say) *v* fork

bigote (bee-*goatay*) *m* moustache

bilingüe (bee-*leeng*-gway) *adj* bilingual

bilis (*bee*-leess) *f* gall, bile

billar (bee-*lᵞahr*) *m* billiards *pl*

billete (bee-*lᵞay*-tay) *m* ticket; ~ **de andén** platform ticket; ~ **de banco** banknote; ~ **gratuito** free ticket

biología (bᵞoa-loa-*khee*-ah) *f* biology

biológico (bᵞoa-*loa*-khee-koa) *adj* biological

bisagra (bee-*sah*-grah) *f* hinge

bizco (*beeth*-koa) *adj* cross-eyed

bizcocho (beeth-*koa*-choa) *m* cookie *nAm*

blanco¹ (*blahng*-koa) *adj* white; blank

blanco² (*blahng*-koa) *m* mark, target

blando (*blahn*-doa) *adj* soft

blanquear (blahng-kay-*ahr*) *v* bleach

bloc (bloak) *mMe* writing-pad

bloque (*bloa*-kay) *m* block; writing-pad

bloquear (bloa-kay-*ahr*) *v* block

blusa (*bloo*-sah) *f* blouse

bobina (boa-*bhee*-nah) *f* spool; ~ **del encendido** ignition coil

bobo (boa-*bhoa*) *adj* silly

boca (*boa*-kah) *f* mouth

bocadillo (boa-kah-*dhee*-lʸoa) *m* sandwich

bocado (boa-*kah*-dhoa) *m* bite

bocina (boa-*thee*-nah) *f* horn, hooter; **tocar la** ~ hoot

boda (*boa*-dhah) *f* wedding

bodega (boa-*dhay*-gah) *f* hold

bofetada (boa-fay-*tah*-dhah) *f* smack, slap

boina (*boi*-nah) *f* beret

bolera (boa-*lay*-rah) *f* bowling alley

boletín meteorológico (boa-lay-*teen* may-tay-oa-roa-*loa*-khee-koa) weather forecast

boleto (boa-*lay*-toa) *mMe* ticket

bolígrafo (boa-*lee*-grah-foa) *m* ballpoint-pen, Biro

Bolivia (boa-*lee*-bhʸah) *f* Bolivia

boliviano (boa-lee-bhʸah-noa) *adj* Bolivian; *m* Bolivian

bolsa (*boal*-sah) *f* bag; stock market, stock exchange; pocket-book, purse; ~ **de hielo** ice-bag; ~ **de papel** paper bag

bolsillo (boal-*see*-lʸoa) *m* pocket

bolso (*boal*-soa) *m* handbag; bag

bollo (*boa*-lʸoa) *m* bun

bomba (*boam*-bah) *f* pump; bomb; ~ **de agua** water pump; ~ **de gasolina** petrol pump; fuel pump *Am*

bombardear (boam-bahr-dhay-*ahr*) *v* bomb

bombear (boam-bay-*ahr*) *v* pump

bomberos (boam-*bay*-roass) *mpl* fire-brigade

bombilla (boam-*bee*-lʸah) *f* light bulb; ~ **de flash** flash-bulb

bombón (boam-*boan*) *m* chocolate; candy *nAm*

bondad (boan-*dahdh*) *f* goodness

bondadoso (boan-dah-*dhoa*-soa) *adj* good-natured, kind

bonito (boa-*nee*-toa) *adj* pretty; fair, nice, lovely

boquerón (boa-kay-*roan*) *m* whitebait

boquilla (boa-*kee*-lʸah) *f* cigarette-holder

bordado (boar-*dhah*-dhoa) *m* embroidery

bordar (boar-*dhahr*) *v* embroider

borde (*boar*-dhay) *m* edge, border; verge, rim, brim; ~ **del camino** wayside

bordillo (boar-*dhee*-lʸoa) *m* curb

a bordo (ah *boar*-doa) aboard

borracho (boa-*rrah*-choa) *adj* drunk

borrar (boa-*rrahr*) *v* erase

borrascoso (boa-rrahss-*koa*-soa) *adj* gusty

borrón (boa-*rroan*) *m* blot

bosque (*boass*-kay) *m* wood, forest

bosquejar (boass-kay-*khahr*) *v* sketch

bosquejo (boass-*kay*-khoa) *m* sketch

bostezar (boass-tay-*thahr*) *v* yawn

bota (*boa*-tah) *f* boot; **botas de esquí** ski boots

botadura (boa-tah-*dhoo*-rah) *f* launching

botánica (boa-*tah*-nee-kah) *f* botany

bote (*boa*-tay) *m* rowing-boat; ~ **a motor** motor-boat

botella (boa-*tay*-lʸah) *f* bottle

botón (boa-*toan*) *m* button; knob, push-button; ~ **del cuello** collar stud

botones (boa-*toa*-nayss) *mpl* bellboy

bóveda (*boa*-bhay-dhah) *f* vault, arch

boxear (boak-say-*ahr*) v box
boya (*boa*-Yah) f buoy
braga (*brah*-gah) f briefs pl; panties pl
bragueta (brah-*gay*-tah) f fly
branquia (*brahng*-kYah) f gill
Brasil (brah-*seel*) m Brazil
brasileño (brah-see-*lay*-ñoa) adj Brazilian; m Brazilian
braza (*brah*-thah) f breaststroke; ~ de mariposa butterfly stroke
brazo (*brah*-thoa) m arm; del ~ arm-in-arm
brea (*bray*-ah) f tar
brecha (*bray*-chah) f breach
bregar (bray-*gahr*) v labour
brema (*bray*-mah) f bream
breve (*bray*-bhay) adj brief; en ~ soon
brezal (bray-*thahl*) m moor
brezo (*bray*-thoa) m heather
brillante (bree-*lYahn*-tay) adj brilliant
brillantina (bree-lYahn-*tee*-nah) f hair cream
brillar (bree-*lYahr*) v glow, *shine
brillo (*bree*-lYoa) m glow, gloss
brincar (breeng-*kahr*) v hop; skip
brindis (*breen*-deess) m toast
brisa (*bree*-sah) f breeze
británico (bree-*tah*-nee-koa) adj British; m Briton
brocha (*broa*-chah) f brush; ~ de afeitar shaving-brush
broche (*broa*-chay) m brooch
broma (*broa*-mah) f joke
bronca (*broang*-kah) f row
bronce (*broan*-thay) m bronze; de ~ bronze
bronquitis (broang-*kee*-teess) f bronchitis
brotar (broa-*tahr*) v bud
bruja (*broo*-khah) f witch
brújula (*broo*-khoo-lah) f compass
brumoso (broo-*moa*-soa) adj foggy; hazy

brutal (broo-*tahl*) adj brutal
bruto (*broo*-toa) adj gross
bucear (boo-thay-*ahr*) v dive
bueno (*bway*-noa) adj good; kind; sound; ¡bueno! well!
buey (bway) m ox
bufanda (boo-*fahn*-dah) f scarf
buffet (boof-*fayt*) m buffet
buhardilla (bwahr-*dee*-lYah) f attic
buho (*boo*-oa) m owl
buitre (*bwee*-tray) m vulture
bujía (boo-*khee*-ah) f sparking-plug
bulbo (*bool*-bhoa) m bulb; light bulb
Bulgaria (bool-*gah*-rYah) f Bulgaria
búlgaro (*bool*-gah-roa) adj Bulgarian; m Bulgarian
bulto (*bool*-toa) m bulk
bulla (*boo*-lYah) f fuss
buque (*boo*-kay) m ship; vessel; ~ a motor launch; ~ cisterna tanker; ~ de guerra man-of-war; ~ velero sailing-boat
burbuja (boor-*boo*-khah) f bubble
burdel (boor-*dhayl*) m brothel
burdo (*boor*-dhoa) adj coarse
burgués (boor-*gayss*) adj middle-class, bourgeois
burla (*boor*-lah) f mockery
burlarse de (boor-*lahr*-say) mock
burocracia (boo-roa-*krah*-thYah) f bureaucracy
burro (*boo*-rroa) m ass, donkey
buscar (booss-*kahr*) v look for; look up, *seek, search; hunt for; *ir a ~ *get, pick up, fetch
búsqueda (*booss*-kay-dhah) f search
busto (*booss*-toa) m bust
butaca (boo-*tah*-kah) f armchair, easy chair; stall; orchestra seat Am
buzón (boo-*thoan*) m pillar-box, letter-box; mailbox nAm

C

caballero (kah-bhah-*l*^{y}*ay*-roa) *m* gentleman; knight

caballitos (kah-bhah-*l*^{y}*ee*-toass) *mpl* merry-go-round

caballo (kah-*bhah*-l^{y}oa) *m* horse; ~ **de carrera** race-horse; ~ **de vapor** horsepower

cabaña (kah-*bhah*-ñah) *f* cabin, hut

cabaret (kah-bhah-*rayt*) *m* cabaret

cabecear (kah-bhay-thay-*ahr*) *v* nod

cabeceo (kah-bhay-*thay*-oa) *m* nod

cabello (kah-*bhay*-l^{y}oa) *m* hair; **suavizante de** ~ conditioner

cabelludo (kah-bhay-*l*^{y}*oo*-dhoa) *adj* hairy

cabeza (kah-*bhay*-thah) *f* head; ~ **de turco** scapegoat; **dolor de** ~ headache

cabezudo (kah-bhay-*thoo*-dhoa) *adj* head-strong

cabina (kah-*bhee*-nah) *f* cabin; booth; ~ **telefónica** telephone booth

cable (*kah*-bhlay) *m* cable

cablegrafiar (kah-bhlay-grah-*f*^{y}*ahr*) *v* cable

cablegrama (kah-bhlay-*grah*-mah) *m* cable

cabo (*kah*-bhoa) *m* cape

cabra (*kah*-bhrah) *f* goat

cabritilla (kah-bhree-*tee*-l^{y}ah) *f* kid

cabrón (kah-*bhroan*) *m* goat

cacahuate (kah-kah-*wah*-tay) *mMe* peanut

cacahuete (kah-kah-*way*-tay) *m* peanut

cacerola (kah-thay-*roa*-lah) *f* saucepan

cachear (kah-chay-*ahr*) *v* search

cachivache (kah-chee-*bhah*-chay) *m* junk

cada (*kah*-dhah) *adj* every, each; ~

uno everyone

cadáver (kah-*dhah*-bhayr) *m* corpse

cadena (kah-*dhay*-nah) *f* chain

cadera (kah-*dhay*-rah) *f* hip

caducado (kah-dhoo-*kah*-dhoa) *adj* expired

*****caer** (kah-*ayr*) *v* *fall; **dejar** ~ drop

café (kah-*fay*) *m* coffee; public house

cafeína (kah-fay-*ee*-nah) *f* caffeine

cafetera filtradora (kah-fay-*tay*-rah feel-trah-*dhoa*-rah) percolator

cafetería (kah-fay-tay-*ree*-ah) *f* snackbar, cafeteria

caída (kah-*ee*-dhah) *f* fall

caja (*kah*-khah) *f* box; crate; paydesk; ~ **de cartón** carton; ~ **de caudales** safe, vault; ~ **de cerillas** match-box; ~ **de colores** paintbox; ~ **de velocidades** gear-box; ~ **fuerte** safe; ~ **metálica** canister

cajero (kah-*khay*-roa) *m* cashier; ~ **automático** cash dispenser, ATM

cajón (kah-*khoan*) *m* drawer

cal (kahl) *f* lime

calambre (kah-*lahm*-bray) *m* cramp

calamidad (kah-lah-mee-*dhahdh*) *f* disaster

calcetín (kahl-thay-*teen*) *m* sock

calcio (*kahl*-th^{y}oa) *m* calcium

calculadora (kahl-koo-lah-*dhoa*-rah) *f* calculator

calcular (kahl-koo-*lahr*) *v* reckon, calculate

cálculo (*kahl*-koo-loa) *m* calculation; ~ **biliar** gallstone

calderilla (kahl-day-*ree*-l^{y}ah) *f* petty cash

calefacción (kah-lay-fahk-*th*^{y}*oan*) *f* heating

calefactor (kah-lay-fahk-*toar*) *m* heater

calendario (kah-layn-*dah*-r^{y}oa) *m* calendar

*****calentar** (kah-layn-*tahr*) *v* warm, heat

calidad (kah-lee-*dhahdh*) *f* quality; **de**

primera ~ first-class

caliente (kah-l^yayn-tay) *adj* warm, hot

calificado (kah-lee-fee-*kah*-dhoa) *adj* qualified

calina (kah-*lee*-nah) *f* haze

calinoso (kah-lee-*noa*-soa) *adj* hazy

calma (*kahl*-mah) *f* calm

calmante (kahl-*mahn*-tay) *m* tranquillizer, sedative

calmar (kahl-*mahr*) *v* calm down; **calmarse** *v* calm down

calor (kah-*loar*) *m* warmth, heat

caloría (kah-loa-*ree*-ah) *f* calorie

calorífero (kah-loa-*ree*-fay-roa) *m* hotwater bottle

calumnia (kah-*loom*-n^yah) *f* slander

calvinismo (kahl-bhee-*neez*-moa) *m* Calvinism

calvo (*kahl*-bhoa) *adj* bald

calzada (kahl-*thah*-dhah) *f* carriageway, causeway; drive

calzado (kahl-*thah*-dhoa) *m* footwear

calzoncillos (kahl-thoan-*thee*-l^yoass) *mpl* pants *pl*, briefs *pl*, drawers; shorts *plAm*

callado (kah-l^yah-dhoa) *adj* silent

callarse (kah-l^yahr-say) *v* *be silent

calle (*kah*-l^yay) *f* street; road; ~ **lateral** side-street; ~ **mayor** main street

callejón (kah-l^yay-*khoan*) *m* alley, lane; ~ **sin salida** cul-de-sac

callo (*kah*-l^yoa) *m* callus; corn

cama (*kah*-mah) *f* bed; ~ **de tijera** camp-bed; cot *nAm*; **camas gemelas** twin beds; ~ **y desayuno** bed and breakfast

camafeo (kah-mah-*fay*-oa) *m* cameo

cámara (*kah*-mah-rah) *f* camera; ~ **fotográfica** camera

camarada (kah-mah-*rah*-dhah) *m* comrade

camarera (kah-mah-*ray*-rah) *f* waitress

camarero (kah-mah-*ray*-roa) *m* waiter; steward; **jefe de camareros** head-waiter

camarón (kah-mah-*roan*) *m* shrimp

camastro (kah-*mahss*-troa) *m* bunk

cambiar (kahm-b^y*ahr*) *v* alter, change; vary; exchange, switch; ~ **de marcha** change gear

cambio (*kahm*-b^yoa) *m* alteration, change, variation; turn; exchange; exchange rate; **oficina de** ~ money exchange

camello (kah-*may*-l^yoa) *m* camel

caminar (kah-mee-*nahr*) *v* *go; hike

caminata (kah-mee-*nah*-tah) *f* walk

camino (kah-*mee*-noa) *m* way; road; **a mitad de** ~ halfway; **borde del** ~ roadside; ~ **de** bound for; ~ **en obras** road up; ~ **principal** main road

camión (kah-m^y*oan*) *m* lorry; truck *nAm*

camioneta (kah-m^yoa-*nay*-tah) *f* van

camisa (kah-*mee*-sah) *f* shirt

camiseta (kah-mee-*say*-tah) *f* undershirt; vest

camisón (kah-mee-*soan*) *m* nightdress

campamento (kahm-pah-*mayn*-toa) *m* camp

campana (kahm-*pah*-nah) *f* bell

campanario (kahm-pah-*nah*-r^yoa) *m* steeple

campaña (kahm-*pah*-ñah) *f* campaign; **catre de** ~ camp-bed

campeón (kahm-pay-*oan*) *m* champion

campesino (kahm-pay-*see*-noa) *m* peasant

camping (*kahm*-peeng) *m* camping site, camping

campo (*kahm*-poa) *m* countryside, country; field; ~ **de aviación** airfield; ~ **de golf** golf-course; ~ **de tenis** tennis-court; **día de** ~ picnic

Canadá (kah-nah-*dhah*) *m* Canada

canadiense (kah-nah-*dh^yayn*-say) *adj*

Canadian; *m* Canadian
canal (kah-*nahl*) *m* canal; channel;
Canal de la Mancha English Channel
canario (kah-*nah*-r^yoa) *m* canary
cancelación (kahn-thay-lah-*th^yoan*) *f* cancellation
cancelar (kahn-thay-*lahr*) *v* cancel
cáncer (*kahn*-thayr) *m* cancer
canción (kahn-*th^yoan*) *f* song
cancha (*kahn*-chah) *f* tennis-court
candado (kahn-*dah*-dhoa) *m* padlock
candela (kahn-*day*-lah) *f* candle
candelabro (kahn-day-*lah*-bhroa) *m* candelabrum
candidato (kahn-dee-*dhah*-toa) *m* candidate
canela (kah-*nay*-lah) *f* cinnamon
cangrejo (kahng-*gray*-khoa) *m* crab
canguro (kahng-*goo*-roa) *m* kangaroo
canica (kah-*nee*-kah) *f* marble
canoa (kah-*noa*-ah) *f* canoe
cansancio (kahn-*sahn*-th^yoa) *m* fatigue
cansar (kahn-*sahr*) *v* tire; **cansado** tired, weary
cantadora (kahn-tah-*dhoa*-rah) *f* singer
cantante (kahn-*tahn*-tay) *m* singer
cantar (kahn-*tahr*) *v* *sing
cántaro (*kahn*-tah-roa) *m* pitcher; jug
cantera (kahn-*tay*-rah) *f* quarry
cantidad (kahn-tee-*dhahdh*) *f* amount, quantity; number; lot
cantina (kahn-*tee*-nah) *f* canteen; *fMe* saloon
canto (*kahn*-toa) *m* singing; edge
caña (*kah*-ñah) *f* cane; **~ de pescar** fishing rod
cañada (kah-*ñah*-dhah) *f* glen
cáñamo (*kah*-ñah-moa) *m* hemp
cañón (kah-*ñoan*) *m* gun; gorge
caos (kah-oass) *m* chaos
caótico (kah-*oa*-tee-koa) *adj* chaotic
capa (*kah*-pah) *f* cloak, cape; layer, deposit

capacidad (kah-pah-thee-*dhahdh*) *f* capacity
capataz (kah-pah-*tahth*) *m* foreman
capaz (kah-*pahth*) *adj* able; capable; ***ser ~ de** *be able to; qualify
capellán (kah-pay-*l^yahn*) *m* chaplain
capilla (kah-*pee*-l^yah) *f* chapel
capital (kah-pee-*tahl*) *m* capital; *adj* capital
capitalismo (kah-pee-tah-*leez*-moa) *m* capitalism
capitán (kah-pee-*tahn*) *m* captain
capitulación (kah-pee-too-lah-*th^yoan*) *f* capitulation
capítulo (kah-*pee*-too-loa) *m* chapter
capó (kah-*poa*) *m* bonnet; hood *nAm*
capricho (kah-*pree*-choa) *m* fancy, whim
cápsula (*kahp*-soo-lah) *f* capsule
captura (kahp-*too*-rah) *f* capture
capturar (kahp-too-*rahr*) *v* capture
capucha (kah-*poo*-chah) *f* hood
capullo (kah-*poo*-l^yoa) *m* bud
caqui (*kah*-kee) *m* khaki
cara (*kah*-rah) *f* face
caracol (kah-rah-*koal*) *m* snail; **~ marino** winkle
carácter (kah-*rahk*-tayr) *m* character
característica (kah-rahk-tay-*reess*-tee-kah) *f* characteristic, feature; quality
característico (kah-rahk-tay-*reess*-tee-koa) *adj* typical, characteristic
caracterizar (kah-rahk-tay-ree-*thahr*) *v* characterize, mark
caramelo (kah-rah-*may*-loa) *m* caramel, toffee, sweet
caravana (kah-rah-*bhah*-nah) *f* caravan; trailer *nAm*
carbón (kahr-*bhoan*) *m* coal; **~ de leña** charcoal
carburador (kahr-bhoo-rah-*dhoar*) *m* carburettor
cárcel (*kahr*-thayl) *f* jail, gaol

carcelero (kahr-thay-*lay*-roa) *m* jailer

cardenal (kahr-dhay-*nahl*) *m* cardinal

cardinal (kahr-dhee-*nahl*) *adj* cardinal

cardo (*kahr*-dhoa) *m* thistle

*****carecer** (kahr-ray-*thayr*) *v* lack

carencia (kah-*rayn*-th⋎ah) *f* want, shortage

carga (*kahr*-gah) *f* charge; cargo, freight, load; batch

cargar (kahr-*gahr*) *v* charge; load

cargo (*kahr*-goa) *m* office; freight

cari (*kah*-ree) *m* curry

caridad (kah-ree-*dhahdh*) *f* charity

carillón (kah-ree-*l⋎oan*) *m* chimes *pl*

cariño (kah-*ree*-ñoa) *m* affection; pet

cariñoso (kah-ree-*ñoa*-soa) *adj* affectionate

carmesí (kahr-may-*see*) *adj* crimson

carnaval (kahr-nah-*bhahl*) *m* carnival

carne (*kahr*-nay) *f* meat; flesh; ~ **de cerdo** pork; ~ **de gallina** gooseflesh; ~ **de ternera** veal; ~ **de vaca** beef

carnero (kahr-*nay*-roa) *m* mutton

carnicero (kahr-nee-*thay*-roa) *m* butcher

caro (*kah*-roa) *adj* expensive, dear

carpa (*kahr*-pah) *f* carp

carpintero (kahr-peen-*tay*-roa) *m* carpenter

carrera (kah-*rray*-rah) *f* career; race; ~ **de caballos** horserace; **pista para carreras** race-track

carretera (kah-rray-*tay*-rah) *f* highway

carretilla (kah-rray-*tee*-l⋎ah) *f* wheelbarrow

carro (*kah*-rroa) *m* cart; *mMe* car; ~ **de gitanos** caravan

carrocería (kah-rroa-thay-*ree*-ah) *f* coachwork

carroza (kah-*rroa*-thah) *f* coach

carta (*kahr*-tah) *f* map; letter; ~ **certificada** registered letter; ~ **de crédito** letter of credit; ~ **de recomen-**

dación letter of recommendation; ~ **de vinos** wine-list; ~ **marina** chart

cartel (kahr-*tayl*) *m* poster, placard

cárter (*kahr*-tayr) *m* crankcase

cartera (kahr-*tay*-rah) *f* bag; satchel; wallet

cartero (kahr-*tay*-roa) *m* postman

cartílago (kahr-*tee*-lah-goa) *m* cartilage

cartón (kahr-*toan*) *m* cardboard; carton; **de** ~ cardboard

cartucho (kahr-*too*-choa) *m* cartridge

casa (*kah*-sah) *f* house; home; **a** ~ home; **ama de** ~ housewife; ~ **de campo** cottage; ~ **de correos** post-office; ~ **del párroco** vicarage; ~ **de pisos** block of flats; apartment house *Am*; ~ **de reposo** rest-home; ~ **flotante** houseboat; ~ **señorial** manor-house; **en** ~ at home; indoors, indoor, home; **gobierno de la** ~ housekeeping

casarse (kah-*sahr*-say) *v* marry

cascada (kahss-*kah*-dhah) *f* waterfall

cascanueces (kahss-kah-*nway*-thayss) *m* nutcrackers *pl*

cáscara (*kahss*-kah-rah) *f* shell; skin; ~ **de nuez** nutshell

casco (*kahss*-koa) *m* helmet; hoof

casero (kah-*say*-roa) *adj* home-made

casi (*kah*-see) *adv* almost, nearly

casimir (kah-see-*meer*) *m* cashmere

casino (kah-*see*-noa) *m* casino

caso (*kah*-soa) *m* event; case; instance; ~ **de urgencia** emergency; **en** ~ **de** in case of; **en ningún** ~ by no means; **en tal** ~ then; **en todo** ~ at any rate, anyway

caspa (*kahss*-pah) *f* dandruff

casquillo (kahss-*kee*-l⋎oa) *m* socket

castaña (kahss-*tah*-ñah) *f* chestnut

castellano (kahss-tay-*l⋎ah*-noa) *adj* Castilian; *m* Castilian

castigar (kahss-tee-*gahr*) v punish
castigo (kahss-*tee*-goa) m penalty, punishment
castillo (kahss-*tee*-l^yoa) m castle
casto (*kahss*-toa) adj chaste; pure
castor (kahss-*toar*) m beaver
por casualidad (poar kah-swah-lee-*dhahdh*) by chance
catacumba (kah-tah-*koom*-bah) f catacomb
catálogo (kah-*tah*-loa-goa) m catalogue
catarro (kah-*tah*-rroa) m catarrh
catástrofe (kah-*tahss*-troa-fay) f disaster, catastrophe, calamity
catedral (kah-tay-*dhrahl*) f cathedral
catedrático (kah-tay-*dhrah*-tee-koa) m professor
categoría (kah-tay-goa-*ree*-ah) f category
católico (kah-*toa*-lee-koa) adj catholic, Roman Catholic
catorce (kah-*toar*-thay) num fourteen
catorceno (kah-toar-*thay*-noa) num fourteenth
caucho (*kou*-choa) m rubber
causa (*kou*-sah) f cause, reason; case; lawsuit; **a ~ de** because of, on account of, for, owing to
causar (kou-*sahr*) v cause
cautela (kou-*tay*-lah) f caution
cautivar (kou-tee-*bhahr*) v fascinate
cavar (kah-*bhahr*) v *dig
caviar (kah-*bh^yahr*) m caviar
cavidad (kah-bhee-*dhahdh*) f cavity
caza (*kah*-thah) f chase, hunt; game; **apeadero de ~** lodge
cazador (kah-thah-*dhoar*) m hunter
cazar (kah-*thahr*) v hunt; chase; **~ en vedado** poach
cebada (thay-*bhah*-dhah) f barley
cebo (*thay*-bhoa) m bait
cebolla (thay-*bhoa*-l^yah) f onion
cebollino (thay-bhoa-l^y*ee*-noa) m

chives pl
cebra (*thay*-bhrah) f zebra
ceder (thay-*dhayr*) v indulge; *give in
cegar (thay-*gahr*) v blind
ceja (*thay*-khah) f eyebrow
celda (*thayl*-dah) f cell
celebración (thay-lay-bhrah-*th^yoan*) f celebration
celebrar (thay-lay-*bhrahr*) v celebrate
célebre (*thay*-lay-bhray) adj famous
celebridad (thay-lay-bhree-*dhahdh*) f celebrity
celeste (thay-*layss*-tay) adj heavenly
celibato (thay-lee-*bhah*-toa) m celibacy
celo (*thay*-loa) m zeal, diligence; **celos** jealousy
celofán (thay-loa-*fahn*) m cellophane
celoso (thay-*loa*-soa) adj zealous, diligent; envious, jealous
célula (*thay*-loo-lah) f cell
cementerio (thay-mayn-*tay*-r^yoa) m churchyard, graveyard, cemetery
cemento (thay-*mayn*-toa) m cement
cena (*thay*-nah) f dinner, supper
cenar (thay-*nahr*) v dine, *eat
cenicero (thay-nee-*thay*-roa) m ashtray
cenit (thay-*neet*) m zenith
ceniza (thay-*nee*-thah) f ash
censura (thayn-*soo*-rah) f censorship
centelleante (thayn-tay-l^y*ay*-ahn-tay) adj sparkling
centígrado (thayn-*tee*-grah-dhoa) adj centigrade
centímetro (thayn-*tee*-may-troa) m centimetre; tape-measure
central (thayn-*trahl*) adj central; **central eléctrica** power-station; **central telefónica** telephone exchange
centralizar (thayn-trah-lee-*thahr*) v centralize
centro (*thayn*-troa) m centre; **~ comercial** shopping centre; **~ de la ciudad** town centre; **~ de recreo** recreation centre

cepillar (thay-pee-/Yahr) v brush

cepillo (thay-pee-lYoa) m brush; ~ **de dientes** toothbrush; ~ **de la ropa** clothes-brush; ~ **para el cabello** hairbrush; ~ **para las uñas** nailbrush

cera (thay-rah) f wax

cerámica (thay-rah-mee-kah) f ceramics pl; crockery, pottery

cerca (thayr-kah) f fence

cerca de (thayr-kah day) near, by; almost

cercano (thayr-kah-noa) adj close, nearby, near

cercar (thayr-kahr) v encircle, surround

cerdo (thayr-dhoa) m pig

cereales (thay-ray-ah-layss) mpl corn

cerebro (thay-ray-bhroa) m brain; **conmoción cerebral** concussion

ceremonia (thay-ray-moa-nYah) f ceremony

cereza (thay-ray-thah) f cherry

cerilla (thay-ree-lYah) f match

cerillo (thay-ree-lYoa) mMe match

cero (thay-roa) m zero, nought

cerradura (thay-rrah-dhoo-rah) f lock; **ojo de la** ~ keyhole

* **cerrar** (thay-rrahr) v close, *shut; fasten; turn off; ~ **con llave** lock

cerrojo (thay-rroa-khoa) m bolt

certificación (thayr-tee-fee-kah-thYoan) f certificate

certificado (thayr-tee-fee-kah-dhoa) m certificate; ~ **de salud** health certificate

certificar (thayr-tee-fee-kahr) v register

cervato (thayr-bhah-toa) m fawn

cervecería (thayr-bhay-thay-ree-ah) f brewery

cerveza (thayr-bhay-thah) f beer; ale

cesar (thay-sahr) v cease, quit, stop, discontinue

césped (thayss-paydh) m lawn; grass

cesta (thayss-tah) f basket

cesto (thayss-toa) m hamper; ~ **para papeles** wastepaper-basket

cicatriz (thee-kah-treeth) f scar

ciclista (thee-kleess-tah) m cyclist

ciclo (thee-kloa) m cycle

ciego (thYay-goa) adj blind

cielo (thYay-loa) m heaven; sky; ~ **raso** ceiling

ciencia (thYayn-thYah) f science

científico (thYayn-tee-fee-koa) adj scientific; m scientist

ciento (thYayn-toa) num hundred; **por** ~ percent

cierre (thYay-rray) m fastener; ~ **relámpago** zipper

cierto (thYayr-toa) adj certain; **por** ~ indeed

ciervo (thYayr-bhoa) m deer

cifra (thee-frah) f number, figure

cigarrillo (thee-gah-rree-lYoa) m cigarette

cigüeña (thee-gway-ñah) f stork

cigüeñal (thee-gway-ñahl) m crankshaft

cilindro (thee-leen-droa) m cylinder; **culata del** ~ cylinder head

cima (thee-mah) f top, summit; hilltop

cinc (theengk) m zinc

cincel (theen-thayl) m chisel

cinco (theeng-koa) num five

cincuenta (theeng-kwayn-tah) num fifty

cine (thee-nay) m pictures

cinematógrafo (thee-nay-mah-toa-grah-foa) m cinema

cinta (theen-tah) f ribbon, tape; ~ **adhesiva** scotch tape, adhesive tape; ~ **de goma** elastic band; ~ **métrica** tape-measure

cintura (theen-too-rah) f waist

cinturón (theen-too-roan) m belt; bypass; ~ **de seguridad** seat-belt

cipo (*thee*-poa) *m* milepost
circo (*theer*-koa) *m* circus
*circuir (theer-*kweer*) *v* encircle
circulación (theer-koo-lah-*th*ᵛ*oan*) *f* circulation
circular (theer-koo-*lahr*) *v* circulate
círculo (*theer*-koo-loa) *m* circle, ring; club
circundante (theer-koon-*dahn*-tay) *adj* surrounding
circundar (theer-koon-*dahr*) *v* circle
circunstancia (theer-koons-*tahn*-th*ʸ*ah) *f* circumstance, condition
ciruela (thee-*rway*-lah) *f* plum; ~ **pasa** prune
cirujano (thee-roo-*khah*-noa) *m* surgeon
cisne (*theez*-nay) *m* swan
cistitis (theess-*tee*-teess) *f* cystitis
cita (*thee*-tah) *f* date, appointment; quotation
citación (thee-tah-*th*ᵛ*oan*) *f* summons
citar (thee-*tahr*) *v* quote
ciudad (th*ʸ*oo-*dahdh*) *f* city, town
ciudadanía (th*ʸ*oo-dhah-dhah-*nee*-ah) *f* citizenship
ciudadano (th*ʸ*oo-dhah-*dhah*-noa) *m* citizen
cívico (*thee*-bhee-koa) *adj* civic
civil (thee-*bheel*) *adj* civilian, civil
civilización (thee-bhee-lee-thah-*th*ᵛ*oan*) *f* civilization
civilizado (thee-bhee-lee-*thah*-dhoa) *adj* civilized
claridad (klah-ree-*dhahdh*) *f* clarity
clarificar (klah-ree-fee-*kahr*) *v* clarify
claro (*klah*-roa) *adj* clear; plain, distinct; serene, bright; *m* clearing
clase (*klah*-say) *f* class; sort; form; classroom; ~ **media** middle class; ~ **turista** tourist class; **de primera** ~ first-rate; **toda** ~ **de** all sorts of
clásico (*klah*-see-koa) *adj* classical
clasificar (klah-see-fee-*kahr*) *v* classify,

assort, sort, arrange
cláusula (*klou*-soo-lah) *f* clause
clavar (klah-*bhahr*) *v* pin
clavicémbalo (klah-bhee-*thaym*-bah-loa) *m* harpsichord
clavícula (klah-*bhee*-koo-lah) *f* collarbone
clavo (*klah*-bhoa) *m* nail
clemencia (klay-*mayn*-th*ʸ*ah) *f* mercy
clérigo (*klay*-ree-goa) *m* clergyman, minister
cliente (kl*ʸ*ayn-tay) *m* client, customer
clima (*klee*-mah) *m* climate
climatizado (klee-mah-tee-*thah*-dhoa) *adj* air-conditioned
clínica (*klee*-nee-kah) *f* clinic
cloro (*kloa*-roa) *m* chlorine
club de yates yacht-club
coagularse (koa-ah-goo-*lahr*-say) *v* coagulate
cobarde (koa-*bhahr*-dhay) *adj* cowardly; *m* coward
cobertizo (koa-bhayr-*tee*-thoa) *m* shed
cobrador (koa-bhrah-*dhoar*) *m* conductor
cobrar (koa-*bhrahr*) *v* cash
cobre (*koa*-bhray) *m* copper, brass; **cobres** *mpl* brassware
cocaína (koa-kah-*ee*-nah) *f* cocaine
cocina (koa-*thee*-nah) *f* kitchen; cooker, stove; ~ **de gas** gas cooker
cocinar (koa-thee-*nahr*) *v* cook
cocinero (koa-thee-*nay*-roa) *m* cook
coco (*koa*-koa) *m* coconut
cocodrilo (koa-koa-*dhree*-l*ʸ*oa) *m* crocodile
cóctel (*koak*-tayl) *m* cocktail
coche (*koa*-chay) *m* car; carriage; ~ **cama** sleeping-car; ~ **comedor** dining-car; ~ **de carreras** sportscar; ~ **Pullman** Pullman
cochecillo (koa-chay-*thee*-l*ʸ*oa) *m* pram; baby carriage *Am*
cochinillo (koa-chee-*nee*-l*ʸ*oa) *m* piglet

codicia (koa-*dhee*-th^yah) *f* greed

codicioso (koa-dhee-*th^yoa*-soa) *adj* greedy

código (*koa*-dhee-goa) *m* code; ~ **postal** zip code *Am*

codo (*koa*-dhoa) *m* elbow

codorniz (koa-dhoar-*neeth*) *f* quail

coger (koa-*khayr*) *v* *catch; *take; **llegar a** ~ *catch

coherencia (koa-ay-*rayn*-th^yah) *f* coherence

cohete (koa-*ay*-tay) *m* rocket

coincidencia (koa-een-thee-*dhayn*-th^yah) *f* concurrence

coincidir (koa-een-thee-*dheer*) *v* coincide

cojear (koa-khay-*ahr*) *v* limp

cojo (*koa*-khoa) *adj* lame

col (koal) *m* cabbage; ~ **de Bruselas** sprouts *pl*

cola (*koa*-lah) *f* queue, file, line; tail; gum, glue; ***hacer** ~ queue

colaboración (koa-lah-bhoa-rah-*th^yoan*) *f* co-operation

colcha (*koal*-chah) *f* counterpane, quilt

colchón (koal-*choan*) *m* mattress

colección (koa-layk-*th^yoan*) *f* collection; ~ **de arte** art collection

coleccionar (koa-layk-th^yoa-*nahr*) *v* gather

coleccionista (koa-layk-th^yoa-*neess*-tah) *m* collector

colectivo (koa-layk-*tee*-bhoa) *adj* collective

colector (koa-layk-*toar*) *m* collector

colega (koa-*lay*-gah) *m* colleague

colegio (koa-*lay*-kh^yoa) *m* college

cólera (*koa*-lay-rah) *f* anger, passion, temper

colérico (koa-*lay*-ree-koa) *adj* hot-tempered

***colgar** (koal-*gahr*) *v* *hang

coliflor (koa-lee-*floar*) *f* cauliflower

colina (koa-*lee*-nah) *f* hill

colisión (koa-lee-*s^yoan*) *f* collision

colmena (koal-*may*-nah) *f* beehive

colmo (*koal*-moa) *m* height

colocar (koa-loa-*kahr*) *v* *lay, place, *put

Colombia (koa-*loam*-b^yah) *f* Colombia

colombiano (koa-loam-*b^yah*-noa) *adj* Colombian; *m* Colombian

colonia (koa-*loa*-n^yah) *f* colony; ~ **veraniega** holiday camp

color (koa-*loar*) *m* colour; ~ **de agua-da** water-colour; **de** ~ coloured

colorado (koa-loa-*rah*-dhoa) *adj* colourful

colorante (koa-loa-*rahn*-tay) *m* colourant

colorete (koa-loa-*ray*-tay) *m* rouge

columna (koa-*loom*-nah) *f* column, pillar; ~ **del volante** steering-column

columpiarse (koa-loom-*p^yahr*-say) *v* *swing

columpio (koa-*loom*-p^yoa) *m* swing; seesaw

collar (koa-*l^yahr*) *m* beads *pl*, necklace; collar

coma (*koa*-mah) *f* comma; *m* coma

comadrona (koa-mah-*dhroa*-nah) *f* midwife

comandante (koa-mahn-*dahn*-tay) *m* commander; captain

comarca (koa-*mahr*-kah) *f* district

comba (*koam*-bah) *f* bend

combate (koam-*bah*-tay) *m* combat, battle, struggle, fight; ~ **de boxeo** boxing match

combatir (koam-bah-*teer*) *v* combat, battle, *fight

combinación (koam-bee-nah-*th^yoan*) *f* combination; slip

combinar (koam-bee-*nahr*) *v* combine

combustible (koam-booss-*tee*-bhlay) *m* fuel; ~ **líquido** fuel oil

comedia (koa-*may*-dh^yah) *f* comedy;

~ **musical** musical

comediante (koa-may-*dh*ʸ*ahn*-tay) *m* comedian

comedor (koa-may-*dhoar*) *m* dining-room; ~ **de gala** banqueting-hall

comentar (koa-mayn-*tahr*) *v* comment

comentario (koa-mayn-*tah*-rʸoa) *m* comment

***comenzar** (koa-mayn-*thahr*) *v* commence, *begin

comer (koa-*mayr*) *v* *eat

comercial (koa-mayr-*th*ʸ*ahl*) *adj* commercial

comerciante (koa-mayr-*th*ʸ*ahn*-tay) *m* merchant; trader, dealer; ~ **al por menor** retailer

comerciar (koa-mayr-*th*ʸ*ahr*) *v* trade

comercio (koa *mayr*-thʸoa) *m* commerce, trade, business; ~ **al por menor** retail trade

comestible (koa-mayss-*tee*-bhlay) *adj* edible

comestibles (koa-mayss-*tee*-bhlayss) *mpl* groceries *pl*; **tienda de ~ finos** delicatessen

cometer (koa-may-*tayr*) *v* commit

cómico (*koa*-mee-koa) *adj* comic, funny; *m* comedian; entertainer

comida (koa-*mee*-dhah) *f* food; meal; ~ **principal** dinner

comidilla (koa-mee-*dhee*-lʸah) *f* hobby-horse

comienzo (koa-*m*ʸ*ayn*-thoa) *m* beginning, start

comillas (koa-*mee*-lʸahss) *fpl* quotation marks

comisaría (koa-mee-sah-*ree*-ah) *f* police-station

comisión (koa-mee-*s*ʸ*oan*) *f* committee, commission

comité (koa-mee-*tay*) *m* committee

comitiva (koa-mee-*tee*-bhah) *f* procession

como (*koa*-moa) *adv* as, like, like; **así**

~ as well as; ~ **máximo** at most; ~ **si** as if

cómo (*koa*-moa) *adv* how

cómoda (*koa*-moa-dhah) *f* chest of drawers; bureau *nAm*

comodidad (koa-moa-dhee-*dhahdh*) *f* comfort, leisure

cómodo (*koa*-moa-dhoa) *adj* convenient, easy

compacto (koam-*pahk*-toa) *adj* compact

compadecerse de (koam-pah-dhay-*thayr*-say) pity

compañero (koam-pah-*ñay*-roa) *m* companion; associate; ~ **de clase** class-mate

compañía (koam-pah-*ñee*-ah) *f* company; society

comparación (koam-pah-rah-*th*ʸ*oan*) *f* comparison

comparar (koam-pah-*rahr*) *v* compare

compartimento (koam-pahr-tee-*mayn*-toa) *m* compartment; ~ **para fumadores** smoking-compartment

compartir (koam-pahr-*teer*) *v* share

compasión (koam-pah-*s*ʸ*oan*) *f* sympathy

compasivo (koam-pah-*see*-bhoa) *adj* sympathetic

compatriota (koam-pah-*tr*ʸ*oa*-tah) *m* countryman

compeler (koam-pay-*layr*) *v* compel

compensación (koam-payn-sah-*th*ʸ*oan*) *f* compensation

compensar (koam-payn-*sahr*) *v* compensate; *make good

competencia (koam-pay-*tayn*-thʸah) *f* competition, rivalry; capacity

competente (koam-pay-*tayn*-tay) *adj* expert, qualified

competidor (koam-pay-tee-*dhoar*) *m* competitor, rival

***competir** (koam-pay-*teer*) *v* compete

compilar (koam-pee-*lahr*) *v* compile

* **complacer** (koam-plah-*thayr*) v
please; *give satisfaction
complejo (koam-*play*-khoa) adj complex; m complex
completamente (koam-play-tah-*mayn*-tay) adv completely, quite
completar (koam-play-*tahr*) v complete; fill in; fill out Am
completo (koam-*play*-toa) adj complete; whole, total, utter; full up
complicado (koam-plee-*kah*-dhoa) adj complicated
cómplice (*koam*-plee-thay) m accessary
complot (koam-*ploat*) m plot
* **componer** (koam-poa-*nayr*) v compose
comportarse (koam-poar-*tahr*-say) v behave, act
composición (koam-poa-see-*th*ʸ*oan*) f composition; essay
compositor (koam-poa-see-*toar*) m composer
compra (*koam*-prah) f purchase; *ir de compras** shop
comprador (koam-prah-*dhoar*) m purchaser, buyer
comprar (koam-*prahr*) v purchase, *buy
comprender (koam-prayn-*dayr*) v *understand; *see, *take; comprise, contain
comprensión (koam-prayn-*s*ʸ*oan*) m understanding
comprobante (koam-proa-*bhahn*-tay) m voucher
* **comprobar** (koam-proa-*bhahr*) v ascertain, diagnose, establish, note; prove
comprometerse (koam-proa-may-*tayr*-say) v engage
compromiso (koam-proa-*mee*-soa) m compromise; engagement
compuerta (koam-*pwayr*-tah) f sluice

común (koa-*moon*) adj common; ordinary; **en ~** joint
comuna (koa-*moo*-nah) f commune
comunicación (koa-moo-nee-kah-*th*ʸ*oan*) f communication
comunicado (koa-moo-nee-*kah*-dhoa) m communiqué, information
comunicar (koa-moo-nee-*kahr*) v communicate, inform
comunidad (koa-moo-nee-*dhahdh*) f congregation
comunismo (koa-moo-*neez*-moa) m communism
comunista (koa-moo-*neess*-tah) m communist
con (koan) prep with; by
* **concebir** (koan-thay-*bheer*) v conceive
conceder (koan-thay-*dhayr*) v extend, grant; award
concentración (koan-thayn-trah-*th*ʸ*oan*) f concentration
concentrarse (koan-thayn-*trahr*-say) v concentrate
concepción (koan-thayp-*th*ʸ*oan*) f conception
concepto (koan-*thayp*-toa) m idea
* **concernir** (koan-thayr-*neer*) v touch, concern; **concerniente a** concerning
concesión (koan-thay-*s*ʸ*oan*) f concession
conciencia (koan-*th*ʸ*ayn*-th*ʸ*ah) f conscience; consciousness
concierto (koan-*th*ʸ*ayr*-toa) m concert
conciso (koan-*thee*-soa) adj concise
* **concluir** (koang-*klweer*) v conclude
conclusión (koang-kloo-*s*ʸ*oan*) f conclusion; issue, ending
* **concordar** (koang-koar-*dhahr*) v agree
concreto (koang-*kray*-toa) adj concrete
concupiscencia (koang-koo-pee-*thayn*-th*ʸ*ah) f lust
concurrido (koang-koo-*rree*-dhoa) adj

busy

concurrir (koang-koo-*rreer*) v coincide; concur

concurso (koang-*koor*-soa) m competition, contest; quiz

concha (*koan*-chah) f shell; sea-shell

condado (koan-*dah*-dhoa) m county

conde (*koan*-day) m count, earl

condena (koan-*day*-nah) f conviction

condenado (koan-day-*nah*-dhoa) m convict

condesa (koan-*day*-sah) f countess

condición (koan-dee-*th*ᵞoan) f condition, term

condicional (koan-dee-th ᵞoa-*nahl*) adj conditional

condimentado (koan-dee-mayn-*tah*-dhoa) adj spiced

* **conducir** (koan-doo-*theer*) v *lead, carry, conduct; *drive

conducta (koan-*dook*-tah) f behaviour, conduct

conducto (koan-*dook*-toa) m pipe

conductor (koan-dook-*toar*) m driver; mMe conductor

conectar (koa-nayk-*tahr*) v connect

conejo (koa-*nay*-khoa) m rabbit; **conejillo de Indias** guinea-pig

conexión (koa-nayk-*s*ᵞoan) f connection

confeccionado (koan-fayk-th ᵞoa-*nah*-dhoa) adj ready-made

confederación (koan-fay-day-day-rah-*th*ᵞoan) f union

conferencia (koan-fay-*rayn*-th ᵞah) f conference; lecture; ~ **interurbana** trunk-call

* **confesarse** (koan-fay-*sahr*-say) v confess

confesión (koan-fay-*s*ᵞoan) f confession

confiable (koan-*f*ᵞah-bhlay) adj trustworthy

confianza (koan-*f*ᵞahn-thah) f faith,

trust, confidence; **indigno de** ~ untrustworthy

confiar (koan-*f*ᵞahr) v commit; ~ **en** trust

confidencial (koan-fee-dhayn-*th*ᵞahl) adj confidential

confirmación (koan-feer-mah-*th*ᵞoan) f confirmation

confirmar (koan-feer-*mahr*) v confirm, acknowledge

confiscar (koan-feess-*kahr*) v confiscate, impound

confitería (koan-fee-tay-*ree*-ah) f sweetshop

confitero (koan-fee-*tay*-roa) m confectioner

confitura (koan-fee-*too*-rah) f marmalade

conflicto (koan-*fleek*-toa) m conflict

conforme (koan-*foar*-may) adj alike; in agreement; ~ **a** according to, in agreement with

conformidad (koan-foar-mee-*dhahdh*) f agreement

confort (koan-*foart*) m comfort

confortable (koan-foar-*tah*-bhlay) adj comfortable; cosy

confundir (koan-foon-*deer*) v *mistake, confuse

confusión (koan-foo-*s*ᵞoan) f confusion; disturbance

confuso (koan-*foo*-soa) adj confused

congelado (koang-khay-*lah*-dhoa) adj frozen; **alimento** ~ frozen food

congelador (koang-khay-lah-*dhoar*) m deep-freeze

congelar (koang-khay-*lahr*) v *freeze

congestión (koang-khayss-*t*ᵞoan) f jam

congregación (koang-gray-gah-*th*ᵞoan) f congregation

congreso (koang-*gray*-soa) m congress

conjetura (koang-khay-*too*-rah) f guess

conjeturar (koang-khay-too-*rahr*) v guess

conjuración (koang-khoo-rah-*th^yoan*) *f* plot

conmemoración (koan-may-moa-rah-*th^yoan*) *f* commemoration

conmovedor (koan-moa-bhay-*dhoar*) *adj* touching

*****conmover** (koan-moa-*bhayr*) *v* move

connotación (koan-noa-tah-*th^yoan*) *f* connotation

*****conocer** (koa-noa-*thayr*) *v* *know

conocido (koa-noa-*thee*-dhoa) *m* acquaintance

conocimiento (koa-noa-thee-*m^yayn*-toa) *m* knowledge

conquista (koang-*keess*-tah) *f* conquest, capture

conquistador (koang-keess-tah-*dhoar*) *m* conqueror

conquistar (koang-keess-*tahr*) *v* conquer, capture

consciente (koan-*th^yayn*-tay) *adj* conscious, aware

consecuencia (koan-say-*kwayn*-th^yah) *f* consequence, result; issue

*****conseguir** (koan-say-*geer*) *v* *get; *make, obtain

consejero (koan-say-*khay*-roa) *m* counsellor; councillor

consejo (koan-*say*-khoa) *m* advice, counsel; council, board

consentimiento (koan-sayn-tee-*m^yayn*-toa) *m* consent; approval

*****consentir** (koan-sayn-*teer*) *v* agree, consent

conserje (koan-*sayr*-khay) *m* concierge, janitor

conservación (koan-sayr-bhah-*th^yoan*) *f* preservation

conservador (koan-sayr-bhah-*dhoar*) *adj* conservative

conservar (koan-sayr-*bhahr*) *v* preserve

conservas (koan-*sayr*-bhahss) *fpl* tinned food

conservatorio (koan-sayr-bhah-*toa*-r^yoa) *m* music academy

considerable (koan-see-dhay-*rah*-bhlay) *adj* considerable

consideración (koan-see-dhay-rah-*th^yoan*) *f* consideration

considerado (koan-see-dhay-*rah*-dhoa) *adj* considerate

considerando (koan-see-dhay-*rahn*-doa) *prep* considering

considerar (koan-see-dhay-*rahr*) *v* regard, consider; *think over; count, reckon

consigna (koan-*seeg*-nah) *f* left luggage office

por consiguiente (poar koan-see-*g^yayn*-tay) consequently

consistir en (koan-seess-*teer*) consist of

*****consolar** (koan-soa-*lahr*) *v* comfort

consorcio (koan-*soar*-th^yoa) *m* concern

conspirar (koans-pee-*rahr*) *v* conspire

constante (koans-*tahn*-tay) *adj* even, constant; steadfast

constar de (koans-*tahr*) consist of

constitución (koans-tee-too-*th^yoan*) *f* constitution

*****constituir** (koans-tee-*tweer*) *v* constitute; represent

construcción (koans-trook-*th^yoan*) *f* construction

*****construir** (koans-*trweer*) *v* construct, *build

consuelo (koan-*sway*-loa) *m* comfort

cónsul (*koan*-sool) *m* consul

consulado (koan-soo-*lah*-dhoa) *m* consulate

consulta (koan-*sool*-tah) *f* consultation

consultar (koan-sool-*tahr*) *v* consult

consultorio (koan-sool-*toa*-r^yoa) *m* surgery

consumidor (koan-soo-mee-*dhoar*) *m* consumer

consumir (koan-soo-*meer*) *v* use up

contacto (koan-*tahk*-toa) *m* contact; touch

contador (koan-tah-*dhoar*) *m* meter

contagioso (koan-tah-*khᵛoa*-soa) *adj* infectious, contagious

contaminación (koan-tah-mee-nah-*thᵛoan*) *f* pollution

*****contar** (koan-*tahr*) *v* count; relate, *tell; ~ con* rely on

contemplar (koan-taym-*plahr*) *v* contemplate

contemporáneo (koan-taym-poa-*rah*-nay-oa) *adj* contemporary; *m* contemporary

contenedor (koan-tay-nay-*dhoar*) *m* container

*****contener** (koan-tay-*nayr*) *v* contain; restrain

contenido (koan-tay-*nee*-dhoa) *m* contents *pl*

contentar (koan-tayn-*tahr*) *v* satisfy

contento (koan-*tayn*-toa) *adj* happy, glad, content, joyful; pleased

contestar (koan-tayss-*tahr*) *v* answer

contienda (koan-*tᵛayn*-dah) *f* dispute

contiguo (koan-*tee*-gwoa) *adj* neighbouring

continental (koan-tee-nayn-*tahl*) *adj* continental

continente (koan-tee-*nayn*-tay) *m* continent

continuación (koan-tee-nwah-*thᵛoan*) *f* sequel

continuamente (koan-tee-nwah-*mayn*-tay) *adv* all the time, continually

continuar (koan-tee-*nwahr*) *v* *go on, *go ahead; carry on, continue, *keep on; *keep

continuo (koan-*tee*-nwoa) *adj* continuous, continual

contorno (koan-*toar*-noa) *m* outline, contour

contra (*koan*-trah) *prep* against, versus

contrabandear (koan-trah-bhahn-day-*ahr*) *v* smuggle

*****contradecir** (koan-trah-dhay-*theer*) *v* contradict

contradictorio (koan-trah-dheek-*toa*-rᵛoa) *adj* contradictory

contrahecho (koan-trah-*ay*-choa) *adj* deformed

contralto (koan-*trahl*-toa) *m* alto

contrario (koan-*trah*-rᵛoa) *adj* opposite, contrary; *m* contrary, reverse; *al ~* on the contrary

contraste (koan-*trahss*-tay) *m* contrast

contratiempo (koan-trah-*tᵛaym*-poa) *m* misfortune

contratista (koan-trah-*teess*-tah) *m* contractor

contrato (koan-*trah*-toa) *m* agreement, contract

contribución (koan-tree-bhoo-*thᵛoan*) *f* contribution

*****contribuir** (koan-tree-*bhweer*) *v* contribute

contrincante (koan-treeng-*kahn*-tay) *m* opponent

control (koan-*troal*) *m* inspection, control

controlar (koan-troa-*lahr*) *v* check, control

controvertible (koan-troa-bhayr-*tee*-bhlay) *adj* controversial

controvertido (koan-troa-bhayr-*tee*-dhoa) *adj* controversial

convencer (koam-bayn-*thayr*) *v* convince, persuade; convict

convencimiento (koam-bayn-thee-*mᵛayn*-toa) *m* conviction

conveniente (koam-bay-*nᵛayn*-tay) *adj* adequate, proper; convenient

convenio (koam-*bay*-nᵛoa) *m* settlement

*****convenir** (koam-bay-*neer*) *v* agree; fit, suit

convento (koam-*bayn*-toa) *m* cloister,

convent; nunnery

conversación (koam-bayr-sah-*th^yoan*) *f* conversation, talk, discussion

*****convertir** (koam-bayr-*teer*) *v* convert; *****convertirse en** turn into

convicción (koam-beek-*th^yoan*) *f* persuasion

convidar (koam-bee-*dhahr*) *v* invite

convulsión (koam-bool-*s^yoan*) *f* convulsion

cónyuges (*koan-^yoo*-khayss) *mpl* married couple

coñac (koa-*ñahk*) *m* cognac

cooperación (koa-oa-pay-rah-*th^yoan*) *f* co-operation

cooperador (koa-oa-pay-rah-*dhoar*) *adj* co-operative

cooperativa (koa-oa-pay-rah-*tee*-bhah) *f* co-operative

cooperativo (koa-oa-pay-rah-*tee*-bhoa) *adj* co-operative

coordinación (koa-oar-dhee-nah-*th^yoan*) *f* co-ordination

coordinar (koa-oar-dhee-*nahr*) *v* co-ordinate

copa (*koa*-pah) *f* cup

copia (*koa*-p^yah) *f* copy, carbon copy

copiar (koa-*p^yahr*) *v* copy

coraje (koa-*rah*-khay) *m* guts

coral (koa-*rahl*) *m* coral

corazón (koa-rah-*thoan*) *m* heart; core

corbata (koar-*bhah*-tah) *f* tie, necktie; ~ **de lazo** bow tie

corbatín (koar-bhah-*teen*) *m* bow tie

corcino (koar-*thee*-noa) *m* fawn

corcho (koar-choa) *m* cork

cordel (koar-*dhayl*) *m* string

cordero (koar-*dhay*-roa) *m* lamb

cordial (koar-*dh^yahl*) *adj* cordial, hearty, sympathetic

cordillera (koar-dhee-*l^yay*-rah) *f* mountain range

cordón (koar-*dhoan*) *m* cord, line; lace, shoe-lace; ~ **de extensión** extension cord; ~ **flexible** flex

cornamenta (koar-nah-*mayn*-tah) *f* antlers *pl*

corneja (koar-*nay*-khah) *f* crow

coro (*koa*-roa) *m* choir

corona (koa-*roa*-nah) *f* crown

coronar (koa-roa-*nahr*) *v* crown

coronel (koa-roa-*nayl*) *m* colonel

corpulento (koar-poo-*layn*-toa) *adj* corpulent, stout

corral (koa-*rrahl*) *m* yard; **aves de** ~ poultry

correa (koa-*rray*-ah) *f* leash, strap; ~ **del ventilador** fan belt; ~ **de reloj** watch-strap

corrección (koa-rrayk-*th^yoan*) *f* correction

correcto (koa-*rrayk*-toa) *adj* correct; right

corredor (koa-rray-*dhoar*) *m* broker; bookmaker; ~ **de casas** house agent

*****corregir** (koa-rray-*kheer*) *v* correct

correo (koa-*rray*-oa) *m* post, mail; ~ **aéreo** airmail; **enviar por** ~ mail; **sello de correos** postage stamp

correr (koa-*rrayr*) *v* *run; dash; flow

correspondencia (koa-rrayss-poan-*dayn*-th^yah) *f* correspondence

corresponder (koa-rrayss-poan-*dayr*) *v* correspond; **corresponderse** *v* correspond

corresponsal (koa-rrayss-poan-*sahl*) *m* correspondent

corrida de toros (koa-*rree*-dhah day toa-roass) *f* bullfight

corriente (koa-*rr^yayn*-tay) *adj* current; regular, customary, plain; *f* current; stream; ~ **alterna** alternating current; ~ **continua** direct current; ~ **de aire** draught

corromper (koa-rroam-*payr*) *v* corrupt

corrupción (koa-rroop-*th^yoan*) *f* corruption

corrupto (koa-*rroop*-toa) *adj* corrupt

corsé (koar-*say*) *m* corset

cortadura (koar-tah-*dhoo*-rah) *f* cut

cortaplumas (koar-tah-*ploo*-mahss) *m* penknife

cortar (koar-*tahr*) *v* *cut; chip, *cut off

corte (*koar*-tay) *f* court

cortés (koar-*tayss*) *adj* civil, courteous, polite

corteza (koar-*tay*-thah) *f* bark; crust

cortijo (koar-*tee*-khoa) *m* farmhouse

cortina (koar-*tee*-nah) *f* curtain

corto (*koar*-toa) *adj* short

cortocircuito (koar-toa-theer-*kwee*-toa) *m* short circuit

cosa (*koa*-sah) *f* thing; **entre otras cosas** among other things

cosecha (koa-*say*-chah) *f* harvest, crop

coser (koa-*sayr*) *v* sew

cosméticos (koaz-*may*-tee-koass) *mpl* cosmetics *pl*

cosquillear (koass-kee-*lyahr*) *v* tickle

costa (*koass*-tah) *f* coast

***costar** (koass-*tahr*) *v* *cost

coste (*koass*-tay) *m* cost

costilla (koass-*tee*-lyah) *f* rib

costoso (koass-*toa*-soa) *adj* expensive

costumbre (koass-*toom*-bray) *f* custom; **costumbres** morals

costura (koass-*too*-rah) *f* seam; **sin ~** seamless

cotidiano (koa-tee-*dhyah*-noa) *adj* everyday

cotorra (koa-*toa*-rrah) *f* parakeet

cráneo (*krah*-nay-oa) *m* skull

cráter (*krah*-tayr) *m* crater

creación (kray-ah-*thyoan*) *f* creation

crear (kray-*ahr*) *v* create

***crecer** (kray-*thayr*) *v* *grow

crecimiento (kray-thee-*myayn*-toa) *m* growth

crédito (*kray*-dhee-toa) *m* credit

crédulo (*kray*-dhoo-loa) *adj* credulous

creencia (kray-*ayn*-thyah) *f* belief

***creer** (kray-*ayr*) *v* believe; guess, reckon

crema (*kray*-mah) *f* cream; **~ de afeitar** shaving-cream; **~ de base** foundation cream; **~ de noche** night-cream; **~ facial** face-cream; **~ hidratante** moisturizing cream; **~ para la piel** skin cream; **~ para las manos** hand cream

cremallera (kray-mah-*lyay*-rah) *f* zip

cremoso (kray-*moa*-soa) *adj* creamy

crepúsculo (kray-*pooss*-koo-loa) *m* twilight, dusk

crespo (*krayss*-poa) *adj* curly

cresta (*krayss*-tah) *f* ridge

creta (*kray*-tah) *f* chalk

criada (*kryah*-dhah) *f* housemaid

criado (*kryah*-dhoa) *m* servant

criar (kryahr) *v* rear; raise

criatura (kryah-*too*-rah) *f* creature; infant

crimen (*kree*-mayn) *m* crime

criminal (kree-mee-*nahl*) *adj* criminal; *m* criminal

criminalidad (kree-mee-nah-lee-*dhahdh*) *f* criminality

crisis (*kree*-seess) *f* crisis

cristal (kreess-*tahl*) *m* crystal; pane; **de ~** crystal

cristiano (kreess-*tyah*-noa) *adj* Christian; *m* Christian

Cristo (*kreess*-toa) Christ

criterio (kree-*tay*-ryoa) *m* criterion

crítica (*kree*-tee-kah) *f* criticism

criticar (kree-tee-*kahr*) *v* criticize

crítico (*kree*-tee-koa) *adj* critical; *m* critic

cromo (*kroa*-moa) *m* chromium

crónica (*kroa*-nee-kah) *f* chronicle

crónico (*kroa*-nee-koa) *adj* chronic

cronológico (kroa-noa-*loa*-khee-koa) *adj* chronological

cruce (*kroo*-thay) *m* crossroads; **~ pa-**

ra peatones pedestrian crossing; crosswalk *nAm*

crucero (kroo-*thay*-roa) *m* cruise

crucificar (kroo-thee-fee-*kahr*) *v* crucify

crucifijo (kroo-thee-*fee*-khoa) *m* crucifix

crucifixión (kroo-thee-feek-sᵛoan) *f* crucifixion

crudo (*kroo*-dhoa) *adj* raw

cruel (krwayl) *adj* harsh, cruel

crujido (kroo-*khee*-dhoa) *m* crack

crujiente (kroo-khᵛayn-tay) *adj* crisp

crujir (kroo-*kheer*) *v* creak, crack

cruz (krooth) *f* cross

cruzada (kroo-*thah*-dhah) *f* crusade

cruzar (kroo-*thahr*) *v* cross

cuadrado (kwah-*dhrah*-dhoa) *adj* square; *m* square

cuadriculado (kwah-dhree-koo-*lah*-dhoa) *adj* chequered

cuadro (*kwah*-dhroa) *m* cadre; picture; **a cuadros** chequered; ~ **de distribución** switchboard

cuál (kwahl) *pron* which

cualidad (kwah-lee-*dhahdh*) *f* property

cualquiera (kwahl-kᵛay-rah) *pron* anyone, anybody; whichever; **cualquier cosa** anything

cuando (*kwahn*-doa) *conj* when; ~ **quiera que** whenever

cuándo (*kwahn*-doa) *adv* when

cuánto (*kwahn*-toa) *adv* how much; how many; **cuanto más … más** the … the; **en cuanto a** as regards

cuarenta (kwah-*rayn*-tah) *num* forty

cuarentena (kwah-rayn-*tay*-nah) *f* quarantine

cuartel (kwahr-*tayl*) *m* barracks *pl*; ~ **general** headquarters *pl*

cuarterón (kwahr-tay-*roan*) *m* panel

cuarto¹ (*kwahr*-toa) *num* fourth; *m* quarter; ~ **de hora** quarter of an hour

cuarto² (*kwahr*-toa) *m* chamber; ~ **de aseo** lavatory; washroom *nAm*; ~ **de baño** bathroom; ~ **de niños** nursery; ~ **para huéspedes** spare room

cuatro (*kwah*-troa) *num* four

Cuba (*koo*-bhah) *f* Cuba

cubano (koo-*bhah*-noa) *adj* Cuban; *m* Cuban

cubierta (koo-bhᵛayr-tah) *f* cover; deck

cubierto (koo-bhᵛayr-toa) *adj* cloudy

cubiertos (koo-bhᵛayr-toass) *mpl* cutlery

cubo (*koo*-bhoa) *m* cube; ~ **de la basura** dustbin

cubrir (koo-*bhreer*) *v* cover

cuclillo (koo-klee-lᵛoa) *m* cuckoo

cuchara (koo-*chah*-rah) *f* spoon; soup-spoon, tablespoon

cucharada (koo-chah-*rah*-dhah) *f* spoonful

cucharadita (koo-chah-rah-*dhee*-tah) *f* teaspoonful

cucharilla (koo-chah-*ree*-lᵛah) *f* tea-spoon

cuchillo (koo-*chee*-lᵛoa) *m* knife

cuello (*kway*-lᵛoa) *m* neck; collar; ~ **de botella** bottleneck

cuenta (*kwayn*-tah) *f* account; bill; check *nAm*; bead; ~ **de banco** bank account; *darse ~ *see

cuento (*kwayn*-toa) *m* story, tale

cuerda (*kwayr*-dhah) *f* cord; string; *dar ~ *wind

cuerno (*kwayr*-noa) *m* horn

cuero (*kway*-roa) *m* leather; ~ **vacuno** cow-hide

cuerpo (*kwayr*-poa) *m* body

cuervo (*kwayr*-bhoa) *m* raven

cuestión (kwayss-tᵛoan) *f* matter, issue, question

cueva (*kway*-bhah) *f* cavern, cave; wine-cellar

cuidado (kwee-*dhah*-dhoa) m care;
*tener ~ watch out, look out
cuidadoso (kwee-dhah-*dhoa*-soa) adj
careful; diligent
cuidar de (kwee-*dhahr*) attend to, look
after, tend, *take care of
culebra (koo-*lay*-bhrah) f snake
culpa (*kool*-pah) f guilt, fault, blame
culpable (kool-*pah*-bhlay) adj guilty
culpar (kool-*pahr*) v blame
cultivar (kool-tee-*bhahr*) v cultivate;
*grow, raise
cultivo (kool-*tee*-bhoa) m cultivation
culto (*kool*-toa) adj cultured; m worship
cultura (kool-*too*-rah) f culture
cultural (kool-too-*rahl*) adj cultural
cumbre (*koom*-bray) f peak
cumpleaños (koom-play-*ah*-ñoass) m
birthday
cumplimentar (koom-plee-mayn-*tahr*)
v compliment
cumplimiento (koom-plee-*mʸayn*-toa)
m compliment
cumplir (koom-*pleer*) v accomplish
cuna (*koo*-nah) f cradle; ~ de viaje
carry-cot
cuneta (koo-*nay*-tah) f ditch; gutter
cuña (*koo*-ñah) f wedge
cuñada (koo-*ñah*-dhah) f sister-in-law
cuñado (koo-*ñah*-dhoa) m brother-in-
law
cuota (*kwoa*-tah) f quota
cupón (koo-*poan*) m coupon
cúpula (*koo*-poo-lah) f dome
cura (*koo*-rah) m priest; f cure
curación (koo-rah-*thʸoan*) f cure, recovery
curandero (koo-rahn-*day*-roa) m quack
curar (koo-*rahr*) v cure, heal; **curarse**
v recover
curato (koo-*rah*-toa) m parsonage
curiosidad (koo-rʸoa-see-*dhahdh*) f
curiosity; sight; curio

curioso (koo-*rʸoa*-soa) adj curious; inquisitive; quaint
cursiva (koor-*see*-bhah) f italics pl
curso (*koor*-soa) m course; lecture; ~
intensivo intensive course
curva (koor-bhah) f turn, curve, bend
curvado (koor-*bhah*-dhoa) adj curved
curvo (*koor*-bhoa) adj crooked, bent
custodia (kooss-*toa*-dhʸah) f custody
cuyo (*koo*-ʸoa) pron whose; of which

CH

chabacano (chah-bhah-*kah*-noa) mMe
apricot
chal (chahl) m shawl
chaleco (chah-*lay*-koa) m waistcoat;
vest nAm; ~ salvavidas lifebelt
chalet (chah-*layt*) m chalet
champán (chahm-*pahn*) m champagne
champú (chahm-*poo*) m shampoo
chantaje (chahn-*tah*-khay) m blackmail; *hacer ~ blackmail
chapa (*chah*-pah) f plate, sheet
chaparrón (chah-pah-*rroan*) m cloud-
burst
chapucero (chah-poo-*thay*-roa) adj
sloppy
chaqueta (chah-*kay*-tah) f jacket; cardigan; ~ ligera blazer
charanga (chah-*rahng*-gah) f brass
band
charco (*chahr*-koa) m puddle
charla (*chahr*-lah) f chat
charlar (chahr-*lahr*) v chat
charlatán (chahr-lah-*tahn*) m chatterbox; quack
charola (chah-*roa*-lah) fMe tray
chasis (chah-*seess*) m chassis
chatarra (chah-*tah*-rrah) f scrap-iron
checo (*chay*-koa) adj Czech; m Czech

cheque (*chay*-kay) *m* cheque; check *nAm*; ~ **de viajero** traveller's cheque

chicle (*chee*-klay) *m* chewing-gum

chico (*chee*-koa) *m* boy; kid

chichón (chee-*choan*) *m* lump

Chile (*chee*-lay) *m* Chile

chileno (chee-*lay*-noa) *adj* Chilean; *m* Chilean

chillar (chee-*lʸahr*) *v* scream, shriek

chillido (chee-*lʸee*-dhoa) *m* scream, shriek

chimenea (chee-may-*nay*-ah) *f* chimney; fireplace

China (*chee*-nah) *f* China

chinche (*cheen*-chay) *f* bug; drawing-pin; thumbtack *nAm*

chinchorro (cheen-*choa*-rroa) *m* dinghy

chino (*chee*-noa) *adj* Chinese; *m* Chinese; *adjMe* curly

chisguete (cheez-*gay*-tay) *m* squirt

chisme (*cheez*-may) *m* gossip; *contar chismes** gossip

chispa (*cheess*-pah) *f* spark

chistoso (cheess-*toa*-soa) *adj* witty, humorous

chocante (choa-*kahn*-tay) *adj* revolting, shocking

chocar (choa-*kahr*) *v* collide, crash, bump; shock; ~ **contra** knock against

chocolate (choa-koa-*lah*-tay) *m* chocolate

chófer (*choa*-fayr) *m* chauffeur

choque (*choa*-kay) *m* crash; shock

chorro (*choa*-rroa) *m* spout, jet

chuleta (choo-*lay*-tah) *f* chop, cutlet

chupar (choo-*pahr*) *v* suck

D

dactilógrafa (dahk-tee-*loa*-grah-fah) *f* typist

dadivoso (dah-dhee-*bhoa*-soa) *adj* liberal

daltoniano (dahl-toa-*nʸah*-noa) *adj* colour-blind

dama (*dah*-mah) *f* lady

danés (dah-*nayss*) *adj* Danish; *m* Dane

dañar (dah-*ñahr*) *v* damage; *hurt*

daño (*dah*-ñoa) *m* mischief; harm; *hacer** ~ *hurt*

dañoso (dah-*ñoa*-soa) *adj* harmful

dar (dahr) *v* *give*; **dado que** supposing that

dátil (*dah*-teel) *m* date

dato (*dah*-toa) *m* data *pl*

de (day) *prep* of; out of, from, off; with

debajo (day-*bhah*-khoa) *adv* underneath, beneath, below; ~ **de** under, beneath, below

debate (day-*bhah*-tay) *m* debate, discussion

debatir (day-bhah-*teer*) *v* discuss

debe (*day*-bhay) *m* debit

deber (day-*bhayr*) *m* duty; *v* *have to*, need to, need; owe; ~ **de** *be* bound to

debido (day-*bhee*-dhoa) *adj* due; proper; ~ **a** owing to

débil (*day*-bheel) *adj* faint, weak, feeble

debilidad (day-bhee-lee-*dhahdh*) *f* weakness

decencia (day-*thayn*-thʸah) *f* decency

decente (day-*thayn*-tay) *adj* decent

decepcionar (day-thayp-thʸoa-*nahr*) *v* *let down*, disappoint

decidir (day-thee-*dheer*) *v* decide; **de-**

cidido resolute

décimo (day-thee-moa) *num* tenth

decimoctavo (day-thee-moak-*tah*-bhoa) *num* eighteenth

decimonono (day-thee-moa-*noa*-noa) *num* nineteenth

decimoséptimo (day-thee-moa-*sayp*-tee-moa) *num* seventeenth

decimosexto (day-thee-moa-*sayks*-toa) *num* sixteenth

*decir (day-*theer*) *v* *say, *tell; ***querer** ~ *mean

decisión (day-thee-s*ʸoan*) *f* decision

decisivo (day-thee-*see*-bhoa) *adj* decisive

declaración (day-klah-rah-*thʸoan*) *f* statement, declaration

declarar (day-klah-*rahr*) *v* state, declare

decoración (day-koa-rah-*thʸoan*) *f* decoration

decorativo (day-koa-rah-*tee*-bhoa) *adj* decorative

decreto (day-*kray*-toa) *m* decree

dedal (day-*dhahl*) *m* thimble

dédalo (*day*-dhah-loa) *m* muddle

dedicar (day-dhee-*kahr*) *v* devote, dedicate

dedo (*day*-dhoa) *m* finger; ~ **auricular** little finger; ~ **del pie** toe

*deducir (day-dhoo-*theer*) *v* infer, deduce; deduct

defecto (day-*fayk*-toa) *m* fault

defectuoso (day-fayk-*twoa*-soa) *adj* defective, faulty

*defender (day-fayn-*dayr*) *v* defend

defensa (day-*fayn*-sah) *f* defence; plea; *fMe* fender

defensor (day-fayn-*soar*) *m* champion

deficiencia (day-fee-*thʸayn*-thʸah) *f* deficiency, shortcoming

déficit (*day*-fee-theet) *m* deficit

definición (day-fee-nee-*thʸoan*) *f* definition

definir (day-fee-*neer*) *v* define; **definido** definite

definitivo (day-fee-nee-*tee*-bhoa) *adj* definitive

deforme (day-*foar*-may) *adj* deformed

dejar (day-*khahr*) *v* *let, *leave; *leave behind, desert; ~ **de** stop

delantal (day-lahn-*tahl*) *m* apron

delante de (day-*lahn*-tay day) before, in front of, ahead of

delegación (day-lay-gah-*thʸoan*) *f* delegation

delegado (day-lay-*gah*-dhoa) *m* delegate

deleitable (day-lay-*tah*-bhlay) *adj* enjoyable

deleite (day-*lay*-tay) *m* delight

deleitoso (day-lay-*toa*-soa) *adj* delightful

deletrear (day-lay-tray-*ahr*) *v* *spell

deletreo (day-lay-*tray*-oa) *m* spelling

delgado (dayl-*gah*-dhoa) *adj* thin

deliberación (day-lee-bhay-rah-*thʸoan*) *f* deliberation

deliberar (day-lee-bhay-*rahr*) *v* deliberate; **deliberado** *adj* deliberate

delicado (day-lee-*kah*-dhoa) *adj* delicate, tender

delicia (day-*lee*-thʸah) *f* joy, delight

delicioso (day-lee-*thʸoa*-soa) *adj* wonderful, delightful, delicious, lovely

delincuente (day-leeng-*kwayn*-tay) *m* criminal

delito (day-*lee*-toa) *m* crime

demanda (day-*mahn*-dah) *f* request; application; demand

demás (day-*mahss*) *adj* remaining

demasiado (day-mah-s*ʸah*-dhoa) *adv* too

democracia (day-moa-*krah*-thʸah) *f* democracy

democrático (day-moa-*krah*-tee-koa) *adj* democratic

*demoler (day-moa-*layr*) *v* demolish

demolición (day-moa-lee-*th^yoan*) *f* demolition

demonio (day-*moa*-n^yoa) *m* devil

demostración (day-moass-trah-*th^yoan*) *f* demonstration

*demostrar (day-moass-*trahr*) *v* demonstrate, *show, prove

*denegar (day-nay-*gahr*) *v* deny

denominación (day-noa-mee-nah-*th^yoan*) *f* denomination

denso (*dayn*-soa) *adj* thick, dense

dentadura postiza (dayn-tah-*dhoo*-rah poass-*tee*-thah) false teeth, denture

dentista (dayn-*teess*-tah) *m* dentist

dentro (*dayn*-troa) *adv* inside; **de ~** within; **~ de** inside, within; into; in

departamento (day-pahr-tah-*mayn*-toa) *m* department; section, division

depender de (day-payn-*dayr*) depend on

dependiente (day-payn-*d^yayn*-tay) *adj* dependant; *m* shop assistant

deporte (day-*poar*-tay) *m* sport; **conjunto de ~** sportswear; **chaqueta de ~** sports-jacket

deportista (day-poar-*teess*-tah) *m* sportsman

depositar (day-poa-see-*tahr*) *v* bank

depósito (day-*poa*-see-toa) *m* deposit; **~ de gasolina** petrol tank

depresión (day-pray-s^yoan*) *f* depression

deprimente (day-pree-*mayn*-tay) *adj* depressing

deprimir (day-pree-*meer*) *v* depress; **deprimido** blue, depressed, low

derecho (day-*ray*-choa) *m* right; law, right, justice, straight; *adj* upright; right-hand; **~ administrativo** administrative law; **~ civil** civil law; **~ comercial** commercial law; **~ electoral** franchise, suffrage; **~ penal** criminal law

derivar de (day-ree-*bhahr*) *be derived from

derramar (day-rrah-*mahr*) *v* *shed

derribar (day-rree-*bhahr*) *v* knock down

derrochador (day-rroa-chah-*dhoar*) *adj* wasteful

derrota (day-*rroa*-tah) *f* defeat

derrotar (day-rroa-*tahr*) *v* defeat

derrumbarse (day-rroom-*bahr*-say) *v* collapse

desabotonar (day-sah-bhoa-toa-*nahr*) *v* unbutton

desacelerar (day-sah-thay-lay-*rahr*) *v* slow down

desacostumbrado (day-sah-koass-toom-*brah*-dhoa) *adj* unaccustomed

desacostumbrar (day-sah-koass-toom-*brahr*) *v* unlearn

desafiar (day-sah-*f^yahr*) *v* dare; challenge

desafilado (day-sah-fee-*lah*-dhoa) *adj* blunt

desafortunado (day-sah-foar-too-*nah*-dhoa) *adj* unlucky, unfortunate

desagradable (day-sah-grah-*dhah*-bhlay) *adj* nasty, disagreeable, unpleasant; unkind

desagradar (day-sah-grah-*dhahr*) *v* displease

desagüe (day-*sah*-gway) *m* sewer, drain

desaliñado (day-sah-lee-*ñah*-doa) *adj* untidy

desamueblado (day-sah-mway-*bhlah*-dhoa) *adj* unfurnished

desánimo (day-*sah*-nee-moa) *m* depression

*desaparecer (day-sah-pah-ray-*thayr*) *v* disappear; vanish

desaparecido (day-sah-pah-ray-*thee*-dhoa) *adj* lost; *m* missing person

desapasionado (day-sah-pah-s^yoa-*nah*-dhoa) *adj* matter-of-fact

*desaprobar (day-sah-proa-*bhahr*) *v*

disapprove

desarrollar (day-sah-rroa-*l*ʸ*ahr*) *v* develop

desarrollo (day-sah-*rroa*-lʸoa) *m* development

desasosiego (day-sah-soa-*s*ʸ*ay*-goa) *m* unrest

desastre (day-*sahss*-tray) *m* disaster, calamity

desastroso (day-sahss-*troa*-soa) *adj* disastrous

desatar (day-sah-*tahr*) *v* *undo, untie, unfasten

desautorizado (day-sou toa-ree-*thah*-dhoa) *adj* unauthorized

desayuno (day-sah-ʸoo-noa) *m* breakfast

descafeinado (dayss-kah-fay-*nah*-dhoa) *adj* decaffeinated

descansar (dayss-kahn-*sahr*) *v* rest; relax

descanso (dayss-*kahn*-soa) *m* rest; break; half-time

descarado (dayss-kah-*rah* dhoa) *adj* bold, impertinent

descargar (dayss-kahr-*gahr*) *v* discharge, unload

descendencia (day-thayn-*dayn*-thʸah) *f* origin

* **descender** (day-thayn-*dhayr*) *v* *fall

descendiente (day-thayn-dʸ*ayn*-tay) *m* descendant

descolorido (dayss-koa-loa-*ree*-dhoa) *adj* discoloured

descompostura (dayss-koam-poass-*too*-rah) *fMe* breakdown

* **desconcertar** (dayss-koan-thayr-*tahr*) *v* overwhelm, embarrass

desconectar (dayss-koa-nayk-*tahr*) *v* disconnect

desconfiado (dayss-koan-fʸ*ah*-dhoa) *adj* suspicious

desconfianza (dayss-koan-fʸ*ahn*-thah) *f* suspicion

desconfiar de (dayss-koan-fʸ*ahr*) *v* mistrust

descongelarse (dayss-koang-khay-*lahr*-say) *v* thaw

* **desconocer** (dayss-koa-noa-*thayr*) *v* not to *know, fail to recognize

desconocido (dayss-koa-noa-*thee*-dhoa) *adj* unknown; unfamiliar

descontento (dayss-koan-*tayn*-toa) *adj* discontented

descorchar (dayss-koar-*chahr*) *v* uncork

descortés (dayss koar-*tayss*) *adj* impolite

describir (dayss-kree-*bheer*) *v* describe

descripción (dayss-kreep-thʸ*oan*) *f* description

descubrimiento (dayss-koo-bhree-mʸ*ayn*-toa) *m* discovery

descubrir (dayss-koo-*bhreer*) *v* discover, detect

descuento (dayss-*kwayn*-toa) *m* discount; ~ **bancario** bank-rate

descuidar (dayss-kwee-*dhahr*) *v* neglect; **descuidado** slovenly

descuido (dayss-*kwee*-dhoa) *m* oversight

desde (*dayz*-dhay) *prep* from; since; ~ **entonces** since; ~ **que** since

desdén (dayz-*dhayn*) *m* disdain

desdichado (dayz-dhee-*chah*-dhoa) *adj* unhappy

deseable (day-say-*ah*-bhlay) *adj* desirable

desear (day-say-*ahr*) *v* desire; wish, want

desecar (day-say-*kahr*) *v* drain

desechable (day-say-*chah*-bhlay) *adj* disposable

desechar (day-say-*chahr*) *v* discard

desecho (day-*say*-choa) *m* refuse

desembarcar (day-saym-bahr-*kahr*) *v* disembark; land

desembocadura (day-saym-boa-kah-

dhoo-rah) f mouth

desempaquetar (day-saym-pah-kay-*tahr*) v unpack

desempeñar (day-saym-pay-*ñahr*) v perform

desempleo (day-saym-*play*-oa) m unemployment

desengaño (day-sayng-*gah*-ñoa) m disappointment

desenvoltura (day-saym-boal-*too*-rah) f ease

* **desenvolver** (day-saym-boal-*bhayr*) v unwrap

deseo (day-*say*-oa) m wish, desire

desertar (day-sayr-*tahr*) v desert

desesperación (day-sayss-pay-rah-*th Yoan*) f despair

desesperado (day-sayss-pay-*rah*-dhoa) adj hopeless, desperate; * **estar ~** despair

desfavorable (dayss-fah-bhoa-*rah*-bhlay) adj unfavourable

desfile (dayss-*fee*-lay) m parade

desgarrar (dayz-gah-*rrahr*) v *tear

desgracia (dayz-*grah*-th Yah) f misfortune

desgraciadamente (dayz-grah-th Yah-dhah-*mayn*-tay) adv unfortunately

* **deshacer** (day-sah-*thayr*) v *undo

deshielo (day-s Yay-loa) m thaw

deshilacharse (day-see-lah-*chahr*-say) v fray

deshonesto (day-soa-*nayss*-toa) adj crooked

deshonor (day-soa-*noar*) m disgrace

deshonra (day-soan-rah) f shame

deshuesar (day-sway-*sahr*) v bone

desierto (day-s Yayr-toa) adj desert; m desert

designar (day-seeg-*nahr*) v designate; appoint

desigual (day-see-*gwahl*) adj unequal, uneven

desinclinado (day-seeng-klee-*nah*-

dhoa) adj unwilling

desinfectante (day-seen-fayk-*tahn*-tay) m disinfectant

desinfectar (day-seen-fayk-*tahr*) v disinfect

desinteresado (day-seen-tay-ray-*sah*-dhoa) adj unselfish

desliz (dayz-*leeth*) m slide; slip

deslizarse (dayz-lee-*thahr*-say) v *slide; slip

deslucido (dayz-loo-*thee*-dhoa) adj dim

deslumbrador (dayz-loom-brah-*dhoar*) adj glaring

desmayarse (dayz-mah-Yahr-say) v faint

desnudarse (dayz-noo-*dhahr*-say) v undress

desnudo (dayz-*noo*-dhoa) adj naked, nude, bare; m nude

desnutrición (dayz-noo-tree-*th Yoan*) f malnutrition

desocupado (day-soa-koo-*pah*-dhoa) adj unoccupied; unemployed

desodorante (day-soa-dhoa-*rahn*-tay) m deodorant

desorden (day-*soar*-dayn) m disorder; mess

despachar (dayss-pah-*chahr*) v dispatch, despatch, *send off

despacho (dayss-*pah*-choa) m study

despedida (dayss-pay-*dhee*-dhah) f parting; departure

* **despedir** (dayss-pay-*dheer*) v dismiss; fire; * **despedirse** v check out

despegar (dayss-pay-*gahr*) v *take off

despegue (dayss-*pay*-gay) m take-off

despensa (dayss-*payn*-sah) f larder

desperdicio (dayss-payr-*dhee*-th Yoa) m litter; waste

despertador (dayss-payr-tah-*dhoar*) m alarm-clock

* **despertar** (dayss-payr-*tahr*) v *wake, *awake; * **despertarse** v wake up

despierto (dayss-p Yayr-toa) adj

awake; vigilant

*desplegar (dayss-play-*gahr*) v unfold; expand

desplomarse (dayss-ploa-*mahr*-say) v collapse

despreciar (dayss-pray-th*y*ahr) v scorn, despise

desprecio (dayss-*pray*-th*y*oa) m scorn, contempt

despreocupado (dayss-pray-oa-koo-*pah*-dhoa) adj carefree

después (dayss-*pwayss*) adv afterwards; then; ~ **de** after; ~ **de que** after

destacado (dayss-tah-*kah*-dhoa) adj outstanding

destacarse (dayss-tah-*kahr*-say) v *stand out

destapar (dayss-tah-*pahr*) v uncover

destartalado (dayss-tahr-tah-*lah*-dhoa) adj ramshackle

destello (dayss-*tay*-l*y*oa) m glare

*desteñirse (dayss-tay-*ñeer*-say) v fade, discolour; **no destiñe** fast-dyed

destinar (dayss-tee-*nahr*) v destine; address

destinatario (dayss-tee-nah-*tah*-r*y*oa) m addressee

destino (dayss-*tee*-noa) m fate, destiny, lot; destination

destornillador (dayss-toar-nee-l*y*ah-*dhoar*) m screw-driver

destornillar (dayss-toar-nee-*l*y*ahr*) v unscrew

destrucción (dayss-trook-th*y*oan) f destruction

*destruir (dayss-*trweer*) v destroy; wreck

desvalorización (dayz-bhah-loa-ree-thah-th*y*oan) f devaluation

desvalorizar (dayz-bhah-loa-ree-*thahr*) v devalue

desvelado (dayz-bhay-*lah*-dhoa) adj

sleepless

desventaja (dayz-bhayn-*tah*-khah) f disadvantage

desviar (dayz-*bh*y*ahr*) v avert; **desviarse** v deviate

desvío (dayz-*bhee*-oa) m detour; diversion

detallado (day-tah-*l*y*ah*-dhoa) adj detailed

detalle (day-*tah*-l*y*ay) m detail; **vender al** ~ retail

detective (day-tayk-*tee*-bhay) m detective

detención (day-tayn-*th*y*oan*) f custody

*detener (day-tay-*nayr*) v detain

detergente (day-tayr-*khayn*-tay) m detergent

determinar (day-tayr-mee-*nahr*) v define, determine; **determinado** definite

detestar (day-tayss-*tahr*) v hate, dislike

detrás (day-*trahss*) adv behind; ~ **de** behind, after

deuda (*day*oo-dhah) f debt

*devolver (day-bhoal-*bhayr*) v *bring back; *send back

día (*dee*-ah) m day; **¡buenos días!** hello!; **de** ~ by day; ~ **de trabajo** working day; ~ **laborable** weekday; **el otro** ~ recently

diabetes (d*y*ah-*bhay*-tayss) f diabetes

diabético (d*y*ah-*bhay*-tee-koa) m diabetic

diablo (*d*y*ah*-bhloa) m devil

diabluras (d*y*ah-*bhloo*-rahss) fpl mischief

diagnosis (d*y*ahg-*noa*-seess) m diagnosis

diagnosticar (d*y*ahg-noass-tee-*kahr*) v diagnose

diagonal (d*y*ah-goa-*nahl*) adj diagonal; f diagonal

dialecto (d*y*ah-*layk*-toa) m dialect

diamante (dᵛah-*mahn*-tay) *m* diamond

diapositiva (dᵛah-poa-see-*tee*-bhah) *f* slide

diario (dᵛah-rᵛoa) *adj* daily; *m* daily, newspaper; diary; **a ~** per day; **~ matutino** morning paper

diarrea (dᵛah-*rray*-ah) *f* diarrhoea

dibujar (dee-bhoo-*khahr*) *v* sketch, *draw

dibujo (dee-*bhoo*-khoa) *m* sketch, drawing; **dibujos animados** cartoon

diccionario (deek-thᵛoa-*nah*-rᵛoa) *m* dictionary

diciembre (dee-*thᵛaym*-bray) December

dictado (deek-*tah*-dhoa) *m* dictation

dictador (deek-tah-*dhoar*) *m* dictator

dictadura (deek-tah-*dhoo*-rah) *f* dictatorship

dictáfono (deek-*tah*-foa-noa) *m* dictaphone

dictar (deek-*tahr*) *v* dictate

dichoso (dee-*choa*-soa) *adj* happy

diecinueve (dᵛay-thee-*nway*-bhay) *num* nineteen

dieciocho (dᵛay-thᵛoa-choa) *num* eighteen

dieciséis (dᵛay-thee-*sayss*) *num* sixteen

diecisiete (dᵛay-thee-sᵛay-tay) *num* seventeen

diente (dᵛayn-tay) *m* tooth; **~ de león** dandelion

diesel (*dee*-sayl) *m* diesel

diestro (dᵛayss-troa) *adj* skilful

diez (dᵛayth) *num* ten

diferencia (dee-fay-*rayn*-thᵛah) *f* difference; contrast, distinction

diferente (dee-fay-*rayn*-tay) *adj* different; unlike

*diferir** (dee-fay-*reer*) *v* vary, differ; delay

difícil (dee-*fee*-theel) *adj* hard, difficult

dificultad (dee-fee-kool-*tahdh*) *f* difficulty

difteria (deef-*tay*-rᵛah) *f* diphtheria

difunto (dee-*foon*-toa) *adj* dead

difuso (dee-*foo*-soa) *adj* dim

digerible (dee-khayss-*tee*-bhlay) *adj* digestible

*digerir** (dee-khay-*reer*) *v* digest

digestión (dee-khayss-*tᵛoan*) *f* digestion

digital (dee-khee-*tahl*) *adj* digital

dignidad (deeg-nee-*dhahdh*) *f* dignity

digno de (*dee*-ño day) worthy of

dilación (dee-lah-*thᵛoan*) *f* delay, respite

diligencia (dee-lee-*khayn*-thᵛah) *f* diligence

diligente (dee-lee-*khayn*-tay) *adj* industrious

*diluir** (dee-*lweer*) *v* dilute

dimensión (dee-mayn-sᵛoan) *f* extent, size

Dinamarca (dee-nah-*mahr*-kah) *f* Denmark

dínamo (*dee*-nah-moa) *f* dynamo

dinero (dee-*nay*-roa) *m* money; **~ contante** cash

dios (dᵛoass) *m* god

diosa (dᵛoa-sah) *f* goddess

diploma (dee-*ploa*-mah) *m* diploma, certificate

diplomático (dee-ploa-*mah*-tee-koa) *m* diplomat

diputado (dee-poo-*tah*-dhoa) *m* deputy; Member of Parliament

dirección (dee-rayk-*thᵛoan*) *f* direction; way; address; leadership, lead; **~ de escena** direction; **~ única** one-way traffic

directamente (dee-rayk-tah-*mayn*-tay) *adv* straight; straight away

directo (dee-*rayk*-toa) *adj* direct

director (dee-rayk-*toar*) *m* director,

manager; conductor; ~ de escuela head teacher, headmaster; principal

directorio telefónico (dee-rayk-*toa*-r^yoa tay-lay-*foa*-nee-koa) *Me* telephone directory

directriz (dee-rayk-*treeth*) *f* directive

dirigir (dee-ree-*kheer*) *v* head; direct

disciplina (dee-thee-*plee*-nah) *f* discipline

discípulo (deess-*thee*-poo-loa) *m* pupil

disco (*deess*-koa) *m* disc; record

disco compacto (*deess*-koa koam-*pahk*-toa) *m* compact disc; **reproductor de ~s ~s** CD player

discreto (deess-*kray*-toa) *adj* inconspicuous

disculpa (deess-*kool*-pah) *f* apology

disculpar (deess-kool-*pahr*) *v* excuse; **disculparse** *v* apologize; ¡disculpe! sorry!

discurso (deess-*koor*-soa) *m* speech

discusión (deess-koo-s^yoan) *f* discussion, argument

discutir (deess koo-*teer*) *v* discuss, deliberate, argue

*****disentir** (dee-sayn-*teer*) *v* disagree

diseñar (dee-say-*ñahr*) *v* design

diseño (dee-*say*-ñoa) *m* design; pattern; **cuaderno de ~** sketch-book

disfraz (deess-*frahth*) *m* disguise

disfrazarse (deess-frah-*thahr*-say) *v* disguise

disfrutar (deess-froo-*tahr*) *v* enjoy

disgustar (deez-gooss-*tahr*) *v* displease

disimular (dee-see-moo-*lahr*) *v* conceal

dislocado (deess-loa-*kah*-dhoa) *adj* dislocated

dislocar (deez-loa-*kahr*) *v* wrench

disminución (deez-mee-noo-th^yoan) *f* decrease

*****disminuir** (deez-mee-*nweer*) *v* reduce, lessen, decrease

*****disolver** (dee-soal-*bhayr*) *v* dissolve

disparar (deess-pah-*rahr*) *v* fire

disparo (deess-*pah*-roa) *m* shot

dispensar (deess-payn-*sahr*) *v* exempt; **~ de** discharge of; ¡dispense usted! sorry!

dispensario (deess-payn-*sah*-r^yoa) *m* health centre

*****disponer** (deess-poa-*nayr*) *v* sort; **~ de** dispose of

disponible (deess-poa-*nee*-bhlay) *adj* available; spare

disposición (deess-poa-see-th^yoan) *f* disposal

dispuesto (deess-*pwayss*-toa) *adj* inclined, willing

disputa (deess-*poo*-tah) *f* dispute, argument, quarrel

disputar (deess-poo-*tahr*) *v* argue, quarrel; dispute

distancia (deess-*tahn*-th^yah) *f* distance; space, way

distinción (deess-teen-*th^yoan*) *f* distinction, difference

distinguido (deess-teeng-*gee*-dhoa) *adj* distinguished, dignified

distinguir (deess-teeng-*geer*) *v* distinguish; **distinguirse** *v* excel

distinto (deess-*teen*-toa) *adj* distinct

distracción (deess-trahk-*th^yoan*) *f* amusement

*****distraer** (deess-trah-*ayr*) *v* distract

distribuidor (deess-tree-bhwee-*dhoar*) *m* distributor

*****distribuir** (deess-tree-*bhweer*) *v* distribute; issue

distrito (deess-*tree*-toa) *m* district; **~ electoral** constituency

disturbio (deess-*toor*-bh^yoa) *m* disturbance

disuadir (dee-swah-*dheer*) *v* dissuade from

diván (dee-*bhahn*) *m* couch

diversión (dee-bhayr-s^yoan) *f* pleasure, fun; diversion, entertainment

diverso (dee-*bhayr*-soa) *adj* diverse

divertido (dee-bhayr-*tee*-dhoa) *adj* amusing, entertaining

*****divertir** (dee-bhayr-*teer*) *v* amuse, entertain

dividir (dee-bhee-*dheer*) *v* divide

divino (dee-*bhee*-noa) *adj* divine

división (dee-bhee-s^y*oan*) *f* division; section

divorciar (dee-bhoar-th^y*ahr*) *v* divorce

divorcio (dee-*bhoar*-th^{y}oa) *m* divorce

dobladillo (doa-bhlah-*dhee*-l^{y}oa) *m* hem

doblar (doa-*bhlahr*) *v* *bend; fold

doble (*doa*-bhlay) *adj* double

doce (*doa*-thay) *num* twelve

docena (doa-*thay*-nah) *f* dozen

doctor (doak-*toar*) *m* doctor

doctrina (doak-*tree*-nah) *f* doctrine

documento (doa-koo-*mayn*-toa) *m* document

*****doler** (doa-*layr*) *v* ache

dolor (doa-*loar*) *m* ache, pain; grief; **dolores** *mpl* labour; **sin ~** painless

dolorido (doa-loa-*ree*-dhoa) *adj* painful

doloroso (doa-loa-*roa*-soa) *adj* sore

domesticado (doa-mayss-tee-*kah*-dhoa) *adj* tame

domesticar (doa-mayss-tee-*kahr*) *v* tame

doméstico (doa-*mayss*-tee-koa) *adj* domestic; **faenas domésticas** housework

domicilio (doa-mee-*thee*-l^{y}oa) *m* domicile

dominación (doa-mee-nah-th^y*oan*) *f* domination

dominante (doa-mee-*nahn*-tay) *adj* leading

dominar (doa-mee-*nahr*) *v* master

domingo (doa-*meeng*-goa) *m* Sunday

dominio (doa-*mee*-n^{y}oa) *m* dominion, rule

don (doan) *m* faculty

donación (doa-nah-th^y*oan*) *f* donation

donante (doa-*nahn*-tay) *m* donor

donar (doa-*nahr*) *v* donate

doncella (doan-*thay*-l^{y}ah) *f* chambermaid

donde (*doan*-day) *conj* where; **en ~ sea** anywhere

dónde (*doan*-day) *adv* where

dondequiera (doan-day-k^y*ay*-rah) *adv* anywhere; **~ que** wherever

dorado (doa-*rah*-dhoa) *adj* gilt; golden

dormido (doar-*mee*-dhoa) *adj* asleep; **quedarse ~** *oversleep

*****dormir** (doar-*meer*) *v* *sleep

dormitorio (doar-mee-toa-r^{y}oa) *m* bedroom; dormitory

dos (doass) *num* two; **~ veces** twice

dosis (*doa*-seess) *f* dose

dotado (doa-*tah*-dhoa) *adj* talented

dragón (drah-*goan*) *m* dragon

drama (*drah*-mah) *m* drama

dramático (drah-*mah*-tee-koa) *adj* dramatic

dramaturgo (drah-mah-*toor*-goa) *m* playwright, dramatist

drenar (dray-*nahr*) *v* drain

droguería (droa-gay-*ree*-ah) *f* chemist's, pharmacy; drugstore *nAm*

ducha (*doo*-chah) *f* shower

duda (*doo*-dhah) *f* doubt; *****poner en ~** query; **sin ~** undoubtedly, without doubt

dudar (doo-*dhahr*) *v* doubt

dudoso (doo-*dhoa*-soa) *adj* doubtful

duelo (*dway*-loa) *m* duel; grief

duende (*dwayn*-dhay) *m* elf

dueña (*dway*-ñah) *f* mistress

dueño (*dway*-ñoa) *m* landlord

dulce (*dool*-thay) *adj* sweet; smooth; *m* sweet; **dulces** cake; sweets; candy *nAm*

duna (*doo*-nah) *f* dune

duodécimo (dwoa-*day*-thee-moa) *num* twelfth

duque (*doo*-kay) *m* duke

duquesa (doo-*kay*-sah) f duchess

duración (doo-rah-*th*ʸ*oan*) f duration

duradero (doo-rah-*dhay*-roa) adj permanent, lasting

durante (doo-*rahn*-tay) prep for, during

durar (doo-*rahr*) v last; continue

duro (*doo*-roa) adj hard; tough

E

ébano (*ay*-bhah-noa) m ebony

eclipse (ay-*kleep*-say) m eclipse

eco (*ay*-koa) m echo

economía (ay-koa-noa-*mee*-ah) f economy

económico (ay-koa-*noa*-mee-koa) adj economic; thrifty, economical; cheap

economista (ay-koa-noa-*meess*-tah) m economist

economizar (ay-koa-noa-mee-*thahr*) v economize

Ecuador (ay-kwah-*dhoar*) m Ecuador

ecuador (ay-kwah-*dhoar*) m equator

ecuatoriano (ay-kwah-toa-*r*ʸ*ah*-noa) m Ecuadorian

eczema (ayk-*thay*-mah) m eczema

echada (ay-*chah*-dhah) f cast

echar (ay-*chahr*) v toss; ~ **al correo** post; ~ **a perder** *spoil; ~ **la culpa** blame

edad (ay-*dhahdh*) f age; **mayor de** ~ of age; **menor de** ~ under age

Edad Media (ay-*dhahdh* may-dhʸah) Middle Ages

edición (ay-dhee-*th*ʸ*oan*) f issue, edition; ~ **de mañana** morning edition

edificar (ay-dhee-fee-*kahr*) v construct

edificio (ay-dhee-*fee*-thʸoa) m construction, building

editor (ay-dhee-*toar*) m publisher

edredón (ay-dhray-*dhoan*) m eiderdown

educación (ay-dhoo-kah-*th*ʸ*oan*) f education

educar (ay-dhoo-*kahr*) v educate, *bring up, raise

efectivamente (ay-fayk-tee-bhah-*mayn*-tay) adv as a matter of fact, in fact

efectivo (ay-fayk-*tee*-bhoa) m cash; *hacer ~ cash

efecto (ay-*fayk*-toa) m effect

efectuar (ay-fayk-*twahr*) v effect; implement

efervescencia (ay-fayr-bhay-*thayn*-thʸah) f fizz

eficacia (ay-fee-*kah*-thʸah) f efficacy

eficaz (ay-fee-*kahth*) adj effective

eficiente (ay-fee-*th*ʸ*ayn*-tay) adj efficient

egipcio (ay-*kheep*-thʸoa) adj Egyptian; m Egyptian

Egipto (ay-*kheep*-toa) m Egypt

egocéntrico (ay-goa-*thayn*-tree-koa) adj self-centred

egoísmo (ay-goa-*eez*-moa) m selfishness

egoísta (ay-goa-*eess*-tah) adj egoistic, selfish

eje (*ay*-khay) m axle

ejecución (ay-khay-koo-*th*ʸ*oan*) f execution

ejecutar (ay-khay-koo-*tahr*) v perform, execute

ejecutivo (ay-khay-koo-*tee*-bhoa) adj executive; m executive

ejemplar (ay-khaym-*plahr*) m copy

ejemplo (ay-*khaym*-ploa) m instance, example; **por** ~ for instance, for example

ejercer (ay-khayr-*thayr*) v exercise

ejercicio (ay-khayr-*thee*-thʸoa) m exercise

ejercitar (ay-khayr-thee-*tahr*) v exercise

ejército (ay-*khayr*-thee-toa) *m* army

ejote (ay-*khoa*-tay) *mMe* bean

el (ayl) *art* (f la; pl los, las) the *art*

él (ayl) *pron* he

elaborar (ay-lah-boa-*rahr*) *v* elaborate

elasticidad (ay-lahss-tee-thee-*dhahdh*) *f* elasticity

elástico (ay-*lahss*-tee-koa) *adj* elastic; *m* rubber band

elección (ay-layk-th*Y*oan) *f* choice, pick, selection; election

electricidad (ay-layk-tree-thee-*dhahdh*) *f* electricity

electricista (ay-layk-tree-*theess*-tah) *m* electrician

eléctrico (ay-*layk*-tree-koa) *adj* electric

electrónico (ay-layk-*troa*-nee-koa) *adj* electronic

elefante (ay-lay-*fahn*-tay) *m* elephant

elegancia (ay-lay-*gahn*-th*Y*ah) *f* elegance

elegante (ay-lay-*gahn*-tay) *adj* smart, elegant

*elegir (ay-lay-*kheer*) *v* elect, select

elemental (ay-lay-mayn-*tahl*) *adj* primary

elemento (ay-lay-*mayn*-toa) *m* element

elevador (ay-lay-bhah-*dhoar*) *mMe* lift; elevator *nAm*

elevar (ay-lay-*bhahr*) *v* elevate

eliminar (ay-lee-mee-*nahr*) *v* eliminate

elogio (ay-*loa*-kh*Y*oa) *m* praise, glory

elucidar (ay-loo-thee-*dhahr*) *v* elucidate

ella (*ay*-l*Y*ah) *pron* she

ello (*ay*-l*Y*oa) *pron* it

ellos (*ay*-l*Y*oass) *pron* they

emancipación (ay-mahn-thee-pah-th*Y*oan) *f* emancipation

embajada (aym-bah-*khah*-dhah) *f* embassy

embajador (aym-bah-khah-*dhoar*) *m* ambassador

embalaje (aym-bah-*lah*-khay) *m* packing

embalar (aym-bah-*lahr*) *v* pack

embalse (aym-*bahl*-say) *m* reservoir

embarazada (aym-bah-rah-*thah*-dhah) *adj* pregnant

embarazoso (aym-bah-rah-*thoa*-soa) *adj* embarrassing, awkward; puzzling

embarcación (aym-bahr-kah-th*Y*oan) *f* vessel; embarkation

embarcar (aym-bahr-*kahr*) *v* embark

embargar (aym-bahr-*gahr*) *v* confiscate

embargo (aym-*bahr*-goa) *m* embargo; sin ~ yet, however, though, still

emblema (aym-*blay*-mah) *m* emblem

emboscada (aym-boass-*kah*-dhah) *f* ambush

embotado (aym-boa-*tah*-dhoa) *adj* dull

embotellamiento (aym-boa-tay-l*Y*ah-m*Y*ayn-toa) *m* traffic jam

embrague (aym-*brah*-gay) *m* clutch

embriagado (aym-br*Y*ah-*gah*-dhoa) *adj* intoxicated

embrollar (aym-broa-*l*Y*ahr*) *v* muddle

embrollo (aym-*broa*-l*Y*oa) *m* muddle

embromar (aym-broa-*mahr*) *v* kid

embudo (aym-*boo*-dhoa) *m* funnel

emergencia (ay-mayr-*khayn*-th*Y*ah) *f* emergency

emigración (ay-mee-*grah*-th*Y*oan) *f* emigration

emigrante (ay-mee-*grahn*-tay) *m* emigrant

emigrar (ay-mee-*grahr*) *v* emigrate

eminente (ay-mee-*nayn*-tay) *adj* outstanding

emisión (ay-mee-s*Y*oan) *f* issue

emisor (ay-mee-*soar*) *m* transmitter

emitir (ay-mee-*teer*) *v* *broadcast; utter

emoción (ay-moa-th*Y*oan) *f* emotion

empalme (aym-*pahl*-may) *m* junction

empapar (aym-pah-*pahr*) *v* soak

empaquetar (aym-pah-kay-*tahr*) v pack up

emparedado (aym-pah-ray-*dhah*-dhoa) m sandwich

emparentado (aym-pah-rayn-*tah*-dhoa) adj related

empaste (aym-*pahss*-tay) m filling

empeñar (aym-pay-*ñahr*) v pawn

empeño (aym-*pay*-ñoa) m pawn; determination

emperador (aym-pay-rah-*dhoar*) m emperor

emperatriz (aym-pay-rah-*treeth*) f empress

*empezar (aym-pay-*thahr*) v *begin, start

empleado (aym-play-*ah*-dhoa) m employee; ~ **de oficina** clerk

emplear (aym-play-*ahr*) v employ; engage

empleo (aym-*play*-oa) m job, employment

emprender (aym-prayn-*dayr*) v *undertake

empresa (aym-*pray*-sah) f undertaking, enterprise; concern, business

*empujar (aym-poo-*khahr*) v push; press

empujón (aym-poo-*khoan*) m push

en (ayn) prep at, in; inside, to

enamorado (ay-nah-moa-*rah*-dhoa) adj in love

enamorarse (aynah-moa-*rahr*-say) v *fall in love

enano (ay-*nah*-noa) m dwarf

encantado (ayng-kahn-*tah*-dhoa) adj delighted

encantador (ayng-kahn-tah-*dhoar*) adj glamorous; charming, enchanting

encantar (ayng-kahn-*tahr*) v delight; bewitch

encanto (ayng-*kahn*-toa) m glamour, charm; spell

encarcelamiento (ayng-kahr-thay-lah-m^yayn-toa) m imprisonment

encarcelar (ayng-kahr-thay-*lahr*) v imprison

encargarse de (ayng-kahr-*gahr*-say) *take over, *take charge of

encargo (ayng-*kahr*-goa) m assignment

encariñado con (ayng-kah-ree-*ñah*-dhoa koan) attached to

encendedor (ayn-thayn-day-*dhoar*) m cigarette-lighter

*encender (ayn-thayn-*dayr*) v *light; turn on, switch on

encendido (ayn-thayn-*dee*-dhoa) m ignition

*encerrar (ayn-thay-*rrahr*) v *shut in; encircle

encía (ayn-*thee*-ah) f gum

enciclopedia (ayn-thee-kloa-*pay*-dh^yah) f encyclopaedia

encima (ayn-*thee*-mah) adv above; over; ~ **de** over, above, on top of

encinta (ayn-*theen*-tah) adj pregnant

encogerse (ayng-koa-*khayr*-say) v *shrink; **no encoge** shrinkproof

*encontrar (ayng-koan-*trahr*) v *come across, *find; ***encontrarse con** *meet, encounter, run into

encorvado (ayng-koar-*bhah*-dhoa) adj curved

encrucijada (ayng-kroo-thee-*khah*-dhah) f crossing, junction

encuentro (ayng-*kwayn*-troa) m meeting, encounter

encuesta (ayng-*kwayss*-tah) f inquiry; enquiry

encurtidos (ayng-koor-*tee*-dhoass) mpl pickles pl

enchufar (ayn-choo-*fahr*) v plug in

enchufe (ayn-*choo*-fay) m plug

endosar (ayn-doa-*sahr*) v endorse

endulzar (ayn-dool-*thahr*) v sweeten

enemigo (ay-nay-*mee*-goa) m enemy

energía (ay-nayr-*khee*-ah) f energy;

power; zest; ~ **nuclear** nuclear energy

enérgico (ay-*nayr*-khee-koa) *adj* energetic

enero (ay-*nay*-roa) January

enfadado (ayn-fah-*dhah*-dhoa) *adj* angry, cross

énfasis (*ayn*-fah-seess) *m* stress

enfatizar (ayn-fah-tee-*thahr*) *v* emphasize

enfermedad (ayn-fayr-may-*dhahdh*) *f* disease; ailment, sickness, illness; ~ **venérea** venereal disease

enfermera (ayn-fayr-*may*-rah) *f* nurse

enfermería (ayn-fayr-may-*ree*-ah) *f* infirmary

enfermizo (ayn-fayr-*mee*-thoa) *adj* unsound

enfermo (ayn-*fayr*-moa) *adj* sick, ill

enfoque (ayn-*foa*-kay) *m* approach

enfrentarse con (ayn-frayn-*tahr*-say) face

enfrente de (ayn-*frayn*-tay day) facing, opposite

engañar (ayng-gah-*ñahr*) *v* cheat, deceive; fool

engaño (ayng-*gah*-ñoa) *m* deceit

engrasar (ayng-grah-*sahr*) *v* grease

enhebrar (ay-nay-*bhrahr*) *v* thread

enigma (ay-*neeg*-mah) *m* mystery, enigma, puzzle

enjuagar (ayng-khwah-*gahr*) *v* rinse

enjuague (ayng-*khwah*-gay) *m* rinse; ~ **bucal** mouthwash

enjugar (ayng-khoo-*gahr*) *v* wipe

enlace (ayn-*lah*-thay) *m* connection, link

enlazar (ayn-lah-*thahr*) *v* link

enmaderado (ayn-mah-dhay-*rah*-dhoa) *m* panelling

enmohecido (ayn-moa-ay-*thee*-dhoa) *adj* mouldy

enojado (ay-noa-*khah*-doa) *adj* angry, cross

enojo (ay-*noa*-khoa) *m* anger

enorme (ay-*noar*-may) *adj* huge, enormous, immense

enrollar (ayn-roa-*lʸahr*) *v* *wind

ensalada (ayn-sah-*lah*-dhah) *f* salad

ensamblar (ayn-sahm-*blahr*) *v* join

ensanchar (ayn-sahn-*chahr*) *v* widen

ensayar (ayn-sah-*ʸahr*) *v* test; rehearse; **ensayarse** *v* practise

ensayo (ayn-*sah*-ʸoa) *m* test; rehearsal; essay

ensenada (ayn-say-*nah*-dhah) *f* inlet, creek

enseñanza (ayn-say-*ñahn*-thah) *f* tuition; teachings *pl*

enseñar (ayn-say-*ñahr*) *v* *teach; *show

ensueño (ayn-*sway*-ñoa) *m* day-dream

entallar (ayn-tah-*lʸahr*) *v* carve

*** entender** (ayn-tayn-*dayr*) *v* conceive; *take

entendimiento (ayn-tayn-dee-*mʸayn*-toa) *m* insight; conception

enteramente (ayn-tay-rah-*mayn*-tay) *adv* completely, entirely, quite

enterar (ayn-tay-*rahr*) *v* inform

entero (ayn-*tay*-roa) *adj* whole, entire

*** enterrar** (ayn-tay-*rrahr*) *v* bury

entierro (ayn-*tʸay*-rroa) *m* burial

entonces (ayn-*toan*-thayss) *adv* then; **de** ~ contemporary

entrada (ayn-*trah*-dhah) *f* entry, entrance, way in; admission; appearance; entrance-fee; **prohibida la** ~ no admittance

entrañas (ayn-*trah*-ñahss) *fpl* insides

entrar (ayn-*trahr*) *v* *go in, enter

entre (*ayn*-tray) *prep* among, amid; between

entreacto (ayn-tray-*ahk*-toa) *m* intermission

entrega (ayn-*tray*-gah) *f* delivery

entregar (ayn-tray-*gahr*) *v* *give; deliver; commit; extradite

entremeses (ayn-tray-*may*-sayss) *mpl* hors-d'œuvre

entrenador (ayn-tray-nah-*dhoar*) *m* coach

entrenamiento (ayn-tray-nah-m^yayn-toa) *m* training

entrenar (ayn-tray-*nahr*) *v* train, drill

entresuelo (ayn-tray-*sway*-loa) *m* mezzanine

entretanto (ayn-tray-*tahn*-toa) *adv* meanwhile, in the meantime

***entretener** (ayn-tray-tay-*nayr*) *v* amuse, entertain

entretenido (ayn-tray-tay-*nee*-dhoa) *adj* entertaining

entretenimiento (ayn-tray-tay-nee-m^yayn-toa) *m* amusement, entertainment

entrevista (ayn-tray-*bheess*-tah) *f* interview

entumecido (ayn-too-may-*thee*-dhoa) *adj* numb

entusiasmo (ayn-too-s^yahz-moa) *m* enthusiasm

entusiasta (ayn-too-s^yahss-tah) *adj* enthusiastic, keen

envenenar (aym-bay-nay-*nahr*) *v* poison

enviado (aym-b^yah-dhoa) *m* envoy

enviar (aym-b^yahr) *v* dispatch, *send

envidia (aym-bee-dh^yah) *f* envy

envidiar (aym-bee-dh^yahr) *v* grudge, envy

envidioso (aym-bee-dh^yoa-soa) *adj* envious

envío (aym-*bee*-oa) *m* expedition, consignment

***envolver** (aym-boal-*bhayr*) *v* wrap; involve

épico (*ay*-pee-koa) *adj* epic

epidemia (ay-pee-*dhay*-m^yah) *f* epidemic

epilepsia (ay-pee-*layp*-s^yah) *f* epilepsy

epílogo (ay-*pee*-loa-goa) *m* epilogue

episodio (ay-pee-*soa*-dheeoa) *m* episode

época (*ay*-poa-kah) *f* period

equilibrio (ay-kee-*lee*-bhr^yoa) *m* balance

equipaje (ay-kee-*pah*-khay) *m* baggage, luggage; ~ **de mano** hand luggage; hand baggage *Am*; **furgón de equipajes** luggage van

equipar (ay-kee-*pahr*) *v* equip

equipo (ay-*kee*-poa) *m* outfit, equipment; gang; team; crew; soccer team

equitación (ay-kee-tah-*th^yoan*) *f* riding

equivalente (ay-kee-bhah-*layn*-tay) *adj* equivalent

equivocación (ay-kee-bhoa-kah-*th^yoan*) *f* misunderstanding, mistake

equivocado (ay-kee-bhoa-*kah*-dhoa) *adj* mistaken

equivocarse (ay-kee-bhoa-*kahr*-say) *v* *be mistaken

equívoco (ay-*kee*-bhoa koa) *adj* ambiguous

era (*ay*-rah) *f* era

erguido (ayr-*gee*-dhoa) *adj* erect

erigir (ay-ree-*kheer*) *v* erect

erizo (ay-*ree*-thoa) *m* hedgehog; ~ **de mar** sea-urchin

***errar** (ay-*rrahr*) *v* err; wander

erróneo (ay-*rroa*-nay-oa) *adj* wrong

error (ay-*rroar*) *m* mistake, error

erudito (ay-roo-*dhee*-toa) *m* scholar

esbelto (ayz-*bhayl*-toa) *adj* slim, slender

escala (ayss-*kah*-lah) *f* scale; ~ **de incendios** fire-escape; ~ **musical** scale

escalar (ayss-kah-*lahr*) *v* ascend

escalera (ayss-kah-*lay*-rah) *f* stairs *pl*, staircase; ~ **de mano** ladder; ~ **móvil** escalator

escalofrío (ayss-kah-loa-*free*-oa) *m* chill, shiver

escama (ayss-*kah*-mah) *f* scale

escándalo (ayss-*kahn*-dah-loa) *m* scandal; offence

Escandinavia (ayss-kahn-dee-*nah*-bhᵛah) *f* Scandinavia

escandinavo (ayss-kahn-dee-*nah*-bhoa) *adj* Scandinavian; *m* Scandinavian

escapar (ayss-kah-*pahr*) *v* escape

escaparate (ayss-kah-pah-*rah*-tay) *m* shop-window

escape (ayss-*kah*-pay) *m* exhaust; **gases de ~** exhaust gases

escaque (ayss-*kah*-kay) *m* check

escarabajo (ayss-kah-rah-*bhah*-khoa) *m* beetle, bug

escarcha (ayss-*kahr*-chah) *f* frost

escarcho (ayss-*kahr*-choa) *m* roach

escarlata (ayss-kahr-*lah*-tah) *adj* scarlet

escarnio (ayss-*kahr*-nᵛoa) *m* scorn

escasez (ayss-kah-*sayth*) *f* scarcity, shortage

escaso (ayss-*kah*-soa) *adj* scarce; minor

escena (ay-*thay*-nah) *f* scene; setting

escenario (ayss-thay-*nah*-rᵛoa) *m* stage

esclavo (ayss-*klah*-bhoa) *m* slave

esclusa (ayss-*kloo*-sah) *f* lock

escoba (ayss-*koa*-bhah) *f* broom

escocés (ayss-koa-*thayss*) *adj* Scottish, Scotch; *m* Scot

Escocia (ayss-*koa*-thᵛah) *f* Scotland

escoger (ayss-koa-*khayr*) *v* *choose, pick

escolta (ayss-*koal*-tah) *f* escort

escoltar (ayss-koal-*tahr*) *v* escort

escombro (ayss-*koam*-broa) *m* mackerel

esconder (ayss-koan-*dayr*) *v* *hide

escribano (ayss-kree-*bhah*-noa) *m* clerk

escribir (ayss-kree-*bheer*) *v* *write; **~ a máquina** type; **papel de ~** notepaper; **por escrito** written, in writing

escrito (ayss-*kree*-toa) *m* writing

escritor (ayss-kree-*toar*) *m* writer

escritorio (ayss-kree-*toa*-rᵛoa) *m* desk, bureau

escritura (ayss-kree-*too*-rah) *f* handwriting

escrupuloso (ayss-kroo-poo-*loa*-soa) *adj* careful

escuadrilla (ayss-kwah-*dhree*-lᵛah) *f* squadron

escuchar (ayss-koo-*chahr*) *v* listen; eavesdrop

escuela (ayss-*kway*-lah) *f* school; **director de ~** head teacher, headmaster; **~ secundaria** secondary school

escultor (ayss-kool-*toar*) *m* sculptor

escultura (ayss-kool-*too*-rah) *f* sculpture

escupir (ayss-koo-*peer*) *v* *spit

escurridor (ayss-koo-rree-*dhoar*) *m* strainer

ese (*ay*-say) *adj* that; **ése** *pron* that

esencia (ay-*sayn*-thᵛah) *f* essence

esencial (ay-sayn-*thᵛahl*) *adj* essential; vital

esfera (ayss-*fay*-rah) *f* sphere; atmosphere

*esforzarse (ayss-foar-*thahr*-say) *v* try, bother

esfuerzo (ayss-*fwayr*-thoa) *m* effort; strain; stress

esgrimir (ayz-gree-*meer*) *v* fence

eslabón (ayz-lah-*bhoan*) *m* link

esmaltado (ayz-mahl-*tah*-dhoa) *adj* enamelled

esmaltar (ayz-mahl-*tahr*) *v* glaze

esmalte (ayz-*mahl*-tay) *m* enamel

esmeralda (ayz-may-*rahl*-dah) *f* emerald

esnórquel (ayz-*noar*-kayl) *m* snorkel

eso (*ay*-soa) *pron* that

espaciar (ayss-pah-*thᵛahr*) *v* space

espacio (ayss-*pah*-thᵛoa) *m* room;

space

espacioso (ayss-pah-*th*ᵞ*oa*-soa) *adj* spacious, roomy, large

espada (ayss-*pah*-dhah) *f* sword

espalda (ayss-*pahl*-dah) *f* back; **dolor de** ~ backache

espantado (ayss-pahn-*tah*-dhoa) *adj* frightened

espantar (ayss-pahn-*tahr*) *v* frighten

espanto (ayss-*pahn*-toa) *m* fright; horror

espantoso (ayss-pahn-*toa*-soa) *adj* dreadful

España (ayss-*pah*-ñah) *f* Spain

español (ayss-pah-*ñoal*) *adj* Spanish; *m* Spaniard

esparadrapo (ayss-pah-rah-*dhrah*-poa) *m* adhesive tape, plaster

esparcir (ayss-pahr-*theer*) *v* scatter, *shed

espárrago (ayss-*pah*-rrah-goa) *m* asparagus

especia (ayss-*pay*-th*ᵞ*ah) *f* spice

especial (ayss-pay-*th*ᵞ*ahl*) *adj* special; peculiar, particular

especialidad (ayss-pay-th*ᵞ*ah-lee-*dhahdh*) *f* speciality

especialista (ayss-pay-th*ᵞ*ah-*leess*-tah) *m* specialist

especializarse (ayss-pay-th*ᵞ*ah-lee-*thahr*-say) *v* specialize; **especializado** skilled

especialmente (ayss-pay-th*ᵞ*ahl-*mayn*-tay) *adv* especially

especie (ayss-*payth*ᵞ*ay*) *f* species, breed

específico (ayss-pay-*thee*-fee-koa) *adj* specific

espécimen (ayss-*pay*-thee-mayn) *m* specimen

espectáculo (ayss-payk-*tah*-koo-loa) *m* spectacle, show; ~ **de variedades** floor show

espectador (ayss-payk-tah-*dhoar*) *m* spectator

espectro (ayss-*payk*-troa) *m* ghost; spectrum

especular (ayss-pay-koo-*lahr*) *v* speculate

espejo (ayss-*pay*-khoa) *m* mirror, looking-glass

espeluznante (ayss-pay-looth-*nahn*-tay) *adj* creepy

espera (ayss-*pay*-rah) *f* waiting

esperanza (ayss-pay-*rahn*-thah) *f* hope; expectation

esperanzado (ayss-pay-rahn-*thah*-dhoa) *adj* hopeful

esperar (ayss-pay-*rahr*) *v* hope; wait; expect, await

espesar (ayss-pay-*sahr*) *v* thicken

espeso (ayss-*pay*-soa) *adj* thick

espesor (ayss-pay-*soar*) *m* thickness

espetón (ayss-pay-*toan*) *m* spit

espía (ayss-*pee*-ah) *m* spy

espiar (ayss-p*ᵞ*ahr) *v* peep

espina (ayss-*pee*-nah) *f* thorn; fishbone; ~ **dorsal** backbone

espinacas (ayss-pee-*nah*-kahss) *fpl* spinach

espinazo (ayss-pee-*nah*-thoa) *m* spine

espirar (ayss-pee-*rahr*) *v* expire

espíritu (ayss-*pee*-ree-too) *m* spirit; ghost

espiritual (ayss-pee-ree-*twahl*) *adj* spiritual

espléndido (ayss-*playn*-dee-dhoa) *adj* splendid; glorious, enchanting, magnificent

esplendor (ayss-playn-*doar*) *m* splendour

esponja (ayss-*poang*-khah) *f* sponge

esposa (ayss-*poa*-sah) *f* wife; **esposas** *fpl* handcuffs *pl*

esposo (ayss-*poa*-soa) *m* husband

espuma (ayss-*poo*-mah) *f* froth, foam, lather

espumante (ayss-poo-*mahn*-tay) *adj*

sparkling
espumar (ayss-poo-*mahr*) *v* foam
esputo (ayss-*poo*-toa) *m* spit
esquela (ayss-*kay*-lah) *f* note
esqueleto (ayss-kay-*lay*-toa) *m* skeleton
esquema (ayss-*kay*-mah) *m* diagram; scheme
esquí (ayss-*kee*) *m* ski; skiing; ~ **acuático** water ski; **salto de** ~ ski-jump
esquiador (ayss-kᵞah-*dhoar*) *m* skier
esquiar (ayss-kᵞahr) *v* ski
esquina (ayss-*kee*-nah) *f* corner
esquivo (ayss-*kee*-bhoa) *adj* shy
estable (ayss-*tah*-bhlay) *adj* permanent, stable
***establecer** (ayss-tah-bhlay-*thayr*) *v* establish
establo (ayss-*tah*-bhloa) *m* stable
estación (ayss-tah-*thᵞoan*) *f* season; station; depot *nAm*; ~ **central** central station; ~ **de servicio** filling station; ~ **terminal** terminal
estacionamiento (ayss-tah-thᵞoa-nah-*mᵞayn*-toa) *m* parking lot *Am*; **derechos de** ~ parking fee
estacionar (ayss-tah-thᵞoa-*nahr*) *v* park; **prohibido estacionarse** no parking
estacionario (ayss-tah-thᵞoa-*nah*-rᵞoa) *adj* stationary
estadio (ayss-*tah*-dhᵞoa) *m* stadium
estadista (ayss-tah-*dheess*-tah) *m* statesman
estadística (ayss-tah-*dheess*-tee-kah) *f* statistics *pl*
Estado (ayss-*tah*-doa) *m* state
estado (ayss-*tah*-dhoa) *m* state, condition
Estados Unidos (ayss-*tah*-dhoass oo-*nee*-dhoass) the States, United States
estafa (ayss-*tah*-fah) *f* swindle
estafador (ayss-tah-fah-*dhoar*) *m* swindler

estafar (ayss-tah-*fahr*) *v* cheat, swindle
estallar (ayss-tah-*lᵞahr*) *v* explode
estambre (ayss-*tahm*-bray) *m/f* worsted
estampa (ayss-*tahm*-pah) *f* engraving
estampilla (ayss-tahm-*pee*-lᵞah) *fMe* stamp
estancia (ayss-*tahn*-thᵞah) *f* stay
estanco (ayss-*tahng*-koa) *m* cigar shop, tobacconist's
estanque (ayss-*tahng*-kay) *m* pond
estanquero (ayss-tahng-*kay*-roa) *m* tobacconist
estante (ayss-*tahn*-tay) *m* shelf
estaño (ayss-*tah*-ñoa) *m* tin; pewter
***estar** (ayss-*tahr*) *v* *be
estatua (ayss-*tah*-twah) *f* statue
estatura (ayss-tah-*too*-rah) *f* figure
este[1] (*ayss*-tay) *m* east
este[2] (*ayss*-tay) *adj* this; **éste** *pron* this
estera (ayss-*tay*-rah) *f* mat
estercolero (ayss-tayr-koa-*lay*-roa) *m* dunghill
estéril (ayss-*tay*-reel) *adj* sterile
esterilizar (ayss-tay-ree-lee-*thahr*) *v* sterilize
estético (ayss-*tay*-tee-koa) *adj* aesthetic
estilo (ayss-*tee*-loa) *m* style
estilográfica (ayss-tee-loa-*grah*-fee-kah) *f* fountain-pen
estima (ayss-*tee*-mah) *f* esteem
estimación (ayss-tee-mah-*thᵞoan*) *f* respect; estimate
estimar (ayss-tee-*mahr*) *v* esteem; estimate
estimulante (ayss-tee-moo-*lahn*-tay) *m* stimulant
estimular (ayss-tee-moo-*lahr*) *v* stimulate; urge
estímulo (ayss-*tee*-moo-loa) *m* impulse
estipulación (ayss-tee-poo-lah-*thᵞoan*)

f stipulation

estipular (ayss-tee-poo-*lahr*) v stipulate

estirar (ayss-tee-*rahr*) v stretch

estirón (ayss-tee-*roan*) m tug

esto (*ayss*-toa) adj this

estola (ayss-*toa*-lah) f stole

estómago (ayss-*toa*-mah-goa) m stomach; **dolor de ~** stomach-ache

estorbar (ayss-toar-*bhahr*) v disturb, embarrass

estornino (ayss-toar-*nee*-noa) m starling

estornudar (ayss-toar-noo-*dhahr*) v sneeze

estrangular (ayss-trahng-goo-*lahr*) v choke, strangle

estrato (ayss-*trah*-toa) m layer

estrechar (ayss-tray-*chahr*) v tighten

estrecho (ayss-*tray*-choa) adj narrow; tight

estrella (ayss-*tray*-lᵞah) f star

estremecido (ayss-tray-may-*thee*-dhoa) adj shivery

estremecimiento (ayss-tray-may-thee-*mᵞayn*-toa) m shudder

estreñido (ayss-tray-*ñee*-dhoa) adj constipated

estreñimiento (ayss-tray-ñee-*mᵞayn*-toa) m constipation

estribo (ayss-*tree*-bhoa) m stirrup

estribor (ayss-tree-*bhoar*) m starboard

estricto (ayss-*treek*-toa) adj strict

estrofa (ayss-*troa*-fah) f stanza

estropeado (ayss-troa-pay-*ah*-dhoa) adj broken; crippled

estropear (ayss-troa-pay-*ahr*) v mess up

estructura (ayss-trook-*too*-rah) f structure; fabric

estuario (ayss-*twah*-rᵞoa) m estuary

estuco (ayss-*too*-koa) m plaster

estuche (ayss-*too*-chay) m case

estudiante (ayss-too-*dhᵞahn*-tay) m student

estudiar (ayss-too-*dhᵞahr*) v study

estudio (ayss-*too*-dhᵞoa) m study

estufa (ayss-*too*-fah) f stove; **~ de gas** gas stove

estupefaciente (ayss-too-pay-fah-*thᵞayn*-tay) m drug

estupendo (ayss-too-*payn*-doa) adj wonderful

estúpido (ayss-*too*-pee-dhoa) adj stupid; dumb

etapa (ay-*tah*-pah) f stage

etcétera (ayt-*thay*-tay-rah) and so on, etcetera

éter (*ay*-tayr) m ether

eternidad (ay-tayr-nee-*dhahdh*) f eternity

eterno (ay-*tayr*-noa) adj eternal

etíope (ay-*tee*-oa-pay) adj Ethiopian; m Ethiopian

Etiopía (ay-tᵞoa-*pᵞah*) f Ethiopia

etiqueta (ay-tee-*kay*-tah) f tag

Europa (ayᵒᵒ-*roa*-pah) f Europe

europeo (ayᵒᵒ-roa-*pay*-oa) adj European; m European

evacuar (ay-bhah-*kwahr*) v evacuate

evaluar (ay-bhah-*lwahr*) v evaluate, estimate

evangelio (ay-bhahng-*khay*-lᵞoa) m gospel

evaporar (ay-bhah-poa-*rahr*) v evaporate

evasión (ay-bhah-*sᵞoan*) f escape

eventual (ay-bhayn-*twahl*) adj eventual; possible

evidente (ay-bhee-*dhayn*-tay) adj evident; self-evident

evidentemente (ay-bhee-dhayn-tay-*mayn*-tay) adv apparently

evitar (ay-bhee-*tahr*) v avoid

evolución (ay-bhoa-loo-*thᵞoan*) f evolution

exactamente (ayk-sahk-tah-*mayn*-tay) adv exactly

exactitud (ayk-sahk-tee-*toodh*) f correctness

exacto (ayk-*sahk*-toa) adj precise, exact, accurate

exagerar (ayk-sah-khay-*rahr*) v exaggerate

examen (ayk-*sah*-mayn) m examination

examinar (ayk-sah-mee-*nahr*) v examine

excavación (ayks-kah-bhah-*th*ʸ*oan*) f excavation

exceder (ayk-thay-*dhayr*) v exceed

excelencia (ayk-thay-*layn*-thʸah) f excellence

excelente (ayk-thay-*layn*-tay) adj excellent, fine

excéntrico (ayk-*thayn*-tree-koa) adj eccentric

excepción (ayk-thayp-*th*ʸ*oan*) f exception

excepcional (ayk-thayp-thʸoa-*nahl*) adj exceptional

excepto (ayk-*thayp*-toa) prep except

excesivo (ayk-thay-*see*-bhoa) adj excessive

exceso (ayk-*thay*-soa) m excess; ~ **de velocidad** speeding

excitación (ayk-thee-tah-*th*ʸ*oan*) f excitement

excitante (ayk-thee-*tahn*-tay) adj exciting

excitar (ayk-thee-*tahr*) v excite

exclamación (ayks-klah-mah-*th*ʸ*oan*) f exclamation

exclamar (ayks-klah-*mahr*) v exclaim

***exclusivamente** (ayks-kloo-see-bhah-*mayn*-tay) adv exclusively, solely

exclusivo (ayks-kloo-*see*-bhoa) adj exclusive

excursión (ayks-koor-*s*ʸ*oan*) f trip, excursion

excusa (ayks-*koo*-sah) f apology, excuse

excusar (ayks-koo-*sahr*) v excuse

exención (ayks-sayn-*th*ʸ*oan*) f exemption

exento (ayk-*sayn*-toa) adj exempt; ~ **de impuestos** duty-free

exhalar (ayk-sah-*lahr*) v exhale

exhausto (ayk-*souss*-toa) adj overtired

exhibir (ayk-see-*bheer*) v exhibit, display

exigencia (ayk-see-*khayn*-thʸah) f demand

exigente (ayk-see-*khayn*-tay) adj particular

exigir (ayk-see-*kheer*) v demand

exiliado (ayk-see-lʸah-dhoa) m exile

exilio (ayk-*see*-lʸoa) m exile

eximir (ayk-see-*meer*) v exempt

existencia (ayk-seess-*tayn*-thʸah) f existence; **existencias** fpl supply, stock; ***tener en** ~ stock

existir (ayk-seess-*teer*) v exist

éxito (*ayk*-see-toa) m success, luck; hit; **de** ~ successful; ***tener** ~ manage, succeed

exorbitante (ayk-soar-bhee-*tahn*-tay) adj prohibitive

exótico (ayk-*soa*-tee-koa) adj exotic

expansión (ayks-pahn-*s*ʸ*oan*) f expansion

expedición (ayks-pay-dhee-*th*ʸ*oan*) f expedition

expediente (ayks-pay-*dh*ʸ*ayn*-tay) m file

experiencia (ayks-pay-*r*ʸ*ayn*-thʸah) f experience

experimentar (ayks-pay-ree-mayn-*tahr*) v experiment; experience; **experimentado** experienced

experimento (ayks-pay-ree-*mayn*-toa) m experiment

experto (ayks-*payr*-toa) m expert

expirar (ayks-pee-*rahr*) v expire

explanada (ayks-plah-*nah*-dhah) *f* esplanade

explicable (ayks-plee-*kah*-bhlay) *adj* accountable

explicación (ayks-plee-kah-*th*ʸ*oan*) *f* explanation

explicar (ayks-plee-*kahr*) *v* explain; account for

explícito (ayks-*plee*-thee-toa) *adj* express, explicit

explorador (ayks-ploa-rah-*dhoar*) *m* scout, boy scout

exploradora (ayks-ploa-rah-*dhoa*-rah) *f* girl guide

explorar (ayks-ploa-*rahr*) *v* explore

explosión (ayks-ploa-s*ʸoan*) *f* explosion, blast; outbreak

explosivo (ayks-ploa-*see*-bhoa) *adj* explosive; *m* explosive

explotar (ayks-ploa-*tahr*) *v* exploit

** **exponer** (ayks-poa-*nayr*) *v* exhibit

exportación (ayks-poar-tah-*th*ʸ*oan*) *f* exportation, export

exportar (ayks-poar-*tahr*) *v* export

exposición (ayks-poa-see-*th*ʸ*oan*) *f* exposition, exhibition, display, show; exposure; ~ **de arte** art exhibition

exposímetro (ayks-poa-*see*-may-troa) *m* exposure meter

expresar (ayks-pray-*sahr*) *v* express

expresión (ayks-pray-s*ʸoan*) *f* expression

expresivo (ayks-pray-*see*-bhoa) *adj* expressive

expreso (ayks-*pray*-soa) *adj* explicit; express; **por** ~ special delivery

expulsar (ayks-pool-*sahr*) *v* chase; expel

exquisito (ayks-kee-*see*-toa) *adj* exquisite; delicious

éxtasis (*ayks*-tah-seess) *m* ecstasy

** **extender** (ayks-tayn-*dayr*) *v* *spread, expand

extenso (ayks-*tayn*-soa) *adj* comprehensive, extensive

extenuar (ayks-tay-*nwahr*) *v* exhaust

exterior (ayks-tay-r*ʸoar*) *adj* external, exterior; *m* exterior, outside

externo (ayks-*tayr*-noa) *adj* outward

extinguir (ayks-teeng-*geer*) *v* extinguish

extintor (ayks-teen-*toar*) *m* fire-extinguisher

extorsión (ayks-toar-s*ʸoan*) *f* extortion

extorsionar (ayks-toar-s*ʸoa*-*nahr*) *v* extort

extra (*ayks*-trah) *adj* extra

extracto (ayks-*trahk*-toa) *m* excerpt

** **extraer** (ayks-trah-*ayr*) *v* extract

extranjero (ayks-trahng-*khay*-roa) *adj* alien, foreign; *m* alien, foreigner; stranger; **en el** ~ abroad

extrañar (ayks-trah-*ñahr*) *v* amaze, surprise; banish

extraño (ayks-*trah*-ñoa) *adj* foreign, strange; peculiar, queer, funny

extraoficial (ayks-trah-oa-fee-*th*ʸ*ahl*) *adj* unofficial

extraordinario (ayks-trah-oar-dhee-*nah*-r*ʸoa*) *adj* extraordinary, exceptional

extravagante (ayks-trah-bhah-*gahn*-tay) *adj* extravagant

extraviar (ayks-trah-*bh*ʸ*ahr*) *v* *mislay

extremo (ayks-*tray*-moa) *adj* extreme; very, utmost; *m* extreme; end

exuberante (ayk-soo-bhay-*rahn*-tay) *adj* exuberant

F

fábrica (*fah*-bhree-kah) *f* factory; works *pl*, mill; ~ **de gas** gasworks

fabricante (fah-bhree-*kahn*-tay) *m* manufacturer

fabricar (fah-bhree-*kahr*) *v* manufacture

fábula (*fah*-bhoo-lah) *f* fable
fácil (*fah*-theel) *adj* easy
facilidad (fah-thee-lee-*dhahdh*) *f* ease; facility
facilitar (fah-thee-lee-*tahr*) *v* facilitate
factible (fahk-*tee*-bhlay) *adj* attainable
factor (fahk-*toar*) *m* factor
factura (fahk-*too*-rah) *f* invoice
facturar (fahk-too-*rahr*) *v* bill
facultad (fah-kool-*tahdh*) *f* faculty
fachada (fah-*chah*-dhah) *f* façade
faisán (figh-*sahn*) *m* pheasant
faja (*fah*-khah) *f* strip; girdle
falda (*fahl*-dah) *f* skirt
faldón (fahl-*doan*) *m* gable
falsificación (fahl-see-fee-kah-*th^yoan*) *f* fake
falsificar (fahl-see-fee-*kahr*) *v* forge, counterfeit
falso (*fahl*-soa) *adj* false; untrue
falta (*fahl*-tah) *f* error; want, lack; offence; **sin ~** without fail
faltar (fahl-*tahr*) *v* fail
fallar (fah-*l^yahr*) *v* fail
*** fallecer** (fah-l^yay-*thayr*) *v* depart
fama (*fah*-mah) *f* fame; **de ~ mundial** world-famous; **de mala ~** notorious
familia (fah-mee-*l^yah*) *f* family
familiar (fah-mee-*l^yahr*) *adj* familiar
famoso (fah-*moa*-soa) *adj* famous
fanal (fah-*nahl*) *m* headlamp
fanático (fah-*nah*-tee-koa) *adj* fanatical
fantasía (fahn-tah-*see*-ah) *f* fantasy
fantasma (fahn-*tahz*-mah) *m* spook, phantom, ghost
fantástico (fahn-*tahss*-tee-koa) *adj* fantastic
farallón (fah-rah-*l^yoan*) *m* cliff
fardo (*fahr*-dhoa) *m* load
farmacéutico (fahr-mah-*thay^{oo}*-tee-koa) *m* chemist
farmacia (fahr-*mah*-th^yah) *f* chemist's,

pharmacy; drugstore *nAm*
farmacología (fahr-mah-koa-loa-*khee*-ah) *f* pharmacology
faro (*fah*-roa) *m* headlight; lighthouse
farol trasero (fah-*roal* trah-*say*-roa) tail-light
farsa (*fahr*-sah) *f* farce
fascismo (fah-*theez*-moa) *m* fascism
fascista (fah-*theess*-tah) *adj* fascist; *m* fascist
fase (*fah*-say) *f* stage, phase
fastidiar (fahss-tee-*dh^yahr*) *v* annoy, bother
fastidioso (fahss-tee-*dh^yoa*-soa) *adj* difficult
fatal (fah-*tahl*) *adj* fatal; mortal
favor (fah-*bhoar*) *m* favour; **a ~ de** on behalf of; **por ~** please
favorable (fah-bhoa-*rah*-bhlay) *adj* favourable
*** favorecer** (fah-bhoa-ray-*thayr*) *v* favour
favorecido (fah-bhoa-ray-*thee*-dhoa) *m* payee
favorito (fah-bhoa-*ree*-toa) *adj* pet; *m* favourite
fe (fay) *f* faith
febrero (fay-*bhray*-roa) February
febril (fay-*bhreel*) *adj* feverish
fecundo (fay-*koon*-doa) *adj* fertile
fecha (*fay*-chah) *f* date
federación (fay-dhay-rah-*th^yoan*) *f* federation
federal (fay-dhay-*rahl*) *adj* federal
felicidad (fay-lee-thee-*dhahdh*) *f* happiness
felicitación (fay-lee-thee-tah-*th^yoan*) *f* congratulation
felicitar (fay-lee-thee-*tahr*) *v* congratulate
feliz (fay-*leeth*) *adj* happy
femenino (fay-may-*nee*-noa) *adj* feminine; female
fenómeno (fay-*noa*-may-noa) *m* phe-

nomenon

feo (*fay*-oa) *adj* ugly

feria (*fay*-r^yah) *f* fair

fermentar (fayr-mayn-*tahr*) *v* ferment

feroz (fay-*roath*) *adj* wild

ferretería (fay-rray-tay-*ree*-ah) *f* hardware store

ferrocarril (fay-rroa-kah-*rreel*) *m* railway; railroad *nAm*

fértil (*fayr*-teel) *adj* fertile

fertilidad (fayr-tee-lee-*dhahdh*) *f* fertility

festival (fayss-tee-*bhahl*) *m* festival

festivo (fayss-*tee*-bhoa) *adj* festive

feudal (fay^{oo}-*dhahl*) *adj* feudal

fiable (f^yah-bhlay) *adj* reliable

fianza (f^yahn-thah) *f* security; bail; deposit

fiasco (f^yahss-koa) *m* failure

fibra (*fee*-bhrah) *f* fibre

ficción (feek-th^yoan) *f* fiction

ficha (*fee*-chah) *f* chip, token

fiebre (f^yay-bhray) *f* fever; ~ **del heno** hay fever

fiel (f^yayl) *adj* faithful, true

fieltro (f^yayl-troa) *m* felt

fiero (f^yay-roa) *adj* fierce

fiesta (f^yayss-tah) *f* feast; party; holiday

figura (fee-*goo*-rah) *f* figure

figurarse (fee-goo-*rahr*-say) *v* imagine

fijador (fee-khah-*dhoar*) *m* setting lotion, hair gel, hair spray

fijar (fee-*khahr*) *v* attach; **fijarse en** mind

fijo (*fee*-khoa) *adj* fixed; permanent

fila (*fee*-lah) *f* row, rank

Filipinas (fee-lee-*pee*-nahss) *fpl* Philippines *pl*

filipino (fee-lee-*pee*-noa) *adj* Philippine; *m* Filipino

filmar (feel-*mahr*) *v* film

filme (*feel*-may) *m* movie

filosofía (fee-loa-soa-*fee*-ah) *f* philos-

ophy

filosófico (fee-loa-*soa*-fee-koa) *adj* philosophical

filósofo (fee-*loa*-soa-foa) *m* philosopher

filtrar (feel-*trahr*) *v* strain

filtro (*feel*-troa) *m* filter; ~ **de aire** air-filter; ~ **del aceite** oil filter

fin (feen) *m* end; aim, purpose; **a ~ de** so that; **al ~** at last

final (fee-*nahl*) *adj* eventual, final; *m* end; **al ~** at last

financiar (fee-nahn-th^yahr) *v* finance

financiero (fee-nahn-*th^yay*-roa) *adj* financial

finanzas (fee-*nahn*-thahss) *fpl* finances *pl*

finca (*feeng*-kah) *f* premises *pl*

fingir (feeng-*kheer*) *v* pretend

finlandés (feen-lahn-*dayss*) *adj* Finnish; *m* Finn

Finlandia (feen-*lahn*-d^yah) *f* Finland

fino (*fee*-noa) *adj* delicate, fine; sheer

firma (*feer*-mah) *f* signature; firm

firmar (feer-*mahr*) *v* sign

firme (*feer*-may) *adj* steady, firm; secure

física (*fee*-see-kah) *f* physics

físico (*fee*-see-koa) *adj* physical; *m* physicist

fisiología (fee-s^yoa-loa-*khee*-ah) *f* physiology

flaco (*flah*-koa) *adj* thin

flamenco (flah-*mayng*-koa) *m* flamingo

flauta (*flou*-tah) *f* flute

flecha (*flay*-chah) *f* arrow

flexible (flayk-*see*-bhlay) *adj* flexible; supple, elastic

flojel (floa-*khayl*) *m* down

flojo (*floa*-khoa) *adj* weak

flor (floar) *f* flower

florista (floa-*reess*-tah) *m* florist

floristería (floa-reess-tay-*ree*-ah) *f*

flower-shop

flota (*floa*-tah) *f* fleet

flotador (floa-tah-*dhoar*) *m* float

flotar (floa-*tahr*) *v* float

fluido (*floo*-ee-dhoa) *adj* fluid; *m* fluid

*fluir (flweer) *v* flow, stream

foca (*foa*-kah) *f* seal

foco (*foa*-koa) *m* focus; *mMe* light bulb

folklore (foal-*kloa*-ray) *m* folklore

folleto (foa-*lᵛay*-toa) *m* brochure

fondo (*foan*-doa) *m* background; ground, bottom; *mMe* slip; **fondos** *mpl* fund

fonético (foa-*nay*-tee-koa) *adj* phonetic

forastero (foa-rahss-*tay*-roa) *m* foreigner; stranger

forma (*foar*-mah) *f* form, shape

formación (foar-mah-*thᵛoan*) *f* formation

formal (foar-*mahl*) *adj* formal

formalidad (foar-mah-lee-*dhahdh*) *f* formality

formar (foar-*mahr*) *v* form, shape; educate

formato (foar-*mah*-toa) *m* size

formidable (foar-mee-*dhah*-bhlay) *adj* huge

fórmula (*foar*-moo-lah) *f* formula

formulario (foar-moo-*lah*-rᵛoa) *m* form; ~ **de matriculación** registration form

forro (*foa*-rroa) *m* lining

fortaleza (foar-tah-*lay*-thah) *f* fortress, fort

fortuna (foar-*too*-nah) *f* fortune

forúnculo (foa-*roong*-koo-loa) *m* boil

*forzar (foar-*thahr*) *v* force; strain

forzosamente (foar-thoa-sah-*mayn*-tay) *adv* by force

foso (*foa*-soa) *m* moat

foto (*foa*-toa) *f* photo

fotocopia (foa-toa-*koa*-pᵛah) *f* photocopy

fotocopiar (foa-toa-koa-*pᵛahr*) *v* photocopy

fotografía (foa-toa-grah-*fee*-ah) *f* photograph; photography; ~ **de pasaporte** passport photograph

fotografiar (foa-toa-grah-*fᵛahr*) *v* photograph

fotógrafo (foa-*toa*-grah-foa) *m* photographer

fracasado (frah-kah-*sah*-dhoa) *adj* unsuccessful

fracaso (frah-*kah*-soa) *m* failure

fracción (frahk-*thᵛoan*) *f* fraction

fractura (frahk-*too*-rah) *f* fracture, break

fracturar (frahk-too-*rahr*) *v* fracture

frágil (*frah*-kheel) *adj* fragile

fragmento (frahg-*mayn*-toa) *m* fragment, piece; extract

frambuesa (frahm-*bway*-sah) *f* raspberry

francés (frahn-*thayss*) *adj* French; *m* Frenchman

Francia (*frahn*-thᵛah) *f* France

franco (*frahng*-koa) *adj* postage paid, post-paid

francotirador (frahng-koa-tee-rah-*dhoar*) *m* sniper

franela (frah-*nay*-lah) *f* flannel

franja (*frahng*-khah) *f* fringe

franqueo (frahng-*kay*-oa) *m* postage

frasco (*frahss*-koa) *m* flask

frase (*frah*-say) *f* sentence; phrase

fraternidad (frah-tayr-nee-*dhahdh*) *f* fraternity

fraude (*frou*-dhay) *m* fraud

frecuencia (fray-*kwayn*-thᵛah) *f* frequency

frecuentar (fray-kwayn-*tahr*) *v* associate with

frecuente (fray-*kwayn*-tay) *adj* frequent

frecuentemente (fray-kwayn-tay-*mayn*-tay) *adv* frequently, often

*fregar (fray-*gahr*) v wash up; scrub

*freír (fray-*eer*) v fry

frenar (fray-*nahr*) v slow down

freno (*fray*-noa) m brake; ~ **de mano** hand-brake; ~ **de pie** foot-brake

frente (*frayn*-tay) f forehead; m front

fresa (*fray*-sah) f strawberry

fresco (*frayss*-koa) adj fresh; chilly, cool

fricción (freek-*th^yoan*) f friction

frigorífico (free-goa-*ree*-fee-koa) m fridge

frío (*free*-oa) adj cold; m cold

frontera (froan-*tay*-rah) f frontier, border; boundary, bound

frotar (froa-*tahr*) v rub

fruta (*froo*-tah) f fruit

fruto (*froo*-toa) m fruit

fuego (*fway*-goa) m fire

fuente (*fwayn*-tay) f source, fountain; dish

fuera (*fway*-rah) adv out; off, away; ~ **de** outside, out of; ~ **de lugar** misplaced; ~ **de temporada** off season

fuerte (*fwayr*-tay) adj powerful, strong; mighty; loud

fuerza (*fwayr*-thah) f force; power, might, energy; strength; ~ **de voluntad** will-power; ~ **motriz** driving force; **fuerzas armadas** military force, armed forces

fugitivo (foo-khee-*tee*-bhoa) m runaway

fumador (foo-mah-*dhoar*) m smoker; **compartimento para fumadores** smoker

fumar (foo-*mahr*) v smoke; **prohibido ~** no smoking

función (foon-*th^yoan*) f function

funcionamiento (foon-th^yoa-nah-m^yayn-toa) m working, operation

funcionar (foon-th^yoa-*nahr*) v work, operate

funcionario (foon-th^yoa-nah-r^yoa) m civil servant

funda (*foon*-dah) f sleeve; ~ **de almohada** pillow-case

fundación (foon-dah-*th^yoan*) f foundation

fundamentado (foon-dah-mayn-*tah*-dhoa) adj well-founded

fundamental (foon-dah-mayn-*tahl*) adj fundamental, basic

fundamento (foon-dah-*mayn*-toa) m basis, base

fundar (foon-*dahr*) v found

fundir (foon-*deer*) v melt

funerales (foo-nay-*rah*-layss) mpl funeral

furgoneta (foor-goa-*nay*-tah) f delivery van

furioso (foo-r^yoa-soa) adj furious

furor (foo-*roar*) m anger, rage

fusible (foo-*see*-bhlay) m fuse

fusil (foo-*seel*) m gun

fusión (foo-s^yoan) f merger

fútbol (*foot*-bhoal) m soccer; football

fútil (*foo*-teel) adj petty

futuro (foo-*too*-roa) adj future

G

gabinete (gah-bhee-*nay*-tay) m cabinet

gafas (*gah*-fahss) fpl goggles pl; ~ **de sol** sun-glasses pl

gaitero (gigh-*tay*-roa) adj gay

galería (gah-lay-*ree*-ah) f gallery; ~ **de arte** art gallery

galgo (*gahl*-goa) m greyhound

galope (gah-*loa*-pay) m gallop

galleta (gah-l^yay-tah) f biscuit

gallina (gah-l^yee-nah) f hen

gallo (*gah*-l^yoa) m cock; ~ **de bosque** grouse

gamba (*gahm*-bah) f prawn

gamuza (gah-*moo*-thah) *f* suede
gana (*gah*-nah) *f* fancy; appetite
ganador (gah-nah-*dhoar*) *adj* winning
ganancia (gah-*nahn*-thᵞah) *f* gain, profit
ganar (gah-*nahr*) *v* gain; *make, earn
ganas (*gah*-nahss) *fpl* desire
gancho (*gahn*-choa) *m* hook
ganga (*gahng*-gah) *f* bargain
garaje (gah-*rah*-khay) *m* garage; **dejar en ~** garage
garante (gah-*rahn*-tay) *m* guarantor
garantía (gah-rahn-*tee*-ah) *f* guarantee
garantizar (gah-rahn-tee-*thahr*) *v* guarantee
garganta (gahr-*gahn*-tah) *f* throat; **dolor de ~** sore throat
garra (*gah*-rrah) *f* claw
garrafa (gah-*rrah*-fah) *f* carafe
garrote (gah-*rroa*-tay) *m* club, cudgel
garza (*gahr*-thah) *f* heron
gas (gahss) *m* gas; **cocina de ~** gas cooker
gasa (*gah*-sah) *f* gauze
gasolina (gah-soa-*lee*-nah) *f* petrol; gasoline *nAm*, gas *nAm*; **~ sin plomo** unleaded petrol; **puesto de ~** petrol station
gastado (gahss-*tah*-dhoa) *adj* worn-out, worn, threadbare
gastar (gahss-*tahr*) *v* *spend; wear out
gasto (*gahss*-toa) *m* expense, expenditure; **gastos de viaje** fare, travelling expenses
gástrico (*gahss*-tree-koa) *adj* gastric
gastrónomo (gahss-*troa*-noa-moa) *m* gourmet
gatear (gah-tay-*ahr*) *v* *creep
gatillo (gah-*tee*-lᵞoa) *m* trigger
gato (*gah*-toa) *m* cat; jack
gaviota (gah-*bhᵞoa*-tah) *f* gull, seagull
gema (*khay*-mah) *f* gem
gemelos (khay-*may*-loass) *mpl* twins

pl; binoculars *pl*; cuff-links *pl*; **~ de campaña** field glasses
*****gemir** (khay-*meer*) *v* groan, moan
generación (khay-nay-rah-*thᵞoan*) *f* generation
generador (khay-nay-rah-*dhoar*) *m* generator
general (khay-nay-*rahl*) *adj* general; universal, public, broad; *m* general; **en ~** in general
generalmente (khay-nay-rahl-*mayn*-tay) *adv* mostly, as a rule
generar (khay-nay-*rahr*) *v* generate
género (*khay*-nay-roa) *m* gender; kind
generosidad (khay-nay-roa-see-*dhahdh*) *f* generosity
generoso (khay-nay-*roa*-soa) *adj* generous, liberal
genial (khay-*nᵞahl*) *adj* genial
genio (*khay*-nᵞoa) *m* genius
genital (khay-nee-*tahl*) *adj* genital
gente (*khayn*-tay) *f* folk; people *pl*
gentil (khayn-*teel*) *adj* gentle
genuino (khay-*nwee*-noa) *adj* genuine
geografía (khay-oa-grah-*fee*-ah) *f* geography
geográfico (khay-oa-*grah*-fee-koa) *adj* geographical
geología (khay-oa-loa-*khee*-ah) *f* geology
geometría (khay-oa-may-*tree*-ah) *f* geometry
gerencial (khay-rayn-*thᵞahl*) *adj* administrative
germen (*khayr*-mayn) *m* germ
gesticular (khayss-tee-koo-*lahr*) *v* gesticulate
gestión (khayss-*tᵞoan*) *f* administration, management
gesto (*khayss*-toa) *m* sign
gigante (khee-*gahn*-tay) *m* giant
gigantesco (khee-gahn-*tayss*-koa) *adj* enormous, gigantic
gimnasia (kheem-*nah*-sᵞah) *f* gymnas-

tics *pl*

gimnasio (kheem-*nah*-s^yoa) *m* gymnasium

gimnasta (kheem-*nahss*-tah) *m* gymnast

ginecólogo (khee-nay-*koa*-loa-goa) *m* gynaecologist

girar (khee-*rahr*) *v* turn

giro (*khee*-roa) *m* draft; ~ **postal** postal order

gitano (khee-*tah*-noa) *m* gipsy

glaciar (glah-th^yahr) *m* glacier

glándula (*glahn*-doo-lah) *f* gland

globo (*gloa*-bhoa) *m* globe; balloon

gloria (*gloa*-r^yah) *f* glory

glorieta (gloa-r^yay-tah) *f* roundabout

glosario (gloa-*sah*-r^yoa) *m* vocabulary

glotón (gloa-*toan*) *adj* greedy

gobernador (goa-bhayr-nah-*dhoar*) *m* governor

gobernante (goa-bhayr-*nahn*-tay) *m* ruler

*****gobernar** (goa-bhayr-*nahr*) *v* reign, rule

gobierno (goa-*bh*^y*ayr*-noa) *m* government, rule; ~ **de la casa** housekeeping

goce (*goa*-thay) *m* enjoyment

gol (goal) *m* goal

golf (goalf) *m* golf; **campo de** ~ golf-links

golfo (*goal*-foa) *m* gulf

golondrina (goa-loan-*dree*-nah) *f* swallow

golosina (goa-loa-*see*-nah) *f* delicacy; **golosinas** sweets; candy *nAm*

golpe (*goal*-pay) *m* blow; knock, bump; *****dar golpes** bump

golpear (goal-pay-*ahr*) *v* *beat, knock, *strike; thump, tap

golpecito (goal-pay-*thee*-toa) *m* tap

gollerías (goa-l^yay-*ree*-ahss) *fpl* delicatessen

goma (*goa*-mah) *f* gum; ~ **de borrar**

eraser, rubber; ~ **de mascar** chewing-gum; ~ **espumada** foam-rubber

góndola (*goan*-doa-lah) *f* gondola

gordo (*goar*-dhoa) *adj* big; fat, stout

gorra (*goa*-rrah) *f* cap

gorrión (goa-*rr*^y*oan*) *m* sparrow

gorro (*goa*-rroa) *m* cap; ~ **de baño** bathing-cap

gota (*goa*-tah) *f* drop; gout

gotear (goa-tay-*ahr*) *v* leak

goteo (goa-*tay*-oa) *m* leak

gótico (*goa*-tee-koa) *adj* Gothic

gozar (goa-*thahr*) *v* enjoy

grabación (grah-bhah-*th*^y*oan*) *f* recording

grabado (grah-*bhah*-dhoa) *m* engraving; picture, print

grabador (grah-bhah-*dhoar*) *m* engraver

grabar (grah-*bhahr*) *v* engrave

gracia (*grah*-th^yah) *f* grace; **de** ~ free, gratis

gracias (*grah*-th^yahss) thank you

gracioso (grah-*th*^y*oa*-soa) *adj* funny, humorous; graceful

grado (*grah*-dhoa) *m* degree; grade; **a tal** ~ so

gradual (grah-*dhwahl*) *adj* gradual

graduar (grah-*dhwahr*) *v* grade; **graduarse** *v* graduate

gráfico (*grah*-fee-koa) *adj* graphic; *m* graph, chart, diagram

gramática (grah-*mah*-tee-kah) *f* grammar

gramatical (grah-mah-tee-*kahl*) *adj* grammatical

gramo (*grah*-moa) *m* gram

Gran Bretaña (grahn bray-*tah*-ñah) Great Britain

grande (*grahn*-day) *adj* big; great, large, major

grandeza (grahn-*day*-thah) *f* greatness; grandness

grandioso (grahn-*d^yoa*-soa) *adj* superb, magnificent

granero (grah-*nay*-roa) *m* barn

granito (grah-*nee*-toa) *m* granite

granizo (grah-*nee*-thoa) *m* hail

granja (*grahng*-khah) *f* farm

granjera (grahng-*khay*-rah) *f* farmer's wife

granjero (grahng-*khay*-roa) *m* farmer

grano (*grah*-noa) *m* grain; corn; pimple

grapa (*grah*-pah) *f* clamp; staple

grasa (*grah*-sah) *f* fat, grease; *fMe* shoe polish

grasiento (grah-*s^yayn*-toa) *adj* fatty, greasy

graso (*grah*-soa) *adj* fat

grasoso (grah-*soa*-soa) *adj* greasy

gratis (*grah*-teess) *adv* free of charge

gratitud (grah-tee-*toodh*) *f* gratitude

grato (*grah*-toa) *adj* enjoyable

gratuito (grah-*twee*-toa) *adj* gratis, free of charge, free

grava (*grah*-bhah) *f* gravel

grave (*grah*-bhay) *adj* grave; bad

gravedad (grah-bhay-*dhahdh*) *f* gravity

Grecia (*gray*-th^yah) *f* Greece

griego (*gr^yay*-goa) *adj* Greek; *m* Greek

grieta (*gr^yay*-tah) *f* cleft, chasm; cave

grifo (*gree*-foa) *m* tap; faucet *nAm*

grillo (*gree*-l^yoa) *m* cricket

gripe (*gree*-pay) *f* influenza, flu

gris (greess) *adj* grey

gritar (gree-*tahr*) *v* cry; yell, scream, shout

grito (*gree*-toa) *m* cry; yell, scream, shout

grosella (groa-*say*-l^yah) *f* currant; ~ **espinosa** gooseberry; ~ **negra** black-currant

grosero (groa-*say*-roa) *adj* gross; coarse, rude, impertinent

grotesco (groa-*tayss*-koa) *adj* ludicrous

grúa (*groo*-ah) *f* crane

gruesa (*grway*-sah) *f* gross

grueso (*grway*-soa) *adj* corpulent

grumo (*groo*-moa) *m* lump

*****gruñir** (groo-*ñeer*) *v* growl

grupo (*groo*-poa) *m* group; party, set, bunch

gruta (*groo*-tah) *f* grotto

guante (*gwahn*-tay) *m* glove

guapo (*gwah*-poa) *adj* handsome

guarda (gwahr-dhah) *m* custodian

guardabarros (gwahr-dhah-*bhah*-rroass) *m* mud-guard

guardabosques (gwahr-dhah-*bhoass*-kayss) *m* forester

guardar (gwahr-*dhahr*) *v* *keep, *put away; guard; ~ **con llave** lock up; **guardarse** *v* beware

guardarropa (gwahr-dhah-*rroa*-pah) *m* wardrobe; cloakroom; checkroom *nAm*

guardería (gwahr-dhay-*ree*-ah) *f* nursery

guardia (*gwahr*-dh^yah) *f* guard; *m* policeman; ~ **personal** bodyguard

guardián (gwahr-*dh^yahn*) *m* attendant, warden; caretaker

guateque (gwah-*tay*-kay) *m* party

guerra (*gay*-rrah) *f* war; ~ **mundial** world war

guía (*gee*-ah) *m* guide; *f* guidebook; ~ **telefónica** telephone directory; telephone book *Am*

guiar (*g^yahr*) *v* guide

guijarro (gee-*khah*-rroa) *m* pebble

guión (*g^yoan*) *m* dash; hyphen

guisante (gee-*sahn*-tay) *m* pea

guisar (gee-*sahr*) *v* cook

guiso (*gee*-soa) *m* dish

guitarra (gee-*tah*-rrah) *f* guitar

gusano (goo-*sah*-noa) *m* worm

gustar (gooss-*tahr*) *v* care for, like; fancy

gusto (*gooss*-toa) *m* taste; **con mucho ~** gladly

gustosamente (gooss-toa-sah-*mayn*-tay) *adv* willingly, gladly

H

* **haber** (ah-*bhayr*) *v* *have
hábil (*ah*-bheel) *adj* able, skilful, skilled
habilidad (ah-bhee-lee-*dhahdh*) *f* ability; skill, art
habitable (ah-bhee-*tah*-bhlay) *adj* inhabitable, habitable
habitación (ah-bhee-tah-*thᵞoan*) *f* room; **~ para huéspedes** guestroom
habitante (ah-bhee-*tahn*-tay) *m* inhabitant
habitar (ah-bhee-*tahr*) *v* inhabit
hábito (*ah*-bhee-toa) *m* habit
habitual (ah-bhee-*twahl*) *adj* habitual
habitualmente (ah-bhee-twahl-*mayn*-tay) *adv* usually
habla (*ah*-bhlah) *f* speech
habladuría (ah-bhlah-dhoo-*ree*-ah) *f* rubbish
hablar (ah-*bhlahr*) *v* *speak, talk
* **hacer** (ah-*thayr*) *v* act; *do; *have, cause to, *make; **hace** ago; *** hacerse** *v* *become; *grow, *go, *get
hacia (*ah*-thᵞah) *prep* at, towards, to; about; **~ abajo** down; **~ adelante** forward; **~ arriba** upwards, up; **~ atrás** backwards
hacienda (ah-*thᵞayn*-dah) *f* estate
hacha (*ah*-chah) *f* axe
hada (*ah*-dhah) *f* fairy; **cuento de hadas** fairytale
halcón (ahl-*koan*) *m* hawk
halibut (ah-lee-*bhoot*) *m* halibut
hallar (ah-*lᵞahr*) *v* *come across

hallazgo (ah-*lᵞahdh*-goa) *m* finding
hamaca (ah-*mah*-kah) *f* hammock
hambre (*ahm*-bray) *f* hunger
hambriento (ahm-*brᵞayn*-toa) *adj* hungry
harina (ah-*ree*-nah) *f* flour
harto de (*ahr*-toa day) fed up with, tired of
hasta (*ahss*-tah) *prep* to, till, until; **~ ahora** so far; **~ que** till
haya (*ah*-ᵞah) *f* beech
hebilla (ay-*bhee*-lᵞah) *f* buckle
hebreo (ay-*bhray*-ua) *m* Hebrew
hechizar (ay-chee-*thahr*) *v* bewitch
hecho (*ay*-choa) *m* fact
* **heder** (ay-*dhayr*) *v* *smell
hediondo (ay-*dhᵞoan*-doa) *adj* smelly
helado (ay-*lah*-dhoa) *adj* freezing; *m* ice-cream
* **helar** (ay-*lahr*) *v* *freeze
hélice (*ay*-lee-thay) *f* propeller
hemorragia (ay-moa-*rrah*-khᵞah) *f* haemorrhage; **~ nasal** nosebleed
hemorroides (ay-moa-*rroi*-dhayss) *fpl* haemorrhoids *pl*, piles *pl*
* **hender** (ayn-*dayr*) *v* *split
hendidura (ayn-dee-*dhoo*-rah) *f* chink, crack
heno (*ay*-noa) *m* hay
heredar (ay-ray-*dhahr*) *v* inherit
hereditario (ay-ray-dhee-*tah*-rᵞoa) *adj* hereditary
herencia (ay-*rayn*-thᵞah) *f* inheritance, legacy
herida (ay-*ree*-dhah) *f* injury, wound
* **herir** (ay-*reer*) *v* injure, wound
hermana (ayr-*mah*-nah) *f* sister
hermano (ayr-*mah*-noa) *m* brother
hermético (ayr-*may*-tee-koa) *adj* airtight
hermoso (ayr-*moa*-soa) *adj* beautiful
hernia (*ayr*-nᵞah) *f* hernia; **~ intervertebral** slipped disc
héroe (*ay*-roa-ay) *m* hero

heroico (ay-*roi*-koa) *adj* heroic
heroísmo (ay-roa-*eez*-moa) *m* heroism
herradura (ay-rrah-*dhoo*-rah) *f* horse-shoe
herramienta (ay-rrah-*mᵞayn*-tah) *f* tool, utensil, implement; **bolsa de herramientas** tool kit
herrería (ay-rray-*ree*-ah) *f* ironworks
herrero (ay-*rray*-roa) *m* smith, blacksmith
herrumbre (ay-*rroom*-bray) *f* rust
* **hervir** (ayr-*bheer*) *v* boil
heterosexual (ay-tay-roa-sayk-*swahl*) *adj* heterosexual
hidalgo (ee-*dhahl*-goa) *m* nobleman
hidrógeno (ee-*dhroa*-khay-noa) *m* hydrogen
hiedra (ᵞay-dhrah) *f* ivy
hielo (ᵞay-loa) *m* ice
hierba (ᵞayr-bhah) *f* herb; **brizna de ~** blade of grass; **mala ~** weed
hierro (ᵞay-rroa) *m* iron; **de ~** iron; **~ fundido** cast iron
hígado (ee-gah-dhoa) *m* liver
higiene (ee-*khᵞay*-nay) *f* hygiene
higiénico (ee-*khᵞay*-nee-koa) *adj* hygienic; **papel ~** toilet-paper
higo (ee-goa) *m* fig
hija (ee-khah) *f* daughter
hijastro (ee-*khahss*-troa) *m* stepchild
hijo (ee-khoa) *m* son
hilar (ee-*lahr*) *v* *spin
hilo (ee-loa) *m* yarn, thread; **~ de zurcir** darning wool
himno (eem-noa) *m* hymn; **~ nacional** national anthem
hinchar (een-*chahr*) *v* inflate; **hincharse** *v* *swell
hinchazón (een-chah-*thoan*) *f* swelling
hipo (ee-poa) *m* hiccup
hipocresía (ee-poa-kray-*see*-ah) *f* hypocrisy
hipócrita (ee-*poa*-kree-tah) *adj* hypocritical; *m* hypocrite

hipódromo (ee-*poa*-dhroa-moa) *m* race-course
hipoteca (ee-poa-*tay*-kah) *f* mortgage
hispanoamericano (eess-pah-noa-ah-may-ree-*kah*-noa) *adj* Spanish-American
histérico (eess-*tay*-ree-koa) *adj* hysterical
historia (eess-*toa*-rᵞah) *f* history; **~ de amor** love-story; **~ del arte** art history
historiador (eess-toa-rᵞah-*dhoar*) *m* historian
histórico (eess-*toa*-ree-koa) *adj* historical, historic
hocico (oa-*thee*-koa) *m* mouth, snout
hogar (oa-*gahr*) *m* hearth
hoja (*oa*-khah) *f* leaf; sheet; blade; **~ de afeitar** razor-blade; **~ de pedido** order-form; **hojas de oro** gold leaf
¡hola! (*oa*-lah) hello!
Holanda (oa-*lahn*-dah) *f* Holland
holandés (oa-lahn-*dayss*) *adj* Dutch; *m* Dutchman
hombre (*oam*-bray) *m* man
hombro (*oam*-broa) *m* shoulder
homenaje (oa-may-*nah*-khay) *m* tribute, homage
homosexual (oa-moa-sayk-*swahl*) *adj* homosexual
hondo (*oan*-doa) *adj* deep
honesto (oa-*nayss*-toa) *adj* honest; honourable, straight
hongo (*oang*-goa) *m* mushroom; toadstool
honor (oa-*noar*) *m* honour; glory
honorable (oa-noa-*rah*-bhlay) *adj* honourable
honorarios (oa-noa-rah-rᵞoass) *mpl* fee
honra (*oan*-rrah) *f* honour
honradez (oan-rah-*dhayth*) *f* honesty
honrado (oan-*rrah*-dhoa) *adj* honest
honrar (oan-*rahr*) *v* honour

hora (*oa*-rah) f hour; ~ **de afluencia** rush-hour; ~ **de llegada** time of arrival; ~ **de salida** time of departure; ~ **punta** peak hour; **horas de consulta** consultation hours; **horas de oficina** office hours, business hours; **horas de visita** visiting hours; **horas hábiles** business hours

horario (oa-*rah*-r^yoa) m schedule; timetable; ~ **de verano** summer time

horca (*oar*-kah) f gallows pl

horizontal (oa-ree-thoan-*tahl*) adj horizontal

horizonte (oa-ree-*thoan*-tay) m horizon

hormiga (oar-*mee*-gah) f ant

hormigón (oar-mee-*goan*) m concrete

hornear (oar-nay-*ahr*) v bake

horno (*oar*-noa) m oven; furnace; ~ **de microonda** microwave oven

horquilla (oar-*kee*-l^yah) f hairpin, hair-grip; bobby pin Am

horrible (oa-*rree*-bhlay) adj horrible; hideous

horror (oa-*rroar*) m horror

horticultura (oar-tee-kool-*too*-rah) f horticulture

hospedar (oass-pay-*dhahr*) v entertain; **hospedarse** v stay

hospedería (oass-pay-dhay-*ree*-ah) f hostel

hospicio (oass-*pee*-th^yoa) m home

hospital (oass-pee-*tahl*) m hospital

hospitalario (oass-pee-tah-*lah*-r^yoa) adj hospitable

hospitalidad (oass-pee-tah-lee-*dhahdh*) f hospitality

hostil (oass-*teel*) adj hostile

hotel (oa-*tayl*) m hotel

hoy (oi) adv today; ~ **en día** nowadays

hoyo (*oa*-^yoa) m pit

hueco (*way*-koa) adj hollow; m gap

huelga (*wayl*-gah) f strike; *estar en ~ *strike

huella (*way*-l^yah) f trace

huérfano (*wayr*-fah-noa) m orphan

huerto (*wayr*-toa) m kitchen garden

hueso (*way*-soa) m bone; stone

huésped (*wayss*-paydh) m guest; lodger, boarder

hueva (*way*-bhah) f roe

huevera (way-*bhay*-rah) f egg-cup

huevo (*way*-bhoa) m egg; **yema de ~** egg-yolk

*huir** (weer) v escape

hule (*oo*-lay) mMe rubber

humanidad (oo-mah-nee-*dhahdh*) f humanity, mankind

humano (oo-*mah*-noa) adj human

humedad (oo-may-*dhahdh*) f moisture, humidity, damp

*humedecer** (oo-may-dhay-*thayr*) v moisten, damp

húmedo (*oo*-may-dhoa) adj moist, humid, damp; wet

humilde (oo-*meel*-day) adj humble

humo (*oo*-moa) m smoke

humor (oo-*moar*) m spirit, mood; humour; **de buen ~** good-tempered, good-humoured

humorístico (oo-moa-*reess*-tee-koa) adj humorous

hundimiento (oon-dee-m^yayn-toa) m ruination

hundirse (oon-*deer*-say) v *sink

húngaro (*oong*-gah-roa) adj Hungarian; m Hungarian

Hungría (oong-*gree*-ah) f Hungary

huracán (oo-rah-*kahn*) m hurricane

hurtar (oor-*tahr*) v *steal

hurto (*oor*-toa) m theft

husmear (oos-may-*ahr*) v scent, *get wind of

I

ibérico (ee-*bhay*-ree-koa) *adj* Iberian

icono (ee-*koa*-noa) *m* icon

ictericia (eek-tay-*ree*-th*y*ah) *f* jaundice

idea (ee-*dhay*-ah) *f* idea

ideal (ee-dhay-*ahl*) *adj* ideal; *m* ideal

idear (ee-dhay-*ahr*) *v* devise

idéntico (ee-*dhayn*-tee-koa) *adj* identical

identidad (ee-dhayn-tee-*dhahdh*) *f* identity; **carnet de** ~ identity card

identificación (ee-dhayn-tee-fee-kah-th*y*oan) *f* identification

identificar (ee-dhayn-tee-fee-*kahr*) *v* identify

idioma (ee-*dh*y*oa*-mah) *m* language

idiomático (ee-dh*y*oa-*mah*-tee-koa) *adj* idiomatic

idiota (ee-*dh*y*oa*-tah) *adj* idiotic; *m* idiot, fool

ídolo (*ee*-dhoa-loa) *m* idol

iglesia (ee-*glay*-s*y*ah) *f* chapel, church

ignorancia (eeg-noa-*rahn*-th*y*ah) *f* ignorance

ignorante (eeg-noa-*rahn*-tay) *adj* ignorant

ignorar (eeg-noa-*rahr*) *v* ignore

igual (ee-*gwahl*) *adj* equal, alike; level, even; **sin** ~ unsurpassed

igualar (ee-gwah-*lahr*) *v* level, equalize; equal

igualdad (ee-gwahl-*dahdh*) *f* equality

igualmente (ee-gwahl-*mayn*-tay) *adv* alike; equally

ilegal (ee-lay-*gahl*) *adj* illegal, unlawful

ilegible (ee-lay-*khee*-bhlay) *adj* illegible

ileso (ee-*lay*-soa) *adj* unhurt

ilimitado (ee-lee-mee-*tah*-dhoa) *adj* unlimited

iluminación (ee-loo-mee-nah-*th*y*oan*) *f* illumination

iluminar (ee-loo-mee-*nahr*) *v* illuminate

ilusión (ee-loo-s*y*oan) *f* illusion

ilustración (ee-looss-trah-*th*y*oan*) *f* illustration; picture

ilustrar (ee-looss-*trahr*) *v* illustrate

ilustre (ee-*looss*-tray) *adj* illustrious

imagen (ee-*mah*-khayn) *f* image, picture; ~ **reflejada** reflection

imaginación (ee-mah-khee-nah-*th*y*oan*) *f* fancy, imagination

imaginar (ee-mah-khee-*nahr*) *v* conceive; **imaginarse** *v* fancy, imagine

imaginario (ee-mah-khee-*nah*-r*y*oa) *adj* imaginary

imitación (ee-mee-tah-*th*y*oan*) *f* imitation

imitar (ee-mee-*tahr*) *v* imitate, copy

impaciente (eem-pah-*th*y*ayn*-tay) *adj* eager, impatient

impar (eem-*pahr*) *adj* odd

imparcial (eem-pahr-*th*y*ahl*) *adj* impartial

impecable (eem-pay-*kah*-bhlay) *adj* faultless

impedimento (eem-pay-dhee-*mayn*-toa) *m* impediment

***impedir** (eem-pay-*dheer*) *v* hinder, impede; restrain, prevent

impeler (eem-pay-*layr*) *v* propel

imperdible (eem-payr-*dhee*-bhlay) *m* safety-pin

imperfección (eem-payr-fayk-*th*y*oan*) *f* fault

imperfecto (eem-payr-*fayk*-toa) *adj* imperfect

imperial (eem-pay-*r*y*ahl*) *adj* imperial

imperio (eem-*pay*-r*y*oa) *m* empire

impermeable (eem-payr-may-*ah*-bhlay) *adj* waterproof, rainproof; *m* raincoat, mackintosh

impersonal (eem-payr-soa-*nahl*) *adj*

impersonal

impertinencia (eem-payr-tee-*nayn*-th^yah) *f* impertinence

impertinente (eem-payr-tee-*nayn*-tay) *adj* bold, impertinent

impetuoso (eem-pay-*twoa*-soa) *adj* violent

implicar (eem-plee-*kahr*) *v* imply; **implicado** involved

imponente (eem-poa-*nayn*-tay) *adj* grand, imposing

imponible (eem-poa-*nee*-bhlay) *adj* dutiable

impopular (eem-poa-poo-*lahr*) *adj* unpopular

importación (eem-poar-tah-*th^yoan*) *f* import

importador (eem-poar-tah-*dhoar*) *m* importer

importancia (eem-poar-*tahn*-th^yah) *f* importance; *****tener ~ matter

importante (eem-poar-*tahn*-tay) *adj* important; considerable, capital, big

importar (eem-poar-*tahr*) *v* import

importuno (eem-poar-*too*-noa) *adj* annoying

imposible (eem-poa-*see*-bhlay) *adj* impossible

impotencia (eem-poa-*tayn*-th^yah) *f* impotence

impotente (eem-poa-*tayn*-tay) *adj* powerless; impotent

impresión (eem-pray-*s^yoan*) *f* impression; ~ **digital** fingerprint

impresionante (eem-pray-s^yoa-*nahn*-tay) *adj* impressive; striking

impresionar (eem-pray-s^yoa-*nahr*) *v* *strike, impress

impreso (eem-*pray*-soa) *m* printed matter

imprevisto (eem-pray-*bheess*-toa) *adj* unexpected, incidental

*****imprimir** (eem-pree-*meer*) *v* print

improbable (eem-proa-*bhah*-bhlay) *adj* unlikely, improbable

ímprobo (*eem*-proa-bhoa) *adj* unfair, dishonest

impropio (eem-*proa*-p^yoa) *adj* improper; wrong

improvisar (eem-proa-bhee-*sahr*) *v* improvise

imprudente (eem-proo-*dhayn*-tay) *adj* unwise

impudente (eem-poo-*dhayn*-tay) *adj* impudent

impuesto (eem-*pwayss*-toa) *m* taxation, tax; Customs duty; ~ **de aduana** Customs duty; **impuestos de importación** import duty; **libre de impuestos** tax-free

impulsivo (eem-pool-*see*-bhoa) *adj* impulsive

impulso (eem-*pool*-soa) *m* urge, impulse

inaccesible (ee-nahk-thay-*see*-bhlay) *adj* inaccessible

inaceptable (ee-nah-thayp-*tah*-bhlay) *adj* unacceptable

inadecuado (ee-nah-dhay-*kwah*-dhoa) *adj* inadequate; unfit, unsuitable

inapreciable (ee-nah-pray-*th^yah*-bhlay) *adj* priceless

incapaz (eeng-kah-*pahth*) *adj* unable, incapable

incendio (een-*thayn*-d^yoa) *m* fire

incidente (een-thee-*dhayn*-tay) *m* incident

incienso (een-*th^yayn*-soa) *m* incense

incierto (een-*th^yayr*-toa) *adj* uncertain

incineración (een-thee-nay-rah-*th^yoan*) *f* cremation

incinerar (een-thee-nay-*rahr*) *v* cremate

incisión (een-thee-*s^yoan*) *f* cut

incitar (een-thee-*tahr*) *v* incite

inclinación (eeng-klee-nah-*th^yoan*) *f* tendency, inclination; incline

inclinar (eeng-klee-*nahr*) v bow; **inclinado** inclined; sloping, slanting; **inclinarse** v *be inclined to; slope, slant

* **incluir** (eeng-*klweer*) v include; enclose; count; **todo incluido** all in

incluso (eeng-*kloo*-soa) adj inclusive, included

incombustible (eeng-koam-booss-*tee*-bhlay) adj fireproof

incomible (eeng-koa-*mee*-bhlay) adj inedible

incomodidad (eeng-koa-moa-dhee-*dhahdh*) f inconvenience

incómodo (eeng-*koa*-moa-dhoa) adj uncomfortable

incompetente (eeng-koam-pay-*tayn*-tay) adj incompetent; unqualified

incompleto (eeng-koam-*play*-toa) adj incomplete

inconcebible (eeng-koan-thay-*bhee*-bhlay) adj inconceivable

incondicional (eeng-koan-dee-th^yoa-*nahl*) adj unconditional

inconsciente (eeng-koan-*th^yayn*-tay) adj unaware; unconscious

inconveniencia (eeng-koam-bay-n^yayn-th^yah) f inconvenience

incorrecto (eeng-koa-*rrayk*-toa) adj incorrect

increíble (eeng-kray-*ee*-bhlay) adj incredible

incrementar (eeng-kray-mayn-*tahr*) v increase

inculto (eeng-*kool*-toa) adj uncultivated; uneducated

incurable (eeng-koo-*rah*-bhlay) adj incurable

indagación (een-dah-gah-*th^yoan*) f inquiry

indagar (een-dah-*gahr*) v query

indecente (een-day-*thayn*-tay) adj indecent

indefenso (een-day-*fayn*-soa) adj un-

protected

indefinido (een-day-fee-*nee*-dhoa) adj indefinite

indemnización (een-daym-nee-thah-*th^yoan*) f compensation, indemnity

independencia (een-day-payn-*dayn*-th^yah) f independence

independiente (een-day-payn-*d^yayn*-tay) adj self-employed, independent

indeseable (een-day-say-*ah*-bhlay) adj undesirable

India (*een*-d^yah) f India

indicación (een-dee-kah-*th^yoan*) f indication

indicador (een-dee-kah-*dhoar*) m trafficator, indicator

indicar (een-dee-*kahr*) v indicate; declare

indicativo (een-dee-kah-*tee*-bhoa) m area code

índice (*een*-dee-thay) m index, table of contents; index finger

indiferencia (een-dee-fay-*rayn*-th^yah) f indifference

indiferente (een-dee-fay-*rayn*-tay) adj indifferent; careless

indígena (een-*dee*-khay-nah) m native

indigestión (een-dee-khayss-*t^yoan*) f indigestion

indignación (een-deeg-nah-*th^yoan*) f indignation

indio (*een*-d^yoa) adj Indian; m Indian

indirecto (een-dee-*rayk*-toa) adj indirect

indispensable (een-deess-payn-*sah*-bhlay) adj essential

indispuesto (een-deess-*pwayss*-toa) adj unwell

individual (een-dee-bhee-*dhwahl*) adj individual

individuo (een-dee-*bhee*-dhwoa) m individual

Indonesia (een-doa-*nay*-s^yah) f Indo-

nesia
indonesio (een-doa-*nay*-s^yoa) *adj* Indonesian; *m* Indonesian
indudable (een-doo-*dhah*-bhlay) *adj* undoubted
indulto (een-*dool*-toa) *m* pardon
industria (een-*dooss*-tr^yah) *f* industry; ingenuity
ineficiente (ee-nay-fee-th^yayn-tay) *adj* inefficient
inerte (ee-*nayr*-tay) *adj* limp
inesperado (ee-nayss-pay-*rah*-dhoa) *adj* unexpected
inestable (ee-nayss-*tah*-bhlay) *adj* unsteady, unstable
inevitable (ee-nay-bhee-*tah*-bhlay) *adj* unavoidable, inevitable
inexacto (ee-nayk-*sahk*-toa) *adj* incorrect, inaccurate; false
inexperto (ee-nayks-*payr*-toa) *adj* inexperienced
inexplicable (ee-nayks-plee-*kah*-bhlay) *adj* unaccountable
infancia (een-*fahn*-th^yah) *f* infancy
infantería (een-fahn-tay-*ree*-ah) *f* infantry
infantil (een-fahn-*teel*) *adj* childlike
infección (een-fayk-th^yoan) *f* infection
infectar (een-fayk-*tahr*) *v* infect; **infectarse** *v* *become septic
inferior (een-fay-r^yoar) *adj* inferior; bottom
infiel (een-f^yayl) *adj* unfaithful
infierno (een-f^yayr-noa) *m* hell
infinidad (een-fee-nee-*dhahdh*) *f* infinity
infinitivo (een-fee-nee-*tee*-bhoa) *m* infinitive
infinito (een-fee-*nee*-toa) *adj* endless, infinite
inflable (een-*flah*-bhlay) *adj* inflatable
inflación (een-flah-th^yoan) *f* inflation
inflamable (een-flah-*mah*-bhlay) *adj* inflammable

inflamación (een-flah-mah-*th^yoan*) *f* inflammation
influencia (een-*flwayn*-th^yah) *f* influence
*** influir** (een-*flweer*) *v* influence
influjo (een-*floo*-khoa) *m* influence
influyente (een-floo-*^yayn*-tay) *adj* influential
información (een-foar-mah-th^yoan) *f* enquiry, information; **oficina de informaciones** inquiry office
informal (een-foar-*mahl*) *adj* informal; casual
informar (een-foar-*mahr*) *v* report, inform; plead; **informarse** *v* inquire
informe (een-*foar*-may) *m* report; **informes** *mpl* information; ***pedir informes** inquire
infortunio (een-foar-*too*-n^yoa) *m* misfortune
infrarrojo (een-frah-*rroa*-khoa) *adj* infra-red
infrecuente (een-fray-*kwayn*-tay) *adj* infrequent
infringir (een-freeng-*kheer*) *v* trespass
ingeniero (eeng-khay-n^yay-roa) *m* engineer
ingenioso (eeng-khay-n^yoa-soa) *adj* ingenious
ingenuo (eeng-*khay*-nwoa) *adj* naïve; simple
Inglaterra (eeng-glah-*tay*-rrah) *f* England; Britain
ingle (*eeng*-glay) *f* groin
inglés (eeng-*glayss*) *adj* English; *m* Englishman; Briton
ingrato (eeng-*grah*-toa) *adj* ungrateful
ingrediente (eeng-gray-dh^yayn-tay) *m* ingredient
ingresar (eeng-gray-*sahr*) *v* deposit
ingreso (eenggray-soa) *m* entry
ingresos (eeng-*gray*-soass) *mpl* revenue, earnings *pl*; income; **impuesto sobre los ~** income-tax

inhabitable (ee-nah-bhee-*tah*-bhlay) *adj* uninhabitable

inhabitado (ee-nah-bhee-*tah*-dhoa) *adj* uninhabited

inhalar (ee-nah-*lahr*) *v* inhale

inicial (ee-nee-*th*ʸ*ahl*) *adj* initial; *f* initial

iniciar (ee-nee-*th*ʸ*ahr*) *v* initiate

iniciativa (ee-nee-th*ʸ*ah-*tee*-bhah) *f* initiative

ininterrumpido (ee-neen-tay-rroom-*pee*-dhoa) *adj* continuous

injusticia (eeng-khooss-*tee*-th*ʸ*ah) *f* injustice

injusto (eeng-*khooss*-toa) *adj* unfair, unjust

inmaculado (een-mah-koo-*lah*-dhoa) *adj* stainless, spotless

inmediatamente (een-may-dh*ʸ*ah-tah-*mayn*-tay) *adv* instantly, immediately

inmediato (een-may-*dh*ʸ*ah*-toa) *adj* immediate, prompt; **de** ~ immediately

inmenso (een-*mayn*-soa) *adj* immense

inmerecido (een-may-ray-*thee*-dhoa) *adj* unearned

inmigración (een-mee-grah-*th*ʸ*oan*) *f* immigration

inmigrante (een-mee-*grahn*-tay) *m* immigrant

inmigrar (een-mee-*grahr*) *v* immigrate

inmodesto (een-moa-*dhayss*-toa) *adj* immodest

inmueble (een-*mway*-bhlay) *m* house

inmundo (een-*moon*-doa) *adj* filthy

inmunidad (een-moo-nee-*dhahdh*) *f* immunity

inmunizar (een-moo-nee-*thahr*) *v* immunize

innato (een-*nah*-toa) *adj* natural

innecesario (een-nay-thay-*sah*-r*ʸ*oa) *adj* unnecessary

innumerable (een-noo-may-*rah*-bhlay) *adj* innumerable

inocencia (ee-noa-*thayn*-th*ʸ*ah) *f* innocence

inocente (ee-noa-*thayn*-tay) *adj* innocent

inoculación (ee-noa-koo-lah-*th*ʸ*oan*) *f* inoculation

inocuo (ee-*noa*-kwoa) *adj* harmless

inoportuno (ee-noa-poar-*too*-noa) *adj* inconvenient; misplaced

inquietarse (eeng-k*ʸ*ay-*tahr*-say) *v* worry

inquieto (een-*k*ʸ*ay*-toa) *adj* restless; uneasy, worried

inquietud (eeng-k*ʸ*ay-*toodh*) *f* unrest; worry

inquilino (eeng-kee-*lee*-noa) *m* tenant

insalubre (een-sah-*loo*-bhray) *adj* unhealthy

insatisfecho (een-sah-teess-*fay*-choa) *adj* dissatisfied

inscribir (eens-kree-*bheer*) *v* enter, book, list; **inscribirse** *v* register, check in

inscripción (eens-kreep-*th*ʸ*oan*) *f* inscription; registration

insecticida (een-sayk-tee-*thee*-dhah) *m* insecticide

insectífugo (een-sayk-*tee*-foo-goa) *m* insect repellent

insecto (een-*sayk*-toa) *m* insect; bug *nAm*

inseguro (een-say-*goo*-roa) *adj* unsafe; doubtful

insensato (een-sayn-*sah*-toa) *adj* senseless

insensible (een-sayn-*see*-bhlay) *adj* insensitive; heartless

insertar (een-sayr-*tahr*) *v* insert

insignificante (een-seeg-nee-fee-*kahn*-tay) *adj* unimportant, petty, insignificant

insípido (een-*see*-pee-dhoa) *adj* tasteless

insistir (een-seess-*teer*) v insist

insolación (een-soa-lah-*th^yoan*) f sunstroke

insolencia (een-soa-*layn*-th^yah) f insolence

insolente (een-soa-*layn*-tay) adj insolent

insólito (een-*soa*-lee-toa) adj uncommon, unusual

insomnio (een-*soam*-n^yoa) m insomnia

insonorizado (een-soa-noa-ree-*thah*-dhoa) adj soundproof

insoportable (een-soa-poar-*tah*-bhlay) adj intolerable

inspección (eens-payk-*th^yoan*) f inspection; ~ **de pasaportes** passport control

inspeccionar (eens-payk-th^yoa-*nahr*) v inspect

inspector (eens-payk-*toar*) m inspector

inspirar (een-spee-*rahr*) v inspire

instalación (eens-tah-lah-*th^yoan*) f installation; plant

instalar (eens-tah-*lahr*) v install; furnish

instantánea (eens-tahn-*tah*-nay-ah) f snapshot

instantáneamente (eens-tahn-tah-nay-ah-*mayn*-tay) adv instantly

instante (eens-*tahn*-tay) m instant; second; **al** ~ instantly

instinto (een-*steen*-toa) m instinct

institución (eens-tee-too-*th^yoan*) f institution, institute

*__instituir__ (eens-tee-*tweer*) v institute

instituto (eens-tee-*too*-toa) m institution, institute

institutor (eens-tee-too-*toar*) m teacher

instrucción (eens-trook-*th^yoan*) f instruction; direction

*__instructivo__ (eens-trook-*tee*-bhoa) adj instructive

instructor (eens-trook-*toar*) m instructor

*__instruir__ (eens-*trweer*) v instruct

instrumento (eens-troo-*mayn*-toa) m instrument; ~ **músico** musical instrument

insuficiente (een-soo-fee-*th^yayn*-tay) adj insufficient

insufrible (een-soo-*free*-bhlay) adj unbearable

insultante (een-sool-*tahn*-tay) adj offensive

insultar (een-sool-*tahr*) v insult; scold, call names

insulto (een-*sool*-toa) m insult

intacto (een-*tahk*-toa) adj intact; unbroken, whole

integral (een-tay-*grahl*) adj integral

integrar (een-tay-*grahr*) v integrate

intelecto (een-tay-*layk*-toa) m intellect

intelectual (een-tay-layk-*twahl*) adj intellectual

inteligencia (een-tay-lee-*khayn* th^yah) f intelligence, brain

inteligente (een-tay-lee-*khayn*-tay) adj intelligent; clever, smart

intención (een-tayn-*th^yoan*) f intention, purpose; *__tener la__ ~ **de** intend

intencionado (een-tayn-th^yoa-*nah*-dhoa) adj on purpose

intencional (een-tayn-th^yoa-*nahl*) adj intentional

intensidad (een-tayn-see-*dhahdh*) f intensity

intenso (een-*tayn*-soa) adj intense

intentar (een-tayn-*tahr*) v attempt, try; intend

intercambiar (een-tayr-kahm-*b^yahr*) v exchange

interés (een-tay-*rayss*) m interest

interesado (een-tay-ray-*sah*-dhoa) adj interested; concerned; m candidate

interesante (een-tay-ray-*sahn*-tay) adj

interesting

interesar (een-tay-ray-*sahr*) v interest

interferencia (een-tayr-fay-*rayn*-th^yah) f interference

interferir (een-tayr-fay-*reer*) v interfere

ínterin (*een*-tay-reen) m interim

interior (een-tay-r^yoar) adj inside, inner; domestic; m interior, inside

intermediario (een-tayr-may-dh^yah-r^yoa) m intermediary

intermedio (een-tayr-*may*-dh^yoa) m interlude

internacional (een-tayr-nah-th^yoa-*nahl*) adj international

internado (een-tayr-*nah*-dhoa) m boarding-school

interno (een-*tayr*-noa) adj internal; resident

interpretar (een-tayr-pray-*tahr*) v interpret

intérprete (een-*tayr*-pray-tay) m interpreter

interrogar (een-tay-rroa-*gahr*) v interrogate

interrogativo (een-tay-rroa-gah-*tee*-bhoa) adj interrogative

interrogatorio (een-tay-rroa-gah-*toa*-r^yoa) m interrogation, examination

interrumpir (een-tay-rroom-*peer*) v interrupt

interrupción (een-tay-rroop-*th^yoan*) f interruption

interruptor (een-tay-rroop-*toar*) m switch

intersección (een-tayr-sayk-*th^yoan*) f intersection

intervalo (een-tayr-*bhah*-loa) m interval

intervención (een-tayr-bhayn-*th^yoan*) f intervention

*intervenir (een-tayr-bhay-*neer*) v intervene

intestino (een-tayss-*tee*-noa) m intestine, gut; ~ **recto** rectum; **intesti-**

nos intestines pl, bowels pl

intimidad (een-tee-mee-*dhahdh*) f privacy

íntimo (*een*-tee-moa) adj intimate; cosy

intoxicación alimentaria (een-toak-see-kah-*th^yoan* ah-lee-mayn-*tah*-r^yah) food poisoning

intransitable (een-trahn-see-*tah*-bhlay) adj impassable

intriga (een-*tree*-gah) f intrigue

introducción (een-troa-dhook-*th^yoan*) f introduction

*introducir (een-troa-dhoo-*theer*) v introduce; *bring up

intruso (een-*troo*-soa) m trespasser

inundación (ee-noon-dah-*th^yoan*) f flood

inusitado (ee-noo-see-*tah*-dhoa) adj unusual

inútil (ee-*noo*-teel) adj useless

inútilmente (ee-noo-teel-*mayn*-tay) adv in vain

invadir (eem-bah-*dheer*) v invade

inválido (eem-*bah*-lee-dhoa) adj invalid, disabled; m invalid

invasión (eem-bah-*s^yoan*) f invasion

invención (eem-bayn-*th^yoan*) f invention

inventar (eem-bayn-*tahr*) v invent

inventario (eem-bayn-*tah*-r^yoa) m inventory

inventivo (eem-bayn-*tee*-bhoa) adj inventive

inventor (eem-bayn-*toar*) m inventor

invernáculo (eem-bayr-*nah*-koo-loa) m greenhouse

invernadero (eem-bayr-nah-*dhay*-roa) m greenhouse

inversión (eem-bayr-*s^yoan*) f investment

inversionista (eem-bayr-s^yoa-*neess*-tah) m investor

inverso (eem-*bayr*-soa) adj reverse

*invertir (eem-bayr-*teer*) v invert; invest

investigación (eem-bayss-tee-gah-*thᵞoan*) f research; investigation, enquiry

investigador (eem-bhayss-tee-gah-*dhoar*) m research worker

investigar (eem-bayss-tee-*gahr*) v investigate, enquire

invierno (eem-*bᵞayr*-noa) m winter; **deportes de** ~ winter sports

invisible (eem-bee-*see*-bhlay) adj invisible

invitación (eem-bee-tah-*thᵞoan*) f invitation

invitado (eem-bee-*tah*-dhoa) m guest

invitar (eem-bee-*tahr*) v invite; ask

inyección (een-ᵞayk-*thᵞoan*) f shot, injection

inyectar (een-ᵞayk-*tahr*) v inject

*ir (eer) v *go; ~ **por** fetch; *irse v *go away

Irak (ee-*rahk*) m Iraq

Irán (ee-*rahn*) m Iran

iraní (ee-rah-*nee*) adj Iranian; m Iranian

iraquí (ee-rah-*kee*) adj Iraqi; m Iraqi

irascible (ee-rahss-*thee*-bhlay) adj irascible, quick-tempered

Irlanda (eer-*lahn*-dah) f Ireland

irlandés (eer-lahn-*dayss*) adj Irish; m Irishman

ironía (ee-roa-*nee*-ah) f irony

irónico (ee-*roa*-nee-koa) adj ironical

irrazonable (ee-rrah-thoa-*nah*-bhlay) adj unreasonable

irreal (ee-rray-*ahl*) adj unreal

irreflexivo (ee-rray-flayk-*see*-bhoa) adj rash

irregular (ee-rray-goo-*lahr*) adj irregular; uneven

irrelevante (ee-rray-lay-*bhahn*-tay) adj insignificant

irreparable (ee-rray-pah-*rah*-bhlay) adj

irreparable

irrevocable (ee-rray-bhoa-*kah*-bhlay) adj irrevocable

irritable (ee-rree-*tah*-bhlay) adj irritable

irritante (ee-rree-*tahn*-tay) adj annoying

irritar (ee-rree-*tahr*) v annoy, irritate

irrompible (ee-rroam-*pee*-bhlay) adj unbreakable

irrupción (ee-rroop-*thᵞoan*) f invasion, raid

isla (*eez*-lah) f island

islandés (eez-lahn-*dayss*) adj Icelandic; m Icelander

Islandia (eez-*lahn*-dᵞah) f Iceland

Israel (eess-rah-*ayl*) m Israel

israelí (eess-rah-ay-*lee*) adj Israeli; m Israeli

istmo (*eest*-moa) m isthmus

Italia (ee-*tah*-lᵞah) f Italy

italiano (ee-tah-*lᵞah*-noa) adj Italian; m Italian

ítem (*ee*-taym) m item

itinerario (ee-tee-nay-*rah*-rᵞoa) m itinerary

izar (ee-*thahr*) v hoist

izquierdo (eeth-*kᵞayr*-dhoa) adj left; left-hand

J

jabón (khah-*bhoan*) m soap; ~ **de afeitar** shaving-soap; ~ **en polvo** soap powder, washing-powder

jade (*khah*-dhay) m jade

jadear (khah-dhay-*ahr*) v pant

jalar (khah-*lahr*) vMe *draw

jalea (khah-*lay*-ah) f jelly

jamás (khah-*mahss*) adv ever

jamón (khah-*moan*) m ham

Japón (khah-*poan*) m Japan

japonés (khah-poa-*nayss*) *adj* Japanese; *m* Japanese

¡jaque! (*khah*-kay) check!

jarabe (khah-*rah*-bhay) *m* syrup

jardín (khahr-*dheen*) *m* garden; ~ **de infancia** kindergarten; ~ **público** public garden; ~ **zoológico** zoological gardens, zoo

jardinero (khahr-dhee-*nay*-roa) *m* gardener

jarra (*khah*-rrah) *f* jar

jaula (*khou*-lah) *f* cage

jefe (*khay*-fay) *m* chief, manager, boss; leader; chieftain; ~ **de cocina** chef; ~ **de estación** stationmaster; ~ **de Estado** head of state; ~ **de gobierno** premier

jengibre (khayng-*khee*-bhray) *m* ginger

jerarquía (khay-rahr-*kee*-ah) *f* hierarchy

jeringa (khay-*reeng*-gah) *f* syringe

jersey (khayr-*say*) *m* jersey; jumper

jinete (khee-*nay*-tay) *m* horseman, rider

jitomate (khee-toa-*mah*-tay) *mMe* tomato

Jordania (khoar-*dhah*-nᵞah) *f* Jordan

jordano (khoar-*dhah*-noa) *adj* Jordanian; *m* Jordanian

jornada (khoar-*nah*-dhah) *f* day trip

joven (*khoa*-bhayn) *adj* young; *m* lad

jovencito (khoa-bhayn-*thee*-toa) *m* teenager

jovial (khoa-*bhᵞahl*) *adj* jolly

joya (*khoa*-ᵞah) *f* jewel, gem

joyería (khoa-ᵞay-*ree*-ah) *f* jewellery

joyero (khoa-ᵞay-roa) *m* jeweller

jubilado (khoo-bhee-*lah*-dhoa) *adj* retired

judía (khoo-*dhee*-ah) *f* bean

judío (khoo-*dhee*-oa) *adj* Jewish; *m* Jew

juego (*khway*-goa) *m* game, play; set; *hacer ~ con match; ~ de bolos

bowling; ~ **de damas** draughts; ~ **de té** tea-set; ~ **electrónico** electronic game

jueves (*khway*-bhayss) *m* Thursday

juez (khwayth) *m* judge

jugada (khoo-*gah*-dhah) *f* move

jugador (khoo-gah-*dhoar*) *m* player

***jugar** (khoo-*gahr*) *v* play

juguete (khoo-*gay*-tay) *m* toy

juguetería (khoo-gay-tay-*ree*-ah) *f* toyshop

juicio (*khwee*-thᵞoa) *m* sense; judgment

julio (*khoo*-lᵞoa) July

junco (*khoong*-koa) *m* rush

jungla (*khoong*-glah) *f* jungle

junio (*khoo*-nᵞoa) June

junquillo (khoong-*kee*-lᵞoa) *m* reed

junta (*khoon*-tah) *f* meeting

juntamente (khoon-tah-*mayn*-tay) *adv* jointly

juntar (khoon-*tahr*) *v* attach; collect; join; **juntarse** *v* gather

junto a (*khoon*-toa ah) beside; next to

juntos (*khoon*-toass) *adv* together

jurado (khoo-*rah*-dhoa) *m* jury

juramento (khoo-rah-*mayn*-toa) *m* vow, oath; *prestar ~ vow

jurar (khoo-*rahr*) *v* *swear

jurídico (khoo-*ree*-dhee-koa) *adj* legal

jurista (khoo-*reess*-tah) *m* lawyer

justamente (khooss-tah-*mayn*-tay) *adv* rightly; just

justicia (khooss-*tee*-thᵞah) *f* justice

justificar (khooss-tee-fee-*kahr*) *v* justify

justo (*khooss*-toa) *adj* fair, just, righteous, right; correct, appropriate, proper

juvenil (khoo-bhay-*neel*) *adj* juvenile

juventud (khoo-bhayn-*toodh*) *f* youth

juzgar (khoodh-*gahr*) *v* judge

K

Kenya (*kay*-n^yah) *m* Kenya
kilogramo (kee-loa-*grah*-moa) *m* kilogram
kilometraje (kee-loa-may-*trah*-khay) *m* distance in kilometres
kilómetro (kee-*loa*-may-troa) *m* kilometre

L

la (lah) *pron* her
laberinto (lah-bhay-*reen*-toa) *m* maze, labyrinth
labio (*lah*-bh^yoa) *m* lip
labor (lah-*bhoar*) *f* labour
laboratorio (lah-bhoa-rah-*toa*-r^yoa) *m* laboratory; ~ **de lenguas** language laboratory
laca (*lah*-kah) *f* lacquer; ~ **para el cabello** hair-spray
ladera (lah-*dhay*-rah) *f* hillside
lado (*lah*-dhoa) *m* side; way; **al** ~ next-door; **al otro** ~ across; **al otro** ~ **de** across
ladrar (lah-*dhrahr*) *v* bay, bark
ladrillo (lah-*dhree*-l^yoa) *m* brick
ladrón (lah-*dhroan*) *m* thief, robber; burglar
lago (*lah*-goa) *m* lake
lágrima (*lah*-gree-mah) *f* tear
laguna (lah-*goo*-nah) *f* lagoon
lamentable (lah-mayn-*tah*-bhlay) *adj* lamentable
lamentar (lah-mayn-*tahr*) *v* lament; grieve
lamer (lah-*mayr*) *v* lick
lámpara (*lahm*-pah-rah) *f* lamp; ~ **para lectura** reading-lamp; ~ **sorda**

hurricane lamp
lana (*lah*-nah) *f* wool; **de** ~ woollen
landa (*lahn*-dhah) *f* heath
langosta (lahng-*goass*-tah) *f* lobster
lanza (*lahn*-thah) *f* spear
lanzamiento (lahn-thah-*m^yayn*-toa) *m* throw
lanzar (lahn-*thahr*) *v* *cast; launch
lápida (*lah*-pee-dhah) *f* gravestone, tombstone
lápiz (*lah*-peeth) *m* pencil; ~ **labial** lipstick; ~ **para las cejas** eye-pencil
largo (*lahr*-goa) *adj* long; **a lo** ~ **de** along, past; **pasar de** ~ pass by
laringitis (lah-reeng-*khee*-teess) *f* laryngitis
¡qué lástima! (kay *lahss*-tee-mah) what a pity!
lata (*lah*-tah) *f* tin, canister, can
lateralmente (lah-tay-rahl-*mayn*-tay) *adv* sideways
latín (lah-*teen*) *m* Latin
latinoamericano (lah too noa-ah-may-ree-*kah*-noa) *adj* Latin-American
latitud (lah-tee-*toodh*) *f* latitude
latón (lah-*toan*) *m* brass
lavable (lah-*bhah*-bhlay) *adj* washable; fast-dyed
lavabo (lah-*bhah*-bhoa) *m* wash-stand
lavabos (lah-*bhah*-bhoass) *mpl* bathroom; ~ **para caballeros** men's room; ~ **para señoras** ladies' room
lavado (lah-*bhah*-dhoa) *m* washing
lavandería (lah-bhahn-day-*ree*-ah) *f* laundry; ~ **de autoservicio** launderette
lavar (lah-*bhahr*) *v* wash
laxante (lahk-*sahn*-tay) *m* laxative
le (lay) *pron* him; her
leal (lay-*ahl*) *adj* true, loyal
lección (layk-th^yoan) *f* lesson
lectura (layk-*too*-rah) *f* reading
leche (*lay*-chay) *f* milk; **batido de** ~ milk-shake

lechería (lay-chay-*ree*-ah) *f* dairy

lechero (lay-*chay*-roa) *m* milkman

lechigada (lay-chee-*gah*-dhah) *f* litter

lechoso (lay-*choa*-soa) *adj* milky

lechuga (lay-*choo*-gah) *f* lettuce

*leer (lay-*ayr*) *v* *read

legación (lay-gah-*th*ʸ*oan*) *f* legation

legal (lay-*gahl*) *adj* legal

legalización (lay-gah-lee-thah-*th*ʸ*oan*) *f* legalization

legible (lay-*khee*-bhlay) *adj* legible

legítimo (lay-*khee*-tee-moa) *adj* legitimate, legal

legumbre (lay-*goom*-bray) *f* vegetable

lejano (lay-*khah*-noa) *adj* remote, far, distant

lejos (*lay*-khoass) *adv* far

lema (*lay*-mah) *f* motto, slogan

lengua (*layng*-gwah) *f* tongue; language; ~ **materna** native language, mother tongue

lenguado (layng-*gwah*-dhoa) *m* sole

lenguaje (layng-*gwah*-khay) *m* speech

lente (*layn*-tay) *m/f* lens; ~ **de aumento** magnifying glass; **lentillas** *fpl* contact lenses

lento (*layn*-toa) *adj* slow; slack

león (lay-*oan*) *m* lion

lepra (*lay*-prah) *f* leprosy

lerdo (*layr*-dhoa) *adj* slow

les (layss) *pron* them

lesión (lay-*s*ʸ*oan*) *f* injury

letra (*lay*-trah) *f* letter

levadura (lay-bhah-*dhoo*-rah) *f* yeast

levantamiento (lay-bhahn-tah-*m*ʸ*ayn*-toa) *m* rise; rising

levantar (lay-bhahn-*tahr*) *v* lift; *bring up; **levantarse** *v* *rise, *get up

leve (*lay*-bhay) *adj* slight

ley (lay) *f* law

leyenda (lay-ʸ*ayn*-dah) *f* legend

liar (*l*ʸ*ahr*) *v* bundle

libanés (lee-bhah-*nayss*) *adj* Lebanese; *m* Lebanese

Líbano (*lee*-bhah-noa) *m* Lebanon

liberación (lee-bhay-rah-*th*ʸ*oan*) *f* liberation; delivery

liberal (lee-bhay-*rahl*) *adj* liberal

liberalismo (lee-bhay-rah-*leez*-moa) *m* liberalism

Liberia (lee-*bhay*-rʸah) *f* Liberia

liberiano (lee-bhay-*r*ʸ*ah*-noa) *adj* Liberian; *m* Liberian

libertad (lee-bhayr-*tahdh*) *f* liberty, freedom

libra (*lee*-bhrah) *f* pound

libranza (lee-*bhrahn*-thah) *f* money order

librar (lee-*bhrahr*) *v* deliver

libre (*lee*-bhray) *adj* free

librería (lee-bhray-*ree*-ah) *f* bookstore

librero (lee-*bhray*-roa) *m* bookseller

libro (*lee*-bhroa) *m* book; ~ **de bolsillo** paperback; ~ **de cocina** cookery-book; ~ **de reclamaciones** complaints book; ~ **de texto** text-book

licencia (lee-*thayn*-th*ʸ*ah) *f* permission, licence; leave

lícito (*lee*-thee-toa) *adj* lawful

licor (lee-*koar*) *m* liqueur

líder (*lee*-dhayr) *m* leader

liebre (*l*ʸ*ay*-bhray) *f* hare

liga (*lee*-gah) *f* union, league

ligero (lee-*khay*-roa) *adj* light; slight

lima (*lee*-mah) *f* file; lime; ~ **para las uñas** nail-file

limitar (lee-mee-*tahr*) *v* limit

límite (*lee*-mee-tay) *m* boundary, limit; ~ **de velocidad** speed limit

limón (lee-*moan*) *m* lemon

limonada (lee-moa-*nah*-dhah) *f* lemonade

limpiaparabrisas (leem-pʸah-pah-rah-*bhree*-sahss) *m* windscreen wiper

limpiapipas (leem-pʸah-*pee*-pahss) *m* pipe cleaner

limpiar (leem-*p*ʸ*ahr*) *v* clean; ~ **en se-**

co dry-clean
limpieza (leem-p^yay-thah) f cleaning
limpio (leem-p^yoa) adj clean
lindo (leen-doa) adj sweet
línea (lee-nay-ah) f line; ~ **de navegación** shipping line; ~ **de pesca** fishing line; ~ **principal** main line
lino (lee-noa) m linen
linterna (leen-tayr-nah) f lantern; torch, flash-light
liquidación (lee-kee-dhah-th^yoan) f clearance sale
líquido (lee-kee-dhoa) adj liquid
liso (lee-soa) adj smooth
lista (leess-tah) f list; ~ **de correos** poste restante; ~ **de espera** waiting-list; ~ **de precios** price-list
listín telefónico (leess-teen tay-lay-foa-nee-koa) telephone directory; telephone book Am
listo (leess-toa) adj bright; clever, smart; ready
litera (lee-tay-rah) f berth
literario (lee-tay-rah-r^yoa) adj literary
literatura (lee-tay-rah-too-rah) f literature
litoral (lee-toa-rahl) m sea-coast
litro (lee-troa) m litre
lo (loa) pron it; ~ **que** what
lobo (loa-bhoa) m wolf
local (loa-kahl) adj local
localidad (loa-kah-lee-dhahdh) f locality; seat
localizar (loa-kah-lee-thahr) v locate
loción (loa-th^yoan) f lotion
loco (loa-koa) adj crazy; mad
locomotora (loa-koa-moa-toa-rah) f engine, locomotive
locuaz (loa-kwahth) adj talkative
locura (loa-koo-rah) f madness, lunacy
lodo (loa-dhoa) m mud
lodoso (loa-dhoa-soa) adj muddy
lógica (loa-khee-kah) f logic
lógico (loa-khee-koa) adj logical

lograr (loa-grahr) v achieve; secure
lona (loa-nah) f canvas; ~ **impermeable** tarpaulin
longitud (loang-khee-toodh) f length; longitude; ~ **de onda** wave-length
longitudinalmente (loang-khee-too-dhee-nahl-mayn-tay) adv lengthways
loro (loa-roa) m parrot
lotería (loa-tay-ree-ah) f lottery
loza (loa-thah) f earthenware; pottery, faience, crockery
lubricación (loo-bhree-kah-th^yoan) f lubrication
lubricar (loo-bhree-kahr) v lubricate
lubrificar (loo-bhree-fee-kahr) v lubricate
lucio (loo-th^yoa) m pike
*lucir (loo-theer) v *shine
lucha (loo-chah) f combat, fight; contest, strife; struggle
luchar (loo-chahr) v struggle, *fight
luego (lway-goa) adv later; ¡hasta luego! so long!
lugar (loo-gahr) m place; spot; **en ~ de** instead of; ~ **de camping** camping site; ~ **de descanso** holiday resort; ~ **de nacimiento** place of birth; ~ **de reunión** meeting-place; *tener ~ *take place
lúgubre (loo-goo-bhray) adj creepy
lujo (loo-khoa) m luxury
lujoso (loo-khoa-soa) adj luxurious
lumbago (loom-bah-goa) m lumbago
luminoso (loo-mee-noa-soa) adj luminous
luna (loo-nah) f moon; ~ **de miel** honeymoon
lunático (loo-nah-tee-koa) adj insane, lunatic
lunes (loo-nayss) m Monday
lúpulo (loo-poo-loa) m hop
lustroso (looss-troa-soa) adj glossy
luto (loo-toa) m mourning
luz (looth) f light; **luces de freno**

brake lights; ~ **de estacionamiento** parking light; ~ **de la luna** moonlight; ~ **del día** daylight; ~ **del sol** sunlight; ~ **lateral** sidelight; ~ **trasera** rear-light

LL

llaga (lʸah-gah) f sore
llama (lʸah-mah) f flame
llamada (lʸah-*mah*-dhah) f call; ~ **local** local call; ~ **telefónica** telephone call
llamar (lʸah-*mahr*) v cry, call; **así llamado** so-called; ~ **por teléfono** phone; **llamarse** v *be called
llano (lʸah-noa) adj flat; level, even, smooth; m plain
llanta (lʸahn-tah) f rim; fMe tire
llave (lʸah-bhay) f key; **ama de llaves** housekeeper; **guardar con** ~ lock up; ~ **de la casa** latchkey; ~ **inglesa** spanner
llegada (lʸay-*gah*-dhah) f arrival; coming
llegar (lʸay-*gahr*) v arrive; ~ **a** attain
llenar (lʸay-*nahr*) v fill; fill in; fill out Am; fill up
lleno (lʸay-noa) adj full
llevar (lʸay-*bhahr*) v *take; *bear, carry; *wear; **llevarse** v *take away
llorar (lʸoa-*rahr*) v cry, *weep
***llover** (lʸoa-*bhayr*) v rain
llovizna (lʸoa-*bheeth*-nah) f drizzle
lluvia (lʸoo-bhʸah) f rain
lluvioso (lʸoo-bhʸoa-soa) adj rainy

M

macizo (mah-*thee*-thoa) adj solid, massive
machacar (mah-chah-*kahr*) v mash
macho (mah-choa) adj male
madera (mah-*dhay*-rah) f wood; **de** ~ wooden; ~ **de construcción** timber
madero (mah-*dhay*-roa) m log
madrastra (mah-*dhrahss*-trah) f stepmother
madre (*mah*-dhray) f mother
madriguera (mah-dhree-*gay*-rah) f den
madrugada (mah-dhroo-*gah*-dhah) f daybreak
madrugar (mah-dhroo-*gahr*) v *rise early
madurez (mah-dhoo-*rayth*) f maturity
maduro (mah-*dhoo*-roa) adj mature, ripe
maestro (mah-*ayss*-troa) m master; schoolteacher, schoolmaster, teacher; ~ **particular** tutor
magia (*mah*-kh ʸah) f magic
mágico (*mah*-khee-koa) adj magic
magistrado (mah-kheess-*trah*-dhoa) m magistrate
magnético (mahg-*nay*-tee-koa) adj magnetic
magneto (mahg-*nay*-toa) m magneto
magnetófono (mahg-nay-*toa*-foa-noa) m tape-recorder
magnífico (mahg-*nee*-fee-koa) adj splendid, gorgeous, magnificent, swell
magro (*mah*-groa) adj lean
magulladura (mah-goo-lʸah-*dhoo*-rah) f bruise
magullar (mah-goo-*lʸahr*) v bruise
maíz (mah-*eeth*) m maize; ~ **en la mazorca** corn on the cob
majestad (mah-khayss-*tahdh*) f majes-

ty

mal (mahl) m harm, evil; wrong; mischief

malaria (mah-lah-rʸah) f malaria

Malasia (mah-lah-sʸah) f Malaysia

malayo (mah-lah-ʸoa) adj Malaysian; m Malay

*maldecir (mahl-day-theer) v curse

maldición (mahl-dee-thʸoan) f curse

maleta (mah-lay-tah) f suitcase, bag

maletín (mah-lay-teen) m grip nAm

malévolo (mah-lay-bhoa-loa) adj spiteful

malicia (mah-lee-thʸah) f mischief

malicioso (mah-lee-thʸoa-soa) adj malicious

maligno (mah-leeg-noa) adj malignant; ill

malo (mah-loa) adj bad; evil, ill

malva (mahl-bhah) adj mauve

malvado (mahl-bhah-dhoa) adj wicked, evil

malla (mah-lʸah) f mesh

mamífero (mah-mee-fay-roa) m mammal

mampara (mahm-pah-rah) f screen

mampostear (mahm-poass-tay-ahr) v *lay bricks

mamut (mah-moot) m mammoth

manada (mah-nah-dhah) f herd

manantial (mah-nahn-tʸahl) m spring

mancuernillas (mahn-kwayr-nee-lʸahss) fplMe cuff-links pl

mancha (mahn-chah) f stain, spot, speck; blot

manchado (mahn-chah-dhoa) adj soiled

manchar (mahn-chahr) v stain

mandar (mahn-dahr) v command; *send; ~ **a buscar** *send for

mandarina (mahn-dah-ree-nah) f mandarin, tangerine

mandato (mahn-dah-toa) m mandate; order

mandíbula (mahn-dee-bhoo-lah) f jaw

mando (mahn-doa) m command

manejable (mah-nay-khah-bhlay) adj handy; manageable

manejar (mah-nay-khahr) v handle

manejo (mah-nay-khoa) m management

manera (mah-nay-rah) f way, manner; **de otra** ~ otherwise

manga (mahng-gah) f sleeve

mango (mahng-goa) m handle

manía (mah-nee-ah) f craze

manicura (mah-nee-koo-rah) f manicure; ***hacer la** ~ manicure

manifestación (mah-nee-fayss-tah-thʸoan) f demonstration; ***hacer una** ~ demonstrate

*manifestar (mah-nee-fayss-tahr) v reveal

maniquí (mah-nee-kee) m model, mannequin

mano (mah-noa) f hand; **de segunda** ~ second-hand; **hecho a** ~ hand-made

mansión (mahn-sʸoan) f mansion

manso (mahn-soa) adj tame

manta (mahn-tah) f blanket

mantel (mahn-tayl) m table-cloth

*mantener (mahn-tay-nayr) v maintain

mantenimiento (mahn-tay-nee-mʸayn-toa) m maintenance

mantequilla (mahn-tay-kee-lʸah) f butter

manual (mah-nwahl) adj manual; m handbook; ~ **de conversación** phrase-book

manuscrito (mah-nooss-kree-toa) m manuscript

manutención (mah-noo-tayn-thʸoan) f upkeep

manzana (mahn-thah-nah) f apple; ~ **de casas** house block Am

mañana (mah-ñah-nah) f morning;

adv tomorrow; **esta ~** this morning

mapa (*mah*-pah) *m* map; **~ de carreteras** road map

maquillaje (mah-kee-*lʸah*-khay) *m* make-up

máquina (*mah*-kee-nah) *f* engine, machine; **~ de afeitar** razor; **~ de billetes** ticket machine; **~ de coser** sewing-machine; **~ de escribir** typewriter; **~ de lavar** washing-machine; **~ tragamonedas** slot-machine

maquinaria (mah-kee-*nah*-rʸah) *f* machinery

mar (mahr) *m* sea; **orilla del ~** seaside, seashore

maravilla (mah-rah-*bhee*-lʸah) *f* marvel

maravillarse (mah-rah-bhee-*lʸahr*-say) *v* marvel

maravilloso (mah-rah-bhee-*lʸoa*-soa) *adj* wonderful, marvellous, fine

marca (*mahr*-kah) *f* brand; mark; **~ de fábrica** trademark

marcar (mahr-*kahr*) *v* mark; score

marco (*mahr*-koa) *m* frame

marcha (*mahr*-chah) *f* march; ***dar ~ atrás** reverse; **~ atrás** reverse

marchar (mahr-*chahr*) *v* march

marea (mah-*ray*-ah) *f* tide

mareado (mah-ray-*ah*-dhoa) *adj* dizzy, giddy; seasick

mareo (mah-*ray*-oa) *m* giddiness; seasickness

marfil (mahr-*feel*) *m* ivory

margarina (mahr-gah-*ree*-nah) *f* margarine

margen (*mahr*-khayn) *m* margin

marido (mah-*ree*-dhoa) *m* husband

marina (mah-*ree*-nah) *f* navy; seascape

marinero (mah-ree-*nay*-roa) *m* sailor

marino (mah-*ree*-noa) *m* seaman

mariposa (mah-ree-*poa*-sah) *f* butterfly

marisco (mah-*reess*-koa) *m* shellfish

marisma (mah-*reez*-mah) *f* swamp

marítimo (mah-*ree*-tee-moa) *adj* maritime

mármol (*mahr*-moal) *m* marble

marqués (mahr-*kayss*) *m* marquis

marroquí (mah-rroa-*kee*) *adj* Moroccan; *m* Moroccan

Marruecos (mah-*rʷay*-koass) *m* Morocco

martes (*mahr*-tayss) *m* Tuesday

martillo (mahr-*tee*-lʸoa) *m* hammer

mártir (*mahr*-teer) *m* martyr

marzo (*mahr*-thoa) March

mas (mahss) *conj* but

más (mahss) *adv* more; plus; **algo ~** some more; **el ~** most; **~ de** over

masa (*mah*-sah) *f* mass; crowd, lot; dough, batter

masaje (mah-*sah*-khay) *m* massage; ***dar ~** massage; **~ facial** face massage

masajista (mah-sah-*kheess*-tah) *m* masseur

máscara (*mahss*-kah-rah) *f* mask; **~ facial** face-pack

masculino (mahss-koo-*lee*-noa) *adj* masculine

masticar (mahss-tee-*kahr*) *v* chew

mástil (*mahss*-teel) *m* mast

matar (mah-*tahr*) *v* kill

mate (*mah*-tay) *adj* mat, dim, dull

matemáticas (mah-tay-*mah*-tee-kahss) *fpl* mathematics

matemático (mah-tay-*mah*-tee-koa) *adj* mathematical

materia (mah-*tay*-rʸah) *f* matter; **~ prima** raw material

material (mah-tay-*rʸahl*) *adj* material, substantial; *m* material

matiz (mah-*teeth*) *m* nuance

matorral (mah-toa-*rrahl*) *m* scrub, bush

matrícula (mah-*tree*-koo-lah) *f* registration number

matrimonial (mah-tree-moa-n^y*ahl*) *adj* matrimonial

matrimonio (mah-tree-*moa*-n^yoa) *m* wedding, marriage; matrimony

matriz (mah-*treeth*) *f* womb

mausoleo (mou-soa-*lay*-oa) *m* mausoleum

máximo (*mahk*-see-moa) *m* maximum

mayo (*mah*-^yoa) May

mayor (may-*^yoar*) *adj* superior, major; main, eldest; *m* major

mayoría (mah-^yoa-*ree*-ah) *f* majority; bulk

mayorista (mah-^yoa-*reess*-tah) *m* wholesale dealer

mayúscula (mah-^y*ooss*-koo-lah) *f* capital letter

mazo (*mah*-thoa) *m* mallet

me (may) *pron* me; myself

mecánico (may-*kah*-nee-koa) *adj* mechanical; *m* mechanic

mecanismo (may-kah-*neez*-moa) *m* mechanism, machinery

mecanografiar (may-kah-noa-grah-f^y*ahr*) *v* type

mecer (may-*thayr*) *v* rock

mecha (*may*-chah) *f* fuse

medalla (may-*dhah*-l^yah) *f* medal

media (*may*-dh^yah) *f* stocking; ~ **pantalón** panty-hose; **medias elásticas** support hose

mediador (may-dh^yah-*dhoar*) *m* mediator

medianamente (may-dh^yah-nah-*mayn*-tay) *adv* fairly

mediano (may-*dh*^yah-noa) *adj* medium

medianoche (may-dh^yah-*noa*-chay) *f* midnight

mediante (may-*dh*^y*ahn*-tay) *adv* by means of

mediar (may-*dh*^y*ahr*) *v* mediate

medicamento (may-dhee-kah-*mayn*-toa) *m* medicine, drug

medicina (may-dhee-*thee*-nah) *f* medicine

médico (*may*-dhee-koa) *adj* medical; *m* doctor, physician; ~ **de cabecera** general practitioner

medida (may-*dhee*-dhah) *f* measure; **hecho a la** ~ made to order, tailormade

medidor (may-dhee-*dhoar*) *m* gauge

medieval (may-dh^yay-*bhahl*) *adj* mediaeval

medio (*may*-dh^yoa) *adj* half; medium; middle; *m* midst, middle; means; **en** ~ **de** amid; ~ **ambiente** milieu, environment

mediocre (may-*dh*^y*oa*-kray) *adj* moderate, poor

mediodía (may-dh^yoa-*dhee*-ah) *m* midday, noon

*** medir** (may-*dheer*) *v* measure

meditación (may-dhee-tah-*th*^y*oan*) *f* meditation

meditar (may-dhee-*tahr*) *v* meditate

Mediterráneo (may-dhee-tay-*rrah*-nay-oa) Mediterranean

médula (*may*-dhoo-lah) *f* marrow

medusa (may-*dhoo*-sah) *f* jelly-fish

mejicano (may-khee-*kah*-noa) *adj* Mexican; *m* Mexican

Méjico (*may*-khee-koa) *m* Mexico

mejilla (may-*khee*-l^yah) *f* cheek

mejillón (may-khee-*l*^y*oan*) *m* mussel

mejor (may-*khoar*) *adj* better; superior

mejora (may-*khoa*-rah) *f* improvement

mejorar (may-khoa-*rahr*) *v* improve

melancolía (may-lahng-koa-*lee*-ah) *f* melancholy

melancólico (may-lahng-*koa*-lee-koa) *adj* sad

melocotón (may-loa-koa-*toan*) *m* peach

melodía (may-loa-*dhee*-ah) f melody

melodioso (may-loa-*dhᵞoa*-soa) adj tuneful

melodrama (may-loa-*dhrah*-mah) m melodrama

melón (may-*loan*) m melon

membrana (maym-*brah*-nah) f diaphragm

memorable (may-moa-*rah*-bhlay) adj memorable

memoria (may-*moa*-rᵞah) f memory; **de ~** by heart

menaje (may-*nah*-khay) m household

mención (mayn-*thᵞoan*) f mention

mencionar (mayn-thᵞoa-*nahr*) v mention

mendigar (mayn-dee-*gahr*) v beg

mendigo (mayn-*dee*-goa) m beggar

menor (may-*noar*) adj minor; junior

menos (*may*-noass) adv less; minus; but; **a ~ que** unless; **por lo ~** at least

menosprecio (may-noass-*pray*-thᵞoa) m contempt

mensaje (mayn-*sah*-khay) m message

mensajero (mayn-sah-*khay*-roa) m messenger

menstruación (mayns-trwah-*thᵞoan*) f menstruation

mensual (mayn-*swahl*) adj monthly

menta (*mayn*-tah) f mint; peppermint

mental (mayn-*tahl*) adj mental

mente (*mayn*-tay) f mind

***mentir** (mayn-*teer*) v lie

mentira (mayn-*tee*-rah) f lie

menú (may-*noo*) m menu

menudo (may-*noo*-dhoa) adj minute, small, tiny; **a ~** often

mercado (mayr-*kah*-dhoa) m market; **~ negro** black market

mercancía (mayr-kahn-*thee*-ah) f merchandise

mercería (mayr-thay-*ree*-ah) f haberdashery

mercurio (mayr-*koo*-rᵞoa) m mercury

***merecer** (may-ray-*thayr*) v merit, deserve

meridional (may-ree-dhᵞoa-*nahl*) adj southern, southerly

merienda (may-rᵞayn-dah) f tea

mérito (*may*-ree-toa) m merit

merluza (mayr-*loo*-thah) f whiting

mermelada (mayr-may-*lah*-dhah) f jam

mes (mayss) m month

mesa (*may*-sah) f table

mesera (may-*say*-rah) fMe waitress

mesero (may-*say*-roa) mMe waiter

meseta (may-*say*-tah) f plateau

meta (*may*-tah) f goal; finish

metal (may-*tahl*) m metal

metálico (may-*tah*-lee-koa) adj metal

meter (may-*tayr*) v *put

meticuloso (may-tee-koo-*loa*-soa) adj precise

metódico (may-*toa*-dhee-koa) adj methodical

método (*may*-toa-dhoa) m method

métrico (*may*-tree-koa) adj metric

metro (*may*-troa) m metre; underground; subway nAm

mezcla (*mayth*-klah) f mixture

mezclar (mayth-*klahr*) v mix; **mezclarse en** interfere with

mezquino (mayth-*kee*-noa) adj narrow-minded, stingy; mean

mezquita (mayth-*kee*-tah) f mosque

mi (mee) adj my

micrófono (mee-*kroa*-foa-noa) m microphone

microscopio (mee-kroass-*koa*-pᵞoa) m microscope

microsurco (mee-kroa-*soor*-koa) m long-playing record

miedo (*mᵞay*-dhoa) m fear, fright; ***tener ~** be afraid

miel (mᵞayl) f honey

miembro (*mᵞaym*-broa) m limb; member

mientras (*mʸayn*-trahss) *conj* whilst, while

miércoles (*mʸayr*-koa-layss) *m* Wednesday

migaja (mee-*gah*-khah) *f* crumb

migraña (mee-*grah*-ñah) *f* migraine

mil (meel) *num* thousand

milagro (mee-*lah*-groa) *m* wonder, miracle

milagroso (mee-lah-*groa*-soa) *adj* miraculous

militar (mee-lee-*tahr*) *adj* military; *m* soldier

milla (*mee*-lʸah) *f* mile

millaje (mee-*lʸah*-khay) *m* mileage

millón (mee-*lʸoan*) *m* million

millonario (mee-lʸoa-nah-*rʸoa*) *m* millionaire

mimar (mee-*mahr*) *v* *spoil

mina (*mee*-nah) *f* mine; pit; ~ **de oro** goldmine

mineral (mee-nay-*rahl*) *m* mineral; ore

minería (moo nay-*ree*-ah) *f* mining

minero (mee-*nay*-roa) *m* miner

miniatura (mee-nʸah-*too*-rah) *f* miniature

mínimo (*mee*-nee-moa) *adj* least

mínimum (*mee*-nee-moom) *m* minimum

ministerio (mee-neess-*tay*-rʸoa) *m* ministry

ministro (mee-*neess*-troa) *m* minister

minoría (mee-noa-*ree*-ah) *f* minority

minorista (mee-noa-*reess*-tah) *m* retailer

minucioso (mee-noo-*thʸoa*-soa) *adj* thorough

minusválido (mee-nooz-*bhah*-lee-*dhoa*) *adj* disabled

minuto (mee-*noo*-toa) *m* minute

mío (*mee*-oa) *pron* mine

miope (*mʸoa*-pay) *adj* short-sighted

mirada (mee-*rah*-dhah) *f* look

mirar (mee-*rahr*) *v* look; watch, view,

look at; stare, gaze

mirlo (*meer*-loa) *m* blackbird

misa (*mee*-sah) *f* Mass

misceláneo (mee-thay-*lah*-nay-oa) *adj* miscellaneous

miserable (mee-say-*rah*-bhlay) *adj* miserable

miseria (mee-*say*-rʸah) *f* misery

misericordia (mee-say-ree-*koar*-dʸah) *f* mercy

misericordioso (mee-say-ree-koar-*dʸoa*-soa) *adj* merciful

misión (mee-*sʸoan*) *f* mission

mismo (*meez*-moa) *adj* same

misterio (meess-*tay*-rʸoa) *m* mystery

misterioso (meess-tay-*rʸoa*-soa) *adj* mysterious; obscure

mitad (mee-*tahdh*) *f* half; **partir por la** ~ halve

mito (*mee*-toa) *m* myth

moción (moa-*thʸoan*) *f* motion

mochila (moa-*chee*-lah) *f* rucksack, knapsack

moda (*moa*-dhah) *f* fashion; **a la** ~ fashionable

modales (moa-*dhah*-layss) *mpl* manners *pl*

modelar (moa-dhay-*lahr*) *v* model

modelo (moa-*dhay*-loa) *m* model

moderado (moa-dhay-*rah*-dhoa) *adj* moderate

moderno (moa-*dhayr*-noa) *adj* modern

modestia (moa-*dhayss*-tʸah) *f* modesty

modesto (moa-*dhayss*-toa) *adj* modest

modificación (moa-dhee-fee-kah-*thʸoan*) *f* change

modificar (moa-dhee-fee-*kahr*) *v* change, modify

modismo (moa-*dheez*-moa) *m* idiom

modista (moa-*dheess*-tah) *f* dressmaker

modo (*moa*-dhoa) *m* fashion, manner; **de cualquier** ~ anyhow; **de ningún** ~ by no means; **de todos modos**

any way: at any rate; **en ~ alguno**
at all; **~ de empleo** directions for
use

mohair (moa-*ayr*) *m* mohair

moho (*moa*-oa) *m* mildew

mojado (moa-*khah*-dhoa) *adj* wet;
moist, damp

mojigato (moa-khee-*gah*-toa) *adj* hypocritical

mojón (moa-*khoan*) *m* landmark

* **moler** (moa-*layr*) *v* *grind

molestar (moa-layss-*tahr*) *v* disturb,
trouble, bother

molestia (moa-*layss*-tʸah) *f* trouble,
nuisance, bother

molesto (moa-*layss*-toa) *adj* troublesome, inconvenient

molinero (moa-lee-*nay*-roa) *m* miller

molino (moa-*lee*-noa) *m* mill; **~ de
viento** windmill

momentáneo (moa-mayn-*tah*-nay-oa)
adj momentary

momento (moa-*mayn*-toa) *m* moment

monarca (moa-*nahr*-kah) *m* monarch,
ruler

monarquía (moa-nahr-*kee*-ah) *f* monarchy

monasterio (moa-nahss-*tay*-rʸoa) *m*
monastery

moneda (moa-*nay*-dhah) *f* currency;
coin; change; **~ extranjera** foreign
currency

monedero (moa-nay-*dhay*-roa) *m*
purse

monetario (moa-nay-*tah*-rʸoa) *adj*
monetary; **unidad monetaria** monetary unit

monja (*moang*-khah) *f* nun

monje (*moang*-khay) *m* monk

mono (*moa*-noa) *m* monkey; overalls
pl

monólogo (moa-*noa*-loa-goa) *m* monologue

monopolio (moa-noa-*poa*-lʸoa) *m*
monopoly

monótono (moa-*noa*-toa-noa) *adj*
monotonous

monstruo (*moans*-trwoa) *m* monster

montaña (moan-*tah*-ñah) *f* mountain

montañismo (moan-tah-*ñeez*-moa) *m*
mountaineering

montañoso (moan-tah-*ñoa*-soa) *adj*
mountainous

montar (moan-*tahr*) *v* mount, *get on;
assemble; *ride

monte (*moan*-tay) *m* mount

montículo (moan-*tee*-koo-loa) *m*
mound

montón (moan-*toan*) *m* heap, stack,
pile

montuoso (moan-*twoa*-soa) *adj* hilly

monumento (moa-noo-*mayn*-toa) *m*
monument; memorial

mora (*moa*-rah) *f* mulberry; blackberry

morado (moa-*rah*-dhoa) *adj* violet

moral (moa-*rahl*) *adj* moral; *f* moral;
spirits

moralidad (moa-rah-lee-*dhahdh*) *f*
morality

mordaza (moar-*dhah*-thah) *f* clamp

mordedura (moar-dhay-*dhoo*-rah) *f*
bite

* **morder** (moar-*dhayr*) *v* *bite

morena (moa-*ray*-nah) *f* brunette

moreno (moa-*ray*-noa) *adj* brown

moretón (moa-ray-*toan*) *m* bruise

morfina (moar-*fee*-nah) *f* morphine,
morphia

* **morir** (moa-*reer*) *v* die

moro (*moa*-roa) *m* Moor

morral (moa-*rrahl*) *m* haversack

morro (*moa*-rroa) *m* pussy-cat

mortal (moar-*tahl*) *adj* mortal; fatal

mosaico (moa-*sigh*-koa) *m* mosaic

mosca (*moass*-kah) *f* fly

mosquitero (moass-kee-*tay*-roa) *m*
mosquito-net

mosquito (moass-*kee*-toa) *m* mosquito

mostaza (moass-*tah*-thah) *f* mustard

mostrador (moass-trah-*dhoar*) *m* counter

* **mostrar** (moass-*trahr*) *v* display, *show

mote (*moa*-tay) *m* nickname

moteado (moa-tay-*ah*-dhoa) *adj* spotted

motel (moa-*tayl*) *m* motel

motín (moa-*teen*) *m* riot

motivo (moa-*tee*-bhoa) *m* motive; cause, occasion

motocicleta (moa-toa-thee-*klay*-tah) *f* motor-cycle; motorbike *nAm*

motoneta (moa-toa-*nay*-tah) *f* scooter

motor (moa-*toar*) *m* motor, engine; ~ **de arranque** starter motor

* **mover** (moa-*bhayr*) *v* move; stir

movible (moa-*bhee*-bhlay) *adj* movable

móvil (*moa*-bheel) *adj* mobile

movimiento (moa-bhee-mᵞ*ayn*-toa) *m* movement, motion

mozo (*moa*-thoa) *m* boy; porter

muchacha (moo-*chah*-chah) *f* girl; maid

muchacho (moo-*chah*-choa) *m* boy; lad

muchedumbre (moo-chay-*dhoom*-bray) *f* crowd

mucho (*moo*-choa) *adv* much; far, very; *adj* much; **con** ~ by far; **muchos** *adj* many

mudanza (moo-*dhahn*-thah) *f* move

mudarse (moo-*dhahr*-say) *v* move; change

mudo (*moo*-dhoa) *adj* mute, dumb

muebles (*mway*-bhlayss) *mpl* furniture

muela (*mway*-lah) *f* molar; **dolor de muelas** toothache

muelle (*mway*-lᵞay) *m* dock, wharf, quay; pier, jetty; spring

muerte (*mwayr*-tay) *f* death

muerto (*mwayr*-toa) *adj* dead

muestra (*mwayss*-trah) *f* sample

mugir (moo-*kheer*) *v* roar

mujer (moo-*khayr*) *f* woman; wife

mújol (*moo*-khoal) *m* mullet

muleta (moo-*lay*-tah) *f* crutch

mulo (*moo*-loa) *m* mule

multa (*mool*-tah) *f* fine; ticket

multiplicación (mool-tee-plee-kah-thᵞ*oan*) *f* multiplication

multiplicar (mool-tee-plee-*kahr*) *v* multiply

multitud (mool-tee-*toodh*) *f* crowd

mundial (moon-dᵞ*ahl*) *adj* world-wide, global

mundo (*moon*-doa) *m* world; **todo el** ~ everyone

municipal (moo-nee-thee-*pahl*) *adj* municipal

municipalidad (moo-nee-thee-pah-lee-*dhahdh*) *f* municipality

muñeca (moo-*ñay*-kah) *f* doll; wrist

muralla (moo-*rah*-lᵞah) *f* wall

muro (*moo*-roa) *m* wall

músculo (*mooss*-koo-loa) *m* muscle

musculoso (mooss-koo-*loa*-soa) *adj* muscular

muselina (moo-say-*lee*-nah) *f* muslin

museo (moo-*say*-oa) *m* museum; ~ **de figuras de cera** waxworks *pl*

musgo (*mooz*-goa) *m* moss

música (*moo*-see-kah) *f* music

musical (moo-see-*kahl*) *adj* musical; **comedia** ~ musical comedy

músico (*moo*-see-koa) *m* musician

muslo (*mooz*-loa) *m* thigh

musulmán (moo-sool-*mahn*) *m* Muslim

mutuo (*moo*-twoa) *adj* mutual

muy (moo^ee) *adv* very, quite

N

nácar (*nah*-kahr) *m* mother-of-pearl

***nacer** (nah-*thayr*) *v* *be born

nacido (nah-*thee*-dhoa) *adj* born

nacimiento (nah-thee-*m*ᵞ*ayn*-toa) *m* birth; rise

nación (nah-th*ᵞoan*) *f* nation

nacional (nah-thᵞoa-*nahl*) *adj* national

nacionalidad (nah-thᵞoa-nah-lee-*dhahdh*) *f* nationality

nacionalizar (nah-thᵞoa-nah-lee-*thahr*) *v* nationalize

nada (*nah*-dhah) nothing; nil

nadador (nah-dhah-*dhoar*) *m* swimmer

nadar (nah-*dhahr*) *v* *swim

nadie (*nah*-dhᵞay) *pron* nobody, no one

naipe (*nigh*-pay) *m* playing-card

nalga (*nahl*-gah) *m* buttock

naranja (nah-*rahng*-khah) *f* orange

narciso (nahr-*thee*-soa) *m* daffodil

narcosis (nahr-*koa*-seess) *f* narcosis

narcótico (nahr-*koa*-tee-koa) *m* narcotic

nariz (nah-*reeth*) *f* nose

narración (nah-rrah-th*ᵞoan*) *f* account

nata (*nah*-tah) *f* cream

natación (nah-tah-th*ᵞoan*) *f* swimming

nativo (nah-*tee*-bhoa) *adj* native

natural (nah-too-*rahl*) *adj* natural; *m* nature

naturaleza (nah-too-rah-*lay*-thah) *f* nature

naturalmente (nah-too-rahl-*mayn*-tay) *adv* naturally

náusea (*nou*-say-ah) *f* nausea, sickness

navaja (nah-*bhah*-khah) *f* pocket-knife

naval (nah-*bhahl*) *adj* naval

navegable (nah-bhay-*gah*-bhlay) *adj* navigable

navegación (nah-bhay-gah-*thᵞoan*) *f* navigation

navegar (nah-bhay-*gahr*) *v* sail; navigate

Navidad (nah-bhee-*dhahdh*) *f* Xmas, Christmas

nebuloso (nay-bhoo-*loa*-soa) *adj* misty

necesario (nay-thay-*sah*-rᵞoa) *adj* necessary; requisite

neceser (nay-thay-*sayr*) *m* toilet case

necesidad (nay-thay-see-*dhahdh*) *f* need, necessity; want; misery

necesitar (nay-thay-see-*tahr*) *v* need

necio (*nay*-thᵞoa) *adj* foolish, silly

***negar** (nay-*gahr*) *v* deny

negativa (nay-gah-*tee*-bhah) *f* refusal

negativo (nay-gah-*tee*-bhoa) *adj* negative; *m* negative

negligencia (nay-glee-*khayn*-thᵞah) *f* neglect

negligente (nay-glee-*khayn*-tay) *adj* neglectful, careless

negociación (nay-goa-thᵞah-*thᵞoan*) *f* negotiation

negociante (nay-goa-*thᵞahn*-tay) *m* dealer

negociar (nay-goa-*thᵞahr*) *v* negotiate

negocio (nay-*goa*-thᵞoa) *m* business; ***hacer negocios con** *deal with; **hombre de negocios** businessman; ~ **fotográfico** camera shop; **viaje de negocios** business trip

negro (*nay*-groa) *adj* black; *m* Negro

neón (nay-*oan*) *m* neon

nervio (*nayr*-bhᵞoa) *m* nerve

nervioso (nayr-*bhᵞoa*-soa) *adj* nervous

neto (*nay*-toa) *adj* net

neumático (nayᵒᵒ-*mah*-tee-koa) *adj* pneumatic; *m* tyre, tire; ~ **de repuesto** spare tyre; ~ **desinflado** flat tyre

neumonía (nayᵒᵒ-moa-*nee*-ah) *f* pneumonia

neuralgia (nayᵒᵒ-*rahl*-khᵞah) *f* neu-

ralgia
neurosis (nay^{oo}-*roa*-seess) *f* neurosis
neutral (nay^{oo}-*trahl*) *adj* neutral
neutro (nay^{oo}-troa) *adj* neuter
*nevar (nay-*bhahr*) *v* snow
nevasca (nay-*bhahss*-kah) *f* snowstorm
nevoso (nay-*bhoa*-soa) *adj* snowy
ni ... ni (nee) neither ... nor
nicotina (nee-koa-*tee*-nah) *f* nicotine
nido (*nee*-dhoa) *m* nest
niebla (*n^yay*-bhlah) *f* mist, fog; haze;
 faro de ~ foglamp
nieta (*n^yay*-tah) *f* granddaughter
nieto (*n^yay*-toa) *m* grandson
nieve (*n^yay*-bhay) *f* snow
Nigeria (nee-*khay*-r^yah) *f* Nigeria
nigeriano (nee-khay-r^y*ah*-noa) *adj* Nigerian; *m* Nigerian
ninguno (neeng-*goo*-noa) *adj* no;
 pron none; **~ de los dos** neither
niñera (nee-*ñay*-rah) *f* nurse
niño (*nee*-ñoa) *m* child; kid
níquel (*nee*-kayl) *m* nickel
nitrógeno (nee-*troa*-khay-noa) *m* nitrogen
nivel (nee-*bhayl*) *m* level; **~ de vida**
 standard of living; **paso a ~** level
 crossing
nivelar (nee-bhay-*lahr*) *v* level
no (noa) not; no; **si ~** otherwise, else
noble (*noa*-bhlay) *adj* noble
nobleza (noa-*bhlay*-thah) *f* nobility
noción (noa-*th^yoan*) *f* notion; idea
nocturno (noak-*toor*-noa) *adj* nightly
noche (*noa*-chay) *f* night; **de ~** overnight, by night; **esta ~** tonight
nogal (noa-*gahl*) *m* walnut
nombramiento (noam-brah-*m^yayn*-toa)
 m appointment, nomination
nombrar (noam-*brahr*) *v* name, mention; appoint, nominate
nombre (*noam*-bray) *m* noun; name;
 denomination; **en ~ de** on behalf
 of, in the name of; **~ de pila** Chris-

tian name, first name
nominación (noa-mee-nah-*th^yoan*) *f*
 nomination
nominal (noa-mee-*nahl*) *adj* nominal
nordeste (noar-*dhayss*-tay) *m* northeast
norma (*noar*-mah) *f* standard
normal (noar-*mahl*) *adj* normal; regular, standard
noroeste (noa-roa-*ayss*-tay) *m* northwest
norte (*noar*-tay) *m* north; **del ~**
 northerly; **polo ~** North Pole
norteño (noar-*tay*-ñoa) *adj* northern
Noruega (noa-*rway*-gah) *f* Norway
noruego (noa-*rway*-goa) *adj* Norwegian; *m* Norwegian
nos (noass) *pron* ourselves
nosotros (noa-*soa*-troass) *pron* we; us
nostalgia (noass-*tahl*-kh^yah) *f* homesickness
nota (*noa*-tah) *f* ticket; note; mark
notable (noa-*tah*-bhlٖlay) *adj* considerable; remarkable, striking, noticeable
notar (noa-*tahr*) *v* notice; note
notario (noa-*tah*-r^yoa) *m* notary
noticia (noa-*tee*-th^yah) *f* news, notice;
 noticias *fpl* news, tidings *pl*
noticiario (noa-tee-*th^yah*-r^yoa) *m*
 news; newsreel
notificar (noa-tee-fee-*kahr*) *v* notify
notorio (noa-*toa*-r^yoa) *adj* well-known
novedad (noa-bhay-*dhahdh*) *f* novelty
novela (noa-*bhay*-lah) *f* novel; **~ policíaca** detective story; **~ por entregas** serial
novelista (noa-bhay-*leess*-tah) *m* novelist
noveno (noa-*bhay*-noa) *num* ninth
noventa (noa-*bhayn*-tah) *num* ninety
novia (*noa*-bh^yah) *f* fiancée; bride
noviazgo (noa-*bh^yahth*-goa) *m* engagement

noviembre (noa-*bhⱽaym*-bray) November

*hacer novillos (ah-*thayr* noa-*bhee*-lⱽoass) play truant

novio (*noa*-bhⱽoa) *m* fiancé; bridegroom

nube (*noo*-bhay) *f* cloud

nublado (noo-*bhlah*-dhoa) *adj* cloudy, overcast

nuca (*noo*-kah) *f* nape of the neck

nuclear (noo-klay-*ahr*) *adj* nuclear

núcleo (*noo*-klay-oa) *m* nucleus; heart, essence, core

nudillo (noo-*dhee*-lⱽoa) *m* knuckle

nudo (*noo*-dhoa) *m* knot; lump; ~ **corredizo** loop

nuestro (*nwayss*-troa) *adj* our

Nueva Zelanda (*nway*-bhah thay-*lahn*-dah) New Zealand

nueve (*nway*-bhay) *num* nine

nuevo (*nway*-bhoa) *adj* new; **de ~** again

nuez (nwayth) *f* nut; ~ **moscada** nutmeg

nulo (*noo*-loa) *adj* invalid, void

numeral (noo-may-*rahl*) *m* numeral

número (*noo*-may-roa) *m* number; digit; quantity; size; act

numeroso (noo-may-*roa*-soa) *adj* numerous

nunca (*noong*-kah) *adv* never

nutritivo (noo-tree-*tee*-bhoa) *adj* nutritious, nourishing

nylon (*nigh*-loan) *m* nylon

O

o (oa) *conj* or; **o ... o** either ... or

oasis (oa-*ah*-seess) *f* oasis

*obedecer (oa-bhay-dhay-*thayr*) *v* obey

obediencia (oa-bhay-*dhⱽayn*-thⱽah) *f* obedience

obediente (oa-bhay-*dhⱽayn*-tay) *adj* obedient

obertura (oa-bhayr-*too*-rah) *f* overture

obesidad (oa-bhay-see-*dhahdh*) *f* fatness

obeso (oa-*bhay*-soa) *adj* corpulent

obispo (oa-*bheess*-poa) *m* bishop

objeción (oabh-khay-*thⱽoan*) *f* objection; ***hacer ~ a** mind

objetar (oabh-khay-*tahr*) *v* object

objetivo (oabh-khay-*tee*-bhoa) *adj* objective; *m* design, objective, target

objeto (oabh-*khay*-toa) *m* object; **objetos de valor** valuables *pl*; **objetos perdidos** lost and found

oblea (oa-*bhlay*-ah) *f* wafer

oblicuo (oa-*bhlee*-kwoa) *adj* slanting

obligar (oa-bhlee-*gahr*) *v* oblige; force

obligatorio (oa-bhlee-gah-*toa*-rⱽoa) *adj* compulsory, obligatory

oblongo (oa-*bhloang*-goa) *adj* oblong

obra (*oa*-bhrah) *f* work; ~ **de arte** work of art; ~ **de teatro** play; ~ **hecha a mano** handwork; ~ **maestra** masterpiece

obrar (oa-*bhrahr*) *v* work; perform

obrero (oa-*bhray*-roa) *m* workman, worker, labourer; ~ **portuario** docker

obsceno (oabh-*thay*-noa) *adj* obscene

obscuridad (oabhs-koo-ree-*dhahdh*) *f* gloom

obscuro (oabhs-*koo*-roa) *adj* dark, obscure

observación (oabh-sayr-bhah-*thⱽoan*) *f* observation; remark; ***hacer una ~** remark

observar (oabh-sayr-*bhahr*) *v* watch, observe, notice, note

observatorio (oabh-sayr-bhah-*toa*-rⱽoa) *m* observatory

obsesión (oabh-say-*sⱽoan*) *f* obsession

obstáculo (oabhs-*tah*-koo-loa) *m* obstacle

no obstante (noa oabhs-*tahn*-tay)
nevertheless

obstinado (oabhs-tee-*nah*-dhoa) *adj*
dogged, obstinate

***obstruir** (oabhs-*trweer*) *v* block

***obtener** (oabh-tay-*nayr*) *v* obtain

obtenible (oabh-tay-*nee*-bhlay) *adj*
available

obtuso (oabh-*too*-soa) *adj* blunt

obvio (*oabh*-bh^yoa) *adj* apparent, obvious

oca (*oa*-kah) *f* goose

ocasión (oa-kah-s^yoan) *f* occasion;
chance

ocasionalmente (oa-kah-s^yoa-nahl-
mayn-tay) *adv* occasionally

ocaso (oa-*kah*-soa) *m* sunset

occidental (oak-thee-dhayn-*tahl*) *adj*
westerly; western

occidente (oak-thee-*dhayn*-tay) *m* west

océano (oa-*thay*-ah-noa) *m* ocean;
Océano Pacífico Pacific Ocean

ocio (*oa*-th^yoa) *m* leisure

ocioso (oa-*th^yoa*-soa) *adj* idle

octavo (oa-*thay*-ah-bhoa) *num* eighth

octubre (oak-*too*-bhray) October

oculista (oa-koo-*leess*-tah) *m* oculist

ocultar (oa-kool-*tahr*) *v* *hide

ocupación (oa-koo-pah-*th^yoan*) *f* occupation; business

ocupante (oa-koo-*pahn*-tay) *m* occupant

ocupar (oa-koo-*pahr*) *v* occupy; *take
up; **ocupado** *adj* engaged, busy;
occupied; **ocuparse de** look after

ocurrencia (oa-koo-*rrayn*-th^yah) *f* idea

ocurrir (oa-koo-*rreer*) *v* occur

ochenta (oa-*chayn*-tah) *num* eighty

ocho (*oa*-choa) *num* eight

odiar (oa-*dh^yahr*) *v* hate

odio (*oa*-dh^yoa) *m* hatred, hate

oeste (oa-*ayss*-tay) *m* west

ofender (oa-fayn-*dayr*) *v* wound,

*hurt, offend, injure

ofensa (oa-*fayn*-sah) *f* offence

ofensivo (oa-fayn-*see*-bhoa) *adj* offensive; *m* offensive

oferta (oa-*fayr*-tah) *f* offer, supply

oficial (oa-fee-*th^yahl*) *adj* official; *m*
officer; ~ **de aduanas** Customs of-
ficer

oficina (oa-fee-*thee*-nah) *f* office; ~ **de
cambio** exchange office; ~ **de colocación** employment exchange; ~
de informaciones information
bureau; ~ **de objetos perdidos** lost
property office

oficinista (oa-fee-thee-*neess*-tah) *m*
clerk

oficio (oa-*fee*-th^yoa) *m* trade

***ofrecer** (oa-fray-*thayr*) *v* offer

oído (oa-*ee*-dhoa) *m* hearing; **dolor
de oídos** earache

***oír** (oa-*eer*) *v* *hear

ojal (oa-*khahl*) *m* buttonhole

ojeada (oa-khay-*ah*-dhah) *f* glimpse,
glance; look

ojear (oa-khay-*ahr*) *v* glance

ojo (*oa*-khoa) *m* eye

ola (*oa*-lah) *f* wave

***oler** (oa-*layr*) *v* *smell

olmo (*oal*-moa) *m* elm

olor (oa-*loar*) *m* smell, odour

olvidadizo (oal-bhee-dhah-*dhee*-thoa)
adj forgetful

olvidar (oal-bhee-*dhahr*) *v* *forget

olla (*oa*-l^yah) *f* pot; kettle; ~ **a presión** pressure-cooker

ombligo (oam-*blee*-goa) *m* navel

omitir (oa-mee-*teer*) *v* *leave out,
omit; fail

omnipotente (oam-nee-poa-*tayn*-tay)
adj omnipotent

once (*oan*-thay) *num* eleven

onceno (oan-*thay*-noa) *num* eleventh

onda (*oan*-dah) *f* wave

ondulación (oan-doo-lah-*th^yoan*) *f*

wave; ~ **permanente** permanent wave

ondulado (oan-doo-*lah*-dhoa) *adj* wavy

ondulante (oan-doo-*lahn*-tay) *adj* undulating

ónix (*oa*-neeks) *m* onyx

ópalo (*oa*-pah-loa) *m* opal

opcional (oap-th^yoa-*nahl*) *adj* optional

ópera (*oa*-pay-rah) *f* opera

operación (oa-pay-rah-*th^yoan*) *f* operation, surgery

operar (oa-pay-*rahr*) *v* operate

opinar (oa-pee-*nahr*) *v* consider

opinión (oa-pee-n^y*oan*) *f* view, opinion

****oponerse** (oa-poa-*nayr*-say) *v* oppose; ~ **a** object to

oportunidad (oa-poar-too-nee-*dhahdh*) *f* chance, opportunity

oportuno (oa-poar-*too*-noa) *adj* convenient

oposición (oa-poa-see-*th^yoan*) *f* opposition

oprimir (oa-pree-*meer*) *v* oppress

óptico (*oap*-tee-koa) *m* optician

optimismo (oap-tee-*meez*-moa) *m* optimism

optimista (oap-tee-*meess*-tah) *adj* optimistic; *m* optimist

óptimo (*oap*-tee-moa) *adj* best

opuesto (oa-*pwayss*-toa) *adj* opposite; averse

oración (oa-rah-*th^yoan*) *f* prayer

oral (oa-*rahl*) *adj* oral

orar (oa-*rahr*) *v* pray

orden (*oar*-dhayn) *f* command; order; *m* method; **de primer** ~ first-rate; ~ **del día** agenda

ordenador (oar-dhay-nah-*dhoar*) *m* computer

ordenar (oar-dhay-*nahr*) *v* arrange; order

ordinario (oar-dhee-*nah*-r^yoa) *adj* simple, ordinary; common, vulgar

oreja (oa-*ray*-khah) *f* ear

orfebre (oar-*fay*-bhray) *m* goldsmith

orgánico (oar-*gah*-nee-koa) *adj* organic

organillo (oar-gah-*nee*-l^yoa) *m* street-organ

organismo (oar-gah-*neez*-moa) *m* organism

organización (oar-gah-nee-thah-*th^yoan*) *f* organization

organizar (oa; -gah-nee-*thahr*) *v* organize; arrange

órgano (*oar*-gah-noa) *m* organ

orgullo (oar-*goo*-l^yoa) *m* pride

orgulloso (oar-goo-*l^yoa*-soa) *adj* proud

orientación (oa-r^yayn-tah-*th^yoan*) *f* orientation

oriental (oa-r^yayn-*tahl*) *adj* eastern, easterly; oriental

orientarse (oa-r^yayn-*tahr*-say) *v* orientate

oriente (oa-r^y*ayn*-tay) *m* Orient

origen (oa-*ree*-khayn) *m* origin

original (oa-ree-khee-*nahl*) *adj* original

originalmente (oa-ree-khee-nahl-*mayn*-tay) *adv* originally

originar (oa-ree-khee-*nahr*) *v* originate

orilla (oa-*ree*-l^yah) *f* bank; shore

orina (oa-*ree*-nah) *f* urine

ornamental (oar-nah-mayn-*tahl*) *adj* ornamental

oro (*oa*-roa) *m* gold

orquesta (oar-*kayss*-tah) *f* orchestra; band

ortodoxo (oar-toa-*dhoak*-soa) *adj* orthodox

os (oass) *pron* you

osar (oa-*sahr*) *v* dare

oscilar (oa-thee-*lahr*) *v* *swing

oscuridad (oass-koo-ree-*dhahdh*) *f* dark

oscuro (oass-*koo*-roa) *adj* dark, dim, obscure

oso (*oa*-soa) *m* bear

ostentación (oass-tayn-tah-*th^yoan*) *f* fuss

ostra (*oass*-trah) *f* oyster

otoño (oa-*toa*-ño-a) *m* autumn; fall *nAm*

otro (*oa*-troa) *adj* other, different; another; ~ **más** another

ovalado (oa-bhah-*lah*-dhoa) *adj* oval

oveja (oa-*bhay*-khah) *f* sheep

overol (oa-bhay-*roal*) *mMe* overalls *pl*

oxidado (oak-see-*dhah*-dhoa) *adj* rusty

oxígeno (oak-*see*-khay-noa) *m* oxygen

oyente (oa-*^yayn*-tay) *m* auditor, listener

P

pabellón (pah-bhay-*l^yoan*) *m* pavilion

*****pacer** (pah-*thayr*) *v* graze

paciencia (pah-*th^yayn*-th^yah) *f* patience

paciente (pah-*th^yayn*-tay) *adj* patient; *m* patient

pacifismo (pah-thee-*feez*-moa) *m* pacifism

pacifista (pah-thee-*feess*-tah) *adj* pacifist; *m* pacifist

*****padecer** (pah-dhay-*thayr*) *v* suffer

padrastro (pah-*dhrahss*-troa) *m* stepfather

padre (*pah*-dhray) *m* father

padres (*pah*-dhrayss) *mpl* parents *pl*; ~ **adoptivos** foster-parents *pl*; ~ **políticos** parents-in-law *pl*

padrino (pah-*dhree*-noa) *m* godfather

paga (*pah*-gah) *f* wages *pl*

pagano (pah-*gah*-noa) *adj* heathen, pagan; *m* heathen, pagan

pagar (pah-*gahr*) *v* *pay; **pagado por adelantado** prepaid; ~ **a plazos** *pay on account

página (*pah*-khee-nah) *f* page

pago (*pah*-goa) *m* payment; **primer** ~ down payment

painel (pigh-*nayl*) *m* panel

país (pah-*eess*) *m* country, land; ~ **natal** native country

paisaje (pigh-*sah*-khay) *m* scenery, landscape

paisano (pigh-*sah*-noa) *m* civilian

Países Bajos (pah-*ee*-sayss -*bah*-khoass) *mpl* the Netherlands

paja (*pah*-khah) *f* straw

pájaro (*pah*-khah-roa) *m* bird

paje (*pah*-khay) *m* page-boy

pala (*pah*-lah) *f* spade, shovel

palabra (pah-*lah*-bhrah) *f* word

palacio (pah-*lah*-th^yoa) *m* palace

palanca (pah-*lahng*-kah) *f* lever; ~ **de cambios** gear lever

palangana (pah-lahng-*gah*-nah) *f* basin; wash-basin

pálido (*pah*-lee-dhoa) *adj* pale; dull; light

palillo (pah-*lee*-l^yoa) *m* toothpick

palma (*pahl*-mah) *f* palm

palo (*pah*-loa) *m* stick; ~ **de golf** golf-club

paloma (pah-*loa*-mah) *f* pigeon

palpable (pahl-*pah*-bhlay) *adj* palpable

palpar (pahl-*pahr*) *v* *feel

palpitación (pahl-pee-tah-*th^yoan*) *f* palpitation

pan (pahn) *m* bread, loaf; ~ **integral** wholemeal bread; ~ **tostado** toast

pana (*pah*-nah) *f* corduroy, velveteen

panadería (pah-nah-dhay-*ree*-ah) *f* bakery

panadero (pah-nah-*dhay*-roa) *m* baker

panecillo (pah-nay-*thee*-l^yoa) *m* roll

pánico (*pah*-nee-koa) *m* panic

pantalones (pahn-tah-*loa*-nayss) *mpl* trousers *pl*; slacks *pl*; pants *plAm*; ~ **cortos** shorts *pl*; ~ **de esquí** ski pants; ~ **de gimnasia** trunks *pl*

pantalla (pahn-*tah*-l^yah) *f* lampshade;

screen
pantano (pahn-*tah*-noa) *m* marsh, bog
pantanoso (pahn-tah-*noa*-soa) *adj* marshy
pantorrilla (pahn-toa-*rree*-lᵛah) *f* calf
pañal (pah-*ñahl*) *m* nappy; diaper *nAm*
pañería (pah-ñay-*ree*-ah) *f* drapery
pañero (pah-*ñay*-roa) *m* draper
paño (*pah*-ñoa) *m* cloth; ~ **higiénico** sanitary towel
pañuelo (pah-*ñway*-loa) *m* handkerchief; ~ **de papel** tissue, Kleenex®
Papa (*pah*-pah) *m* pope
papa (*pah*-pah) *fMe* potato
papá (pah-*pah*) *m* dad
papaíto (pah-pah-*ee*-toa) *m* daddy
papel (pah-*payl*) *m* paper; **de ~** paper; ~ **carbón** carbon paper; ~ **de envolver** wrapping paper; ~ **de escribir** writing-paper; ~ **de estaño** tinfoil; ~ **de lija** sandpaper; ~ **higiénico** toilet-paper; ~ **para cartas** notepaper; ~ **para mecanografiar** typing paper; ~ **pintado** wallpaper; ~ **secante** blotting paper
papelería (pah-pay-lay-*ree*-ah) *f* stationery; stationer's
paperas (pah-*pay*-rahss) *fpl* mumps
paquete (pah-*kay*-tay) *m* packet, package, parcel; bundle
Paquistán (pah-keess-*tahn*) *m* Pakistan
paquistaní (pah-keess-tah-*nee*) *adj* Pakistani; *m* Pakistani
par (pahr) *adj* even; *m* pair
para (*pah*-rah) *prep* to, for; to, in order to; ~ **con** towards; ~ **que** what for
parabrisas (pah-rah-*bhree*-sahss) *m* windscreen; windshield *nAm*
parachoques (pah-rah-*choa*-kayss) *m* fender, bumper
parada (pah-*rah*-dhah) *f* parade; stop;

~ **de taxis** taxi rank; taxi stand *Am*
parado (pah-*rah*-dhoa) *adjMe* erect
parador (pah-rah-*dhoar*) *m* roadhouse
parafina (pah-rah-*fee*-nah) *f* paraffin
paraguas (pah-*rah*-gwahss) *m* umbrella
paraíso (pah-rah-*ee*-soa) *m* paradise
paralelo (pah-rah-*lay*-loa) *adj* parallel; *m* parallel
paralítico (pah-rah-*lee*-tee-koa) *adj* lame
paralizar (pah-rah-lee-*thahr*) *v* paralise
pararse (pah-*rahr*-say) *v* halt; pull up
parcela (pahr-*thay*-lah) *f* plot
parcial (pahr-*thᵛahl*) *adj* partial
parecer (pah-ray-*thayr*) *m* view, opinion
*****parecer** (pah-ray-*thayr*) *v* appear, seem, look
parecido (pah-ray-*thee*-dhoa) *adj* alike; **bien ~** good-looking
pared (pah-*raydh*) *f* wall
pareja (pah-*ray*-khah) *f* couple; partner
pariente (pah-rᵛ*ayn*-tay) *m* relative, relation
parlamentario (pahr-lah-mayn-*tah*-rᵛoa) *adj* parliamentary
parlamento (pahr-lah-*mayn*-toa) *m* parliament
párpado (*pahr*-pah-dhoa) *m* eyelid
parque (*pahr*-kay) *m* park; ~ **de estacionamiento** car park; ~ **de reserva zoológica** game reserve; ~ **nacional** national park
parquímetro (pahr-*kee*-may-troa) *m* parking meter
párrafo (*pah*-rrah-foa) *m* paragraph
parrilla (pah-*rree*-lᵛah) *f* grill; grillroom; **asar en ~** grill
parroquia (pah-*rroa*-kᵛah) *f* parish
parsimonioso (pahr-see-moa-*nᵛoa*-soa) *adj* economical
parte (*pahr*-tay) *f* part; share; **en al-**

guna ~ somewhere; **en ninguna** ~ nowhere; **en** ~ partly; **otra** ~ elsewhere; ~ **posterior** rear; ~ **superior** top, top side; **por otra** ~ besides; **por todas partes** everywhere, throughout

participante (pahr-tee-thee-*pahn*-tay) *m* participant

participar (pahr-tee-thee-*pahr*) *v* participate

particular (pahr-tee-koo-*lahr*) *adj* private; particular; **en** ~ specially, in particular

particularidad (pahr-tee-koo-lah-ree-*dhahdh*) *f* detail; peculiarity

partida (pahr-*tee*-dhah) *f* departure

partido (pahr-*tee*-dhoa) *m* side, party; match; ~ **de fútbol** football match

partir (pahr-*teer*) *v* *leave, depart, pull out, *set out; **a** ~ **de** as from; from

parto (*pahr*-toa) *m* childbirth, delivery

párvulo (*pahr*-bhoo-loa) *m* toddler; **escuela de párvulos** kindergarten

pasa (*pah*-sah) *f* raisin; ~ **de Corinto** currant

pasado (pah-*sah*-dhoa) *adj* past; *m* past

pasaje (pah-*sah*-khay) *m* passage

pasajero (pah-sah-*khay*-roa) *m* passenger

pasaporte (pah-sah-*poar*-tay) *m* passport

pasar (pah-*sahr*) *v* happen; *go through; pass; *spend; ~ **por alto** overlook; **pasarse sin** spare

pasarela (pah-sah-*ray*-lah) *f* gangway

Pascua (*pahss*-kwah) Easter

paseante (pah-say-*ahn*-tay) *m* walker

pasear (pah-say-*ahr*) *v* walk, stroll

paseo (pah-*say*-oa) *m* stroll; ride; promenade

pasillo (pah-*see*-l^yoa) *m* corridor; aisle

pasión (pah-s^yoan) *f* passion

pasivo (pah-*see*-bhoa) *adj* passive

paso (*pah*-soa) *m* step, pace; move, gait; crossing; mountain pass; **de** ~ **casual**; ~ **a nivel** crossing; **prioridad de** ~ right of way; **prohibido el** ~ no entry

pasta (*pahss*-tah) *f* paste; ~ **dentífrica** toothpaste

pastel (pahss-*tayl*) *m* cake

pastelería (pahss-tay-lay-*ree*-ah) *f* pastry, cake; pastry shop

pastilla (pahss-*tee*-l^yah) *f* tablet

pastor (pahss-*toar*) *m* shepherd; clergyman, parson, rector

pata (*pah*-tah) *f* paw; leg

patada (pah-*tah*-dhah) *f* kick

patata (pah-*tah*-tah) *f* potato; **patatas fritas** chips

patear (pah-tay-*ahr*) *v* kick; stamp

patente (pah-*tayn*-tay) *f* patent

patillas (pah-*tee*-l^yahss) *fpl* whiskers *pl*, sideburns *pl*

patín (pah-*teen*) *m* skate; scooter

patinaje (pah-tee-*nah*-khay) *m* skating

patinar (pah-tee-*nahr*) *v* skate; skid

pato (*pah*-toa) *m* duck

patria (*pah*-tr^yah) *f* native country, fatherland

patriota (pah-tr^yoa-tah) *m* patriot

patrón (pah-*troan*) *m* boss, master; employer; landlord

patrona (pah-*troa*-nah) *f* landlady

patrulla (pah-*troo*-l^yah) *f* patrol

patrullar (pah-troo-*l^yahr*) *v* patrol

paulatinamente (pou-lah-tee-nah-*mayn*-tay) *adv* gradually

pausa (*pou*-sah) *f* pause; *hacer una ~ pause

pavimentar (pah-bhee-mayn-*tahr*) *v* pave

pavimento (pah-bhee-*mayn*-toa) *m* pavement

pavo (*pah*-bhoa) *m* peacock; turkey

payaso (pah-^yah-soa) *m* clown

paz (pahth) *f* peace; quiet

peaje (pay-*ah*-khay) *m* toll

peatón (pay-ah-*toan*) *m* pedestrian; **prohibido para los peatones** no pedestrians

pecado (pay-*kah*-dhoa) *m* sin

pecio (*pay*-thⁱoa) *m* wreck

peculiar (pay-koo-lⁱ*ahr*) *adj* peculiar

pecho (*pay*-choa) *m* chest; bosom

pedal (pay-*dhahl*) *m* pedal

pedazo (pay-*dhah*-thoa) *m* piece; scrap

pedernal (pay-dhayr-*nahl*) *m* flint

pedicuro (pay-dhee-*koo*-roa) *m* chiropodist, pedicure

pedido (pay-*dhee*-dhoa) *m* order

*pedir (pay-*dheer*) *v* beg; order; charge

pegajoso (pay-gah-*khoa*-soa) *adj* sticky

pegar (pay-*gahr*) *v* smack, slap, *hit; *stick, paste; **pegarse** *v* *burn

peinado (pay-*nah*-dhoa) *m* hair-do

peinar (pay-*nahr*) *v* comb

peine (*pay*-nay) *m* comb; ~ **de bolsillo** pocket-comb

pelar (pay-*lahr*) *v* peel

peldaño (payl-*dah*-ñoa) *m* step

pelea (pay-*lay*-ah) *f* battle

peletero (pay-lay-*tay*-roa) *m* furrier

pelícano (pay-*lee*-kah-noa) *m* pelican

película (pay-*lee*-koo-lah) *f* film; ~ **en colores** colour film

peligro (pay-*lee*-groa) *m* danger; peril, risk; distress

peligroso (pay-lee-*groa*-soa) *adj* dangerous; perilous

pelmazo (payl-*mah*-thoa) *m* bore

pelota (pay-*loa*-tah) *f* ball

peluca (pay-*loo*-kah) *f* wig

peluquero (pay-loo-*kay*-roa) *m* hairdresser

pelvis (*payl*-bheess) *m* pelvis

pellizcar (pay-lⁱ*eeth*-*kahr*) *v* pinch

pena (*pay*-nah) *f* sorrow; pains; penalty; ~ **de muerte** death penalty

pendiente (payn-dⁱ*ayn*-tay) *adj* slanting; *m* earring, pendant; *f* gradient, slope

penetrar (pay-nay-*trahr*) *v* penetrate

penicilina (pay-nee-thee-*lee*-nah) *f* penicillin

península (pay-*neen*-soo-lah) *f* peninsula

pensador (payn-sah-*dhoar*) *m* thinker

pensamiento (payn-sah-mⁱ*ayn*-toa) *m* idea, thought

*pensar (payn-*sahr*) *v* *think; ~ **en** *think of

pensativo (payn-sah-*tee*-bhoa) *adj* thoughtful

pensión (payn-sⁱ*oan*) *f* guest-house, pension, boarding-house; board; ~ **alimenticia** alimony; ~ **completa** full board, board and lodging

Pentecostés (payn-tay-koass-*tayss*) *m* Whitsun

peña (*pay*-ñah) *f* boulder

peón (pay-*oan*) *m* pawn

peor (pay-*oar*) *adj* worse; *adv* worse

pepino (pay-*pee*-noa) *m* cucumber

pepita (pay-*pee*-tah) *f* pip

pequeño (pay-*kay*-ñoa) *adj* small, little; petty, minor

pera (*pay*-rah) *f* pear

perca (*payr*-kah) *f* perch, bass

percepción (payr-thayp-thⁱ*oan*) *f* perception

perceptible (payr-thayp-*tee*-bhlay) *adj* perceptible, noticeable

percibir (payr-thee-*bheer*) *v* perceive

percha (*payr*-chah) *f* hanger, coat-hanger, peg; hat rack

*perder (payr-*dhayr*) *v* *lose; miss; waste

pérdida (*payr*-dhee-dhah) *f* loss

perdiz (payr-*dheeth*) *f* partridge

perdón (payr-*dhoan*) *m* pardon;

grace; **¡perdón!** sorry!

perdonar (payr-dhoa-*nahr*) v *forgive

perecedero (pay-ray-thay-*dhay*-roa) *adj* perishable

*****perecer** (pay-ray-*thayr*) v perish

peregrinación (pay-ray-gree-nah-th^yoan) *f* pilgrimage

peregrino (pay-ray-*gree*-noa) *m* pilgrim

perejil (pay-ray-*kheel*) *m* parsley

perezoso (pay-ray-*thoa*-soa) *adj* lazy

perfección (payr-fayk-th^yoan) *f* perfection

perfecto (payr-*fayk*-toa) *adj* perfect; faultless

perfil (payr-*feel*) *m* profile

perfume (payr-*foo*-may) *m* perfume; scent

periódico (pay-r^yoa-dhee-koa) *adj* periodical; *m* periodical, paper; **vendedor de periódicos** newsagent

periodismo (pay-r^yoa-*deez*-moa) *m* journalism

periodista (pay-r^yoa-*dheess*-tah) *m* journalist

período (pay-*ree*-oa-dhoa) *m* period, term

perito (pay-*ree*-toa) *m* expert, connoisseur

perjudicar (payr-khoo-dhee-*kahr*) v harm

perjudicial (payr-khoo-dhee-th^yahl) *adj* harmful, hurtful

perjuicio (payr-*khwee*-th^yoa) *m* harm, damage

perjurio (payr-*khoo*-r^yoa) *m* perjury

perla (*payr*-lah) *f* pearl

*****permanecer** (payr-mah-nay-*thayr*) v remain

permanente (payr-mah-*nayn*-tay) *adj* permanent; **planchado** ~ permanent press

permiso (payr-*mee*-soa) *m* permission, authorization; permit, licence; ~ **de**

conducir driving licence; ~ **de pesca** fishing licence; ~ **de residencia** residence permit; ~ **de trabajo** work permit; labor permit *Am*

permitir (payr-mee-*teer*) v permit, allow; enable; **permitirse** v afford

perno (*payr*-noa) *m* bolt

pero (*pay*-roa) *conj* yet, only, but

peróxido (pay-*roak*-see-dhoa) *m* peroxide

perpendicular (payr-payn-dee-koo-*lahr*) *adj* perpendicular

perpetuo (payr-*pay*-twoa) *adj* perpetual

perra (*pay*-rrah) *f* bitch

perrera (pay-*rray*-rah) *f* kennel

perro (*pay*-rroa) *m* dog; ~ **lazarillo** guide-dog

persa (*payr*-sah) *adj* Persian; *m* Persian

*****perseguir** (payr-say-*geer*) v pursue

perseverar (payr-say-bhay-*rahr*) v *keep up

Persia (*payr*-s^yah) *f* Persia

persiana (payr-s^y*ah*-nah) *f* shutter, blind

persistir (payr-seess-*teer*) v insist

persona (payr-*soa*-nah) *f* person; **por** ~ per person

personal (payr-soa-*nahl*) *adj* personal, private; *m* personnel, staff

personalidad (payr-soa-nah-lee-dhahdh) *f* personality

perspectiva (payrs-payk-*tee*-bhah) *f* perspective; prospect

persuadir (payr-swah-dheer) v persuade

*****pertenecer** (payr-tay-nay-*thayr*) v belong

pertenencias (payr-tay-*nayn*-th^yahss) *fpl* belongings *pl*

pertinaz (payr-tee-*nahth*) *adj* obstinate

pesado (pay-*sah*-dhoa) *adj* heavy

pesadumbre (pay-sah-*dhoom*-bray) *f*

grief
pesar (pay-*sahr*) v weigh; **a ~ de** despite, in spite of

pesca (*payss*-kah) f fishing; fishing industry

pescadería (payss-kah-dhay-*ree*-ah) f fish shop

pescador (payss-kah-*dhoar*) m fisherman

pescar (payss-*kahr*) v fish; **~ con caña** angle

pesebre (pay-*say*-bhray) m manger

pesimismo (pay-see-*meez*-moa) m pessimism

pesimista (pay-see-*meess*-tah) adj pessimistic; m pessimist

pésimo (*pay*-see-moa) adj worst; terrible

peso (*pay*-soa) m weight; burden

pestaña (payss-*tah*-ñah) f eyelash

petaca (pay-*tah*-kah) f pouch; tobacco pouch

pétalo (*pay*-tah-loa) m petal

petición (pay-tee-*th*y*oan*) f petition

petirrojo (pay-tee-*rroa*-khoa) m robin

petróleo (pay-*troa*-lay-oa) m petroleum, oil; **~ lampante** kerosene; **pozo de ~** oil-well; **refinería de ~** oil-refinery

pez (payth) m fish

piadoso (p*y*ah-*dhoa*-soa) adj pious

pianista (p*y*ah-*neess*-tah) m pianist

piano (p*y*ah-noa) m piano; **~ de cola** grand piano

picadero (pee-kah-*dhay*-roa) m riding-school

picadura (pee-kah-*dhoo*-rah) f sting, bite; cigarette tobacco

picante (pee-*kahn*-tay) adj spicy, savoury

picar (pee-*kahr*) v itch; mince; *sting

pícaro (*pee*-kah-roa) m rascal

picazón (pee-kah-*thoan*) f itch

pico (*pee*-koa) m beak; peak; pick-

axe
pie (p*y*ay) m foot; **a ~ on foot**; walking; **de ~** upright; *estar de ~ *stand; **~ de cabra** crowbar

piedad (p*y*ay-*dhahdh*) f pity; *tener **~ de** pity

piedra (p*y*ay-dhrah) f stone; **de ~** stone; **~ miliar** milestone; **~ pómez** pumice stone; **~ preciosa** stone

piel (p*y*ayl) f skin; fur, hide; peel; **de ~** leather; **~ de cerdo** pigskin

pierna (p*y*ayr-nah) f leg

pieza (p*y*ay-thah) f part; **de dos piezas** two-piece; **~ de repuesto** spare part; **~ en un acto** one-act play

pijama (pee-*khah*-mah) m pyjamas pl

pilar (pee-*lahr*) m pillar

píldora (*peel*-doa-rah) f pill

pileta (pee-*lay*-tah) f sink

piloto (pee-*loa*-toa) m pilot

pillo (*pee*-l*y*oa) m rascal

pimienta (pee-m*y*ayn-tah) f pepper

pincel (peen-*thayl*) m paint-brush

pinchado (peen-*chah*-dhoa) adj punctured

pinchar (peen-*chahr*) v prick

pinchazo (peen-*chah*-thoa) m puncture

pingüino (peeng-*gwee*-noa) m penguin

pino (*pee*-noa) m fir-tree

pintar (peen-*tahr*) v paint

pintor (peen-*toar*) m painter

pintoresco (peen-toa-*rayss*-koa) adj picturesque, scenic

pintura (peen-*too*-rah) f paint; painting; **~ al óleo** oil-painting

pinzas (*peen*-thahss) fpl tweezers pl

pinzón (peen-*thoan*) m finch

piña (*pee*-ñah) f pineapple

pío (*pee*-oa) adj pious

piojo (p*y*oa-khoa) m louse

pionero (p*y*oa-*nay*-roa) m pioneer

pipa (*pee*-pah) f pipe

pirata (pee-*rah*-tah) m pirate

pisar (pee-*sahr*) v step

piscina (pee-*thee*-nah) f swimming pool

piso (*pee*-soa) m storey, floor; flat; apartment *nAm*; ~ **bajo** ground floor

pista (*peess*-tah) f ring; track; lane; ~ **de aterrizaje** runway; ~ **de patinaje** skating-rink; ~ **para carreras** race-course

pistola (peess-*toa*-lah) f pistol

pistón (peess-*toan*) m piston

pitillera (pee-tee-*l*Yay-rah) f cigarette-case

pizarra (pee-*thah*-rrah) f slate; blackboard

placa (*plah*-kah) f registration plate

placer (plah-*thayr*) m pleasure

* **placer** (plah-*thayr*) v please

plaga (*plah*-gah) f plague

plan (plahn) m plan, project

plancha (*plahn*-chah) f iron; **no precisa** ~ wash and wear, drip-dry

planchar (plahn-*chahr*) v iron; press

planeador (plah-nay-ah-*dhoar*) m glider

planear (plah-nay-*ahr*) v plan

planeta (plah-*nay*-tah) m planet

planetario (plah-nay-*tah*-rYoa) m planetarium

plano (*plah*-noa) adj level, even, plane; m plan, map; **primer** ~ foreground

planta (*plahn*-tah) f plant

plantación (plahn-tah-*th*Yoan) f plantation

plantar (plahn-*tahr*) v plant

plantear (plahn-tay-*ahr*) v *put

plástico (*plahss*-tee-koa) m plastic; **de** ~ plastic

plata (*plah*-tah) f silver; **de** ~ silver; ~ **labrada** silverware

plátano (*plah*-tah-noa) m banana

platero (plah-*tay*-roa) m silversmith

platija (plah-*tee*-khah) f plaice

platillo (plah-*tee*-lYoa) m saucer

platino (plah-*tee*-noa) m platinum

plato (*plah*-toa) m dish, plate; course; ~ **para sopa** soup-plate

playa (*plah*-Yah) f beach; ~ **de veraneo** seaside resort; ~ **para nudistas** nudist beach

plaza (*plah*-thah) f square; ~ **de mercado** market-place; ~ **de toros** bullring; ~ **fuerte** stronghold

plazo (*plah*-thoa) m term; instalment; **compra a plazos** hire-purchase

pleamar (play-ah-*mahr*) f high tide

* **plegar** (play-*gahr*) v crease

pliegue (*pl*Yay-gay) m crease, fold

plomero (ploa-*may*-roa) m plumber

plomo (*ploa*-moa) m lead

pluma (*ploo*-mah) f feather; pen

plural (ploo-*rahl*) m plural

población (poa-bhlah-*th*Yoan) f population

pobre (*poa*-bhray) adj poor

pobreza (poa-*bhray*-thah) f poverty

poco (*poa*-koa) adj little; m bit; **dentro de** ~ presently; **pocos** adj few; **un** ~ some

poder (poa-*dhayr*) m power; authority

* **poder** (poa-*dhayr*) v *be able to, *can; *might, *may

poderoso (poa-dhay-*roa*-soa) adj powerful

podrido (poa-*dhree*-dhoa) adj rotten

poema (poa-*ay*-mah) m poem; ~ **épico** epic

poesía (poa-ay-*see*-ah) f poetry

poeta (poa-*ay*-tah) m poet

poético (poa-*ay*-tee-koa) adj poetic

polaco (poa-*lah*-koa) adj Polish; m Pole

polea (poa-*lay*-ah) f pulley

policía (poa-lee-*thee*-ah) f police pl

polifacético (poa-lee-fah-*thay*-tee-koa) adj all-round

polilla (poa-lee-l^yah) f moth

polio (poa-l^yoa) f polio

poliomielitis (poa-l^yoa-m^yay-lee-teess) f polio

política (poa-lee-tee-kah) f policy; politics

político (poa-lee-tee-koa) adj political; m politician

póliza (poa-lee-thah) f policy

Polonia (poa-loa-n^yah) f Poland

polución (poa-loo-th^yoan) f pollution

polvera (poal-bhay-rah) f powder compact

polvo (poal-bhoa) m dust; powder; grit; ~ **facial** face-powder; ~ **para los dientes** toothpowder; ~ **para los pies** foot powder

pólvora (poal-bhoa-rah) f gunpowder

polvoriento (poal-bhoa-r^yayn-toa) adj dusty

pollero (poa-l^yay-roa) m poulterer

pollo (poa-l^yoa) m chicken

pomelo (poa-may-loa) m grapefruit

pómulo (poa-moo-loa) m cheek-bone

ponderado (poan-day-rah-dhoa) adj sober

*poner (poa-nayr) v place, *lay, *put, *set; ***ponerse** v *put on

pony (poa-nee) m pony

popelín (poa-pay-leen) m poplin

popular (poa-poo-lahr) adj popular; vulgar; **canción** ~ folk song; **danza** ~ folk-dance

populoso (poa-poo-loa-soa) adj populous

por (poar) prep by; for; via; times

porcelana (poar-thay-lah-nah) f china, porcelain

porcentaje (poar-thayn-tah-khay) m percentage

porción (poar-th^yoan) f portion, helping

porque (poar-kay) conj because, for, as; **por qué** why

porra (poa-rrah) f club

portabagajes (poar-tah-bah-khah-gayss) m luggage rack

portador (poar-tah-dhoar) m bearer

portaequipajes (poar-tah-ay-kee-pah-khayss) m boot; trunk nAm

portafolio (poar-tah-foa-l^yoa) m attaché case, briefcase

portaligas (poar-tah-lee-gahss) m suspender belt

portátil (poar-tah-teel) adj portable

portero (poar-tay-roa) m doorman, door-keeper, porter; goalkeeper

pórtico (poar-tee-koa) m arcade

portilla (poar-tee-l^yah) f porthole

portón (poar-toan) m gate

Portugal (poar-too-gahl) m Portugal

portugués (poar-too-gayss) adj Portuguese; m Portuguese

porvenir (poar-bhay-neer) m future

posada (poa-sah-dhah) f inn

posadero (poa-sah-dhay-roa) m inn-keeper

*poseer (poa-say-ayr) v own, possess

posesión (poa-say-s^yoan) f possession

posibilidad (poa-see-bhee-lee-dhahdh) f possibility

posible (poa-see-bhlay) adj possible

posición (poa-see-th^yoan) f position

positiva (poa-see-tee-bhah) f positive, print

positivo (poa-see-tee-bhoa) adj positive

postal ilustrada (poass-tahl ee-looss-trah-dhah) picture postcard

poste (poass-tay) m post, pole; ~ **de farol** lamp-post; ~ **de indicador** signpost

posterior (poass-tay-r^yoar) adj subsequent

postizo (poass-tee-thoa) m hair piece

postre (poass-tray) m dessert

potable (poa-tah-bhlay) adj for drinking

potencia (poa-*tayn*-thᵞah) *f* capacity; power

pozo (*poa*-thoa) *m* well; ~ **de petróleo** oil-well

práctica (*prahk*-tee-kah) *f* practice

prácticamente (*prahk*-tee-kah-mayntay) *adv* practically

practicar (prahk-tee-*kahr*) *v* practise

práctico (*prahk*-tee-koa) *adj* practical; business-like; *m* pilot

prado (*prah*-dhoa) *m* meadow, pasture

precario (pray-*kah*-rᵞoa) *adj* critical, precarious

precaución (pray-kou-*thᵞoan*) *f* precaution

precaverse (pray-kah-*bhayr*-say) *v* beware

precedente (pray-thay-*dhayn*-tay) *adj* previous, preceding, last

preceder (pray-thay-*dhayr*) *v* precede

precio (*pray*-thᵞoa) *m* price; charge, cost, rate; ~ **de compra** purchase price; ~ **del billete** fare

precioso (pray-*thᵞoa*-soa) *adj* precious; lovely

precipicio (pray-thee-*pee*-thᵞoa) *m* precipice

precipitación (pray-thee-pee-tah-*thᵞoan*) *f* precipitation

precipitarse (pray-thee-pee-*tahr*-say) *v* rush; crash; **precipitado** *adj* rash

preciso (pray-*thee*-soa) *adj* precise; very

predecesor (pray-dhay-thay-*soar*) *m* predecessor

*   **predecir** (pray-dhay-*theer*) *v* predict

predicar (pray-dhee-*kahr*) *v* preach

preferencia (pray-fay-*rayn*-thᵞah) *f* preference

preferible (pray-fay-*ree*-bhlay) *adj* preferable

*   **preferir** (pray-fay-*reer*) *v* prefer; **preferido** *adj* favourite

prefijo (pray-*fee*-khoa) *m* prefix

pregunta (pray-*goon*-tah) *f* question; query, inquiry

preguntar (pray-goon-*tahr*) *v* ask; enquire; **preguntarse** *v* wonder

prejuicio (pray-*khwee*-thᵞoa) *m* prejudice

preliminar (pray-lee-mee-*nahr*) *adj* preliminary

prematuro (pray-mah-*too*-roa) *adj* premature

premio (*pray*-mᵞoa) *m* award, prize; ~ **de consolación** consolation prize

prender (prayn-*dayr*) *v* attach

prensa (*prayn*-sah) *f* press; **conferencia de** ~ press conference

preocupación (pray-oa-koo-pah-*thᵞoan*) *f* concern, anxiety, worry; trouble

preocupado (pray-oa-koo-*pah*-dhoa) *adj* concerned, anxious

preocuparse de (pray-oa-koo-*pahr*-say) *v* care about

preparación (pray-pah-rah-*thᵞoan*) *f* preparation

preparado (pray-pah-*rah*-dhoa) *adj* prepared, ready

preparar (pray-pah-*rahr*) *v* prepare; cook

preposición (pray-poa-see-*thᵞoan*) *f* preposition

presa (*pray*-sah) *f* dam

prescindir (pray-theen-*deer*) *v* omit; disregard; **prescindiendo de** apart from

prescribir (prayss-kree-*bheer*) *v* prescribe

prescripción (prayss-kreep-*thᵞoan*) *f* prescription

presencia (pray-*sayn*-thᵞah) *f* presence

presenciar (pray-sayn-*thᵞahr*) *v* witness

presentación (pray-sayn-tah-*thᵞoan*) *f* introduction

presentar (pray-sayn-*tahr*) *v* introduce,

present; offer; **presentarse** v report

presente (pray-*sayn*-tay) *adj* present; *m* present

preservativo (pray-sayr-bhah-*tee*-bhoa) *m* condom

preservar (pray-sayr-*bhahr*) *v* preserve

presidente (pray-see-*dhayn*-tay) *m* president, chairman

presidir (pray-see-*dheer*) *v* preside at

presión (pray-*s*ʸoan) *f* pressure; ~ **atmosférica** atmospheric pressure; ~ **del aceite** oil pressure; ~ **del neumático** tyre pressure

preso (*pray*-soa) *m* prisoner; **coger ~** capture

prestamista (prayss-tah-*meess*-tah) *m* pawnbroker

préstamo (*prayss*-tah-moa) *m* loan

prestar (prayss-*tahr*) *v* *lend; ~ **atención a** attend to, *pay attention to; **tomar prestado** borrow

prestigio (prayss-*tee*-kh*ʸoa) *m* prestige

presumible (pray-soo-*mee*-bhlay) *adj* presumable

presumido (pray-soo-*mee*-dhoa) *adj* presumptuous

presumir (pray-soo-*meer*) *v* assume; boast

presuntuoso (pray-soon-*twoa*-soa) *adj* conceited; presumptuous

presupuesto (pray-soo-*pwayss*-toa) *m* budget

pretender (pray-tayn-*dayr*) *v* claim

pretensión (pray-tayn-*s*ʸoan) *f* claim

pretexto (pray-*tayks*-toa) *m* pretext, pretence

*****prevenir** (pray-bhay-*neer*) *v* anticipate, prevent

preventivo (pray-bhayn-*tee*-bhoa) *adj* preventive

*****prever** (pray-*bhayr*) *v* anticipate

previo (*pray*-bhʸoa) *adj* previous

previsión (pray-bhee-*s*ʸoan) *f* outlook, forecast

prima (*pree*-mah) *f* cousin; premium

primario (pree-*mah*-rʸoa) *adj* primary

primavera (pree-mah-*bhay*-rah) *f* springtime, spring

primero (pree-*may*-roa) *num* first; *adj* foremost; primary

primitivo (pree-mee-*tee*-bhoa) *adj* primitive

primo (*pree*-moa) *m* cousin

primordial (pree-moar-*dh*ʸahl) *adj* primary

princesa (preen-*thay*-sah) *f* princess

principal (preen-thee-*pahl*) *adj* principal; chief, main, cardinal; *m* principal

principalmente (preen-thee-pahl-*mayn*-tay) *adv* mainly

príncipe (*preen*-thee-pay) *m* prince

principiante (preen-thee-*p*ʸahn-tay) *m* beginner, learner

principio (preen-*thee*-pʸoa) *m* principle; **al ~** at first

prioridad (prʸoa-ree-*dhahdh*) *f* priority

prisa (*pree*-sah) *f* haste, speed, hurry; *dar ~ *speed; *darse ~ hurry; **de ~** in a hurry

prisión (pree-*s*ʸoan) *f* prison

prisionero (pree-sʸoa-*nay*-roa) *m* prisoner; ~ **de guerra** prisoner of war

prismáticos (preez-*mah*-tee-koass) *mpl* binoculars *pl*

privado (pree-*bhah*-dhoa) *adj* private

privar de (pree-*bhahr*) deprive of

privilegio (pree-bhee-*lay*-kh*ʸoa) *m* privilege

probable (proa-*bhah*-bhlay) *adj* probable; likely

probablemente (proa-bhah-bhlay-*mayn*-tay) *adv* probably

probador (proa-bhah-*dhoar*) *m* fitting room

*****probar** (proa-*bhahr*) *v* attempt; test; taste; *****probarse** *v* try on

problema (proa-*bhlay*-mah) *m* problem, question

procedencia (proa-thay-*dhayn*-th*Y*ah) *f* origin

proceder (proa-thay-*dhayr*) *v* proceed

procedimiento (proa-thay-dhee-*mY ayn*-toa) *m* procedure; process

procesión (proa-thay-*sY oan*) *f* procession

proceso (proa-*thay*-soa) *m* process, trial, lawsuit

proclamar (proa-klah-*mahr*) *v* proclaim

procurador (proa-koo-rah-*dhoar*) *m* solicitor

procurar (proa-koo-*rahr*) *v* furnish

pródigo (*proa*-dhee-goa) *adj* lavish

producción (proa-dhook-*thY oan*) *f* production, output; ~ **en serie** mass production

*producir (proa-dhoo-*theer*) *v* produce

producto (proa-*dhook*-toa) *m* product, produce

productor (proa-dhook-*toar*) *m* producer

profano (proa-*fah*-noa) *m* layman

profesar (proa-fay-*sahr*) *v* confess

profesión (proa-fay-*sY oan*) *f* profession

profesional (proa-fay-sY oa-*nahl*) *adj* professional

profesor (proa-fay-*soar*) *m* master, teacher; professor

profesora (proa-fay-*soa*-rah) *f* teacher

profeta (proa-*fay*-tah) *m* prophet

profundidad (proa-foon-dee-*dhahdh*) *f* depth

profundo (proa-*foon*-doa) *adj* low; profound

programa (proa-*grah*-mah) *m* programme

progresista (proa-gray-*seess*-tah) *adj* progressive

progresivo (proa-gray-*see*-bhoa) *adj* progressive

progreso (proa-*gray*-soa) *m* progress

prohibición (proa-ee-bhee-*thY oan*) *f* prohibition

prohibido (proa-ee-*bhee*-dhoa) *adj* prohibited

prohibir (proa-ee-*bheer*) *v* prohibit, *forbid

prolongación (proa-loang-gah-*thY oan*) *f* prolongation

prolongar (proa-loang-*gahr*) *v* extend

promedio (proa-*may*-dh*Y*oa) *adj* average; *m* average, mean; **en** ~ on the average

promesa (proa-*may*-sah) *f* promise

prometer (proa-may-*tayr*) *v* promise

prometido (proa-may-*tee*-dhoa) *adj* engaged

promoción (proa-moa-*thY oan*) *f* promotion

promontorio (proa-moan-*toa*-r*Y*oa) *m* headland

*promover (proa-moa-*bhayr*) *v* promote

pronombre (proa-*noam*-bray) *m* pronoun

pronosticar (proa-noass-tee-*kahr*) *v* forecast

pronto (*proan*-toa) *adj* prompt; *adv* soon, shortly; **tan** ~ **como** as soon as

pronunciación (proa-noon-th*Y*ah-*thY oan*) *f* pronunciation

pronunciar (proa-noon-*thY ahr*) *v* pronounce

propaganda (proa-pah-*gahn*-dah) *f* propaganda

propicio (proa-*pee*-th*Y*oa) *adj* favourable; well-disposed

propiedad (proa-p*Y*ay-*dhahdh*) *f* property; estate

propietario (proa-p*Y*ay-*tah*-r*Y*oa) *m* owner, proprietor; landlord

propina (proa-*pee*-nah) *f* gratuity, tip

propio (*proa*-p*Y*oa) *adj* own

*proponer (proa-poa-*nayr*) *v* propose

proporción (proa-poar-*th*ʸ*oan*) *f* proportion

proporcional (proa-poar-th*ʸ*oa-*nahl*) *adj* proportional

proporcionar (proa-poar-th*ʸ*oa-*nahr*) *v* adjust; procure

propósito (proa-*poa*-see-toa) *m* purpose; **a** ~ by the way

propuesta (proa-*pwayss*-tah) *f* proposition, proposal

prórroga (*proa*-rroa-gah) *f* extension

prosa (*proa*-sah) *f* prose

*proseguir (proa-say-*geer*) *v* proceed, continue, carry on

prospecto (proass-*payk*-toa) *m* prospectus

prosperidad (proass-pay-ree-*dhahdh*) *f* prosperity

próspero (*proass*-pay-roa) *adj* prosperous

prostituta (proass-tee-*too*-tah) *f* prostitute

protección (proa-tayk-*th*ʸ*oan*) *f* protection

proteger (proa-tay-*khayr*) *v* protect

proteína (proa-tay-ee-nah) *f* protein

protesta (proa-*tayss*-tah) *f* protest

protestante (proa-tayss-*tahn*-tay) *adj* Protestant

protestar (proa-tayss-*tahr*) *v* protest

provechoso (proa-bhay-*choa*-soa) *adj* profitable

*proveer (proa-bhay-*ayr*) *v* provide; ~ **de** furnish with

proverbio (proa-*bhayr*-bhʸoa) *m* proverb

provincia (proa-*bheen*-thʸah) *f* province

provincial (proa-bheen-*thʸahl*) *adj* provincial

provisional (proa-bhee-sʸoa-*nahl*) *adj* provisional, temporary

provisiones (proa-bhee-sʸoa-nayss) *fpl* provisions *pl*

provocar (proa-bhoa-*kahr*) *v* cause

próximamente (*proak*-see-mah-mayn-tay) *adv* shortly

próximo (*proak*-see-moa) *adj* next

proyectar (proa-ʸayk-*tahr*) *v* project

proyecto (proa-ʸayk-toa) *m* project, scheme

proyector (proa-ʸayk-*toar*) *m* spotlight

prudente (proo-*dhayn*-tay) *adj* cautious, wary, gentle

prueba (*prway*-bhah) *f* experiment, trial, test; proof, token, evidence; **a** ~ on approval

prurito (proo-*ree*-toa) *m* itch

psicoanalista (see-koa-ah-nah-*leess*-tah) *m* analyst, psychoanalyst

psicología (see-koa-loa-*khee*-ah) *f* psychology

psicológico (see-koa-*loa*-khee-koa) *adj* psychological

psicólogo (see-*koa*-loa-goa) *m* psychologist

psiquiatra (see-kʸah-trah) *m* psychiatrist

psíquico (*see*-kee-koa) *adj* psychic

publicación (poo-bhlee-kah-*th*ʸ*oan*) *f* publication

publicar (poo-bhlee-*kahr*) *v* publish

publicidad (poo-bhlee-thee-*dhahdh*) *f* advertising, publicity

público (*poo*-bhlee-koa) *adj* public; *m* public

pueblo (*pway*-bhloa) *m* nation, people; village

puente (*pwayn*-tay) *m* bridge; ~ **colgante** suspension bridge; ~ **levadizo** drawbridge; ~ **superior** main deck

puerta (*pwayr*-tah) *f* door; ~ **corrediza** sliding door; ~ **giratoria** revolving door

puerto (*pwayr*-toa) *m* harbour, port; ~ **de mar** seaport

pues (pwayss) *conj* since

puesta (*pwayss*-tah) *f* bet

puesto (loo-*gahr*) *m* spot; job, post, position; stand, stall, booth; ~ **de gasolina** service station; gas station *Am*; ~ **de libros** bookstand

puesto que (*pwayss*-toa kay) because, since

pulcro (*pool*-kroa) *adj* neat

pulgar (pool-*gahr*) *m* thumb

pulir (poo-*leer*) *v* polish

pulmón (pool-*moan*) *m* lung

pulóver (poo-*loa*-bhayr) *m* pullover

púlpito (*pool*-pee-toa) *m* pulpit

pulpo (*pool*-poa) *m* octopus

pulsera (pool-*say*-rah) *f* bracelet, bangle

pulso (*pool*-soa) *m* pulse

pulverizador (pool-bhay-ree-thah-*dhoar*) *m* atomizer

punta (*poon*-tah) *f* tip, point

puntiagudo (poon-tʸah-*goo*-dhoa) *adj* pointed

puntilla (poon-*tee*-lʸah) *f* lace

punto (*poon*-toa) *m* point; item, issue; period, full stop; stitch; **géneros de** ~ hosiery; *hacer* ~ *knit; ~ **de congelación** freezing-point; ~ **de partida** starting-point; ~ **de vista** point of view; ~ **y coma** semicolon

puntual (poon-*twahl*) *adj* punctual

punzada (poon-*thah*-dhah) *f* stitch

punzar (poon-*thahr*) *v* pierce

puñado (poo-*ñah*-dhoa) *m* handful

puñetazo (poo-ñay-*tah*-thoa) *m* punch; *dar puñetazos* punch

puño (*poo*-ñoa) *m* fist; cuff

pupitre (poo-*pee*-tray) *m* desk

purasangre (poo-rah-*sahng*-gray) *adj* thoroughbred

puro (*poo*-roa) *adj* pure; clean, neat, sheer; *m* cigar

purpúreo (poor-*poo*-ray-oa) *adj* purple

pus (pooss) *f* pus

Q

que (kay) *pron* who, which, that; *conj* that; as, than

qué (kay) *pron* what; *adv* how

quebradizo (kay-bhrah-*dhee*-thoa) *adj* crisp

quebrantar (kay-bhrahn-*tahr*) *v* *break

*quebrar** (kay-*bhrahr*) *v* crack, *break, *burst

quedar (kay-*dhahr*) *v* remain; **quedarse** *v* remain, stay

queja (*kay*-khah) *f* complaint

quejarse (kay-*khahr*-say) *v* complain

quemadura (kay-mah-*dhoo*-rah) *f* burn; ~ **del sol** sunburn

quemar (kay-*mahr*) *v* *burn

*querer** (kay-*rayr*) *v* *will, want; like, *be fond of

querida (kay-*ree*-dhah) *f* sweetheart; mistress

querido (kay-*ree*-dhoa) *adj* beloved, dear; precious; *m* darling

queso (*kay*-soa) *m* cheese

quien (kʸayn) *pron* who; **a** ~ whom

quienquiera (kʸayng-*kʸay*-rah) *pron* whoever

quieto (*kʸay*-toa) *adj* still, quiet; *estarse* ~ *keep quiet

quilate (kee-*lah*-tay) *m* carat

quilla (*kee*-lʸah) *f* keel

química (*kee*-mee-kah) *f* chemistry

químico (*kee*-mee-koa) *adj* chemical

quincalla (keeng-*kah*-lʸah) *f* hardware

quince (*keen*-thay) *num* fifteen

quincena (keen-*thay*-nah) *f* fortnight

quinceno (keen-*thay*-noa) *num* fifteenth

quinina (kee-*nee*-nah) *f* quinine

quinta (*keen*-tah) *f* country house

quinto[1] (*keen*-toa) *num* fifth

quinto[2] (*keen*-toa) *m* conscript

quiosco (k*Y*oass-koa) *m* kiosk; ~ **de periódicos** newsstand

quitamanchas (kee-tah-*mahn*-chahss) *m* cleaning fluid, stain remover

quitar (kee-*tahr*) *v* *take away

quitasol (kee-tah-*soal*) *m* sunshade

quizás (kee-*thahss*) *adv* maybe, perhaps

R

rábano (*rah*-bhah-noa) *m* radish; ~ **picante** horseradish

rabia (*rah*-bh*Y*ah) *f* rage; rabies

rabiar (rah-*bh*Y*ahr*) *v* rage

rabioso (rah-*bh*Y*oa*-soa) *adj* mad

racial (rah-*th*Y*ahl*) *adj* racial

ración (rah-*th*Y*oan*) *f* ration

radiador (rah-dh*Y*ah-*dhoar*) *m* radiator

radical (rah-dhee-*kahl*) *adj* radical

radio (*rah*-dh*Y*oa) *m* radius; spoke; *f* wireless, radio

radiografía (rah-dh*Y*oa-grah-*fee*-ah) *f* X-ray

radiografiar (rah-dh*Y*oa-grah-*f*Y*ahr*) *v* X-ray

raedura (rah-ay-*dhoo*-rah) *f* scratch; *hacer raeduras scratch

ráfaga (*rah*-fah-gah) *f* gust, blow

raíz (rah-*eeth*) *f* root

rallar (rah-*l*Y*ahr*) *v* grate

rama (*rah*-mah) *f* branch, bough

ramita (rah-*mee*-tah) *f* twig

ramo (*rah*-moa) *m* bouquet, bunch

rampa (*rahm*-pah) *f* ramp

rana (*rah*-nah) *f* frog

rancio (*rahn*-th*Y*oa) *adj* rancid

rancho (*rahn*-choa) *mMe* farmhouse

rango (*rahng*-goa) *m* rank

ranura (rah-*noo*-rah) *f* slot

rápidamente (rah-pee-dah-mayn-tay) *adv* soon

rapidez (rah-pee-*dhayth*) *f* speed

rápido (*rah*-pee-dhoa) *adj* fast, rapid, quick; **rápidos de río** rapids *pl*

raqueta (rah-*kay*-tah) *f* racquet

raro (*rah*-roa) *adj* uncommon, rare; strange, odd; **raras veces** rarely

rascacielos (rahss-kah-*th*Y*ay*-loass) *m* skyscraper

rascar (rahss-*kahr*) *v* scratch

rasgar (rahz-*gahr*) *v* rip

rasgo (*rahz*-goa) *m* trait; feature; ~ **característico** characteristic

rasgón (rahz-*goan*) *m* tear

rasguño (rahz-*goo*-ño-a) *m* scratch

raso (*rah*-soa) *adj* bare; *m* satin

raspar (rahss-*pahr*) *v* scrape

rastrear (rahss-tray-*ahr*) *v* trace

rastrillo (rahss-*tree*-l*Y*oa) *m* rake

rastro (*rahss*-troa) *m* trail

rasurarse (rah-soo-*rahr*-say) *v* shave

rata (*rah*-tah) *f* rat

rato (*rah*-toa) *m* while

ratón (rah-*toan*) *m* mouse

raya (*rah*-*Y*ah) *f* line, stripe; crease; parting

rayado (rah-*Y*ah-dhoa) *adj* striped

rayador (rah-*Y*ah-*dhoar*) *m* grater

rayo (*rah*-*Y*oa) *m* beam, ray

rayón (rah-*Y*oan) *m* rayon

raza (*rah*-thah) *f* race; breed

razón (rah-*thoan*) *f* wits *pl*, sense, reason; **no *tener** ~ *be wrong*; **tener** ~ * be right

razonable (rah-thoa-*nah*-bhlay) *adj* reasonable

razonar (rah-thoa-*nahr*) *v* reason

reacción (ray-ahk-*th*Y*oan*) *f* reaction

reaccionar (ray-ahk-th*Y*oa-*nahr*) *v* react

real (ray-*ahl*) *adj* factual, true, substantial; royal

realidad (ray-ah-lee-*dhahdh*) *f* reality;

en ~ actually, as a matter of fact

realizable (ray-ah-lee-*thah*-bhlay) *adj* feasible, realizable

realización (ray-ah-lee-thah-*th^yoan*) *f* achievement

realizar (ray-ah-lee-*thahr*) *v* realize; carry out

rebaja (ray-*bhah*-khah) *f* reduction, rebate; **rebajas** *fpl* sales

rebajar (ray-bhah-*khahr*) *v* lower, reduce

rebaño (ray-*bhah*-ñoa) *m* flock

rebelde (ray-*bhayl*-day) *m* rebel

rebelión (ray-bhay-l^y*oan*) *f* revolt, rebellion

recado (ray-*kah*-dhoa) *m* errand

recambio (ray-*kahm*-b^yoa) *m* spare part

recepción (ray-thayp-*th^yoan*) *f* reception

recepcionista (ray-thayp-th^yoa-*neess*-tah) *f* receptionist

receptáculo (ray-thayp-*tah*-koo-loa) *m* container

receptor (ray-thayp-*toar*) *m* receiver

receta (ray-*thay*-tah) *f* recipe

recibir (ray-thee-*bheer*) *v* receive

recibo (ray-*thee*-bhoa) *m* voucher, receipt; **oficina de** ~ reception office

reciclable (ray-thee-*clah*-bhlay) *adj* recyclable

reciclar (ray-thee-*clahr*) *v* recycle

recién (ray-*th^yayn*) *adv* recently

reciente (ray-*th^yayn*-tay) *adj* recent

recientemente (ray-th^yayn-tay-*mayn*-tay) *adv* lately, recently

recíproco (ray-*thee*-proa-koa) *adj* mutual

recital (ray-thee-*tahl*) *m* recital

reclamar (ray-klah-*mahr*) *v* claim

recluta (ray-*kloo*-tah) *m* recruit

recoger (ray-koa-*khayr*) *v* pick up, pick; collect, gather; *overtake

recogida (ray-koa-*khee*-dhah) *f* collec-

tion

recomendación (ray-koa-mayn-dah-*th^yoan*) *f* recommendation

*   **recomendar** (ray-koa-mayn-*dahr*) *v* recommend

*   **recomenzar** (ray-koa-mayn-*thahr*) *v* recommence

recompensa (ray-koam-*payn*-sah) *f* prize, reward

recompensar (ray-koam-payn-*sahr*) *v* reward

reconciliación (ray-koan-thee-l^yah-*th^yoan*) *f* reconciliation

*   **reconocer** (ray-koa-noa-*thayr*) *v* recognize; admit, confess, acknowledge; realize

reconocimiento (ray-koa-noa-thee-m^yayn-toa) *m* recognition; check-up

récord (*ray*-koardh) *m* record

*   **recordar** (ray-koar-*dhahr*) *v* remind; *think of

recorrer (ray-koa-*rrayr*) *v* cross

recortar (ray-koar-*tahr*) *v* trim

recreación (ray-kray-ah-*th^yoan*) *f* recreation

recreo (ray-*kray*-oa) *m* recreation; **patio de** ~ playground

recriar (ray-kr^y*ahr*) *v* *breed

rectangular (rayk-tahng-goo-*lahr*) *adj* rectangular

rectángulo (rayk-*tahng*-goo-loa) *m* oblong, rectangle

rectificación (rayk-tee-fee-kah-*th^yoan*) *f* correction

recto (*rayk*-toa) *adj* erect

rector (rayk-*toar*) *m* rector

rectoría (rayk-toa-*ree*-ah) *f* rectory

recuerdo (ray-*kwayr*-dhoa) *m* remembrance, memory; souvenir

recuperación (ray-koo-pay-rah-*th^yoan*) *f* revival

recuperar (ray-koo-pay-*rahr*) *v* recover

rechazar (ray-chah-*thahr*) *v* reject, turn down

red (raydh) *f* net; network; **~ de carreteras** road system; **~ de pescar**
fishing net

redacción (ray-dhahk-*th*ʸoan) *f* word-
ing; editorial staff

redactar (ray-dhahk-*tahr*) *v* *make up;
*draw up

redactor (ray-dhahk-*toar*) *m* editor

redecilla (ray-dhay-*thee*-lʸah) *f* hair-
net

redimir (ray-dhee-*meer*) *v* redeem

rédito (*ray*-dhee-toa) *m* interest

redondeado (ray-dhoan-day-*ah*-dhoa)
adj rounded

redondo (ray-*dhoan*-doa) *adj* round

reducción (ray-dhook-*th*ʸoan) *f* reduction, rebate

*reducir (ray-dhoo-*theer*) *v* *cut, decrease, reduce

reembolsar (ray-aym-boal-*sahr*) *v*
reimburse

reemplazar (ray-aym-plah-*thahr*) *v* replace

reemprender (ray-aym-prayn-*dayr*) *v*
resume

reexpedir (ray-ayks-pay-*dheer*) *v* forward

referencia (ray-fay-*rayn*-thʸah) *f* reference; **punto de ~** landmark

*referir (ray-fay-*reer*) *v* refer; narrate

refinería (ray-fee-nay-*ree*-ah) *f* refinery

reflector (ray-flayk-*toar*) *m* reflector;
searchlight

reflejar (ray-flay-*khahr*) *v* reflect

reflejo (ray-*flay*-khoa) *m* reflection

reflexionar (ray-flayk-sʸoa-*nahr*) *v*
*think

Reforma (ray-*foar*-mah) *f* reformation

refractario (ray-frahk-*tah*-rʸoa) *adj*
fireproof

refrenar (ray-fray-*nahr*) *v* curb

refrescar (ray-frayss-*kahr*) *v* refresh

refresco (ray-*frayss*-koa) *m* refreshment

refrigerador (ray-free-khay-rah-*dhoar*)
m fridge, refrigerator

refugio (ray-*foo*-khʸoa) *m* cover, shelter

refunfuñar (ray-foon-foo-*ñahr*) *v*
grumble

regalar (ray-gah-*lahr*) *v* present

regaliz (ray-gah-*leeth*) *m* liquorice

regalo (ray-*gah*-loa) *m* present, gift

regata (ray-*gah*-tah) *f* regatta

regatear (ray-gah-tay-*ahr*) *v* bargain

régimen (*ray*-khee-mayn) *m* (pl regi-
menes) régime; government, rule;
diet

regimiento (ray-khee-*m*ʸayn-toa) *m*
regiment

región (ray-*kh*ʸoan) *f* region; zone,
country, area

regional (ray-khʸoa-*nahl*) *adj* regional

*regir (ray-*kheer*) *v* govern, rule

registrar (ray-kheess-*trahr*) *v* book, record

registro (ray-*kheess*-troa) *m* record

regla (*ray*-glah) *f* rule; regulation;
ruler; **en ~** in order; **por ~ general**
as a rule

reglamento (ray-glah-*mayn*-toa) *m*
regulation

regocijo (ray-goa-*thee*-khoa) *m* joy

regordete (ray-goar-*dhay*-tay) *adj*
plump

regresar (ray-gray-*sahr*) *v* *go back,
*get back

regreso (ray-*gray*-soa) *m* return; **viaje
de ~** return journey; **vuelo de ~** return flight

regulación (ray-goo-lah-*th*ʸoan) *f* regulation

regular (ray-goo-*lahr*) *v* regulate; *adj*
regular

rehabilitación (ray-ah-bhee-lee-tah-
*th*ʸoan) *f* rehabilitation

rehén (ray-*ayn*) *m* hostage

rehusar (rayᵒᵒ-*sahr*) *v* refuse; reject

reina (ray-nah) f queen
reinado (ray-nah-dhoa) m reign
reino (ray-noa) m kingdom
reintegrar (rayn-tay-grahr) v *repay, refund
reintegro (rayn-tay-groa) m repayment, refund
* **reír** (ray-eer) v laugh
reivindicación (ray-bheen-dee-kah-thᵞoan) f claim
reivindicar (ray-bheen-dee-kahr) v claim
reja (ray-khah) f grate; fence, gate
rejilla (roy-khee-lᵞah) f luggage rack
relación (ray-lah-thᵞoan) f connection, relation; reference; report
relacionar (ray-lah-thᵞoa-nahr) v relate
relajación (ray-lah-khah-thᵞoan) f relaxation
relajado (ray-lah-khah-dhoa) adj easy-going
relámpago (ray-lahm-pah-goa) m lightning; flash
relatar (ray-lah-tahr) v report
relativo (ray-lah-tee-bhoa) adj comparative, relative; ~ **a** regarding
relato (ray-lah-toa) m tale
relevar (ray-lay-bhahr) v relieve
relieve (ray-lᵞay-bhay) m relief
religión (ray-lee-khᵞoan) f religion
religioso (ray-lee-khᵞoa-soa) adj religious
reliquia (ray-lee-kᵞah) f relic
reloj (ray-loakh) m clock; watch; ~ **de bolsillo** pocket-watch; ~ **de pulsera** wrist-watch
relojero (ray-loa-khay-roa) m watchmaker
reluciente (ray-loo-thᵞayn-tay) adj bright
* **relucir** (ray-loo-theer) v *shine
rellenado (ray-lᵞay-nah-doa) adj stuffed

relleno (ray-lᵞay-noa) m stuffing; filling
remanente (ray-mah-nayn-tay) m remnant
remar (ray-mahr) v row
remedio (ray-may-dhᵞoa) m remedy
* **remendar** (ray-mayn-dahr) v mend; patch
remesa (ray-may-sah) f remittance
remitir (ray-mee-teer) v remit; ~ **a** refer to
remo (ray-moa) m paddle, oar
remoción (ray-moa-thᵞoan) f removal
remojar (ray-moa-khahr) v soak
remolacha (ray-moa-lah-chah) f beetroot, beet
remolcador (ray-moal-kah-dhoar) m tug
remolcar (ray-moal-kahr) v tug, tow
remolque (ray-moal-kay) m trailer
remoto (ray-moa-toa) adj remote, faraway, far-off
* **remover** (ray-moa-bhayr) v remove
remuneración (ray-moo-nay-rah-thᵞoan) f remuneration
remunerar (ray-moo-nay-rahr) v remunerate
Renacimiento (ray-nah-thee-mᵞayn-toa) m Renaissance
rendición (rayn-dee-thᵞoan) f surrender
* **rendir** (rayn-deer) v *pay; ~ **homenaje** honour; * **rendirse** v surrender
renglón (rayng-gloan) m line
reno (ray-noa) m reindeer
renombre (ray-noam-bray) m reputation
* **renovar** (ray-noa-bhahr) v renew
renta (rayn-tah) f revenue
rentable (rayn-tah-bhlay) adj paying
renunciar (ray-noon-thᵞahr) v *give up
* **reñir** (ray-ñeer) v dispute, quarrel
reparación (ray-pah-rah-thᵞoan) f reparation; repair

reparar (ray-pah-*rahr*) v repair, mend

repartir (ray-pahr-*teer*) v divide, deal, share out

reparto (ray-*pahr*-toa) m delivery; **camioneta de** ~ pick-up van

repelente (ray-pay-*layn*-tay) adj repellent, revolting

repentinamente (ray-payn-tee-nah-*mayn*-tay) adv suddenly

repertorio (ray-payr-*toa*-rᵛoa) m repertory

repetición (ray-pay-tee-*thᵛoan*) f repetition

repetidamente (ray-pay-tee-dhah-*mayn*-tay) adv again and again

* repetir (ray-pay-*teer*) v repeat

repleto (ray-*play*-toa) adj crowded

reportero (ray-poar-*tay*-roa) m reporter

reposado (ray-poa-*sah*-dhoa) adj restful

reposo (ray-*poa*-soa) m rest

reprender (ray-prayn-*dayr*) v reprimand, scold

representación (ray-pray-sayn-tah-*thᵛoan*) f representation; show, performance

representante (ray-pray-sayn-*tahn*-tay) m agent

representar (ray-pray-sayn-*tahr*) v represent

representativo (ray-pray-sayn-tah-*tee*-bhoa) adj representative

reprimir (ray-pree-*meer*) v suppress

* reprobar (ray-proa-*bhahr*) v reject

reprochar (ray-proa-*chahr*) v reproach

reproche (ray-*proa*-chay) m reproach, blame

reproducción (ray-proa-dhook-*thᵛoan*) f reproduction

* reproducir (ray-proa-dhoo-*theer*) v reproduce

reptil (rayp-*teel*) m reptile

república (ray-*poo*-bhlee-kah) f republic

republicano (ray-poo-bhlee-*kah*-noa) adj republican

repuesto (ray-*pwayss*-toa) m store; refill

repugnancia (ray-poog-*nahn*-thᵛah) f dislike

repugnante (ray-poog-*nahn*-tay) adj repellent, disgusting, revolting

repulsivo (ray-pool-*see*-bhoa) adj repulsive

reputación (ray-poo-tah-*thᵛoan*) f reputation, fame

requerimiento (ray-kay-ree-*mᵛayn*-toa) m requirement

* requerir (ray-kay-*reer*) v require, demand

resaca (ray-*sah*-kah) f undercurrent; hangover

resbaladizo (rayz-bhah-lah-*dhee*-thoa) adj slippery

resbalar (rayz-bhah-*lahr*) v slip, glide

rescatar (rayss-kah-*tahr*) v rescue

rescate (rayss-*kah*-tay) m rescue; ransom

* resentirse por (ray-sayn-*teer*-say) resent

reseña (ray-*say*-ñah) f review

reserva (ray-*sayr*-bhah) f qualification; reserve; booking; **de** ~ spare

reservación (ray-sayr-bhah-*thᵛoan*) f reservation, booking

reservar (ray-sayr-*bhahr*) v engage; reserve, book

resfriado (rayss-*frᵛah*-dhoa) m cold

resfriarse (rayss-*frᵛahr*-say) v catch a cold

residencia (ray-see-*dhayn*-thᵛah) f residence

residente (ray-see-*dhayn*-tay) adj resident; m resident

residir (ray-see-*dheer*) v reside

residuo (ray-*see*-dhwoa) m remnant

resignación (ray-seeg-nah-*thᵛoan*) f resignation

resignar (ray-seeg-*nahr*) v resign
resina (ray-*see*-nah) f resin
resistencia (ray-seess-*tayn*-thᵛah) f resistance
resistir (ray-seess-*teer*) v resist
resolución (ray-soa-loo-*thᵛoan*) f resolution
***resolver** (ray-soal-*bhayr*) v solve
***resonar** (ray-soa-*nahr*) v sound
respectivo (rayss-payk-*tee*-bhoa) adj respective
respecto a (rayss-*payk*-toa ah) about, regarding
respetable (rayss-pay-*tah*-bhlay) adj respectable
respetar (rayss-pay-*tahr*) v respect
respeto (rayss-*pay*-toa) m respect, esteem, regard
respetuoso (rayss-pay-*twoa*-soa) adj respectful
respiración (rayss-pee-rah-*thᵛoan*) f respiration, breathing
respirar (rayss-pee-*rahr*) v breathe
***resplandecer** (rayss-plahn-day-*thayr*) v *shine
resplandor (rayss-plahn-*doar*) m glare
responder (rayss-poan-*dayr*) v reply, answer
responsabilidad (rayss-poan-sah-bhee-lee-*dhahdh*) f responsibility; liability
responsable (rayss-poan-*sah*-bhlay) adj responsible; liable
respuesta (rayss-*pwayss*-tah) f reply, answer
***restablecerse** (rayss-tah-bhlay-*thayr*-say) v recover
restablecimiento (rayss-tah-bhlay-thee-*mᵛayn*-toa) m recovery
restante (rayss-*tahn*-tay) adj remaining
restar (rayss-*tahr*) v subtract
restaurante (rayss-tou-*rahn*-tay) m restaurant; ~ **de autoservicio** self-service restaurant

resto (*rayss*-toa) m rest; remnant, remainder
restricción (rayss-treek-*thᵛoan*) f restriction; qualification
resuelto (ray-*swayl*-toa) adj resolute, determined
resultado (ray-sool-*tah*-dhoa) m result; issue, outcome, effect
resultar (ray-sool-*tahr*) v result; prove
resumen (ray-*soo*-mayn) m résumé, survey, summary
retardar (ray-tahr-*dhahr*) v delay
***retener** (ray-tay-*nayr*) v *hold
retina (ray-*tee*-nah) f retina
retirar (ray-tee-*rahr*) v *withdraw
reto (*ray*-toa) m challenge
retrasado (ray-trah-*sah*-dhoa) adj late
retraso (ray-*trah*-soa) m delay
retrato (ray-*trah*-toa) m portrait
retrete (ray-*tray*-tay) m toilet
retroceso (ray-troa-*thay*-soa) m recession
retumbo (ray-*toom*-boa) m roar
reumatismo (rayᵒᵒ-mah-*teez*-moa) m rheumatism
reunión (rayᵒᵒ-*nᵛoan*) f meeting, assembly, rally
reunir (rayᵒᵒ-*neer*) v join, assemble; reunite
revelación (ray-bhay-lah-*thᵛoan*) f revelation
revelar (ray-bhay-*lahr*) v reveal; *give away; develop
revendedor (ray-bhayn-day-*dhoar*) m retailer
***reventar** (ray-bhayn-*tahr*) v crack, *burst
reventón (ray-bhayn-*toan*) m blow-out
reverencia (ray-bhay-*rayn*-thᵛah) f respect
reverso (ray-*bhayr*-soa) m reverse
revés (ray-*bhayss*) m reverse; **al** ~ the other way round; upside-down; inside out

revisar (ray-bhee-*sahr*) v revise, over-haul

revisión (ray-bhee-s*ᵞoan*) f revision

revisor (ray-bhee-*soar*) m ticket collector

revista (ray-*bheess*-tah) f journal; review, magazine; revue; ~ **mensual** monthly magazine

revocar (ray-bhoa-*kahr*) v recall

revolución (ray-bhoa-loo-*th*ᵞoan) f revolution

revolucionar (ray-bhoa-loo-th*ᵞoa-nahr*) v revolution

revolucionario (ray-bhoa-loo-th*ᵞoa-nah-r*ᵞoa) adj revolutionary

***revolver** (ray-bhoal-*bhayr*) v stir

revólver (ray-*bhoal*-bhayr) m revolver, gun

revuelta (ray-*bhwayl*-tah) f revolt

rey (ray) m king

rezar (ray-*thahr*) v pray

riada (r*ᵞah*-dhah) f flood

ribera (ree-*bhay*-rah) f riverside, river bank, shore

rico (ree-*koa*) adj rich; wealthy; nice, enjoyable, tasty

ridiculizar (ree-dhee-koo-lee-*thahr*) v ridicule

ridículo (ree-*dhee*-koo-loa) adj ridiculous, ludicrous

riesgo (r*ᵞayz*-goa) m hazard, chance, risk

rigoroso (ree-goa-*roa*-soa) adj severe

riguroso (ree-goo-*roa*-soa) adj bleak

rima (*ree*-mah) f rhyme

rímel (ree-*mayl*) m mascara

rincón (reeng-*koan*) m angle

rinoceronte (ree-noa-thay-*roan*-tay) m rhinoceros

riña (*ree*-ñah) f dispute

riñón (ree-*ñoan*) m kidney

río (*ree*-oa) m river; ~ **abajo** downstream; ~ **arriba** upstream

riqueza (ree-*kay*-thah) f riches pl, wealth

risa (*ree*-sah) f laughter, laugh

ritmo (*reet*-moa) m rhythm; pace

rival (ree-*bhahl*) m rival

rivalidad (ree-bhah-lee-*dhahdh*) f rivalry

rivalizar (ree-bhah-lee-*thahr*) v rival

rizador (ree-thah-*dhoar*) m curling-tongs pl; **rizadores** mpl hair rollers

rizar (ree-*thahr*) v curl

rizo (*ree*-thoa) m curl

robar (roa-*bhahr*) v rob; burgle

roble (roa-bhlay) m oak

robo (*roa*-bhoa) m robbery, theft

robusto (roa-*bhooss*-toa) adj solid, robust

roca (*roa*-kah) f rock

rocío (roa-*thee*-oa) m dew

rocoso (roa-*koa*-soa) adj rocky

rodaballo (roa-dhah-*bhah*-l*ᵞoa) m brill

***rodar** (roa-*dhahr*) v roll

rodear (roa-dhay-*ahr*) v circle, surround; by-pass

rodilla (roa-*dhee*-l*ᵞah) f knee

***rogar** (roa-*gahr*) v ask

rojo (*roa*-khoa) adj red

rollo (*roa*-l*ᵞoa) m roll

romano (roa-*mah*-noa) adj Roman

Romanticismo (roa-mahn-tee-*theez*-moa) m Romanticism

romántico (roa-*mahn*-tee-koa) adj romantic

rompecabezas (roam-pay-kah-*bhay*-thahss) m puzzle; jigsaw puzzle

romper (roam-*payr*) v *break

roncar (roang-*kahr*) v snore

ronco (*roang*-koa) adj hoarse

ropa (*roa*-pah) f clothes pl; ~ **blanca** linen; ~ **de cama** bedding; ~ **interior** underwear; ~ **interior de mujer** lingerie; ~ **sucia** washing, laundry

rosa (*roa*-sah) f rose; adj rose

rosado (roa-*sah*-dhoa) adj pink

rosario (roa-*sah*-r ᵞoa) *m* beads *pl*, rosary

rostro (*roas*-troa) *m* face

rota (*roa*-tah) *f* rattan

roto (*roa*-toa) *adj* broken

rótula (*roa*-too-lah) *f* kneecap

rotular (roa-too-*lahr*) *v* label

rótulo (*roa*-too-loa) *m* label

rozadura (roa-thah-*dhoo*-rah) *f* graze

rubí (roo-*bhee*) *m* ruby

rubia (*roo*-bh ᵞah) *f* blonde

rubio (*roo*-bh ᵞoa) *adj* fair

ruborizarse (roo-bhoa-ree-*thahr*-say) blush

rubricar (roo-bhree-*kahr*) *v* initial

rueda (*rway*-dhah) *f* wheel; **patinaje de ruedas** roller-skating; ~ **de repuesto** spare wheel

ruego (*rway*-goa) *m* request

rugido (roo-*khee*-dhoa) *m* roar

rugir (roo-*kheer*) *v* roar

ruibarbo (rwee-*bhahr*-bhoa) *m* rhubarb

ruido (*rwee*-dhoa) *m* noise

ruidoso (rwee-*dhoa*-soa) *adj* noisy

ruina (*rwee*-nah) *f* ruins; ruin, destruction

ruinoso (rwee-*noa*-soa) *adj* dilapidated

ruiseñor (rwee-say-*ñoar*) *m* nightingale

ruleta (roo-*lay*-tah) *f* roulette

rulo (*roo*-loa) *m* curler

Rumania (roo-*mah*-n ᵞah) *f* Rumania

rumano (roo-*mah*-noa) *adj* Rumanian; *m* Rumanian

rumbo (*room*-boa) *m* course

rumor (roo-*moar*) *m* rumour

rural (roo-*rahl*) *adj* rural

Rusia (*roo*-s ᵞah) *f* Russia

ruso (*roo*-soa) *adj* Russian; *m* Russian

rústico (*rooss*-tee-koa) *adj* rustic

ruta (*roo*-tah) *f* route; ~ **principal** thoroughfare

rutina (roo-*tee*-nah) *f* routine

S

sábado (*sah*-bhah-dhoa) *m* Saturday

sábana (*sah*-bhah-nah) *f* sheet

sabañón (sah-bhah-*ñoan*) *m* chilblain

*****saber** (sah-*bhayr*) *v* *know; *be able to; **a** ~ namely; ~ **a** taste

sabiduría (sah-bhee-dhoo-*ree*-ah) *f* wisdom

sabio (*sah*-bh ᵞoa) *adj* wise

sabor (sah-*bhoar*) *m* flavour

sabroso (sah-*bhroa*-soa) *adj* savoury, tasty

sacacorchos (sah-kah-*koar*-choass) *mpl* corkscrew

sacapuntas (sah-kah-*poon*-tahss) *m* pencil-sharpener

sacar (sah-*kahr*) *v* *take out; *draw; ~ **brillo** brush

sacarina (sah-kah-*ree*-nah) *f* saccharin

sacerdote (sah-thayr-*dhoa*-tay) *m* priest

saco (*sah*-koa) *m* sack; *mMe* jacket; ~ **de compras** shopping bag; ~ **de dormir** sleeping-bag

sacrificar (sah-kree-fee-*kahr*) *v* sacrifice

sacrificio (sah-kree-*fee*-th ᵞoa) *m* sacrifice

sacrilegio (sah-kree-*lay*-kh ᵞoa) *m* sacrilege

sacristán (sah-kreess-*tahn*) *m* sexton

sacudir (sah-koo-*dheer*) *v* *shake

sagrado (sah-*grah*-dhoa) *adj* sacred

sainete (sigh-*nay*-tay) *m* farce

sal (sahl) *f* salt; **sales de baño** bath salts

sala (*sah*-lah) *f* hall; ~ **de conciertos** concert hall; ~ **de espera** waiting-room; ~ **de estar** sitting-room, liv-

ing-room; ~ **de lectura** reading-room; ~ **para fumar** smoking-room
salado (sah-*lah*-dhoa) *adj* salty
salario (sah-*lah*-rʸoa) *m* pay
salchicha (sahl-*chee*-chah) *f* sausage
saldo (*sahl*-doa) *m* balance
salero (sah-*lay*-roa) *m* salt-cellar
salida (sah-*lee*-dhah) *f* issue, exit, way out; ~ **de emergencia** emergency exit
*****salir** (sah-*leer*) *v* *go out; appear
saliva (sah-*lee*-bhah) *f* spit
salmón (sahl-*moan*) *m* salmon
salón (sah-*loan*) *m* salon, lounge, drawing-room; ~ **de baile** ball-room; ~ **de belleza** beauty parlour; ~ **de demostraciones** showroom; ~ **de té** tea-shop
salpicadera (sahl-pee-kah-*dhay*-rah) *fMe* mud-guard
salpicar (sahl-pee-*kahr*) *v* splash
salsa (*sahl*-sah) *f* sauce; gravy
saltamontes (sahl-tah-*moan*-tayss) *m* grasshopper
saltar (sahl-*tahr*) *v* jump, *leap; skip
salto (*sahl*-toa) *m* jump, leap, hop
salud (sah-*loodh*) *f* health
saludable (sah-loo-*dhah*-bhlay) *adj* wholesome
saludar (sah-loo-*dhahr*) *v* greet; salute
saludo (sah-*loo*-dhoa) *m* greeting
salvador (sahl-bhah-*dhoar*) *m* saviour
salvaje (sahl-*bhah*-khay) *adj* wild, savage; fierce, desert
salvar (sahl-*bhahr*) *v* save
sanatorio (sah-nah-*toa*-rʸoa) *m* sanatorium
sandalia (sahn-*dah*-lʸah) *f* sandal; **sandalias de gimnasia** gym shoes
sandía (sahn-*dee*-ah) *f* watermelon
sangrar (sahng-*grahr*) *v* *bleed
sangre (*sahng*-gray) *f* blood
sangriento (sahng-*grʸayn*-toa) *adj* bloody

sanitario (sah-nee-*tah*-rʸoa) *adj* sanitary
sano (*sah*-noa) *adj* healthy, well
santo (*sahn*-toa) *adj* holy; *m* saint; ~ **y seña** password
santuario (sahn-*twah*-rʸoa) *m* shrine
sapo (*sah*-poa) *m* toad
sarampión (sah-rahm-*pʸoan*) *m* measles
sardina (sahr-*dhee*-nah) *f* sardine
sartén (sahr-*tayn*) *f* pan; frying-pan
sastre (*sahss*-tray) *m* tailor
satélite (sah-*tay*-lee-tay) *m* satellite
satisfacción (sah-teess-fahk-*thʸoan*) *f* satisfaction
*****satisfacer** (sah-teess-fah-*thayr*) *v* satisfy; **satisfecho** satisfied
saudí (sou-*dhee*) *adj* Saudi Arabian
sauna (*sou*-nah) *f* sauna
sazonar (sah-thoa-*nahr*) *v* flavour
se (say) *pron* himself; herself; yourselves; themselves
secadora (say-kah-*dhoa*-rah) *f* dryer
secar (say-*kahr*) *v* dry
sección (sayk-*thʸoan*) *f* section; agency
seco (*say*-koa) *adj* dry
secretaria (say-kray-*tah*-rʸah) *f* secretary
secretario (say-kray-*tah*-rʸoa) *m* secretary; clerk
secreto (say-*kray*-toa) *adj* secret; *m* secret
sector (sayk-*toar*) *m* sector
secuencia (say-*kwayn*-thʸah) *f* shot
secuestrador (say-kwayss-trah-*dhoar*) *m* hijacker
secundario (say-koon-*dah*-rʸoa) *adj* secondary; minor
sed (saydh) *f* thirst
seda (*say*-dhah) *f* silk
sede (*say*-dhay) *f* seat
sediento (say-*dhʸayn*-toa) *adj* thirsty
sedoso (say-*dhoa*-soa) *adj* silken

*seducir (say-dhoo-*theer*) *v* seduce

en seguida (ayn say-*gee*-dhah) straight away, at once, presently

*seguir (say-*geer*) *v* follow; **~ el paso** *keep up with; **todo seguido** straight on, straight ahead

según (say-*goon*) *prep* according to

segundo (say-*goon*-doa) *num* second; *m* second

seguramente (say-goo-rah-*mayn*-tay) *adv* surely

seguridad (say-goo-ree-*dhahdh*) *f* security, safety; **cinturón de ~** safety-belt

seguro (say-*goo*-roa) *adj* safe; sure; *m* insurance; **póliza de ~** insurance policy; **~ de viaje** travel insurance; **~ de vida** life insurance

seis (sayss) *num* six

selección (say-layk-*th*ʸoan) *f* selection; choice

seleccionado (say-layk-thʸoa-*nah*-dhoa) *adj* select

seleccionar (say-layk-thʸoa-*nahr*) *v* select

selecto (say-*layk*-toa) *adj* select

selva (*sayl*-bhah) *f* jungle, forest

selvoso (sayl-*bhoa*-soa) *adj* wooded

sellar (say-*l*ʸahr) *v* stamp

sello (*say*-lʸoa) *m* stamp; seal

semáforo (say-*mah*-foa-roa) *m* traffic light

semana (say-*mah*-nah) *f* week; **fin de ~** weekend

semanal (say-mah-*nahl*) *adj* weekly

*sembrar (saym-*brahr*) *v* *sow

semejante (say-may-*khahn*-tay) *adj* like

semejanza (say-may-*khahn*-thah) *f* resemblance, similarity

semi- (*say*-mee) semi-

semicírculo (say-mee-*theer*-koo-loa) *m* semicircle

semilla (say-*mee*-lʸah) *f* seed

senado (say-*nah*-dhoa) *m* senate

senador (say-nah-*dhoar*) *m* senator

sencillo (sayn-*thee*-lʸoa) *adj* plain

senda (*sayn*-dah) *f* footpath

sendero (sayn-*day*-roa) *m* trail

senil (say-*neel*) *adj* senile

seno (*say*-noa) *m* bosom; breast

sensación (sayn-sah-*th*ʸoan) *f* sensation; feeling

sensacional (sayn-sah-thʸoa-*nahl*) *adj* sensational

sensato (sayn-*sah*-toa) *adj* sensible; down-to-earth

sensibilidad (sayn-see-bhee-lee-*dhahdh*) *f* sensibility

sensible (sayn-*see*-bhlay) *adj* sensitive; perceptible

sensitivo (sayn-see-*tee*-bhoa) *adj* sensitive

*sentarse (sayn-*tahr*-say) *v* *sit down; ***estar sentado** *sit; ***sentar bien** *become

sentencia (sayn-*tayn*-thʸah) *f* sentence, verdict

sentenciar (sayn-tayn-*th*ʸahr) *v* sentence

sentido (sayn-*tee*-dhoa) *m* sense; reason; **~ del honor** sense of honour; **sin ~** meaningless

sentimental (sayn-tee-mayn-*tahl*) *adj* sentimental

sentimiento (sayn-tee-*m*ʸayn-toa) *m* sentiment

*sentir (sayn-*teer*) *v* *feel, sense; regret

seña (*say*-ñah) *f* sign; **señas personales** description

señal (say-*ñahl*) *f* signal, sign, indication; *m* token, tick; ***hacer señales** signal; wave; **~ de alarma** distress signal

señalar (say-ñah-*lahr*) *v* tick off, indicate

señor (say-*ñoar*) *m* mister; sir

señora (say-ñoa-rah) f lady; mistress; madam

señorita (say-ñoa-ree-tah) f miss

separación (say-pah-rah-thⱽoan) f division

separadamente (say-pah-rah-dhah-mayn-tay) adv apart

separado (say-pah-rah-dhoa) adj separate; **por ~** apart, separately

separar (say-pah-rahr) v separate, part; divide; detach

septentrional (sayp-tayn-trⱽoa-nahl) adj north

septicemia (sayp-tee-thay-mⱽah) f blood-poisoning

séptico (sayp-tee-koa) adj septic

septiembre (sayp-tⱽaym-bray) September

séptimo (sayp-tee-moa) num seventh

sepulcro (say-pool-kroa) m sepulchre

sepultura (say-pool-too-rah) f grave

sequía (say-kee-ah) f drought

ser (sayr) m being, creature; **~ humano** human being

*ser (sayr) v *be

sereno (say-ray-noa) adj serene

serie (say-rⱽay) f series; sequence

seriedad (say-rⱽay-dhahdh) f seriousness, gravity

serio (say-rⱽoa) adj serious

sermón (sayr-moan) m sermon

serpentear (sayr-payn-tay-ahr) v *wind

serrín (say-rreen) m sawdust

servicial (sayr-bhee-thⱽahl) adj helpful

servicio (sayr-bhee-thⱽoa) m service; service charge; **~ de habitación** room service; **~ de mesa** dinner-service; **~ postal** postal service

servilleta (sayr-bhee-lⱽay-tah) f napkin, serviette; **~ de papel** paper napkin

*servir (sayr-bheer) v serve; attend on, wait on; *be of use

sesenta (say-sayn-tah) num sixty

sesión (say-sⱽoan) f session

seta (say-tah) f mushroom

setenta (say-tayn-tah) num seventy

seto (say-toa) m hedge

severo (say-bhay-roa) adj harsh, strict, severe

sexo (sayk-soa) m sex

sexto (sayks-toa) num sixth

sexual (sayk-swahl) adj sexual

sexualidad (sayk-swah-lee-dhahdh) f sexuality; sex

si (see) conj if; in case; whether; **si ... o** whether ... or; **~ bien** though

sí (see) yes

siamés (sⱽah-mayss) adj Siamese; m Siamese

SIDA (see-dhah) m AIDS

siempre (sⱽaym-pray) adv ever, always

sien (sⱽayn) f temple

sierra (sⱽay-rrah) f saw

siesta (sⱽayss-tah) f nap

siete (sⱽay-tay) num seven

sifón (see-foan) m siphon, syphon

siglo (see-gloa) m century

significado (seeg-nee-fee-kah-dhoa) m meaning

significar (seeg-nee-fee-kahr) v *mean

significativo (seeg-nee-fee-kah-tee-bhoa) adj significant

signo (seeg-noa) m sign; **~ de interrogación** question mark

siguiente (see-gⱽayn-tay) adj following

sílaba (see-lah-bhah) f syllable

silbar (seel-bhahr) v whistle

silbato (seel-bhah-toa) m whistle

silenciador (see-layn-thⱽah-dhoar) m silencer

silencio (see-layn-thⱽoa) m stillness, quiet, silence

silencioso (see-layn-thⱽoa-soa) adj silent

silla (see-lⱽah) f chair; saddle; **~ de ruedas** wheelchair; **~ de tijera**

deck chair

sillón (see-*lYoan*) *m* armchair

simbólico (seem-*boa*-lee-koa) *adj* symbolic

símbolo (*seem*-boa-loa) *m* symbol

similar (see-mee-*lahr*) *adj* similar

simpatía (seem-pah-*tee*-ah) *f* sympathy

simpático (seem-*pah*-tee-koa) *adj* nice, pleasant; obliging

simple (*seem*-play) *adj* simple

simular (see-moo-*lahr*) *v* simulate

simultáneo (see-mool-*tah*-nay-oa) *adj* simultaneous

sin (seen) *prep* without

sinagoga (see-nah-*goa*-gah) *f* synagogue

sincero (seen-*thay*-roa) *adj* sincere; open, honest

sindicato (seen-dee-*kah*-toa) *m* trade-union

sinfonía (seen-foa-*nee*-ah) *f* symphony

singular (seeng-goo-*lahr*) *adj* singular, queer; *m* singular

siniestro (see-*nYayss*-troa) *adj* ominous, sinister

sino (*see*-noa) *conj* but

sinónimo (see-*noa*-nee-moa) *m* synonym

sintético (seen-*tay*-tee-koa) *adj* synthetic

síntoma (*seen*-toa-mah) *m* symptom

sintonizar (seen-toa-nee-*thahr*) *v* tune in

siquiera (see-*kYay*-rah) *adv* at least; *conj* even though

sirena (see-*ray*-nah) *f* siren; mermaid

Siria (*see*-rYah) *f* Syria

sirio (*see*-rYoa) *adj* Syrian; *m* Syrian

sirviente (seer-*bhYayn*-tay) *m* domestic; boy

sistema (seess-*tay*-mah) *m* system; ~ **decimal** decimal system; ~ **de lubricación** lubrication system; ~ **de**

refrigeración cooling system

sistemático (seess-tay-*mah*-tee-koa) *adj* systematic

sitio (*see*-tYoa) *m* site; seat, room; siege

situación (see-twah-*thYoan*) *f* situation

situado (see-*twah*-dhoa) *adj* situated

situar (see-*twahr*) *v* locate

slogan (*sloa*-gahn) *m* slogan

smoking (*smoa*-keeng) *m* dinner-jacket; tuxedo *nAm*

soberano (soa-bhay-*rah*-noa) *m* sovereign

soberbio (soa-*bhayr*-bhYoa) *adj* superb

sobornar (soa-bhoar-*nahr*) *v* bribe

soborno (soa-*bhoar*-noa) *m* bribery

sobra (*soa*-bhrah) *f* surplus

sobrar (soa-*bhrahr*) *v* *be left over; *be in plenty

sobre (*soa*-bhray) *prep* on, upon; *m* envelope

sobrecubierta (soa-bhray-koo-*bhYayr*-tah) *f* jacket

sobreexcitado (soa-bhray-ayk-thee-*tah*-dhoa) *adj* overstrung

sobrepeso (soa-bhray-*pay*-soa) *m* overweight

sobretasa (soa-bhray-*tah*-sah) *f* surcharge

sobretodo (soa-bhray-*toa*-dhoa) *m* coat, topcoat

sobrevivir (soa-bhray-bhee-*bheer*) *v* survive

sobrina (soa-*bhree*-nah) *f* niece

sobrino (soa-*bhree*-noa) *m* nephew

sobrio (*soa*-bhrYoa) *adj* sober

social (soa-*thYahl*) *adj* social

socialismo (soa-thYah-*leez*-moa) *m* socialism

socialista (soa-thYah-*leess*-tah) *adj* socialist; *m* socialist

sociedad (soa-thYay-*dhahdh*) *f* community, society; company

socio (*soa*-thYoa) *m* associate; partner

socorro (soa-*koa*-rroa) *m* aid; **puesto de** ~ first-aid post
soda (*soa*-dhah) *f* soda-water
sofá (soa-*fah*) *m* sofa
sofocante (soa-foa-*kahn*-tay) *adj* stuffy
sofocarse (soa-foa-*kahr*-say) *v* choke
soga (*soa*-gah) *f* rope
sol (soal) *m* sun; **tomar el** ~ sunbathe
solamente (soa-lah-*mayn*-tay) *adv* merely, only
solapa (soa-*lah*-pah) *f* lapel
soldado (soal-*dah*-dhoa) *m* soldier
soldador (soal-dah-*dhoar*) *m* soldering-iron
soldadura (soal-dah-*dhoo*-rah) *f* joint
*soldar** (soal-*dahr*) *v* solder; weld
soleado (soa-lay-*ah*-dhoa) *adj* sunny
soledad (soa-lay-*dhahdh*) *f* solitude
solemne (soa-*laym*-nay) *adj* solemn
*soler** (soa-*layr*) *v* would
solicitar (soa-lee-thee-*tahr*) *v* request; ~ **un puesto** apply
solicitud (soa-lee-thee-*toodh*) *f* application
sólido (*soa*-lee-dhoa) *adj* solid, firm; *m* solid
solitario (soa-lee-*tah*-rʸoa) *adj* lonely
solo (*soa*-loa) *adj* only, single
sólo (*soa*-loa) *adv* alone; only
*soltar** (soal-*tahr*) *v* loosen
soltero (soal-*tay*-roa) *adj* single; *m* bachelor
solterona (soal-tay-*roa*-nah) *f* spinster
soluble (soa-*loo*-bhlay) *adj* soluble
solución (soa-loo-*thʸoan*) *f* solution
sombra (*soam*-brah) *f* shade; shadow; ~ **para los ojos** eye-shadow
sombreado (soam-bray-*ah*-dhoa) *adj* shady
sombrerera (soam-bray-*ray*-rah) *f* milliner
sombrero (soam-*bray*-roa) *m* hat
sombrío (soam-*bree*-oa) *adj* sombre, gloomy

someter (soa-may-*tayr*) *v* subject; **someterse** *v* submit
somnífero (soam-*nee*-fay-roa) *m* sleeping-pill
*sonar** (soa-*nahr*) *v* sound; *ring
sonido (soa-*nee*-dhoa) *m* sound
sonreír (soan-ray-*eer*) *v* smile
sonrisa (soan-*ree*-sah) *f* smile
*soñar** (soa-*ñahr*) *v* *dream
soñoliento (soa-ñoa-*lʸayn*-toa) *adj* sleepy
sopa (*soa*-pah) *f* soup
soplar (soa-*plahr*) *v* *blow
soportar (soa-poar-*tahr*) *v* *bear, endure, sustain; support
sóquet (*soa*-kayt) *mMe* socket
sorbo (*soar*-bhoa) *m* sip
sórdido (*soar*-dhee-dhoa) *adj* filthy
sordo (*soar*-dhoa) *adj* deaf
sorprender (soar-prayn-*dayr*) *v* surprise; *catch
sorpresa (soar-*pray*-sah) *f* surprise; astonishment
sorteo (soar-*tay*-oa) *m* draw
sosegado (soa-say-*gah*-dhoa) *adj* sedate
soso (*soa*-soa) *adj* dull, boring; tasteless
sospecha (soass-*pay*-chah) *f* suspicion
sospechar (soass-pay-*chahr*) *v* suspect
sospechoso (soass-pay-*choa*-soa) *adj* suspicious; **persona sospechosa** suspect
sostén (soass-*tayn*) *m* brassiere, bra
*sostener** (soass-tay-*nayr*) *v* support, *hold up
sota (*soa*-tah) *f* knave
sótano (*soa*-tah-noa) *m* basement; cellar
soto (*soa*-toa) *m* grove
starter (*stahr*-tayr) *m* choke
su (soo) *adj* his; her; their
suahili (swah-*ee*-lee) *m* Swahili

suave (*swah*-bhay) *adj* mild, mellow; gentle

subacuático (soo-bhah-*kwah*-tee-koa) *adj* underwater

subalterno (soo-bhahl-*tayr*-noa) *adj* subordinate

subasta (soo-*bhahss*-tah) *f* auction

súbdito (*soobh*-dhee-toa) *m* subject

subestimar (soo-bhayss-tee-*mahr*) *v* underestimate

subida (soo-*bhee*-dhah) *f* climb, rise, ascent

subir (soo-*bheer*) *v* *rise, ascend; *get on

súbito (*soo*-bhee-toa) *adj* sudden

sublevación (soo-bhlay-bhah-*thᵞoan*) *f* rebellion

sublevarse (soo-bhlay-*bhahr*-say) *v* revolt

subordinado (soo-bhoar-dhee-*nah*-dhoa) *adj* subordinate

subrayar (soobh-rah-ᵞ*ahr*) *v* underline

subsidio (soobh-*see*-dhᵞoa) *m* subsidy

substancia (soobhs-*tahn*-thᵞah) *f* substance

substantivo (soobh-stahn-*tee*-bhoa) *m* noun

substituir (soobhs-tee-*tweer*) *v* replace

subterráneo (soobh-tay-*rrah*-nay-oa) *adj* underground

subtítulo (soobh-*tee*-too-loa) *m* subtitle

suburbano (soo-bhoor-*bhah*-noa) *adj* suburban; *m* commuter

suburbio (soo-*bhoor*-bhᵞoa) *m* suburb

subvención (soobh-bhayn-*thᵞoan*) *f* grant

subyugar (soobh-ᵞoo-*gahr*) *v* overwhelm

suceder (soo-thay-*dhayr*) *v* happen, occur; succeed

sucesión (soo-thay-*sᵞoan*) *f* sequence

suceso (soo-*thay*-soa) *m* event

suciedad (soo-thᵞay-*dhahdh*) *f* dirt; muck

sucio (*soo*-thᵞoa) *adj* dirty; unclean, foul

sucumbir (soo-koom-*beer*) *v* succumb

sucursal (soo-koor-*sahl*) *f* branch

sudar (soo-*dhahr*) *v* perspire, sweat

sudeste (soo-*dhayss*-tay) *m* south-east

sudoeste (soo-dhoa-*ayss*-tay) *m* south-west

sudor (soo-*dhoar*) *m* perspiration, sweat

Suecia (*sway*-thᵞah) *f* Sweden

sueco (*sway*-koa) *adj* Swedish; *m* Swede

suegra (*sway*-grah) *f* mother-in-law

suegro (*sway*-groa) *m* father-in-law

suela (*sway*-lah) *f* sole

sueldo (*swayl*-doa) *m* salary, pay; **aumento de** ~ rise; raise *nAm*

suelo (*sway*-loa) *m* soil, earth; floor

suelto (*swayl*-toa) *adj* loose

sueño (*sway*-ñoa) *m* sleep; dream

suero (*sway*-roa) *m* serum

suerte (*swayr*-tay) *f* luck; fortune, lot; chance; **mala** ~ bad luck

suéter (*sway*-tayr) *m* sweater

suficiente (soo-fee-*thᵞayn*-tay) *adj* enough, sufficient; *ser ~ *do

sufragio (soo-*frah*-khᵞoa) *m* suffrage

sufrimiento (soo-free-*mᵞayn*-toa) *m* affliction, sorrow, suffering

sufrir (soo-*freer*) *v* suffer

sugerir (soo-khay-*reer*) *v* suggest

sugestión (soo-khayss-*tᵞoan*) *f* suggestion

suicidio (swee-*thee*-dhᵞoa) *m* suicide

Suiza (*swee*-thah) *f* Switzerland

suizo (*swee*-thoa) *adj* Swiss; *m* Swiss

sujetador (soo-khay-tah-*dhoar*) *m* brassiere, bra

sujeto (soo-*khay*-toa) *m* subject; theme

sujeto a (soo-*khay*-toa ah) liable to,

subject to

suma (soo-mah) f amount, sum

sumar (soo-mahr) v add; amount to

sumario (soo-mah-rʸoa) m summary

suministrar (soo-mee-neess-trahr) v furnish, supply

suministro (soo-mee-neess-troa) m supply

a lo sumo (soo-moa) at most

superar (soo-pay-rahr) v exceed, *outdo

superficial (soo-payr-fee-thʸahl) adj superficial

superficie (soo-payr-fee-thʸay) f surface; area

superfluo (soo-payr-flwoa) adj superfluous, redundant

superior (soo-pay-rʸoar) adj superior, upper; top

superlativo (soo-payr-lah-tee-bhoa) adj superlative; m superlative

supermercado (soo-payr-mayr-kah-dhoa) m supermarket

superstición (soo-payrs-tee-thʸoan) f superstition

supervisar (soo-payr-bhee-sahr) v supervise

supervisión (soo-payr-bhee-sʸoan) f supervision

supervisor (soo-payr-bhee-soar) m supervisor

supervivencia (soo-payr-bhee-bhayn-thʸah) f survival

suplemento (soo-play-mayn-toa) m supplement

suplicar (soo-plee-kahr) v beg

*suponer** (soo-poa-nayr) v assume, suppose

supositorio (soo-poa-see-toa-rʸoa) m suppository

supremo (soo-pray-moa) adj supreme

suprimir (soo-pree-meer) v discontinue

por supuesto (poar soo-pwayss-toa)

naturally, of course

sur (soor) m south; **polo ~** South Pole

surco (soor-koa) m groove

surgir (soor-kheer) v *arise

surtido (soor-tee-dhoa) m assortment

suscribir (sooss-kree-bheer) v sign

suscripción (sooss-kreep-thʸoan) f subscription

suscrito (sooss-kree-toa) m undersigned

suspender (sooss-payn-dayr) v suspend; *ser suspendido** fail

suspensión (sooss-payn-sʸoan) f suspension

suspicacia (sooss-pee-kah-thʸah) f suspicion

suspicaz (sooss-pee-kahth) adj suspicious

sustancia (sooss-tahn-thʸah) f substance

sustancial (sooss-tahn-thʸahl) adj substantial

sustento (sooss-tayn-toa) m livelihood

*sustituir** (sooss-tee-tweer) v substitute

sustituto (sooss-tee-too-toa) m deputy, substitute

susto (sooss-toa) m scare

susurrar (soo-soo-rrahr) v whisper

susurro (soo-soo-rroa) m whisper

sutil (soo-teel) adj subtle

sutura (soo-too-rah) f stitch; *hacer una ~** sew up

suyo (soo-ʸoa) pron his

T

tabaco (tah-bhah-koa) m tobacco; **~ de pipa** pipe tobacco

taberna (tah-bhayr-nah) f public house, pub; tavern; **moza de ~**

barmaid

tabique (tah-*bhee*-kay) *m* partition

tabla (*tah*-bhlah) *f* board; chart, table; ~ **de conversión** conversion chart; ~ **para surf** surf-board

tablero (tah-*bhlay*-roa) *m* board; ~ **de ajedrez** checkerboard *nAm*; ~ **de damas** draught-board; ~ **de instrumentos** dashboard

tablón (tah-*bhloan*) *m* plank

tabú (tah-*bhoo*) *m* taboo

tacón (tah-*koan*) *m* heel

táctica (*tahk*-tee-kah) *f* tactics *pl*

tacto (*tahk*-toa) *m* touch

tailandés (tigh-lahn-*dayss*) *adj* Thai; *m* Thai

Tailandia (tigh-*lahn*-d ͮ ah) *f* Thailand

tajada (tah-*khah*-dhah) *f* slice

tajar (tah-*khahr*) *v* chop

tal (tahl) *adj* such; **con ~ que** provided that; ~ **como** such as

taladrar (tah-lah-*dhrahr*) drill, bore

taladro (tah-*lah*-dhroa) *m* drill

talco (*tahl*-koa) *m* talc powder

talento (tah-*layn*-toa) *m* gift, talent

talentoso (tah-layn-*toa*-soa) *adj* gifted

talismán (tah-leez-*mahn*) *m* lucky charm

talón (tah-*loan*) *m* heel; counterfoil, stub

talonario (tah-loa-*nah*-r ͮ oa) *m* chequebook; check-book *nAm*

talla (*tah*-l ͮ ah) *f* wood-carving, carving

tallar (tah-*l ͮ ahr*) *v* carve

taller (tah-*l ͮ ayr*) *m* workshop

tallo (*tah*-l ͮ oa) *m* stem

tamaño (tah-*mah*-ño-a) *m* size; ~ **extraordinario** outsize

también (tahm-*b ͮ ayn*) *adv* too, also, as well; **así** ~ likewise

tambor (tahm-*boar*) *m* drum; ~ **del freno** brake drum

tamiz (tah-*meeth*) *m* sieve

tamizar (tah-mee-*thahr*) *v* sift, sieve

tampoco (tahm-*poa*-koa) *adv* not ... either

tan (tahn) *adv* so, such

tangible (tahng-*khee*-bhlay) *adj* tangible

tanque (*tahng*-kay) *m* tank

tanteo (tahn-*tay*-oa) *m* score

tanto (*tahn*-toa) *adv* as much; as; **por lo ~** therefore; **por ~** so; **tanto ... como** both ... and

tapa (*tah*-pah) *f* lid, top, cover; appetizer

tapiz (tah-*peeth*) *m* tapestry

tapizar (tah-pee-*thahr*) *v* upholster

tapón (tah-*poan*) *m* stopper, cork; tampon

taquigrafía (tah-kee-grah-*fee*-ah) *f* shorthand

taquígrafo (tah-*kee*-grah-foa) *m* stenographer

taquilla (tah-*kee*-l ͮ ah) *f* box-office

tararear (tah-rah-ray-*ahr*) *v* hum

tardanza (tahr-*dhahn*-thah) *f* delay

tarde (*tahr*-dhay) *f* afternoon; evening

tardío (tahr-*dhee*-oa) *adj* late

tarea (tah-*ray*-ah) *f* duty, task; job

tarifa (tah-*ree*-fah) *f* rate; ~ **nocturna** night rate

tarjeta (tahr-*khay*-tah) *f* card; ~ **de crédito** credit card; charge plate *Am*; ~ **de temporada** season-ticket; ~ **de visita** visiting-card; ~ **postal** postcard, card; ~ **postal ilustrada** picture postcard; ~ **verde** green card

tarta (*tahr*-tah) *f* cake

taxi (*tahk*-see) *m* cab, taxi

taxímetro (tahk-*see*-may-troa) *m* taximeter

taxista (tahk-*seess*-tah) *m* cab-driver, taxi-driver

taza (*tah*-thah) *f* cup; mug; ~ **de té** teacup

tazón (tah-*thoan*) *m* bowl, basin

te (tay) *pron* yourself

té (tay) *m* tea

teatro (tay-*ah*-troa) *m* drama; theatre; ~ **de la ópera** opera house; ~ **de variedades** music-hall, variety theatre; ~ **guiñol** puppet-show

tebeo (tay-*bhay*-oa) *m* comics *pl*

técnica (*tayk*-nee-kah) *f* technique

técnico (*tayk*-nee-koa) *adj* technical; *m* technician

tecnología (tayk-noa-loa-*khee*-ah) *f* technology

techo (*tay*-choa) *m* roof; ~ **de paja** thatched roof

teja (*tay*-khah) *f* tile

tejedor (tay-khay-*dhoar*) *m* weaver

tejer (tay-*khayr*) *v* *weave

tejido (tay-*khee*-dhoa) *m* fabric, tissue, material

tela (*tay*-lah) *f* cloth; ~ **para toallas** towelling

telaraña (tay-lah-*rah*-ñah) *f* spider's web

telefax (tay-lay-*fahks*) *m* fax; **mandar un** ~ send a fax

telefonear (tay-lay-foa-nay-*ahr*) *v* phone; call up *Am*

telefonista (tay-lay-foa-*neess*-tah) *f* telephonist, telephone operator

teléfono (tay-*lay*-foa-noa) *m* phone, telephone; **llamar por** ~ ring up

telegrafiar (tay-lay-grah-*fʸahr*) *v* telegraph

teleobjetivo (tay-lay-oabh-khay-*tee*-bhoa) *m* telephoto lens

telepatía (tay-lay-pah-*tee*-ah) *f* telepathy

telesilla (tay-lay-*see*-lʸah) *m* ski-lift

televisión (tay-lay-bhee-*sʸoan*) *f* television; ~ **por cable** cable television; ~ **por satélite** satellite television

televisor (tay-lay-bhee-*soar*) *m* televi-

sion set

télex (*tay*-layks) *m* telex

telón (tay-*loan*) *m* curtain

tema (*tay*-mah) *m* theme

*temblar** (taym-*bhlahr*) *v* tremble, shiver

temer (tay-*mayr*) *v* fear, dread

temor (tay-*moar*) *m* fear, dread

temperamento (taym-pay-rah-*mayn*-toa) *m* temperament

temperatura (taym-pay-rah-*too*-rah) *f* temperature; ~ **ambiente** room temperature

tempestad (taym-payss-*tahdh*) *f* tempest

tempestuoso (taym-payss-*twoa*-soa) *adj* stormy

templo (*taym*-ploa) *m* temple

temporada (taym-poa-*rah*-dhah) *f* season; **apogeo de la** ~ high season; ~ **baja** low season

temporal (taym-poa-*rahl*) *adj* temporary

temprano (taym-*prah*-noa) *adj* early

tenazas (tay-*nah*-thahss) *f* tongs *pl*, pincers *pl*

tendencia (tayn-*dayn*-thʸah) *f* tendency

*tender a** (tayn-*dayr*) tend; *tender-se** *v* *lie down

tendero (tayn-*day*-roa) *m* shopkeeper; tradesman

tendón (tayn-*doan*) *m* sinew, tendon

tenedor (tay-nay-*dhoar*) *m* fork

*tener** (tay-*nayr*) *v* *have; *keep, *hold; ~ **que** *must; *ought to, *should, *shall; *be obliged to; **tenga usted** here you are

teniente (tay-*nʸayn*-tay) *m* lieutenant

tenis (*tay*-neess) *m* tennis; ~ **de mesa** ping-pong, table tennis

tensión (tayn-*sʸoan*) *f* strain, pressure, tension; ~ **arterial** blood pressure

tenso (*tayn*-soa) *adj* tense

tentación (tayn-tah-*th*Yoan) *f* temptation

*****tentar** (tayn-*tahr*) *v* tempt

tentativa (tayn-tah-*tee*-bhah) *f* attempt, try

tentempié (tayn-taym-*p*Yay) *m* snack

*****teñir** (tay-*ñeer*) *v* dye

teología (tay-oa-loa-*khee*-ah) *f* theology

teoría (tay-oa-*ree*-ah) *f* theory

teórico (tay-*oa*-ree-koa) *adj* theoretical

terapia (tay-*rah*-pYah) *f* therapy

tercero (tayr-*thay*-roa) *num* third

terciopelo (tayr-thYoa-*pay*-loa) *m* velvet

terilene (tay-ree-*lay*-nay) *m* terylene

terminación (tayr-mee-nah-*th*Yoan) *f* finish

terminar (tayr-mee-*nahr*) *v* end, finish; accomplish; **terminarse** *v* expire, end

término (*tayr*-mee-noa) *m* term; issue

termo (*tayr*-moa) *m* vacuum flask, thermos flask

termómetro (tayr-*moa*-may-troa) *m* thermometer

termostato (tayr-moass-*tah*-toa) *m* thermostat

ternero (tayr-*nay*-roa) *m* calf

ternura (tayr-*noo*-rah) *f* tenderness

terraplén (tay-rrah-*playn*) *m* embankment

terraza (tay-*rrah*-thah) *f* terrace

terremoto (tay-rray-*moa*-toa) *m* earthquake

terreno (tay-*rray*-noa) *m* terrain; field, grounds

terrible (tay-*rree*-bhlay) *adj* frightful; awful, horrible, terrible, dreadful

territorio (tay-rree-*toa*-rYoa) *m* territory

terrón (tay-*rroan*) *m* lump

terror (tay-*rroar*) *m* terror; terrorism

terrorismo (tay-rroa-*reez*-moa) *m* terrorism

terrorista (tay-rroa-*reess*-tah) *m* terrorist

tesis (*tay*-seess) *f* thesis

Tesorería (tay-soa-ray-*ree*-ah) *f* treasury

tesorero (tay-soa-*ray*-roa) *m* treasurer

tesoro (tay-*soa*-roa) *m* treasure

testamento (tayss-tah-*mayn*-toa) *m* will

testarudo (tayss-tah-*roo*-dhoa) *adj* pigheaded, stubborn

testigo (tayss-*tee*-goa) *m* witness; ~ **de vista** eye-witness

testimoniar (tayss-tee-moa-*n*Yahr) *v* testify

testimonio (tayss-tee-*moa*-nYoa) *m* testimony

tetera (tay-*tay*-rah) *f* teapot

textil (tayks-*teel*) *m* textile

texto (*tayks*-toa) *m* text

textura (tayks-*too*-rah) *f* texture

tez (tayth) *f* complexion

ti (tee) *pron* you

tía (*tee*-ah) *f* aunt

tibio (*tee*-bhYoa) *adj* tepid, lukewarm

tiburón (tee-bhoo-*roan*) *m* shark

tiempo (*t*Yaym-poa) *m* time; weather; **a** ~ in time; ~ **libre** spare time

tienda (*t*Yayn-dah) *f* shop; tent

tierno (*t*Yayr-noa) *adj* gentle, tender

tierra (*t*Yay-rrah) *f* earth; ground, soil; land; **en** ~ ashore; ~ **baja** lowlands *pl*; ~ **firme** mainland

tieso (*t*Yay-soa) *adj* stiff

tifus (*tee*-fooss) *m* typhoid

tigre (*tee*-gray) *m* tiger

tijeras (tee-*khay*-rahss) *fpl* scissors *pl*; ~ **para las uñas** nail-scissors *pl*

tilo (*tee*-loa) *m* limetree, lime

timbre (*teem*-bray) *m* tone; bell; doorbell; *mMe* postage stamp

timidez (tee-mee-*dhayth*) *f* timidity, shyness

tímido (tee-mee-dhoa) *adj* timid, embarrassed, shy

timón (tee-*moan*) *m* helm, rudder

timonel (tee-moa-*nayl*) *m* steersman

timonero (tee-moa-*nay*-roa) *m* helmsman

tímpano (*teem*-pah-noa) *m* ear-drum

tinta (*teen*-tah) *f* ink

tintorería (teen-toa-ray-*ree*-ah) *f* dry-cleaner's

tintura (teen-*too*-rah) *f* dye

tío (*tee*-oa) *m* uncle

típico (*tee*-pee-koa) *adj* typical, characteristic

tipo (*tee*-poa) *m* type; fellow, guy

tirada (tee-*rah*-dhah) *f* issue

tirano (tee-*rah*-noa) *m* tyrant

tirantes (tee-*rahn*-tayss) *mpl* braces *pl*; suspenders *plAm*

tirar (tee-*rahr*) *v* pull; *throw; *shoot

tiritar (tee-ree-*tahr*) *v* shiver

tiro (*tee*-roa) *m* shot

tirón (tee-*roan*) *m* wrench

titular (tee-too-*lahr*) *m* headline

título (*tee*-too-loa) *m* heading, title; degree

toalla (toa-*ah*-lᵞah) *f* towel; ~ **de baño** bath towel

tobera (toa-*bhay*-rah) *f* nozzle

tobillo (toa-*bhee*-lᵞoa) *m* ankle

tobogán (toa-bhoa-*gahn*) *m* slide

tocadiscos (toa-kah-*deess*-koass) *m* record-player

tocador (toa-kah-*dhoar*) *m* dressing-table; powder-room; **artículos de** ~ toiletry

tocante a (toa-*kahn*-tay ah) regarding

tocar (toa-*kahr*) *v* touch, *hit; play; **no** ~ *keep off

tocino (toa-*thee*-noa) *m* bacon

todavía (toa-dhah-*bhee*-ah) *adv* still, however

todo (*toa*-dhoa) *adj* all; entire; *pron* everything; **sobre** ~ most of all, es-

sentially, especially; **todos** *pron* everybody

toldo (*toal*-doa) *m* awning

tolerable (toa-lay-*rah*-bhlay) *adj* tolerable

tomar (toa-*mahr*) *v* *catch; *take; ~ **el pelo** tease

tomate (toa-*mah*-tay) *m* tomato

tomillo (toa-*mee*-lᵞoa) *m* thyme

tomo (*toa*-moa) *m* volume

tonada (toa-*nah*-dhah) *f* tune

tonel (toa-*nayl*) *m* barrel, cask

tonelada (toa-nay-*lah*-dhah) *f* ton

tónico (*toa*-nee-koa) *m* tonic; ~ **para el cabello** hair tonic

tono (*toa*-noa) *m* tone; note; shade

tontería (toan-tay-*ree*-ah) *f* nonsense, rubbish; *decir **tonterías** talk rubbish

tonto (*toan*-toa) *adj* foolish; *m* fool

topetar (toa-pay-*tahr*) *v* bump

topetón (toa-pay-*toan*) *m* bump

toque (*toa*-kay) *m* touch

torcedura (toar-thay-*dhoo*-rah) *f* sprain

*torcer** (toar-*thayr*) *v* twist; *torcerse** *v* sprain

tordo (*toar*-dhoa) *m* thrush

tormenta (toar-*mayn*-tah) *f* storm

tormento (toar-*mayn*-toa) *m* torment

tormentoso (toar-mayn-*toa*-soa) *adj* thundery

tornar (toar-*nahr*) *v* return

torneo (toar-*nay*-oa) *m* tournament

tornillo (toar-*nee*-lᵞoa) *m* screw

en torno (ayn *toar*-noa) about, around

en torno de (ayn *toar*-noa day) round, around

toro (*toa*-roa) *m* bull

toronja (toa-*roan*-khah) *fMe* grapefruit

torpe (*toar*-pay) *adj* clumsy, awkward

torre (*toa*-rray) *f* tower

torsión (toar-*s*ᵞ*oan*) *f* twist

tortilla (toar-*tee*-lᵞah) *f* omelette

tortuga (toar-*too*-gah) *f* turtle

tortuoso (toar-*twoa*-soa) *adj* winding

tortura (toar-*too*-rah) *f* torture

torturar (toar-too-*rahr*) *v* torture

tos (toass) *f* cough

toser (toa-*sayr*) *v* cough

tostado (toass-*tah*-dhoa) *adj* tanned

total (toa-*tahl*) *adj* total; overall, utter; *m* total; whole; **en ~** altogether

totalitario (toa-tah-lee-*tah*-r^yoa) *adj* totalitarian

totalizador (toa-tah-lee-thah-*dhoar*) *m* totalizator

totalmente (toa-tahl-*mayn*-tay) *adv* completely, altogether, wholly

tóxico (*toak*-see-koa) *adj* toxic

trabajar (trah-bhah-*khahr*) *v* work

trabajo (trah-*bhah*-khoa) *m* work, labour; difficulty; **~ manual** handicraft

tractor (trahk-*toar*) *m* tractor

tradición (trah-dhee-*th*^y*oan*) *f* tradition

tradicional (trah-dhee-th^yoa-*nahl*) *adj* traditional

traducción (trah-dhook-*th*^y*oan*) *f* translation

*****traducir** (trah-dhoo-*theer*) *v* translate

traductor (trah-dhook-*toar*) *m* translator

*****traer** (trah-*ayr*) *v* *bring

tragar (trah-*gahr*) *v* swallow

tragedia (trah-*khay*-dh^yah) *f* drama, tragedy

trágico (*trah*-khee-koa) *adj* tragic

traición (trigh-*th*^y*oan*) *f* treason

traicionar (trigh-th^yoa-*nahr*) *v* betray

traidor (trigh-*dhoar*) *m* traitor

tráilla (trah-ee-l^yah) *f* lead

traje (*trah*-khay) *m* suit; gown; robe; **~ de baño** bathing-suit; **~ de etiqueta** evening dress; **~ del país** national dress; **~ de malla** tights *pl*; **~ pantalón** pant-suit

trama (*trah*-mah) *f* plot

trampa (*trahm*-pah) *f* trap; hatch

tranquilidad (trahng-kee-lee-*dhahdh*) *f* tranquillity

tranquilizar (trahng-kee-lee-*thahr*) *v* reassure

tranquilo (trahng-*kee*-loa) *adj* tranquil, quiet, calm; peaceful

transacción (trahn-sahk-*th*^y*oan*) *f* transaction, deal; **volumen de transacciones** turnover

transatlántico (trahn-saht-*lahn*-tee-koa) *adj* transatlantic

transbordador (trahnz-bhoar-dhah-*dhoar*) *m* ferry-boat; **~ de trenes** train ferry

transcurrir (trahns-koo-*rrer*) *v* pass

transeúnte (trahn-say-*oon*-tay) *m* passer-by

*****transferir** (trahns-fay-*reer*) *v* transfer

transformador (trahns-foar-mah-*dhoar*) *m* transformer

transformar (trahns-foar-*mahr*) *v* transform

transgredir (trahnz-gray-*deer*) *v* offend

transición (trahn-see-*th*^y*oan*) *f* transition

tránsito (*trahn*-see-toa) *m* traffic

transmisión (trahnz-mee-s^y*oan*) *f* transmission, broadcast

transmitir (trahnz-mee-*teer*) *v* transmit

transparente (trahns-pah-*rayn*-tay) *adj* transparent

transpiración (trahns-pee-rah-*th*^y*oan*) *f* perspiration

transpirar (trahns-pee-*rahr*) *v* perspire

transportar (trahns-poar-*tahr*) *v* transport; ship

transporte (trahns-*poar*-tay) *m* transportation, transport

tranvía (trahm-*bee*-ah) *m* tram; streetcar *nAm*

trapo (*trah*-poa) *m* rag; **~ de cocina** tea-cloth

tras (trahss) *prep* behind

* hacer trasbordo (ah-*thayr* trahz-*bhoar*-dhoa) change

trasero (trah-*say*-roa) *m* bottom

trasladar (trahz-lah-*dhahr*) *v* move

traslúcido (trahz-*loo*-thee-dhoa) *adj* sheer

trastornado (trahss-toar-*nah*-dhoa) *adj* upset

trastornar (trahss-toar-*nahr*) *v* upset

trastos (*trahss*-toass) *mpl* litter

tratado (trah-*tah*-dhoa) *m* essay; treaty

tratamiento (trah-tah-*m^yayn*-toa) *m* treatment; **~ de belleza** beauty treatment

tratar (trah-*tahr*) *v* handle, treat; **~ con** *deal with

trato (*trah*-toa) *m* intercourse

a través de (ah trah-*bhayss day*) across, through

travesía (trah-bhay-*see*-ah) *f* crossing, passage

travieso (trah-*bh^yay*-soa) *adj* naughty, bad; mischievous

trazar (trah-*thahr*) *v* sketch

trébol (*tray*-bhoal) *m* clover, shamrock

trece (*tray*-thay) *num* thirteen

treceno (tray-*thay*-noa) *num* thirteenth

trecho (*tray*-choa) *m* stretch

treinta (*trayn*-tah) *num* thirty

treintavo (trayn-*tah*-bhoa) *num* thirtieth

tremendo (tray-*mayn*-doa) *adj* awful, terrible; tremendous, terrific

trementina (tray-mayn-*tee*-nah) *f* turpentine

tren (trayn) *m* train; **~ de cercanías** stopping train; **~ de mercancías** goods train; **~ de pasajeros** passenger train; **~ directo** through train; **~ expreso** express train; **~ nocturno** night train; **~ ómnibus** local train

trenza (*trayn*-thah) *f* twine

trepar (tray-*pahr*) *v* climb

tres (trayss) *num* three

triangular (tr^yahng-goo-*lahr*) *adj* triangular

triángulo (tr^yahng-goo-loa) *m* triangle

tribu (*tree*-bhoo) *m* tribe

tribuna (tree-*bhoo*-nah) *f* stand

tribunal (tree-bhoo-*nahl*) *m* court, law court

trigal (tree-*gahl*) *m* cornfield

trigo (*tree*-goa) *m* grain, corn; wheat

trimestral (tree-mayss-*trahl*) *adj* quarterly

trimestre (tree-*mayss*-tray) *m* quarter

trinchar (treen-*chahr*) *v* carve

trineo (tree-*nay*-oa) *m* sleigh, sledge

triste (*treess*-tay) *adj* sad

tristeza (treess-*tay*-thah) *f* sorrow, sadness

triturar (tree-too-*rahr*) *v* *grind

triunfante (tr^yoon-*fahn*-tay) *adj* triumphant

triunfar (tr^yoon-*fahr*) *v* triumph

triunfo (tr^yoon-foa) *m* triumph

* trocar (troa-*kahr*) *v* swap

trolebús (troa-lay-*bhooss*) *m* trolleybus

trompeta (troam-*pay*-tah) *f* trumpet

tronada (troa-*nah*-dhah) *f* thunderstorm

* tronar (troa-*nahr*) *v* thunder

tronco (*troang*-koa) *m* trunk

trono (*troa*noa) *m* throne

tropas (*troa*-pahss) *fpl* troops *pl*

* tropezarse (troa-pay-*thahr*-say) *v* stumble

tropical (troa-pee-*kahl*) *adj* tropical

trópicos (*troa*-pee-koass) *mpl* tropics *pl*

trozo (*troa*-thoa) *m* chunk, morsel, bit; fragment, passage

truco (*troo*-koa) *m* trick

trucha (*troo*-chah) *f* trout

trueno (_trway_-noa) _m_ thunder
tu (too) _adj_ your
tú (too) _pron_ you
tuberculosis (too-bhayr-koo-_loa_-seess) _f_ tuberculosis
tubo (_too_-bhoa) _m_ tube
tuerca (_twayr_-kah) _f_ nut
tulipán (too-lee-_pahn_) _m_ tulip
tumba (_toom_-bah) _f_ tomb
tumor (too-_moar_) _m_ growth, tumour
tunecino (too-nay-_thee_-noa) _adj_ Tunisian; _m_ Tunisian
túnel (_too_-nayl) _m_ tunnel
Túnez (_too_-nayth) _m_ Tunisia
túnica (_too_-nee-kah) _f_ tunic
turbar (toor-_bhahr_) _v_ embarrass
turbera (toor-_bhay_-rah) _f_ moor
turbina (toor-_bhee_-nah) _f_ turbine
turco (_toor_-koa) _adj_ Turkish; _m_ Turk
turismo (too-_reez_-moa) _m_ tourism
turista (too-_reess_-tah) _m_ tourist; **oficina para turistas** tourist office
turno (_toor_-noa) _m_ turn; shift
Turquía (toor-_kee_-ah) _f_ Turkey
turrón (too-_rroan_) _m_ nougat
tutela (too-_tay_-lah) _f_ custody
tutor (too-_toar_) _m_ tutor; guardian
tuyos (_too_-Yoass) _adj_ your

U

ubicación (oo-bhee-kah-_th_Yoan) _f_ situation, location
ujier (oo-kh_Y_ayr) _m_ bailiff
úlcera (_ool_-thay-rah) _f_ ulcer, sore; ~ **gástrica** gastric ulcer
ulterior (ool-tay-r_Y_oar) _adj_ further
últimamente (_ool_-tee-mah-mayn-tay) _adv_ lately
último (_ool_-tee-moa) _adj_ ultimate; last
ultraje (ool-_trah_-khay) _m_ outrage
.ramar (ool-trah-_mahr_) _adv_ overseas

ultravioleta (ool-trah-bh_Y_oa-_lay_-tah) _adj_ ultraviolet
umbral (oom-_brahl_) _m_ threshold
un (oon) _art_ a
unánime (oo-_nah_-nee-may) _adj_ likeminded, unanimous
ungüento (oong-_gwayn_-toa) _m_ ointment, salve
únicamente (_oo_-nee-kah-mayn-tay) _adv_ exclusively
único (_oo_-nee-koa) _adj_ unique, sole
unidad (oo-nee-_dhahdh_) _f_ unity; unit
unido (oo-_nee_-dhoa) _adj_ joint
uniforme (oo-nee-_foar_-may) _adj_ uniform; _m_ uniform
unilateral (oo-nee-lah-tay-_rahl_) _adj_ one-sided
unión (oo-n_Y_oan) _f_ union
Unión Europea (oo-n_Y_oan ay°°-roa-pay-ah) European Union
unir (oo-_neer_) _v_ unite; combine; **unirse a** join
universal (oo-nee-bhayr-_sahl_) _adj_ universal
universidad (oo-nee-bhayr-see-_dhahdh_) _f_ university
universo (oo-nee-_bhayr_-soa) _m_ universe
uno (_oo_-noa) _num_ one; _pron_ one; **unos** _adj_ some; _pron_ some
uña (_oo_-ñah) _f_ nail
urbano (oor-_bhah_-noa) _adj_ urban
urgencia (oor-_khayn_-th_Y_ah) _f_ urgency; emergency; **botiquín de ~** first-aid kit
urgente (oor-_khayn_-tay) _adj_ pressing, urgent
urraca (oo-_rrah_-kah) _f_ magpie
Uruguay (oo-roo-_gwigh_) _m_ Uruguay
uruguayo (oo-roo-_gwah_-Yoa) _adj_ Uruguayan; _m_ Uruguayan
usar (oo-_sahr_) _v_ use
uso (_oo_-soa) _m_ use, usage
usted (ooss-_taydh_) _pron_ you; **a ~**

you; **de** ~ your

usual (oo-*swahl*) *adj* common, customary, usual

usuario (oo-*swah*-rᵛoa) *m* user

utensilio (oo-tayn-*see*-lᵛoa) *m* utensil

útil (*oo*-teel) *adj* useful

utilidad (oo-tee-lee-*dhahdh*) *f* utility, use

utilizable (oo-tee-lee-*thah*-bhlay) *adj* usable

utilizar (oo-tee-lee-*thahr*) *v* utilize

uvas (*oo*-bhahss) *fpl* grapes *pl*

V

vaca (*bah*-kah) *f* cow

vacaciones (bah-kah-*th*ᵛoa-nayss) *fpl* holiday, vacation; **de** ~ on holiday

vacante (bah-*kahn*-tay) *adj* vacant; *f* vacancy

vaciar (bah-*th*ᵛahr) *v* empty; vacate

vacilante (bah-thee-lahn-tay) *adj* unsteady, shaky

vacilar (bah-thee-*lahr*) *v* hesitate; falter

vacío (bah-*thee*-oa) *adj* empty; *m* vacuum

vacunación (bah-koo-nah-*th*ᵛoan) *f* vaccination

vacunar (bah-koo-*nahr*) *v* vaccinate, inoculate

vadear (bah-dhay-*ahr*) *v* wade

vado (*bah*-dhoa) *m* ford

vagabundear (bah-gah-bhoon-day-*ahr*) *v* tramp, roam

vagabundo (bah-gah-*bhoon*-doa) *m* tramp

vagancia (bah-*gahn*-thᵛah) *f* vagrancy

vagar (bah-*gahr*) *v* wander

vago (*bah*-goa) *adj* vague; faint, dim; idle

vagón (bah-*goan*) *m* waggon, carriage; coach

vainilla (bigh-*nee*-lᵛah) *f* vanilla

vale (*bah*-lay) *m* banknote

***valer** (bah-*layr*) *v* *be worth; ~ **la pena** *be worth-while

valiente (bah-*l*ᵛayn-tay) *adj* courageous, plucky, brave

valija (bah-*lee*-khah) *f* case

valioso (bah-*l*ᵛoa-soa) *adj* valuable

valor (bah-*loar*) *m* worth, value; courage; **bolsa de valores** stock exchange; **sin** ~ worthless

vals (bahls) *m* waltz

valuar (bah-*lwahr*) *v* value; appreciate

válvula (*bahl*-bhoo-lah) *f* valve

valle (*bah*-lᵛay) *m* valley

vanidoso (bah-nee-*dhoa*-soa) *adj* vain

vano (*bah*-noa) *adj* idle, vain; **en** ~ in vain

vapor (bah-*poar*) *m* steam, vapour; steamer; ~ **de línea** liner

vaporizador (bah-poa-ree-thah-*dhoar*) *m* atomizer

vaqueros (bah-*kay*-roass) *mpl* jeans *pl*

variable (bah-*r*ᵛah-bhlay) *adj* variable

variación (bah-*r*ᵛah-*th*ᵛoan) *f* variation

variado (bah-*r*ᵛah-dhoa) *adj* varied

variar (bah-*r*ᵛahr) *v* vary

varice (*bah*-ree-thay) *f* varicose vein

varicela (bah-ree-*thay*-lah) *f* chicken-pox

variedad (bah-*r*ᵛay-*dhahdh*) *f* variety; **espectáculo de variedades** variety show

varios (*bah*-rᵛoass) *adj* various, several

vaselina (bah-say-*lee*-nah) *f* vaseline

vasija (bah-*see*-khah) *f* vessel

vaso (*bah*-soa) *m* glass; mug, tumbler; vase; ~ **sanguíneo** blood-vessel

vasto (*bahss*-toa) *adj* wide, vast; extensive

vatio (*bah*-tᵛoa) *m* watt

vecindad (bay-theen-*dahdh*) *f* neighbourhood, vicinity

vecindario (bay-theen-*dah*-r^yoa) *m* community

vecino (bay-*thee*-noa) *adj* neighbouring; *m* neighbour

vegetación (bay-khay-tah-*th^yoan*) *f* vegetation

vegetariano (bay-khay-tah-r^y*ah*-noa) *m* vegetarian

vehículo (bay-*ee*-koo-loa) *m* vehicle

veinte (*bayn*-tay) *num* twenty

vejez (bay-*khayth*) *f* old age

vejiga (bay-*khee*-gah) *f* bladder

vela (*bay*-lah) *f* sail; **deporte de ~** yachting

velo (*bay*-loa) *m* veil

velocidad (bay-loa-thee-*dhahdh*) *f* speed; rate; gear; **límite de ~** speed limit; **~ de cruce** cruising speed

velocímetro (bay-loa-*thee*-may-troa) *m* speedometer

veloz (bay-*loath*) *adj* swift

vena (*bay*-nah) *f* vein

vencedor (bayn-thay-*dhoar*) *m* winner

vencer (bayn-*thayr*) *v* *overcome, conquer; *win

vencimiento (bayn-thee-m^y*ayn*-toa) *m* expiry

vendaje (bayn-*dah*-khay) *m* bandage

vendar (bayn-*dahr*) *v* dress

vendedor (bayn-day-*dhoar*) *m* salesman

vendedora (bayn-day-*dhoa*-rah) *f* salesgirl

vender (bayn-*dayr*) *v* *sell; **~ al detalle** retail

vendible (bayn-*dee*-bhlay) *adj* saleable

vendimia (bayn-*dee*-m^yah) *f* vintage

veneno (bay-*nay*-noa) *m* poison

venenoso (bay-nay-*noa*-soa) *adj* poisonous

venerable (bay-nay-*rah*-bhlay) *adj* venerable

venerar (bay-nay-*rahr*) *v* worship

venezolano (bay-nay-thoa-*lah*-noa) *adj* Venezuelan; *m* Venezuelan

Venezuela (bay-nay-*thway*-lah) *f* Venezuela

venganza (bayng-*gahn*-thah) *f* revenge

venidero (bay-nee-*dhay*-roa) *adj* oncoming

*venir** (bay-*neer*) *v* *come

venta (*bayn*-tah) *f* sale; **de ~** for sale; **~ al por mayor** wholesale

ventaja (bayn-*tah*-khah) *f* benefit, advantage; profit; lead

ventajoso (bayn-tah-*khoa*-soa) *adj* advantageous

ventana (bayn-*tah*-nah) *f* window; **~ de la nariz** nostril

ventarrón (bayn-tah-*rroan*) *m* gale

ventilación (bayn-tee-lah-*th^yoan*) *f* ventilation

ventilador (bayn-tee-lah-*dhoar*) *m* fan, ventilator

ventilar (bayn-tee-*lahr*) *v* ventilate

ventisca (bhayn-*teess*-kah) *f* blizzard

ventoso (bayn-*toa*-soa) *adj* windy

*ver** (bayr) *v* *see, notice

veranda (bay-*rahn*-dah) *f* veranda

verano (bay-*rah*-noa) *m* summer; **pleno ~** midsummer

verbal (bayr-*bhahl*) *adj* verbal

verbo (*bayr*-bhoa) *m* verb

verdad (bayr-*dhahdh*) *f* truth

verdaderamente (bayr-dhah-dhay-rah-*mayn*-tay) *adv* really

verdadero (bayr-dhah-*dhay*-roa) *adj* true; real, very; actual

verde (*bayr*-dhay) *adj* green

verdulero (bayr-dhoo-*lay*-roa) *m* greengrocer

veredicto (bay-ray-*dheek*-toa) *m* verdict

vergel (*bayr*-gayl) *m* orchard

vergüenza (bayr-*gwayn*-thah) *f* shame;

¡qué vergüenza! shame!

verídico (bay-*ree*-dhee-koa) *adj* truthful

verificar (bay-ree-fee-*kahr*) *v* check, verify

verosímil (bay-roa-*see*-meel) *adj* credible

versión (bayr-sʸoan) *f* version

verso (*bayr*-soa) *m* verse

*verter (bayr-*tayr*) *v* pour; *spill

vertical (bayr-tee-*kahl*) *adj* vertical

vértigo (*bayr*-tee-goa) *m* dizziness, vertigo

vestíbulo (bayss-*tee*-bhoo-loa) *m* hall, lobby; foyer

vestido (bayss-*tee*-dhoa) *m* frock, dress; **vestidos** *mpl* clothes *pl*

*vestir (bayss-*teer*) *v* dress; ***vestirse** *v* dress

vestuario (bayss-*twah*-rʸoa) *m* wardrobe; dressing-room

veterinario (bay-tay-ree-*nah*-rʸoa) *m* veterinary surgeon

vez (bayth) *f* time; **alguna ~** some time; **a veces** sometimes; **de ~ en cuando** occasionally, now and then; **otra ~** again, once more; **pocas veces** seldom; **una ~** once

vía (*bee*-ah) *f* track; **~ del tren** railroad *nAm*; **~ navegable** waterway

viaducto (bʸah-*dhook*-toa) *m* viaduct

viajar (bʸah-*khahr*) *v* travel

viaje (*bʸah*-khay) *m* journey; trip, voyage

viajero (bʸah-*khay*-roa) *m* traveller

vibración (bee-bhrah-*thʸoan*) *f* vibration

vibrar (bee-*bhrahr*) *v* tremble, vibrate

vicario (bee-*kah*-rʸoa) *m* vicar

vicepresidente (bee-thay-pray-see-*dhayn*-tay) *m* vice-president

vicioso (bee-*thʸoa*-soa) *adj* vicious

víctima (*beek*-tee-mah) *f* casualty, victim

victoria (beek-*toa*-rʸah) *f* victory

vida (*bee*-dhah) *f* life; lifetime; **en ~** alive; **~ privada** privacy

videocámara (bee-dhay-oa-*kah*-mah-rah) *f* video camera

videocasete (bee-dhay-oa-kah-*say*-tay) *m* video cassette

videograbadora (bee-dhay-oa-grah-bhah-*dhoa*-rah) *f* video recorder

vidrio (*bee*-dhrʸoa) *m* glass; **de ~** glass; **~ de color** stained glass

viejo (*bʸay*-khoa) *adj* old; ancient, aged; stale

viento (*bʸayn*-toa) *m* wind

vientre (*bʸayn*-tray) *m* belly

viernes (*bʸayr*-nayss) *m* Friday

vigente (bee-*khayn*-tay) *adj* valid

vigésimo (bee-*khay*-see-moa) *num* twentieth

vigilar (bee-khee-*lahr*) *v* watch, patrol

vigor (bee-*goar*) *m* strength; stamina

villa (*bee*-lʸah) *f* villa

villano (bee-*lʸah*-noa) *m* villain

vinagre (bee-*nah*-gray) *m* vinegar

vino (*bee*-noa) *m* wine

viña (*bee*-ñah) *f* vineyard

violación (bʸoa-lah-*thʸoan*) *f* violation

violar (bʸoa-*lahr*) *v* assault, rape

violencia (bʸoa-*layn*-thʸah) *f* violence

violento (bʸoa-*layn*-toa) *adj* violent; fierce, severe

violeta (bʸoa-*lay*-tah) *f* violet

violín (bʸoa-*leen*) *m* violin

virgen (*beer*-khayn) *f* virgin

virtud (beer-*toodh*) *f* virtue

visado (bee-*sah*-dhoa) *m* visa

visar (bee-*sahr*) *v* endorse

visibilidad (bee-see-bhee-lee-*dhahdh*) *f* visibility

visible (bee-*see*-bhlay) *adj* visible

visión (bee-sʸoan) *f* vision

visita (bee-*see*-tah) *f* visit, call

visitante (bee-see-*tahn*-tay) *m* visitor

visitar (bee-see-*tahr*) *v* visit, call on

vislumbrar (beez-loom-*brahr*) v glimpse

vislumbre (beez-*loom*-bray) m glimpse

visón (bee-*soan*) m mink

visor (bee-*soar*) m view-finder

vista (*beess*-tah) f sight; view; **punto de ~** outlook

vistoso (beess-*toa*-soa) adj striking

vital (bee-*tahl*) adj vital

vitamina (bee-tah-*mee*-nah) f vitamin

vitrina (bee-*tree*-nah) f show-case

viuda (bⁿoo-dhah) f widow

viudo (bⁿoo-dhoa) m widower

vivaz (bee-*bhahth*) adj active

vivero (bee-*bhay*-roa) m nursery

vivienda (bee-*bhⁿayn*-dah) f house

vivir (bee-*bheer*) v live; experience

vivo (bee-bhoa) adj alive, live; brisk, vivid, lively

vocabulario (boa-kah-bhoo-*lah*-rⁿoa) m vocabulary

vocación (boa-kah-*thⁿoan*) f vocation

vocal (boa-*kahl*) f vowel, adj vocal

vocalista (boa-kah-*leess*-tah) m vocalist

volante (boa-*lahn*-tay) m steering-wheel

*****volar** (boa-*lahr*) v *fly

volatería (boa-lah-tay-*ree*-ah) f fowl

volcán (boal-*kahn*) m volcano

voltaje (boal-*tah*-khay) m voltage

voltio (*boal*-tⁿoa) m volt

volumen (boa-*loo*-mayn) m volume

voluminoso (boa-loo-mee-*noa*-soa) adj bulky; big

voluntad (boa-loon-*tahdh*) f will; **buena ~** goodwill

voluntario (boa-loon-*tah*-rⁿoa) adj voluntary; m volunteer

*****volver** (boal-*bhayr*) v return, turn back; turn over, turn, turn round; **~ a casa** *go home; *****volverse** v turn round

vomitar (boa-mee-*tahr*) v vomit

vosotros (boa-*soa*-troass) pron you

votación (boa-tah-*thⁿoan*) f vote

votar (boa-*tahr*) v vote

voto (*boa*-toa) m vote; vow

voz (boath) f voice; cry; **en ~ alta** aloud

vuelo (*bway*-loa) m flight; **~ fletado** charter flight; **~ nocturno** night flight

vuelta (*bwayl*-tah) f return journey, way back; tour; turning, turn; round; **ida y ~** round trip Am

vuestro (*bwayss*-troa) adj your

vulgar (bool-*gahr*) adj vulgar

vulnerable (bool-nay-*rah*-bhlay) adj vulnerable

Y

y (ee) conj and

ya (ⁿah) adv already; **~ no** no longer; **~ que** as

*****yacer** (ⁿah-*thayr*) v *lie

yacimiento (ⁿah-thee-*mⁿayn*-toa) m deposit

yate (ⁿah-tay) m yacht

yegua (ⁿay-gwah) f mare

yema (ⁿay-mah) f yolk

yerno (ⁿayr-noa) m son-in-law

yeso (ⁿay-soa) m plaster

yo (ⁿoa) pron I

yodo (ⁿoa-dhoa) m iodine

yugo (ⁿoo-goa) m yoke

Z

zafiro (thah-*fee*-roa) *m* sapphire
zanahoria (thah-nah-*oa*-r^yah) *f* carrot
zanja (*thahng*-khah) *f* ditch
zapatería (thah-pah-tay-*ree*-ah) *f* shoe-shop
zapatero (thah-pah-*tay*-roa) *m* shoe-maker
zapatilla (thah-pah-*tee*-l^yah) *f* slipper
zapato (thah-*pah*-toa) *m* shoe; **zapatos de gimnasia** plimsolls *pl*; sneakers *plAm*; **zapatos de tenis**

tennis shoes
zatara (thah-*tah*-rah) *f* raft
zodíaco (thoa-*dhee*-ah-koa) *m* zodiac
zona (*thoa*-nah) *f* zone; area; ~ **industrial** industrial area
zoología (thoa-oa-loa-*khee*-ah) *f* zoology
zorro (*thoa*-rroa) *m* fox
zueco (*thway*-koa) *m* wooden shoe
zumo (*thoo*-moa) *m* juice; squash
zumoso (thoo-*moa*-soa) *adj* juicy
zurcir (thoor-*theer*) *v* darn
zurdo (*thoor*-dhoa) *adj* left-handed
zurra (*thoo*-rrah) *f* spanking

Menu Reader

Food

a caballo steak topped with two eggs
acedera sorrel
aceite oil
aceituna olive
achicoria endive (US chicory)
(al) adobo marinated
aguacate avocado (pear)
ahumado smoked
ajiaceite garlic mayonnaise
ajiaco bogotano chicken soup with potatoes
(al) ajillo cooked in garlic and oil
ajo garlic
al, a la in the style of, with
albahaca basil
albaricoque apricot
albóndiga spiced meat- or fishball
alcachofa artichoke
alcaparra caper
aliñado seasoned
alioli garlic mayonnaise
almeja clam, cockle
almejas a la marinera cooked in hot, pimento sauce
almendra almond
  ~ **garrapiñada** sugared almond
almíbar syrup
almuerzo lunch
alubia bean

anchoa anchovy
anguila eel
angula baby eel
anticucho beef heart grilled on a skewer with green peppers
apio celery
a punto medium (done)
arenque herring
  ~ **en escabeche** marinated, pickled herring
arepa flapjack made of maize (corn)
arroz rice
  ~ **blanco** boiled, steamed
  ~ **escarlata** with tomatoes and prawns
  ~ **a la española** with chicken liver, pork, tomatoes, fish stock
  ~ **con leche** rice pudding
  ~ **primavera** with spring vegetables
  ~ **a la valenciana** with vegetables, chicken, shellfish (and sometimes eel)
asado roast
  ~ **antiguo a la venezolana mechado** roast beef stuffed with capers
asturias a strong, fermented cheese with a sharp flavour

atún tunny (US tuna)
avellana hazelnut
azafrán saffron
azúcar sugar
bacalao cod
~ **a la vizcaína** with green peppers, potatoes, tomato sauce
barbo barbel (fish)
batata sweet potato, yam
becada woodcock
berberecho cockle
berenjena aubergine (US eggplant)
berraza parsnip
berro cress
berza cabbage
besugo sea bream
bien hecho well-done
biftec, bistec beef steak
bizcocho sponge cake, sponge finger (US ladyfinger)
~ **borracho** cake steeped in rum (or wine) and syrup
bizcotela glazed biscuit (US cookie)
blando soft
bocadillo 1) sandwich 2) sweet (Colombia)
bollito, bollo roll, bun
bonito a kind of tunny (US tuna)
boquerón 1) anchovy 2) whitebait
(en) brocheta (on a) skewer
budín blancmange, custard
buey ox
buñuelo 1) doughnut 2) fritter with ham, mussels and prawns (sometimes flavoured with brandy)
burgos a popular soft, creamy cheese named after the Spanish province of its origin
butifarra spiced sausage
caballa fish of the mackerel family
cabeza de ternera calf's head

cabra goat
cabrales blue-veined goat's-milk cheese
cabrito kid
cacahuete peanut
cachelos diced potatoes boiled with cabbage, paprika, garlic, bacon, *chorizo* sausage
calabacín vegetable marrow, courgette (US zucchini)
calabaza pumpkin
calamar squid
calamares a la romana squids fried in batter
caldereta de cabrito kid stew (often cooked in red wine)
caldillo de congrio conger-eel soup with tomatoes and potatoes
caldo consommé
~ **gallego** meat and vegetable broth
callos tripe (often served in pimento sauce)
~ **a la madrileña** in piquant sauce with *chorizo* sausage and tomatoes
camarón shrimp
canela cinnamon
cangrejo de mar crab
cangrejo de río crayfish
cantarela chanterelle mushroom
caracol snail
carbonada criolla baked pumpkin stuffed with diced beef
carne meat
~ **asada al horno** roast meat
~ **molida** minced beef
~ **a la parrilla** charcoal-grilled steak
~ **picada** minced beef
carnero mutton
carpa carp
casero home made

castaña chestnut

castañola sea perch

(a la) catalana with onions, parsley, tomatoes and herbs

caza game

(a la) cazadora with mushrooms, spring onions, herbs in wine

cazuela de cordero lamb stew with vegetables

cebolla onion

cebolleta chive

cebrero blue-veined cheese of creamy texture with a pale, yellow rind; sharp taste

cena dinner, supper

centolla spider-crab, served cold

cerdo pork

cereza cherry

ceviche fish marinated in lemon and lime juice

cigala Dublin Bay prawn

cincho a hard cheese made from sheep's milk

ciruela plum

~ **pasa** prune

cocido 1) cooked, boiled 2) stew of beef with ham, fowl, chick peas, potatoes and vegetables (the broth is eaten first)

cochifrito de cordero highly seasoned stew of lamb or kid

codorniz quail

col cabbage

~ **de Bruselas** brussels sprout

coliflor cauliflower

comida meal

compota stewed fruit

conejo rabbit

confitura jam

congrio conger eel

consomé al jerez chicken broth with sherry

copa nuria egg-yolk and egg-white, whipped and served with jam

corazón de alcachofa artichoke heart

corazonada heart stewed in sauce

cordero lamb

~ **recental** spring lamb

cortadillo small pancake with lemon

corzo deer

costilla chop

crema 1) cream or mousse

~ **batida** whipped cream

~ **española** dessert of milk, eggs, fruit jelly

~ **nieve** frothy egg-yolk, sugar, rum (or wine)

crema 2) soup

criadillas (de toro) glands (of bull)

(a la) criolla with green peppers, spices and tomatoes

croqueta croquette, fish or meat dumpling

crudo raw

cubierto cover charge

cuenta bill (US check)

curanto dish consisting of seafood, vegetables and suck(l)ing pig, all cooked in an earthen well, lined with charcoal

chabacano apricot

chalote shallot

champiñón mushroom

chancho adobado pork braised with sweet potatoes, orange and lemon juice

chanfaina goat's liver and kidney stew, served in a thick sauce

chanquete whitebait

chile chili pepper

chiles en nogada green peppers stuffed with whipped cream and nut sauce

chimichurri hot parsley sauce

chipirón small squid

chopa a kind of sea bream

chorizo pork sausage, highly seasoned with garlic and paprika

chuleta cutlet

chupe de mariscos scallops served with a creamy sauce and gratinéed with cheese

churro sugared tubular fritter

damasco variety of apricot

dátil date

desayuno breakfast

dorada gilt-head

dulce sweet
 ~ **de naranja** marmalade

durazno peach

embuchado stuffed with meat

embutido spicy sausage

empanada pie or tart with meat or fish filling
 ~ **de horno** dough filled with minced meat, similar to ravioli

empanadilla small patty stuffed with seasoned meat or fish

empanado breaded

emperador swordfish

encurtido pickle

enchilada a maizeflour (US cornmeal) pancake *(tortilla)* stuffed and usually served with vegetable garnish and sauce
 ~ **roja** sausage-filled maizeflour pancake dipped into a red sweet-pepper sauce
 ~ **verde** maizeflour pancake stuffed with meat or fowl and braised in a green-tomato sauce

endibia chicory (US endive)

eneldo dill

ensalada salad
 ~ **común** green
 ~ **de frutas** fruit salad
 ~ **(a la) primavera** spring
 ~ **valenciana** with green peppers, lettuce and oranges

ensaladilla rusa diced cold vegetables with mayonnaise

entremés appetizer, hors-d'oeuvre

erizo de mar sea urchin

(en) escabeche marinated, pickled
 ~ **de gallina** chicken marinated in vinegar

escarcho red gurnard (fish)

escarola endive (US chicory)

espalda shoulder

(a la) española with tomatoes

espárrago asparagus

especia spice

especialidad de la casa chef's speciality

espinaca spinach

esqueixada mixed fish salad

(al) estilo de in the style of

estofado stew(ed)

estragón tarragon

fabada (asturiana) stew of pork, beans, bacon and sausage

faisán pheasant

fiambres cold meat (US cold cuts)

fideo thin noodle

filete steak
 ~ **de lomo** fillet steak (US tenderloin)
 ~ **de res** beef steak
 ~ **de lenguado empanado** breaded fillet of sole

(a la) flamenca with onions, peas, green peppers, tomatoes and spiced sausage

flan caramel mould, custard

frambuesa raspberry

(a la) francesa sautéed in butter

fresa strawberry
 ~ **de bosque** wild

fresco fresh, chilled

fresón large strawberry

fricandó veal bird, thin slice of meat rolled in bacon and braised

frijol bean

frijoles refritos fried mashed beans

frío cold

frito 1) fried 2) fry
~ **de patata** deep-fried potato croquette

fritura fry
~ **mixta** meat, fish or vegetables deep-fried in batter

fruta fruit
~ **escarchada** crystallized (US candied) fruit

galleta salted or sweet biscuit (US cracker or cookie)
~ **de nata** cream biscuit (US sandwich cookie)

gallina hen
~ **de Guinea** guinea fowl

gallo cockerel

gamba shrimp
~ **grande** prawn

gambas con mayonesa shrimp cocktail

ganso goose

garbanzo chick pea

gazpacho seasoned broth made of raw onions, garlic, tomatoes, cucumber and green pepper; served chilled

(a la) gitanilla with garlic

gordo fatty, rich (of food)

granada pomegranate

grande large

(al) gratín gratinéed

gratinado gratinéed

grelo turnip greens

grosella currant
~ **espinosa** gooseberry
~ **negra** blackcurrant
~ **roja** redcurrant

guacamole a purée of avocado and spices used as a dip, in a salad, for a *tortilla* filling or as a garnish

guarnición garnish, trimming

guayaba guava (fruit)

guinda sour cherry

guindilla chili pepper

guisado stew(ed)

guisante green pea

haba broad bean

habichuela verde French bean (US green bean)

hamburguesa hamburger

hayaca central maizeflour (US cornmeal) pancake, usually with a minced-meat filling

helado ice-cream, ice

hervido 1) boiled 2) stew of beef and vegetables (Latin America)

hielo ice

hierba herb

hierbas finas finely chopped mixture of herbs

hígado liver

higo fig

hinojo fennel

hongo mushroom

(al) horno baked

hortaliza greens

hueso bone

huevo egg
~ **cocido** boiled
~ **duro** hard-boiled
~ **escalfado** poached
~ **a la española** stuffed with tomatoes and served with cheese sauce
~ **a la flamenca** baked with asparagus, peas, peppers, onions, tomatoes and sausage
~ **frito** fried
~ **al nido** egg-yolk placed into small, soft roll, fried, then covered with egg-white
~ **pasado por agua** soft-boiled
~ **revuelto** scrambled

~ **con tocino** bacon and egg

humita boiled maize (US corn) with tomatoes, green peppers, onions and cheese

(a la) inglesa 1) underdone (of meat) 2) boiled 3) served with boiled vegetables

jabalí wild boar

jalea jelly

jamón ham

  ~ **cocido** boiled (often referred to as *jamón de York*)

  ~ **en dulce** boiled and served cold

  ~ **gallego** smoked and cut thinly

  ~ **serrano** cured and cut thinly

(a la) jardinera with carrots, peas and other vegetables

jengibre ginger

(al) jerez braised in sherry

judía bean

  ~ **verde** French bean (US green bean)

jugo gravy, meat juice

  en su ~ in its own juice

juliana with shredded vegetables

jurel variety of mackerel

lacón shoulder of pork

  ~ **curado** salted pork

lamprea lamprey

langosta spiny lobster

langostino Norway lobster, Dublin Bay prawn

laurel bay leaf

lechón suck(l)ing pig

lechuga lettuce

legumbre vegetable

lengua tongue

lenguado sole, flounder

  ~ **frito** fried fillet of sole on bed of vegetables

lenteja lentil

liebre hare

~ **estofada** jugged hare

lima 1) lime 2) sweet lime (Latin America)

limón lemon

lista de platos menu

lista de vinos wine list

lobarro a variety of bass

lombarda red cabbage

lomo loin

longaniza long, highly seasoned sausage

lonja slice of meat

lubina bass

macarrones macaroni

(a la) madrileña with *chorizo* sausage, tomatoes and paprika

magras al estilo de Aragón cured ham in tomato sauce

maíz maize (US corn)

(a la) mallorquina usually refers to highly seasoned fish and shellfish

manchego hard cheese from La Mancha, made from sheep's milk, white or golden-yellow in colour

maní peanut

mantecado 1) small butter cake 2) custard ice-cream

mantequilla butter

manzana apple

  ~ **en dulce** in honey

(a la) marinera usually with mussels, onions, tomatoes, herbs and wine

marisco seafood

matambre rolled beef stuffed with vegetables

mayonesa mayonnaise

mazapán marzipan, almond paste

mejillón mussel

mejorana marjoram

melaza treacle, molasses

melocotón peach

membrillo quince
menestra boiled green vegetable soup
  ~ **de pollo** chicken and vegetable soup
menta mint
menú menu
  ~ **del día** set menu
  ~ **turístico** tourist menu
menudillos giblets
merengue meringue
merienda snack
merluza hake
mermelada jam
mezclado mixed
miel honey
(a la) milanesa with cheese, generally baked
minuta menu
mixto mixed
mole poblano chicken served with a sauce of chili peppers, spices and chocolate
molusco mollusc (snail, mussel, clam)
molleja sweetbread
mora mulberry
morcilla black pudding (US blood sausage)
morilla morel mushroom
moros y cristianos rice and black beans with diced ham, garlic, green peppers and herbs
mostaza mustard
mújol mullet
nabo turnip
naranja orange
nata cream
  ~ **batida** whipped cream
natillas custard
  ~ **al limón** lemon cream
níspola medlar (fruit)
nopalito young cactus leaf served with salad dressing

nuez nut
  ~ **moscada** nutmeg
olla stew
  ~ **gitana** vegetable stew
  ~ **podrida** stew made of vegetables, meat, fowl and ham
ostra oyster
oveja ewe
pabellón criollo beef in tomato sauce garnished with beans, rice and bananas
paella consists basically of saffron rice with assorted seafood and sometimes meat
  ~ **alicantina** with green peppers, onions, tomatoes, artichokes and fish
  ~ **catalana** with sausages, pork, squid, tomatoes, red sweet peppers and peas
  ~ **marinera** with fish, shellfish and meat
  ~ **(a la) valenciana** with chicken, shrimps, peas, tomatoes, mussels and garlic
palmito palm heart
palta avocado (pear)
pan bread
panecillo roll
papa potato
papas a la huancaína with cheese and green peppers
(a la) parrilla grilled
parrillada mixta mixed grill
pasado done, cooked
  bien ~ well-done
  poco ~ underdone (US rare)
pastas noodles, macaroni, spaghetti
pastel cake, pie
  ~ **de choclo** maize with minced beef, chicken, raisins and olives
pastelillo small tart
pata trotter (US foot)

patatas potatoes
  ~ **fritas** fried; usually chips (US french fries)
  ~ **(a la) leonesa** with onions
  ~ **nuevas** new
pato duck, duckling
pavo turkey
pechuga breast (of fowl)
pepinillo gherkin (US pickle)
pepino cucumber
(en) pepitoria stewed with onions, green peppers and tomatoes
pera pear
perca perch
percebe barnacle (shellfish)
perdiz partridge
  ~ **en escabeche** cooked in oil with vinegar, onions, parsley, carrots and green pepper; served cold
  ~ **estofada** stewed and served with a white-wine sauce
perejil parsley
perifollo chervil
perilla a firm, bland cheese
pescadilla whiting
pescado fish
pez espada swordfish
picadillo minced meat, hash
picado minced
picante sharp, spicy, highly seasoned
picatoste deep-fried slice of bread
pichoncillo young pigeon (US squab)
pierna leg
pimentón chili pepper
pimienta pepper
pimiento sweet pepper
  ~ **morrón** red (sweet) pepper
pincho moruno grilled meat (often kidneys) on a skewer, sometimes served with spicy sauces
pintada guinea fowl

piña pineapple
pisto diced and sautéed vegetables: mainly aubergines, green peppers and tomatoes; served cold
(a la) plancha grilled on a girdle
plátano banana
plato plate, dish, portion
  ~ **típico de la región** regional speciality
pollito spring chicken
pollo chicken
  ~ **pibil** simmered in fruit juice and spices
polvorón hazelnut biscuit (US cookie)
pomelo grapefruit
porción portion
porotos granados shelled beans served with pumpkin and maize (US corn)
postre dessert, sweet
potaje vegetable soup
puchero stew
puerro leek
pulpo octopus
punta de espárrago asparagus tip
punto de nieve dessert of whipped cream with beaten egg-whites
puré de patatas mashed potatoes
queso cheese
quisquilla shrimp
rábano radish
  ~ **picante** horse-radish
raja slice or portion
rallado grated
rape angler fish
ravioles ravioli
raya skate, ray
rebanada slice
rebozado breaded or fried in batter
recargo extra charge
rehogada sautéed

relleno stuffed
remolacha beetroot
repollo cabbage
requesón a fresh-curd cheese
riñón kidney
róbalo haddock
rodaballo turbot, flounder
(a la) romana dipped in batter and fried
romero rosemary
roncal cheese made from sheep's milk; close grained and hard in texture with a few small holes; piquant flavour
ropa vieja cooked, left-over meat and vegetables, covered with tomatoes and green peppers
rosbif roast beef
rosquilla doughnut
rubio red mullet
ruibarbo rhubarb
sal salt
salado salted, salty
salchicha small pork sausage for frying
salchichón salami
salmón salmon
salmonete red mullet
salsa sauce
  ~ **blanca** white
  ~ **española** brown sauce with herbs, spices and wine
  ~ **mayordoma** butter and parsley
  ~ **picante** hot pepper
  ~ **romana** bacon or ham, egg, cream (sometimes flavoured with nutmeg)
  ~ **tártara** tartar
  ~ **verde** parsley
salsifí salsify
salteado sauté(ed)
salvia sage
san simón a firm, bland cheese

resembling *perilla*; shiny yellow rind
sandía watermelon
sardina sardine, pilchard
sémola semolina
sencillo plain
sepia cuttlefish
servicio service
  ~ **(no) incluido** (not) included
sesos brains
seta mushroom
sobrasada salami
solomillo fillet steak (US tenderloin)
sopa soup
  ~ **(de) cola de buey** oxtail
  ~ **sevillana** a highly spiced fish soup
suave soft
suflé soufflé
suizo bun
surtido assorted
taco wheat or maizeflour (US cornmeal) pancake usually with a meat filling and garnished with a spicy sauce
tajada slice
tallarín noodle
tamal a pastry dough of coarsely ground maizeflour with meat or fruit filling, steamed in maizehusks (US corn husks)
tapa appetizer, snack
tarta cake, tart
  ~ **helada** ice-cream tart
ternera veal
tocino bacon
  ~ **de cielo** 1) caramel mould 2) custard-filled cake
tomate tomato
tomillo thyme
tordo thrush
toronja variety of grapefruit
tortilla 1) omelet 2) a type of

pancake made with maizeflour (US cornmeal)

~ **de chorizo** with pieces of a spicy sausage

~ **a la española** with onions, potatoes and seasoning

~ **a la francesa** plain

~ **gallega** potatoes with ham, red sweet peppers and peas

~ **a la jardinera** with mixed, diced vegetables

~ **al ron** rum

tortita waffle

tortuga turtle

tostada toast

tripas tripe

trucha trout

~ **frita a la asturiana** floured and fried in butter, garnished with lemon

trufa truffle

turrón nougat

ulloa a soft cheese from Galicia, rather like a mature camembert

uva grape

~ **pasa** raisin

vaca salada corned beef

vainilla vanilla

(a la) valenciana with rice, toma-

toes and garlic

variado varied, assorted

varios sundries

venado venison

venera scallop, coquille St. Jacques

verdura greens

vieira scallop

villalón a cheese from sheep's milk

vinagre vinegar

vinagreta a piquant vinegar dressing (vinaigrette) to accompany salads

(a la) ~ marinated in oil and vinegar or lemon juice with mixed herbs

(a la) vizcaína with green peppers, tomatoes, garlic and paprika

yema egg-yolk

yemas a dessert of whipped egg-yolks and sugar

zanahoria carrot

zarzamora blackberry

zarzuela savoury stew of assorted fish and shellfish

~ **de mariscos** seafood stew

~ **de pescado** selection of fish served with a highly seasoned sauce

~ **de verduras** vegetable stew

Drinks

abocado sherry made from a blend of sweet and dry wines

agua water

aguardiente spirits

Alicante this region to the south

of Valencia produces a large quantity of red table wine and some good rosé, particularly from Yecla

Amontillado medium-dry sherry,

light amber in colour, with a nutty flavour

Andalucía a drink of dry sherry and orange juice

Angélica a Basque herb liqueur similar to yellow Chartreuse

anís aniseed liqueur

Anís del Mono a Calatonian aniseed liqueur

anís seco aniseed brandy

anisado an aniseed-based soft drink which may be slightly alcoholic

batido milk shake

bebida drink

Bobadilla Gran Reserva a wine-distilled brandy

botella bottle

  media ~ half bottle

café coffee

  ~ **cortado** small cup of strong coffee with a dash of milk or cream

  ~ **descafeinado** coffeine-free

  ~ **exprés** espresso

  ~ **granizado** iced (white)

  ~ **con leche** white

  ~ **negro/solo** black

Calisay a quinine-flavoured liqueur

Carlos I a wine-distilled brandy

Cataluña Catalonia; this region southwest of Barcelona is known for its *xampañ*, bearing little resemblance to the famed French sparkling wine

Cazalla an aniseed liqueur

cerveza beer

  ~ **de barril** draught (US draft)

  ~ **dorada** light

  ~ **negra** dark

cola de mono a blend of coffee, milk, rum and *pisco*

coñac 1) French Cognac 2) term

applied to any Spanish wine-distilled brandy

Cordoníu a brand-name of Catalonian sparkling wine locally referred to as *xampañ* (champagne)

cosecha harvest; indicates the vintage of wine

crema de cacao cocoa liqueur, crème de cacao

Cuarenta y Tres an egg liqueur

Cuba libre rum and Coke

champán, champaña 1) French Champagne 2) term applied to any Spanish sparkling wine

chicha de manzana apple brandy

Chinchón an aniseed liqueur

chocolate chocolate drink

  ~ **con leche** hot chocolate with milk

Dulce dessert wine

Fino dry sherry wine, very pale and straw-coloured

Fundador a wine-distilled brandy

Galicia this Atlantic coastal region has good table wines

gaseosa fizzy (US carbonated) water

ginebra gin

gran vino term found on Chilean wine labels to indicate a wine of exceptional quality

granadina pomegranate syrup mixed with wine or brandy

horchata de almendra (or **de chufa**) drink made from ground almonds (or Jerusalem artichoke)

Jerez 1) sherry 2) the Spanish region near the Portuguese border, internationally renowned for its *Jerez*

jugo fruit juice

leche milk

limonada lemonade, lemon

squash

Málaga 1) dessert wine 2) the region in the south of Spain, is particularly noted for its dessert wine

Manzanilla dry sherry, very pale and straw-coloured

margarita *tequila* with lime juice

Montilla a dessert wine from near Cordoba, often drunk as an aperitif

Moscatel fruity dessert wine

naranjada orangeade

Oloroso sweet, dark sherry, drunk as dessert wine, resembles brown cream sherry

Oporto port (wine)

pisco grape brandy

ponche crema egg-nog liquor

Priorato the region south of Barcelona produces good quality red and white wine but also a dessert wine, usually called *Priorato* but renamed *Tarragona* when it is exported

refresco a soft drink

reservado term found on Chilean wine labels to indicate a wine of exceptional quality

Rioja the northern region near the French border is considered to produce Spain's best wines—especially red; some of the finest Rioja wines resemble good Bordeaux wines

ron rum

sangría a mixture of red wine, ice, orange, lemon, brandy and sugar

sangrita *tequila* with tomato, orange and lime juices

sidra cider

sol y sombra a blend of wine-distilled brandy and aniseed liqueur

sorbete (iced) fruit drink

té tea

tequila brandy made from agave (US aloe)

tinto 1) red wine 2) black coffee with sugar (Colombia)

Tío Pepe a brand-name sherry

Triple Seco an orange liqueur

Valdepeñas the region south of Madrid is an important wine-producing area

vermú vermouth

Veterano Osborne a wine-distilled brandy

vino wine
  ~ **blanco** white
  ~ **clarete** rosé
  ~ **común** table wine
  ~ **dulce** dessert
  ~ **espumoso** sparkling
  ~ **de mesa** table wine
  ~ **del país** local wine
  ~ **rosado** rosé
  ~ **seco** dry
  ~ **suave** sweet
  ~ **tinto** red

xampañ Catalonian sparkling wine

Yerba mate South American holly tea

zumo juice

Mini-Grammar

Articles

Nouns in Spanish are either masculine or feminine. Articles agree in gender and number with the noun.

1. Definite article (the):

	singular		plural
	singular		plural
masc.	**el tren**	the train	**los trenes**
fem.	**la casa**	the house	**las casas**

2. Indefinite article (a/an):

masc.	**un lápiz**	a pencil	**unos lápices**
fem.	**una carta**	a letter	**unas cartas**

Nouns

1. Most nouns which end in **o** are masculine. Those ending in **a** are generally feminine.

2. Normally, nouns which end in a vowel add **s** to form the plural; nouns ending in a consonant add **es**.

3. To show possession, use the preposition **de** (of).

el fin de la fiesta	the end of the party
el príncipio del* mes	the beginning of the month
las maletas de los viajeros	the travellers' suitcases
los ojos de las niñas	the girls' eyes
la habitación de Roberto	Robert's room

Adjectives

1. Adjectives agree with the noun in gender and number. If the masculine form ends in **o** the feminine ends in **a**. As a rule, the adjective comes after the noun.

el niño pequeño	the small boy
la niña pequeña	the small girl

If the masculine form ends in **e** or with a consonant, the feminine keeps in general the same form.

el muro/la casa grande	the big wall/house
el mar/la flor azul	the blue sea/flower

2. Most adjectives form their plurals in the same way as nouns.

un coche inglés	an English car
dos coches ingleses	two English cars

3. Possessive adjectives: They agree with the thing possessed, not with the possessor.

---

* (**del** is the contraction of **de + el**)

	sing.	plur.
my	**mi**	**mis**
your (fam.)	**tu**	**tus**
your (polite form)	**su**	**sus**
his/her/its	**su**	**sus**
our	**nuestro(a)**	**nuestros(as)**
your	**vuestro(a)**	**vuestros(as)**
their	**su**	**sus**

su hijo	*his* or *her* son
su habitación	*his* or *her* or *their* room
sus maletas	*his* or *her* or *their* suitcases

4. Comparative and superlative: These are formed by adding **más** (more) or **menos** (less) and **lo más** or **lo menos**, respectively, before the adjective.

alto	high	**más alto**	**lo más alto**

Adverbs

These are generally formed by adding **-mente** to the feminine form of the adjective (if it differs from the masculine); otherwise to the masculine.

cierto(a)	sure	**fácil**	easy
ciertamente	surely	**fácilmente**	easily

Possessive pronouns

	sing.	plur.
mine	**mío(a)**	**míos(as)**
yours (fam. sing.)	**tuyo(a)**	**tuyos(as)**
yours (polite form)	**suyo(a)**	**suyos(as)**
his/hers/its	**suyo(a)**	**suyos(as)**
ours	**nuestro(a)**	**nuestros(as)**
yours (fam. pl.)	**vuestro(a)**	**vuestros(as)**
theirs	**suyo(a)**	**suyos(as)**

Demonstrative pronouns

	masc.	fem.	neut.
this	**éste**	**ésta**	**esto**
these	**éstos**	**éstas**	**estos**
that	**ése/aquél**	**ésa/aquélla**	**eso/aquello**
those	**ésos/aquéllos**	**ésas/aquéllas**	**esos/aquellos**

The above masculine and feminine forms are also used as demonstrative adjectives, but accents are dropped. The two forms for "that" designate difference in place; **ése** means "that one", **aquél** "that one over there".

Esos libros no me gustan.	I don't like those books.
Eso no me gusta.	I don't like that.

Personal pronouns

	subject	direct object	indirect object
I	**yo**	**me**	**me**
you	**tú**	**te**	**te**
you	**usted**	**lo**	**le**
he	**él**	**lo**	**le**
she	**ella**	**la**	**le**
it	**él/ella**	**lo/la**	**le**
we	**nosotros(as)**	**nos**	**nos**
you	**vosotros(as)**	**os**	**os**
	ustedes	**los**	**les**
they	**ellos(as)**	**los**	**les**

Subject pronouns are generally omitted, except in the polite form (**usted, ustedes**) which corresponds to "you". **Tú** (sing.) and **vosotros** (plur.) are used when talking to relatives, close friends and children and between young people; **usted** and the plural **ustedes** (often abbreviated to **Vd./Vds.**) are used in all other cases.

Negatives

Negatives are formed by placing **no** before the verb.

Es nuevo.   It's new.   **No es nuevo.**   It's not new.

Questions

In Spanish, questions are often formed by changing the intonation of your voice. Very often, the personal pronoun is left out, both in affirmative sentences and in questions.

Hablo español.   I speak Spanish.
¿Habla español?   Do you speak Spanish?

Note the double question mark used in Spanish.
The same is true of exclamation marks.

¡Qué tarde se hace!   How late it's getting!

Verbs

Below are some examples of Spanish verbs in the three regular conjugations, grouped by families according to their infinitive endings, -ar, -er and -ir. Verbs which do not follow the conjugations below are considered irregular (see irregular verb list). Note that there are some verbs which follow the regular conjugation of the category they belong to, but present some minor changes in spelling. Examples: *tocar, toque; cargar, cargue.* The personal pronoun is not generally expressed, since the verb endings clearly indicate the person.

		1st conj.	2nd conj.	3rd conj.
Infinitive		am **ar** *(to love)*	tem **er** *(to fear)*	viv **ir** *(to live)*
Present	(yo)	am **o**	tem **o**	viv **o**
	(tú)	am **as**	tem **es**	viv **es**
	(él)	am **a**	tem **e**	viv **e**
	(nosotros)	am **amos**	tem **emos**	viv **imos**
	(vosotros)	am **áis**	tem **éis**	viv **ís**
	(ellos)	am **an**	tem **en**	viv **en**
Imperfect	(yo)	am **aba**	tem **ía**	viv **ía**
	(tú)	am **abas**	tem **ías**	viv **ías**
	(él)	am **aba**	tem **ía**	viv **ía**
	(nosotros)	am **ábamos**	tem **íamos**	viv **íamos**
	(vosotros)	am **abais**	tem **íais**	viv **íais**
	(ellos)	am **aban**	tem **ían**	viv **ían**
Past. def.	(yo)	am **é**	tem **í**	viv **í**
	(tú)	am **aste**	tem **iste**	viv **iste**
	(él)	am **ó**	tem **ió**	viv **ió**
	(nosotros)	am **amos**	tem **imos**	viv **imos**
	(vosotros)	am **asteis**	tem **isteis**	viv **isteis**
	(ellos)	am **aron**	tem **ieron**	viv **ieron**
Future	(yo)	am **aré**	tem **eré**	viv **iré**
	(tú)	am **arás**	tem **erás**	viv **irás**
	(él)	am **ará**	tem **erá**	viv **irá**
	(nosotros)	am **aremos**	tem **eremos**	viv **iremos**
	(vosotros)	am **aréis**	tem **eréis**	viv **iréis**
	(ellos)	am **arán**	tem **erán**	viv **irán**
Conditional	(yo)	am **aría**	tem **ería**	viv **iría**
	(tú)	am **arías**	tem **erías**	viv **irías**
	(él)	am **aría**	tem **ería**	viv **iría**
	(nosotros)	am **aríamos**	tem **eríamos**	viv **iríamos**
	(vosotros)	am **aríais**	tem **eríais**	viv **iríais**
	(ellos)	am **arían**	tem **erían**	viv **irían**
Subj. Pres.	(yo)	am **e**	tem **a**	viv **a**
	(tú)	am **es**	tem **as**	viv **as**
	(él)	am **e**	tem **a**	viv **a**
	(nosotros)	am **emos**	tem **amos**	viv **amos**
	(vosotros)	am **éis**	tem **áis**	viv **áis**
	(ellos)	am **en**	tem **an**	viv **an**

| Pres. Part./Gerund | am **ando** | tem **iendo** | viv **iendo** |
| Past. Part. | am **ado** | tem **ido** | viv **ido** |

Auxiliary verbs

The verb **to have** is translated either by *haber* or by *tener*. *Haber* is the auxiliary (e.g. he has gone) and *tener* (see list of irregular verbs) is a transitive verb, which conveys the idea of possession (e.g. she has a house).

The verb **to be** is translated either by *ser* or *estar*. *Ser* is used as an auxiliary verb to form the passive (e.g. they are understood) and to express an intrinsic quality of a fundamental characteristic (e.g. man is mortal). *Estar* (see list of irregular verbs) expresses a state or an attitude, whether lasting or not, of a thing or a person (e.g. she is hungry).

	haber *(to have)*		**ser** *(to be)*	
	Present	*Imperfect*	*Present*	*Imperfect*
(yo)	he	había	soy	era
(tú)	has	habías	eres	eras
(él)	ha	había	es	era
(nosotros)	hemos	habíamos	somos	éramos
(vosotros)	habéis	habíais	sois	erais
(ellos)	han	habían	son	eran
	Future	*Conditional*	*Future*	*Conditional*
(yo)	habré	habría	seré	sería
(tú)	habrás	habrías	serás	serías
(él)	habrá	habría	será	sería
(nosotros)	habremos	habríamos	seremos	seríamos
(vosotros)	habréis	habríais	seréis	seríais
(ellos)	habrán	habrían	serán	serían
	Present subjunctive	*Present perfect*	*Present subjunctive*	*Present perfect*
(yo)	haya	he habido	sea	he sido
(tú)	hayas	has habido	seas	has sido
(él)	haya	ha habido	sea	ha sido
(nosotros)	hayamos	hemos habido	seamos	hemos sido
(vosotros)	hayáis	habéis habido	seáis	habéis sido
(ellos)	hayan	han habido	sean	han sido
	Present participle	*Past participle*	*Present participle*	*Past participle*
	habiendo	habido	siendo	sido

Irregular verbs

Below is a list of the verbs and tenses commonly used in spoken Spanish. In the listing, a) stands for the present tense, b) for the imperfect, c) for the past def., d) for the future, e) for the present participle and f) for the past participle. The only forms given below are the irregular ones commonly used. There can be other irregular forms, but they are considered rare. In tenses other than present, all persons can be regularly formed from the first person. Unless otherwise indicated, verbs with prefixes (*ad-*, *ante-*, *com-*, *con-*, *de-*, *des-*, *dis-*, *en-*, *ex-*, *im-*, *pos-*, *pre-*, *pro-*, *re-*, *sobre-*, *sub-*, *tras-*, etc.) are conjugated like the stem verb.

abstenerse *refrain*	→tener
acertar *guess*	→cerrar
acontecer *happen*	→agradecer
acordar *agree ; decide*	→contar
acostarse *lie down*	→contar
acrecentar *increase ; advance*	→cerrar
adormecer *put to sleep*	→agradecer
adquirir *acquire*	a) adquiero, adquieres, adquiere, adquirimos, adquirís, adquieren; b) adquiría; c) adquirí; d) adquiriré; e) adquiriendo; f) adquirido
advertir *notice*	→sentir
agradecer *thank*	a) agradezco, agradeces, agradece, agradecemos, agradecéis, agradecen; b) agradecía; c) agradecí; d) agradeceré; e) agradeciendo; f) agradecido
alentar *encourage*	→cerrar
almorzar *have lunch*	→contar
amanecer *dawn*	→agradecer
andar *walk*	a) ando, andas, anda, andamos, andáis, andan; b) andaba; c) anduve; d) andaré; e) andando; f) andado
anochecer *begin to get dark*	→agradecer
apetecer *want*	→agradecer
apostar *bet*	→contar
apretar *tighten, squeeze*	→cerrar

arrendar
let, lease, rent
→cerrar

arrepentirse
repent, regret
→sentir

ascender
climb, reach
→perder

atenerse
obey; rely on
→tener

atravesar
cross, pierce
→cerrar

atribuir
attribute
→instruir

aventar
fan, air
→cerrar

avergonzar
put to shame, embarrass
→contar

bendecir
bless
→decir

caber
contain; fit
a) quepo, cabes, cabe, cabemos, cabéis, caben;
b) cabía; c) cupe; d) cabré; e) cabiendo; f) cabido

caer
fall
a) caigo, caes, cae, caemos, caéis, caen; b) caía;
c) caí; d) caeré; e) cayendo; f) caído

calentar
heat
→cerrar

carecer
lack
→agradecer

cegar
blind
→cerrar

cerrar
close
a) cierro, cierras, cierra, cerramos, cerráis, cierran;
b) cerraba; c) cerré; d) cerraré; e) cerrando; f) cerrado

cocer
boil
a) cuezo, cueces, cuece, cocemos, cocéis, cuecen;
b) cocía; c) cocí; d) coceré; e) cociendo; f) cocido

colar
strain; filter
→contar

colgar
hang
→contar

comenzar
begin
→cerrar

competir
compete
→pedir

concebir
conceive
→pedir

concernir →sentir
concern

concluir →instruir
conclude, finish

concordar →contar
agree, reconcile

conducir →traducir
drive

conferir →sentir
confer

confesar →cerrar
confess

conocer a) conozco, conoces, conoce, conocemos, conocéis,
know conocen; b) conocía; c) conocí; d) conoceré;
e) conociendo; f) conocido

consolar →contar
console, comfort

constituir →instruir
constitute, be

construir →instruir
build, erect

contar a) cuento, cuentas, cuenta, contamos, contáis, cuentan;
count, bear in mind b) contaba; c) conté; d) contaré; e) contando;
f) contado

contribuir →instruir
contribute

convertir →sentir
convert

corregir →pedir
correct

costar →contar
cost

crecer →agradecer
grow, rise

dar a) doy, das, da, damos, dais, dan; b) daba; c) di;
give d) daré; e) dando; f) dado

decir a) digo, dices, dice, decimos, decís, dicen; b) decía;
say c) dije; d) diré e) diciendo; f) dicho

deducir →traducir
deduce

defender →perder
defend

derretir →pedir
melt

descender
descend, let down →perder

descollar
be outstanding →contar

desconcertar
damage; upset →cerrar

despertar
awaken, revive →cerrar

desterrar
banish →cerrar

destituir
deprive, dismiss →instruir

destruir
destroy →instruir

desvanecer
make disappear,
take out →agradecer

diferir
defer →sentir

digerir
digest →sentir

diluir
dilute →instruir

discernir
discern →sentir

disminuir
diminish →instruir

disolver
dissolve →morder

distribuir
distribute →instruir

divertir
entertain, distract →sentir

doler
hurt →morder

dormir
sleep a) duermo, duermes, duerme, dormimos, dormís
duermen; b) dormía; c) dormí; d) dormiré;
e) durmiendo; f) dormido

elegir
elect, choose →pedir

embestir
assault →pedir

empezar
begin, start →cerrar

enaltecer →agradecer
exalt, praise

enardecer →agradecer
excite ; inflame

encender →perder
light, ignite

encomendar →cerrar
entrust

encontrar →contar
find

engrandecer →agradecer
enlarge, exaggerate

enloquecer →agradecer
madden

enmendar →cerrar
emend, correct

enmudecer →agradecer
silence

enorgullecer →agradecer
fill with pride

enriquecer →agradecer
enrich

ensangrentar →cerrar
stain with blood

ensoberbecer →agradecer
make proud

ensordecer →agradecer
deafen

enternecer →agradecer
soften ; affect

enterrar →cerrar
bury

entristecer →agradecer
sadden

envejecer →agradecer
age

errar →cerrar
miss ; wander

escarmentar →cerrar
chastise, punish

escarnecer →agradecer
scoff

establecer →agradecer
establish

estar *be*	a) estoy, estás, está, estamos, estáis, están; b) estaba; c) estuve; d) estaré; e) estando; f) estado
estremecer *shake*	→agradecer
excluir *exclude*	→instruir
fallecer *die*	→agradecer
favorecer *favour*	→agradecer
florecer *blossom*	→agradecer
fluir *flow*	→instruir
fortalecer *strengthen*	→agradecer
forzar *compel, force*	→contar
fregar *wash up ; scrub*	→cerrar
freír *fry*	→reír
gemir *groan*	→pedir
gobernar *govern*	→cerrar
gruñir *grunt*	a) gruño, gruñes, gruñe, gruñimos, gruñís, gruñen; b) gruñía ;c) gruñí; d) gruñiré; e) gruñiendo; f) gruñido
haber *have*	a) he, has, ha, hemos, habéis, han; b) había; c) hube; d) habré; e) habiendo; f) habido
hacer *make*	a) hago, haces, hace, hacemos, hacéis, hacen; b) hacía; c) hice; d) haré; e) haciendo; f) hecho
heder *stink*	→perder
helar *freeze*	→cerrar
hender *crack*	→perder
herir *injure*	→sentir
hervir *boil*	→sentir
huir *escape*	→instruir

humedecer *humidify*	→agradecer
incluir *include*	→instruir
inducir *induce*	→traducir
ingerir *swallow; consume*	→sentir
instituir *institute*	→instruir
instruir *instruct*	a) instruyo, instruyes, instruye, instruimos, instruís, instruyen; b) instruía; c) instruí; d) instruiré; e) instruyendo; f) instruido
introducir *introduce*	→traducir
invertir *invest*	→sentir
ir *go*	a) voy, vas, va, vamos, vais, van; b) iba; c) fui; d) iré; e) yendo; f) ido
jugar *play*	a) juego, juegas, juega, jugamos, jugáis, juegan; b) jugaba; c) jugué; d) jugaré; e) jugando; f) jugado
lucir *shine*	a) luzco, luces, luce, lucimos, lucís, lucen; b) lucía; c) lucí; d) luciré; e) luciendo; f) lucido
llover *rain*	a) llueve; b) llovía; c) llovió; d) lloverá; e) lloviendo; f) llovido
manifestar *manifest*	→cerrar
mantener *maintain*	→tener
medir *measure*	→pedir
mentir *tell a lie*	→sentir
merecer *deserve*	→agradecer
merendar *have tea, snack*	→cerrar
moler *grind*	→morder
morder *bite*	a) muerdo, muerdes, muerde, mordemos, mordéis, muerden; b) mordía; c) mordí; d) morderé; e) mordiendo; f) mordido
morir *die*	→dormir

mostrar *show*	→contar
mover *move*	→morder
nacer *be born*	a) nazco, naces, nace, nacemos, nacéis, nacen; b) nacía; c) nací; d) naceré; e) naciendo; f) nacido
negar *deny*	→cerrar
nevar *snow*	a) nieva; b) nevaba; c) nevó; d) nevará; e) nevando; f) nevado
obedecer *obey*	→agradecer
obscurecer *darken*	→agradecer
obstruir *obstruct*	→instruir
obtener *obtain*	→tener
ofrecer, *offer*	→agradecer
oír *hear, listen*	a) oigo, oyes, oye, oímos, oís, oyen; b) oía; c) oí; d) oiré; e) oyendo; f) oído
oler *smell*	→morder
pacer *graze*	→nacer
padecer *suffer*	→agradecer
parecer *seem*	→agradecer
pedir *ask for, request*	a) pido, pides, pide, pedimos, pedís, piden; b) pedía; c) pedí; d) pediré; e) pidiendo; f) pedido
pensar *think*	→cerrar
perder *lose*	a) pierdo, pierdes, pierde, perdemos, perdéis, pierden; b) perdía; c) perdí; d) perderé; e) perdiendo; f) perdido
perecer *perish*	→agradecer
permanecer *stay*	→agradecer
pertenecer *belong to*	→agradecer
pervertir *pervert*	→sentir

placer *please*	a) plazco, places, place, placemos, placéis, placen; b) placía; c) plací; d) placeré; e) placiendo; f) placido
plegar *fold*	→cerrar
poblar *populate*	→contar
poder *can, be able*	a) puedo, puedes, puede, podemos, podéis, pueden; b) podía; c) pude; d) podré; e) pudiendo; f) podido
poner *put*	a) pongo, pones, pone, ponemos, ponéis, ponen; b) ponía; c) puse; d) pondré; e) poniendo; f) puesto
preferir *prefer*	→sentir
probar *try*	→contar
producir *produce*	→traducir
proferir *utter*	→sentir
quebrar *break*	→cerrar
querer *want, wish*	a) quiero, quieres, quiere, queremos, queréis, quieren; b) quería; c) quise; d) querré; e) queriendo; f) querido
recomendar *recommend*	→cerrar
recordar *remember*	→contar
reducir *reduce*	→traducir
referir *refer, relate*	→sentir
regar *water*	→cerrar
regir *govern*	→pedir
reir *laugh*	a) río, ríes, ríe, reímos, reís, ríen; b) reía; c) reí; d) reiré; e) riendo; f) reído
remendar *mend*	→cerrar
rendir *produce ; overcome*	→pedir
renovar *renew*	→contar
reñir *scold ; quarrel*	→teñir

repetir *repeat*	→pedir
requerir *request*	→sentir
resolver *resolve*	→morder
resplandecer *shine*	→agradecer
restituir *restore, return*	→instruir
retribuir *pay ; reward*	→instruir
reventar *burst*	→cerrar
robustecer *strengthen*	→agradecer
rodar *drive ; roll*	→contar
rogar *beg, plead*	→contar
saber *know*	a) sé, sabes, sabe, sabemos, sabéis, saben;)b sabía; c) supe; d) sabré; e) sabiendo; f) sabido
salir *go out*	a) salgo, sales, sale, salimos, salís, salen; b) salía; c) salí; d) saldré; e) saliendo; f) salido
satisfacer *satisfy*	→hacer
seducir *seduce*	→traducir
seguir *follow*	→pedir
sembrar *sow*	→cerrar
sentar *sit, seat*	→cerrar
sentir *feel*	a) siento, sientes, siente, sentimos, sentís, sienten; b) sentía; c) sentí; d) sentiré; e) sintiendo; f) sentido
ser. *be*	a) soy, eres, es, somos, sois, son; b) era c) fui; d) seré; e) siendo; f) sido
servir *serve*	→pedir
soldar *solder ; join*	→contar
soler *be used to*	a) suelo, sueles, suele, solemos, soléis, suelen; b) solía; c) solí; e) soliendo; f) solido

soltar   →contar
release; loosen

sonar   →contar
ring, sound

soñar   →contar
dream

sugerir   →sentir
suggest

sustituir   →instruir
substitute

temblar   →cerrar
tremble

tender   →perder
stretch, extend

tener   a) tengo, tienes, tiene, tenemos, tenéis, tienen; b) tenía;
have (got)   c) tuve; d) tendré; e) teniendo; f) tenido

tentar   →cerrar
touch; try

teñir   a) tiño, tiñes, tiñe, teñimos, teñís, tiñen; b) teñía;
dye   c) teñí; d) teñiré; e) tiñiendo; f) teñido

torcer   →cocer
twist

tostar   →contar
roast

traducir   a) traduzco, traduces, traduce, traducimos, traducís,
translate   traducen; b) traducía; c) traduje; d) traduciré;
    e) traduciendo; f) traducido

traer   a) traigo, traes, trae, traemos, traéis, traen; b) traía;
bring   c) traje; d) traeré; e) trayendo; f) traído

transferir   →sentir
transfer

trocar   →contar
(ex)change

tronar   a) trueno, truenas, truena, tronamos, tronáis, truenan;
thunder   b) tronaba; c) troné; d) tronaré; e) tronando; f) tronado

tropezar   →cerrar
stumble

valer   a) valgo, vales, vale, valemos, valéis, valen; b) valía;
protect; be worth   c) valí; d) valdré; e) valiendo; f) valido

venir   a) vengo, vienes, viene, venimos, venís, vienen; b) venía;
come   c) vine; d) vendré; e) viniendo; f) venido

ver   a) veo, ves, ve, vemos, veis, ven; b) veía; c) vi; d) veré;
see   e) viendo; f) visto

verter   →perder
pour ; spill

vestir   →pedir
dress

volar   →contar
fly

volcar   →contar
tip over

volver   →morder
(re)turn

yacer   →nacer
lie, rest

zambullir   a) zambullo, zambulles, zambulle, zambullimos,
plunge   zambullís, zambullen; b) zambullía; c) zambullí;
        d) zambulliré; e) zambullendo; f) zambullido

Spanish Abbreviations

a.C.	*antes de Cristo*	B.C.
A.C.	*año de Cristo*	A.D.
admón.	*administración*	administration
A.L.A.L.C.	*Asociación Latino-Americana de Libre Comercio*	Latin American Free Trade Association
apdo.	*apartado de correos*	P.O. Box
Av./Avda.	*Avenida*	avenue
Barna.	*Barcelona*	Barcelona
C/	*Calle*	street, road
c/c.	*cuenta corriente*	current account
Cía.	*Compañía*	company
ct(s).	*céntimo(s)*	1/100 of a peseta
cta.	*cuenta*	account; bill
cte.	*corriente*	inst., of this month
CV.	*caballos de vapor*	horsepower
D.	*Don*	courtesy title for gentlemen, only used together with the Christian name
D.ª	*Doña*	courtesy title for ladies, only used together with the Christian name
dcha.	*derecha*	right (direction)
D.N.I.	*Documento Nacional de Identidad*	identity card
d.v.	*días de visita*	open days
EE.UU.	*Estados Unidos*	USA
Exc.ª	*Excelencia*	Your Excellency
f.c.	*ferrocarril*	railway
G.C.	*Guardia Civil*	Spanish police force
gral.	*general*	general
h.	*hora*	hour
hab.	*habitantes*	inhabitants, population
hnos.	*hermanos*	brothers (in firms)
íd.	*ídem*	ditto
igla.	*iglesia*	church
izq./izqda.	*izquierda*	left (direction)
lic.	*licenciado*	licentiate; lawyer
M.I.T.	*Ministerio de Información y Turismo*	Spanish Ministry of Information and Tourism
Mons.	*Monseñor*	Roman Catholic title (approx. Your Grace)

N.ª S.ª	*Nuestra Señora*	Our Lady, Virgin Mary
n.º/núm.	*número*	number
O.E.A.	*Organización de Estados Americanos*	Organization of American States
P.	*Padre*	Father (ecclesiastical title)
pág.	*página*	page
P.D.	*posdata*	P.S.
p.ej.	*por ejemplo*	e.g.
P.P.	*porte pagado*	postage paid
pta(s).	*peseta(s)*	peseta(s)
P.V.P.	*precio de venta al público*	retail price
R.A.C.E.	*Real Automóvil Club de España*	Royal Automobile Association of Spain
R.A.E.	*Real Academia Española*	Royal Academy of the Spanish Language
R.C.	*Real Club…*	Royal… Association
RENFE	*Red Nacional de los Ferrocarriles Españoles*	Spanish National Railways
R.M.	*Reverenda Madre*	Mother Superior, abbess
R.P.	*Reverendo Padre*	Reverend Father (title for Catholic priests and abbots)
Rte.	*Remite, Remitente*	sender (of a letter)
RTVE	*Radio Televisión Española*	Spanish Radio and Television Corporation
S./Sto./ Sta.	*San/Santo/Santa*	saint
S.A.	*Sociedad Anónima*	Ltd., Inc.
S.A.R.	*Su Alteza Real*	His/Her Royal Highness
s.a.s.s.	*su atento y seguro servidor*	approx. Yours faithfully
S.E.	*Su Excelencia*	His Excellency
sgte.	*siguiente*	following
S.M.	*Su Majestad*	His/Her Majesty
Sr.	*Señor*	Mr.
Sra.	*Señora*	Mrs.
S.R.C.	*se ruega contestación*	please reply
Sres./Srs.	*Señores*	Sirs, Gentlemen
Srta.	*Señorita*	Miss
S.S.	*Su Santidad*	His Holiness
Ud./Vd.	*Usted*	you (singular)
Uds./Vds.	*Ustedes*	you (plural)
Vda.	*viuda*	widow
v.g./v.gr.	*verbigracia*	e.g.

Numerals

Cardinal numbers		Ordinal numbers	
0	cero	1.°	primero
1	uno	2.°	segundo
2	dos	3.°	tercero
3	tres	4.°	cuarto
4	cuatro	5.°	quinto
5	cinco	6.°	sexto
6	seis	7.°	séptimo
7	siete	8.°	octavo
8	ocho	9.°	noveno (nono)
9	nueve	10.°	décimo
10	diez	11.°	undécimo
11	once	12.°	duodécimo
12	doce	13.°	decimotercero
13	trece	14.°	decimocuarto
14	catorce	15.°	decimoquinto
15	quince	16.°	decimosexto
16	dieciséis	17.°	decimoséptimo
17	diecisiete	18.°	decimoctavo
18	dieciocho	19.°	decimonoveno
19	diecinueve	20.°	vigésimo
20	veinte	21.°	vigésimo primero
21	veintiuno	22.°	vigésimo segundo
30	treinta	30.°	trigésimo
31	treinta y uno	40.°	cuadragésimo
40	cuarenta	50.°	quincuagésimo
50	cincuenta	60.°	sexagésimo
60	sesenta	70.°	septuagésimo
70	setenta	80.°	octogésimo
80	ochenta	90.°	nonagésimo
90	noventa	100.°	centésimo
100	ciento (cien)	230.°	ducentésimo trigésimo
101	ciento uno	300.°	tricentésimo
230	doscientos treinta	400.°	cuadringentésimo
500	quinientos	500.°	quingentésimo
700	setecientos	600.°	sexcentésimo
900	novecientos	700.°	septingentésimo
1.000	mil	800.°	octingentésimo
100.000	cien mil	900.°	noningentésimo
1.000.000	un millón	1.000.°	milésimo

Time

Although official time in Spain is based on the 24-hour clock, the 12-hour system is used in conversation.

In some Latin American countries you can specify *a.m.* or *p.m.* as in English, but it is far more common to add *de la mañana, de la tarde* or *de la noche* as in Spain.

Thus:

las ocho de la mañana	8 a.m.
la una de la tarde	1 p.m.
las ocho de la noche	8 p.m.

Days of the Week

domingo	Sunday	*jueves*	Thursday
lunes	Monday	*viernes*	Friday
martes	Tuesday	*sábado*	Saturday
miércoles	Wednesday		

Some Basic Phrases	**Algunas expresiones útiles**
Please.	Por favor.
Thank you very much.	Muchas gracias.
Don't mention it.	No hay de qué.
Good morning.	Buenos días.
Good afternoon.	Buenas tardes.
Good evening.	Buenas noches.
Good night.	Buenas noches (despedida).
Good-bye.	Adiós.
See you later.	Hasta luego.
Where is/Where are…?	¿Dónde está/Dónde están…?
What do you call this?	¿Cómo se llama esto?
What does that mean?	¿Qué quiere decir eso?
Do you speak English?	¿Habla usted inglés?
Do you speak German?	¿Habla usted alemán?
Do you speak French?	¿Habla usted francés?
Do you speak Spanish?	¿Habla usted español?
Do you speak Italian?	¿Habla usted italiano?
Could you speak more slowly, please?	¿Puede usted hablar más despacio, por favor?
I don't understand.	No comprendo.
Can I have…?	¿Puede darme…?
Can you show me…?	¿Puede usted enseñarme…?
Can you tell me…?	¿Puede usted decirme…?
Can you help me, please?	¿Puede usted ayudarme, por favor?
I'd like…	Quisiera…
We'd like…	Quisiéramos…
Please give me…	Por favor, déme…
Please bring me…	Por favor, tráigame…
I'm hungry.	Tengo hambre.
I'm thirsty.	Tengo sed.
I'm lost.	Me he perdido.
Hurry up!	¡Dése prisa!

There is/There are...   Hay...
There isn't/There aren't...   No hay...

Arrival

Llegada

Your passport, please.   Su pasaporte, por favor.

Have you anything to declare?   ¿Tiene usted algo que declarar?

No, nothing at all.   No, nada en absoluto.

Can you help me with my luggage,   ¿Puede usted ayudarme con mi
please?   equipaje, por favor?

Where's the bus to the centre of   ¿Dónde está el autobús que va al
town, please?   centro, por favor?

This way, please.   Por aquí, por favor.

Where can I get a taxi?   ¿Dónde puedo coger un taxi?

What's the fare to...?   ¿Cuánto es la tarifa a...?

Take me to this address, please.   Lléveme a esta dirección, por
                                      favor.

I'm in a hurry.   Tengo mucha prisa.

Hotel

Hotel

My name is...   Me llamo...

Have you a reservation?   ¿Ha hecho usted una reserva?

I'd like a room with a bath.   Quisiera una habitación con
                                      baño.

What's the price per night?   ¿Cuánto cuesta por noche?

May I see the room?   ¿Puedo ver la habitación?

What's my room number, please?   ¿Cuál es el número de mi habita-
                                      ción, por favor?

There's no hot water.   No hay agua caliente.

May I see the manager, please?   ¿Puedo ver al director, por favor?

Did anyone telephone me?   ¿Me ha llamado alguien?

Is there any mail for me?   ¿Hay correo para mí?

May I have my bill (check),   ¿Puede darme mi cuenta,
please?   por favor?

Eating out	**Restaurante**
Do you have a fixed-price menu?	¿Tiene usted un menú de precio fijo?
May I see the menu?	¿Puedo ver la carta?
May we have an ashtray, please?	¿Nos puede traer un cenicero, por favor?
Where's the toilet, please?	¿Dónde están los servicios, por favor?
I'd like an hors d'œuvre (starter).	Quisiera un entremés.
Have you any soup?	¿Tiene usted sopa?
I'd like some fish.	Quisiera pescado.
What kind of fish do you have?	¿Qué clases de pescado tiene usted?
I'd like a steak.	Quisiera un bistec.
What vegetables have you got?	¿Qué verduras tiene usted?
Nothing more, thanks.	Nada más, gracias.
What would you like to drink?	¿Qué le gustaría beber?
I'll have a beer, please.	Tomaré una cerveza, por favor.
I'd like a bottle of wine.	Quisiera una botella de vino.
May I have the bill (check), please?	¿Podría darme la cuenta, por favor?
Is service included?	¿Está incluido el servicio?
Thank you, that was a very good meal.	Gracias. Ha sido una comida muy buena.

Travelling	**Viajes**
Where's the railway station, please?	¿Dónde está la estación de ferrocarril, por favor?
Where's the ticket office, please?	¿Dónde está la taquilla, por favor?
I'd like a ticket to...	Quisiera un billete para...
First or second class?	¿Primera o segunda clase?
First class, please.	Primera clase, por favor.
Single or return (one way or roundtrip)?	¿Ida, o ida y vuelta?

Do I have to change trains?	¿Tengo que transbordar?
What platform does the train for… leave from?	¿De qué andén sale el tren para…?
Where's the nearest underground (subway) station?	¿Dónde está la próxima estación de Metro?
Where's the bus station, please?	¿Dónde está la estación de autobuses, por favor?
When's the first bus to…?	¿Cuándo sale el primer autobús para…?
Please let me off at the next stop.	Por favor, deténgase en la próxima parada.

Relaxing

Diversiones

What's on at the cinema (movies)?	¿Qué dan en el cine?
What time does the film begin?	¿A qué hora empieza la película?
Are there any tickets for tonight?	¿Quedan entradas para esta noche?
Where can we go dancing?	¿Dónde se puede ir a bailar?

Meeting people

Presentaciones – Citas

How do you do.	Buenos días Señora/ Señorita/Señor.
How are you?	¿Cómo está usted?
Very well, thank you. And you?	Muy bien, gracias. ¿Y usted?
May I introduce…?	¿Me permite presentarle a…?
My name is…	Me llamo…
I'm very pleased to meet you.	Tanto gusto (en conocerle).
How long have you been here?	¿Cuánto tiempo lleva usted aquí?
It was nice meeting you.	Ha sido un placer conocerle.
Do you mind if I smoke?	¿Le molesta si fumo?
Do you have a light, please?	¿Tiene usted fuego, por favor?
May I get you a drink?	¿Me permite invitarle a una bebida (una copa)?
May I invite you for dinner tonight?	¿Me permite invitarle a cenar esta noche?
Where shall we meet?	¿Dónde quedamos citados?

Shops, stores and services	**Comercios y servicios**
Where's the nearest bank, please?	Dónde está el banco más cercano, por favor?
Where can I cash some travellers' cheques?	¿Dónde puedo cambiar unos cheques de viaje?
Can you give me some small change, please?	¿Puede usted darme algún dinero suelto, por favor?
Where's the nearest chemist's (pharmacy)?	¿Dónde está la farmacia más cercana?
How do I get there?	¿Cómo podría ir hasta allí?
Is it within walking distance?	¿Se puede ir andando?
Can you help me, please?	¿Puede usted atenderme, por favor?
How much is this? And that?	¿Cuánto cuesta éste? ¿Y ése?
It's not quite what I want.	No es exactamente lo que quiero.
I like it.	Me gusta.
Can you recommend something for sunburn?	¿Podría recomendarme algo para las quemaduras del sol?
I'd like a haircut, please.	Quisiera cortarme el pelo, por favor.
I'd like a manicure, please.	Quisiera una manicura, por favor.

Street directions	**Direcciones**
Can you show me on the map where I am?	¿Puede enseñarme en el mapa dónde estoy?
You are on the wrong road.	Está usted equivocado de camino.
Go/Walk straight ahead.	Siga todo derecho.
It's on the left/on the right.	Está a la izquierda/a la derecha.

Emergencies	**Urgencias**
Call a doctor quickly.	Llame a un médico rápidamente.
Call an ambulance.	Llame a una ambulancia.
Please call the police.	Llame a la policía, por favor.

inglés-español

english-spanish

Abreviaturas

adj	adjetivo	*n*	nombre
adv	adverbio		(sustantivo)
Am	inglés americano	*nAm*	nombre
art	artículo		(inglés americano)
conj	conjunción	*num*	numeral
f	femenino	*p*	tiempo pasado
fMe	femenino (mexicano)	*pl*	plural
fpl	femenino plural	*plAm*	plural (inglés americano)
fplMe	femenino plural	*pp*	participio pasado
	(mexicano)	*pr*	tiempo presente
m	masculino	*pref*	prefijo
Me	mexicano	*prep*	preposición
mMe	masculino (mexicano)	*pron*	pronombre
mpl	masculino plural	*v*	verbo
mplMe	masculino plural	*vAm*	verbo (inglés americano)
	(mexicano)	*vMe*	verbo (mexicano)

Introducción

Este diccionario ha sido concebido para resolver de la mejor manera posible sus problemas prácticos de lenguaje. Se han suprimido las informaciones lingüísticas innecesarias. Los vocablos se suceden en un estricto orden alfabético, sin tener en cuenta si la palabra es simple o compuesta, o si se trata de una expresión formada por dos o más términos separados. Como única excepción, algunas expresiones idiomáticas están colocadas en orden alfabético, considerando para ello la palabra más característica. Cuando un término principal va seguido de otras palabras, expresiones o locuciones, éstas se hallan anotadas también en orden alfabético.

Cada palabra va seguida de una transcripción fonética (véase la guía de pronunciación). Después de la transcripción fonética se encuentra una indicación de la parte de la oración a la que pertenece el vocablo. Cuando una palabra puede desempeñar distintos oficios en la oración, las diferentes traducciones se dan una a continuación de la otra, precedidas de la indicación correspondiente.

Se indica el plural de los nombres cuando son irregulares y en algunos otros casos dudosos.

Cuando haya que repetir una palabra para formar el plural irregular o en las series de palabras se usa la tilde (~) para representar el vocablo principal.

En los plurales irregulares de las palabras compuestas sólo se escribe la parte que cambia, mientras que la parte invariable se representa por un guión (-).

Un asterisco (*) colocado antes de un verbo indica que dicho verbo es irregular. Para más detalles puede consultar la lista de los verbos irregulares.

Las palabras de este diccionario están escritas en su forma inglesa. La forma y significado americanos están señalados como tales (véase la lista de abreviaturas empleadas en el texto).

Guía de pronunciación

Cada vocablo principal de esta parte del diccionario va acompañado de una transcripción fonética destinada a indicar la pronunciación. Esta representación fonética debe leerse como si se tratara del idioma español hablado en Castilla. A continuación figuran tan solo las letras y los símbolos ambiguos o particularmente difíciles de comprender.

Cada sílaba está separada por un guión y la que lleva el acento está impresa en letra *bastardilla*.

Por supuesto, los sonidos de dos lenguas rara vez coinciden exactamente, pero siguiendo con atención nuestras explicaciones, el lector de habla española llegará a pronunciar las palabras extranjeras de manera que pueda ser comprendido. A fin de facilitar su tarea, algunas veces nuestras transcripciones simplifican ligeramente el sistema fonético del idioma, sin dejar por ello de reflejar las diferencias de sonido esenciales.

Consonantes

b	como en **b**ueno
d	como en **d**ía
ð	como **d** en rui**d**o
dʒ	como la **ll** argentina, precedida por una **d**
gh	como **g** en **g**ato
h	sonido que es una espiración suave
ng	como **n** en bla**n**co
r	ponga la lengua en la misma posición que para pronunciar ʒ (véase más abajo), luego abra ligeramente la boca y baje la lengua
s	sonido siempre suave y sonoro como en mi**s**mo
ʃ	como **ch** en mu**ch**o, pero sin la **t** inicial que compone el sonido
v	más o menos como en la**v**a; sonido que se obtiene colocando los dientes incisivos superiores sobre el labio inferior y expulsando suavemente el aire
ʒ	como la **ll** argentina

Vocales y diptongos

æ	sonido que combina el de la **a** en c**a**so con el de la **e** en sab**e**r
ê	como **e** en sab**e**r
o	como **o** en p**o**r
ö	vocal neutra; sonido parecido al de la **a** española, pero con los labios extendidos

1) Las vocales largas están impresas a doble.

2) Las letras situadas más arriba que las otras (por ej.: ^{u}i, u^{ö}) deben pronunciarse con menor intensidad y rápidamente.

3) Algunas palabras inglesas toman del francés las vocales nasales, que están indicadas con un símbolo de vocal mas **ng** (por ej.: a**ng**). Este signo **ng** *no* se debe pronunciar y sólo sirve para indicar la nasalidad de la vocal precedente. Las vocales nasales se pronuncian con la boca y la nariz simultáneamente.

Pronunciación americana

Nuestra transcripción representa la pronunciación de Gran Bretaña. Aunque existen notables variaciones regionales en la lengua americana, ésta presenta en general algunas diferencias importantes respecto al inglés de Gran Bretaña.

He aquí algunos ejemplos:

1) La **r**, delante de una consonante o al final de una palabra, siempre se pronuncia, lo cual es contrario a la costumbre inglesa.

2) En muchas palabras (por ej.: *ask*, *castle*, *laugh*, etc.) la **aa** se transforma en **ææ**.

3) El sonido inglés **o** se pronuncia **a** o también **oo**.

4) En palabras como *duty*, *tune*, *new*, etc., el sonido **y** se omite a menudo antes de **uu**.

5) Por último, el acento tónico de algunas palabras puede variar considerablemente.

A

a (ei,ö) *art* (an) un *art*

abbey (æ-bi) *n* abadía *f*

abbreviation (ö-brii-vi-*ei*-ʃön) *n* abreviatura *f*

aberration (æ-bö-*rei*-ʃön) *n* anomalía *f*

ability (ö-*bi*-lö-ti) *n* habilidad *f*

able (*ei*-böl) *adj* capaz; hábil; *be ~ to *ser capaz de; *saber, *poder

abnormal (æb-*noo*-möl) *adj* anormal

aboard (ö-*bood*) *adv* a bordo

abolish (ö-*bo*-liʃ) *v* abolir

abortion (ö-*boo*-ʃön) *n* aborto *m*

about (ö-*baut*) *prep* acerca de; respecto a; alrededor de; *adv* hacia, aproximadamente; en torno

above (ö-*bav*) *prep* encima de; *adv* encima

abroad (ö-*brood*) *adv* en el extranjero

abscess (æb-ssêss) *n* absceso *m*

absence (æb-ssönss) *n* ausencia *f*

absent (æb-ssönt) *adj* ausente

absolutely (æb-ssö-luut-li) *adv* absolutamente

abstain from (öb-*sstein*) *abstenerse de

abstract (æb-sstrækt) *adj* abstracto

absurd (öb-*ssööd*) *adj* absurdo

abundance (ö-*ban*-dönss) *n* abundancia *f*

abundant (ö-*ban*-dönt) *adj* abundante

abuse (ö-*byuuss*) *n* abuso *m*

abyss (ö-*biss*) *n* abismo *m*

academy (ö-*kæ*-dö-mi) *n* academia *f*

accelerate (ök-*ssê*-lö-reit) *v* acelerar

accelerator (ök-*ssê*-lö-rei-tö) *n* acelerador *m*

accent (æk-ssönt) *n* acento *m*

accept (ök-*ssêpt*) *v* aceptar

access (æk-ssêss) *n* acceso *m*

accessary (ök-*ssê*-ssö-ri) *n* cómplice *m*

accessible (ök-*ssê*-ssö-böl) *adj* accesible

accessories (ök-*ssê*-ssö-ris) *pl* accesorios *mpl*

accident (æk-ssi-dönt) *n* accidente *m*

accidental (æk-ssi-*dên*-töl) *adj* accidental

accommodate (ö-*ko*-mö-deit) *v* acomodar

accommodation (ö-ko-mö-*dei*-ʃön) *n* acomodación *f*, alojamiento *m*

accompany (ö-*kam*-pö-ni) *v* acompañar

accomplish (ö-*kam*-pliʃ) *v* terminar; cumplir

in accordance with (in ö-*koo*-dönss ᵁið) con arreglo a

according to (ö-*koo*-ding tuu) según; conforme a

account (ö-*kaunt*) *n* cuenta *f*; narración *f*; ~ **for** explicar; **on** ~ **of** a causa de

accountable (ö-*kaun*-tö-böl) *adj* explicable

accurate (*æ*-kyu-röt) *adj* exacto

accuse (ö-*kyuus*) *v* acusar

accused (ö-*kyuusd*) *n* acusado *m*

accustom (ö-*ka*-sstöm) *v* acostumbrar; **accustomed** acostumbrado

ache (eik) *v* *doler; *n* dolor *m*

achieve (ö-*chiiv*) *v* alcanzar; lograr

achievement (ö-*chiiv*-mönt) *n* realización *f*

acid (*æ*-ssid) *n* ácido *m*

acknowledge (ök-*no*-lidʒ) *v* *reconocer; admitir; confirmar

acne (*æk*-ni) *n* acné *m*

acorn (*ei*-koon) *n* bellota *f*

acquaintance (ö-*kʷein*-tönss) *n* conocido *m*

acquire (ö-*kʷaiᵒ*) *v* *adquirir

acquisition (*æ*-kʷi-si-ʃön) *n* adquisición *f*

acquittal (ö-*kʷi*-töl) *n* absolución *f*

across (ö-*kross*) *prep* a través de; al otro lado de; *adv* al otro lado

act (ækt) *n* acto *m*; número *m*; *v* actuar, *hacer; comportarse

action (*æk*-ʃön) *n* acción *f*

active (*æk*-tiv) *adj* activo; vivaz

activity (æk-*ti*-vö-ti) *n* actividad *f*

actor (*æk*-tö) *n* actor *m*

actress (*æk*-triss) *n* actriz *f*

actual (*æk*-chu-öl) *adj* verdadero

actually (*æk*-chu-ö-li) *adv* en realidad

acute (ö-*kyuut*) *adj* agudo

adapt (ö-*dæpt*) *v* adaptar

adaptor (ö-*dæpt*-tö) *n* adaptador *m*

add (æd) *v* sumar, adicionar; añadir

addition (ö-*di*-ʃön) *n* adición *f*

additional (ö-*di*-ʃö-nöl) *adj* adicional; accesorio

address (ö-*drêss*) *n* dirección *f*; *v*

destinar; dirigirse a

addressee (æ-drê-*ssii*) *n* destinatario *m*

adequate (*æ*-di-kʷöt) *adj* adecuado; conveniente

adjective (*æ*-dʒik-tiv) *n* adjetivo *m*

adjourn (ö-*dʒöön*) *v* aplazar

adjust (ö-*dʒasst*) *v* ajustar

administer (öd-*mi*-ni-sstö) *v* administrar

administration (öd-mi-ni-*sstrei*-ʃön) *n* administración *f*; gestión *f*

administrative (öd-*mi*-ni-sströ-tiv) *adj* gerencial; administrativo; ~ **law** derecho administrativo

admiral (*æd*-mö-röl) *n* almirante *m*

admiration (æd-mö-*rei*-ʃön) *n* admiración *f*

admire (öd-*maiᵒ*) *v* admirar

admission (öd-*mi*-ʃön) *n* entrada *f*; admisión *f*

admit (öd-*mit*) *v* admitir; *reconocer

admittance (öd-*mi*-tönss) *n* admisión *f*; **no** ~ prohibida la entrada

adopt (ö-*dopt*) *v* adoptar

adorable (ö-*doo*-rö-böl) *adj* adorable

adult (*æ*-dalt) *n* adulto *m*; *adj* adulto

advance (öd-*vaanss*) *n* adelanto *m*; anticipo *m*; *v* avanzar; anticipar; **in** ~ por adelantado

advanced (öd-*vaansst*) *adj* avanzado

advantage (öd-*vaan*-tidʒ) *n* ventaja *f*

advantageous (æd-vön-*tei*-dʒöss) *adj* ventajoso

adventure (öd-*vên*-chö) *n* aventura *f*

adverb (*æd*-vööb) *n* adverbio *m*

advertisement (öd-*vöö*-tiss-mönt) *n* anuncio *m*

advertising (*æd*-vö-tai-sing) *n* publicidad *f*

advice (öd-*vaiss*) *n* consejo *m*

advise (öd-*vais*) *v* aconsejar

advocate (*æd*-vö-köt) *n* abogado *m*

aerial (*êᵒ*-ri-öl) *n* antena *f*

aeroplane (ê^ö-rö-plein) n avión m

affair (ö-fê^ö) n asunto m; amorío m

affect (ö-fêkt) v afectar

affected (ö-fêk-tid) adj afectado

affection (ö-fêk-ʃön) n afección f; cariño m

affectionate (ö-fêk-ʃö-nit) adj cariñoso

affiliated (ö-fi-li-ei-tid) adj afiliado

affirmative (ö-föö-mö-tiv) adj afirmativo

affliction (ö-flik-ʃön) n sufrimiento m

afford (ö-food) v permitirse

afraid (ö-freid) adj angustioso, asustado; *be ~ *tener miedo

Africa (æ-fri-kö) África f

African (æ-fri-kön) adj africano

after (aaf-tö) prep después de; detrás de; conj después de que

afternoon (aaf-tö-nuun) n tarde f

afterwards (aaf-tö-ᵘöds) adv después

again (ö-ghên) adv otra vez; de nuevo; ~ and again repetidamente

against (ö-ghênsst) prep contra

age (eidʒ) n edad f; vejez f; of ~ mayor de edad; under ~ menor de edad

aged (ei-dʒid) adj viejo; anciano

agency (ei-dʒön-ssi) n agencia f; sección f

agenda (ei-dʒên-dö) n orden del día

agent (ei-dʒönt) n agente m, representante m

aggressive (ö-ghrê-ssiv) adj agresivo

ago (ö-ghou) adv hace

agrarian (ö-ghrê^ö-ri-ön) adj agrario, agrícola

agree (ö-ghrii) v *convenir, *concordar; *consentir; *acordar

agreeable (ö-ghrii-ö-böl) adj agradable

agreement (ö-ghrii-mönt) n contrato m; acuerdo m; conformidad f

agriculture (æ-ghri-kal-chö) n agricul-

tura f

ahead (ö-hêd) adv adelante; ~ of delante de; *go ~ continuar; straight ~ todo seguido

aid (eid) n socorro m; v asistir, ayudar

AIDS (eids) n SIDA m

ailment (eil-mönt) n enfermedad f

aim (eim) n fin m; ~ at apuntar; aspirar a

air (ê^ö) n aire m; v airear

air-conditioning (ê^ö-kön-di-ʃö-ning) n aire acondicionado; air-conditioned adj climatizado

aircraft (ê^ö-kraaft) n (pl ~) avión m

airfield (ê^ö-fiild) n campo de aviación

airline (ê^ö-lain) n aerolínea f

airmail (ê^ö-meil) n correo aéreo

airplane (ê^ö-plein) nAm avión m

airport (ê^ö-poot) n aeropuerto m

air-sickness (ê^ö-ssik-nöss) n mal de las alturas

airtight (ê^ö-tait) adj hermético

airy (ê^ö-ri) adj airoso

aisle (ail) n nave lateral; pasillo m

alarm (ö-laam) n alarma f; v alarmar

alarm-clock (ö-laam-klok) n despertador m

album (æl-böm) n álbum m

alcohol (æl-kö-hol) n alcohol m

alcoholic (æl-kö-ho-lik) adj alcohólico

ale (eil) n cerveza f

algebra (æl-dʒi-brö) n álgebra f

Algeria (æl-dʒi^ö-ri-ö) Argelia f

Algerian (æl-dʒi^ö-ri-ön) adj argelino

alien (ei-li-ön) n extranjero m; adj extranjero

alike (ö-laik) adj igual, parecido; adv igualmente

alimony (æ-li-mö-ni) n pensión alimenticia

alive (ö-laiv) adj en vida, vivo

all (ool) adj todo; ~ in todo incluido; ~ right! ¡bien!; at ~ en modo algu-

no
allergy (æ-lö-dʒi) *n* alergia *f*
alley (æ-li) *n* callejón *m*
alliance (ö-*lai*-önss) *n* alianza *f*
allot (ö-*lot*) *v* asignar
allow (ö-*lau*) *v* permitir, autorizar; ~ **to** autorizar a; ***be allowed** *estar autorizado
allowance (ö-*lau*-önss) *n* asignación *f*
all-round (ool-*raund*) *adj* polifacético
almanac (*ool*-mö-næk) *n* almanaque *m*
almond (*aa*-mönd) *n* almendra *f*
almost (*ool*-mousst) *adv* casi; cerca de
alone (ö-*loun*) *adv* sólo
along (ö-*long*) *prep* a lo largo de
aloud (ö-*laud*) *adv* en voz alta
alphabet (*æl*-fö-bêt) *n* abecedario *m*
already (ool-*rê*-di) *adv* ya
also (*ool*-ssou) *adv* también; asimismo
altar (*ool*-tö) *n* altar *m*
alter (*ool*-tö) *v* cambiar, alterar
alteration (ool-tö-*rei*-jön) *n* cambio *m*, alteración *f*
alternate (*ool*-töö-nöt) *adj* alternativo
alternative (*ool*-*töö*-nö-tiv) *n* alternativa *f*
although (ool-*ðou*) *conj* aunque
altitude (*æl*-ti-tyuud) *n* altitud *f*
alto (*æl*-tou) *n* (pl ~s) contralto *m*
altogether (ool-tö-*ghê*-ðö) *adv* totalmente; en total
always (*ool*-ᵘeis) *adv* siempre
am (æm) *v* (pr be)
amaze (ö-*meis*) *v* extrañar, asombrar
amazement (ö-*meis*-mönt) *n* asombro *m*
ambassador (æm-*bæ*-ssö-dö) *n* embajador *m*
amber (*æm*-bö) *n* ámbar *m*
ambiguous (æm-*bi*-ghyu-öss) *adj* ambiguo; equívoco
ambition (æm-bi-*jön*) *n* ambición *f*

ambitious (æm-*bi*-jöss) *adj* ambicioso
ambulance (*æm*-byu-lönss) *n* ambulancia *f*
ambush (*æm*-buʃ) *n* emboscada *f*
America (ö-*mê*-ri-kö) América *f*
American (ö-*mê*-ri-kön) *adj* americano
amethyst (*æ*-mi-zisst) *n* amatista *f*
amid (ö-*mid*) *prep* entre; en medio de
ammonia (ö-*mou*-ni-ö) *n* amoníaco *m*
amnesty (*æm*-ni-ssti) *n* amnistía *f*
among (ö-*mang*) *prep* entre; ~ **other things** entre otras cosas
amount (ö-*maunt*) *n* cantidad *f*; suma *f*; ~ **to** sumar
amuse (ö-*myuus*) *v* *divertir, *entretener
amusement (ö-*myuus*-mönt) *n* distracción *f*, entretenimiento *m*
amusing (ö-*myuu*-sing) *adj* divertido
anaemia (ö-*nii*-mi-ö) *n* anemia *f*
anaesthesia (æ-niss-*zii*-si-ö) *n* anestesia *f*
anaesthetic (æ-niss-*zê*-tik) *n* anestésico *m*
analyse (*æ*-nö-lais) *v* analizar
analysis (ö-*næ*-lö-ssiss) *n* (pl -ses) análisis *f*
analyst (*æ*-nö-lisst) *n* analista *m*; psicoanalista *m*
anarchy (*æ*-nö-ki) *n* anarquía *f*
anatomy (ö-*næ*-tö-mi) *n* anatomía *f*
ancestor (*æn*-ssê-sstö) *n* antepasado *m*
anchor (*æng*-kö) *n* ancla *f*
anchovy (*æn*-chö-vi) *n* anchoa *f*
ancient (*ein*-jönt) *adj* viejo, antiguo; anticuado
and (ænd, önd) *conj* y
angel (*ein*-dʒöl) *n* ángel *m*
anger (*æng*-ghö) *n* cólera *f*, enojo *m*; furor *m*
angle (*æng*-ghöl) *v* pescar con caña; *n* ángulo *m*

angry (æng-ghri) *adj* enfadado, enojado

animal (æ-ni-möl) *n* animal *m*

ankle (æng-köl) *n* tobillo *m*

annex[1] (æ-nêkss) *n* anexo *m*

annex[2] (ö-nêkss) *v* anexar

anniversary (æ-ni-*vöö*-ssö-ri) *n* aniversario *m*

announce (ö-*nauns*) *v* anunciar

announcement (ö-*nauns*-mönt) *n* anuncio *m*

annoy (ö-*noi*) *v* irritar, fastidiar; aburrir

annoyance (ö-*noi*-önss) *n* aburrimiento *m*

annoying (ö-*noi*-ing) *adj* irritante, importuno

annual (æ-nyu-öl) *adj* anual; *n* anuario *m*

per annum (pör æ-nöm) al año

anonymous (ö-*no*-ni-möss) *adj* anónimo

another (ö-*na*-ðö) *adj* otro más; otro

answer (*aan*-ssö) *v* responder a; *n* respuesta *f*

ant (ænt) *n* hormiga *f*

anthology (æn-*zo*-lö-dʒi) *n* antología *f*

antibiotic (æn-ti-bai-*o*-tik) *n* antibiótico *m*

anticipate (æn-*ti*-ssi-peit) *v* *prever; *prevenir

antifreeze (æn-ti-friis) *n* anticongelante *m*

antipathy (æn-*ti*-pö-zi) *n* antipatía *f*

antique (æn-*tiik*) *adj* antiguo; *n* antigualla *f*; ~ **dealer** anticuario *m*

antiquity (æn-*ti*-kuö-ti) *n* Antigüedad *f*; **antiquities** *pl* antigüedades *fpl*

antiseptic (æn-ti-*ssêp*-tik) *n* antiséptico *m*

antlers (*ænt*-lös) *pl* cornamenta *f*

anxiety (æng-*sai*-ö-ti) *n* preocupación *f*

anxious (ængk-ʃöss) *adj* ansioso; preocupado

any (*ê*-ni) *adj* alguno

anybody (*ê*-ni-bo-di) *pron* cualquiera

anyhow (*ê*-ni-hau) *adv* de cualquier modo

anyone (*ê*-ni-ᵘan) *pron* cualquiera

anything (*ê*-ni-zing) *pron* cualquier cosa

anyway (*ê*-ni-ᵘei) *adv* en todo caso

anywhere (*ê*-ni-ᵘêᵃ) *adv* en donde sea; dondequiera

apart (ö-*paat*) *adv* por separado, separadamente; ~ **from** prescindiendo de

apartment (ö-*paat*-mönt) *nAm* apartamento *m*; piso *m*; ~ **house** *Am* casa de pisos

aperitif (o-pê-rö-tiv) *n* aperitivo *m*

apologize (ö-*po*-lö-dʒais) *v* disculparse

apology (ö-*po*-lö-dʒi) *n* excusa *f*, disculpa *f*

apparatus (æ-pö-*rei*-töss) *n* aparato *m*

apparent (ö-*pæ*-rönt) *adj* aparente; obvio

apparently (ö-*pæ*-rönt-li) *adv* por lo visto; evidentemente

apparition (æ-pö-*ri*-ʃön) *n* aparición *f*

appeal (ö-*piil*) *n* apelación *f*

appear (ö-*piᵃ*) *v* *parecer; *salir; *aparecer

appearance (ö-*piᵃ*-rönss) *n* apariencia *f*; aspecto *m*; entrada *f*

appendicitis (ö-pên-di-*ssai*-tiss) *n* apendicitis *f*

appendix (ö-*pên*-dikss) *n* (pl -dices, -dixes) apéndice *m*

appetite (æ-pö-tait) *n* apetito *m*

appetizer (æ-pö-tai-sö) *n* tapa *f*

appetizing (æ-pö-tai-sing) *adj* apetitoso

applause (ö-*ploos*) *n* aplauso *m*

apple (æ-pöl) *n* manzana *f*

appliance (ö-*plai*-önss) *n* aparato *m*

application (æ-pli-*kei*-ſön) *n* aplicación *f*; demanda *f*; solicitud *f*

apply (ö-*plai*) *v* aplicar; solicitar un puesto; aplicarse a

appoint (ö-*point*) *v* designar, nombrar

appointment (ö-*point*-mönt) *n* cita *f*; nombramiento *m*

appreciate (ö-*prii*-ſi-eit) *v* valuar; apreciar

appreciation (ö-prii-ſi-*ei*-ſön) *n* aprecio *m*

approach (ö-*prouch*) *v* acercarse; *n* enfoque *m*; acceso *m*

appropriate (ö-*prou*-pri-öt) *adj* justo, apropiado, adecuado

approval (ö-*pruu*-völ) *n* aprobación *f*; consentimiento *m*, acuerdo *m*; **on ~** a prueba

approve (ö-*pruuv*) *v* *aprobar; ~ of* *estar de acuerdo con

approximate (ö-*prok*-ssi-möt) *adj* aproximado

approximately (ö-*prok*-ssi-möt-li) *adv* aproximadamente

apricot (*ei*-pri-kot) *n* albaricoque *m*; chabacano *mMe*

April (*ei*-pröl) abril

apron (*ei*-prön) *n* delantal *m*

Arab (æ-röb) *adj* árabe

arbitrary (*aa*-bi-trö-ri) *adj* arbitrario

arcade (aa-*keid*) *n* pórtico *m*, arcada *f*

arch (aach) *n* arco *m*; bóveda *f*

archaeologist (aa-ki-*o*-lö-dʒisst) *n* arqueólogo *m*

archaeology (aa-ki-*o*-lö-dʒi) *n* arqueología *f*

archbishop (aach-*bi*-ſöp) *n* arzobispo *m*

arched (aacht) *adj* arqueado

architect (*aa*-ki-tëkt) *n* arquitecto *m*

architecture (*aa*-ki-tëk-chö) *n* arquitectura *f*

archives (*aa*-kaivs) *pl* archivo *m*

are (aa) *v* (pr be)

area (*êᵒ*-ri-ö) *n* región *f*; zona *f*; superficie *f*; **~ code** indicativo *m*

Argentina (aa-dʒön-*tii*-nö) Argentina *f*

Argentinian (aa-dʒön-*ti*-ni-ön) *adj* argentino

argue (*aa*-ghyuu) *v* argumentar, discutir; disputar

argument (*aa*-ghyu-mönt) *n* argumento *m*; discusión *f*; disputa *f*

arid (æ-rid) *adj* árido

***arise** (ö-*rais*) *v* surgir

arithmetic (ö-*riz*-mö-tik) *n* aritmética *f*

arm (aam) *n* brazo *m*; arma *f*; *v* armar

armchair (*aam*-chêᵒ) *n* butaca *f*, sillón *m*

armed (aamd) *adj* armado; **~ forces** fuerzas armadas

armour (*aa*-mö) *n* armadura *f*

army (*aa*-mi) *n* ejército *m*

aroma (ö-*rou*-mö) *n* aroma *m*

around (ö-*raund*) *prep* alrededor de, en torno de; *adv* en torno

arrange (ö-*reindʒ*) *v* clasificar, ordenar; organizar

arrangement (ö-*reindʒ*-mönt) *n* arreglo *m*

arrest (ö-*rêsst*) *v* arrestar; *n* arresto *m*

arrival (ö-*rai*-völ) *n* llegada *f*

arrive (ö-*raiv*) *v* llegar

arrow (æ-rou) *n* flecha *f*

art (aat) *n* arte *m/f*; habilidad *f*; **~ collection** colección de arte; **~ exhibition** exposición de arte; **~ gallery** galería de arte; **~ history** historia del arte; **arts and crafts** artes industriales; **~ school** academia de bellas artes

artery (*aa*-tö-ri) *n* arteria *f*

artichoke (*aa*-ti-chouk) *n* alcachofa *f*

article (*aa*-ti-köl) *n* artículo *m*

artifice (aa-ti-fiss) n artificio m
artificial (aa-ti-fi-ʃöl) adj artificial
artist (aa-tisst) n artista m/f
artistic (aa-ti-sstik) adj artístico
as (æs) conj como; tanto; que; ya
que, porque; ~ from a partir de; ~
if como si
asbestos (æs-bê-sstoss) n asbesto m
ascend (ö-ssênd) v subir; escalar
ascent (ö-ssênt) n subida f
ascertain (æ-ssö-tein) v *comprobar;
asegurarse de
ash (æʃ) n ceniza f
ashamed (ö-ʃeimd) adj avergonzado;
*be ~ *avergonzarse
ashore (ö-ʃoo) adv en tierra
ashtray (æʃ-trei) n cenicero m
Asia (ei-ʃö) Asia f
Asian (ei-ʃön) adj asiático
aside (ö-ssaid) adv aparte
ask (aassk) v preguntar; *rogar; invitar
asleep (ö-ssliip) adj dormido
asparagus (ö-sspæ-rö-ghöss) n espárrago m
aspect (æ-sspêkt) n aspecto m
asphalt (æss-fælt) n asfalto m
aspire (ö-sspaiⁿ) v aspirar
aspirin (æ-sspö-rin) n aspirina f
ass (æss) n burro m
assassination (ö-ssæ-ssi-nei-ʃön) n
asesinato m
assault (ö-ssoolt) v atacar; violar
assemble (ö-ssêm-böl) v reunir; montar
assembly (ö-ssêm-bli) n reunión f,
asamblea f
assignment (ö-ssain-mönt) n encargo
m
assign to (ö-ssain) asignar a; *atribuir a
assist (ö-ssisst) v asistir
assistance (ö-ssi-sstönss) n auxilio
m; apoyo m, asistencia f

assistant (ö-ssi-sstönt) n asistente m
associate¹ (ö-ssou-ʃi-öt) n compañero
m, asociado m; aliado m; socio m
associate² (ö-ssou-ʃi-eit) v asociar; ~
with frecuentar
association (ö-ssou-ssi-ei-ʃön) n asociación f
assort (ö-ssoot) v clasificar
assortment (ö-ssoot-mönt) n surtido
m
assume (ö-ssyuum) v *suponer, presumir
assure (ö-ʃuⁿ) v asegurar
asthma (æss-mö) n asma f
astonish (ö-ssto-niʃ) v asombrar
astonishing (ö-ssto-ni-ʃing) adj asombroso
astonishment (ö-ssto-niʃ-mönt) n sorpresa f
astronomy (ö-sstro-nö-mi) n astronomía f
asylum (ö-ssai-löm) n asilo m
at (æt) prep en, a; hacia
ate (êt) v (p eat)
atheist (ei-zi-isst) n ateo m
athlete (æz-liit) n atleta m
athletics (æz-lê-tikss) pl atletismo m
Atlantic (öt-læn-tik) Atlántico m
atmosphere (æt-möss-fiⁿ) n atmósfera f; esfera f, ambiente m
atom (æ-töm) n átomo m
atomic (ö-to-mik) adj atómico
atomizer (æ-tö-mai-sö) n vaporizador
m; aerosol m, pulverizador m
attach (ö-tæch) v prender; fijar; juntar; attached to encariñado con
attack (ö-tæk) v atacar; n ataque m
attain (ö-tein) v llegar a
attainable (ö-tei-nö-böl) adj factible;
alcanzable
attempt (ö-têmpt) v intentar; *probar; n tentativa f
attend (ö-tênd) v asistir a; ~ on *servir; ~ to cuidar de, *atender a;

prestar atención a
attendance (ö-*tên*-dönss) *n* asistencia *f*
attendant (ö-*tên*-dönt) *n* guardián *m*
attention (ö-*tén*-ʃön) *n* atención *f*; *pay* ~ prestar atención
attentive (ö-*tên*-tiv) *adj* atento
attic (*æ*-tik) *n* buhardilla *f*
attitude (*æ*-ti-tyuud) *n* actitud *f*
attorney (ö-*töö*-ni) *n* abogado *m*
attract (ö-*trækt*) *v* *atraer
attraction (ö-*træk*-ʃön) *n* atracción *f*
attractive (ö-*træk*-tiv) *adj* atractivo
auburn (*oo*-bön) *adj* castaño
auction (*ook*-ʃön) *n* subasta *f*
audible (*oo*-di-böl) *adj* audible
audience (*oo*-di-önss) *n* auditorio *m*
auditor (*oo*-di-tö) *n* oyente *m*
auditorium (oo-di-*too*-ri-öm) *n* aula *f*
August (*oo*-ghösst) agosto
aunt (aant) *n* tía *f*
Australia (o-*sstrei*-li-ö) Australia *f*
Australian (o-*sstrei*-li-ön) *adj* australiano
Austria (*o*-sstri-ö) Austria *f*
Austrian (*o*-sstri-ön) *adj* austríaco
authentic (oo-*zên*-tik) *adj* auténtico
author (*oo*-zö) *n* autor *m*
authoritarian (oo-zo-ri-*tê*ᵒ-ri-ön) *adj* autoritario
authority (oo-*zo*-rö-ti) *n* autoridad *f*; poder *m*
authorization (oo-zö-rai-*sei*-ʃön) *n* autorización *f*; permiso *m*
automatic (oo-tö-*mæ*-tik) *adj* automático; ~ **teller** cajero automático
automation (oo-tö-*mei*-ʃön) *n* automatización *f*
automobile (*oo*-tö-mö-biil) *n* automóvil *m*; ~ **club** automóvil club
autonomous (oo-*to*-nö-möss) *adj* autónomo
autopsy (*oo*-to-pssi) *n* autopsia *f*
autumn (*oo*-töm) *n* otoño *m*

available (ö-*vei*-lö-böl) *adj* adquirible, obtenible, disponible
avalanche (*æ*-vö-laanʃ) *n* avalancha *f*
avaricious (æ-vö-*ri*-föss) *adj* avaro
avenue (*æ*-vö-nyuu) *n* avenida *f*
average (*æ*-vö-ridʒ) *adj* promedio; *n* promedio *m*; **on the** ~ en promedio
averse (ö-*vööss*) *adj* opuesto
aversion (ö-*vöö*-ʃön) *n* aversión *f*
avert (ö-*vööt*) *v* desviar
avoid (ö-*void*) *v* evitar
await (ö-*ᵘeit*) *v* esperar
awake (ö-*ᵘeik*) *adj* despierto
awake (ö-*ᵘeik*) *v* *despertar
award (ö-*ᵘood*) *n* premio *m*; *v* conceder
aware (ö-*ᵘêᵒ*) *adj* consciente
away (ö-*ᵘei*) *adv* fuera; *go* ~ *irse
awful (*oo*-föl) *adj* terrible, tremendo
awkward (*oo*-kᵘöd) *adj* embarazoso; torpe
awning (*oo*-ning) *n* toldo *m*
axe (ækss) *n* hacha *f*
axle (*æk*-ssöl) *n* eje *m*

B

baby (*bei*-bi) *n* bebé *m*; ~ **carriage** *Am* cochecillo *m*
babysitter (*bei*-bi-ssi-tö) *n* babysitter *m*
bachelor (*bæ*-chö-lö) *n* soltero *m*
back (bæk) *n* espalda *f*; *adv* atrás; *go* ~ regresar
backache (*bæ*-keik) *n* dolor de espalda
backbone (*bæk*-boun) *n* espina dorsal
background (*bæk*-ghraund) *n* fondo *m*; antecedentes *mpl*
backwards (*bæk*-ᵘöds) *adv* hacia atrás

bacon (*bei*-kön) *n* tocino *m*

bacterium (bæk-*tii*-ri-öm) *n* (pl -ria) bacteria *f*

bad (bæd) *adj* malo; grave; travieso

bag (bægh) *n* bolsa *f*; bolso *m*, cartera *f*; maleta *f*

baggage (*bæ*-ghidʒ) *n* equipaje *m*; **hand ~** *Am* equipaje de mano

bail (beil) *n* fianza *f*

bailiff (*bei*-lif) *n* ujier *m*

bait (beit) *n* cebo *m*

bake (beik) *v* hornear

baker (*bei*-kö) *n* panadero *m*

bakery (*bei*-kö-ri) *n* panadería *f*

balance (*bæ*-lönss) *n* equilibrio *m*; balance *m*; saldo *m*

balcony (*bæl*-kö-ni) *n* balcón *m*

bald (boold) *adj* calvo

ball (bool) *n* pelota *f*; baile *m*

ballet (*bæ*-lei) *n* ballet *m*

balloon (bö-*luun*) *n* globo *m*

ballpoint-pen (*bool*-point-pên) *n* bolígrafo *m*

ballroom (*bool*-ruum) *n* salón de baile

bamboo (bæm-*buu*) *n* (pl ~s) bambú *m*

banana (bö-*naa*-nö) *n* plátano *m*

band (bænd) *n* orquesta *f*; banda *f*

bandage (*bæn*-didʒ) *n* vendaje *m*

bandit (*bæn*-dit) *n* bandido *m*

bangle (*bæng*-ghöl) *n* pulsera *f*

banisters (*bæ*-ni-sstöss) *pl* baranda *f*

bank (bængk) *n* orilla *f*; banco *m*; *v* depositar; **~ account** cuenta de banco

banknote (*bæng*k-nout) *n* vale *m*, billete de banco

bank-rate (*bæng*k-reit) *n* descuento bancario

bankrupt (*bæng*k-rapt) *adj* en quiebra

banner (*bæ*-nö) *n* bandera *f*

banquet (*bæng*-kʷit) *n* banquete *m*

banqueting-hall (*bæng*-kʷi-ting-hool) *n* comedor de gala

baptism (*bæp*-ti-söm) *n* bautismo *m*, bautizo *m*

baptize (bæp-*tais*) *v* bautizar

bar (baa) *n* bar *m*; barra *f*; barrote *m*

barber (*baa*-bö) *n* barbero *m*

bare (bêᵒ) *adj* desnudo; raso

barely (*bêᵒ*-li) *adv* apenas

bargain (*baa*-ghin) *n* ganga *f*; *v* regatear

baritone (*bæ*-ri-toun) *n* barítono *m*

bark (baak) *n* corteza *f*; *v* ladrar

barley (*baa*-li) *n* cebada *f*

barmaid (*baa*-meid) *n* moza de taberna

barman (*baa*-mön) *n* (pl -men) barman *m*

barn (baan) *n* granero *m*

barometer (bö-*ro*-mi-tö) *n* barómetro *m*

baroque (bö-*rok*) *adj* barroco

barracks (*bæ*-rökss) *pl* cuartel *m*

barrel (*bæ*-röl) *n* tonel *m*, barril *m*

barrier (*bæ*-ri-ö) *n* barrera *f*

barrister (*bæ*-ri-sstö) *n* abogado *m*

bartender (*baa*-tên-dö) *n* barman *m*

base (beiss) *n* base *f*; fundamento *m*; *v* basar

baseball (*beiss*-bool) *n* béisbol *m*

basement (*beiss*-mönt) *n* sótano *m*

basic (*bei*-ssik) *adj* fundamental

basilica (bö-*si*-li-kö) *n* basílica *f*

basin (*bei*-ssön) *n* tazón *m*, palangana *f*

basis (*bei*-ssiss) *n* (pl bases) fundamento *m*, base *f*

basket (*baa*-sskit) *n* cesta *f*

bass¹ (beiss) *n* bajo *m*

bass² (bæss) *n* (pl ~) perca *f*

bastard (*baa*-sstöd) *n* bastardo *m*; descarado *m*

batch (bæch) *n* carga *f*

bath (baaz) *n* baño *m*; **~ salts** sales de baño; **~ towel** toalla de baño

bathe (beið) v bañarse
bathing-cap (bei-ðing-kæp) n gorro de baño
bathing-suit (bei-ðing-ssuut) n traje de baño
bathing-trunks (bei-ðing-trangkss) n bañador m
bathrobe (baaz-roub) n bata de baño
bathroom (baaz-ruum) n cuarto de baño; lavabos mpl; baño mMe
batter (bæ-tö) n masa f
battery (bæ-tö-ri) n batería f; acumulador m
battle (bæ-töl) n batalla f; pelea f, combate m; v combatir
bay (bei) n bahía f; v ladrar
*be (bii) v *estar, *ser
beach (biich) n playa f; nudist ~ playa para nudistas
bead (biid) n cuenta f; beads pl collar m; rosario m
beak (biik) n pico m
beam (biim) n rayo m; viga f
bean (biin) n judía f; ejote mMe
bear (bêô) n oso m
*bear (bêô) v llevar; aguantar; soportar
beard (biôd) n barba f
bearer (bêô-rö) n portador m
beast (biisst) n animal m; ~ of prey animal de presa
*beat (biit) v batir, golpear
beautiful (byuu-ti-föl) adj hermoso
beauty (byuu-ti) n belleza f; ~ parlour salón de belleza; ~ salon salón de belleza; ~ treatment tratamiento de belleza
beaver (bii-vö) n castor m
because (bi-kos) conj porque; puesto que; ~ of a causa de
*become (bi-kam) v *hacerse; *sentar bien
bed (bêd) n cama f; ~ and board pensión completa; ~ and breakfast cama y desayuno

bedding (bê-ding) n ropa de cama
bedroom (bêd-ruum) n dormitorio m
bee (bii) n abeja f
beech (bii-ch) n haya f
beef (biif) n carne de vaca
beehive (bii-haiv) n colmena f
been (biin) v (pp be)
beer (biô) n cerveza f
beet (biit) n remolacha f
beetle (bii-töl) n escarabajo m
beetroot (biit-ruut) n remolacha f
before (bi-foo) prep antes de; delante de; conj antes de que; adv antes
beg (bêgh) v mendigar; suplicar; *pedir
beggar (bê-ghö) n mendigo m
*begin (bi-ghin) v *empezar; *comenzar
beginner (bi-ghi-nö) n principiante m
beginning (bi-ghi-ning) n comienzo m
on behalf of (on bi-haaf ov) en nombre de; a favor de
behave (bi-heiv) v comportarse
behaviour (bi-hei-vyö) n conducta f
behind (bi-haind) prep detrás de; adv detrás
beige (beiʒ) adj beige
being (bii-ing) n ser m
Belgian (bêl-dʒön) adj belga
Belgium (bêl-dʒöm) Bélgica f
belief (bi-liif) n creencia f
believe (bi-liiv) v *creer
bell (bêl) n campana f; timbre m
bellboy (bêl-boi) n botones mpl
belly (bê-li) n vientre m
belong (bi-long) v *pertenecer
belongings (bi-long-ings) pl pertenencias fpl
beloved (bi-lavd) adj querido
below (bi-lou) prep debajo de; bajo; adv debajo
belt (bêlt) n cinturón m
bench (bênch) n banco m

bend (bênd) *n* comba *f*, curva *f*

***bend** (bênd) *v* doblar; ~ **down** bajarse

beneath (bi-*niiz*) *prep* debajo de; *adv* debajo

benefit (*bê*-ni-fit) *n* beneficio *m*; ventaja *f*; *v* aprovechar

bent (bênt) *adj* (pp bend) curvo

beret (*bê*-rei) *n* boina *f*

berry (*bê*-ri) *n* baya *f*

berth (bööz) *n* litera *f*

beside (bi-*ssaid*) *prep* junto a

besides (bi-*ssaids*) *adv* además; por otra parte; *prep* además de

best (bêsst) *adj* óptimo

bet (bêt) *n* apuesta *f*; puesta *f*

***bet** (bêt) *v* *apostar

betray (bi-*trei*) *v* traicionar

better (*bê*-tö) *adj* mejor

between (bi-*tᵘiin*) *prep* entre

beverage (*bê*-vö-ridʒ) *n* bebida *f*

beware (bi-ᵘê*ö*) *v* precaverse, guardarse

bewitch (bi-ᵘ*ich*) *v* hechizar, encantar

beyond (bi-*yond*) *prep* más allá de; además de; *adv* más allá

bible (*bai*-böl) *n* biblia *f*

bicycle (*bai*-ssi-köl) *n* bicicleta *f*; biciclo *m*

big (bigh) *adj* grande; voluminoso; gordo; importante

bile (bail) *n* bilis *f*

bilingual (bai-*ling*-ghᵘöl) *adj* bilingüe

bill (bil) *n* cuenta *f*; *v* facturar

billiards (*bil*-yöds) *pl* billar *m*

***bind** (baind) *v* atar

binding (*bain*-ding) *n* atadura *f*

binoculars (bi-*no*-kyö-lös) *pl* prismáticos *mpl*; gemelos *mpl*

biology (bai-*o*-lö-dʒi) *n* biología *f*

birch (bööch) *n* abedul *m*

bird (bööd) *n* pájaro *m*

Biro (*bai*-rou) *n* bolígrafo *m*

birth (bööz) *n* nacimiento *m*

birthday (*bööz*-dei) *n* cumpleaños *m*

biscuit (*biss*-kit) *n* galleta *f*

bishop (*bi*-jöp) *n* obispo *m*

bit (bit) *n* trozo *m*; poco *m*

bitch (bich) *n* perra *f*

bite (bait) *n* bocado *m*; mordedura *f*; picadura *f*

***bite** (bait) *v* *morder

bitter (*bi*-tö) *adj* amargo

black (blæk) *adj* negro; ~ **market** mercado negro

blackberry (*blæk*-bö-ri) *n* mora *f*

blackbird (*blæk*-bööd) *n* mirlo *m*

blackboard (*blæk*-bood) *n* pizarra *f*

black-currant (blæk-*ka*-rönt) *n* grosella negra

blackmail (*blæk*-meil) *n* chantaje *m*; *v* *hacer chantaje

blacksmith (*blæk*-ssmiz) *n* herrero *m*

bladder (*blæ*-dö) *n* vejiga *f*

blade (bleid) *n* hoja *f*; ~ **of grass** brizna de hierba

blame (bleim) *n* culpa *f*; reproche *m*; *v* echar la culpa, culpar

blank (blængk) *adj* blanco

blanket (*blæng*-kit) *n* manta *f*

blast (blaasst) *n* explosión *f*

blazer (*blei*-sö) *n* chaqueta de sport, chaqueta ligera

bleach (bliich) *v* blanquear

bleak (bliik) *adj* riguroso

***bleed** (bliid) *v* sangrar; chupar la sangre

bless (blêss) *v* *bendecir

blessing (*blê*-ssing) *n* bendición *f*

blind (blaind) *n* persiana *f*; *adj* ciego; *v* *cegar

blister (*bli*-sstö) *n* ampolla *f*

blizzard (*bli*-söd) *n* ventisca *f*

block (blok) *v* *obstruir, bloquear; *n* bloque *m*; ~ **of flats** casa de pisos

blonde (blond) *n* rubia *f*

blood (blad) *n* sangre *f*; ~ **pressure** tensión arterial

blood-poisoning (*blad*-poi-sö-ning) *n* septicemia *f*

blood-vessel (*blad*-vê-ssöl) *n* vaso sanguíneo

blot (blot) *n* borrón *m* ; mancha *f* ; **blotting paper** papel secante

blouse (blaus) *n* blusa *f*

blow (blou) *n* golpe *m* ; ráfaga *f*

***blow** (blou) *v* soplar

blow-out (*blou*-aut) *n* reventón *m*

blue (bluu) *adj* azul; deprimido

blunt (blant) *adj* desafilado; obtuso

blush (blaʃ) *v* ruborizarse

board (bood) *n* tabla *f* ; tablero *m* ; pensión *f* ; consejo *m* ; ~ **and lodging** pensión completa

boarder (*boo*-dö) *n* huésped *m*

boarding-house (*boo*-ding-hauss) *n* pensión *f*

boarding-school (*boo*-ding-sskuul) *n* internado *m*

boast (bousst) *v* presumir

boat (bout) *n* barco *m*, barca *f*

body (*bo*-di) *n* cuerpo *m*

bodyguard (*bo*-di-ghaad) *n* guardia personal

bog (bogh) *n* pantano *m*

boil (boil) *v* *hervir; *n* forúnculo *m*

bold (bould) *adj* audaz; impertinente, descarado

Bolivia (bö-*li*-vi-ö) Bolivia *f*

Bolivian (bö-*li*-vi-ön) *adj* boliviano

bolt (boult) *n* cerrojo *m* ; perno *m*

bomb (bom) *n* bomba *f* ; *v* bombardear

bond (bond) *n* obligación *f*

bone (boun) *n* hueso *m* ; espina *f* ; *v* deshuesar

bonnet (*bo*-nit) *n* capó *m*

book (buk) *n* libro *m* ; *v* reservar; inscribir, registrar

booking (*bu*-king) *n* reservación *f*, reserva *f*

bookmaker (*buk*-mei-kö) *n* corredor *m*

bookseller (*buk*-ssê-lö) *n* librero *m*

bookstand (*buk*-sstænd) *n* puesto de libros

bookstore (*buk*-sstoo) *n* librería *f*

boot (buut) *n* bota *f* ; portaequipajes *m*

booth (buuð) *n* puesto *m* ; cabina *f*

border (*boo*-dö) *n* frontera *f* ; borde *m*

bore[1] (boo) *v* aburrir; taladrar; *n* pelmazo *m*

bore[2] (boo) *v* (p bear)

boring (*boo*-ring) *adj* aburrido

born (boon) *adj* nacido

borrow (*bo*-rou) *v* tomar prestado; tomar

bosom (*bu*-söm) *n* pecho *m* ; seno *m*

boss (boss) *n* jefe *m*, patrón *m*

botany (*bo*-tö-ni) *n* botánica *f*

both (bouz) *adj* ambos; **both ... and** tanto ... como

bother (*bo*-ðö) *v* fastidiar, molestar; *esforzarse; *n* molestia *f*

bottle (*bo*-töl) *n* botella *f* ; ~ **opener** destapador de botellas; **hot-water** ~ calorífero *m*

bottleneck (*bo*-töl-nêk) *n* cuello de botella

bottom (*bo*-töm) *n* fondo *m* ; trasero *m* ; *adj* inferior

bough (bau) *n* rama *f*

bought (boot) *v* (p, pp buy)

boulder (*boul*-dö) *n* peña *f*

bound (baund) *n* frontera *f* ; *be ~ to** deber de; ~ **for** camino de

boundary (*baun*-dö-ri) *n* límite *m* ; frontera *f*

bouquet (bu-*kei*) *n* ramo *m*

bourgeois (*buᵒ*-ȝ*u*aa) *adj* burgués

boutique (bu-*tiik*) *n* boutique *f*

bow[1] (bau) *v* inclinar

bow[2] (bou) *n* arco *m* ; ~ **tie** corbata de lazo, corbatín *m*

bowels (bau⁰ls) *pl* intestinos *mpl*

bowl (boul) *n* tazón *m*

bowling (*bou*-ling) *n* bowling *m*, juego de bolos; ~ **alley** bolera *f*

box¹ (bokss) *v* boxear; **boxing match** combate de boxeo

box² (bokss) *n* caja *f*

box-office (*bokss*-o-fiss) *n* taquilla *f*

boy (boi) *n* muchacho *m*; chico *m*, mozo *m*; sirviente *m*; ~ **scout** explorador *m*

bra (braa) *n* sujetador *m*, sostén *m*

bracelet (*breiss*-lit) *n* pulsera *f*

braces (*brei*-ssis) *pl* tirantes *mpl*

brain (brein) *n* cerebro *m*; inteligencia *f*

brain-wave (*brein*-ᵘeiv) *n* ocurrencia *f*

brake (breik) *n* freno *m*; ~ **drum** tambor del freno; ~ **lights** luces de freno

branch (braanch) *n* rama *f*; sucursal *f*

brand (brænd) *n* marca *f*

brand-new (brænd-*nyuu*) *adj* flamante

brass (braass) *n* latón *m*; cobre *m*, cobre amarillo; ~ **band** *n* charanga *f*

brassiere (bræ-siⁿ) *n* sujetador *m*, sostén *m*

brassware (*braass*-ᵘêⁿ) *n* cobres *mpl*

brave (breiv) *adj* valiente

Brazil (brö-*sil*) Brasil *m*

Brazilian (brö-*sil*-yön) *adj* brasileño

breach (briich) *n* brecha *f*

bread (brêd) *n* pan *m*; **wholemeal** ~ pan integral

breadth (brêdz) *n* ancho *m*

break (breik) *n* fractura *f*; descanso *m*

*break (breik) *v* *quebrar, quebrantar; ~ **down** averiarse; analizar

breakdown (*breik*-daun) *n* avería *f*; descompostura *fMe*

breakfast (*brêk*-fösst) *n* desayuno *m*

bream (briim) *n* (pl ~) brema *f*

breast (brêsst) *n* seno *m*

breaststroke (*brêsst*-sstrouk) *n* braza *f*

breath (brêz) *n* aliento *m*; aire *m*

breathe (briið) *v* respirar

breathing (*brii*-ðing) *n* respiración *f*

breed (briid) *n* raza *f*; especie *f*

*breed (briid) *v* recriar

breeze (briis) *n* brisa *f*

brew (bruu) *v* fabricar cerveza

brewery (*bruu*-ö-ri) *n* cervecería *f*

bribe (braib) *v* sobornar

bribery (*brai*-bö-ri) *n* soborno *m*

brick (brik) *n* ladrillo *m*

bricklayer (*brik*-leiⁿ) *n* albañil *m*

bride (braid) *n* novia *f*

bridegroom (*braid*-ghruum) *n* novio *m*

bridge (bridʒ) *n* puente *m*; bridge *m*

brief (briif) *adj* breve

briefcase (*briif*-keiss) *n* portafolio *m*

briefs (briifss) *pl* braga *f*, calzoncillos *mpl*

bright (brait) *adj* claro; reluciente; listo

brill (bril) *n* rodaballo *m*

brilliant (*bril*-yönt) *adj* brillante

brim (brim) *n* borde *m*

*bring (bring) *v* *traer; ~ **back** *devolver; ~ **up** educar; *introducir, levantar

brisk (brissk) *adj* vivo

Britain (*bri*-tön) Inglaterra *f*

British (*bri*-tiʃ) *adj* británico

Briton (*bri*-tön) *n* británico *m*; inglés *m*

broad (brood) *adj* ancho; amplio; general

broadcast (*brood*-kaasst) *n* transmisión *f*

*broadcast (*brood*-kaasst) *v* emitir

brochure (brou-ʃuⁿ) *n* folleto *m*

broke¹ (brouk) *v* (p break)

broke² (brouk) *adj* arruinado

broken (*brou*-kön) *adj* (pp break) estropeado, roto

broker (*brou*-kö) *n* corredor *m*

bronchitis (brong-*kai*-tiss) *n* bronquitis *f*

bronze (brons) *n* bronce *m*; *adj* de bronce

brooch (brouch) *n* broche *m*

brook (bruk) *n* arroyo *m*

broom (bruum) *n* escoba *f*

brothel (*bro*-zöl) *n* burdel *m*

brother (*bra*-ðö) *n* hermano *m*

brother-in-law (*bra*-ðö-rin-loo) *n* (pl brothers-) cuñado *m*

brought (broot) *v* (p, pp bring)

brown (braun) *adj* moreno

bruise (bruus) *n* moretón *m*, magulladura *f*; *v* magullar

brunette (bruu-*nêt*) *n* morena *f*

brush (braʃ) *n* cepillo *m*; brocha *f*; *v* sacar brillo, cepillar

brutal (*bruu*-töl) *adj* brutal

bubble (*ba*-böl) *n* burbuja *f*

bucket (*ba*-kit) *n* balde *m*

buckle (*ba*-köl) *n* hebilla *f*

bud (bad) *n* capullo *m*

budget (*ba*-dʒit) *n* presupuesto *m*

buffet (*bu*-fei) *n* buffet *m*

bug (bagh) *n* chinche *f*; escarabajo *m*; *nAm* insecto *m*

***build** (bild) *v* *construir

building (*bil*-ding) *n* edificio *m*

bulb (balb) *n* bulbo *m*; **light** ~ bombilla *f*; foco *mMe*

Bulgaria (bal-*ghêᵒ*-ri-ö) Bulgaria *f*

Bulgarian (bal-*ghêᵒ*-ri-ön) *adj* búlgaro

bulk (balk) *n* bulto *m*; mayoría *f*

bulky (*bal*-ki) *adj* voluminoso

bull (bul) *n* toro *m*

bullet (*bu*-lit) *n* bala *f*

bullfight (*bul*-fait) *n* corrida de toros

bullring (*bul*-ring) *n* plaza de toros

bump (bamp) *v* topetar; chocar; *dar golpes; *n* golpe *m*, topetón *n*

bumper (*bam*-pö) *n* parachoques *m*

bumpy (*bam*-pi) *adj* lleno de baches

bun (ban) *n* bollo *m*

bunch (banch) *n* ramo *m*; grupo *m*

bundle (*ban*-döl) *n* paquete *m*; *v* atar, liar

bunk (bangk) *n* camastro *m*

buoy (boi) *n* boya *f*

burden (*böö*-dön) *n* peso *m*

bureau (*byuᵒ*-rou) *n* (pl ~x, ~s) escritorio *m*; *nAm* cómoda *f*

bureaucracy (byuᵒ-*ro*-krö-ssi) *n* burocracia *f*

burglar (*böö*-ghlö) *n* ladrón *m*

burgle (*böö*-ghöl) *v* robar

burial (*bê*-ri-öl) *n* entierro *m*

burn (böön) *n* quemadura *f*

***burn** (böön) *v* quemar; pegarse

***burst** (böösst) *v* *reventar; *quebrar

bury (*bê*-ri) *v* *enterrar

bus (bass) *n* autobús *m*

bush (buʃ) *n* matorral *m*

business (*bis*-nöss) *n* negocios *mpl*, comercio *m*; empresa *f*, negocio *m*; ocupación *f*; asunto *m*; ~ **hours** horas hábiles, horas de oficina; ~ **trip** viaje de negocios; **on** ~ por asuntos de negocio

business-like (*bis*-niss-laik) *adj* práctico

businessman (*bis*-nöss-mön) *n* (pl -men) hombre de negocios

bust (basst) *n* busto *m*

bustle (*ba*-ssöl) *n* agitación *f*

busy (*bi*-si) *adj* ocupado; concurrido, atareado

but (bat) *conj* mas; pero; *prep* menos

butcher (*bu*-chö) *n* carnicero *m*

butter (*ba*-tö) *n* mantequilla *f*

butterfly (*ba*-tö-flai) *n* mariposa *f*; ~ **stroke** braza de mariposa

buttock (*ba*-tök) *n* nalga *m*

button (*ba*-tön) *n* botón *m*; *v* abrochar

buttonhole (*ba*-tön-houl) *n* ojal *m*

***buy** (bai) *v* comprar; *adquirir

buyer (*bai*-ö) *n* comprador *m*

by (bai) *prep* por; con; cerca de

by-pass (*bai*-paass) *n* cinturón *m*; *v* rodear

C

cab (kæb) *n* taxi *m*

cabaret (*kæ*-bö-rei) *n* cabaret *m*

cabbage (*kæ*-bidʒ) *n* col *m*

cab-driver (*kæb*-drai-vö) *n* taxista *m*

cabin (*kæ*-bin) *n* cabina *f*; cabaña *f*

cabinet (*kæ*-bi-nöt) *n* gabinete *m*

cable (*kei*-böl) *n* cable *m*; cablegrama *m*; *v* cablegrafiar

café (*kæ*-fei) *n* bar *m*

cafeteria (kæ-fö-*ti^ö*-ri-ö) *n* cafetería *f*

caffeine (*kæ*-fiin) *n* cafeína *f*

cage (keidʒ) *n* jaula *f*

cake (keik) *n* pastel *m*; pastelería *f*, tarta *f*, dulces

calamity (kö-*læ*-mö-ti) *n* desastre *m*, catástrofe *f*

calcium (*kæl*-ssi-öm) *n* calcio *m*

calculate (*kæl*-kyu-leit) *v* calcular

calculation (kæl-kyu-*lei*-ʃön) *n* cálculo *m*

calculator (*kæl*-kyu-lei-tö) *n* calculadora *f*

calendar (*kæ*-lön-dö) *n* calendario *m*

calf (kaaf) *n* (pl calves) ternero *m*; pantorrilla *f*; ~ **skin** becerro *m*

call (kool) *v* llamar; *n* llamada *f*; visita *f*; *be called llamarse; ~ names insultar; ~ on visitar; ~ up *Am* telefonear

callus (*kæ*-löss) *n* callo *m*

calm (kaam) *adj* tranquilo; ~ **down** calmar

calorie (*kæ*-lö-ri) *n* caloría *f*

Calvinism (*kæl*-vi-ni-söm) *n* calvinismo *m*

came (keim) *v* (p come)

camel (*kæ*-möl) *n* camello *m*

cameo (*kæ*-mi-ou) *n* (pl ~s) camafeo *m*

camera (*kæ*-mö-rö) *n* cámara fotográfica; cámara *f*; ~ **shop** negocio fotográfico

camp (kæmp) *n* campamento *m*; *v* acampar

campaign (kæm-*pein*) *n* campaña *f*

camp-bed (kæmp-*bêd*) *n* catre de campaña, cama de tijera

camper (*kæm*-pö) *n* acampador *m*

camping (*kæm*-ping) *n* camping *m*; ~ **site** camping *m*, lugar de camping

camshaft (*kæm*-ʃaaft) *n* árbol de levas

can (kæn) *n* lata *f*; ~ **opener** abrelatas *m*

***can** (kæn) *v* *poder

Canada (*kæ*-nö-dö) Canadá *m*

Canadian (kö-*nei*-di-ön) *adj* canadiense

canal (kö-*næl*) *n* canal *m*

canary (kö-*nê^ö*-ri) *n* canario *m*

cancel (*kæn*-ssöl) *v* cancelar; anular

cancellation (kæn-ssö-*lei*-ʃön) *n* cancelación *f*

cancer (*kæn*-ssö) *n* cáncer *m*

candelabrum (kæn-dö-*laa*-bröm) *n* (pl -bra) candelabro *m*

candidate (*kæn*-di-döt) *n* candidato *m*, interesado *m*

candle (*kæn*-döl) *n* candela *f*

candy (*kæn*-di) *nAm* bombón *m*; dulces, golosinas

cane (kein) *n* caña *f*; bastón *m*

canister (*kæ*-ni-sstö) *n* caja metálica, lata *f*

canoe (kö-*nuu*) *n* canoa *f*

canteen (kæn-*tiin*) *n* cantina *f*

canvas (*kæn*-vöss) *n* lona *f*

cap (kæp) *n* gorra *f*, gorro *m*

capable (*kei*-pö-böl) *adj* capaz

capacity (kö-*pæ*-ssö-ti) *n* capacidad

f; potencia *f*; competencia *f*
cape (keip) *n* capa *f*; cabo *m*
capital (kæ-pi-töl) *n* capital *f*; capital *m*; *adj* importante, capital; ~ **letter** mayúscula *f*
capitalism (kæ-pi-tö-li-söm) *n* capitalismo *m*
capitulation (kö-pi-tyu-*lei*-ʃön) *n* capitulación *f*
capsule (kæp-ssyuul) *n* cápsula *f*
captain (kæp-tin) *n* capitán *m*; comandante *m*
capture (kæp-chö) *v* coger preso, capturar; conquistar; *n* captura *f*; conquista *f*
car (kaa) *n* coche *m*; carro *m Me*; ~ **hire** alquiler de coches; ~ **park** parque de estacionamiento
carafe (kö-*ræf*) *n* garrafa *f*
caramel (kæ-rö-möl) *n* caramelo *m*
carat (kæ-röt) *n* quilate *m*
caravan (kæ-rö-væn) *n* caravana *f*; carro de gitanos
carburettor (kaa-byu-*rê*-tö) *n* carburador *m*
card (kaad) *n* tarjeta *f*; tarjeta postal
cardboard (kaad-bood) *n* cartón *m*; *adj* de cartón
cardigan (kaa-di-ghön) *n* chaqueta *f*
cardinal (kaa-di-nöl) *n* cardenal *m*; *adj* cardinal, principal
care (kêᵒ) *n* cuidado *m*; ~ **about** preocuparse de; ~ **for** gustar; *take ~ of cuidar de
career (kö-*riᵒ*) *n* carrera *f*
carefree (kêᵒ-frii) *adj* despreocupado
careful (kêᵒ-föl) *adj* cuidadoso; escrupuloso
careless (kêᵒ-löss) *adj* indiferente, negligente
caretaker (kêᵒ-tei-kö) *n* guardián *m*
cargo (kaa-ghou) *n* (pl ~es) carga *f*
carnival (kaa-ni-völ) *n* carnaval *m*
carp (kaap) *n* (pl ~) carpa *f*

carpenter (kaa-pin-tö) *n* carpintero *m*
carpet (kaa-pit) *n* alfombra *f*
carriage (kæ-ridʒ) *n* vagón *m*; coche *m*, carruaje *m*
carriageway (kæ-ridʒ-ᵘei) *n* calzada *f*
carrot (kæ-röt) *n* zanahoria *f*
carry (kæ-ri) *v* llevar; *conducir; ~ **on** continuar; *proseguir; ~ **out** realizar
carry-cot (kæ-ri-kot) *n* cuna de viaje
cart (kaat) *n* carro *m*
cartilage (kaa-ti-lidʒ) *n* cartílago *m*
carton (kaa-tön) *n* caja de cartón; cartón *m*
cartoon (kaa-*tuun*) *n* dibujos animados
cartridge (kaa-tridʒ) *n* cartucho *m*
carve (kaav) *v* trinchar; entallar, tallar
carving (kaa-ving) *n* talla *f*
case (keiss) *n* caso *m*; causa *f*; valija *f*; estuche *m*; **attaché** ~ portafolio *m*; **in** ~ si; **in** ~ **of** en caso de
cash (kæʃ) *n* dinero contante, efectivo *m*; *v* cobrar,*hacer efectivo; ~ **dispenser** cajero automático
cashier (kæ-*ʃiᵒ*) *n* cajero *m*; cajera *f*
cashmere (kæʃ-miᵒ) *n* casimir *f*
casino (kö-*ssii*-nou) *n* casino *m*
cask (kaassk) *n* barril *m*, tonel *m*
cast (kaasst) *n* echada *f*
***cast** (kaasst) *v* lanzar; **cast iron** hierro fundido
castle (kaa-ssöl) *n* castillo *m*
casual (kæ-ʒu-öl) *adj* informal; de paso, por casualidad
casualty (kæ-ʒu-öl-ti) *n* víctima *f*
cat (kæt) *n* gato *m*
catacomb (kæ-tö-koum) *n* catacumba *f*
catalogue (kæ-tö-logh) *n* catálogo *m*
catarrh (kö-*taa*) *n* catarro *m*
catastrophe (kö-*tæ*-sströ-fi) *n* catástrofe *f*

*catch (kæch) v coger; sorprender

category (kǽ-ti-ghö-ri) n categoría f

cathedral (kö-zii-dröl) n catedral f

catholic (kǽ-zö-lik) adj católico

cattle (kǽ-töl) pl ganado m

caught (koot) v (p, pp catch)

cauliflower (ko-li-flauᵒ) n coliflor f

cause (koos) v causar; provocar; n causa f; motivo m; ~ **to** *hacer

causeway (koos-ᵘei) n calzada f

caution (koo-∫ön) n cautela f; v *advertir

cautious (koo-∫öss) adj prudentc

cave (keiv) n cueva f; grieta f

cavern (kǽ-vön) n cueva f

caviar (kǽ-vi-aa) n caviar m

cavity (kǽ-vö-ti) n cavidad f

cease (ssiiss) v cesar

ceiling (ssii-ling) n cielo raso

celebrate (ssê-li-breit) v celebrar

celebration (ssê-li-brei-∫ön) n celebración f

celebrity (ssi-lê-brö-ti) n cclcbridad f

celery (ssê-lö-ri) n apio m

celibacy (ssê-li-bö-ssi) n celibato m

cell (ssêl) n celda f

cellar (ssê-lö) n sótano m

cellophane (ssê-lö-fein) n celofán m

cement (ssi-mênt) n cemento m

cemetery (ssê-mi-tri) n cementerio m

censorship (ssên-ssö-∫ip) n censura f

centigrade (ssên-ti-ghreid) adj centígrado

centimetre (ssên-ti-mii-tö) n centímetro m

central (ssên-tröl) adj central; ~ **heating** calefacción central; ~ **station** estación central

centralize (ssên-trö-lais) v centralizar

centre (ssên-tö) n centro m

century (ssên-chö-ri) n siglo m

ceramics (ssi-rǽ-mikss) pl cerámica f

ceremony (ssê-rö-mö-ni) n ceremonia f

certain (ssöö-tön) adj cierto

certificate (ssö-ti-fi-köt) n certificado m; certificación f, acta f, diploma m

chain (chein) n cadena f

chair (chêᵒ) n silla f

chairman (chêᵒ-mön) n (pl -men) presidente m

chalet (∫æ-lei) n chalet m

chalk (chook) n creta f

challenge (chæ-löndʒ) v desafiar; n reto m

chamber (cheim-bö) n cuarto m

chambermaid (cheim-bö-meid) n doncella f

champagne (∫æm-pein) n champán m

champion (chæm-pyön) n campeón m; defensor m

chance (chaanss) n azar m; oportunidad f, ocasión f; riesgo m; suerte f; **by** ~ por casualidad

change (cheindʒ) v modificar, cambiar; mudarse; *hacer trasbordo; n modificación f, cambio m; moneda f

channel (chæ-nöl) n canal m; **English Channel** Canal de la Mancha

chaos (kei-oss) n caos m

chaotic (kei-o-tik) adj caótico

chap (chæp) n hombre m

chapel (chæ-pöl) n iglesia f, capilla f

chaplain (chæ-plin) n capellán m

character (kæ-rök-tö) n carácter m

characteristic (kæ-rök-tö-ri-sstik) adj típico, característico; n característica f; rasgo característico

characterize (kæ-rök-tö-rais) v caracterizar

charcoal (chaa-koul) n carbón de leña

charge (chaadʒ) v *pedir; cargar; acusar; n precio m; carga f; acusación f; ~ **plate** Am tarjeta de crédito; **free of** ~ gratuito; **in** ~ **of** encargado de; ***take** ~ **of** encargarse de

charity (*chæ*-rö-ti) *n* caridad *f*

charm (chaam) *n* encanto *m*; amuleto *m*

charming (*chaa*-ming) *adj* encantador

chart (chaat) *n* tabla *f*; gráfico *m*; carta marina; **conversion** ~ tabla de conversión

chase (cheiss) *v* cazar; expulsar, ahuyentar; *n* caza *f*

chasm (*kæ*-söm) *n* grieta *f*

chassis (*fæ*-ssi) *n* (pl ~) chasis *m*

chaste (cheisst) *adj* casto

chat (chæt) *v* charlar; *n* charla *f*

chatterbox (*chæ*-tö-bokss) *n* charlatán *m*

chauffeur (*fou*-fö) *n* chófer *m*

cheap (chiip) *adj* barato; económico

cheat (chiit) *v* engañar; estafar

check (chêk) *v* controlar, verificar; *n* escaque *m*; *nAm* cuenta *f*; cheque *m*; **check!** ¡jaque!; ~ **in** inscribirse; ~ **out** *despedirse

check-book (*chêk*-buk) *nAm* talonario *m*

checkerboard (*chê*-kö-bood) *nAm* tablero de ajedrez

checkroom (*chêk*-ruum) *nAm* guardarropa *m*

check-up (*chê*-kap) *n* reconocimiento *m*

cheek (chiik) *n* mejilla *f*

cheek-bone (*chiik*-boun) *n* pómulo *m*

cheer (chiö) *v* aclamar; ~ **up** alegrar

cheerful (*chiö*-föl) *adj* alegre

cheese (chiis) *n* queso *m*

chef (fêf) *n* jefe de cocina

chemical (*kê*-mi-köl) *adj* químico

chemist (*kê*-misst) *n* farmacéutico *m*; **chemist's** farmacia *f*; droguería *f*

chemistry (*kê*-mi-sstri) *n* química *f*

cheque (chêk) *n* cheque *m*

cheque-book (*chêk*-buk) *n* talonario *m*

chequered (*chê*-köd) *adj* a cuadros, cuadriculado

cherry (*chê*-ri) *n* cereza *f*

chess (chêss) *n* ajedrez *m*

chest (chêsst) *n* pecho *m*; arca *f*; ~ **of drawers** cómoda *f*

chestnut (*chêss*-nat) *n* castaña *f*

chew (chuu) *v* masticar

chewing-gum (*chuu*-ing-gham) *n* goma de mascar, chicle *m*

chic (fik) *adj* elegante

chicken (*chi*-kin) *n* pollo *m*

chickenpox (*chi*-kin-pokss) *n* varicela *f*

chief (chiif) *n* jefe *m*; *adj* principal

chiefly (*chiif*-li) *adv* sobre todo

chieftain (*chiif*-tön) *n* jefe *m*

chilblain (*chil*-blein) *n* sabañón *m*

child (chaild) *n* (pl children) niño *m*

childbirth (*chaild*-bööz) *n* parto *m*

childhood (*chaild*-hud) *n* infancia *f*

Chile (*chi*-li) Chile *m*

Chilean (*chi*-li-ön) *adj* chileno

chill (chil) *n* escalofrío *m*

chilly (*chi*-li) *adj* fresco

chimes (chaims) *pl* carillón *m*

chimney (*chim*-ni) *n* chimenea *f*

chin (chin) *n* barbilla *f*

China (*chai*-nö) China *f*

china (*chai*-nö) *n* porcelana *f*

Chinese (chai-*niis*) *adj* chino

chink (chingk) *n* hendidura *f*

chip (chip) *n* astilla *f*; ficha *f*; *v* cortar, astillar; **chips** patatas fritas

chiropodist (ki-*ro*-pö-disst) *n* pedicuro *m*

chisel (*chi*-söl) *n* cincel *m*

chives (chaivs) *pl* cebollino *m*

chlorine (*kloo*-riin) *n* cloro *m*

chocolate (*cho*-klöt) *n* chocolate *m*; bombón *m*

choice (choiss) *n* elección *f*; selección *f*

choir (k^{u}ai^ö) *n* coro *m*

choke (chouk) v sofocarse; estrangular; n starter m

*choose (chuus) v escoger

chop (chop) n chuleta f; v tajar

Christ (kraisst) Cristo

christen (kri-ssön) v bautizar

christening (kri-ssö-ning) n bautizo m

Christian (kriss-chön) adj cristiano; ~ name nombre de pila

Christmas (kriss-möss) Navidad f

chromium (krou-mi-öm) n cromo m

chronic (kro-nik) adj crónico

chronological (kro-nö-lo-dʒi-köl) adj cronológico

chuckle (cha-köl) v *reírse entre dientes

chunk (changk) n trozo m

church (chööch) n iglesia f

churchyard (chööch-yaad) n cementerio m

cigar (ssi-ghaa) n puro m; ~ shop estanco m

cigarette (ssi-ghö-rêt) n cigarrillo m; ~ tobacco picadura f

cigarette-case (ssi-ghö-rêt-keiss) n pitillera f

cigarette-holder (ssi-ghö-rêt-houl-dö) n boquilla f

cigarette-lighter (ssi-ghö-rêt-lai-tö) n encendedor m

cinema (ssi-nö-mö) n cinematógrafo m

cinnamon (ssi-nö-mön) n canela f

circle (ssöö-köl) n círculo m; balcón m; v rodear, circundar

circulation (ssöö-kyu-lei-ʃön) n circulación f; circulación de la sangre

circumstance (ssöö-köm-sstænss) n circunstancia f

circus (ssöö-köss) n circo m

citizen (ssi-ti-sön) n ciudadano m

citizenship (ssi-ti-sön-ʃip) n ciudadanía f

city (ssi-ti) n ciudad f

civic (ssi-vik) adj cívico

civil (ssi-völ) adj civil; cortés; ~ law derecho civil; ~ servant funcionario m

civilian (ssi-vil-yön) adj civil; n paisano m

civilization (ssi-vö-lai-sei-ʃön) n civilización f

civilized (ssi-vö-laisd) adj civilizado

claim (kleim) v reivindicar, reclamar; afirmar; n reivindicación f, pretensión f

clamp (klæmp) n mordaza f; grapa f

clap (klæp) v aplaudir

clarify (klæ-ri-fai) v aclarar, clarificar

class (klaass) n clase f

classical (klæ-ssi-köl) adj clásico

classify (klæ-ssi-fai) v clasificar

class-mate (klaass-meit) n compañero de clase

classroom (klaass-ruum) n clase f

clause (kloos) n cláusula f

claw (kloo) n garra f

clay (klei) n arcilla f

clean (kliin) adj puro, limpio; v limpiar

cleaning (klii-ning) n limpieza f; ~ fluid quitamanchas m

clear (kliö) adj claro; v limpiar

clearing (kliö-ring) n claro m

cleft (klêft) n grieta f

clergyman (klöö-dʒi-mön) n (pl -men) pastor m; clérigo m

clerk (klaak) n empleado de oficina, oficinista m; escribano m; secretario m

clever (klê-vö) adj inteligente; astuto, listo

client (klai-önt) n cliente m

cliff (klif) n acantilado m, farallón m

climate (klai-mit) n clima m

climb (klaim) v trepar; n subida f

clinic (kli-nik) n clínica f

cloak (klouk) n capa f

cloakroom (*klouk*-ruum) *n* guardarropa *m*

clock (klok) *n* reloj *m*; **at ... o'clock** a las ...

cloister (*kloi*-sstö) *n* convento *m*

close¹ (klous) *v* *cerrar

close² (klouss) *adj* cercano

closet (*klo*-sit) *n* armario *m*

cloth (kloz) *n* tela *f*; paño *m*

clothes (klouðs) *pl* ropa *f*, vestidos *mpl*

clothes-brush (*klouðs*-braʃ) *n* cepillo de la ropa

clothing (*klou*-ðing) *n* vestido *m*

cloud (klaud) *n* nube *f*

cloud-burst (*klaud*-böösst) *n* chaparrón *m*

cloudy (*klau*-di) *adj* cubierto, nublado

clover (*klou*-vö) *n* trébol *m*

clown (klaun) *n* payaso *m*

club (klab) *n* club *m*; círculo *m*, asociación *f*; porra *f*, garrote *m*

clumsy (*klam*-si) *adj* torpe

clutch (klach) *n* embrague *m*; apretón *m*

coach (kouch) *n* autobús *m*; vagón *m*; carroza *f*; entrenador *m*

coachwork (*kouch*-ᵁöök) *n* carrocería *f*

coagulate (kou-*æ*-ghyu-leit) *v* coagularse

coal (koul) *n* carbón *m*

coarse (kooss) *adj* burdo; grosero

coast (kousst) *n* costa *f*

coat (kout) *n* sobretodo *m*, abrigo *m*

coat-hanger (*kout*-hæng-ö) *n* percha *f*

cobweb (*kob*-ᵁêb) *n* tela de araña

cocaine (kou-*kein*) *n* cocaína *f*

cock (kok) *n* gallo *m*

cocktail (*kok*-teil) *n* cóctel *m*

coconut (*kou*-kö-nat) *n* coco *m*

cod (kod) *n* (pl ~) bacalao *m*

code (koud) *n* código *m*

coffee (*ko*-fi) *n* café *m*

cognac (*ko*-nyæk) *n* coñac *m*

coherence (kou-*hi*ᵈ-rönss) *n* coherencia *f*

coin (koin) *n* moneda *f*

coincide (kou-in-*ssaid*) *v* coincidir

cold (kould) *adj* frío; *n* frío *m*; resfriado *m*; **catch a ~** resfriarse

collapse (kö-*læpss*) *v* desplomarse, derrumbarse

collar (*ko*-lö) *n* collar *m*; cuello *m*; **~ stud** botón del cuello

collarbone (*ko*-lö-boun) *n* clavícula *f*

colleague (*ko*-liigh) *n* colega *m*

collect (kö-*lêkt*) *v* juntar; recoger; *hacer una colecta

collection (kö-*lêk*-ʃön) *n* colección *f*; recogida *f*

collective (kö-*lêk*-tiv) *adj* colectivo

collector (kö-*lêk*-tö) *n* coleccionista *m*; colector *m*

college (*ko*-lidʒ) *n* colegio *m*

collide (kö-*laid*) *v* chocar

collision (kö-*li*-ʒön) *n* colisión *f*

Colombia (kö-*lom*-bi-ö) Colombia *f*

Colombian (kö-*lom*-bi-ön) *adj* colombiano

colonel (*köö*-nöl) *n* coronel *m*

colony (*ko*-lö-ni) *n* colonia *f*

colour (*ka*-lö) *n* color *m*; *v* colorear; **~ film** película en colores

colourant (*ka*-lö-rönt) *n* colorante *m*

colour-blind (*ka*-lö-blaind) *adj* daltoniano

coloured (*ka*-löd) *adj* de color

colourful (*ka*-lö-föl) *adj* colorado, lleno de color

column (*ko*-löm) *n* columna *f*

coma (*kou*-mö) *n* coma *m*

comb (koum) *v* peinar; *n* peine *m*

combat (*kom*-bæt) *n* lucha *f*, combate *m*; *v* combatir

combination (kom-bi-*nei*-ʃön) *n* combinación *f*

combine (köm-*bain*) *v* combinar; unir

*come (kam) v *venir; ~ across *encontrar; hallar

comedian (kö-mii-di-ön) n comediante m; cómico m

comedy (ko-mö-di) n comedia f; musical ~ comedia musical

comfort (kam-föt) n comodidad f, confort m; consuelo m; v *consolar

comfortable (kam-fö-tö-böl) adj confortable

comic (ko-mik) adj cómico

comics (ko-mikss) pl tebeo m

coming (ka-ming) n llegada f

comma (ko-mö) n coma f

command (kö-maand) v mandar; n orden f

commander (kö-maan-dö) n comandante m

commemoration (kö-mê-mö-rei-jön) n conmemoración f

commence (kö-mênss) v *comenzar

comment (ko-mênt) n comentario m; v comentar

commerce (ko-mööss) n comercio m

commercial (kö-möö-jöl) adj comercial; n anuncio publicitario; ~ law derecho comercial

commission (kö-mi-jön) n comisión f

commit (kö-mit) v confiar, entregar; cometer

committee (kö-mi-ti) n comisión f, comité m

common (ko-mön) adj común; usual; ordinario

commune (ko-myuun) n comuna f

communicate (kö-myuu-ni-keit) v comunicar

communication (kö-myuu-ni-kei-jön) n comunicación f

communiqué (kö-myuu-ni-kei) n comunicado m

communism (ko-myu-ni-söm) n comunismo m

community (kö-myuu-nö-ti) n sociedad f, vecindario m

commuter (kö-myuu-tö) n suburbano m

compact (kom-pækt) adj compacto

compact disc (kom-pækt dissk) n disco compacto m; ~ player reproductor de discos compactos

companion (köm-pæ-nyön) n compañero m

company (kam-pö-ni) n compañía f; sociedad f

comparative (köm-pæ-rö-tiv) adj relativo

compare (köm-pêö) v comparar

comparison (köm-pæ-ri-ssön) n comparación f

compartment (köm-paat-mönt) n compartimento m

compass (kam-pöss) n brújula f

compel (köm-pêl) v compeler

compensate (kom-pön-sseit) v compensar

compensation (kom-pön-ssei-jön) n compensación f; indemnización f

compete (köm-piit) v *competir

competition (kom-pö-ti-jön) n concurso m; competencia f

competitor (köm-pê-ti-tör) n competidor m

compile (köm-pail) v compilar

complain (köm-plein) v quejarse

complaint (köm-pleint) n queja f

complete (köm-pliit) adj completo; v completar

completely (köm-pliit-li) adv enteramente, totalmente, completamente

complex (kom-plêkss) n complejo m; adj complejo

complexion (köm-plêk-jön) n tez f

complicated (kom-pli-kei-tid) adj complicado

compliment (kom-pli-mönt) n cumpli-

miento *m*; *v* cumplimentar
compose (köm-*pous*) *v* *componer
composer (köm-*pou*-sö) *n* compositor *m*
composition (kom-pö-*si*-ʃön) *n* composición *f*
comprehensive (kom-pri-*hên*-ssiv) *adj* extenso
comprise (köm-*prais*) *v* comprender
compromise (*kom*-prö-mais) *n* compromiso *m*
compulsory (köm-*pal*-ssö-ri) *adj* obligatorio
computer (köm-*pyu*-tö) *n* ordenador *m*
comrade (*kom*-reid) *n* camarada *m*
conceal (kön-*ssiil*) *v* disimular
conceited (kön-*ssii*-tid) *adj* presuntuoso
conceive (kön-*ssiiv*) *v* *concebir, *entender; imaginar
concentrate (*kon*-ssön-treit) *v* concentrarse
concentration (kon-ssön-*trei*-ʃön) *n* concentración *f*
concern (kön-*ssöön*) *v* *concernir, atañer; *n* preocupación *f*; asunto *m*; empresa *f*, consorcio *m*
concerned (kön-*ssöönd*) *adj* preocupado; interesado
concerning (kön-*ssöö*-ning) *prep* en lo que se refiere a, concerniente a
concert (*kon*-ssöt) *n* concierto *m*; ~ **hall** sala de conciertos
concession (kön-*ssê*-ʃön) *n* concesión *f*
concierge (kong-ssi-*ê*ᵒʒ) *n* conserje *m*
concise (kön-*ssaiss*) *adj* conciso
conclusion (köng-*kluu*-ʒön) *n* conclusión *f*
concrete (*kong*-kriit) *adj* concreto; *n* hormigón *m*
concurrence (köng-*ka*-rönss) *n* coincidencia *f*

concussion (köng-*ka*-ʃön) *n* conmoción cerebral
condemn (kön-*dêm*) *v* condenar
condition (kön-*di*-ʃön) *n* condición *f*; estado *m*; circunstancia *f*
conditional (kön-*di*-ʃö-nöl) *adj* condicional
conditioner (kön-*di*-ʃö-nöl) *n* suavizante de cabello *m*
condom (*kon*-dom) *n* preservativo *m*
conduct (*kon*-dakt) *n* conducta *f*
conductor (kön-*dak*-tö) *n* cobrador *m*; director *m*; conductor *m Me*
conference (*kon*-fö-rönss) *n* conferencia *f*
confess (kön-*fêss*) *v* *reconocer; *confesarse; profesar
confession (kön-*fê*-ʃön) *n* confesión *f*
confidence (*kon*-fi-dönss) *n* confianza *f*
confident (*kon*-fi-dönt) *adj* lleno de confianza
confidential (kon-fi-*dên*-ʃöl) *adj* confidencial
confirm (kön-*fööm*) *v* confirmar
confirmation (kon-fö-*mei*-ʃön) *n* confirmación *f*
confiscate (*kon*-fi-sskeit) *v* embargar, confiscar
conflict (*kon*-flikt) *n* conflicto *m*
confuse (kön-*fyuus*) *v* confundir; **confused** *adj* confuso
confusion (kön-*fyuu*-ʒön) *n* confusión *f*
congratulate (köng-*ghræ*-chu-leit) *v* felicitar
congratulation (köng-ghræ-chu-*lei*-ʃön) *n* felicitación *f*
congregation (kong-ghri-*ghei*-ʃön) *n* comunidad *f*, congregación *f*
congress (*kong*-ghröss) *n* congreso *m*
connect (kö-*nêkt*) *v* conectar
connection (kö-*nêk*-ʃön) *n* relación *f*; conexión *f*; enlace *m*

connoisseur (ko-nö-*ssöö*) n perito m

connotation (ko-nö-*tei*-ʃön) n connotación f

conquer (*kong*-kö) v conquistar; vencer

conqueror (*kong*-kö-rö) n conquistador m

conquest (*kong*-kᵘêsst) n conquista f

conscience (*kon*-ʃönss) n conciencia f

conscious (*kon*-ʃöss) adj consciente

consciousness (*kon*-ʃöss-nöss) n conciencia f

conscript (*kon*-sskript) n quinto m

consent (kön-*ssênt*) v *consentir; n consentimiento m

consequence (*kon*-ssi-kᵘönss) n consecuencia f

consequently (*kon*-ssi-kᵘönt-li) adv por consiguiente

conservative (kön-*ssöö*-vö-tiv) adj conservador

consider (kön-*ssi*-dö) v considerar; opinar

considerable (kön-*ssi* dö-rö-böl) adj considerable; importante, notable

considerate (kön-*ssi*-dö-röt) adj considerado

consideration (kön-ssi-dö-*rei*-ʃön) n consideración f; atención f

considering (kön-*ssi*-dö-ring) prep considerando

consignment (kön-*ssain*-mönt) n envío m

consist of (kön-*ssisst*) constar de

conspire (kön-*sspaiᵒ*) v conspirar

constant (*kon*-sstönt) adj constante

constipated (*kon*-ssti-pei-tid) adj estreñido

constipation (kon-ssti-*pei*-ʃön) n estreñimiento m

constituency (kön-*ssti*-chu-ön-ssi) n distrito electoral

constitution (kon-ssti-*tyuu*-ʃön) n constitución f

construct (kön-*sstrakt*) v *construir; edificar

construction (kön-*sstrak*-ʃön) n construcción f; edificio m

consul (*kon*-ssöl) n cónsul m

consulate (*kon*-ssyu-löt) n consulado m

consult (kön-*ssalt*) v consultar

consultation (kön-ssöl-*tei*-ʃön) n consulta f; ~ hours n horas de consulta

consumer (kön-*ssyuu*-mö) n consumidor m

contact (*kon*-tækt) n contacto m; v *ponerse en contacto con; ~ lenses lentillas fpl

contagious (kön-*tei*-dʒöss) adj contagioso

contain (kön-*tein*) v *contener; comprender

container (kön-*tei*-nö) n receptáculo m; contenedor m

contemporary (kön *têm*-pö-rö-ri) adj contemporáneo; de entonces; n contemporáneo m

contempt (kön-*têmpt*) n desprecio m, menosprecio m

content (kön-*tênt*) adj contento

contents (*kon*-têntss) pl contenido m

contest (*kon*-têsst) n lucha f; concurso m

continent (*kon*-ti-nönt) n continente m

continental (kon-ti-*nên*-töl) adj continental

continual (kön-*ti*-nyu-öl) adj continuo

continue (kön-*ti*-nyuu) v continuar; *proseguir, durar

continuous (kön-*ti*-nyu-öss) adj continuo, ininterrumpido

contour (*kon*-tuᵒ) n contorno m

contraceptive (kon-trö-*ssêp*-tiv) n anticonceptivo m

contract¹ (*kon*-trækt) n contrato m

contract[2] (kön-*trækt*) *v* atrapar

contractor (kön-*træk*-tö) *n* contratista *m*

contradict (kon-trö-*dikt*) *v* *contradecir

contradictory (kon-trö-*dik*-tö-ri) *adj* contradictorio

contrary (*kon*-trö-ri) *n* contrario *m*; *adj* contrario; **on the ~** al contrario

contrast (*kon*-traasst) *n* contraste *m*; diferencia *f*

contribution (kon-tri-*byuu*-ʃön) *n* contribución *f*

control (kön-*troul*) *n* control *m*; *v* controlar

controversial (kon-trö-*vöö*-ʃöl) *adj* controvertido, controvertible

convenience (kön-*vii*-nyönss) *n* comodidad *f*

convenient (kön-*vii*-nyönt) *adj* cómodo; adecuado, conveniente

convent (*kon*-vönt) *n* convento *m*

conversation (kon-vö-*ssei*-ʃön) *n* conversación *f*

convert (kön-*vööt*) *v* *convertir

convict[1] (kön-*vikt*) *v* convencer

convict[2] (*kon*-vikt) *n* condenado *m*

conviction (kön-*vik*-ʃön) *n* convencimiento *m*; condena *f*

convince (kön-*vinss*) *v* convencer

convulsion (kön-*val*-ʃön) *n* convulsión *f*

cook (kuk) *n* cocinero *m*; *v* cocinar; guisar, preparar

cooker (*ku*-kö) *n* cocina *f*; **gas ~** cocina de gas

cookery-book (*ku*-kö-ri-buk) *n* libro de cocina

cookie (*ku*-ki) *nAm* bizcocho *m*

cool (kuul) *adj* fresco; **cooling system** sistema de refrigeración

co-operation (kou-o-pö-*rei*-ʃön) *n* cooperación *f*; colaboración *f*

co-operative (kou-o-pö-rö-tiv) *adj*

**cooperativo; cooperador; *n* cooperativa *f*

co-ordinate (kou-*oo*-di-neit) *v* coordinar

co-ordination (kou-oo-di-*nei*-ʃön) *n* coordinación *f*

copper (*ko*-pö) *n* cobre *m*

copy (*ko*-pi) *n* copia *f*; ejemplar *m*; *v* copiar; imitar; **carbon ~** copia *f*

coral (*ko*-röl) *n* coral *m*

cord (kood) *n* cuerda *f*; cordón *m*

cordial (*koo*-di-öl) *adj* cordial

corduroy (*koo*-dö-roi) *n* pana *f*

core (koo) *n* núcleo *m*; corazón *m*

cork (kook) *n* corcho *m*; tapón *m*

corkscrew (*kook*-sskruu) *n* sacacorchos *mpl*

corn (koon) *n* grano *m*; cereales *mpl*, trigo *m*; callo *m*; **~ on the cob** maíz en la mazorca

corner (*koo*-nö) *n* esquina *f*

cornfield (*koon*-fiild) *n* trigal *m*

corpse (koopss) *n* cadáver *m*

corpulent (*koo*-pyu-lönt) *adj* corpulento; grueso, obeso

correct (kö-*rêkt*) *adj* correcto, justo; *v* *corregir

correction (kö-*rêk*-ʃön) *n* corrección *f*; rectificación *f*

correctness (kö-*rêkt*-nöss) *n* exactitud *f*

correspond (ko-ri-*sspond*) *v* corresponderse; corresponder

correspondence (ko-ri-*sspon*-dönss) *n* correspondencia *f*

correspondent (ko-ri-*sspon*-dönt) *n* corresponsal *m*

corridor (*ko*-ri-doo) *n* pasillo *m*

corrupt (kö-*rapt*) *adj* corrupto; *v* corromper

corruption (kö-*rap*-ʃön) *n* corrupción *f*

corset (*koo*-ssit) *n* corsé *m*

cosmetics (kos-*mê*-tikss) *pl* productos

cosméticos, cosméticos *mpl*

cost (kosst) *n* coste *m*; precio *m*

***cost** (kosst) *v* *costar

cosy (*kou*-si) *adj* íntimo, confortable

cot (kot) *nAm* cama de tijera

cottage (*ko*-tidʒ) *n* casa de campo

cotton (*ko*-tön) *n* algodón *m*; de algodón

cotton-wool (*ko*-tön-ᵘul) *n* algodón *m*

couch (kauch) *n* diván *m*

cough (kof) *n* tos *f*; *v* toser

could (kud) *v* (p can)

council (*kaun*-ssöl) *n* consejo *m*

councillor (*kaun*-ssö-lö) *n* consejero *m*

counsel (*kaun*-ssöl) *n* consejo *m*

counsellor (*kaun*-ssö-lö) *n* consejero *m*

count (kaunt) *v* *contar; adicionar; *incluir; considerar; *n* conde *m*

counter (*kaun*-tö) *n* mostrador *m*; barra *f*

counterfeit (*kaun*-tö-fiit) *v* falsificar

counterfoil (*kaun*-tö-foil) *n* talón *m*

counterpane (*kaun*-tö-pein) *n* colcha *f*

countess (*kaun*-tiss) *n* condesa *f*

country (*kan*-tri) *n* país *m*; campo *m*; región *f*; ~ **house** quinta *f*

countryman (*kan*-tri-mön) *n* (pl -men) compatriota *m*

countryside (*kan*-tri-ssaid) *n* campo *m*

county (*kaun*-ti) *n* condado *m*

couple (*ka*-pöl) *n* pareja *f*

coupon (*kuu*-pon) *n* cupón *m*

courage (*ka*-ridʒ) *n* valor *m*

courageous (kö-*rei*-dʒöss) *adj* valiente

course (kooss) *n* rumbo *m*; plato *m*; curso *m*; **intensive** ~ curso intensivo; **of** ~ por supuesto

court (koot) *n* tribunal *m*; corte *f*

courteous (*köö*-ti-öss) *adj* cortés

cousin (*ka*-sön) *n* prima *f*, primo *m*

cover (*ka*-vö) *v* cubrir; *n* refugio *m*;

tapa *f*; cubierta *f*; ~ **charge** precio del cubierto

cow (kau) *n* vaca *f*

coward (*kau*-öd) *n* cobarde *m*

cowardly (*kau*-öd-li) *adj* cobarde

cow-hide (*kau*-haid) *n* cuero vacuno

crab (kræb) *n* cangrejo *m*

crack (kræk) *n* crujido *m*; hendidura *f*; *v* crujir; *quebrar, *reventar

cradle (*krei*-döl) *n* cuna *f*

cramp (kræmp) *n* calambre *m*

crane (krein) *n* grúa *f*

crankcase (*krængk*-keiss) *n* cárter *m*

crankshaft (*krængk*-ʃaaft) *n* cigüeñal *m*

crash (kræʃ) *n* choque *m*; *v* chocar; precipitarse; ~ **barrier** barrera de protección

crate (kreit) *n* caja *f*

crater (*krei*-tö) *n* cráter *m*

crawl (krool) *v* arrastrarse; *n* crawl *m*

craze (kreis) *n* manía *f*

crazy (*krei*-si) *adj* loco

creak (kriik) *v* crujir

cream (kriim) *n* crema *f*; nata *f*; *adj* de color crema

creamy (*krii*-mi) *adj* cremoso

crease (kriiss) *v* *plegar; *n* raya *f*; pliegue *m*

create (kri-*eit*) *v* crear

creature (*krii*-chö) *n* criatura *f*; ser *m*

credible (*krê*-di-böl) *adj* verosímil

credit (*krê*-dit) *n* crédito *m*; *v* acreditar; ~ **card** tarjeta de crédito

creditor (*krê*-di-tö) *n* acreedor *m*

credulous (*krê*-dyu-löss) *adj* crédulo

creek (kriik) *n* ensenada *f*

***creep** (kriip) *v* gatear

creepy (*krii*-pi) *adj* lúgubre, espeluznante

cremate (kri-*meit*) *v* incinerar

cremation (kri-*mei*-ʃön) *n* incineración *f*

crew (kruu) *n* equipo *m*

cricket (*kri*-kit) *n* cricquet *m*; grillo *m*

crime (kraim) *n* crimen *m*

criminal (*kri*-mi-nöl) *n* delincuente *m*, criminal *m*; *adj* criminal; ~ **law** derecho penal

criminality (kri-mi-*næ*-lö-ti) *n* criminalidad *f*

crimson (*krim*-sön) *adj* carmesí

crippled (*kri*-pöld) *adj* estropeado

crisis (*krai*-ssiss) *n* (pl crises) crisis *f*

crisp (krissp) *adj* crujiente, quebradizo

critic (*kri*-tik) *n* crítico *m*

critical (*kri*-ti-köl) *adj* crítico; precario

criticism (*kri*-ti-ssi-söm) *n* crítica *f*

criticize (*kri*-ti-ssais) *v* criticar

crochet (krou-ʃei) *v* *hacer croché

crockery (kro-kö-ri) *n* cerámica *f*, loza *f*

crocodile (*kro*-kö-dail) *n* cocodrilo *m*

crooked (*kru*-kid) *adj* torcido, curvo; deshonesto

crop (krop) *n* cosecha *f*

cross (kross) *v* *atravesar; *adj* enojado, enfadado; *n* cruz *f*

cross-eyed (*kross*-aid) *adj* bizco

crossing (*kro*-ssing) *n* travesía *f*; encrucijada *f*; paso *m*; paso a nivel

crossroads (*kross*-rouds) *n* cruce *m*

crosswalk (*kross*-ᵘook) *nAm* cruce para peatones

crow (krou) *n* corneja *f*

crowbar (*krou*-baa) *n* pie de cabra

crowd (kraud) *n* masa *f*, muchedumbre *f*

crowded (*krau*-did) *adj* animado; repleto

crown (kraun) *n* corona *f*; *v* coronar

crucifix (*kruu*-ssi-fikss) *n* crucifijo *m*

crucifixion (kruu-ssi-*fik*-ʃön) *n* crucifixión *f*

crucify (*kruu*-ssi-fai) *v* crucificar

cruel (kruᵒl) *adj* cruel

cruise (kruus) *n* crucero *m*

crumb (kram) *n* migaja *f*

crusade (kruu-*sseid*) *n* cruzada *f*

crust (krasst) *n* corteza *f*

crutch (krach) *n* muleta *f*

cry (krai) *v* llorar; gritar; llamar; *n* grito *m*; voz *f*

crystal (*kri*-sstöl) *n* cristal *m*; *adj* de cristal

Cuba (*kyuu*-bö) Cuba *f*

Cuban (*kyuu*-bön) *adj* cubano

cube (kyuub) *n* cubo *m*

cuckoo (*ku*-kuu) *n* cuclillo *m*

cucumber (*kyuu*-köm-bö) *n* pepino *m*

cuddle (*ka*-döl) *v* acariciar

cudgel (*ka*-dȝöl) *n* garrote *m*

cuff (kaf) *n* puño *m*

cuff-links (*kaf*-lingkss) *pl* gemelos *mpl*; mancuernillas *fplMe*

cul-de-sac (*kal*-dö-ssæk) *n* callejón sin salida

cultivate (*kal*-ti-veit) *v* cultivar

culture (*kal*-chö) *n* cultura *f*

cultured (*kal*-chöd) *adj* culto

cunning (*ka*-ning) *adj* astuto

cup (kap) *n* taza *f*; copa *f*

cupboard (*ka*-böd) *n* armario *m*

curb (kööb) *n* bordillo *m*; *v* refrenar

cure (kyuᵒ) *v* curar; *n* cura *f*; curación *f*

curio (*kyuᵒ*-ri-ou) *n* (pl ~s) curiosidad *f*

curiosity (kyuᵒ-ri-*o*-ssö-ti) *n* curiosidad *f*

curious (*kyuᵒ*-ri-öss) *adj* curioso

curl (kööl) *v* rizar; *n* rizo *m*

curler (*köö*-lö) *n* rulo *m*

curling-tongs (*köö*-ling-tongs) *pl* rizador *m*

curly (*köö*-li) *adj* crespo; chino *adjMe*

currant (*ka*-rönt) *n* pasa de Corinto; grosella *f*

currency (*ka*-rön-ssi) *n* moneda *f*; **foreign** ~ moneda extranjera

current (*ka*-rönt) *n* corriente *f*; *adj* corriente; **alternating** ~ corriente alterna; **direct** ~ corriente continua

curry (*ka*-ri) *n* cari *m*

curse (kööss) *v* *maldecir; *n* maldición *f*

curtain (*köö*-tön) *n* cortina *f*; telón *m*

curve (kööv) *n* curva *f*

curved (köövd) *adj* curvado, encorvado

cushion (*ku*-jön) *n* almohadón *m*

custodian (ka-*sstou*-di-ön) *n* guarda *m*

custody (*ka*-sstö di) *n* detención *f*; custodia *f*; tutela *f*

custom (*ka*-sstöm) *n* costumbre *f*

customary (*ka*-sstö-mö-ri) *adj* usual, corriente, acostumbrado

customer (*ka*-sstö-mö) *n* cliente *m*

Customs (*ka*-sstöms) *pl* aduana *f*; ~ **duty** impuesto *m*; ~ **officer** oficial de aduanas

cut (kat) *n* incisión *f*; cortadura *f*

*cut (kat) *v* cortar; *reducir; ~ off cortar

cutlery (*kat*-lö-ri) *n* cubiertos *mpl*

cutlet (*kat*-löt) *n* chuleta *f*

cycle (*ssai*-köl) *n* biciclo *m*; bicicleta *f*; ciclo *m*

cyclist (*ssai*-klisst) *n* ciclista *m*

cylinder (*ssi*-lin-dö) *n* cilindro *m*; ~ **head** culata del cilindro

Cyprus (*ssai*-prös) Chipre *f*

cystitis (ssi-*sstai*-tiss) *n* cistitis *f*

Czech (chêk) *adj* checo

D

dad (dæd) *n* papá *m*

daddy (*dæ*-di) *n* papaíto *m*

daffodil (*dæ*-fö-dil) *n* narciso *m*

daily (*dei*-li) *adj* diario; *n* diario *m*

dairy (*dê*-ri) *n* lechería *f*

dam (dæm) *n* presa *f*; dique *m*

damage (*dæ*-midʒ) *n* perjuicio *m*; *v* dañar

damp (dæmp) *adj* húmedo; mojado; *n* humedad *f*; *v* *humedecer

dance (daanss) *v* bailar; *n* baile *m*

dandelion (*dæn*-di-lai-ön) *n* diente de león

dandruff (*dæn*-dröf) *n* caspa *f*

Dane (dein) *n* danés *m*

danger (*dein*-dʒö) *n* peligro *m*

dangerous (*dein*-dʒö-röss) *adj* peligroso

Danish (*dei*-niʃ) *adj* danés

dare (dêᵒ) *v* atreverse, osar; desafiar

daring (*dêᵒ*-ring) *adj* atrevido

dark (daak) *adj* oscuro, obscuro; *n* oscuridad *f*

darling (*daa*-ling) *n* amor *m*, querido *m*

darn (daan) *v* zurcir

dash (dæʃ) *v* correr; *n* guión *m*

dashboard (*dæʃ*-bood) *n* tablero de instrumentos

data (*dei*-tö) *pl* dato *m*

date¹ (deit) *n* fecha *f*; cita *f*; *v* datar; **out of** ~ anticuado

date² (deit) *n* dátil *m*

daughter (*doo*-tö) *n* hija *f*

dawn (doon) *n* alba *f*; aurora *f*

day (dei) *n* día *m*; **by** ~ de día; ~ **trip** jornada *f*; **per** ~ a diario; **the** ~ **before yesterday** anteayer

daybreak (*dei*-breik) *n* amanecer *m*

daylight (*dei*-lait) *n* luz del día

dead (dêd) *adj* muerto; difunto

deaf (dêf) *adj* sordo

deal (diil) *n* transacción *f*

*deal (diil) *v* repartir; ~ **with** *v* tratar con; *hacer negocios con

dealer (*dii*-lö) *n* negociante *m*, comerciante *m*

dear (diᵒ) *adj* querido; caro; amado

death (dêz) n muerte f; ~ **penalty** pena de muerte

debate (di-*beit*) n debate m

debit (*dé*-bit) n debe m

debt (dêt) n deuda f

decaffeinated (dii-*kæ*-fi-nei-tid) adj descafeinado

deceit (di-*ssiit*) n engaño m

deceive (di-*ssiiv*) v engañar

December (di-*ssêm*-bö) diciembre

decency (*dii*-ssön-ssi) n decencia f

decent (*dii*-ssönt) adj decente

decide (di-*ssaid*) v decidir

decision (di-*ssi*-3ön) n decisión f

deck (dêk) n cubierta f; ~ **cabin** camarote en cubierta; ~ **chair** silla de tijera

declaration (dê-klö-*rei*-[ön) n declaración f

declare (di-*klêᵒ*) v declarar; indicar

decoration (dê-kö-*rei*-[ön) n decoración f

decrease (dii-*kriiss*) v *reducir; *disminuir; n disminución f

dedicate (*dê*-di-keit) v dedicar

deduce (di-*dyuuss*) v *deducir

deduct (di-*dakt*) v *deducir

deed (diid) n acción f, acto m

deep (diip) adj hondo

deep-freeze (diip-*friis*) n congelador m

deer (diᵒ) n (pl ~) ciervo m

defeat (di-*fiit*) v derrotar; n derrota f

defective (di-*fêk*-tiv) adj defectuoso

defence (di-*fênss*) n defensa f

defend (di-*fênd*) v *defender

deficiency (di-*fi*-[ön-ssi) n deficiencia f

deficit (*dê*-fi-ssit) n déficit m

define (di-*fain*) v definir, determinar

definite (*dê*-fi-nit) adj determinado; definido

definition (dê-fi-*ni*-[ön) n definición f

deformed (di-*foomd*) adj contrahecho, deforme

degree (di-*ghrii*) n grado m; título m

delay (di-*lei*) v retardar; *diferir; n retraso m, tardanza f; dilación f

delegate (*dê*-li-ghöt) n delegado m

delegation (dê-li-*ghei*-[ön) n delegación f

deliberate¹ (di-*li*-bö-reit) v discutir, deliberar

deliberate² (di-*li*-bö-röt) adj deliberado

deliberation (di-li-bö-*rei*-[ön) n deliberación f

delicacy (*dê*-li-kö-ssi) n golosina f

delicate (*dê*-li-köt) adj delicado; fino

delicatessen (dê-li-kö-*tê*-ssön) n gollerías fpl; tienda de comestibles finos

delicious (di-*li*-[öss) adj exquisito, delicioso

delight (di-*lait*) n delicia f, deleite m; v encantar

delightful (di-*lait*-föl) adj delicioso, deleitoso

deliver (di-*li*-vö) v entregar; librar

delivery (di-*li*-vö-ri) n entrega f, reparto m; parto m; liberación f; ~ **van** furgoneta f

demand (di-*maand*) v *requerir, exigir; n exigencia f; demanda f

democracy (di-*mo*-krö-ssi) n democracia f

democratic (dê-mö-*kræ*-tik) adj democrático

demolish (di-*mo*-li[) v *demoler

demolition (dê-mö-*li*-[ön) n demolición f

demonstrate (*dê*-mön-sstreit) v *demostrar; *hacer una manifestación

demonstration (dê-mön-*sstrei*-[ön) n manifestación f; demostración f

den (dên) n madriguera f

Denmark (*dên*-maak) Dinamarca f

denomination (di-no-mi-*nei*-[ön) n denominación f

dense (dênss) *adj* denso

dent (dênt) *n* abolladura *f*

dentist (*dén*-tisst) *n* dentista *m*

denture (*dên*-chö) *n* dentadura postiza

deny (di-*nai*) *v* *negar; *denegar

deodorant (dii-*ou*-dö-rönt) *n* desodorante *m*

depart (di-*paat*) *v* partir; *fallecer

department (di-*paat*-mönt) *n* departamento *m*; ~ **store** grandes almacenes

departure (di-*paa*-chö) *n* despedida *f*, partida *f*

dependant (di-*pên*-dönt) *adj* dependiente

depend on (di-*pênd*) depender de

deposit (di-*po*-sit) *n* depósito *m*; fianza *f*; capa *f*, yacimiento *m*; *v* ingresar

depository (di-*po*-si-tö-ri) *n* almacén *m*

depot (*dê*-pou) *n* almacén *m*; *nAm* estación *f*

depress (di-*préss*) *v* deprimir

depression (di-*prê*-ʃön) *n* desánimo *m*; depresión *f*

deprive of (di-*praiv*) privar de

depth (dêpz) *n* profundidad *f*

deputy (*dê*-pyu-ti) *n* diputado *m*; sustituto *m*

descend (di-*ssênd*) *v* *descender

descendant (di-*ssên*-dönt) *n* descendiente *m*

descent (di-*ssênt*) *n* bajada *f*

describe (di-*sskraib*) *v* describir

description (di-*sskrip*-ʃön) *n* descripción *f*; señas personales

desert[1] (*dê*-söt) *n* desierto *m*; *adj* salvaje, desierto

desert[2] (di-*sööt*) *v* desertar; dejar

deserve (di-*sööv*) *v* *merecer

design (di-*sain*) *v* diseñar; *n* diseño *m*; objetivo *m*

designate (*dê*-sigh-neit) *v* designar

desirable (di-*sai*ᵒ-rö-böl) *adj* deseable

desire (di-*sai*ᵒ) *n* deseo *m*; ganas *fpl*; *v* anhelar, desear

desk (dêssk) *n* escritorio *m*; pupitre *m*

despair (di-*sspê*ᵒ) *n* desesperación *f*; *v* *estar desesperado

despatch (di-*sspæch*) *v* despachar

desperate (*dê*-sspö-röt) *adj* desesperado

despise (di-*sspais*) *v* despreciar

despite (di-*sspait*) *prep* a pesar de

dessert (di-*sööt*) *n* postre *m*

destination (dê-ssti-*nei*-ʃön) *n* destino *m*

destine (*dê*-sstin) *v* destinar

destiny (*dê*-ssti-ni) *n* destino *m*

destroy (di-*sstroi*) *v* *destruir

destruction (di-*sstrak*-ʃön) *n* destrucción *f*; ruina *f*

detach (di-*tæch*) *v* separar

detail (*dii*-teil) *n* particularidad *f*, detalle *m*

detailed (*dii*-teild) *adj* detallado

detect (di-*têkt*) *v* descubrir

detective (di-*têk*-tiv) *n* detective *m*; ~ **story** novela policíaca

detergent (di-*töö*-dʒönt) *n* detergente *m*

determine (di-*töö*-min) *v* determinar

determined (di-*töö*-mind) *adj* resuelto

detour (*dii*-tuᵒ) *n* desvio *m*

devaluation (dii-væl-yu-*ei*-ʃön) *n* desvalorización *f*

devalue (dii-*væl*-yuu) *v* desvalorizar

develop (di-*vê*-löp) *v* desarrollar; revelar

development (di-*vê*-löp-mönt) *n* desarrollo *m*

deviate (*dii*-vi-eit) *v* desviarse

devil (*dê*-völ) *n* diablo *m*

devise (di-*vais*) *v* idear

devote (di-*vout*) *v* dedicar

dew (dyuu) *n* rocío *m*
diabetes (dai-ö-*bii*-tiis) *n* diabetes *f*
diabetic (dai-ö-*bê*-tik) *n* diabético *m*
diagnose (dai-ögh-*nous*) *v* diagnosticar; *comprobar
diagnosis (dai-ögh-*nou*-ssiss) *n* (pl -ses) diagnosis *m*
diagonal (dai-æ-ghö-nöl) *n* diagonal *f*; *adj* diagonal
diagram (*dai*-ö-ghræm) *n* esquema *m*; gráfico *m*
dialect (*dai*-ö-lêkt) *n* dialecto *m*
diamond (*dai*-ö-mönd) *n* diamante *m*
diaper (*dai*-ö-pö) *nAm* pañal *m*
diaphragm (*dai*-ö-fræm) *n* membrana *f*
diarrhoea (dai-ö-*ri*-ö) *n* diarrea *f*
diary (*dai*-ö-ri) *n* agenda *f*; diario *m*
dictaphone (*dik*-tö-foun) *n* dictáfono *m*
dictate (dik-*teit*) *v* dictar
dictation (dik-*tei*-jön) *n* dictado *m*
dictator (dik-*tei*-tö) *n* dictador *m*
dictionary (*dik*-jö-nö-ri) *n* diccionario *m*
did (did) *v* (p do)
die (dai) *v* *morir
diesel (*dii*-söl) *n* diesel *m*
diet (*dai*-öt) *n* régimen *m*
differ (*di*-fö) *v* *diferir
difference (*di*-fö-rönss) *n* diferencia *f*; distinción *f*
different (*di*-fö-rönt) *adj* diferente; otro'
difficult (*di*-fi-költ) *adj* difícil; fastidioso
difficulty (*di*-fi-köl-ti) *n* dificultad *f*; trabajo *m*
* **dig** (digh) *v* cavar
digest (di-*dʒêsst*) *v* *digerir
digestible (di-*dʒê*-sstö-böl) *adj* digerible
digestion (di-*dʒêss*-chön) *n* digestión *f*

digit (*di*-dʒit) *n* número *m*
digital (*di*-dʒi-töl) *adj* digital
dignified (*digh*-ni-faid) *adj* distinguido
dilapidated (di-*læ*-pi-dei-tid) *adj* ruinoso
diligence (*di*-li-dʒönss) *n* celo *m*, diligencia *f*
diligent (*di*-li-dʒönt) *adj* celoso, cuidadoso
dilute (dai-*lyuut*) *v* *diluir
dim (dim) *adj* deslucido, mate; oscuro, vago, difuso
dine (dain) *v* cenar
dinghy (*ding*-ghi) *n* chinchorro *m*
dining-car (*dai*-ning-kaa) *n* coche comedor
dining-room (*dai*-ning-ruum) *n* comedor *m*
dinner (*di*-nö) *n* comida principal; cena *f*
dinner-jacket (*di*-nö-dʒæ-kit) *n* smoking *m*
dinner-service (*di*-nö-ssöö-viss) *n* servicio de mesa
diphtheria (dif-*ziºº*-ri-ö) *n* difteria *f*
diploma (di-*plou*-mö) *n* diploma *m*
diplomat (*di*-plö-mæt) *n* diplomático *m*
direct (di-*rêkt*) *adj* directo; *v* dirigir; administrar
direction (di-*rêk*-jön) *n* dirección *f*; instrucción *f*; dirección de escena; administración *f*; **directions for use** modo de empleo
directive (di-*rêk*-tiv) *n* directriz *f*
director (di-*rêk*-tö) *n* director *m*; director de escena
dirt (dööt) *n* suciedad *f*
dirty (*döö*-ti) *adj* sucio
disabled (di-*ssei*-böld) *adj* minusválido, inválido
disadvantage (di-ssöd-*vaan*-tidʒ) *n* desventaja *f*
disagree (di-ssö-*ghrii*) *v* no *estar de

acuerdo, *disentir

disagreeable (di-ssö-*ghrii*-ö-böl) *adj* desagradable

disappear (di-ssö-*piº*) *v* *desaparecer

disappoint (di-ssö-*point*) *v* decepcionar

disappointment (di-ssö-*point*-mönt) *n* desengaño *m*

disapprove (di-ssö-*pruuv*) *v* *desaprobar

disaster (di-*saa*-sstö) *n* desastre *m*; catástrofe *f*, calamidad *f*

disastrous (di-*saa*-sströss) *adj* desastroso

disc (dissk) *n* disco *m*; **slipped ~** hernia intervertebral

discard (di-*sskaad*) *v* desechar

discharge (diss-*chaadʒ*) *v* descargar; **~ of** dispensar de

discipline (*di*-ssi-plin) *n* disciplina *f*

discolour (di-*sska*-lö) *v* *desteñirse*; **discoloured** descolorido

disconnect (di-sskö-*nêkt*) *v* desconectar

discontented (di-sskön-*tên*-tid) *adj* descontento

discontinue (di-sskön-*ti*-nyuu) *v* suprimir, cesar

discount (*di*-sskaunt) *n* descuento *m*

discover (di-*sska*-vö) *v* descubrir

discovery (di-*sska*-vö-ri) *n* descubrimiento *m*

discuss (di-*sskass*) *v* discutir; debatir

discussion (di-*sska*-ʃön) *n* discusión *f*; conversación *f*, debate *m*

disease (di-*siis*) *n* enfermedad *f*

disembark (di-ssim-*baak*) *v* desembarcar

disgrace (diss-*ghreiss*) *n* deshonor *m*

disguise (diss-*ghais*) *v* disfrazarse; *n* disfraz *m*

disgusting (diss-*gha*-ssting) *adj* repugnante, asqueroso

dish (diʃ) *n* plato *m*; fuente *f*; guiso *m*

dishonest (di-*sso*-nisst) *adj* ímprobo

disinfect (di-ssin-*fêkt*) *v* desinfectar

disinfectant (di-ssin-*fêk*-tönt) *n* desinfectante *m*

dislike (di-*sslaik*) *v* detestar, no gustar; *n* repugnancia *f*, aversión *f*, antipatía *f*

dislocated (*di*-sslö-kei-tid) *adj* dislocado

dismiss (diss-*miss*) *v* *despedir

disorder (di-*ssoo*-dö) *n* desorden *m*

dispatch (di-*sspæch*) *v* enviar, despachar

display (di-*ssp
lei*) *v* exhibir; *mostrar; *n* exposición *f*

displease (di-*sspliis*) *v* disgustar, desagradar

disposable (di-*sspou*-sö-böl) *adj* desechable

disposal (di-*sspou*-söl) *n* disposición *f*

dispose of (di-*sspous*) *disponer de

dispute (di-*sspyuut*) *n* disputa *f*; riña *f*, contienda *f*; *v* *reñir, disputar

dissatisfied (di-*ssæ*-tiss-faid) *adj* insatisfecho

dissolve (di-*solv*) *v* *disolver

dissuade from (di-ssᵘ*eid*) disuadir

distance (*di*-sstönss) *n* distancia *f*; **~ in kilometres** kilometraje *m*

distant (*di*-sstönt) *adj* lejano

distinct (di-*sstingkt*) *adj* claro; distinto

distinction (di-*sstingk*-ʃön) *n* distinción *f*, diferencia *f*

distinguish (di-*ssting*-ghᵘiʃ) *v* distinguir

distinguished (di-*ssting*-ghᵘiʃt) *adj* distinguido

distress (di-*sstrêss*) *n* peligro *m*; **~ signal** señal de alarma

distribute (di-*sstri*-byuut) *v* *distribuir

distributor (di-*sstri*-byu-tö) *n* distribuidor *m*

district (*di*-sstrikt) *n* distrito *m*; comarca *f*; barrio *m*

disturb (di-*sstööb*) *v* estorbar, molestar

disturbance (di-*sstöö*-bönss) *n* disturbio *m*; confusión *f*

ditch (dich) *n* zanja *f*, cuneta *f*

dive (daiv) *v* bucear

diversion (dai-*vöö*-jön) *n* desvío *m*; diversión *f*

divide (di-*vaid*) *v* dividir; repartir; separar

divine (di-*vain*) *adj* divino

division (di-*vi*-ʒön) *n* división *f*; separación *f*; departamento *m*

divorce (di-*vooss*) *n* divorcio *m*; *v* divorciar

dizziness (*di*-si-nöss) *n* vértigo *m*

dizzy (*di*-si) *adj* mareado

*do (duu) *v* *hacer; *ser suficiente

dock (dok) *n* dock *m*; muelle *m*; *v* atracar

docker (*do*-kö) *n* obrero portuario

doctor (*dok*-tö) *n* médico *m*; doctor *m*

document (*do*-kyu-mönt) *n* documento *m*

dog (dogh) *n* perro *m*

dogged (*do*-ghid) *adj* obstinado

doll (dol) *n* muñeca *f*

dome (doum) *n* cúpula *f*

domestic (dö-*mê*-sstik) *adj* doméstico; interior; *n* sirviente *m*

domicile (*do*-mi-ssail) *n* domicilio *m*

domination (do-mi-*nei*-jön) *n* dominación *f*

dominion (dö-*mi*-nyön) *n* dominio *m*

donate (dou-*neit*) *v* donar

donation (dou-*nei*-jön) *n* donación *f*

done (dan) *v* (pp do)

donkey (*dong*-ki) *n* burro *m*

donor (*dou*-nö) *n* donante *m*

door (doo) *n* puerta *f*; **revolving ~** puerta giratoria; **sliding ~** puerta corrediza

doorbell (*doo*-bêl) *n* timbre *m*

door-keeper (*doo*-kii-pö) *n* portero *m*

doorman (*doo*-mön) *n* (pl -men) portero *m*

dormitory (*doo*-mi-tri) *n* dormitorio *m*

dose (douss) *n* dosis *f*

dot (dot) *n* punto *m*

double (*da*-böl) *adj* doble

doubt (daut) *v* dudar; *n* duda *f*; **without ~** sin duda

doubtful (*daut*-föl) *adj* dudoso; inseguro

dough (dou) *n* masa *f*

down[1] (daun) *adv* abajo; hacia abajo; *adj* abatido; *prep* a lo largo de, debajo de; **~ payment** primer pago

down[2] (daun) *n* flojel *m*

downpour (*daun*-poo) *n* aguacero *m*

downstairs (daun-*sstê*ºs) *adv* abajo

downstream (daun-*sstriim*) *adv* río abajo

down-to-earth (daun-tu-*ööz*) *adj* sensato

downwards (*daun*-ºöds) *adv* hacia abajo

dozen (*da*-sön) *n* (pl ~, ~s) docena *f*

draft (draaft) *n* giro *m*

drag (drægh) *v* arrastrar

dragon (*dræ*-ghön) *n* dragón *m*

drain (drein) *v* desecar; drenar; *n* desagüe *m*

drama (*draa*-mö) *n* drama *m*; tragedia *f*; teatro *m*

dramatic (drö-*mæ*-tik) *adj* dramático

dramatist (*dræ*-mö-tisst) *n* dramaturgo *m*

drank (drængk) *v* (p drink)

draper (*drei*-pö) *n* pañero *m*

drapery (*drei*-pö-ri) *n* pañería *f*

draught (draaft) *n* corriente de aire; **draughts** juego de damas

draught-board (*draaft*-bood) *n* tablero

de damas

draw (droo) *n* sorteo *m*

*draw (droo) *v* dibujar; arrastrar; sacar; jalar *vMe*; ~ **up** redactar

drawbridge (*droo*-bridƷ) *n* puente levadizo

drawer (*droo*-ö) *n* cajón *m*; **drawers** calzoncillos *mpl*

drawing (*droo*-ing) *n* dibujo *m*

drawing-pin (*droo*-ing-pin) *n* chinche *f*

drawing-room (*droo*-ing-ruum) *n* salón *m*

dread (drêd) *v* temer; *n* temor *m*

dreadful (*drêd*-föl) *adj* terrible, espantoso

dream (driim) *n* sueño *m*

*dream (driim) *v* *soñar

dress (drèss) *v* *vestir; *vestirse; vendar; *n* vestido *m*

dressing-gown (*drê*-ssing-ghaun) *n* bata *f*

dressing-room (*drê*-ssing-ruum) *n* vestuario *m*

dressing-table (*drê*-ssing-tei-böl) *n* tocador *m*

dressmaker (*drêss*-mei-kö) *n* modista *f*

drill (dril) *v* taladrar; entrenar; *n* taladro *m*

drink (dringk) *n* aperitivo *m*, bebida *f*

*drink (dringk) *v* beber

drinking-water (*dring*-king-ᵘoo-tö) *n* agua potable

drip-dry (drip-*drai*) *adj* no precisa plancha

drive (draiv) *n* calzada *f*; paseo en coche

*drive (draiv) *v* *conducir

driver (*drai*-vö) *n* conductor *m*

drizzle (*dri*-söl) *n* llovizna *f*

drop (drop) *v* dejar caer; *n* gota *f*

drought (draut) *n* sequía *f*

drown (draun) *v* ahogar; ***be**

drowned ahogarse

drug (dragh) *n* estupefaciente *m*; medicamento *m*

drugstore (*dragh*-sstoo) *nAm* droguería *f*, farmacia *f*; almacén *m*

drum (dram) *n* tambor *m*

drunk (drangk) *adj* (pp drink) borracho

dry (drai) *adj* seco; *v* secar

dry-clean (drai-*kliin*) *v* limpiar en seco

dry-cleaner's (drai-*klii*-nös) *n* tintorería *f*

dryer (*drai*-ö) *n* secadora *f*

duchess (da-chiss) *n* duquesa *f*

duck (dak) *n* pato *m*

due (dyuu) *adj* aguardado; adeudado; debido

dues (dyuus) *pl* derechos *mpl*

dug (dagh) *v* (p, pp dig)

duke (dyuuk) *n* duque *m*

dull (dal) *adj* aburrido; pálido, mate; embotado

dumb (dam) *adj* mudo; atontado, estúpido

dune (dyuun) *n* duna *f*

dung (dang) *n* abono *m*

dunghill (*dang*-hil) *n* estercolero *m*

duration (dyu-*rei*-jön) *n* duración *f*

during (*dyu*ö-ring) *prep* durante

dusk (dassk) *n* crepúsculo *m*

dust (dasst) *n* polvo *m*

dustbin (*dasst*-bin) *n* cubo de la basura

dusty (*da*-ssti) *adj* polvoriento

Dutch (dach) *adj* holandés

Dutchman (*dach*-mön) *n* (pl -men) holandés *m*

dutiable (*dyuu*-ti-ö-böl) *adj* imponible

duty (*dyuu*-ti) *n* deber *m*; tarea *f*; arancel *m*; **Customs** ~ impuesto de aduana

duty-free (dyuu-ti-*frii*) *adj* exento de impuestos

dwarf (dᵘoof) *n* enano *m*

dye (dai) *v* *teñir; *n* tintura *f*
dynamo (*dai*-nö-mou) *n* (pl ~s) dínamo *f*
dysentery (*di*-sson-tri) *n* disentería *f*

E

each (iich) *adj* cada; ~ **other** el uno al otro
eager (*ii*-ghö) *adj* ansioso, impaciente
eagle (*ii*-ghöl) *n* águila *m*
ear (iö) *n* oreja *f*
earache (*iö*-reik) *n* dolor de oídos
ear-drum (*iö*-dram) *n* tímpano *m*
earl (ööl) *n* conde *m*
early (*öö*-li) *adj* temprano
earn (öön) *v* ganar
earnest (*öö*-nisst) *n* seriedad *f*
earnings (*öö*-nings) *pl* ingresos *mpl*, ganancias *fpl*
earring (*iö*-ring) *n* pendiente *m*
earth (ööz) *n* tierra *f*; suelo *m*
earthenware (*öö*-zön-ᵘêö) *n* loza *f*
earthquake (*ööz*-kᵘeik) *n* terremoto *m*
ease (iis) *n* desenvoltura *f*, facilidad *f*; bienestar *m*
east (iisst) *n* este *m*
Easter (*ii*-sstö) Pascua
easterly (*ii*-sstö-li) *adj* oriental
eastern (*ii*-sstön) *adj* oriental
easy (*ii*-si) *adj* fácil; cómodo; ~ **chair** butaca *f*
easy-going (*ii*-si-ghou-ing) *adj* relajado
*__eat__ (iit) *v* comer; cenar
eavesdrop (*iivs*-drop) *v* escuchar
ebony (*ê*-bö-ni) *n* ébano *m*
eccentric (ik-*ssên*-trik) *adj* excéntrico
echo (*ê*-kou) *n* (pl ~es) eco *m*
eclipse (i-*klipss*) *n* eclipse *m*
economic (ii-kö-*no*-mik) *adj* económico

economical (ii-kö-*no*-mi-köl) *adj* parsimonioso, económico
economist (i-*ko*-nö-misst) *n* economista *m*
economize (i-*ko*-nö-mais) *v* economizar
economy (i-*ko*-nö-mi) *n* economía *f*
ecstasy (*êk*-sstö-si) *n* éxtasis *m*
Ecuador (*ê*-kᵘö-doo) Ecuador *m*
Ecuadorian (ê-kᵘö-*doo*-ri-ön) *n* ecuatoriano *m*
eczema (*êk*-ssi-mö) *n* eczema *m*
edge (êdȝ) *n* borde *m*
edible (*ê*-di-böl) *adj* comestible
edition (i-*di*-fön) *n* edición *f*; **morning** ~ edición de mañana
editor (*ê*-di-tö) *n* redactor *m*
educate (*ê*-dȝu-keit) *v* formar, educar
education (ê-dȝu-*kei*-fön) *n* educación *f*
eel (iil) *n* anguila *f*
effect (i-*fêkt*) *n* resultado *m*, efecto *m*; *v* efectuar; **in** ~ en realidad
effective (i-*fêk*-tiv) *adj* eficaz
efficient (i-*fi*-fönt) *adj* eficiente
effort (*ê*-föt) *n* esfuerzo *m*
egg (êgh) *n* huevo *m*
egg-cup (*êgh*-kap) *n* huevera *f*
eggplant (*êgh*-plaant) *n* berenjena *f*
egg-yolk (*êgh*-youk) *n* yema de huevo
egoistic (ê-ghou-*i*-sstik) *adj* egoísta
Egypt (*ii*-dȝipt) Egipto *m*
Egyptian (i-*dȝip*-fön) *adj* egipcio
eiderdown (*ai*-dö-daun) *n* edredón *m*
eight (eit) *num* ocho
eighteen (ei-*tiin*) *num* dieciocho
eighteenth (ei-*tiinz*) *num* decimoctavo
eighth (eitz) *num* octavo
eighty (*ei*-ti) *num* ochenta
either (*ai*-öö) *pron* cualquiera de los dos; **either ... or** o ... o, bien ... bien

elaborate (i-*læ*-bö-reit) *v* elaborar

elastic (i-*læ*-sstik) *adj* elástico; flexible; ~ **band** cinta de goma

elasticity (ê-læ-*ssti*-ssö-ti) *n* elasticidad *f*

elbow (*êl*-bou) *n* codo *m*

elder (*êl*-dö) *adj* mayor

elderly (*êl*-dö-li) *adj* anciano

eldest (*êl*-disst) *adj* mayor

elect (i-*lêkt*) *v* *elegir

election (i-*lêk*-ʃön) *n* elección *f*

electric (i-*lêk*-trik) *adj* eléctrico; ~ **razor** afeitadora eléctrica

electrician (i-lêk-*tri*-ʃön) *n* electricista *m*

electricity (i-lêk-*tri*-ssö-ti) *n* electricidad *f*

electronic (i-lêk-*tro*-nik) *adj* electrónico; ~ **game** juego electrónico

elegance (ê-li-ghönss) *n* elegancia *f*

elegant (ê-li-ghönt) *adj* elegante

element (ê-li-mönt) *n* elemento *m*

elephant (ê-li-fönt) *n* elefante *m*

elevator (ê-li-vei-to) *nAm* ascensor *m*; elevador *mMe*

eleven (i-*lê*-vön) *num* once

eleventh (i-*lê*-vönz) *num* onceno

elf (êlf) *n* (pl elves) duende *m*

eliminate (i-*li*-mi-neit) *v* eliminar

elm (êlm) *n* olmo *m*

else (êlss) *adv* si no

elsewhere (êl-ss*u*ê*ö) *adv* otra parte

elucidate (i-*luu*-ssi-deit) *v* elucidar

emancipation (i-mæn-ssi-*pei*-ʃön) *n* emancipación *f*

embankment (im-*bængk*-mönt) *n* terraplén *m*

embargo (êm-*baa*-ghou) *n* (pl ~es) embargo *m*

embark (im-*baak*) *v* embarcar

embarkation (êm-baa-*kei*-ʃön) *n* embarcación *f*

embarrass (im-*bæ*-röss) *v* turbar; *desconcertar; estorbar; **embar-**

rassed tímido

embassy (*êm*-bö-ssi) *n* embajada *f*

emblem (*êm*-blöm) *n* emblema *m*

embrace (im-*breiss*) *v* abrazar; *n* abrazo *m*

embroider (im-*broi*-dö) *v* bordar

embroidery (im-*broi*-dö-ri) *n* bordado *m*

emerald (ê-mö-röld) *n* esmeralda *f*

emergency (i-*möö*-dʒön-ssi) *n* caso de urgencia, urgencia *f*; emergencia *f*; ~ **exit** salida de emergencia

emigrant (ê-mi-ghrönt) *n* emigrante *m*

emigrate (ê-mi-ghreit) *v* emigrar

emigration (ê-mi-*ghrei*-ʃön) *n* emigración *f*

emotion (i-*mou*-ʃön) *n* emoción *f*

emperor (*êm*-pö-rö) *n* emperador *m*

emphasize (*êm*-fö-ssais) *v* enfatizar, acentuar

empire (*êm*-paiö) *n* imperio *m*

employ (im-*ploi*) *v* emplear

employee (êm-ploi-*ii*) *n* empleado *m*

employer (im-*ploi*-ö) *n* patrón *m*

employment (im-*ploi*-mönt) *n* empleo *m*; ~ **exchange** oficina de colocación

empress (*êm*-priss) *n* emperatriz *f*

empty (*êmp*-ti) *adj* vacío; *v* vaciar

enable (i-*nei*-böl) *v* permitir

enamel (i-*næ*-möl) *n* esmalte *m*

enamelled (i-*næ*-möld) *adj* esmaltado

enchanting (in-*chaan*-ting) *adj* espléndido, encantador

encircle (in-*ssöö*-köl) *v* *circuir, cercar; *encerrar

enclose (ing-*klous*) *v* *incluir

enclosure (ing-*klou*-ʒö) *n* anexo *m*

encounter (ing-*kaun*-tö) *v* *encontrarse con; *n* encuentro *m*

encourage (ing-*ka*-ridʒ) *v* *alentar

encyclopaedia (ên-ssai-klö-*pii*-di-ö) *n* enciclopedia *f*

end (ênd) *n* fin *m*, extremo *m*; final *m*; *v* terminar, acabar; terminarse

ending (*én*-ding) *n* conclusión *f*

endless (*énd*-löss) *adj* infinito

endorse (in-*dooss*) *v* visar, endosar

endure (in-*dyu*ô) *v* soportar

enemy (*é*-nö-mi) *n* enemigo *m*

energetic (ê-nö-*dȝê*-tik) *adj* enérgico

energy (*é*-nö-dȝi) *n* energía *f*; fuerza *f*

engage (ing-*gheidȝ*) *v* emplear; reservar; comprometerse; **engaged** prometido; ocupado

engagement (ing-*gheidȝ*-mönt) *n* noviazgo *m*; compromiso *m*; ~ **ring** anillo de esponsales

engine (*én*-dȝin) *n* máquina *f*, motor *m*; locomotora *f*

engineer (ên-dȝi-*ni*ô) *n* ingeniero *m*

England (*ing*-ghlönd) Inglaterra *f*

English (*ing*-ghliʃ) *adj* inglés

Englishman (*ing*-ghliʃ-mön) *n* (pl - men) inglés *m*

engrave (ing-*ghreiv*) *v* grabar

engraver (ing-*ghrei*-vö) *n* grabador *m*

engraving (ing-*ghrei*-ving) *n* estampa *f*; grabado *m*

enigma (i-*nigh*-mö) *n* enigma *m*

enjoy (in-*dȝoi*) *v* disfrutar, gozar

enjoyable (in-*dȝoi*-ö-böl) *adj* agradable, grato, deleitable; rico

enjoyment (in-*dȝoi*-mönt) *n* goce *m*

enlarge (in-*laadȝ*) *v* ampliar

enlargement (in-*laadȝ*-mönt) *n* ampliación *f*

enormous (i-*noo*-möss) *adj* gigantesco, enorme

enough (i-*naf*) *adv* bastante; *adj* suficiente

enquire (ing-*k*u*ai*ô) *v* preguntar; investigar

enquiry (ing-*k*u*ai*ô-ri) *n* información *f*; investigación *f*; encuesta *f*

enter (*én*-tö) *v* entrar; inscribir

enterprise (*én*-tö-prais) *n* empresa *f*

entertain (ên-tö-*tein*) *v* *divertir, *entretener; hospedar

entertainer (ên-tö-*tei*-nö) *n* cómico *m*

entertaining (ên-tö-*tei*-ning) *adj* divertido, entretenido

entertainment (ên-tö-*tein*-mönt) *n* diversión *f*, entretenimiento *m*

enthusiasm (in-*zyuu*-si-æ-söm) *n* entusiasmo *m*

enthusiastic (in-zyuu-si-æ-sstik) *adj* entusiasta

entire (in-*tai*ô) *adj* todo, entero

entirely (in-*tai*ô-li) *adv* enteramente

entrance (*én*-trönss) *n* entrada *f*; acceso *m*

entrance-fee (*én*-trönss-fii) *n* entrada *f*

entry (*én*-tri) *n* entrada *f*, ingreso *m*; anotación *f*; **no** ~ prohibido el paso

envelope (*én*-vö-loup) *n* sobre *m*

envious (*én*-vi-öss) *adj* envidioso, celoso

environment (in-*vai*ô-rön-mönt) *n* medio ambiente; alrededores *mpl*

envoy (*én*-voi) *n* enviado *m*

envy (*én*-vi) *n* envidia *f*; *v* envidiar

epic (*é*-pik) *n* poema épico; *adj* épico

epidemic (ê-pi-*dé*-mik) *n* epidemia *f*

epilepsy (*é*-pi-lêp-ssi) *n* epilepsia *f*

epilogue (*é*-pi-logh) *n* epílogo *m*

episode (*é*-pi-ssoud) *n* episodio *m*

equal (*ii*-k*ö*l) *adj* igual; *v* igualar

equality (i-*k*u*ö*-lö-ti) *n* igualdad *f*

equalize (*ii*-k*ö*-lais) *v* igualar

equally (*ii*-k*ö*-li) *adv* igualmente

equator (i-*k*u*ei*-tö) *n* ecuador *m*

equip (i-*k*u*ip*) *v* equipar

equipment (i-*k*u*ip*-mönt) *n* equipo *m*

equivalent (i-*k*u*i*-vö-lönt) *adj* equivalente

eraser (i-*rei*-sö) *n* goma de borrar

erect (i-*rêkt*) *v* erigir; *adj* erguido, recto; parado *adjMe*

err (öö) v *errar

errand (ê-rönd) n recado m

error (ê-rö) n falta f, error m

escalator (ê-sskö-lei-tö) n escalera móvil

escape (i-sskeip) v escaparse; *huir, escapar; n evasión f

escort¹ (ê-sskoot) n escolta f

escort² (i-sskoot) v escoltar

especially (i-sspê-[ö-li]) adv sobre todo, especialmente

essay (ê-ssei) n ensayo m; tratado m, composición f

essence (ê-ssönss) n esencia f; núcleo m

essential (i-ssên-[öl]) adj indispensable; esencial

essentially (i-ssên-[ö-li]) adv sobre todo

establish (i-sstæ-bli[) v *establecer; *comprobar

estate (i-ssteit) n propiedad f

esteem (i-sstiim) n respeto m, estima f; v estimar

estimate¹ (ê-ssti-meit) v evaluar, estimar

estimate² (ê-ssti-möt) n estimación f

estuary (êss-chu-ö-ri) n estuario m

etcetera (êt-ssê-tö-rö) etcétera

etching (ê-ching) n aguafuerte f

eternal (i-töö-nöl) adj eterno

eternity (i-töö-nö-ti) n eternidad f

ether (ii-zö) n éter m

Ethiopia (i-zi-ou-pi-ö) Etiopía f

Ethiopian (i-zi-ou-pi-ön) adj etíope

Europe (yu⁰-röp) Europa f

European (yu⁰-rö-pii-ön) adj europeo

European Union (yu⁰-rö-pii-ön yuu-nyön) Unión Europea

evacuate (i-væ-kyu-eit) v evacuar

evaluate (i-væl-yu-eit) v evaluar

evaporate (i-væ-pö-reit) v evaporar

even (ii-vön) adj llano, plano, igual; constante; par; adv aun

evening (iiv-ning) n tarde f; ~ **dress** traje de etiqueta

event (i-vênt) n acontecimiento m; caso m

eventual (i-vên-chu-öl) adj eventual; final

ever (ê-vö) adv jamás; siempre

every (êv-ri) adj cada

everybody (êv-ri-bo-di) pron todos

everyday (êv-ri-dei) adj cotidiano

everyone (êv-ri-ᵘan) pron cada uno, todo el mundo

everything (êv-ri-zing) pron todo

everywhere (êv-ri-ᵘê̂⁰) adv por todas partes

evidence (ê-vi-dönss) n prueba f

evident (ê-vi-dönt) adj evidente

evil (ii-völ) n mal m; adj malo, malvado

evolution (ii-vö-luu-[ön]) n evolución f

exact (igh-sækt) adj exacto

exactly (igh-sækt-li) adv exactamente

exaggerate (igh-sæ-dʒo-reit) v exagerar

examination (igh-sæ-mi-nei-[ön]) n examen m; interrogatorio m

examine (igh-sæ-min) v examinar

example (igh-saam-pöl) n ejemplo m; for ~ por ejemplo

excavation (êkss-kö-vei-[ön]) n excavación f

exceed (ik-ssiid) v exceder; superar

excel (ik-ssêl) v distinguirse

excellent (êk-ssö-lönt) adj excelente

except (ik-ssêpt) prep excepto

exception (ik-ssêp-[ön]) n excepción f

exceptional (ik-ssêp-[ö-nöl]) adj extraordinario, excepcional

excerpt (êk-ssööpt) n extracto m

excess (ik-ssêss) n exceso m

excessive (ik-ssê-ssiv) adj excesivo

exchange (ikss-cheindʒ) v intercambiar, cambiar; n cambio m; bolsa f; ~ **office** oficina de cambio; ~

rate cambio *m*

excite (ik-*ssait*) *v* excitar

excitement (ik-*ssait*-mönt) *n* agitación *f*, excitación *f*

exciting (ik-*ssai*-ting) *adj* excitante

exclaim (ik-*sskleim*) *v* exclamar

exclamation (êk-ssklö-*mei*-ſön) *n* exclamación *f*

exclude (ik-*sskluud*) *v* *excluir

exclusive (ik-*sskluu*-ssiv) *adj* exclusivo

exclusively (ik-*sskluu*-ssiv-li) *adv* exclusivamente, únicamente

excursion (ik-*ssköö*-ſön) *n* excursión *f*

excuse¹ (ik-*sskyuuss*) *n* excusa *f*

excuse² (ik-*sskyuus*) *v* excusar, disculpar

execute (*êk*-ssi-kyuut) *v* ejecutar

execution (êk-ssi-*kyuu*-ſön) *n* ejecución *f*

executioner (êk-ssi-*kyuu*-ſö-nö) *n* verdugo *m*

executive (igh-*sê*-kyu-tiv) *adj* ejecutivo; *n* poder ejecutivo; ejecutivo *m*

exempt (igh-*ʒêmpt*) *v* dispensar, eximir; *adj* exento

exemption (igh-*sêmp*-ſön) *n* exención *f*

exercise (*êk*-ssö-ssais) *n* ejercicio *m*; *v* ejercitar; ejercer

exhale (êkss-*heil*) *v* exhalar

exhaust (igh-*soosst*) *n* tubo de escape, escape *m*; *v* extenuar; ~ **gases** gases de escape

exhibit (igh-*si*-bit) *v* *exponer; exhibir

exhibition (êk-ssi-*bi*-ſön) *n* exposición *f*

exile (*êk*-ssail) *n* exilio *m*; exiliado *m*

exist (igh-*sisst*) *v* existir

existence (igh-*si*-sstönss) *n* existencia *f*

exit (*êk*-ssit) *n* salida *f*

exotic (igh-*so*-tik) *adj* exótico

expand (ik-*sspænd*) *v* *extender; *desplegar

expect (ik-*sspêkt*) *v* aguardar, esperar

expectation (êk-sspêk-*tei*-ſön) *n* esperanza *f*

expedition (êk-ssp*ö*-*di*-ſön) *n* envío *m*; expedición *f*

expel (ik-*sspêl*) *v* expulsar

expenditure (ik-*sspên*-di-chö) *n* gasto *m*

expense (ik-*sspênss*) *n* gasto *m*

expensive (ik-*sspên*-ssiv) *adj* caro; costoso

experience (ik-*sspi*ᵒ-ri-önss) *n* experiencia *f*; *v* experimentar, vivir; **experienced** experimentado

experiment (ik-*sspê*-ri-mönt) *n* prueba *f*, experimento *m*; *v* experimentar

expert (*êk*-sspööt) *n* perito *m*, experto *m*; *adj* competente

expire (ik-*sspai*ᵒ) *v* expirar, terminarse; espirar; **expired** caducado

expiry (ik-*sspai*ᵒ-ri) *n* vencimiento *m*

explain (ik-*ssplein*) *v* explicar

explanation (êk-ssplö-*nei*-ſön) *n* aclaración *f*, explicación *f*

explicit (ik-*sspli*-ssit) *adj* expreso, explícito

explode (ik-*ssploud*) *v* estallar

exploit (ik-*ssploit*) *v* abusar de, explotar

explore (ik-*ssploo*) *v* explorar

explosion (ik-*ssplou*-ʒön) *n* explosión *f*

explosive (ik-*ssplou*-ssiv) *adj* explosivo; *n* explosivo *m*

export¹ (ik-*sspoot*) *v* exportar

export² (*êk*-sspoot) *n* exportación *f*

exportation (êk-sspoo-*tei*-ſön) *n* exportación *f*

exports (*êk*-sspootss) *pl* exportación *f*

exposition (êk-sspö-*si*-ſön) *n* exposición *f*

exposure (ik-*sspou*-ʒö) *n* exposición *f*; ~ **meter** exposímetro *m*

express (ik-*sspréss*) v expresar; *adj* expreso; explícito; ~ **train** tren expreso

expression (ik-*ssprê*-ʃön) n expresión f

exquisite (ik-*ssk^ui*-sit) *adj* exquisito

extend (ik-*sstênd*) v prolongar; ampliar; conceder

extension (ik-*sstên*-ʃön) n prórroga f; ampliación f; extensión f; ~ **cord** cordón de extensión

extensive (ik-*sstên*-ssiv) *adj* extenso; vasto

extent (ik-*sstênt*) n dimensión f

exterior (êk-*ssti^o*-ri-ö) *adj* exterior; n exterior m

external (êk-*sstöö*-nöl) *adj* exterior

extinguish (ik-*ssting*-gh^uiʃ) v extinguir, apagar

extort (ik-*sstoot*) v extorsionar

extortion (ik-*sstoo*-ʃön) n extorsión f

extra (ik-*sströ*) *adj* extra

extract[1] (ik-*sstrækt*) v *extraer

extract[2] (êk-*sstrækt*) n fragmento m

extradite (êk-*sströ*-dait) v entregar

extraordinary (ik-*sstroo*-dön-ri) *adj* extraordinario

extravagant (ik-*sströ*-vö-ghönt) *adj* exagerado, extravagante

extreme (ik-*sstriim*) *adj* extremo; n extremo m

exuberant (igh-*syuu*-bö-rönt) *adj* exuberante

eye (ai) n ojo m

eyebrow (*ai*-brau) n ceja f

eyelash (*ai*-læʃ) n pestaña f

eyelid (*ai*-lid) n párpado m

eye-pencil (*ai*-pên-ssöl) n lápiz para las cejas

eye-shadow (*ai*-ʃæ-dou) n sombra para los ojos

eye-witness (*ai*-^uit-nöss) n testigo de vista

F

fable (*fei*-böl) n fábula f

fabric (*fæ*-brik) n tejido m; estructura f

façade (fö-*ssaad*) n fachada f

face (feiss) n cara f; v enfrentarse con; ~ **massage** masaje facial; **facing** enfrente de

face-cream (*feiss*-kriim) n crema facial

face-pack (*feiss*-pæk) n máscara facial

face-powder (*feiss*-pau-dö) n polvo facial

facility (fö-*ssi*-lö-ti) n facilidad f

fact (fækt) n hecho m; **in** ~ efectivamente

factor (*fæk*-tö) n factor m

factory (*fæk*-tö-ri) n fábrica f

factual (*fæk*-chu-öl) *adj* real

faculty (*fæ*-köl-ti) n facultad f; don m, aptitud f

fad (fæd) n antojo m

fade (feid) v *desteñirse

faience (fai-*angss*) n loza f

fail (feil) v fallar; faltar; omitir; *ser suspendido; **without** ~ sin falta

failure (*feil*-yö) n fracaso m; fiasco m

faint (feint) v desmayarse; *adj* débil, vago

fair (fê^ö) n feria f; *adj* justo; rubio; bonito

fairly (*fê^ö*-li) *adv* bastante, medianamente

fairy (*fê^ö*-ri) n hada f

fairytale (*fê^ö*-ri-teil) n cuento de hadas

faith (feiz) n fe f; confianza f

faithful (*feiz*-ful) *adj* fiel

fake (feik) n falsificación f

fall (fool) n caída f; *nAm* otoño m

***fall** (fool) v *caer

false (foolss) *adj* falso; inexacto; ~

teeth dentadura postiza
falter (*fool*-tö) v vacilar; balbucear
fame (feim) n fama f; reputación f
familiar (fö-*mil*-yö) adj familiar
family (*fæ*-mö-li) n familia f; ~ **name** apellido m
famous (*fei*-möss) adj famoso
fan (fæn) n ventilador m; abanico m; admirador m; ~ **belt** correa del ventilador
fanatical (fö-*næ*-ti-köl) adj fanático
fancy (*fæn*-ssi) v gustar, antojarse; imaginarse; n capricho m; imaginación f
fantastic (fæn-*tæ*-sstik) adj fantástico
fantasy (*fæn*-tö-si) n fantasía f
far (faa) adj lejano; adv mucho; **by** ~ con mucho; **so** ~ hasta ahora
far-away (faa-rö-ʊei) adj remoto
farce (faass) n sainete m, farsa f
fare (fêʰ) n gastos de viaje, precio del billete; alimento m
farm (faam) n granja f
farmer (*faa*-mö) n granjero m; **farmer's wife** granjera f
farmhouse (*faam*-hauss) n cortijo m; rancho mMe
far-off (faa-rof) adj remoto
fascinate (*fæ*-ssi-neit) v cautivar
fascism (*fæ*-ʃi-söm) n fascismo m
fascist (*fæ*-ʃisst) adj fascista
fashion (*fæ*-ʃön) n moda f; modo m
fashionable (*fæ*-ʃö-nö-böl) adj a la moda
fast (faasst) adj rápido; firme
fast-dyed (faasst-*daid*) adj lavable, no destiñe
fasten (*faa*-ssön) v atar; *cerrar
fastener (*faa*-ssö-nö) n cierre m
fat (fæt) adj graso, gordo; n grasa f
fatal (*fei*-töl) adj fatal, mortal
fate (feit) n destino m
father (*faa*-ðö) n padre m
father-in-law (*faa*-ðö-rin-loo) n (pl fa-

thers-) suegro m
fatherland (*faa*-ðö-lönd) n patria f
fatness (*fæt*-nöss) n obesidad f
fatty (*fæ*-ti) adj grasiento
faucet (*foo*-ssit) nAm grifo m
fault (foolt) n culpa f; imperfección f, defecto m
faultless (*foolt*-löss) adj impecable; perfecto
faulty (*fool*-ti) adj defectuoso
favour (*fei*-vö) n favor m; v *favorecer
favourable (*fei*-vö-rö-böl) adj favorable
favourite (*fei*-vö-rit) n favorito m; adj preferido
fax (fakss) n telefax m; **send a** ~ mandar un telefax
fear (fiʰ) n temor m, miedo m; v temer
feasible (*fii*-sö-böl) adj realizable
feast (fiisst) n fiesta f
feat (fiit) n gran trabajo
feather (*fê*-ðö) n pluma f
feature (*fii*-chö) n característica f; rasgo m
February (*fê*-bru-ö-ri) febrero
federal (*fê*-dö-röl) adj federal
federation (fê-dö-*rei*-ʃön) n federación f
fee (fii) n honorarios mpl
feeble (*fii*-böl) adj débil
***feed** (fiid) v alimentar; **fed up with** harto de
***feel** (fiil) v *sentir; palpar; ~ **like** antojarse
feeling (*fii*-ling) n sensación f
fell (fêl) v (p fall)
fellow (*fê*-lou) n tipo m
felt¹ (fêlt) n fieltro m
felt² (fêlt) v (p, pp feel)
female (*fii*-meil) adj femenino
feminine (*fê*-mi-nin) adj femenino
fence (fênss) n cerca f; reja f; v es-

grimir

fender (*fên*-dö) *n* parachoques *m*; defensa *fMe*

ferment (föö-*mênt*) *v* fermentar

ferry-boat (*fê*-ri-bout) *n* transbordador *m*

fertile (*föö*-tail) *adj* fértil

festival (*fê*-ssti-völ) *n* festival *m*

festive (*fê*-sstiv) *adj* festivo

fetch (fêch) *v* *ir por; *ir a buscar

feudal (*fyuu*-döl) *adj* feudal

fever (*fii*-vö) *n* fiebre *f*

feverish (*fii*-vö-rif) *adj* febril

few (fyuu) *adj* pocos

fiancé (fi-*ang*-ssei) *n* novio *m*

fiancée (fi-*ang*-ssei) *n* novia *f*

fibre (*fai*-bö) *n* fibra *f*

fiction (*fik*-fön) *n* ficción *f*

field (fiild) *n* campo *m*; terreno *m*; ~ **glasses** gemelos de campaña

fierce (fi°ss) *adj* fiero; salvaje, violento

fifteen (fif-*tiin*) *num* quince

fifteenth (fif-*tiinz*) *num* quinceno

fifth (fifz) *num* quinto

fifty (*fif*-ti) *num* cincuenta

fig (figh) *n* higo *m*

fight (fait) *n* combate *m*, lucha *f*

***fight** (fait) *v* combatir, luchar

figure (*fi*-ghö) *n* estatura *f*, figura *f*; cifra *f*

file (fail) *n* lima *f*; expediente *m*; cola *f*

Filipino (fi-li-*pii*-nou) *n* filipino *m*

fill (fil) *v* llenar; ~ **in** completar, llenar; **filling station** estación de servicio; ~ **out** *Am* completar, llenar; ~ **up** llenar

filling (*fi*-ling) *n* empaste *m*; relleno *m*

film (film) *n* película *f*; *v* filmar

filter (*fil*-tö) *n* filtro *m*

filthy (*fil*-zi) *adj* sórdido, inmundo

final (*fai*-nöl) *adj* final

finance (fai-*nænss*) *v* financiar

finances (fai-*næn*-ssis) *pl* finanzas *fpl*

financial (fai-*næn*-föl) *adj* financiero

finch (finch) *n* pinzón *m*

***find** (faind) *v* *encontrar

fine (fain) *n* multa *f*; *adj* fino; bello; excelente, maravilloso; ~ **arts** bellas artes

finger (*fing*-ghö) *n* dedo *m*; **little** ~ dedo auricular

fingerprint (*fing*-ghö-print) *n* impresión digital

finish (*fi*-nif) *v* terminar; *n* terminación *f*; meta *f*; **finished** acabado

Finland (*fin*-lönd) Finlandia *f*

Finn (fin) *n* finlandés *m*

Finnish (*fi*-nif) *adj* finlandés

fire (fai°) *n* fuego *m*; incendio *m*; *v* disparar; *despedir

fire-alarm (*fai°*-rö-laam) *n* alarma de incendio

fire-brigade (*fai°*-bri-gheid) *n* bomberos *mpl*

fire-escape (*fai°*-ri-sskeip) *n* escala de incendios

fire-extinguisher (*fai°*-rik-ssting-gh*u*i-fö) *n* extintor *m*

fireplace (*fai°*-pleiss) *n* chimenea *f*

fireproof (*fai°*-pruuf) *adj* incombustible; refractario

firm (fööm) *adj* firme; sólido; *n* firma *f*

first (föösst) *num* primero; **at** ~ antes; al principio; ~ **name** nombre de pila

first-aid (föösst-*eid*) *n* primeros auxilios; ~ **kit** botiquín de urgencia; ~ **post** puesto de socorro

first-class (föösst-*klaass*) *adj* de primera calidad

first-rate (föösst-*reit*) *adj* de primer orden, de primera clase

fir-tree (*föö*-trii) *n* pino *m*

fish[1] (fif) *n* (pl ~, ~es) pez *m*; ~

shop pescadería f
fish² (fiʃ) v pescar; **fishing gear** avíos de pesca; **fishing fly** mosca artificial; **fishing hook** anzuelo m; **fishing licence** permiso de pesca; **fishing line** línea de pesca; **fishing net** red de pescar; **fishing rod** caña de pescar; **fishing tackle** aparejo de pesca
fishbone (fiʃ-boun) n espina f
fisherman (fi-ʃö-mön) n (pl -men) pescador m
fist (fisst) n puño m
fit (fit) adj apropiado; n ataque m; v convenir; **fitting room** probador m
five (faiv) num cinco
fix (fikss) v arreglar
fixed (fiksst) adj fijo
fizz (fis) n efervescencia f
fjord (fyood) n fiordo m
flag (flægh) n bandera f
flame (fleim) n llama f
flamingo (flö-ming-ghou) n (pl ~s, ~es) flamenco m
flannel (flæ-nöl) n franela f
flash (flæʃ) n relámpago m
flash-bulb (flæʃ-balb) n bombilla de flash
flash-light (flæʃ-lait) n linterna f
flask (flaassk) n frasco m; **thermos ~** termo m
flat (flæt) adj llano; n piso m; **~ tyre** neumático desinflado
flavour (flei-vö) n sabor m; v sazonar
fleet (fliit) n flota f
flesh (fleʃ) n carne f
flew (fluu) v (p fly)
flex (flêkss) n cordón flexible
flexible (flêk-ssi-böl) adj flexible
flight (flait) n vuelo m; **charter ~** vuelo fletado
flint (flint) n pedernal m
float (flout) v flotar; n flotador m

flock (flok) n rebaño m
flood (flad) n inundación f; riada f
floor (floo) n suelo m; piso m; **~ show** espectáculo de variedades
florist (flo-risst) n florista m
flour (flauö) n harina f
flow (flou) v correr, *fluir
flower (flauö) n flor f
flowerbed (flauö-bêd) n arriate m
flower-shop (flauö-ʃop) n floristería f
flown (floun) v (pp fly)
flu (fluu) n gripe f
fluent (fluu-önt) adj con soltura
fluid (fluu-id) adj fluido; n fluido m
flute (fluut) n flauta f
fly (flai) n mosca f; bragueta f
*fly (flai) v *volar
foam (foum) n espuma f; v espumar
foam-rubber (foum-ra-bö) n goma espumada
focus (fou-köss) n foco m
fog (fogh) n niebla f
foggy (fo-ghi) adj brumoso
foglamp (fogh-læmp) n faro de niebla
fold (fould) v doblar; n pliegue m
folk (fouk) n gente f; **~ song** canción popular
folk-dance (fouk-daanss) n danza popular
folklore (fouk-loo) n folklore m
follow (fo-lou) v *seguir; **following** adj siguiente
*be fond of (bii fond ov) *querer
food (fuud) n comida f; alimento m; **~ poisoning** intoxicación alimentaria
foodstuffs (fuud-sstafss) pl artículos alimenticios
fool (fuul) n idiota m, tonto m; v engañar
foolish (fuu-liʃ) adj necio, tonto; absurdo
foot (fut) n (pl feet) pie m; **~ powder** polvo para los pies; **on ~** a pie

football (*fut*-bool) *n* fútbol *m* ; ~ **match** partido de fútbol

foot-brake (*fut*-breik) *n* freno de pie

footpath (*fut*-paaz) *n* senda *f*

footwear (*fut*-ᵘê⁰) *n* calzado *m*

for (foo, fö) *prep* para; durante; a causa de, por; *conj* porque

*****forbid** (fö-*bid*) *v* prohibir

force (fooss) *v* obligar, *forzar; *n* fuerza *f*; **by** ~ forzosamente; **driving** ~ fuerza motriz

ford (food) *n* vado *m*

forecast (*foo*-kaasst) *n* previsión *f*; *v* pronosticar

foreground (*foo*-ghraund) *n* primer plano

forehead (*fo*-rêd) *n* frente *f*

foreign (*fo*-rin) *adj* extranjero; extraño

foreigner (*fo*-ri-nö) *n* extranjero *m*; forastero *m*

foreman (*foo*-mön) *n* (pl -men) capataz *m*

foremost (*foo*-mousst) *adj* primero

foresail (*foo*-sseil) *n* foque *m*

forest (*fo*-risst) *n* selva *f*, bosque *m*

forester (*fo*-ri-sstö) *n* guardabosques *m*

forge (food3) *v* falsificar

*****forget** (fö-*ghêt*) *v* olvidar

forgetful (fö-*ghêt*-föl) *adj* olvidadizo

*****forgive** (fö-*ghiv*) *v* perdonar

fork (fook) *n* tenedor *m*; bifurcación *f*; *v* bifurcarse

form (foom) *n* forma *f*; formulario *m*; clase *f*; *v* formar

formal (*foo*-möl) *adj* formal

formality (foo-*mæ*-lö-ti) *n* formalidad *f*

former (*foo*-mö) *adj* antiguo; anterior; **formerly** antes

formula (*foo*-myu-lö) *n* (pl ~e, ~s) fórmula *f*

fort (foot) *n* fortaleza *f*

fortnight (*foot*-nait) *n* quincena *f*

fortress (*foo*-triss) *n* fortaleza *f*

fortunate (*foo*-chö-nöt) *adj* afortunado

fortune (*foo*-chuun) *n* fortuna *f*; suerte *f*

forty (*foo*-ti) *num* cuarenta

forward (*foo*-ᵘöd) *adv* hacia adelante, adelante; *v* reexpedir

foster-parents (*fo*-sstö-pê⁰-röntss) *pl* padres adoptivos

fought (foot) *v* (p, pp fight)

foul (faul) *adj* sucio; vil

found¹ (faund) *v* (p, pp find)

found² (faund) *v* fundar

foundation (faun-*dei*-ʃön) *n* fundación *f*; ~ **cream** crema de base

fountain (*faun*-tin) *n* fuente *f*

fountain-pen (*faun*-tin-pên) *n* estilográfica *f*

four (foo) *num* cuatro

fourteen (foo-*tiin*) *num* catorce

fourteenth (foo-*tiinz*) *num* catorceno

fourth (fooz) *num* cuarto

fowl (faul) *n* (pl ~s, ~) volatería *f*

fox (fokss) *n* zorro *m*

foyer (foi-ei) *n* vestíbulo *m*

fraction (*fræk*-ʃön) *n* fracción *f*

fracture (*fræk*-chö) *v* fracturar; *n* fractura *f*

fragile (*fræ*-d3ail) *adj* frágil

fragment (*frægh*-mönt) *n* fragmento *m*; trozo *m*

frame (freim) *n* marco *m*; armadura *f*

France (fraanss) Francia *f*

franchise (*fræn*-chais) *n* derecho electoral

fraternity (frö-*töö*-nö-ti) *n* fraternidad *f*

fraud (frood) *n* fraude *m*

fray (frei) *v* deshilacharse

free (frii) *adj* libre; gratuito; ~ **of charge** gratis; ~ **ticket** billete gratuito

freedom (*frii*-döm) *n* libertad *f*

*freeze (friis) *v* *helar; congelar

freezing (*frii*-sing) *adj* helado

freezing-point (*frii*-sing-point) *n* punto de congelación

freight (freit) *n* carga *f*, cargo *m*

French (frênch) *adj* francés

Frenchman (*frênch*-mön) *n* (pl -men) francés *m*

frequency (*frii*-kᵘön-ssi) *n* frecuencia *f*

frequent (*frii*-kᵘönt) *adj* frecuente

fresh (frêʃ) *adj* fresco; ~ **water** agua dulce

friction (*frik*-ʃön) *n* fricción *f*

Friday (*frai*-di) viernes *m*

fridge (fridʒ) *n* frigorífico *m*, refrigerador *m*

friend (frênd) *n* amigo *m*; amiga *f*

friendly (*frênd*-li) *adj* amable; amistoso

friendship (*frênd*-ʃip) *n* amistad *f*

fright (frait) *n* miedo *m*, espanto *m*

frighten (*frai*-tön) *v* espantar

frightened (*frai*-tönd) *adj* espantado; ***be** ~ asustarse

frightful (*frait*-föl) *adj* terrible

fringe (frindʒ) *n* franja *f*

frock (frok) *n* vestido *m*

frog (frogh) *n* rana *f*

from (from) *prep* desde; de; a partir de

front (frant) *n* frente *m*; **in** ~ **of** delante de

frontier (*fran*-tiᵒ) *n* frontera *f*

frost (frosst) *n* escarcha *f*

froth (froz) *n* espuma *f*

frozen (*frou*-sön) *adj* congelado; ~ **food** alimento congelado

fruit (fruut) *n* fruta *f*; fruto *m*

fry (frai) *v* *freír

frying-pan (*frai*-ing-pæn) *n* sartén *f*

fuel (*fyuu*-öl) *n* combustible *m*; ~ **pump** *Am* bomba de gasolina

full (ful) *adj* lleno; ~ **board** pensión completa; ~ **stop** punto *m*; ~ **up** completo

fun (fan) *n* diversión *f*

function (*fangk*-ʃön) *n* función *f*

fund (fand) *n* fondos *mpl*

fundamental (fan-dö-*mên*-töl) *adj* fundamental

funeral (*fyuu*-nö-röl) *n* funerales *mpl*

funnel (*fa*-nöl) *n* embudo *m*

funny (*fa*-ni) *adj* gracioso, cómico; extraño

fur (föö) *n* piel *f*; ~ **coat** abrigo de pieles; **furs** piel *f*

furious (*fyu*ᵒ-ri-öss) *adj* furioso

furnace (*föö*-niss) *n* horno *m*

furnish (*föö*-niʃ) *v* suministrar, procurar; instalar, amueblar; ~ **with** *proveer de

furniture (*föö*-ni-chö) *n* muebles *mpl*

furrier (*fa*-ri-ö) *n* peletero *m*

further (*föö*-ðö) *adj* más lejos; ulterior

furthermore (*föö*-ðö-moo) *adv* además

furthest (*föö*-ðisst) *adj* el más alejado

fuse (fyuus) *n* fusible *m*; mecha *f*

fuss (fass) *n* bulla *f*; ostentación *f*, alharaca *f*

future (*fyuu*-chö) *n* porvenir *m*; *adj* futuro

G

gable (*ghei*-böl) *n* faldón *m*

gadget (*ghæ*-dʒit) *n* accesorio *m*

gaiety (*ghei*-ö-ti) *n* alegría *f*

gain (ghein) *v* ganar; *n* ganancia *f*

gait (gheit) *n* paso *m*

gale (gheil) *n* ventarrón *m*

gall (ghool) *n* bilis *f*; ~ **bladder** vesícula biliar

gallery (*ghæ*-lö-ri) *n* galería *f*

gallop (*ghæ*-löp) *n* galope *m*

gallows (*ghæ*-lous) *pl* horca *f*

gallstone (*ghool*-sstoun) *n* cálculo biliar

game (gheim) *n* juego *m*; caza *f*; ~ **reserve** parque de reserva zoológica

gang (ghæng) *n* banda *f*; equipo *m*

gangway (*ghæng*-ᵘei) *n* pasarela *f*

gaol (dzeil) *n* cárcel *f*

gap (ghæp) *n* hueco *m*

garage (*ghæ*-raaz) *n* garaje *m*; *v* dejar en garaje

garbage (*ghaa*-bidz) *n* basura *f*

garden (*ghaa*-dön) *n* jardín *m*; **public** ~ jardín público; **zoological gardens** jardín zoológico

gardener (*ghaa*-dö-nö) *n* jardinero *m*

gargle (*ghaa*-ghöl) *v* *hacer gárgaras

garlic (*ghaa*-lik) *n* ajo *m*

gas (ghæss) *n* gas *m*; *nAm* gasolina *f*; ~ **cooker** cocina de gas; ~ **station** *Am* puesto de gasolina; ~ **stove** estufa de gas

gasoline (*ghæ*-ssö-liin) *nAm* gasolina *f*

gastric (*ghæ*-sstrik) *adj* gástrico; ~ **ulcer** úlcera gástrica

gasworks (*ghæss*-ᵘöökss) *n* fábrica de gas

gate (gheit) *n* portón *m*; reja *f*

gather (*ghæ*-ðö) *v* coleccionar; juntarse; recoger

gauge (gheidz) *n* medidor *m*

gauze (ghoos) *n* gasa *f*

gave (gheiv) *v* (p give)

gay (ghei) *adj* alegre; gaitero

gaze (gheis) *v* mirar

gazetteer (ghæ-sö-*ti*ö) *n* diccionario geográfico

gear (ghiᵒ) *n* velocidad *f*; aparejo *m*; **change** ~ cambiar de marcha; ~ **lever** palanca de cambios

gear-box (*ghi*ᵒ-bokss) *n* caja de veloci-

dades

gem (dzêm) *n* joya *f*, gema *f*; alhaja *f*

gender (*dzê*n-dö) *n* género *m*

general (*dzê*-nö-röl) *adj* general; *n* general *m*; ~ **practitioner** médico de cabecera; **in** ~ en general

generate (*dzê*-nö-reit) *v* generar

generation (dzê-nö-*rei*-jön) *n* generación *f*

generator (*dzê*-nö-rei-tör) *n* generador *m*

generosity (dzê-nö-*ro*-ssö-ti) *n* generosidad *f*

generous (*dzê*-nö-röss) *adj* generoso

genital (*dzê*-ni-töl) *adj* genital

genius (*dzii*-ni-öss) *n* genio *m*

gentle (*dzê*n-töl) *adj* gentil; tierno, suave; prudente

gentleman (*dzê*n-töl-mön) *n* (pl -men) caballero *m*

genuine (*dzê*-nyu-in) *adj* genuino

geography (dzi-*o*-ghrö-fi) *n* geografía *f*

geology (dzi-*o*-lö-dzi) *n* geología *f*

geometry (dzi-*o*-mö-tri) *n* geometría *f*

germ (dzööm) *n* germen *m*

German (*dzöö*-mön) *adj* alemán

Germany (*dzöö*-mö-ni) Alemania *f*

gesticulate (dzi-*ssti*-kyu-leit) *v* gesticular

***get** (ghêt) *v* *conseguir; *ir a buscar; *hacerse; ~ **back** regresar; ~ **off** apearse; ~ **on** subir, montar; adelantar; ~ **up** levantarse

ghost (ghousst) *n* fantasma *m*; espíritu *m*

giant (*dzai*-önt) *n* gigante *m*

giddiness (*ghi*-di-nöss) *n* mareo *m*

giddy (*ghi*-di) *adj* mareado

gift (ghift) *n* regalo *m*; talento *m*

gifted (*ghif*-tid) *adj* talentoso

gigantic (dzai-*ghæn*-tik) *adj* gigantesco

giggle (*ghi*-ghöl) *v* *soltar risitas

gill (ghil) *n* branquia *f*

gilt (ghilt) *adj* dorado

ginger (*dʒin*-dʒö) *n* jengibre *m*

gipsy (*dʒip*-ssi) *n* gitano *m*

girdle (*ghöö*-döl) *n* faja *f*

girl (ghööl) *n* muchacha *f*; ~ **guide** exploradora *f*

****give** (ghiv) *v* *dar; entregar; ~ **away** revelar; ~ **in** ceder; ~ **up** renunciar

glacier (*ghlæ*-ssi-ö) *n* glaciar *m*

glad (ghlæd) *adj* alegre, contento; **gladly** con mucho gusto, gustosamente

gladness (*ghlæd*-nöss) *n* alegría *f*

glamorous (*ghlæ*-mö-röss) *adj* encantador

glamour (*ghlæ*-mö) *n* encanto *m*

glance (ghlaanss) *n* ojeada *f*; *v* ojear

gland (ghlænd) *n* glándula *f*

glare (ghlêᵒ) *n* destello *m*; resplandor *m*

glaring (*ghlêᵒ*-ring) *adj* deslumbrador

glass (ghlaass) *n* vaso *m*; vidrio *m*; de vidrio; **glasses** anteojos *mpl*; **magnifying** ~ lente de aumento

glaze (ghleis) *v* esmaltar

glen (ghlên) *n* cañada *f*

glide (ghlaid) *v* resbalar

glider (*ghlai*-dö) *n* planeador *m*

glimpse (ghlimpss) *n* vislumbre *m*; ojeada *f*; *v* vislumbrar

global (*ghlou*-böl) *adj* mundial

globe (ghloub) *n* globo *m*

gloom (ghluum) *n* obscuridad *f*

gloomy (*ghluu*-mi) *adj* sombrío

glorious (*ghloo*-ri-öss) *adj* espléndido

glory (*ghloo*-ri) *n* gloria *f*; honor *m*, elogio *m*

gloss (ghloss) *n* brillo *m*

glossy (*ghlo*-ssi) *adj* lustroso

glove (ghlav) *n* guante *m*

glow (ghlou) *v* brillar; *n* brillo *m*

glue (ghluu) *n* cola *f*

****go** (ghou) *v* *ir; caminar; *hacerse; ~ **ahead** continuar; ~ **away** *irse; ~ **back** regresar; ~ **home** *volver a casa; ~ **in** entrar; ~ **on** continuar; ~ **out** *salir; ~ **through** pasar

goal (ghoul) *n* meta *f*; gol *m*

goalkeeper (*ghoul*-kii-pö) *n* portero *m*

goat (ghout) *n* cabrón *m*, cabra *f*

god (ghod) *n* dios *m*

goddess (*gho*-diss) *n* diosa *f*

godfather (*ghod*-faa-ðö) *n* padrino *m*

goggles (*gho*-ghöls) *pl* gafas *fpl*

gold (ghould) *n* oro *m*; ~ **leaf** hojas de oro

golden (*ghoul*-dön) *adj* dorado

goldmine (*ghould*-main) *n* mina de oro

goldsmith (*ghould*-ssmiz) *n* orfebre *m*

golf (gholf) *n* golf *m*

golf-club (*gholf*-klab) *n* palo de golf

golf-course (*gholf*-kooss) *n* campo de golf

golf-links (*gholf*-lingkss) *n* campo de golf

gondola (*ghon*-dö-lö) *n* góndola *f*

gone (ghon) *adv* (pp go) ido

good (ghud) *adj* bueno

good-bye! (ghud-*bai*) ¡adiós!

good-humoured (ghud-*hyuu*-möd) *adj* de buen humor

good-looking (ghud-*lu*-king) *adj* bien parecido

good-natured (ghud-*nei*-chöd) *adj* bondadoso

goods (ghuds) *pl* mercancías *fpl*, bienes *mpl*; ~ **train** tren de mercancías

good-tempered (ghud-*têm*-pöd) *adj* de buen humor

goodwill (ghud-ᵘ*il*) *n* buena voluntad

goose (ghuuss) *n* (pl geese) oca *f*

gooseberry (*ghus*-bö-ri) *n* grosella espinosa

goose-flesh (*ghuuss*-flêʃ) *n* carne de

gallina

gorge (ghood3) *n* cañón *m*

gorgeous (ghoo-d3öss) *adj* magnífico

gospel (*gho*-sspöl) *n* evangelio *m*

gossip (*gho*-ssip) *n* chisme *m*; *v* *contar chismes

got (ghot) *v* (p, pp get)

Gothic (*gho*-zik) *adj* gótico

gourmet (*ghu⁶*-mei) *n* gastrónomo *m*

gout (ghaut) *n* gota *f*

govern (*gha*-vön) *v* *regir

governess (*gha* vö niss) *n* aya *f*

government (*gha*-vön-mönt) *n* régimen *m*, gobierno *m*

governor (*gha*-vö-nö) *n* gobernador *m*

gown (ghaun) *n* traje *m*

grace (ghreiss) *n* gracia *f*; perdón *m*

graceful (ghreiss-föl) *adj* gracioso

grade (ghreid) *n* grado *m*; *v* graduar

gradient (*ghrei*-di-önt) *n* pendiente *f*

gradual (*ghræ*-d3u öl) *adj* gradual; **gradually** *adv* paulatinamente

graduate (*ghræ*-d3u-eit) *v* graduarse

grain (ghrein) *n* grano *m*, trigo *m*

gram (ghræm) *n* gramo *m*

grammar (*ghræ*-mö) *n* gramática *f*

grammatical (ghrö-*mæ*-ti-köl) *adj* gramatical

grand (ghrænd) *adj* imponente

granddad (*ghræn*-dæd) *n* abuelo *m*

granddaughter (*ghræn*-doo-tö) *n* nieta *f*

grandfather (*ghræn*-faa-ðö) *n* abuelo *m*

grandmother (*ghræn*-ma-ðö) *n* abuela *f*

grandparents (*ghræn*-pê⁶-röntss) *pl* abuelos *mpl*

grandson (*ghræn*-ssan) *n* nieto *m*

granite (*ghræ*-nit) *n* granito *m*

grant (ghraant) *v* conceder; *n* subvención *f*, beca *f*

grapefruit (*ghreip*-fruut) *n* pomelo *m*; toronja *fMe*

grapes (ghreipss) *pl* uvas *fpl*

graph (ghræf) *n* gráfico *m*

graphic (*ghræ*-fik) *adj* gráfico

grasp (ghraassp) *v* agarrar; *n* agarre *m*

grass (ghraass) *n* césped *m*

grasshopper (*ghraass*-ho-pö) *n* saltamontes *m*

grate (ghreit) *n* reja *f*; *v* rallar

grateful (*ghreit*-föl) *adj* agradecido

grater (*ghrei*-tö) *n* rayador *m*

gratis (*ghræ*-tiss) *adj* gratuito

gratitude (*ghræ*-ti-tyuud) *n* gratitud *f*

gratuity (ghrö-*tyuu*-ö-ti) *n* propina *f*

grave (ghreiv) *n* sepultura *f*; *adj* grave

gravel (*ghræ*-völ) *n* grava *f*

gravestone (*ghreiv*-sstoun) *n* lápida *f*

graveyard (*ghreiv*-yaad) *n* cementerio *m*

gravity (*ghræ*-vö-ti) *n* gravedad *f*; seriedad *f*

gravy (*ghrei*-vi) *n* salsa *f*

graze (ghreis) *v* *pacer; *n* rozadura *f*

grease (ghriiss) *n* grasa *f*; *v* engrasar

greasy (*ghrii*-ssi) *adj* grasiento, graso-so

great (ghreit) *adj* grande; **Great Britain** Gran Bretaña

Greece (ghriiss) Grecia *f*

greed (ghriid) *n* codicia *f*

greedy (*ghrii*-di) *adj* codicioso; glotón

Greek (ghriik) *adj* griego

green (ghriin) *adj* verde; ~ **card** tarjeta verde

greengrocer (*ghriin*-ghrou-ssö) *n* verdulero *m*

greenhouse (*ghriin*-hauss) *n* invernadero *m*, invernáculo *m*

greens (ghriinss) *pl* legumbres *fpl*

greet (ghriit) *v* saludar

greeting (*ghrii*-ting) *n* saludo *m*

grey (ghrei) *adj* gris
greyhound (*ghrei*-haund) *n* galgo *m*
grief (ghriif) *n* pesadumbre *f*; aflicción *f*, dolor *m*
grieve (ghriiv) *v* *estar afligido
grill (ghril) *n* parrilla *f*; *v* asar en parrilla
grill-room (*ghril*-ruum) *n* parrilla *f*
grin (ghrin) *v* *sonreír; *n* sonrisa sardónica
***grind** (ghraind) *v* *moler; triturar
grip (ghrip) *v* *asir; *n* agarradero *m*, agarre *m*; *nAm* maletín *m*
grit (ghrit) *n* polvo *m*
groan (ghroun) *v* *gemir
grocer (*ghrou*-ssö) *n* abacero *m*; abarrotero *mMe*; **grocer's** abacería *f*; abarrotería *fMe*
groceries (*ghrou*-ssö-ris) *pl* comestibles *mpl*
groin (ghroin) *n* ingle *f*
groove (ghruuv) *n* surco *m*
gross¹ (ghrouss) *n* (pl ~) gruesa *f*
gross² (ghrouss) *adj* grosero; bruto
grotto (*ghro*-tou) *n* (pl ~es, ~s) gruta *f*
ground¹ (ghraund) *n* fondo *m*, tierra *f*; ~ **floor** piso bajo; **grounds** terreno *m*
ground² (ghraund) *v* (p, pp grind)
group (ghruup) *n* grupo *m*
grouse (ghrauss) *n* (pl ~) gallo de bosque
grove (ghrouv) *n* soto *m*
***grow** (ghrou) *v* *crecer; cultivar; *hacerse
growl (ghraul) *v* *gruñir
grown-up (*ghroun*-ap) *adj* adulto; *n* adulto *m*
growth (ghrouz) *n* crecimiento *m*; tumor *m*
grudge (ghradʒ) *v* envidiar
grumble (*ghram*-böl) *v* refunfuñar
guarantee (ghæ-rön-*tii*) *n* garantía *f*;

v garantizar
guarantor (ghæ-rön-*too*) *n* garante *m*
guard (ghaad) *n* guardia *f*; *v* guardar
guardian (*ghaa*-di-ön) *n* tutor *m*
guess (ghêss) *v* adivinar; *creer, conjeturar; *n* conjetura *f*
guest (ghêsst) *n* huésped *m*, invitado *m*
guest-house (*ghêsst*-hauss) *n* pensión *f*
guest-room (*ghêsst*-ruum) *n* habitación para huéspedes
guide (ghaid) *n* guía *m*; *v* guiar
guidebook (*ghaid*-buk) *n* guía *f*
guide-dog (*ghaid*-dogh) *n* perro lazarillo
guilt (ghilt) *n* culpa *f*
guilty (*ghil*-ti) *adj* culpable
guinea-pig (*ghi*-ni-pigh) *n* conejillo de Indias
guitar (ghi-*taa*) *n* guitarra *f*
gulf (ghalf) *n* golfo *m*
gull (ghal) *n* gaviota *f*
gum (gham) *n* encía *f*; goma *f*; cola *f*
gun (ghan) *n* fusil *m*, revólver *m*; cañón *m*
gunpowder (*ghan*-pau-dö) *n* pólvora *f*
gust (ghasst) *n* ráfaga *f*
gusty (*gha*-ssti) *adj* borrascoso
gut (ghat) *n* intestino *m*; **guts** coraje *m*
gutter (*gha*-tö) *n* cuneta *f*
guy (ghai) *n* tipo *m*
gymnasium (dʒim-*nei*-si-öm) *n* (pl ~s, -sia) gimnasio *m*
gymnast (*dʒim*-næsst) *n* gimnasta *m*
gymnastics (dʒim-*næ*-sstikss) *pl* gimnasia *f*
gynaecologist (ghai-nö-*ko*-lö-dʒisst) *n* ginecólogo *m*

H

haberdashery (*hæ*-bö-dæ-ʃö-ri) *n* mercería *f*

habit (*hæ*-bit) *n* hábito *m*

habitable (*hæ*-bi-tö-böl) *adj* habitable

habitual (hö-*bi*-chu-öl) *adj* habitual

had (hæd) *v* (p, pp have)

haddock (*hæ*-dök) *n* (pl ~) bacalao *m*

haemorrhage (*hê*-mö-ridʒ) *n* hemorragia *f*

haemorrhoids (*hê*-mö-roids) *pl* hemorroides *fpl*

hail (heil) *n* granizo *m*

hair (hê⁰) *n* cabello *m*; ~ **cream** brillantina *f*; ~ **gel** gel fijador de cabello; ~ **piece** postizo *m*; ~ **rollers** rizadores *mpl*; ~ **tonic** tónico para el cabello

hairbrush (*hê⁰*-braʃ) *n* cepillo para el cabello

haircut (*hê⁰*-kat) *n* corte de pelo

hair-do (*hê⁰*-duu) *n* peinado *m*

hairdresser (*hê⁰*-drê-ssö) *n* peluquero *m*

hair-dryer (*hê⁰*-drai-ö) *n* secador para el pelo

hair-grip (*hê⁰*-ghrip) *n* horquilla *f*

hair-net (*hê⁰*-nêt) *n* redecilla *f*

hairpin (*hê⁰*-pin) *n* horquilla *f*

hair-spray (*hê⁰*-ssprei) *n* laca para el cabello

hairy (*hê⁰*-ri) *adj* cabelludo

half¹ (haaf) *adj* medio

half² (haaf) *n* (pl halves) mitad *f*

half-time (haaf-*taim*) *n* descanso *m*

halfway (haaf-*ᵘei*) *adv* a mitad de camino

halibut (*hæ*-li-böt) *n* (pl ~) halibut *m*

hall (hool) *n* vestíbulo *m*; sala *f*

halt (hoolt) *v* pararse

halve (haav) *v* partir por la mitad

ham (hæm) *n* jamón *m*

hamlet (*hæm*-löt) *n* aldea *f*

hammer (*hæ*-mö) *n* martillo *m*

hammock (*hæ*-mök) *n* hamaca *f*

hamper (*hæm*-pö) *n* cesto *m*

hand (hænd) *n* mano *f*; *v* alargar; ~ **cream** crema para las manos

handbag (*hænd*-bægh) *n* bolso *m*

handbook (*hænd*-buk) *n* manual *m*

hand-brake (*hænd*-breik) *n* freno de mano

handcuffs (*hænd*-kafss) *pl* esposas *fpl*

handful (*hænd*-ful) *n* puñado *m*

handicraft (*hæn*-di-kraaft) *n* trabajo manual; artesanía *f*

handkerchief (*hæng*-kö-chif) *n* pañuelo *m*

handle (*hæn*-döl) *n* mango *m*; *v* manejar; tratar

hand-made (hænd-*meid*) *adj* hecho a mano

handshake (*hænd*-ʃeik) *n* apretón de manos

handsome (*hæn*-ssöm) *adj* guapo

handwork (*hænd*-ᵘöök) *n* obra hecha a mano

handwriting (*hænd*-rai-ting) *n* escritura *f*

handy (*hæn*-di) *adj* manejable

*hang (hæng) *v* *colgar

hanger (*hæng*-ö) *n* percha *f*

hangover (*hæng*-ou-vö) *n* resaca *f*

happen (*hæ*-pön) *v* suceder, pasar

happening (*hæ*-pö-ning) *n* acontecimiento *m*

happiness (*hæ*-pi-nöss) *n* felicidad *f*

happy (*hæ*-pi) *adj* contento, feliz

harbour (haa-bö) *n* puerto *m*

hard (haad) *adj* duro; difícil; **hardly** apenas

hardware (haad-ᵘê⁰) *n* quincalla *f*; ~ **store** ferretería *f*

hare (hê⁰) *n* liebre *f*

harm (haam) *n* perjuicio *m*; mal *m*,

daño m; v perjudicar

harmful (*haam*-fŏl) *adj* perjudicial, dañoso

harmless (*haam*-löss) *adj* inocuo

harmony (*haa*-mö-ni) *n* armonía *f*

harp (haap) *n* arpa *f*

harpsichord (*haap*-ssi-kood) *n* clavicémbalo *m*

harsh (haaʃ) *adj* áspero; severo; cruel

harvest (*haa*-visst) *n* cosecha *f*

has (hæs) *v* (pr have)

haste (heisst) *n* prisa *f*

hasten (*hei*-ssön) *v* apresurarse

hasty (*hei*-ssti) *adj* apresurado

hat (hæt) *n* sombrero *m*; ~ **rack** percha *f*

hatch (hæch) *n* trampa *f*

hate (heit) *v* detestar; odiar; *n* odio *m*

hatred (*hei*-trid) *n* odio *m*

haughty (*hoo*-ti) *adj* altivo

haul (hool) *v* arrastrar

***have** (hæv) *v* *haber, *tener; *hacer; ~ **to** deber

haversack (*hæ*-vö-ssæk) *n* morral *m*

hawk (hook) *n* azor *m*; halcón *m*

hay (hei) *n* heno *m*; ~ **fever** fiebre del heno

hazard (*hæ*-söd) *n* riesgo *m*

haze (heis) *n* calina *f*; niebla *f*

hazelnut (*hei*-söl-nat) *n* avellana *f*

hazy (*hei*-si) *adj* calinoso; brumoso

he (hii) *pron* él

head (hĕd) *n* cabeza *f*; *v* dirigir; ~ **of state** jefe de Estado; ~ **teacher** director de escuela

headache (*hĕ*-deik) *n* dolor de cabeza

heading (*hĕ*-ding) *n* título *m*

headlamp (*hĕd*-læmp) *n* fanal *m*

headland (*hĕd*-lönd) *n* promontorio *m*

headlight (*hĕd*-lait) *n* faro *m*

headline (*hĕd*-lain) *n* titular *m*

headmaster (hĕd-*maa*-sstö) *n* director

de escuela

headquarters (hĕd-*kᵘoo*-tös) *pl* cuartel general

head-strong (*hĕd*-sstrong) *adj* cabezudo

head-waiter (hĕd-ᵘ*ei*-tö) *n* jefe de camareros

heal (hiil) *v* curar

health (hĕlz) *n* salud *f*; ~ **centre** dispensario *m*; ~ **certificate** certificado de salud

healthy (*hĕl*-zi) *adj* sano

heap (hiip) *n* montón *m*

***hear** (hiö) *v* *oír

hearing (*hiö*-ring) *n* oído *m*

heart (haat) *n* corazón *m*; núcleo *m*; **by ~** de memoria; ~ **attack** ataque cardíaco

heartburn (*haat*-böön) *n* acidez *f*

hearth (haaz) *n* hogar *m*

heartless (*haat*-löss) *adj* insensible

hearty (*haa*-ti) *adj* cordial

heat (hiit) *n* calor *m*; *v* *calentar; **heating pad** almohada eléctrica

heater (*hii*-tö) *n* calefactor *m*; **immersion ~** calentador de inmersión

heath (hiiz) *n* landa *f*

heathen (*hii*-ðön) *n* pagano *m*

heather (*hĕ*-ðö) *n* brezo *m*

heating (*hii*-ting) *n* calefacción *f*

heaven (*hĕ*-vön) *n* cielo *m*

heavy (*hĕ*-vi) *adj* pesado

Hebrew (*hii*-bruu) *n* hebreo *m*

hedge (hĕdʒ) *n* seto *m*

hedgehog (*hĕdʒ*-hogh) *n* erizo *m*

heel (hiil) *n* talón *m*; tacón *m*

height (hait) *n* altura *f*; colmo *m*, apogeo *m*

hell (hĕl) *n* infierno *m*

hello! (hĕ-*lou*) ¡hola!; ¡buenos días!

helm (hĕlm) *n* timón *m*

helmet (*hĕl*-mit) *n* casco *m*

helmsman (*hĕlms*-mön) *n* timonero *m*

help (hĕlp) *v* ayudar; *n* ayuda *f*

helper (*hêl*-pö) *n* ayudante *m*
helpful (*hélp*-föl) *adj* servicial
helping (*hêl*-ping) *n* porción *f*
hem (hêm) *n* dobladillo *m*
hemp (hêmp) *n* cáñamo *m*
hen (hên) *n* gallina *f*
henceforth (hênss-*fooz*) *adv* de ahora en adelante
her (höö) *pron* la, le; *adj* su
herb (hööb) *n* hierba *f*
herd (hööd) *n* manada *f*
here (hi*ö*) *adv* acá; ~ **you are** tenga usted
hereditary (hi-*rê*-di-tö-ri) *adj* hereditario
hernia (*höö*-ni-ö) *n* hernia *f*
hero (*hi*ö-rou) *n* (pl ~es) héroe *m*
heron (*hê*-rön) *n* garza *f*
herring (*hê*-ring) *n* (pl ~, ~s) arenque *m*
herself (höö-*ssêlf*) *pron* se; ella misma
hesitate (*hê*-ṣi-teit) *v* vacilar
heterosexual (hê-tö-rö-*ssêk*-ʃu-öl) *adj* heterosexual
hiccup (*hi*-kap) *n* hipo *m*
hide (haid) *n* piel *f*
***hide** (haid) *v* esconder
hideous (*hi*-di-öss) *adj* horrible
hierarchy (*hai*ö-raa-ki) *n* jerarquía *f*
high (hai) *adj* alto
highway (*hai*-ᵘei) *n* carretera *f*; *nAm* autopista *f*
hijack (*hai*-dʒæk) *v* apresar
hijacker (*hai*-dʒæ-kö) *n* secuestrador *m*
hike (haik) *v* caminar
hill (hil) *n* colina *f*
hillside (*hil*-ssaid) *n* ladera *f*
hilltop (*hil*-top) *n* cima *f*
hilly (*hi*-li) *adj* montuoso
him (him) *pron* le
himself (him-*ssêlf*) *pron* se; él mismo
hinder (*hin*-dö) *v* *impedir

hinge (hindʒ) *n* bisagra *f*
hip (hip) *n* cadera *f*
hire (hai*ö*) *v* alquilar; **for** ~ de alquiler
hire-purchase (hai*ö*-*pöö*-chöss) *n* compra a plazos
his (his) *adj* su
historian (hi-*sstoo*-ri-ön) *n* historiador *m*
historic (hi-*ssto*-rik) *adj* histórico
historical (hi-*ssto*-ri-köl) *adj* histórico
history (*hi*-ssto-ri) *n* historia *f*
hit (hit) *n* éxito *m*
***hit** (hit) *v* pegar; tocar, *acertar
hitchhike (*hich*-haik) *v* *hacer autostop
hitchhiker (*hich*-hai-kö) *n* autoestopista *m*
hoarse (hooss) *adj* ronco
hobby (*ho*-bi) *n* afición *f*
hobby-horse (*ho*-bi-hooss) *n* comidilla *f*
hockey (*ho*-ki) *n* hockey *m*
hoist (hoisst) *v* izar
hold (hould) *n* bodega *f*
***hold** (hould) *v* *tener; *retener; ~ **on** agarrarse; ~ **up** *sostener
hold-up (*houl*-dap) *n* atraco *m*
hole (houl) *n* bache *m*, agujero *m*
holiday (*ho*-lö-di) *n* vacaciones *fpl*; fiesta *f*; ~ **camp** colonia veraniega; ~ **resort** lugar de descanso; **on** ~ de vacaciones
Holland (*ho*-lönd) Holanda *f*
hollow (*ho*-lou) *adj* hueco
holy (*hou*-li) *adj* santo
homage (*ho*-midʒ) *n* homenaje *m*
home (houm) *n* casa *f*; hospicio *m*; *adv* en casa, a casa; **at** ~ en casa
home-made (houm-*meid*) *adj* casero
homesickness (*houm*-ssik-nöss) *n* nostalgia *f*
homosexual (hou-mö-*ssêk*-ʃu-öl) *adj* homosexual

honest (*o*-nisst) *adj* honesto; sincero
honesty (*o*-ni-ssti) *n* honradez *f*
honey (*ha*-ni) *n* miel *f*
honeymoon (*ha*-ni-muun) *n* luna de miel
honour (*o*-nö) *n* honor *m*; *v* honrar, *rendir homenaje
honourable (*o*-nö-rö-böl) *adj* honorable; honesto
hood (hud) *n* capucha *f*; *nAm* capó *m*
hoof (huuf) *n* casco *m*
hook (huk) *n* gancho *m*
hoot (huut) *v* tocar la bocina
hooter (*huu*-tö) *n* bocina *f*
hoover (*huu*-vö) *v* pasar el aspirador
hop[1] (hop) *v* brincar; *n* salto *m*
hop[2] (hop) *n* lúpulo *m*
hope (houp) *n* esperanza *f*; *v* esperar
hopeful (*houp*-föl) *adj* esperanzado
hopeless (*houp*-löss) *adj* desesperado
horizon (hö-*rai*-sön) *n* horizonte *m*
horizontal (ho-ri-*son*-töl) *adj* horizontal
horn (hoon) *n* cuerno *m*; bocina *f*
horrible (*ho*-ri-böl) *adj* horrible; terrible, atroz
horror (*ho*-rö) *n* espanto *m*, horror *m*
hors-d'œuvre (oo-*döövr*) *n* entremeses *mpl*
horse (hooss) *n* caballo *m*
horseman (*hooss*-mön) *n* (pl -men) jinete *m*
horsepower (*hooss*-pauö) *n* caballo de vapor
horserace (*hooss*-reiss) *n* carrera de caballos
horseradish (*hooss*-ræ-diʃ) *n* rábano picante
horseshoe (*hooss*-ʃuu) *n* herradura *f*
horticulture (*hoo*-ti-kal-chö) *n* horticultura *f*
hosiery (*hou*-ʒö-ri) *n* géneros de punto

hospitable (*ho*-sspi-tö-böl) *adj* hospitalario
hospital (*ho*-sspi-töl) *n* hospital *m*
hospitality (ho-sspi-*tæ*-lö-ti) *n* hospitalidad *f*
host (housst) *n* anfitrión *m*
hostage (*ho*-sstidʒ) *n* rehén *m*
hostel (*ho*-sstöl) *n* hospedería *f*
hostess (*hou*-sstiss) *n* azafata *f*
hostile (*ho*-sstail) *adj* hostil
hot (hot) *adj* caliente
hotel (hou-*têl*) *n* hotel *m*
hot-tempered (hot-*têm*-pöd) *adj* colérico
hour (auö) *n* hora *f*
hourly (*auö*-li) *adj* a cada hora
house (hauss) *n* casa *f*; vivienda *f*; inmueble *m*; ~ **agent** corredor de casas; ~ **block** *Am* manzana de casas; **public** ~ café *m*
houseboat (*hauss*-bout) *n* casa flotante
household (*hauss*-hould) *n* menaje *m*
housekeeper (*hauss*-kii-pö) *n* ama de llaves
housekeeping (*hauss*-kii-ping) *n* gobierno de la casa
housemaid (*hauss*-meid) *n* criada *f*
housewife (*hauss*-ᵘaif) *n* ama de casa
housework (*hauss*-ᵘöök) *n* faenas domésticas
how (hau) *adv* cómo; qué; ~ **many** cuánto; ~ **much** cuánto
however (hau-*ê*-vö) *conj* todavía, sin embargo
hug (hagh) *v* abrazar; *n* abrazo *m*
huge (hyuudʒ) *adj* formidable, enorme
hum (ham) *v* tararear
human (*hyu*-mön) *adj* humano; ~ **being** ser humano
humanity (hyu-*mæ*-nö-ti) *n* humanidad *f*
humble (*ham*-böl) *adj* humilde

humid (*hyuu*-mid) *adj* húmedo

humidity (hyu-*mi*-dö-ti) *n* humedad *f*

humorous (*hyuu*-mö-röss) *adj* chistoso, gracioso, humorístico

humour (*hyuu*-mö) *n* humor *m*

hundred (*han*-dröd) *n* ciento

Hungarian (hang-*ghêê*-ri-ön) *adj* húngaro

Hungary (*hang*-ghö-ri) Hungría *m*

hunger (*hang*-ghö) *n* hambre *f*

hungry (*hang*-ghri) *adj* hambriento

hunt (hant) *v* cazar; *n* caza *f*; ~ **for** buscar

hunter (*han*-tö) *n* cazador *m*

hurricane (*ha*-ri-kön) *n* huracán *m*; ~ **lamp** lámpara sorda

hurry (*ha*-ri) *v* *darse prisa, apresurarse; *n* prisa *f*; **in a** ~ de prisa

*__hurt__ (hööt) *v* *hacer daño, dañar; ofender

hurtful (*hööt*-föl) *adj* perjudicial

husband (*has*-bönd) *n* esposo *m*, marido *m*

hut (hat) *n* cabaña *f*

hydrogen (*hai*-drö-dӡön) *n* hidrógeno *m*

hygiene (*hai*-dӡiin) *n* higiene *f*

hygienic (hai-*dӡii*-nik) *adj* higiénico

hymn (him) *n* himno *m*

hyphen (*hai*-fön) *n* guión *m*

hypocrisy (hi-*po*-krö-ssi) *n* hipocresía *f*

hypocrite (*hi*-pö-krit) *n* hipócrita *m*

hypocritical (hi-pö-*kri*-ti-köl) *adj* hipócrita, mojigato

hysterical (hi-*sstê*-ri-köl) *adj* histérico

I

I (ai) *pron* yo

ice (aiss) *n* hielo *m*

ice-bag (*aiss*-bægh) *n* bolsa de hielo

ice-cream (*aiss*-kriim) *n* helado *m*

Iceland (*aiss*-lönd) Islandia *f*

Icelander (*aiss*-lön-dö) *n* islandés *m*

Icelandic (aiss-*læn*-dik) *adj* islandés

icon (*ai*-kon) *n* icono *m*

idea (ai-*diº*) *n* idea *f*; pensamiento *m*; noción *f*, concepto *m*

ideal (ai-*diºl*) *adj* ideal; *n* ideal *m*

identical (ai-*dên*-ti-köl) *adj* idéntico

identification (ai-dên-ti-fi-*kei*-ʃön) *n* identificación *f*

identify (ai-*dên*-ti-fai) *v* identificar

identity (ai-*dên*-tö-ti) *n* identidad *f*; ~ **card** carnet de identidad

idiom (*i*-di-öm) *n* modismo *m*

idiomatic (i-di-ö-*mæ*-tik) *adj* idiomático

idiot (*i*-di-öt) *n* idiota *m*

idiotic (i-di-*o*-tik) *adj* idiota

idle (*ai*-döl) *adj* ocioso; vago; vano

idol (*ai*-döl) *n* ídolo *m*

if (if) *conj* si

ignition (igh-*ni*-ʃön) *n* encendido *m*; ~ **coil** bobina del encendido

ignorant (*igh*-nö-rönt) *adj* ignorante

ignore (igh-*noo*) *v* ignorar

ill (il) *adj* enfermo; malo; maligno

illegal (i-*lii*-ghöl) *adj* ilegal

illegible (i-*lê*-dӡö-böl) *adj* ilegible

illiterate (i-*li*-tö-röt) *n* analfabeto *m*

illness (*il*-nöss) *n* enfermedad *f*

illuminate (i-*luu*-mi-neit) *v* iluminar

illumination (i-luu-mi-*nei*-ʃön) *n* iluminación *f*

illusion (i-*luu*-ӡön) *n* ilusión *f*

illustrate (*i*-lö-sstreit) *v* ilustrar

illustration (i-lö-*sstrei*-ʃön) *n* ilustración *f*

image (*i*-midӡ) *n* imagen *f*

imaginary (i-*mæ*-dӡi-nö-ri) *adj* imaginario

imagination (i-*mæ*-dӡi-*nei*-ʃön) *n* imaginación *f*

imagine (i-*mæ*-dӡin) *v* imaginarse; fi-

gurarse
imitate (*i*-mi-teit) *v* imitar
imitation (i-mi-*tei*-ſön) *n* imitación *f*
immediate (i-*mii*-dyöt) *adj* inmediato
immediately (i-*mii*-dyöt-li) *adv* inmediatamente, de inmediato
immense (i-*mênss*) *adj* inmenso, enorme
immigrant (*i*-mi-ghrönt) *n* inmigrante *m*
immigrate (*i*-mi-ghreit) *v* inmigrar
immigration (i-mi-*ghrei*-ſön) *n* inmigración *f*
immodest (i-*mo*-disst) *adj* inmodesto
immunity (i-*myuu*-nö-ti) *n* inmunidad *f*
immunize (*i*-myu-nais) *v* inmunizar
impartial (im-*paa*-ſöl) *adj* imparcial
impassable (im-*paa*-ssö-böl) *adj* intransitable
impatient (im-*pei*-ſönt) *adj* impaciente
impede (im-*piid*) *v* *impedir
impediment (im-*pê*-di-mönt) *n* impedimento *m*
imperfect (im-*pöö*-fikt) *adj* imperfecto
imperial (im-*piⁿ*-ri-öl) *adj* imperial
impersonal (im-*pöö*-ssö-nöl) *adj* impersonal
impertinence (im-*pöö*-ti-nönss) *n* impertinencia *f*
impertinent (im-*pöö*-ti-nönt) *adj* grosero, descarado, impertinente
implement[1] (*im*-pli-mönt) *n* herramienta *f*
implement[2] (*im*-pli-mênt) *v* efectuar
imply (im-*plai*) *v* implicar
impolite (im-pö-*lait*) *adj* descortés
import[1] (im-*poot*) *v* importar
import[2] (*im*-poot) *n* importación *f*; ~ **duty** impuestos de importación
importance (im-*poo*-tönss) *n* importancia *f*
important (im-*poo*-tönt) *adj* impor-

tante
importer (im-*poo*-tö) *n* importador *m*
imposing (im-*pou*-sing) *adj* imponente
impossible (im-*po*-ssö-böl) *adj* imposible
impotence (*im*-pö-tönss) *n* impotencia *f*
impotent (*im*-pö-tönt) *adj* impotente
impound (im-*paund*) *v* confiscar
impress (im-*prêss*) *v* impresionar
impression (im-*prê*-ſön) *n* impresión *f*
impressive (im-*prê*-ssiv) *adj* impresionante
imprison (im-*pri*-sön) *v* encarcelar
imprisonment (im-*pri*-sön-mönt) *n* encarcelamiento *m*
improbable (im-*pro*-bö-böl) *adj* improbable
improper (im-*pro*-pö) *adj* impropio
improve (im-*pruuv*) *v* mejorar
improvement (im-*pruuv*-mönt) *n* mejora *f*
improvise (*im*-prö-vais) *v* improvisar
impudent (*im*-pyu-dönt) *adj* impudente
impulse (*im*-palss) *n* impulso *m*; estímulo *m*
impulsive (im-*pal*-ssiv) *adj* impulsivo
in (in) *prep* en; dentro de; *adv* adentro
inaccessible (i-næk-*ssê*-ssö-böl) *adj* inaccesible
inaccurate (i-*næ*-kyu-röt) *adj* inexacto
inadequate (i-*næ*-di-kᵘöt) *adj* inadecuado
incapable (ing-*kei*-pö-böl) *adj* incapaz
incense (*in*-ssênss) *n* incienso *m*
incident (*in*-ssi-dönt) *n* incidente *m*
incidental (in-ssi-*dên*-töl) *adj* imprevisto
incite (in-*ssait*) *v* incitar
inclination (ing-kli-*nei*-ſön) *n* inclinación *f*
incline (ing-*klain*) *n* inclinación *f*

inclined (ing-*klaind*) *adj* dispuesto, inclinado; *be ~ to* v inclinarse
include (ing-*kluud*) v *incluir
inclusive (ing-*kluu*-ssiv) *adj* incluso
income (*ing*-köm) n ingresos *mpl*
income-tax (*ing*-köm-tækss) n impuesto sobre los ingresos
incompetent (ing-*kom*-pö-tönt) *adj* incompetente
incomplete (in-köm-*pliit*) *adj* incompleto
inconceivable (ing-kön-*ssii*-vö-böl) *adj*
inconcebible
inconspicuous (ing-kön-*sspi*-kyu-öss)
adj discreto
inconvenience (ing-kön-*vii*-nyönss) n
incomodidad f, inconveniencia f
inconvenient (ing-kön-*vii*-nyönt) *adj*
inoportuno; molesto
incorrect (ing-kö-*rêkt*) *adj* inexacto,
incorrecto
increase[1] (ing-*kriiss*) v aumentar; incrementar, *acrecentarse
increase[2] (*Ing*-kriiss) n aumento m
incredible (ing-*krê*-dö-böl) *adj* increíble
incurable (ing-*kyuᵒ*-rö-böl) *adj* incurable
indecent (in-*dii*-ssönt) *adj* indecente
indeed (in-*diid*) *adv* por cierto
indefinite (in-*dê*-fi-nit) *adj* indefinido
indemnity (in-*dêm*-nö-ti) n indemnización f
independence (in-di-*pên*-dönss) n independencia f
independent (in-di-*pên*-dönt) *adj* independiente; autónomo
index (*in*-dêkss) n índice m; ~ finger
índice m
India (*in*-di-ö) India f
Indian (*in*-di-ön) *adj* indio; n indio m
indicate (*in*-di-keit) v señalar, indicar
indication (in-di-*kei*-jön) n señal f, indicación f

indicator (*in*-di-kei-tö) n indicador m
indifferent (in-*di*-fö-rönt) *adj* indiferente
indigestion (in-di-*dʒêss*-chön) n indigestión f
indignation (in-digh-*nei*-jön) n indignación f
indirect (in-di-*rêkt*) *adj* indirecto
individual (in-di-*vi*-dʒu-öl) *adj* aparte,
individual; n individuo m
Indonesia (in-dö-*nii*-si-ö) Indonesia f
Indonesian (in-dö-*nii*-si-ön) *adj* indonesio
indoor (*in*-doo) *adj* en casa
indoors (in-*doos*) *adv* en casa
indulge (in-*daldʒ*) v ceder
industrial (in-*da*-sstri-öl) *adj* industrial; ~ area zona industrial
industrious (in-*da*-sstri-öss) *adj* diligente
industry (*in*-dö-sstri) n industria f
inedible (i-*nê*-di-böl) *adj* incomible
inefficient (i-ni-*fi*-jönt) *adj* ineficiente
inevitable (i-*nê*-vi-tö-böl) *adj* inevitable
inexpensive (i-nik-*sspên*-ssiv) *adj* barato
inexperienced (i-nik-*sspiᵒ*-ri-önsst) *adj*
inexperto
infant (*in*-fönt) n criatura f
infantry (*in*-fön-tri) n infantería f
infect (in-*fêkt*) v infectar
infection (in-*fêk*-jön) n infección f
infectious (in-*fêk*-jöss) *adj* contagioso
infer (in-*föö*) v *deducir
inferior (in-*fiᵒ*-ri-ö) *adj* inferior
infinite (*in*-fi-nöt) *adj* infinito
infinitive (in-*fi*-ni-tiv) n infinitivo m
infirmary (in-*föö*-mö-ri) n enfermería
f
inflammable (in-*flæ*-mö-böl) *adj* inflamable
inflammation (in-flö-*mei*-jön) n inflamación f

inflatable (in-*flei*-tö-böl) *adj* inflable
inflate (in-*fleit*) *v* hinchar
inflation (in-*flei*-Jön) *n* inflación *f*
influence (*in*-flu-önss) *n* influencia *f*; *v* *influir
influential (in-flu-*ên*-Jöl) *adj* influyente
influenza (in-flu-*ên*-sö) *n* gripe *f*
inform (in-*foom*) *v* informar; comunicar
informal (in-*foo*-möl) *adj* informal
information (in-fö-*mei*-Jön) *n* información *f*; informes *mpl*, comunicado *m*; ~ **bureau** oficina de informaciones
infra-red (in-frö-*rêd*) *adj* infrarrojo
infrequent (in-*frii*-kᵘönt) *adj* infrecuente
ingredient (ing-*ghrii*-di-önt) *n* ingrediente *m*
inhabit (in-*hæ*-bit) *v* habitar
inhabitable (in-*hæ*-bi-tö-böl) *adj* habitable
inhabitant (in-*hæ*-bi-tönt) *n* habitante *m*
inhale (in-*heil*) *v* inhalar
inherit (in-*hê*-rit) *v* heredar
inheritance (in-*hê*-ri-tönss) *n* herencia *f*
initial (i-*ni*-Jöl) *adj* inicial; *n* inicial *f*; *v* rubricar
initiative (i-*ni*-Jö-tiv) *n* iniciativa *f*
inject (in-*dʒêkt*) *v* inyectar
injection (in-*dʒêk*-Jön) *n* inyección *f*
injure (*in*-dʒö) *v* *herir; ofender
injury (*in*-dʒö-ri) *n* herida *f*; lesión *f*
injustice (in-*dʒa*-sstiss) *n* injusticia *f*
ink (ingk) *n* tinta *f*
inlet (*in*-lêt) *n* ensenada *f*
inn (in) *n* posada *f*
inner (*i*-nö) *adj* interior; ~ **tube** cámara de aire
inn-keeper (*in*-kii-pö) *n* posadero *m*
innocence (*i*-nö-ssönss) *n* inocencia *f*

innocent (*i*-nö-ssönt) *adj* inocente
inoculate (i-*no*-kyu-leit) *v* vacunar
inoculation (i-no-kyu-*lei*-Jön) *n* inoculación *f*
inquire (ing-kᵘ*ai*ᵒ) *v* informarse, *pedir informes
inquiry (ing-kᵘ*ai*ᵒ-ri) *n* pregunta *f*, indagación *f*; encuesta *f*; ~ **office** oficina de informaciones
inquisitive (ing-kᵘ*i*-sö-tiv) *adj* curioso
insane (in-*ssein*) *adj* lunático
inscription (in-*sskrip*-Jön) *n* inscripción *f*
insect (*in*-ssêkt) *n* insecto *m*; ~ **repellent** insectífugo *m*
insecticide (in-*ssêk*-ti-ssaid) *n* insecticida *m*
insensitive (in-*ssên*-ssö-tiv) *adj* insensible
insert (in-*ssööt*) *v* insertar
inside (in-*ssaid*) *n* interior *m*; *adj* interior; *adv* adentro; dentro; *prep* en, dentro de; ~ **out** al revés; **insides** entrañas *fpl*
insight (*in*-ssait) *n* entendimiento *m*
insignificant (in-ssigh-*ni*-fi-könt) *adj* insignificante; irrelevante; baladí
insist (in-*ssisst*) *v* insistir; persistir
insolence (*in*-ssö-lönss) *n* insolencia *f*
insolent (*in*-ssö-lönt) *adj* insolente
insomnia (in-*ssom*-ni-ö) *n* insomnio *m*
inspect (in-*sspêkt*) *v* inspeccionar
inspection (in-*sspêk*-Jön) *n* inspección *f*; control *m*
inspector (in-*sspêk*-tö) *n* inspector *m*
inspire (in-*sspai*ᵒ) *v* inspirar
install (in-*sstool*) *v* instalar
installation (in-sstö-*lei*-Jön) *n* instalación *f*
instalment (in-*sstool*-mönt) *n* plazo *m*
instance (*in*-sstönss) *n* ejemplo *m*; caso *m*; **for** ~ por ejemplo
instant (*in*-sstönt) *n* instante *m*

instantly (*in*-sstönt-li) *adv* instantáneamente, inmediatamente, al instante

instead of (in-*sstêd* ov) en lugar de

instinct (*in*-sstingkt) *n* instinto *m*

institute (*in*-ssti-tyuut) *n* instituto *m*; institución *f*; *v* *instituir

institution (in-ssti-*tyuu*-Jön) *n* instituto *m*, institución *f*

instruct (in-*sstrakt*) *v* *instruir

instruction (in-*sstrak*-Jön) *n* instrucción *f*

instructive (in-*sstrak*-tiv) *adj* instructivo

instructor (in-*sstrak*-tö) *n* instructor *m*

instrument (*in*-sstru-mönt) *n* instrumento *m*; **musical** ~ instrumento músico

insufficient (in-ssö-*fi*-Jönt) *adj* insuficiente

insulate (*in*-ssyu-leit) *v* aislar

insulation (in-ssyu-*lei*-Jön) *n* aislamiento *m*

insulator (*in*-ssyu-lei-tö) *n* aislador *m*

insult[1] (in-*ssalt*) *v* insultar

insult[2] (*in*-ssalt) *n* insulto *m*

insurance (in-*Juô*-rönss) *n* seguro *m*; ~ **policy** póliza de seguro

insure (in-*Juô*) *v* asegurar

intact (in-*tækt*) *adj* intacto

intellect (*in*-tö-lêkt) *n* intelecto *m*

intellectual (in-tö-*lêk*-chu-öl) *adj* intelectual

intelligence (in-*tê*-li-dʒönss) *n* inteligencia *f*

intelligent (in-*tê*-li-dʒönt) *adj* inteligente

intend (in-*tênd*) *v* intentar, *tener la intención de

intense (in-*tênss*) *adj* intenso

intention (in-*tên*-Jön) *n* intención *f*

intentional (in-*tên*-J-nöl) *adj* intencional

intercourse (*in*-tö-kooss) *n* trato *m*

interest (*in*-trösst) *n* interés *m*; rédito *m*; *v* interesar

interesting (*in*-trö-ssting) *adj* interesante

interfere (in-tö-*fiô*) *v* interferir; ~ **with** mezclarse en

interference (in-tö-*fiô*-rönss) *n* interferencia *f*

interim (*in*-tö-rim) *n* interin *m*

interior (in-*tiô*-ri-ö) *n* interior *m*

interlude (*in*-tö-luud) *n* intermedio *m*

intermediary (in tö-*mii*-dyö-ri) *n* intermediario *m*

intermission (in-tö-*mi*-Jön) *n* entreacto *m*

internal (in-*töö*-nöl) *adj* interno

international (in-tö-*næ*-Jö-nöl) *adj* internacional

interpret (in-*töö*-prit) *v* interpretar

interpreter (in-*töö*-pri-tö) *n* intérprete *m*

interrogate (in *tê*-rö-gheit) *v* interrogar

interrogation (in-tê-rö-*ghei*-Jön) *n* interrogatorio *m*

interrogative (in-tö-*ro*-ghö-tiv) *adj* interrogativo

interrupt (in-tö-*rapt*) *v* interrumpir

interruption (in-tö-*rap*-Jön) *n* interrupción *f*

intersection (in-tö-*ssêk*-Jön) *n* intersección *f*

interval (*in*-tö-völ) *n* intervalo *m*

intervene (in-tö-*viin*) *v* *intervenir

interview (*in*-tö-vyuu) *n* entrevista *f*

intestine (in-*tê*-sstin) *n* intestino *m*

intimate (*in*-ti-möt) *adj* íntimo

into (*in*-tu) *prep* dentro de

intolerable (in-*to*-lö-rö-böl) *adj* insoportable

intoxicated (in-*tok*-ssi-kei-tid) *adj* embriagado

intrigue (in-*triigh*) *n* intriga *f*

introduce (in-trö-*dyuuss*) *v* presentar;
*introducir

introduction (in-trö-*dak*-ʃön) *n* presentación *f*; introducción *f*

invade (in-*veid*) *v* invadir

invalid¹ (*in*-vö-liid) *n* inválido *m*; *adj*
inválido

invalid² (in-*væ*-lid) *adj* nulo

invasion (in-*vei*-ӡön) *n* irrupción *f*, invasión *f*

invent (in-*vênt*) *v* inventar

invention (in-*vên*-ʃön) *n* invención *f*

inventive (in-*vên*-tiv) *adj* inventivo

inventor (in-*vên*-tö) *n* inventor *m*

inventory (*in*-vön-tri) *n* inventario *m*

invert (in-*vööt*) *v* *invertir

invest (in-*vêsst*) *v* *invertir

investigate (in-*vê*-ssti-gheit) *v* investigar

investigation (in-vê-ssti-*ghei*-ʃön) *n*
investigación *f*

investment (in-*vêsst*-mönt) *n* inversión *f*

investor (in-*vê*-sstö) *n* inversionista *m*

invisible (in-*vi*-sö-böl) *adj* invisible

invitation (in-vi-*tei*-ʃön) *n* invitación *f*

invite (in-*vait*) *v* invitar, convidar

invoice (*in*-voiss) *n* factura *f*

involve (in-*volv*) *v* *envolver; **involved** implicado

inwards (*in*-ᵘöds) *adv* hacia adentro

iodine (*ai*-ö-diin) *n* yodo *m*

Iran (i-*raan*) Irán *m*

Iranian (i-*rei*-ni-ön) *adj* iraní

Iraq (i-*raak*) Irak *m*

Iraqi (i-*raa*-ki) *adj* iraquí

irascible (i-*ræ*-ssi-böl) *adj* irascible

Ireland (*aiᵒ*-lönd) Irlanda *f*

Irish (*aiᵒ*-riʃ) *adj* irlandés

Irishman (*aiᵒ*-riʃ-mön) *n* (pl -men) irlandés *m*

iron (*ai*-ön) *n* hierro *m*; plancha *f*; de
hierro; *v* planchar

ironical (ai-*ro*-ni-köl) *adj* irónico

ironworks (*ai*-ön-ᵘöökss) *n* herrería *f*

irony (*aiᵒ*-rö-ni) *n* ironía *f*

irregular (i-*rê*-ghyu-lö) *adj* irregular

irreparable (i-*rê*-pö-rö-böl) *adj* irreparable

irrevocable (i-*rê*-vö-kö-böl) *adj* irrevocable

irritable (*i*-ri-tö-böl) *adj* irritable

irritate (*i*-ri-teit) *v* irritar

is (is) *v* (pr be)

island (*ai*-lönd) *n* isla *f*

isolate (*ai*-ssö-leit) *v* aislar

isolation (ai-ssö-*lei*-ʃön) *n* aislamiento
m

Israel (*is*-reil) Israel *m*

Israeli (is-*rei*-li) *adj* israelí

issue (*i*-ʃuu) *v* *distribuir; *n* emisión
f, tirada *f*, edición *f*; cuestión *f*,
punto *m*; consecuencia *f*, resultado
m, conclusión *f*, término *m*; salida
f

isthmus (*iss*-möss) *n* istmo *m*

it (it) *pron* lo

Italian (i-*tæl*-yön) *adj* italiano

italics (i-*tæ*-likss) *pl* cursiva *f*

Italy (*i*-tö-li) Italia *f*

itch (ich) *n* picazón *f*; prurito *m*; *v*
picar

item (*ai*-töm) *n* ítem *m*; punto *m*

itinerant (ai-*ti*-nö-rönt) *adj* ambulante

itinerary (ai-*ti*-nö-rö-ri) *n* itinerario *m*

ivory (*ai*-vö-ri) *n* marfil *m*

ivy (*ai*-vi) *n* hiedra *f*

J

jack (dӡæk) *n* gato *m*

jacket (*dӡæ*-kit) *n* americana *f*, chaqueta *f*; sobrecubierta *f*; saco *mMe*

jade (dӡeid) *n* jade *m*

jail (dӡeil) *n* cárcel *f*

jailer (*dӡei*-lö) *n* carcelero *m*

jam (dʒæm) *n* mermelada *f*; congestión *f*

janitor (*dʒæ*-ni-tö) *n* conserje *m*

January (*dʒæ*-nyu-ö-ri) enero

Japan (dʒö-*pæn*) Japón *m*

Japanese (dʒæ-pö-*niis*) *adj* japonés

jar (dʒaa) *n* jarra *f*

jaundice (*dʒoon*-diss) *n* ictericia *f*

jaw (dʒoo) *n* mandíbula *f*

jealous (*dʒê*-löss) *adj* celoso

jealousy (*dʒê*-lö-ssi) *n* celos *m*

jeans (dʒiins) *pl* vaqueros *mpl*

jelly (*dʒê*-li) *n* jalea *f*

jelly-fish (*dʒê*-li-fiʃ) *n* medusa *f*

jersey (*dʒöö*-si) *n* jersey *m*

jet (dʒêt) *n* chorro *m*; avión a reacción

jetty (*dʒê*-ti) *n* muelle *m*

Jew (dʒuu) *n* judío *m*

jewel (*dʒuu*-öl) *n* joya *f*

jeweller (*dʒuu*-ö-lö) *n* joyero *m*

jewellery (*dʒuu*-öl-ri) *n* joyería *f*

Jewish (*dʒuu*-iʃ) *adj* judío

job (dʒob) *n* tarea *f*; puesto *m*, empleo *m*

jockey (*dʒo*-ki) *n* jockey *m*

join (dʒoin) *v* juntar; unirse a, asociarse a; ensamblar, reunir

joint (dʒoint) *n* articulación *f*; soldadura *f*; *adj* unido, en común

jointly (*dʒoint*-li) *adv* juntamente

joke (dʒouk) *n* broma *f*

jolly (*dʒo*-li) *adj* jovial

Jordan (*dʒoo*-dön) Jordania *f*

Jordanian (dʒoo-*dei*-ni-ön) *adj* jordano

journal (*dʒöö*-nöl) *n* revista *f*

journalism (*dʒöö*-nö-li-söm) *n* periodismo *m*

journalist (*dʒöö*-nö-lisst) *n* periodista *m*

journey (*dʒöö*-ni) *n* viaje *m*

joy (dʒoi) *n* delicia *f*, regocijo *m*

joyful (*dʒoi*-föl) *adj* contento, alegre

jubilee (*dʒuu*-bi-lii) *n* aniversario *m*

judge (dʒadʒ) *n* juez *m*; *v* juzgar

judgment (*dʒadʒ*-mönt) *n* juicio *m*

jug (dʒagh) *n* cántaro *m*

juggernaut (*dʒagh*-ö-noot) *n* camión grande *m*

juice (dʒuuss) *n* zumo *m*

juicy (*dʒuu*-ssi) *adj* zumoso

July (dʒu-*lai*) julio

jump (dʒamp) *v* saltar; *n* salto *m*

jumper (*dʒam*-pö) *n* jersey *m*

junction (*dʒangk*-ʃön) *n* encrucijada *f*; empalme *m*

June (dʒuun) junio

jungle (*dʒang*-ghöl) *n* selva *f*, jungla *f*

junior (*dʒuu*-nyö) *adj* menor;
~ **school** escuela primaria

junk (dʒangk) *n* cachivache *m*

jury (*dʒuᵒ*-ri) *n* jurado *m*

just (dʒasst) *adj* justo; *adv* apenas; justamente

justice (*dʒa*-sstiss) *n* derecho *m*; justicia *f*

juvenile (*dʒuu*-vö-nail) *adj* juvenil

K

kangaroo (kæng-ghö-*ruu*) *n* canguro *m*

keel (kiil) *n* quilla *f*

keen (kiin) *adj* entusiasta; agudo

* **keep** (kiip) *v* *tener; guardar; continuar; ~ **away from** *mantenerse alejado de; ~ **off** no tocar; ~ **on** continuar; ~ **quiet** *estarse quieto; ~ **up** perseverar; ~ **up with** *seguir el paso

keg (kêgh) *n* barrilete *m*

kennel (*kê*-nöl) *n* perrera *f*; perrera *m*

Kenya (*kê*-nyö) Kenya *m*

kerosene (*kê*-rö-ssiin) *n* petróleo lampante

kettle (*kê*-töl) *n* olla *f*

key (kii) *n* llave *f*

keyhole (*kii*-houl) *n* ojo de la cerradura

khaki (*kaa*-ki) *n* caqui *m*

kick (kik) *v* patear; *n* patada *f*

kick-off (ki-*kof*) *n* saque inicial

kid (kid) *n* niño *m*, chico *m*; cabritilla *f*; *v* embromar

kidney (*kid*-ni) *n* riñón *m*

kill (kil) *v* matar

kilogram (*ki*-lö-ghræm) *n* kilogramo *m*

kilometre (*ki*-lö-mii-tö) *n* kilómetro *m*

kind (kaind) *adj* amable, bondadoso; bueno; *n* género *m*

kindergarten (*kin*-dö-ghaa-tön) *n* escuela de párvulos, jardín de infancia

king (king) *n* rey *m*

kingdom (*king*-döm) *n* reino *m*

kiosk (*kii*-ossk) *n* quiosco *m*

kiss (kiss) *n* beso *m*; *v* besar

kit (kit) *n* avíos *mpl*

kitchen (*ki*-chin) *n* cocina *f*; ~ **garden** huerto *m*

Kleenex® (*klii*-nêkss) *n* pañuelo de papel

knapsack (*næp*-ssæk) *n* mochila *f*

knave (neiv) *n* sota *f*

knee (nii) *n* rodilla *f*

kneecap (*nii*-kæp) *n* rótula *f*

*kneel (niil) *v* arrodillarse

knew (nyuu) *v* (p know)

knickers (*ni*-kös) *pl* braga *f*

knife (naif) *n* (pl knives) cuchillo *m*

knight (nait) *n* caballero *m*

*knit (nit) *v* *hacer punto

knob (nob) *n* botón *m*

knock (nok) *v* golpear; *n* golpe *m*; ~ **against** chocar contra; ~ **down** derribar

knot (not) *n* nudo *m*; *v* anudar

*know (nou) *v* *saber, *conocer

knowledge (*no*-lidʒ) *n* conocimiento *m*

knuckle (*na*-köl) *n* nudillo *m*

L

label (*lei*-böl) *n* rótulo *m*; *v* rotular

laboratory (lö-*bo*-rö-tö-ri) *n* laboratorio *m*

labour (*lei*-bö) *n* trabajo *m*, labor *f*; dolores *mpl*; *v* ajetrearse, bregar; **labor permit** *Am* permiso de trabajo

labourer (*lei*-bö-rö) *n* obrero *m*

labour-saving (*lei*-bö-ssei-ving) *adj* economizador de trabajo

labyrinth (*læ*-bö-rinz) *n* laberinto *m*

lace (leiss) *n* puntilla *f*; cordón *m*

lack (læk) *n* falta *f*; *v* *carecer

lacquer (*læ*-kö) *n* laca *f*

lad (læd) *n* joven *m*, muchacho *m*

ladder (*læ*-dö) *n* escalera de mano

lady (*lei*-di) *n* señora *f*; **ladies' room** lavabos para señoras

lagoon (lö-*ghuun*) *n* laguna *f*

lake (leik) *n* lago *m*

lamb (læm) *n* cordero *m*

lame (leim) *adj* paralítico, cojo

lamentable (*læ*-mön-tö-böl) *adj* lamentable

lamp (læmp) *n* lámpara *f*

lamp-post (*læmp*-pousst) *n* poste de farol

lampshade (*læmp*-ʃeid) *n* pantalla *f*

land (lænd) *n* país *m*, tierra *f*; *v* aterrizar; desembarcar

landlady (*lænd*-lei-di) *n* patrona *f*

landlord (*lænd*-lood) *n* propietario *m*, dueño *m*; patrón *m*

landmark (*lænd*-maak) *n* punto de referencia; mojón *m*

landscape (*lænd*-sskeip) *n* paisaje *m*

lane (lein) *n* callejón *m*; pista *f*

language (*læng*-gh^uidʒ) *n* lengua *f*; ~ **laboratory** laboratorio de lenguas

lantern (*læn*-tön) *n* linterna *f*

lapel (lö-*pél*) *n* solapa *f*

larder (*laa*-dö) *n* despensa *f*

large (laadʒ) *adj* grande; espacioso

lark (laak) *n* alondra *f*

laryngitis (læ-rin-*dʒai*-tiss) *n* laringitis *f*

last (laasst) *adj* último; precedente; *v* durar; **at** ~ al fin; al final

lasting (*laa*-ssting) *adj* duradero

latchkey (*læch*-kii) *n* llave de la casa

late (leit) *adj* tardío; retrasado

lately (*leit*-li) *adv* últimamente, recientemente

lather (*laa*-ðö) *n* espuma *f*

Latin America (*læ*-tin ö-*mê*-ri-kö) América Latina

Latin-American (læ-tin-ö-*mê*-ri-kön) *adj* latinoamericano

latitude (*læ*-ti-tyuud) *n* latitud *f*

laugh (laaf) *v* *reír; *n* risa *f*

laughter (*laaf*-tö) *n* risa *f*

launch (loonch) *v* lanzar; *n* buque a motor

launching (*loon*-ching) *n* botadura *f*

launderette (loon-dö-*rêt*) *n* lavandería de autoservicio

laundry (*loon*-dri) *n* lavandería *f*; ropa sucia

lavatory (*læ*-vö-tö-ri) *n* cuarto de aseo

lavish (*læ*-viʃ) *adj* pródigo

law (loo) *n* ley *f*; derecho *m*; ~ **court** tribunal *m*

lawful (*loo*-föl) *adj* lícito

lawn (loon) *n* césped *m*

lawsuit (*loo*-ssuut) *n* proceso *m*, causa *f*

lawyer (*loo*-yö) *n* abogado *m*; jurista *m*

laxative (*læk*-ssö-tiv) *n* laxante *m*

***lay** (lei) *v* colocar, *poner; ~ **bricks** mampostear

layer (lei^ö) *n* capa *f*

layman (*lei*-mön) *n* profano *m*

lazy (*lei*-si) *adj* perezoso

lead¹ (liid) *n* ventaja *f*; dirección *f*; trailla *f*

lead² (lêd) *n* plomo *m*

***lead** (liid) *v* *conducir

leader (*lii*-dö) *n* jefe *m*, líder *m*

leadership (*lii*-dö-ʃip) *n* dirección *f*

leading (*lii*-ding) *adj* dominante, principal

leaf (liif) *n* (pl leaves) hoja *f*

league (liigh) *n* liga *f*

leak (liik) *v* gotear; *n* goteo *m*

leaky (*lii*-ki) *adj* que tiene escapes

lean (liin) *adj* magro

***lean** (liin) *v* apoyarse

leap (liip) *n* salto *m*

***leap** (liip) *v* saltar

leap-year (*liip*-yl^ö) *n* año bisiesto

***learn** (löön) *v* aprender

learner (*löö*-nö) *n* principiante *m*

lease (liiss) *n* contrato de arrendamiento; arrendamiento *m*; *v* *arrendar, alquilar

leash (liiʃ) *n* correa *f*

least (liisst) *adj* mínimo, menos; **at** ~ por lo menos

leather (*lê*-ðö) *n* cuero *m*; de piel

leave (liiv) *n* licencia *f*

***leave** (liiv) *v* partir, dejar; ~ **out** omitir

Lebanese (lê-bö-*niis*) *adj* libanés

Lebanon (*lê*-bö-nön) *n* Líbano *m*

lecture (*lêk*-chö) *n* curso *m*, conferencia *f*

left¹ (lêft) *adj* izquierdo

left² (lêft) *v* (p, pp leave)

left-hand (*lêft*-hænd) *adj* izquierdo, de izquierda

left-handed (lêft-*hæn*-did) *adj* zurdo

leg (lêgh) *n* pata *f*, pierna *f*

legacy (*lê*-ghö-ssi) *n* herencia *f*

legal (*lii*-ghöl) *adj* legítimo, legal; jurídico

legalization (lii-ghö-lai-*sei*-ʃön) *n* legalización *f*

legation (li-*ghei*-ʃön) *n* legación *f*

legible (*lê*-dʒi-böl) *adj* legible

legitimate (li-*dʒi*-ti-möt) *adj* legítimo

leisure (*lê*-ʒö) *n* ocio *m*; comodidad *f*

lemon (*lê*-mön) *n* limón *m*

lemonade (lê-mö-*neid*) *n* limonada *f*

*****lend** (lênd) *v* prestar

length (lêngz) *n* longitud *f*

lengthen (*lêng*-zön) *v* alargar

lengthways (*lêngz*-ᵘeis) *adv* longitudinalmente

lens (lêns) *n* lente *m/f*; **telephoto ~** teleobjetivo *m*; **zoom ~** lente de foco regulable

leprosy (*lê*-prö-ssi) *n* lepra *f*

less (lêss) *adv* menos

lessen (*lê*-ssön) *v* *disminuir

lesson (*lê*-ssön) *n* lección *f*

*****let** (lêt) *v* dejar; alquilar; **~ down** decepcionar

letter (*lê*-tö) *n* carta *f*; letra *f*; **~ of credit** carta de crédito; **~ of recommendation** carta de recomendación

letter-box (*lê*-tö-bokss) *n* buzón *m*

lettuce (*lê*-tiss) *n* lechuga *f*

level (*lê*-völ) *adj* igual; plano, llano; *n* nivel *m*; *v* igualar, nivelar; **~ crossing** paso a nivel

lever (*lii*-vö) *n* palanca *f*

Levis (*lii*-vais) *pl* jeans *mpl*

liability (lai-ö-*bi*-lö-ti) *n* responsabilidad *f*

liable (*lai*-ö-böl) *adj* responsable; **~ to** sujeto a

liberal (*li*-bö-röl) *adj* liberal; generoso, dadivoso

liberation (li-bö-*rei*-ʃön) *n* liberación *f*

Liberia (lai-*biᵒ*-ri-ö) Liberia *f*

Liberian (lai-*biᵒ*-ri-ön) *adj* liberiano

liberty (*li*-bö-ti) *n* libertad *f*

library (*lai*-brö-ri) *n* biblioteca *f*

licence (*lai*-ssönss) *n* licencia *f*; permiso *m*; **driving ~** permiso de conducir

license (*lai*-ssönss) *v* autorizar

lick (lik) *v* lamer

lid (lid) *n* tapa *f*

lie (lai) *v* *mentir; *n* mentira *f*

*****lie** (lai) *v* *yacer; **~ down** *tenderse

life (laif) *n* (pl lives) vida *f*; **~ insurance** seguro de vida

lifebelt (*laif*-bêlt) *n* chaleco salvavidas

lifetime (*laif*-taim) *n* vida *f*

lift (lift) *v* levantar; *n* ascensor *m*; elevador *mMe*

light (lait) *n* luz *f*; *adj* ligero; pálido; **~ bulb** bulbo *m*

*****light** (lait) *v* *encender

lighter (*lai*-tö) *n* encendedor *m*

lighthouse (*lait*-hauss) *n* faro *m*

lighting (*lai*-ting) *n* alumbrado *m*

lightning (*lait*-ning) *n* relámpago *m*

like (laik) *v* *querer; gustar; *adj* semejante; *conj* como

likely (*lai*-kli) *adj* probable

like-minded (laik-*main*-did) *adj* unánime

likewise (*laik*-ᵘais) *adv* así también, asimismo

lily (*li*-li) *n* azucena *f*

limb (lim) *n* miembro *m*

lime (laim) *n* cal *f*; tilo *m*; lima *f*

limetree (*laim*-trii) *n* tilo *m*

limit (*li*-mit) *n* límite *m*; *v* limitar

limp (limp) *v* cojear; *adj* inerte

line (lain) *n* renglón *m*; raya *f*; cordón *m*; línea *f*; cola *f*

linen (*li*-nin) *n* lino *m*; ropa blanca

liner (*lai*-nö) *n* vapor de línea

lingerie (*long*-ʒö-rii) *n* ropa interior de

mujer

lining (*lai*-ning) n forro m

link (lingk) v enlazar; n enlace m; eslabón m

lion (*lai*-ön) n león m

lip (lip) n labio m

lipsalve (*lip*-ssaav) n manteca de cacao

lipstick (*lip*-sstik) n lápiz labial

liqueur (li-*kyu*ö) n licor m

liquid (*li*-kᵘid) adj líquido; n líquido m

liquor (*li*-kö) n bebidas alcohólicas

liquorice (*li*-kö-riss) n regaliz m

list (lisst) n lista f; v inscribir

listen (*li*-ssön) v escuchar

listener (*liss*-nö) n oyente m

literary (*li*-trö-ri) adj literario

literature (*li*-trö-chö) n literatura f

litre (*lii*-tö) n litro m

litter (*li*-tö) n desperdicio m; trastos mpl; lechigada f

little (*li*-töl) adj pequeño; poco

live¹ (liv) v vivir

live² (laiv) adj vivo

livelihood (*laiv*-li-hud) n sustento m

lively (*laiv*-li) adj vivo

liver (*li*-vö) n hígado m

living-room (*li*-ving-ruum) n sala de estar, living m

load (loud) n carga f; fardo m; v cargar

loaf (louf) n (pl loaves) pan m

loan (loun) n préstamo m

lobby (*lo*-bi) n vestíbulo m

lobster (*lob*-sstö) n langosta f

local (*lou*-köl) adj local; ~ call llamada local; ~ train tren ómnibus

locality (lou-*kæ*-lö-ti) n localidad f

locate (lou-*keit*) v localizar

location (lou-*kei*-fön) n ubicación f

lock (lok) v *cerrar con llave; n cerradura f; esclusa f; ~ up guardar con llave

locomotive (lou-kö-*mou*-tiv) n locomotora f

lodge (lodʒ) v alojar; n apeadero de caza

lodger (*lo*-dʒö) n huésped m

lodgings (*lo*-dʒĩngs) pl alojamiento m

log (logh) n madero m

logic (*lo*-dʒik) n lógica f

logical (*lo*-dʒi-köl) adj lógico

lonely (*loun*-li) adj solitario

long (long) adj largo; ~ for anhelar; no longer ya no

longing (*long*-ing) n anhelo m

longitude (*lon*-dʒi-tyuud) n longitud f

look (luk) v mirar; *parecer, *tener aires de; n ojeada f, mirada f; aspecto m; ~ after ocuparse de, cuidar de; ~ at mirar; ~ for buscar; ~ out prestar atención, *tener cuidado; ~ up buscar

looking-glass (*lu*-king-ghlaass) n espejo m

loop (luup) n nudo corredizo

loose (luuss) adj suelto

loosen (*luu*-ssön) v *soltar

lord (lood) n lord m

lorry (*lo*-ri) n camión m

*lose (luus) v *perder

loss (loss) n pérdida f

lost (losst) adj perdido; desaparecido; ~ and found objetos perdidos; ~ property office oficina de objetos perdidos

lot (lot) n suerte f, destino m; masa f, cantidad f

lotion (*lou*-fön) n loción f; after-shave ~ loción para después de afeitarse

lottery (*lo*-tö-ri) n lotería f

loud (laud) adj fuerte

loud-speaker (laud-*sspii*-kö) n altavoz m

lounge (laundʒ) n salón m

louse (lauss) n (pl lice) piojo m

love (lav) *v* amar; *n* amor *m*; **in** ~ enamorado

lovely (*lav*-li) *adj* delicioso, precioso, bonito

lover (*la*-vö) *n* amante *m*

love-story (*lav*-sstoo-ri) *n* historia de amor

low (lou) *adj* bajo; profundo; deprimido; ~ **tide** bajamar *f*

lower (*lou*-ö) *v* bajar; rebajar; arriar; *adj* inferior

lowlands (*lou*-lönds) *pl* tierra baja

loyal (*loi*-öl) *adj* leal

lubricate (*luu*-bri-keit) *v* lubrificar, lubricar

lubrication (luu-bri-*kei*-fön) *n* lubricación *f*; ~ **oil** aceite lubricante; ~ **system** sistema de lubricación

luck (lak) *n* éxito *m*, suerte *f*; azar *m*

lucky (*la*-ki) *adj* afortunado; ~ **charm** talismán *m*

ludicrous (*luu*-di-kröss) *adj* ridículo, grotesco

luggage (*la*-ghidʒ) *n* equipaje *m*; **hand** ~ equipaje de mano; **left** ~ **office** consigna *f*; ~ **rack** portabagajes *m*, rejilla *f*; ~ **van** furgón de equipajes

lukewarm (*luuk*-ᵘoom) *adj* tibio

lumbago (lam-*bei*-ghou) *n* lumbago *m*

luminous (*luu*-mi-nöss) *adj* luminoso

lump (lamp) *n* nudo *m*, grumo *m*, terrón *m*; chichón *m*; ~ **of sugar** terrón de azúcar; ~ **sum** suma global

lumpy (*lam*-pi) *adj* apelmazado

lunacy (*luu*-nö-ssi) *n* locura *f*

lunatic (*luu*-nö-tik) *n* lunático; *n* alienado *m*

lunch (lanch) *n* almuerzo *m*

luncheon (*lan*-chön) *n* almuerzo *m*

lung (lang) *n* pulmón *m*

lust (lasst) *n* concupiscencia *f*

luxurious (lagh-ʒuᵒ-ri-öss) *adj* lujoso

luxury (*lak*-fö-ri) *n* lujo *m*

M

machine (mö-*fiin*) *n* aparato *m*, máquina *f*

machinery (mö-*fii*-nö-ri) *n* maquinaria *f*; mecanismo *m*

mackerel (*mæ*-kröl) *n* (pl ~) escombro *m*

mackintosh (*mæ*-kin-tof) *n* impermeable *m*

mad (mæd) *adj* loco; rabioso

madam (*mæ*-döm) *n* señora *f*

madness (*mæd*-nöss) *n* locura *f*

magazine (mæ-ghö-*siin*) *n* revista *f*

magic (*mæ*-dʒik) *n* magia *f*; *adj* mágico

magician (mö-*dʒi*-fön) *n* prestidigitador *m*

magistrate (*mæ*-dʒi-sstreit) *n* magistrado *m*

magnetic (mægh-*nê*-tik) *adj* magnético

magneto (mægh-*nii*-tou) *n* (pl ~s) magneto *m*

magnificent (mægh-*ni*-fi-ssönt) *adj* magnífico; grandioso, espléndido

magpie (*mægh*-pai) *n* urraca *f*

maid (meid) *n* muchacha *f*

maiden name (*mei*-dön neim) apellido de soltera

mail (meil) *n* correo *m*; *v* enviar por correo

mailbox (*meil*-bokss) *nAm* buzón *m*

main (mein) *adj* principal; mayor; ~ **deck** puente superior; ~ **line** línea principal; ~ **road** camino principal; ~ **street** calle mayor

mainland (*mein*-lönd) *n* tierra firme

mainly (*mein*-li) *adv* principalmente

mains (meins) *pl* conducción principal

maintain (mein-*tein*) v *mantener

maintenance (*mein*-tö-nönss) n mantenimiento m

maize (meis) n maíz m

major (*mei*-dʒö) adj grande; mayor; n mayor m

majority (mö-*dʒo*-rö-ti) n mayoría f

*make** (meik) v *hacer; ganar; *conseguir; ~ **do with** arreglarse con; ~ **good** compensar; ~ **up** redactar

make-up (*mei*-kap) n maquillaje m

malaria (mö-*lê*ᵒ-ri-ö) n malaria f

Malay (mö-*lei*) n malayo m

Malaysia (mö-*lei*-si-ö) Malasia f

Malaysian (mö-*lei*-si-ön) adj malayo

male (meil) adj macho

malicious (mö-*li*-ʃöss) adj malicioso

malignant (mö-*ligh*-nönt) adj maligno

mallet (*mæ*-lit) n mazo m

malnutrition (mæl-nyu-*tri*-ʃön) n desnutrición f

mammal (*mæ*-möl) n mamífero m

mammoth (*mæ*-möz) n mamut m

man (mæn) n (pl men) hombre m; **men's room** lavabos para caballeros

manage (*mæ*-nidʒ) v administrar; *tener éxito

manageable (*mæ*-ni-dʒö-böl) adj manejable

management (*mæ*-nidʒ-mönt) n manejo m; gestión f

manager (*mæ*-ni-dʒö) n jefe m, director m

mandarin (*mæn*-dö-rin) n mandarina f

mandate (*mæn*-deit) n mandato m

manger (*mein*-dʒö) n pesebre m

manicure (*mæ*-ni-kyuᵒ) n manicura f; v *hacer la manicura

mankind (mæn-*kaind*) n humanidad f

mannequin (*mæ*-nö-kin) n maniquí m

manner (*mæ*-nö) n modo m, manera f; **manners** pl modales mpl

man-of-war (mæ-növ-ᵘ*oo*) n buque de guerra

manor-house (*mæ*-nö-hauss) n casa señorial

mansion (*mæn*-ʃön) n mansión f

manual (*mæ*-nyu-öl) adj manual

manufacture (mæ-nyu-*fæk*-chö) v fabricar

manufacturer (mæ-nyu-*fæk*-chö-rö) n fabricante m

manure (mö-*nyu*ᵒ) n abono m

manuscript (*mæ*-nyu-sskript) n manuscrito m

many (*mê*-ni) adj muchos

map (mæp) n carta f; mapa m; plano m

maple (*mei*-pöl) n arce m

marble (*maa*-böl) n mármol m; canica f

March (maach) marzo

march (maach) v marchar; n marcha f

mare (mê*ᵒ*) n yegua f

margarine (maa-dʒö-*riin*) n margarina f

margin (*maa*-dʒin) n margen m

maritime (*mæ*-ri-taim) adj marítimo

mark (maak) v marcar; caracterizar; n marca f; nota f; blanco m

market (*maa*-kit) n mercado m

market-place (*maa*-kit-pleiss) n plaza de mercado

marmalade (*maa*-mö-leid) n confitura f

marriage (*mæ*-ridʒ) n matrimonio m

marrow (*mæ*-rou) n médula f

marry (*mæ*-ri) v casarse; **married couple** cónyuges mpl

marsh (maaʃ) n pantano m

marshy (*maa*-ʃi) adj pantanoso

martyr (*maa*-tö) n mártir m

marvel (*maa*-völ) n maravilla f; v maravillarse

marvellous (*maa*-vö-löss) adj maravilloso

mascara (mæ-*sskaa*-rö) *n* rímel *m*

masculine (*mæ*-sskyu-lin) *adj* masculino

mash (mæʃ) *v* machacar

mask (maassk) *n* máscara *f*

Mass (mæss) *n* misa *f*

mass (mæss) *n* masa *f*; ~ **production** producción en serie

massage (*mæ*-ssaaʒ) *n* masaje *m*; *v* *dar masaje

masseur (mæ-*ssöö*) *n* masajista *m*

massive (*mæ*-ssiv) *adj* macizo

mast (maasst) *n* mástil *m*

master (maa-sstö) *v* maestro *m*; patrón *m*; profesor *m*; *v* dominar

masterpiece (*maa*-sstö-piiss) *n* obra maestra

mat (mæt) *n* estera *f*; *adj* mate, apagado

match (mæch) *n* cerilla *f*; partido *m*; cerillo *mMe*; *v* *hacer juego con

match-box (*mæch*-bokss) *n* caja de cerillas

material (mö-*ti*ᵒ-ri-öl) *n* material *m*; tejido *m*; *adj* material

mathematical (mæ-zö-*mæ*-ti-köl) *adj* matemático

mathematics (mæ-zö-*mæ*-tikss) *n* matemáticas *fpl*

matrimonial (mæ-tri-*mou*-ni-öl) *adj* matrimonial

matrimony (*mæ*-tri-mö-ni) *n* matrimonio *m*

matter (*mæ*-tö) *n* materia *f*; asunto *m*, cuestión *f*; *v* *tener importancia; **as a** ~ **of fact** efectivamente, en realidad

matter-of-fact (mæ-tö-röv-*fækt*) *adj* desapasionado

mattress (*mæ*-tröss) *n* colchón *m*

mature (mö-*tyu*ᵒ) *adj* maduro

maturity (mö-*tyu*ᵒ-rö-ti) *n* madurez *f*

mausoleum (moo-ssö-*lii*-öm) *n* mau-

soleo *m*

mauve (mouv) *adj* malva

May (mei) mayo

* **may** (mei) *v* *poder

maybe (*mei*-bii) *adv* quizás

mayor (mê⁶) *n* alcalde *m*

maze (meis) *n* laberinto *m*

me (mii) *pron* me

meadow (*mê*-dou) *n* prado *m*

meal (miil) *n* comida *f*

mean (miin) *adj* mezquino; *n* promedio *m*

* **mean** (miin) *v* significar; *querer decir

meaning (*mii*-ning) *n* significado *m*

meaningless (*mii*-ning-löss) *adj* sin sentido

means (miins) *n* medio *m*; **by no** ~ en ningún caso, de ningún modo

in the meantime (in ðö *miin*-taim) entretanto

meanwhile (*miin*-ᵘail) *adv* entretanto

measles (*mii*-söls) *n* sarampión *m*

measure (*mê*-ʒö) *v* *medir; *n* medida *f*

meat (miit) *n* carne *f*

mechanic (mi-*kæ*-nik) *n* mecánico *m*

mechanical (mi-*kæ*-ni-köl) *adj* mecánico

mechanism (*mê*-kö-ni-söm) *n* mecanismo *m*

medal (*mê*-döl) *n* medalla *f*

mediaeval (mê-di-*ii*-völ) *adj* medieval

mediate (*mii*-di-eit) *v* mediar

mediator (*mii*-di-ei-tö) *n* mediador *m*

medical (*mê*-di-köl) *adj* médico

medicine (*mêd*-ssin) *n* medicamento *m*; medicina *f*

meditate (*mê*-di-teit) *v* meditar

Mediterranean (mê-di-tö-*rei*-ni-ön) Mediterráneo

medium (*mii*-di-öm) *adj* mediano, medio

* **meet** (miit) *v* *encontrarse con

meeting (*mii*-ting) *n* asamblea *f*, reunión *f*; encuentro *m*

meeting-place (*mii*-ting-pleiss) *n* lugar de reunión

melancholy (*mê*-löng-kö-li) *n* melancolía *f*

mellow (*mê*-lou) *adj* suave

melodrama (*mê*-lö-draa-mö) *n* melodrama *m*

melody (*mê*-lö-di) *n* melodía *f*

melon (*mê*-lön) *n* melón *m*

melt (mêlt) *v* fundir

member (*mêm*-bö) *n* miembro *m*; **Member of Parliament** diputado *m*

membership (*mêm*-bö-ſip) *n* afiliación *f*

memo (*mê*-mou) *n* (pl ~s) apunte *m*

memorable (*mê*-mö-rö-böl) *adj* memorable

memorial (mö-*moo*-ri-öl) *n* monumento *m*

memorize (*mê*-mö-rais) *v* aprenderse de memoria

memory (*mê*-mö-ri) *n* memoria *f*; recuerdo *m*

mend (mênd) *v* reparar, *remendar

menstruation (mên-sstru-*ei*-ſön) *n* menstruación *f*

mental (*mên*-töl) *adj* mental

mention (*mên*-ſön) *v* nombrar, mencionar; *n* mención *f*

menu (*mê*-nyuu) *n* menú *m*

merchandise (*möö*-chön-dais) *n* mercancía *f*

merchant (*möö*-chönt) *n* comerciante *m*

merciful (*möö*-ssi-föl) *adj* misericordioso

mercury (*möö*-kyu-ri) *n* mercurio *m*

mercy (*möö*-ssi) *n* misericordia *f*, clemencia *f*

mere (miö) *adj* puro

merely (*miö*-li) *adv* solamente

merger (*möö*-dӡö) *n* fusión *f*

merit (*mê*-rit) *v* *merecer; *n* mérito *m*

mermaid (*möö*-meid) *n* sirena *f*

merry (*mê*-ri) *adj* alegre

merry-go-round (*mê*-ri-ghou-raund) *n* caballitos *mpl*

mesh (mêſ) *n* malla *f*

mess (mêss) *n* desorden *m*; ~ **up** estropear

message (*mê*-ssidӡ) *n* mensaje *m*

messenger (*mê*-ssin-dӡö) *n* mensajero *m*

metal (*mê*-töl) *n* metal *m*; metálico

meter (*mii*-tö) *n* contador *m*

method (*mê*-zöd) *n* método *m*; orden *m*

methodical (mö-*zo*-di-köl) *adj* metódico

methylated spirits (*mê*-zö-lei-tid *sspi*-ritss) alcohol de quemar

metre (*mii*-tö) *n* metro *m*

metric (*mô* trik) *adj* métrico

Mexican (*mêk*-ssi-kön) *adj* mejicano; *n* mejicano *m*

Mexico (*mêk*-ssi-kou) Méjico *m*

mezzanine (*mê*-sö-niin) *n* entresuelo *m*

microphone (*mai*-krö-foun) *n* micrófono *m*

midday (*mid*-dei) *n* mediodía *m*

middle (*mi*-döl) *n* medio *m*; *adj* medio; **Middle Ages** Edad Media; ~ **class** clase media; **middle-class** *adj* burgués

midnight (*mid*-nait) *n* medianoche *f*

midst (midsst) *n* medio *m*

midsummer (*mid*-ssa-mö) *n* pleno verano

midwife (*mid*-ᵘaif) *n* (pl -wives) comadrona *f*

might (mait) *n* fuerza *f*

*** might** (mait) *v* *poder

mighty (*mai*-ti) *adj* fuerte

migraine (*mi*-ghrein) *n* migraña *f*

mild (maild) *adj* suave

mildew (*mil*-dyu) *n* moho *m*

mile (mail) *n* milla *f*

mileage (*mai*-lidʒ) *n* millaje *m*

milepost (*mail*-pousst) *n* cipo *m*

milestone (*mail*-sstoun) *n* piedra miliar

milieu (*mii*-lyöö) *n* medio ambiente

military (*mi*-li-tö-ri) *adj* militar; ~ **force** fuerzas armadas

milk (milk) *n* leche *f*

milkman (*milk*-mön) *n* (pl -men) lechero *m*

milk-shake (*milk*-ʃeik) *n* batido de leche

milky (*mil*-ki) *adj* lechoso

mill (mil) *n* molino *m*; fábrica *f*

miller (*mi*-lö) *n* molinero *m*

milliner (*mi*-li-nö) *n* sombrerera *f*

million (*mil*-yön) *n* millón *m*

millionaire (mil-yö-*nêᵒ*) *n* millonario *m*

mince (minss) *v* picar

mind (maind) *n* mente *f*; *v* *hacer objeción a; fijarse en, *tener cuidado con

mine (main) *n* mina *f*

miner (*mai*-nö) *n* minero *m*

mineral (*mi*-nö-röl) *n* mineral *m*; ~ **water** agua mineral

miniature (*min*-yö-chö) *n* miniatura *f*

minimum (*mi*-ni-möm) *n* mínimum *m*

mining (*mai*-ning) *n* minería *f*

minister (*mi*-ni-sstö) *n* ministro *m*; clérigo *m*; **Prime Minister** Presidente de Consejo de ministros

ministry (*mi*-ni-sstri) *n* ministerio *m*

mink (mingk) *n* visón *m*

minor (*mai*-nö) *adj* pequeño, escaso, menor; secundario; *n* menor de edad

minority (mai-*no*-rö-ti) *n* minoría *f*

mint (mint) *n* menta *f*

minus (*mai*-nöss) *prep* menos

minute¹ (*mi*-nit) *n* minuto *m*; **minutes** actas

minute² (mai-*nyuut*) *adj* menudo

miracle (*mi*-rö-köl) *n* milagro *m*

miraculous (mi-*ræ*-kyu-löss) *adj* milagroso

mirror (*mi*-rö) *n* espejo *m*

misbehave (miss-bi-*heiv*) *v* portarse mal

miscarriage (miss-*kæ*-ridʒ) *n* aborto *m*

miscellaneous (mi-ssö-*lei*-ni-öss) *adj* misceláneo

mischief (*miss*-chif) *n* diabluras *fpl*; mal *m*, daño *m*, malicia *f*

mischievous (*miss*-chi-völl) *adj* travieso

miserable (*mi*-sö-rö-böl) *adj* miserable

misery (*mi*-sö-ri) *n* miseria *f*; necesidad *f*

misfortune (miss-*foo*-chên) *n* contratiempo *m*, infortunio *m*

*mislay (miss-*lei*) *v* extraviar

misplaced (miss-*pleisst*) *adj* inoportuno; fuera de lugar

mispronounce (miss-prö-*naunss*) *v* pronunciar mal

miss¹ (miss) señorita *f*

miss² (miss) *v* *perder

missing (*mi*-ssing) *adj* que falta; ~ **person** desaparecido *m*

mist (misst) *n* niebla *f*

mistake (mi-*ssteik*) *n* error *m*, equivocación *f*

*mistake (mi-*ssteik*) *v* confundir

mistaken (mi-*sstei*-kön) *adj* equivocado; *be ~ equivocarse

mister (*mi*-sstö) *n* señor *m*

mistress (*mi*-sströss) *n* señora *f*; dueña *f*; querida *f*

mistrust (miss-*trasst*) *v* desconfiar de

misty (*mi*-ssti) *adj* nebuloso

*misunderstand (mi-ssan-dö-*sstænd*)

v comprender mal

misunderstanding (mi-ssan-dö-*sstæn*-ding) *n* equivocación *f*

misuse (miss-*yuuss*) *n* abuso *m*

mittens (*mi*-töns) *pl* guantes *mpl*

mix (mikss) *v* mezclar; ~ **with** alternar con

mixed (miksst) *adj* mezclado

mixer (*mik*-ssö) *n* batidora *f*

mixture (*mikss*-chö) *n* mezcla *f*

moan (moun) *v* *gemir

moat (mout) *n* foso *m*

mobile (*mou*-bail) *adj* móvil

mock (mok) *v* burlarse de

mockery (*mo*-kö-ri) *n* burla *f*

model (*mo*-döl) *n* modelo *m*; maniquí *m*; *v* modelar

moderate (*mo*-dö-röt) *adj* moderado; mediocre

modern (*mo*-dön) *adj* moderno

modest (*mo*-disst) *adj* modesto

modesty (*mo*-di-ssti) *n* modestia *f*

modify (*mo*-di-fai) *v* modificar

mohair (*mou*-hëö) *n* mohair *m*

moist (moisst) *adj* mojado, húmedo

moisten (*moi*-ssön) *v* *humedecer

moisture (*moiss*-chö) *n* humedad *f*; **moisturizing cream** crema hidratante

molar (*mou*-lö) *n* muela *f*

moment (*mou*-mönt) *n* momento *m*

momentary (*mou*-mön-tö-ri) *adj* momentáneo

monarch (*mo*-nök) *n* monarca *m*

monarchy (*mo*-nö-ki) *n* monarquía *f*

monastery (*mo*-nö-sstri) *n* monasterio *m*

Monday (*man*-di) lunes *m*

monetary (*ma*-ni-tö-ri) *adj* monetario; ~ **unit** unidad monetaria

money (*ma*-ni) *n* dinero *m*; ~ **exchange** oficina de cambio; ~ **order** libranza *f*

monk (mangk) *n* monje *m*

monkey (*mang*-ki) *n* mono *m*

monologue (*mo*-no-logh) *n* monólogo *m*

monopoly (mö-*no*-pö-li) *n* monopolio *m*

monotonous (mö-*no*-tö-nöss) *adj* monótono

month (manz) *n* mes *m*

monthly (*manz*-li) *adj* mensual; ~ **magazine** revista mensual

monument (*mo*-nyu-mönt) *n* monumento *m*

mood (muud) *n* humor *m*

moon (muun) *n* luna *f*

moonlight (*muun*-lait) *n* luz de la luna

moor (muö) *n* brezal *m*, turbera *f*

moose (muuss) *n* (pl ~, ~s) alce *m*

moped (*mou*-pêd) *n* bicimotor *m*

moral (*mo*-röl) *n* moral *f*; *adj* moral; **morals** costumbres

morality (mö-*ræ*-lö-ti) *n* moralidad *f*

more (moo) *adj* más; **once** ~ otra vez

moreover (moo-*rou*-vö) *adv* además

morning (*moo*-ning) *n* mañana *f*; ~ **paper** diario matutino

Moroccan (mö-*ro*-kön) *adj* marroquí

Morocco (mö-*ro*-kou) Marruecos *m*

morphia (*moo*-fi-ö) *n* morfina *f*

morphine (*moo*-fiin) *n* morfina *f*

morsel (*moo*-ssöl) *n* trozo *m*

mortal (*moo*-töl) *adj* fatal, mortal

mortgage (*moo*-ghid3) *n* hipoteca *f*

mosaic (mö-*sei*-ik) *n* mosaico *m*

mosque (mossk) *n* mezquita *f*

mosquito (mö-*sskii*-tou) *n* (pl ~es) mosquito *m*

mosquito-net (mö-*sskii*-tou-nêt) *n* mosquitero *m*

moss (moss) *n* musgo *m*

most (mousst) *adj* el más; **at** ~ a lo sumo, como máximo; ~ **of all** sobre todo

mostly (*mousst*-li) *adv* generalmente

motel (mou-*têl*) *n* motel *m*

moth (moz) *n* polilla *f*

mother (*ma*-ðö) *n* madre *f*; ~ **tongue** lengua materna

mother-in-law (*ma*-ðö-rin-loo) *n* (pl mothers-) suegra *f*

mother-of-pearl (ma-ðö-röv-*pööl*) *n* nácar *m*

motion (*mou*-∫ön) *n* movimiento *m*; moción *f*

motive (*mou*-tiv) *n* motivo *m*

motor (*mou*-tö) *n* motor *m*; *v* *ir en coche; **starter** ~ motor de arranque

motorbike (*mou*-tö-baik) *nAm* motocicleta *f*

motor-boat (*mou*-tö-bout) *n* bote a motor

motor-car (*mou*-tö-kaa) *n* automóvil *m*

motor-cycle (*mou*-tö-ssai-köl) *n* motocicleta *f*

motoring (*mou*-tö-ring) *n* automovilismo *m*

motorist (*mou*-tö-risst) *n* automovilista *m*

motorway (*mou*-tö-ᵘei) *n* autopista *f*

motto (*mo*-tou) *n* (pl ~es, ~s) lema *f*

mouldy (*moul*-di) *adj* enmohecido

mound (maund) *n* montículo *m*

mount (maunt) *v* montar; *n* monte *m*

mountain (*maun*-tin) *n* montaña *f*; ~ **pass** paso *m*; ~ **range** cordillera *f*

mountaineering (maun-ti-*niö*-ring) *n* montañismo *m*

mountainous (*maun*-ti-nöss) *adj* montañoso

mourning (*moo*-ning) *n* luto *m*

mouse (mauss) *n* (pl mice) ratón *m*

moustache (mö-*sstaa*∫) *n* bigote *m*

mouth (mauz) *n* boca *f*; hocico *m*; desembocadura *f*

mouthwash (*mauz*-ᵘo∫) *n* enjuague bucal

movable (*muu*-vö-böl) *adj* movible

move (muuv) *v* *mover; trasladar;

mudarse; *conmover; *n* jugada *f*, paso *m*; mudanza *f*

movement (*muuv*-mönt) *n* movimiento *m*

movie (*muu*-vi) *n* filme *m*

much (mach) *adj* mucho; **as** ~ tanto

muck (mak) *n* suciedad *f*

mud (mad) *n* lodo *m*

muddle (*ma*-döl) *n* dédalo *m*, embrollo *m*; *v* embrollar

muddy (*ma*-di) *adj* lodoso

mud-guard (*mad*-ghaad) *n* guardabarros *m*; salpicadera *fMe*

mug (magh) *n* vaso *m*, taza *f*

mulberry (*mal*-bö-ri) *n* mora *f*

mule (myuul) *n* mulo *m*

mullet (*ma*-lit) *n* mújol *m*

multiplication (mal-ti-pli-*kei*-∫ön) *n* multiplicación *f*

multiply (*mal*-ti-plai) *v* multiplicar

mumps (mampss) *n* paperas *fpl*

municipal (myuu-*ni*-ssi-pöl) *adj* municipal

municipality (myuu-ni-ssi-*pæ*-lö-ti) *n* municipalidad *f*

murder (*möö*-dö) *n* asesinato *m*; *v* asesinar

murderer (*möö*-dö-rö) *n* asesino *m*

muscle (*ma*-ssöl) *n* músculo *m*

muscular (*ma*-sskyu-lö) *adj* musculoso

museum (myuu-*sii*-öm) *n* museo *m*

mushroom (*ma*∫-ruum) *n* seta *f*; hongo *m*

music (*myuu*-sik) *n* música *f*; ~ **academy** conservatorio *m*

musical (*myuu*-si-köl) *adj* musical; *n* comedia musical

music-hall (*myuu*-sik-hool) *n* teatro de variedades

musician (myuu-*si*-∫ön) *n* músico *m*

muslin (*mas*-lin) *n* muselina *f*

mussel (*ma*-ssöl) *n* mejillón *m*

must (masst) *v* *tener que

mustard (*ma*-sstöd) *n* mostaza *f*

mute (myuut) *adj* mudo

mutiny (*myuu*-ti-ni) *n* amotinamiento *m*

mutton (*ma*-tön) *n* carnero *m*

mutual (*myuu*-chu-öl) *adj* mutuo, recíproco

my (mai) *adj* mi

myself (mai-*sêlf*) *pron* me; yo mismo

mysterious (mi-*ssti⁰*-ri-öss) *adj* misterioso

mystery (*mi*-sstö-ri) *n* enigma *m*, misterio *m*

myth (miz) *n* mito *m*

N

nail (neil) *n* uña *f*; clavo *m*

nailbrush (*neil*-braʃ) *n* cepillo para las uñas

nail-file (*neil*-fail) *n* lima para las uñas

nail-polish (*neil*-po-liʃ) *n* barniz para las uñas

nail-scissors (*neil*-ssi-sös) *pl* tijeras para las uñas

naïve (naa-*iiv*) *adj* ingenuo

naked (*nei*-kid) *adj* desnudo

name (neim) *n* nombre *m*; *v* nombrar; **in the ~ of** en nombre de

namely (*neim*-li) *adv* a saber

nap (næp) *n* siesta *f*

napkin (*næp*-kin) *n* servilleta *f*

nappy (*næ*-pi) *n* pañal *m*

narcosis (naa-*kou*-ssiss) *n* (pl -ses) narcosis *f*

narcotic (naa-*ko*-tik) *n* narcótico *m*

narrow (*næ*-rou) *adj* angosto, estrecho

narrow-minded (næ-rou-*main*-did) *adj* mezquino

nasty (*naa*-ss.i) *adj* antipático, desagradable

nation (*nei*-ʃön) *n* nación *f*; pueblo *m*

national (*næ*-ʃö-nöl) *adj* nacional; del Estado; **~ anthem** himno nacional; **~ dress** traje del país; **~ park** parque nacional

nationality (næ-ʃö-*næ*-lö-ti) *n* nacionalidad *f*

nationalize (*næ*-ʃö-nö-lais) *v* nacionalizar

native (*nei*-tiv) *n* indígena *m*; *adj* nativo; **~ country** patria *f*, país natal; **~ language** lengua materna

natural (*næ*-chö-röl) *adj* natural; innato

naturally (*næ*-chö-rö-li) *adv* naturalmente, por supuesto

nature (*nei*-chö) *n* naturaleza *f*; natural *m*

naughty (*noo*-ti) *adj* travieso

nausea (*noo*-ssi-ö) *n* náusea *f*

naval (*nei*-völ) *adj* naval

navel (*nei*-völ) *n* ombligo *m*

navigable (*næ*-vi-ghö-böl) *adj* navegable

navigate (*næ*-vi-gheit) *v* navegar

navigation (næ-vi-*ghei*-ʃön) *n* navegación *f*

navy (*nei*-vi) *n* marina *f*

near (ni⁰) *prep* cerca de; *adj* cercano

nearby (ni⁰-bai) *adj* cercano

nearly (*ni⁰*-li) *adv* casi

neat (niit) *adj* pulcro; puro

necessary (*nê*-ssö-ssö-ri) *adj* necesario

necessity (nö-*ssê*-ssö-ti) *n* necesidad *f*

neck (nêk) *n* cuello *m*; **nape of the ~** nuca *f*

necklace (*nêk*-löss) *n* collar *m*

necktie (*nêk*-tai) *n* corbata *f*

need (niid) *v* deber, necesitar; *n* necesidad *f*; **~ to** deber

needle (*nii*-döl) *n* aguja *f*

needlework (*nii*-döl-ᵘöök) *n* labor de aguja

negative (*nê*-ghö-tiv) *adj* negativo; *n*

negativo *m*

neglect (ni-*ghlêkt*) *v* descuidar; *n* negligencia *f*

neglectful (ni-*ghlêkt*-föl) *adj* negligente

negligee (nê-ghli-ʒei) *n* bata suelta

negotiate (ni-*ghou*-ʃi-eit) *v* negociar

negotiation (ni-ghou-ʃi-*ei*-ʃön) *n* negociación *f*

Negro (*nii*-ghrou) *n* (pl ~es) negro *m*

neighbour (*nei*-bö) *n* vecino *m*

neighbourhood (*nei*-bö-hud) *n* vecindad *f*

neighbouring (*nei*-bö-ring) *adj* contiguo, vecino

neither (*nai*-ðö) *pron* ninguno de los dos; **neither ... nor** ni ... ni

neon (*nii*-on) *n* neón *m*

nephew (*nê*-fyuu) *n* sobrino *m*

nerve (nööv) *n* nervio *m*; audacia *f*

nervous (*nöö*-vöss) *adj* nervioso

nest (nêsst) *n* nido *m*

net (nêt) *n* red *f*; *adj* neto

the Netherlands (*nê*-ðö-lönds) Países Bajos *mpl*

network (*nêt*-ᵘöök) *n* red *f*

neuralgia (nyu⁶-*ræl*-dʒö) *n* neuralgia *f*

neurosis (nyu⁶-*rou*-ssiss) *n* neurosis *f*

neuter (*nyuu*-tö) *adj* neutro

neutral (*nyuu*-tröl) *adj* neutral

never (*nê*-vö) *adv* nunca

nevertheless (nê-vö-ðö-*lêss*) *adv* no obstante

new (nyuu) *adj* nuevo; **New Year** año nuevo

news (nyuus) *n* noticiario *m*, noticia *f*; noticias *fpl*

newsagent (*nyuu*-sei-dʒönt) *n* vendedor de periódicos

newspaper (*nyuus*-pei-pö) *n* diario *m*

newsreel (*nyuus*-riil) *n* noticiario *m*

newsstand (*nyuus*-sstænd) *n* quiosco de periódicos

New Zealand (nyuu *sii*-lönd) Nueva Zelanda

next (nêksst) *adj* próximo; ~ **to** junto a

next-door (nêksst-*doo*) *adv* al lado

nice (naiss) *adj* agradable, bonito, ameno; rico; simpático

nickel (*ni*-köl) *n* níquel *m*

nickname (*nik*-neim) *n* mote *m*

nicotine (*ni*-kö-tiin) *n* nicotina *f*

niece (niiss) *n* sobrina *f*

Nigeria (nai-*dʒi*⁶-ri-ö) Nigeria *f*

Nigerian (nai-*dʒi*⁶-ri-ön) *adj* nigeriano

night (nait) *n* noche *f*; **by ~** de noche; ~ **flight** vuelo nocturno; ~ **rate** tarifa nocturna; ~ **train** tren nocturno

nightclub (*nait*-klab) *n* cabaret *m*

night-cream (*nait*-kriim) *n* crema de noche

nightdress (*nait*-drêss) *n* camisón *m*

nightingale (*nai*-ting-gheil) *n* ruiseñor *m*

nightly (*nait*-li) *adj* nocturno

nil (nil) nada

nine (nain) *num* nueve

nineteen (nain-*tiin*) *num* diecinueve

nineteenth (nain-*tiinz*) *num* decimonono

ninety (*nain*-ti) *num* noventa

ninth (nainz) *num* noveno

nitrogen (*nai*-trö-dʒön) *n* nitrógeno *m*

no (nou) no; *adj* ninguno; ~ **one** nadie

nobility (nou-*bi*-lö-ti) *n* nobleza *f*

noble (*nou*-böl) *adj* noble

nobody (*nou*-bo-di) *pron* nadie

nod (nod) *n* cabeceo *m*; *v* cabecear

noise (nois) *n* ruido *m*; alboroto *m*

noisy (*noi*-si) *adj* ruidoso

nominal (*no*-mi-nöl) *adj* nominal

nominate (*no*-mi-neit) *v* nombrar

nomination (no-mi-*nei*-ʃör) *n* nominación *f*; nombramiento *m*

none (nan) *pron* ninguno

nonsense (*non*-ssönss) *n* tontería *f*

noon (nuun) *n* mediodía *m*

normal (*noo*-möl) *adj* normal

north (nooz) *n* norte *m*; *adj* septentrional; **North Pole** polo norte

north-east (nooz-*iisst*) *n* nordeste *m*

northerly (*noo*-ðö-li) *adj* del norte

northern (*noo*-ðön) *adj* norteño

north-west (nooz-*u*êsst) *n* noroeste *m*

Norway (*noo*-u̯ei) Noruega *f*

Norwegian (noo-*u̯ii*-dʒön) *adj* noruego

nose (nous) *n* nariz *f*

nosebleed (*nous*-bliid) *n* hemorragia nasal

nostril (*no*-sstril) *n* ventana de la nariz

not (not) *adv* no

notary (*nou*-tö-ri) *n* notario *m*

note (nout) *n* apunte *m*, esquela *f*; nota *f*; tono *m*; *v* notar; observar, *comprobar

notebook (*nout*-buk) *n* libreta de apuntes

noted (*nou*-tid) *adj* afamado

notepaper (*nout*-pei-pö) *n* papel de escribir, papel para cartas

nothing (*na*-zing) *n* nada *f*, nada *f*

notice (*nou*-tiss) *v* observar, notar, *advertir; *ver; *n* aviso *m*, noticia *f*; atención *f*

noticeable (*nou*-ti-ssö-böl) *adj* perceptible; notable

notify (*nou*-ti-fai) *v* notificar

notion (*nou*-ʃön) *n* noción *f*

notorious (nou-*too*-ri-öss) *adj* de mala fama

nougat (*nuu*-ghaa) *n* turrón *m*

nought (noot) *n* cero *m*

noun (naun) *n* nombre *m*, substantivo *m*

nourishing (*na*-ri-ʃing) *adj* nutritivo

novel (*no*-völ) *n* novela *f*

novelist (*no*-vö-lisst) *n* novelista *m*

November (nou-*vêm*-bö) noviembre

now (nau) *adv* ahora; actualmente; ~ **and then** de vez en cuando

nowadays (*nau*-ö-deis) *adv* hoy en día

nowhere (*nou*-u̯êô) *adv* en ninguna parte

nozzle (*no*-söl) *n* tobera *f*

nuance (nyuu-*angss*) *n* matiz *m*

nuclear (*nyuu*-kli-ö) *adj* nuclear; ~ **energy** energía nuclear

nucleus (*nyuu*-kli-öss) *n* núcleo *m*

nude (nyuud) *adj* desnudo; *n* desnudo *m*

nuisance (*nyuu*-ssönss) *n* molestia *f*

numb (nam) *adj* entumecido; aterido

number (*nam*-bö) *n* número *m*; cifra *f*; cantidad *f*

numeral (*nyuu*-mö-röl) *n* numeral *m*

numerous (*nyuu*-mö-röss) *adj* numeroso

nun (nan) *n* monja *f*

nunnery (*na*-nö-ri) *n* convento *m*

nurse (nööss) *n* enfermera *f*; niñera *f*; *v* *atender a; amamantar

nursery (*nöö*-ssö-ri) *n* cuarto de niños; guardería *f*; vivero *m*

nut (nat) *n* nuez *f*; tuerca *f*

nutcrackers (*nat*-kræ-kös) *pl* cascanueces *m*

nutmeg (*nat*-mêgh) *n* nuez moscada

nutritious (nyuu-*tri*-ʃöss) *adj* nutritivo

nutshell (*nat*-ʃêl) *n* cáscara de nuez

nylon (*nai*-lon) *n* nylon *m*

O

oak (ouk) *n* roble *m*

oar (oo) *n* remo *m*

oasis (ou-*ei*-ssiss) *n* (pl oases) oasis *f*

oath (ouz) *n* juramento *m*

oats (outss) *pl* avena *f*

obedience (ö-*bii*-di-önss) *n* obediencia *f*

obedient (ö-*bii*-di-önt) *adj* obediente
obey (ö-*bei*) *v* *obedecer
object[1] (*ob*-dʒikt) *n* objeto *m*
object[2] (öb-*dʒêkt*) *v* objetar; ~ to *oponerse a
objection (öb-*dʒêk*-ʃön) *n* objeción *f*
objective (öb-*dʒêk*-tiv) *adj* objetivo; *n* objetivo *m*
obligatory (ö-*bli*-ghö-tö-ri) *adj* obligatorio
oblige (ö-*blaidʒ*) *v* obligar; *be obliged to *estar obligado a; *tener que
obliging (ö-*blai*-dʒing) *adj* simpático
oblong (*ob*-long) *adj* oblongo; *n* rectángulo *m*
obscene (öb-*ssiin*) *adj* obsceno
obscure (öb-*sskyuᵒ*) *adj* obscuro, misterioso, oscuro
observation (ob-sö-*vei*-ʃön) *n* observación *f*
observatory (öb-*söö*-vö-tri) *n* observatorio *m*
observe (öb-*sööv*) *v* observar
obsession (öb-*ssê*-ʃön) *n* obsesión *f*
obstacle (*ob*-sstö-köl) *n* obstáculo *m*
obstinate (*ob*-ssti-nöt) *adj* obstinado; pertinaz
obtain (öb-*tein*) *v* *conseguir, *obtener
obtainable (öb-*tei*-nö-böl) *adj* adquirible
obvious (*ob*-vi-öss) *adj* obvio
occasion (ö-*kei*-ʒön) *n* ocasión *f*; motivo *m*
occasionally (ö-*kei*-ʒö-nö-li) *adv* de vez en cuando, ocasionalmente
occupant (*o*-kyu-pönt) *n* ocupante *m*
occupation (o-kyu-*pei*-ʃön) *n* ocupación *f*
occupy (*o*-kyu-pai) *v* ocupar
occur (ö-*köö*) *v* suceder, ocurrir, *acontecer
occurrence (ö-*ka*-rönss) *n* aconteci-

miento *m*
ocean (*ou*-ʃön) *n* océano *m*
October (ok-*tou*-bö) octubre
octopus (ok-tö-pöss) *n* pulpo *m*
oculist (*o*-kyu-lisst) *n* oculista *m*
odd (od) *adj* raro; impar
odour (*ou*-dö) *n* olor *m*
of (ov, öv) *prep* de
off (of) *adv* fuera; *prep* de
offence (ö-*fênss*) *n* falta *f*; ofensa *f*, escándalo *m*
offend (ö-*fênd*) *v* ofender; transgredir
offensive (ö-*fên*-ssiv) *adj* ofensivo; insultante; *n* ofensivo *m*
offer (*o*-fö) *v* *ofrecer; presentar; *n* oferta *f*
office (*o*-fiss) *n* oficina *f*; cargo *m*; ~ hours horas de oficina
officer (*o*-fi-ssö) *n* oficial *m*
official (ö-*fi*-ʃöl) *adj* oficial
off-licence (*of*-lai-ssönss) *n* almacén de licores
often (*o*-fön) *adv* a menudo, frecuentemente
oil (oil) *n* aceite *m*; petróleo *m*; fuel ~ combustible líquido); ~ filter filtro del aceite; ~ pressure presión del aceite
oil-painting (oil-*pein*-ting) *n* pintura al óleo
oil-refinery (*oil*-ri-fai-nö-ri) *n* refinería de petróleo
oil-well (*oil*-ᵘêl) *n* pozo de petróleo
oily (*oi*-li) *adj* aceitoso
ointment (*oint*-mönt) *n* ungüento *m*
okay! (ou-*kei*) ¡de acuerdo!
old (ould) *adj* viejo; ~ age vejez *f*
old-fashioned (ould-*fæ*-ʃönd) *adj* anticuado
olive (*o*-liv) *n* aceituna *f*; ~ oil aceite de oliva
omelette (*om*-löt) *n* tortilla *f*
ominous (*o*-mi-nöss) *adj* siniestro
omit (ö-*mit*) *v* omitir

omnipotent (om-*ni*-pö-tönt) *adj* omnipotente

on (on) *prep* sobre; a

once (ᵘanss) *adv* una vez; **at** ~ en seguida; ~ **more** otra vez

oncoming (*on*-ka-ming) *adj* venidero

one (ᵘan) *num* uno; *pron* uno

oneself (ᵘan-*sélf*) *pron* uno mismo

onion (*a*-nyön) *n* cebolla *f*

only (*oun*-li) *adj* solo; *adv* sólo, solamente; *conj* pero

onwards (*on*-ᵘöds) *adv* adelante

onyx (*o*-nikss) *n* ónix *m*

opal (*ou*-pöl) *n* ópalo *m*

open (*ou*-pön) *v* abrir; *adj* abierto; sincero

opening (*ou*-pö-ning) *n* abertura *f*

opera (*o*-pö-rö) *n* ópera *f*; ~ **house** teatro de la ópera

operate (*o*-pö-reit) *v* operar, funcionar

operation (o-pö-*rei*-jön) *n* funcionamiento *m*; operación *f*

operator (*o*-pö-rei-tö) *n* telefonista *f*

operetta (o-pö-*ré*-tö) *n* opereta *f*

opinion (ö-*pi*-nyön) *n* parecer *m*, opinión *f*

opponent (ö-*pou*-nönt) *n* contrincante *m*

opportunity (o-pö-*tyuu*-nö-ti) *n* oportunidad *f*

oppose (ö-*pous*) *v* *oponerse

opposite (*o*-pö-sit) *prep* enfrente de; *adj* contrario, opuesto

opposition (o-pö-*si*-jön) *n* oposición *f*

oppress (ö-*préss*) *v* oprimir

optician (op-*ti*-jön) *n* óptico *m*

optimism (*op*-ti-mi-söm) *n* optimismo *m*

optimist (*op*-ti-misst) *n* optimista *m*

optimistic (op-ti-*mi*-sstik) *adj* optimista

optional (*op*-jö-nöl) *adj* opcional

or (oo) *conj* o

oral (*oo*-röl) *adj* oral

orange (*o*-rindʒ) *n* naranja *f*; *adj* de color naranja

orchard (*oo*-chöd) *n* vergel *m*

orchestra (*oo*-ki-sströ) *n* orquesta *f*; ~ **seat** *Am* butaca *f*

order (*oo*-dö) *v* ordenar; *pedir; *n* orden *m*; orden *f*, mandato *m*; pedido *m*; **in** ~ en regla; **in** ~ **to** para; **made to** ~ hecho a la medida; **out of** ~ averiado; **postal** ~ giro postal

order form (*oo*-dö-foom) *n* hoja de pedido

ordinary (*oo*-dön-ri) *adj* común, ordinario

ore (oo) *n* mineral *m*

organ (*oo*-ghön) *n* órgano *m*

organic (oo-*ghæ*-nik) *adj* orgánico

organization (oo-ghö-nai-*sei*-jön) *n* organización *f*

organize (*oo*-ghö-nais) *v* organizar

Orient (*oo*-ri-önt) *n* oriente *m*

oriental (oo-ri-*én*-töl) *adj* oriental

orientate (*oo*-ri-ön-teit) *v* orientarse

origin (*o*-ri-dʒin) *n* origen *m*; descendencia *f*, procedencia *f*

original (ö-*ri*-dʒi-nöl) *adj* auténtico, original

originally (ö-*ri*-dʒi-nö-li) *adv* originalmente

orlon (*oo*-lon) *n* orlón *m*

ornament (*oo*-nö-mönt) *n* adorno *m*

ornamental (oo-nö-*mên*-töl) *adj* ornamental

orphan (*oo*-fön) *n* huérfano *m*

orthodox (*oo*-zö-dokss) *adj* ortodoxo

ostrich (*o*-sstrich) *n* avestruz *m*

other (*a*-ðö) *adj* otro

otherwise (*a*-ðö-ᵘais) *conj* si no; *adv* de otra manera

* ought to (oot) *tener que

our (auᵒ) *adj* nuestro

ourselves (auᵒ-*sélvs*) *pron* nos; no-

sotros mismos
out (aut) *adv* fuera; ~ **of** fuera de, de
outbreak (*aut*-breik) *n* explosión *f*
outcome (*aut*-kam) *n* resultado *m*
***outdo** (aut-*duu*) *v* superar
outdoors (aut-*doos*) *adv* afuera
outer (*au*-tö) *adj* exterior
outfit (*aut*-fit) *n* equipo *m*
outline (*aut*-lain) *n* contorno *m*; *v* bosquejar
outlook (*aut*-luk) *n* previsión *f*; punto de vista
output (*aut*-put) *n* producción *f*
outside (aut-*ssaid*) *adv* afuera; *prep* fuera de; *n* exterior *m*
outsize (*aut*-ssais) *n* tamaño extraordinario
outskirts (*aut*-ssköötss) *pl* afueras *fpl*
outstanding (aut-*sstæn*-ding) *adj* eminente, destacado
outward (*aut*-ᵘöd) *adj* externo
outwards (*aut*-ᵘöds) *adv* hacia afuera
oval (*ou*-völ) *adj* ovalado
oven (*a*-vön) *n* horno *m*; **microwave** ~ horno de microonda
over (*ou*-vö) *prep* encima de; más de; *adv* encima; abajo; *adj* acabado; ~ **there** allá
overall (*ou*-vö-rool) *adj* total
overalls (*ou*-vö-rools) *pl* mono *m*; overol *mMe*
overcast (*ou*-vö-kaasst) *adj* nublado
overcoat (*ou*-vö-kout) *n* abrigo *m*
***overcome** (ou-vö-*kam*) *v* vencer
overdue (*ou*-vö-*dyuu*) *adj* atrasado
overgrown (ou-vö-*ghroun*) *adj* cubierto de verdor
overhaul (ou-vö-*hool*) *v* revisar
overhead (ou-vö-*hêd*) *adv* en alto
overlook (ou-vö-*luk*) *v* pasar por alto
overnight (*ou*-vö-*nait*) *adv* de noche
overseas (ou-vö-*ssiis*) *adj* ultramar
oversight (*ou*-vö-ssait) *n* descuido *m*
***oversleep** (ou-vö-*ssliip*) *v* quedarse dormido

overstrung (ou-vö-*sstrang*) *adj* sobreexcitado
***overtake** (ou-vö-*teik*) *v* recoger; **no overtaking** prohibido adelantar
over-tired (ou-vö-*tai*ᵒd) *adj* exhausto
overture (*ou*-vö-chö) *n* obertura *f*
overweight (*ou*-vö-ᵘeit) *n* sobrepeso *m*
overwhelm (ou-vö-ᵘêlm) *v* *desconcertar, subyugar
overwork (ou-vö-ᵘöök) *v* trabajar demasiado
owe (ou) *v* deber; **owing to** a causa de, debido a
owl (aul) *n* buho *m*
own (oun) *v* *poseer; *adj* propio
owner (*ou*-nö) *n* propietario *m*
ox (okss) *n* (pl oxen) buey *m*
oxygen (*ok*-ssi-dჳön) *n* oxígeno *m*
oyster (*oi*-sstö) *n* ostra *f*

P

pace (peiss) *n* andares *mpl*; paso *m*; ritmo *m*
Pacific Ocean (pö-*ssi*-fik *ou*-ʃön) Océano Pacífico
pacifism (*pæ*-ssi-fi-söm) *n* pacifismo *m*
pacifist (*pæ*-ssi-fisst) *n* pacifista *m*
pack (pæk) *v* embalar; ~ **up** empaquetar
package (*pæ*-kidჳ) *n* paquete *m*
packet (*pæ*-kit) *n* paquete *m*
packing (*pæ*-king) *n* embalaje *m*
pad (pæd) *n* almohadilla *f*; bloque *m*
paddle (*pæ*-döl) *n* remo *m*
padlock (*pæd*-lok) *n* candado *m*
pagan (*pei*-ghön) *adj* pagano; *n* pagano *m*
page (peidჳ) *n* página *f*

page-boy (*peidʒ*-boi) *n* paje *m*

pail (peil) *n* balde *m*

pain (pein) *n* dolor *m*; **pains** pena *f*

painful (*pein*-föl) *adj* dolorido

painless (*pein*-löss) *adj* sin dolor

paint (peint) *n* pintura *f*; *v* pintar

paint-box (*peint*-bokss) *n* caja de colores

paint-brush (*peint*-braʃ) *n* pincel *m*

painter (*pein*-tö) *n* pintor *m*

painting (*pein*-ting) *n* pintura *f*

pair (pêö) *n* par *m*

Pakistan (paa-ki-*sstaan*) Paquistán *m*

Pakistani (paa-ki-*sstaa*-ni) *adj* paquistaní

palace (*pæ*-löss) *n* palacio *m*

pale (peil) *adj* pálido

palm (paam) *n* palma *f*

palpable (*pæl*-pö-böl) *adj* palpable

palpitation (pæl-pi-*tei*-ʃön) *n* palpitación *f*

pan (pæn) *n* sartén *f*

pane (pein) *n* cristal *m*

panel (*pæ*-nöl) *n* painel *m*, cuarterón *m*

panelling (*pæ*-nö-ling) *n* enmaderado *m*

panic (*pæ*-nik) *n* pánico *m*

pant (pænt) *v* jadear

panties (*pæn*-tis) *pl* braga *f*

pants (pæntss) *pl* calzoncillos *mpl*; *plAm* pantalones *mpl*

pant-suit (*pænt*-ssuut) *n* traje pantalón

panty-hose (*pæn*-ti-hous) *n* media pantalón

paper (*pei*-pö) *n* papel *m*; periódico *m*; de papel; **carbon ~** papel carbón; **~ bag** bolsa de papel; **~ napkin** servilleta de papel; **typing ~** papel para mecanografiar; **wrapping ~** papel de envolver

paperback (*pei*-pö-bæk) *n* libro de bolsillo

paper-knife (*pei*-pö-naif) *n* abrecartas *m*

parade (pö-*reid*) *n* parada *f*, desfile *m*

paraffin (*pæ*-rö-fin) *n* parafina *f*

paragraph (*pæ*-rö-ghraaf) *n* párrafo *m*

parakeet (*pæ*-rö-kiit) *n* cotorra *f*

paralise (*pæ*-rö-lais) *v* paralizar

parallel (*pæ*-rö-lêl) *adj* paralelo; *n* paralelo *m*

parcel (*paa*-ssöl) *n* paquete *m*

pardon (*paa*-dön) *n* perdón *m*; indulto *m*

parents (*pêö*-röntss) *pl* padres *mpl*

parents-in-law (*pêö*-röntss-in-loo) *pl* padres políticos

parish (*pæ*-riʃ) *n* parroquia *f*

park (paak) *n* parque *m*; *v* estacionar

parking (*paa*-king) *n* aparcamiento *m*; **no ~** prohibido estacionarse; **~ fee** derechos de estacionamiento; **~ light** luz de estacionamiento; **~ lot** *Am* estacionamiento *m*; **~ meter** parquímetro *m*; **~ zone** zona de aparcamiento

parliament (*paa*-lö-mönt) *n* parlamento *m*

parliamentary (paa-lö-*mên*-tö-ri) *adj* parlamentario

parrot (*pæ*-röt) *n* loro *m*

parsley (*paa*-ssli) *n* perejil *m*

parson (*paa*-ssön) *n* pastor *m*

parsonage (*paa*-ssö-nidʒ) *n* curato *m*

part (paat) *n* parte *f*; pieza *f*; *v* separar; **spare ~** recambio *m*

partial (*paa*-ʃöl) *adj* parcial

participant (paa-*ti*-ssi-pönt) *n* participante *m*

participate (paa-*ti*-ssi-peit) *v* participar

particular (pö-*ti*-kyu-lö) *adj* especial, particular; exigente; **in ~** en particular

parting (*paa*-ting) *n* despedida *f*; raya *f*

partition (paa-*ti*-ʃön) *n* tabique *m*

partly (*paat*-li) *adv* en parte

partner (*paat*-nö) *n* pareja *f*; socio *m*

partridge (*paa*-tridʒ) *n* perdiz *f*

party (*paa*-ti) *n* partido *m*; guateque *m*, fiesta *f*; grupo *m*

pass (paass) *v* transcurrir, pasar; *aprobar; ~ by pasar de largo; ~ through *atravesar

passage (*pæ*-ssidʒ) *n* pasaje *m*; travesía *f*; trozo *m*

passenger (*pæ*-ssön-dʒö) *n* pasajero *m*; ~ train tren de pasajeros

passer-by (paa-ssö-*bai*) *n* transeúnte *m*

passion (*pæ*-ʃön) *n* pasión *f*; cólera *f*

passionate (*pæ*-ʃö-nöt) *adj* apasionado

passive (*pæ*-ssiv) *adj* pasivo

passport (*paass*-poot) *n* pasaporte *m*; ~ control inspección de pasaportes; ~ photograph fotografía de pasaporte

password (*paass*-ᵁööd) *n* santo y seña

past (paasst) *n* pasado *m*; *adj* pasado; transcurrido; *prep* a lo largo de, más allá de

paste (peisst) *n* pasta *f*; *v* pegar

pastry (*pei*-sstri) *n* pastelería *f*; ~ shop pastelería *f*

pasture (*paass*-chö) *n* prado *m*

patch (pæch) *v* *remendar

patent (*pei*-tönt) *n* patente *f*

path (paaz) *n* senda *f*

patience (*pei*-ʃönss) *n* paciencia *f*

patient (*pei*-ʃönt) *adj* paciente; *n* paciente *m*

patriot (*pei*-tri-öt) *n* patriota *m*

patrol (pö-*troul*) *n* patrulla *f*; *v* patrullar; vigilar

pattern (*pæ*-tön) *n* diseño *m*

pause (poos) *n* pausa *f*; *v* *hacer una pausa

pave (peiv) *v* pavimentar

pavement (*peiv*-mönt) *n* acera *f*; pavimento *m*

pavilion (pö-*vil*-yön) *n* pabellón *m*

paw (poo) *n* pata *f*

pawn (poon) *v* empeñar; *n* peón *m*

pawnbroker (*poon*-brou-kö) *n* prestamista *m*

pay (pei) *n* salario *m*, sueldo *m*

*pay (pei) *v* pagar; *rendir; ~ attention to prestar atención a; paying rentable; ~ off amortizar; ~ on account pagar a plazos

pay-desk (*pei*-dêssk) *n* caja *f*

payee (pei-*ii*) *n* favorecido *m*

payment (*pei*-mönt) *n* pago *m*

pea (pii) *n* guisante *m*

peace (piiss) *n* paz *f*

peaceful (*piiss*-föl) *adj* tranquilo

peach (piich) *n* melocotón *m*

peacock (*pii*-kok) *n* pavo *m*

peak (piik) *n* pico *m*; cumbre *f*; ~ hour hora punta; ~ season apogeo de la temporada

peanut (*pii*-nat) *n* cacahuete *m*; cacahuate *mMe*

pear (pêᵒ) *n* pera *f*

pearl (pööl) *n* perla *f*

peasant (*pê*-sönt) *n* campesino *m*

pebble (*pê*-böl) *n* guijarro *m*

peculiar (pi-*kyuul*-yö) *adj* extraño; especial, peculiar

peculiarity (pi-kyuu-li-æ-rö-ti) *n* particularidad *f*

pedal (*pê*-döl) *n* pedal *m*

pedestrian (pi-*dê*-sstri-ön) *n* peatón *m*; no pedestrians prohibido para los peatones; ~ crossing cruce para peatones

pedicure (*pê*-di-kyuᵒ) *n* pedicuro *m*

peel (piil) *v* pelar; *n* piel *f*

peep (piip) *v* espiar

peg (pêgh) *n* percha *f*

pelican (*pê*-li-kön) *n* pelícano *m*

pelvis (*pêl*-viss) *n* pelvis *m*

pen (pên) *n* pluma *f*

penalty (*pê*-nöl-ti) *n* pena *f*; castigo *m*; ~ **kick** penalty *m*

pencil (*pên*-ssöl) *n* lápiz *m*

pencil-sharpener (*pên*-ssöl-ʃaap-nö) *n* sacapuntas *m*

pendant (*pên*-dönt) *n* pendiente *m*

penetrate (*pê*-ni-treit) *v* penetrar

penguin (*pêng*-ghⁿin) *n* pingüino *m*

penicillin (pê-ni-*ssi*-lin) *n* penicilina *f*

peninsula (pö-*nin*-ssyu-lö) *n* península *f*

penknife (*pên*-naif) *n* (pl -knives) cortaplumas *m*

pension[1] (*pang*-ssi-ong) *n* pensión *f*

pension[2] (*pên*-ʃön) *n* pensión *f*

people (*pii*-pöl) *pl* gente *f*; *n* pueblo *m*

pepper (*pê*-pö) *n* pimienta *f*

peppermint (*pê*-pö-mint) *n* menta *f*

perceive (pö-*ssiiv*) *v* percibir

percent (pö-*ssênt*) *n* por ciento

percentage (pö-*ssên*-tidʒ) *n* porcentaje *m*

perceptible (pö-*ssêp*-ti-böl) *adj* perceptible

perception (pö-*ssêp*-ʃön) *n* percepción *f*

perch (pööch) (pl ~) perca *f*

percolator (*pöö*-kö-lei-tö) *n* cafetera filtradora

perfect (*pöö*-fikt) *adj* perfecto

perfection (pö-*fêk*-ʃön) *n* perfección *f*

perform (pö-*foom*) *v* ejecutar, desempeñar

performance (pö-*foo*-mönss) *n* representación *f*

perfume (*pöö*-fyuum) *n* perfume *m*

perhaps (pö-*hæpss*) *adv* quizás

peril (*pê*-ril) *n* peligro *m*

perilous (*pê*-ri-löss) *adj* peligroso

period (*piⁱ*-ri-öd) *n* época *f*, período *m*; punto *m*

periodical (piⁱ-ri-*o*-di-köl) *n* periódico

m; *adj* periódico

perish (*pê*-riʃ) *v* *perecer

perishable (*pê*-ri-ʃö-böl) *adj* perecedero

perjury (*pöö*-dʒö-ri) *n* perjurio *m*

permanent (*pöö*-mö-nönt) *adj* duradero, permanente; estable, fijo; ~ **press** planchado permanente; ~ **wave** ondulación permanente

permission (pö-*mi*-ʃön) *n* permiso *m*, autorización *f*; licencia *f*

permit[1] (pö-*mit*) *v* permitir

permit[2] (*pöö*-mit) *n* permiso *m*

peroxide (pö-*rok*-ssaid) *n* peróxido *m*

perpendicular (pöö-pön-*di*-kyu-lö) *adj* perpendicular

Persian (*pöö*-ʃön) *adj* persa

person (*pöö*-ssön) *n* persona *f*; **per** ~ por persona

personal (*pöö*-ssö-nöl) *adj* personal

personality (öö-ssö-*næ*-lö-ti) *n* personalidad *f*

personnel (pöö-ssö-*nêl*) *n* personal *m*

perspective (pö-*sspêk*-tiv) *n* perspectiva *f*

perspiration (pöö-sspö-*rei*-ʃön) *n* transpiración *f*, sudor *m*

perspire (pö-*sspaiⁿ*) *v* transpirar, sudar

persuade (pö-*ssⁿeid*) *v* persuadir; convencer

persuasion (pö-*ssⁿei*-ʒön) *n* convicción *f*

pessimism (*pê*-ssi-mi-söm) *n* pesimismo *m*

pessimist (*pê*-ssi-misst) *n* pesimista *m*

pessimistic (pê-ssi-*mi*-sstik) *adj* pesimista

pet (pêt) *n* animal doméstico; cariño *m*; favorito

petal (*pê*-töl) *n* pétalo *m*

petition (pi-*ti*-ʃön) *n* petición *f*

petrol (*pê*-tröl) *n* gasolina *f*; **unleaded** ~ gasolina sin plomo; ~ **pump**

bomba de gasolina; ~ **station** puesto de gasolina; ~ **tank** depósito de gasolina

petroleum (pi-*trou*-li-öm) *n* petróleo *m*

petty (*pê*-ti) *adj* pequeño, fútil, insignificante; ~ **cash** calderilla *f*

pewit (*pii*-ᵁit) *n* avefría *f*

pewter (*pyuu*-tö) *n* estaño *m*

phantom (*fæn*-töm) *n* fantasma *m*

pharmacology (faa-mö-*ko*-lö-dʒi) *n* farmacología *f*

pharmacy (*faa*-mö-ssi) *n* farmacia *f*; droguería *f*

pheasant (*fê*-sönt) *n* faisán *m*

Philippine (*fi*-li-pain) *adj* filipino

Philippines (*fi*-li-piins) *pl* Filipinas *fpl*

philosopher (fi-*lo*-ssö-fö) *n* filósofo *m*

philosophy (fi-*lo*-ssö-fi) *n* filosofía *f*

phone (foun) *n* teléfono *m*; *v* llamar por teléfono, telefonear

phonetic (fö-*nê*-tik) *adj* fonético

photo (*fou*-tou) *n* (pl ~s) foto *f*

photocopy (*fou*-tö-ko-pi) *n* fotocopia *f*; *v* fotocopiar

photograph (*fou*-tö-ghraaf) *n* fotografía *f*; *v* fotografiar

photographer (fö-*to*-ghrö-fö) *n* fotógrafo *m*

photography (fö-*to*-ghrö-fi) *n* fotografía *f*

phrase (freis) *n* frase *f*

phrase-book (*freis*-buk) *n* manual de conversación

physical (*fi*-si-köl) *adj* físico

physician (fi-*si*-jön) *n* médico *m*

physicist (*fi*-si-ssisst) *n* físico *m*

physics (*fi*-sikss) *n* física *f*

physiology (fi-si-*o*-lö-dʒi) *n* fisiología *f*

pianist (*pii*-ö-nisst) *n* pianista *m*

piano (pi-*æ*-nou) *n* piano *m*; **grand ~** piano de cola

pick (pik) *v* recoger; escoger; *n* elec-

ción *f*; ~ **up** recoger; *ir a buscar; pick-up van camioneta de reparto

pick-axe (*pi*-kækss) *n* pico *m*

pickles (*pi*-köls) *pl* encurtidos *mpl*

picnic (*pik*-nik) *n* día de campo; *v* *hacer un día de campo

picture (*pik*-chö) *n* cuadro *m*; ilustración *f*, grabado *m*; imagen *f*; ~ **postcard** tarjeta postal ilustrada, postal ilustrada; **pictures** cine *m*

picturesque (pik-chö-*rêssk*) *adj* pintoresco

piece (piiss) *n* fragmento *m*, pedazo *m*

pier (piö) *n* muelle *m*

pierce (piöss) *v* punzar

pig (pigh) *n* cerdo *m*

pigeon (*pi*-dʒön) *n* paloma *f*

pig-headed (pigh-*hê*-did) *adj* testarudo

piglet (*pigh*-löt) *n* cochinillo *m*

pigskin (*pigh*-sskin) *n* piel de cerdo

pike (paik) (pl ~) lucio *m*

pile (pail) *n* montón *m*; *v* amontonar; **piles** *pl* hemorroides *fpl*

pilgrim (*pil*-ghrim) *n* peregrino *m*

pilgrimage (*pil*-ghri-midʒ) *n* peregrinación *f*

pill (pil) *n* píldora *f*

pillar (*pi*-lö) *n* columna *f*, pilar *m*

pillar-box (*pi*-lö-bokss) *n* buzón *m*

pillow (*pi*-lou) *n* almohadón *m*, almohada *f*

pillow-case (*pi*-lou-keiss) *n* funda de almohada

pilot (*pai*-löt) *n* piloto *m*; práctico *m*

pimple (*pim*-pöl) *n* grano *m*

pin (pin) *n* alfiler *m*; *v* clavar; **bobby ~** *Am* horquilla *f*

pincers (*pin*-ssös) *pl* tenazas *fpl*

pinch (pinch) *v* pellizcar

pineapple (*pai*-næ-pöl) *n* piña *f*

ping-pong (*ping*-pong) *n* tenis de mesa

pink (pingk) *adj* rosado

pioneer (pai-ö-*ni*ᵒ) *n* pionero *m*

pious (*pai*-öss) *adj* pío

pip (pip) *n* pepita *f*

pipe (paip) *n* pipa *f*; conducto *m*; ~ **cleaner** limpiapipas *m*; ~ **tobacco** tabaco de pipa

pirate (*pai*ᵒ-röt) *n* pirata *m*

pistol (*pi*-sstöl) *n* pistola *f*

piston (*pi*-sstön) *n* pistón *m*; ~ **ring** aro de émbolo

piston-rod (*pi*-sstön-rod) *n* biela *f*

pit (pit) *n* hoyo *m*; mina *f*

pitcher (*pi*-chö) *n* cántaro *m*

pity (*pi*-ti) *n* piedad *f*; *v* *tener piedad de, compadecerse de; **what a pity!** ¡qué lástima!

placard (*plæ*-kaad) *n* cartel *m*

place (pleiss) *n* lugar *m*; *v* *poner, colocar; ~ **of birth** lugar de nacimiento; *take ~ *tener lugar

plague (pleigh) *n* plaga *f*

plaice (pleiss) (pl ~) platija *f*

plain (plein) *adj* claro; corriente, sencillo; *n* llano *m*

plan (plæn) *n* plan *m*; plano *m*; *v* planear

plane (plein) *adj* plano; *n* avión *m*; ~ **crash** accidente aéreo

planet (*plæ*-nit) *n* planeta *m*

planetarium (plæ-ni-*tê*ᵒ-ri-öm) *n* planetario *m*

plank (plængk) *n* tablón *m*

plant (plaant) *n* planta *f*; instalación *f*; *v* plantar

plantation (plæn-*tei*-ʃön) *n* plantación *f*

plaster (*plaa*-sstö) *n* estuco *m*, yeso *m*; esparadrapo *m*

plastic (*plæ*-sstik) *adj* de plástico; *n* plástico *m*

plate (pleit) *n* plato *m*; chapa *f*

plateau (*plæ*-tou) *n* (pl ~x, ~s) meseta *f*

platform (*plæt*-foom) *n* andén *m*; ~ **ticket** billete de andén

platinum (*plæ*-ti-nöm) *n* platino *m*

play (plei) *v* *jugar; tocar; *n* juego *m*; obra de teatro; **one-act** ~ pieza en un acto; ~ **truant** *hacer novillos

player (plei ᵒ) *n* jugador *m*

playground (*plei*-ghraund) *n* patio de recreo

playing-card (*plei*-ing-kaad) *n* naipe *m*

playwright (*plei*-rait) *n* dramaturgo *m*

plea (plii) *n* defensa *f*

plead (pliid) *v* informar

pleasant (*plê*-sönt) *adj* agradable, simpático

please (pliis) por favor; *v* *placer; **pleased** contento; **pleasing** agradable

pleasure (*plê*-ʒö) *n* placer *m*, diversión *f*

plentiful (*plên*-ti-föl) *adj* abundante

plenty (*plên*-ti) *n* abundancia *f*

pliers (plaiᵒs) *pl* alicates *mpl*

plimsolls (*plim*-ssöls) *pl* zapatos de gimnasia

plot (plot) *n* conjuración *f*, complot *m*; trama *f*; parcela *f*

plough (plau) *n* arado *m*; *v* arar

plucky (*pla*-ki) *adj* valiente

plug (plagh) *n* enchufe *m*; ~ **in** enchufar

plum (plam) *n* ciruela *f*

plumber (*pla*-mö) *n* plomero *m*

plump (plamp) *adj* regordete

plural (*plu*ᵒ-röl) *n* plural *m*

plus (plass) *prep* más

pneumatic (nyuu-*mæ*-tik) *adj* neumático

pneumonia (nyuu-*mou*-ni-ö) *n* neumonía *f*

poach (pouch) *v* cazar en vedado

pocket (*po*-kit) *n* bolsillo *m*

pocket-book (*po*-kit-buk) *n* bolsa *f*

pocket-comb (*po*-kit-koum) *n* peine de bolsillo

pocket-knife (*po*-kit-naif) *n* (pl -knives) navaja *f*

pocket-watch (*po*-kit-ᵘoch) *n* reloj de bolsillo

poem (*pou*-im) *n* poema *m*

poet (*pou*-it) *n* poeta *m*

poetry (*pou*-i-tri) *n* poesía *f*

point (point) *n* punto *m*; punta *f*; *v* señalar con el dedo; ~ **of view** punto de vista; ~ **out** apuntar

pointed (*poin*-tid) *adj* puntiagudo

poison (*poi*-sön) *n* veneno *m*; *v* envenenar

poisonous (*poi*-sö-nöss) *adj* venenoso

Poland (*pou*-lönd) Polonia *f*

Pole (poul) *n* polaco *m*

pole (poul) *n* poste *m*

police (pö-*liiss*) *pl* policía *f*

policeman (pö-*liiss*-mön) *n* (pl -men) agente de policía, guardia *m*

police-station (pö-*liiss*-sstei-ʃön) *n* comisaría *f*

policy (*po*-li-ssi) *n* política *f*; póliza *f*

polio (*pou*-li-ou) *n* polio *f*, poliomielitis *f*

Polish (*pou*-liʃ) *adj* polaco *m*

polish (*po*-liʃ) *v* pulir

polite (pö-*lait*) *adj* cortés

political (pö-*li*-ti-köl) *adj* político

politician (po-li-*ti*-ʃön) *n* político *m*

politics (*po*-li-tikss) *n* política *f*

pollution (pö-*luu*-ʃön) *n* contaminación *f*, polución *f*

pond (pond) *n* estanque *m*

pony (*pou*-ni) *n* pony *m*

poor (puᵒ) *adj* pobre; mediocre

pope (poup) *n* Papa *m*

poplin (*po*-plin) *n* popelín *m*

pop music (pop *myuu*-sik) música pop

poppy (*po*-pi) *n* amapola *f*; adormidera *f*

popular (*po*-pyu-lö) *adj* popular

population (po-pyu-*lei*-ʃön) *n* población *f*

populous (*po*-pyu-löss) *adj* populoso

porcelain (*poo*-ssö-lin) *n* porcelana *f*

porcupine (*poo*-kyu-pain) *n* puerco espín

pork (pook) *n* carne de cerdo

port (poot) *n* puerto *m*; babor *m*

portable (*poo*-tö-böl) *adj* portátil

porter (*poo*-tö) *n* mozo *m*; portero *m*

porthole (*poot*-houl) *n* portilla *f*

portion (*poo*-ʃön) *n* porción *f*

portrait (*poo*-trit) *n* retrato *m*

Portugal (*poo*-tyu-ghöl) Portugal *m*

Portuguese (poo-tyu-*ghiis*) *adj* portugués

position (pö-*si*-ʃön) *n* posición *f*; actitud *f*; puesto *m*

positive (*po*-sö-tiv) *adj* positivo; *n* positiva *f*

possess (pö-*séss*) *v* *poseer; possessed *adj* poseído

possession (pö-*sé*-ʃön) *n* posesión *f*; possessions bienes *mpl*

possibility (po-ssö-*bi*-lö-ti) *n* posibilidad *f*

possible (*po*-ssö-böl) *adj* posible; eventual

post (pousst) *n* poste *m*; puesto *m*; correo *m*; *v* echar al correo; post-office casa de correos

postage (*pou*-sstidʒ) *n* franqueo *m*; ~ **paid** franco; ~ **stamp** sello de correos; timbre *mMe*

postcard (*pousst*-kaad) *n* tarjeta postal; tarjeta postal ilustrada

poster (*pou*-sstö) *n* cartel *m*, poster *m*

poste restante (pousst rê-*sstangt*) lista de correos

postman (*pousst*-mön) *n* (pl -men) cartero *m*

post-paid (pousst-*peid*) *adj* franco

postpone (pö-*sspoun*) *v* aplazar

pot (pot) *n* olla *f*

potato (pö-*tei*-tou) *n* (pl ~es) patata *f*; papa *f Me*

pottery (*po*-tö-ri) *n* cerámica *f*; loza *f*

pouch (pauch) *n* petaca *f*

poulterer (*poul*-tö-rö) *n* pollero *m*

poultry (*poul*-tri) *n* aves de corral

pound (paund) *n* libra *f*

pour (poo) *v* *verter

poverty (*po*-vö-ti) *n* pobreza *f*

powder (*pau*-dö) *n* polvo *m*; ~ compact polvera *f*; talc ~ talco *m*

powder-puff (*pau*-dö-paf) *n* borla para empolvarse

powder-room (*pau*-dö-ruum) *n* tocador *m*

power (pauö) *n* fuerza *f*, energía *f*; poder *m*; potencia *f*

powerful (*pauö*-föl) *adj* poderoso; fuerte

powerless (*pauö*-löss) *adj* impotente

power-station (*pauö*-sstei-jön) *n* central eléctrica

practical (*præk*-ti-köl) *adj* práctico

practically (*præk*-tɪ-klɪ) *adv* prácticamente

practice (*præk*-tiss) *n* práctica *f*

practise (*præk*-tiss) *v* practicar; ensayarse

praise (preis) *v* alabar; *n* elogio *m*

pram (præm) *n* cochecillo *m*

prawn (proon) *n* gamba *f*

pray (prei) *v* orar

prayer (preˆ*ö*) *n* oración *f*

preach (priich) *v* predicar

precarious (pri-*keˆö*-ri-öss) *adj* precario

precaution (pri-*koo*-jön) *n* precaución *f*

precede (pri-*ssiid*) *v* preceder

preceding (pri-*ssii*-ding) *adj* precedente

precious (*preˆ*-jöss) *adj* precioso; querido

precipice (*preˆ*-ssi-piss) *n* precipicio *m*

precipitation (pri-ssi-pi-*tei*-jön) *n* precipitación *f*

precise (pri-*ssaiss*) *adj* preciso, exacto; meticuloso

predecessor (*prii*-di-ssè-ssö) *n* predecesor *m*

predict (pri-*dikt*) *v* *predecir

prefer (pri-*föö*) *v* *preferir

preferable (*preˆ*-fö-rö-böl) *adj* preferible

preference (*preˆ*-fö-rönss) *n* preferencia *f*

prefix (*prii*-fikss) *n* prefijo *m*

pregnant (*prêgh*-nönt) *adj* encinta, embarazada

prejudice (*preˆ*-dʒö-diss) *n* prejuicio *m*

preliminary (pri-*li*-mi-nö-ri) *adj* preliminar

premature (*preˆ*-mö-chuˆö) *adj* prematuro

premier (*prêm*-iˆö) *n* jefe de gobierno

premises (*preˆ*-mi-ssis) *pl* finca *f*

premium (*prii*-mi-öm) *n* prima *f*

prepaid (prii-*peid*) *adj* pagado por adelantado

preparation (prê-pö-*rei*-jön) *n* preparación *f*

prepare (pri-*pêˆö*) *v* preparar

preposition (prê-pö-*si*-jön) *n* preposición *f*

prescribe (pri-*sskraib*) *v* prescribir

prescription (pri-*sskrip*-jön) *n* prescripción *f*

presence (*prê*-sönss) *n* presencia *f*

present¹ (*prê*-sönt) *n* regalo *m*, presente *m*; *adj* actual; presente

present² (pri-*sênt*) *v* presentar

presently (*prê*-sönt-li) *adv* en seguida, dentro de poco

preservation (prê-sö-*vei*-jön) *n* conservación *f*

preserve (pri-*sööv*) *v* preservar; conservar

president (*prê*-si-dönt) *n* presidente *m*

press (prèss) *n* prensa *f*; *v* empujar, *apretar; planchar; ~ **conference** conferencia de prensa

pressing (prê-ssing) *adj* urgente

pressure (prê-ʃö) *n* presión *f*; tensión *f*; **atmospheric** ~ presión atmosférica

pressure-cooker (prê-ʃö-ku-kö) *n* olla a presión

prestige (prê-sstiiʒ) *n* prestigio *m*

presumable (pri-syuu-mö-böl) *adj* presumible

presumptuous (pri-samp-ʃöss) *adj* presuntuoso; presumido

pretence (pri-tênss) *n* pretexto *m*

pretend (pri-ténd) *v* fingir

pretext (prii-têksst) *n* pretexto *m*

pretty (pri-ti) *adj* bonito; *adv* bastante

prevent (pri-vênt) *v* *impedir; *prevenir

preventive (pri-vên-tiv) *adj* preventivo

previous (prii-vi-öss) *adj* precedente, anterior, previo

pre-war (prii-ᵘoo) *adj* de la preguerra

price (praiss) *n* precio *m*; *v* fijar el precio

priceless (praiss-löss) *adj* inapreciable

price-list (praiss-lisst) *n* lista de precios

prick (prik) *v* pinchar

pride (praid) *n* orgullo *m*

priest (priisst) *n* cura *m*

primary (prai-mö-ri) *adj* primario; primero, primordial; elemental

prince (prinss) *n* príncipe *m*

princess (prin-ssêss) *n* princesa *f*

principal (prin-ssö-pöl) *adj* principal; *n* director de escuela, principal *m*

principle (prin-ssö-pöl) *n* principio *m*

print (print) *v* *imprimir; *n* positiva *f*; grabado *m*; **printed matter** impreso *m*

prior (prai⁶) *adj* anterior

priority (prai-o-rö-ti) *n* prioridad *f*

prison (pri-sön) *n* prisión *f*

prisoner (pri-sö-nö) *n* preso *m*, prisionero *m*; ~ **of war** prisionero de guerra

privacy (prai-vö-ssi) *n* intimidad *f*, vida privada

private (prai-vit) *adj* particular, privado; personal

privilege (pri-vi-lidʒ) *n* privilegio *m*

prize (praiss) *n* premio *m*; recompensa *f*

probable (pro-bö-böl) *adj* probable

probably (pro-bö-bli) *adv* probablemente

problem (pro-blöm) *n* problema *m*

procedure (prö-ssii-dʒö) *n* procedimiento *m*

proceed (prö-ssiid) *v* *proseguir; proceder

process (prou-ssêss) *n* procedimiento *m*, proceso *m*

procession (prö-ssê-ʃön) *n* procesión *f*, comitiva *f*

proclaim (prö-kleim) *v* proclamar

produce¹ (prö-dyuuss) *v* *producir

produce² (prod-yuuss) *n* producto *m*

producer (prö-dyuu-ssö) *n* productor *m*

product (pro-dakt) *n* producto *m*

production (prö-dak-ʃön) *n* producción *f*

profession (prö-fê-ʃön) *n* profesión *f*

professional (prö-fê-ʃö-nöl) *adj* profesional

professor (prö-fê-ssö) *n* profesor *m*

profit (pro-fit) *n* beneficio *m*, ganancia *f*; ventaja *f*; *v* aprovechar

profitable (pro-fi-tö-böl) *adj* provechoso

profound (prö-faund) *adj* profundo

programme (prou-ghræm) *n* programa *m*

progress¹ (prou-ghrêss) *n* progreso *m*

progress² (prö-*ghréss*) v progresar

progressive (prö-*ghré*-ssiv) adj progresista; progresivo

prohibit (prö-*hi*-bit) v prohibir

prohibition (prou-i-*bi*-ſön) n prohibición f

prohibitive (prö-*hi*-bi-tiv) adj exorbitante

project (*pro*-dʒékt) n plan m, proyecto m

promenade (pro-mö-*naad*) n paseo m

promise (*pro*-miss) n promesa f; v prometer

promote (prö-*mout*) v *promover

promotion (prö-*mou*-ſön) n promoción f

prompt (prompt) adj inmediato, pronto

pronoun (*prou*-naun) n pronombre m

pronounce (prö-*naunss*) v pronunciar

pronunciation (prö-nan-ssi-*ei*-ſön) n pronunciación f

proof (pruuf) n prueba f

propaganda (pro pö-*ghæn*-dö) n propaganda f

propel (prö-*pêl*) v impeler

propeller (prö-*pê*-lö) n hélice f

proper (*pro*-pö) adj justo; debido, conveniente, apropiado

property (*pro*-pö-ti) n propiedad f; cualidad f

prophet (*pro*-fit) n profeta m

proportion (prö-*poo*-ſön) n proporción f

proportional (prö-*poo*-ſö-nöl) adj proporcional

proposal (prö-*pou*-söl) n propuesta f

propose (prö-*pous*) v *proponer

proposition (pro-pö-*si*-ſön) n propuesta f

proprietor (prö-*prai*-ö-tö) n propietario m

prospect (*pro*-sspékt) n perspectiva f

prospectus (prö-*sspêk*-töss) n pros-

pecto m

prosperity (pro-*sspê*-rö-ti) n prosperidad f

prosperous (*pro*-sspö-röss) adj próspero

prostitute (*pro*-ssti-tyuut) n prostituta f

protect (prö-*têkt*) v proteger

protection (prö-*têk*-ſön) n protección f

protein (*prou*-tiin) n proteina f

protest¹ (*prou*-têsst) n protesta f

protest² (prö-*têsst*) v protestar

Protestant (*pro*-ti-sstönt) adj protestante

proud (praud) adj orgulloso

prove (pruuv) v *demostrar, *comprobar; resultar

proverb (*pro*-vööb) n proverbio m

provide (prö-*vaid*) v *proveer; **provided that** con tal que

province (*pro*-vinss) n provincia f

provincial (prö-*vin*-ſöl) adj provincial

provisional (prö-*vi*-ʒö-nöl) adj provisional

provisions (prö-*vi*-ʒöns) pl provisiones fpl

prune (pruun) n ciruela pasa

psychiatrist (ssai-*kai*-ö-trisst) n psiquiatra m

psychic (*ssai*-kik) adj psíquico

psychoanalyst (ssai-kou-*æ*-nö-lisst) n psicoanalista m

psychological (ssai-ko-*lo*-dʒi-köl) adj psicológico

psychologist (ssai-*ko*-lö-dʒisst) n psicólogo m

psychology (ssai-*ko*-lö-dʒi) n psicología f

pub (pab) n taberna f

public (*pa*-blik) adj público; general; n público m; ~ **garden** jardín público; ~ **house** taberna f

publication (pa-bli-*kei*-ſön) n publica-

ción f
publicity (pa-*bli*-ssö-ti) n publicidad f
publish (*pa*-bliʃ) v publicar
publisher (*pa*-bli-ʃö) n editor m
puddle (*pa*-döl) n charco m
pull (pul) v tirar; ~ **out** partir; ~ **up** pararse
pulley (*pu*-li) n (pl ~s) polea f
Pullman (*pul*-mön) n coche Pullman
pullover (*pu*-lou-vö) n pulóver m
pulpit (*pul*-pit) n púlpito m
pulse (palss) n pulso m
pump (pamp) n bomba f; v bombear
punch (panch) v *dar puñetazos; n puñetazo m
punctual (*pangk*-chu-öl) adj puntual
puncture (*pangk*-chö) n pinchazo m
punctured (*pangk*-chöd) adj pinchado
punish (*pa*-niʃ) v castigar
punishment (*pa*-niʃ-mönt) n castigo m
pupil (*pyuu*-pöl) n alumno m
puppet-show (*pa*-pit-ʃou) n teatro guiñol
purchase (*pöö*-chöss) v comprar; n compra f; ~ **price** precio de compra; ~ **tax** impuesto sobre la venta
purchaser (*pöö*-chö-ssö) n comprador m
pure (pyuᵒ) adj casto, puro
purple (*pöö*-pöl) adj purpúreo
purpose (*pöö*-pöss) n propósito m, fin m, intención f; **on** ~ intencionado
purse (pööss) n bolsa f, monedero m
pursue (pö-*ssyuu*) v *perseguir
pus (pass) n pus f
push (puʃ) n empujón m; v empujar
push-button (*puʃ*-ba-tön) n botón m
***put** (put) v colocar, *poner; meter; plantear; ~ **away** guardar; ~ **off** aplazar; ~ **on** *ponerse; ~ **out** apagar
puzzle (*pa*-söl) n rompecabezas m;

enigma m; v confundir; **jigsaw** ~ rompecabezas m
puzzling (*pas*-ling) adj embarazoso
pyjamas (pö-*dʒaa*-mös) pl pijama m

Q

quack (kᵘæk) n curandero m, charlatán m
quail (kᵘeil) n (pl ~, ~s) codorniz f
quaint (kᵘeint) adj curioso; anticuado
qualification (kᵘo-li-fi-*kei*-ʃön) n aptitud f; reserva f, restricción f
qualified (kᵘo-li-faid) adj calificado; competente
qualify (kᵘo-li-fai) v *ser capaz de, *ser apto para
quality (kᵘo-lö-ti) n calidad f; característica f
quantity (kᵘon-tö-ti) n cantidad f; número m
quarantine (kᵘo-rön-tiin) n cuarentena f
quarrel (kᵘo-röl) v disputar, *reñir; n disputa f
quarry (kᵘo-ri) n cantera f
quarter (kᵘoo-tö) n cuarto m; trimestre m; barrio m; ~ **of an hour** cuarto de hora
quarterly (kᵘoo-tö-li) adj trimestral
quay (kii) n muelle m
queen (kᵘiin) n reina f
queer (kᵘiᵒ) adj singular, extraño
query (kᵘiᵒ-ri) n pregunta f; v indagar; *poner en duda
question (kᵘêss-chön) n pregunta f; cuestión f, problema m; v interrogar; *poner en duda; ~ **mark** signo de interrogación
queue (kyuu) n cola f; v *hacer cola
quick (kᵘik) adj rápido
quick-tempered (kᵘik-*têm*-pöd) adj

irascible

quiet (k^{u}ai-öt) *adj* quieto, tranquilo; *n* silencio *m*, paz *f*

quilt (k^{u}ilt) *n* colcha *f*

quinine (k^{u}i-*niin*) *n* quinina *f*

quit (k^{u}it) *v* cesar

quite (k^{u}ait) *adv* enteramente, completamente; bastante; muy

quiz (k^{u}is) *n* (pl ~zes) concurso *m*

quota (k^{u}ou-tö) *n* cuota *f*

quotation (k^{u}ou-*tei*-jön) *n* cita *f*; ~ **marks** comillas *fpl*

quote (k^{u}out) *v* citar

R

rabbit (*ræ*-bit) *n* conejo *m*

rabies (*rei*-bis) *n* rabia *f*

race (reiss) *n* carrera *f*; raza *f*

race-course (*reiss*-kooss) *n* pista para carreras, hipódromo *m*

race-horse (*reiss*-hooss) *n* caballo de carrera

race-track (*reiss*-træk) *n* pista para carreras

racial (*rei*-jöl) *adj* racial

racket (*ræ*-kit) *n* alboroto *m*

racquet (*ræ*-kit) *n* raqueta *f*

radiator (*rei*-di-ei-tö) *n* radiador *m*

radical (*ræ*-di-köl) *adj* radical

radio (*rei*-di-ou) *n* radio *f*

radish (*ræ*-dij) *n* rábano *m*

radius (*rei*-di-öss) *n* (pl radii) radio *m*

raft (raaft) *n* zatara *f*

rag (rægh) *n* trapo *m*

rage (reidʒ) *n* furor *m*, rabia *f*; *v* rabiar

raid (reid) *n* irrupción *f*

rail (reil) *n* barandilla *f*, barrera *f*

railing (*rei*-ling) *n* barandilla *f*

railroad (*reil*-roud) *nAm* vía del tren, ferrocarril *m*

railway (*reil*-^{u}ei) *n* ferrocarril *m*

rain (rein) *n* lluvia *f*; *v* *llover

rainbow (*rein*-bou) *n* arco iris

raincoat (*rein*-kout) *n* impermeable *m*

rainproof (*rein*-pruuf) *adj* impermeable

rainy (*rei*-ni) *adj* lluvioso

raise (reis) *v* alzar; aumentar; educar, cultivar, criar; recaudar; *nAm* aumento de sueldo

raisin (*rei*-sön) *n* pasa *f*

rake (reik) *n* rastrillo *m*

rally (*ræ*-li) *n* reunión *f*

ramp (ræmp) *n* rampa *f*

ramshackle (*ræm*-ʃæ-köl) *adj* destartalado

rancid (*ræn*-ssid) *adj* rancio

rang (ræng) *v* (p ring)

range (reindʒ) *n* alcance *m*

range-finder (*reindʒ*-fain-dö) *n* telémetro *m*

rank (rængk) *n* rango *m*; fila *f*

ransom (*ræn*-ssöm) *n* rescate *m*

rape (reip) *v* violar

rapid (*ræ*-pid) *adj* rápido

rapids (*ræ*-pids) *pl* rápidos de río

rare (rê^ö) *adj* raro

rarely (*rê^ö*-li) *adv* raras veces

rascal (*raa*-ssköl) *n* pícaro *m*, pillo *m*

rash (ræʃ) *n* erupción *f*; *adj* precipitado, irreflexivo

raspberry (*raas*-bö-ri) *n* frambuesa *f*

rat (ræt) *n* rata *f*

rate (reit) *n* precio *m*, tarifa *f*; velocidad *f*; **at any** ~ de todos modos, en todo caso; ~ **of exchange** cambio *m*

rather (*raa*-ðö) *adv* bastante; más bien

ration (*ræ*-jön) *n* ración *f*

rattan (*ræ*-tæn) *n* rota *f*

raven (*rei*-vön) *n* cuervo *m*

raw (roo) *adj* crudo; ~ **material** materia prima

ray (rei) *n* rayo *m*

rayon (*rei*-on) *n* rayón *m*

razor (*rei*-sö) *n* máquina de afeitar

razor-blade (*rei*-sö-bleid) *n* hoja de afeitar

reach (riich) *v* alcanzar; *n* alcance *m*

reaction (ri-*æk*-∫ön) *n* reacción *f*

* read (riid) *v* *leer

reading (*rii*-ding) *n* lectura *f*

reading-lamp (*rii*-ding-læmp) *n* lámpara para lectura

reading-room (*rii*-ding-ruum) *n* sala de lectura

ready (*rê*-di) *adj* preparado, listo

ready-made (*rê*-di-*meid*) *adj* confeccionado

real (riºl) *adj* verdadero

reality (ri-*æ*-lö-ti) *n* realidad *f*

realizable (*riº*-lai-sö-böl) *adj* realizable

realize (*riº*-lais) *v* *reconocer; realizar

really (*riº*-li) *adv* verdaderamente, en realidad; de veras

rear (riº) *n* parte posterior; *v* criar

rear-light (riº-*lait*) *n* luz trasera

reason (*rii*-sön) *n* causa *f*, razón *f*; sentido *m*; *v* razonar

reasonable (*rii*-sö-nö-böl) *adj* razonable

reassure (rii-ö-*ſuº*) *v* tranquilizar

rebate (*rii*-beit) *n* reducción *f*, rebaja *f*

rebellion (ri-*bêl*-yön) *n* sublevación *f*, rebelión *f*

recall (ri-*kool*) *v* *acordarse; llamar; revocar

receipt (ri-*ssiit*) *n* recibo *m*

receive (ri-*ssiiv*) *v* recibir

receiver (ri-*ssii*-vö) *n* receptor *m*

recent (*rii*-ssönt) *adj* reciente

recently (*rii*-ssönt-li) *adv* el otro día, recientemente

reception (ri-*ssêp*-∫ön) *n* recepción *f*; acogida *f*; ~ **office** oficina de reci-

bo

receptionist (ri-*ssêp*-∫ö-nisst) *n* recepcionista *f*

recession (ri-*ssê*-∫ön) *n* retroceso *m*

recipe (*rê*-ssi-pi) *n* receta *f*

recital (ri-*ssai*-töl) *n* recital *m*

reckon (*rê*-kön) *v* calcular; considerar; *creer

recognition (rê-kögh-*ni*-∫ön) *n* reconocimiento *m*

recognize (*rê*-kögh-nais) *v* *reconocer

recollect (rê-kö-*lêkt*) *v* *acordarse

recommence (rii-kö-*mênss*) *v* *recomenzar

recommend (rê-kö-*mênd*) *v* *recomendar; aconsejar

recommendation (rê-kö-mên-*dei*-∫ön) *n* recomendación *f*

reconciliation (rê-kön-ssi-li-*ei*-∫ön) *n* reconciliación *f*

record[1] (*rê*-kood) *n* disco *m*; récord *m*; registro *m*; **long-playing** ~ microsurco *m*

record[2] (ri-*kood*) *v* registrar

recorder (ri-*koo*-dö) *n* magnetófono *m*

recording (ri-*koo*-ding) *n* grabación *f*

record-player (*rê*-kood-pleiº) *n* tocadiscos *m*

recover (ri-*ka*-vö) *v* recuperar; *restablecerse, curarse

recovery (ri-*ka*-vö-ri) *n* curación *f*, restablecimiento *m*

recreation (rê-kri-*ei*-∫ön) *n* recreación *f*, recreo *m*; ~ **centre** centro de recreo; ~ **ground** terreno de recreo público

recruit (ri-*kruut*) *n* recluta *m*

rectangle (*rêk*-tæng-ghöl) *n* rectángulo *m*

rectangular (rêk-*tæng*-ghyu-lö) *adj* rectangular

rector (*rêk*-tö) *n* pastor *m*, rector *m*

rectory (*rêk*-tö-ri) *n* rectoría *f*

rectum (*rêk*-töm) *n* intestino recto

recyclable (ri-*ssai*-klö-böl) *adj* reciclable

recycle (ri-*ssai*-köl) *v* reciclar

red (rêd) *adj* rojo

redeem (ri-*diim*) *v* redimir

reduce (ri-*dyuuss*) *v* *reducir, *disminuir, rebajar

reduction (ri-*dak*-∫ön) *n* rebaja *f*, reducción *f*

redundant (ri-*dan*-dönt) *adj* superfluo

reed (riid) *n* junquillo *m*

reef (riif) *n* arrecife *m*

reference (*rêf*-rönss) *n* refcrencia *f*; relación *f*; **with ~ to** con respecto a

refer to (ri-*föö*) remitir a

refill (*rii*-fil) *n* repuesto *m*

refinery (ri-*fai*-nö-ri) *n* refinería *f*

reflect (ri-*flêkt*) *v* reflejar

reflection (ri-*flêk*-∫ön) *n* reflejo *m*; imagen reflejada

refresh (ri-*frê∫*) *v* refrescar

refreshment (ri-*frê∫*-mönt) *n* refresco *m*

refrigerator (ri-*fri*-dʒö-rei-tö) *n* refrigerador *m*

refund[1] (ri-*fand*) *v* reintegrar

refund[2] (*rii*-fand) *n* reintegro *m*

refusal (ri-*fyuu*-söl) *n* negativa *f*

refuse[1] (ri-*fyuus*) *v* rehusar

refuse[2] (*rê*-fyuuss) *n* desecho *m*

regard (ri-*ghaad*) *v* considerar; *n* respeto *m*; **as regards** en cuanto a, por lo que se refiere a

regarding (ri-*ghaa*-ding) *prep* relativo a, tocante a; respecto a

regatta (ri-*ghæ*-tö) *n* regata *f*

régime (rei-*ʒiim*) *n* régimen *m*

region (*rii*-dʒön) *n* región *f*

regional (*rii*-dʒö-nöl) *adj* regional

register (*rê*-dʒi-sstö) *v* inscribirse; certificar; **registered letter** carta certificada

registration (rê-dʒi-*sstrei*-∫ön) *n* inscripción *f*; ~ **form** formulario de matriculación; ~ **number** matrícula *f*; ~ **plate** placa *f*

regret (ri-*ghrêt*) *v* *sentir; *n* arrepentimiento *m*

regular (*rê*-ghyu-lö) *adj* regular; corriente, normal

regulate (*rê*-ghyu-leit) *v* regular

regulation (rê-ghyu-*lei*-∫ön) *n* reglamento *m*, regulación *f*; regla *f*

rehabilitation (rii-hö-bi-li-*tei*-∫ön) *n* rehabilitación *f*

rehearsal (ri-*höö*-ssöl) *n* ensayo *m*

rehearse (ri-*hööss*) *v* ensayar

reign (rein) *n* reinado *m*; *v* *gobernar

reimburse (rii-im-*bööss*) *v* reembolsar

reindeer (*rein*-diᵒ) *n* (pl ~) reno *m*

reject (ri-*dʒêkt*) *v* rehusar, rechazar; *reprobar

relate (ri-*leit*) *v* *contar

related (ri-*lei*-tid) *adj* emparentado

relation (ri-*lei*-∫ön) *n* relación *f*; pariente *m*

relative (*rê*-lö-tiv) *n* pariente *m*; *adj* relativo

relax (ri-*lækss*) *v* descansar

relaxation (ri-læk-*ssei*-∫ön) *n* relajación *f*

reliable (ri-*lai*-ö-böl) *adj* fiable

relic (*rê*-lik) *n* reliquia *f*

relief (ri-*liif*) *n* alivio *m*; ayuda *f*; relieve *m*

relieve (ri-*liiv*) *v* relevar

religion (ri-*li*-dʒön) *n* religión *f*

religious (ri-*li*-dʒöss) *adj* religioso

rely on (ri-*lai*) *contar con

remain (ri-*mein*) *v* quedarse; quedar

remainder (ri-*mein*-dö) *n* resto *m*

remaining (ri-*mei*-ning) *adj* demás, restante

remark (ri-*maak*) *n* observación *f*; *v* *hacer una observación

remarkable (ri-*maa*-kö-böl) *adj* notable

remedy (rê-mö-di) n remedio m
remember (ri-mêm-bö) v *acordarse
remembrance (ri-mêm-brönss) n recuerdo m
remind (ri-maind) v *recordar
remit (ri-mit) v remitir
remittance (ri-mi-tönss) n remesa f
remnant (rêm-nönt) n resto m, residuo m, remanente m
remote (ri-mout) adj remoto, lejano
removal (ri-muu-völ) n remoción f
remove (ri-muuv) v *remover
remunerate (ri-myuu-nö-reit) v remunerar
remuneration (ri-myuu-nö-rei-ʃön) n remuneración f
renew (ri-nyuu) v *renovar; alargar
rent (rênt) v alquilar; n alquiler m
repair (ri-pêö) v arreglar, reparar; n reparación f
reparation (rê-pö-rei-ʃön) n reparación f
*repay (ri-pei) v reintegrar
repayment (ri-pei-mönt) n reintegro m
repeat (ri-piit) v *repetir
repellent (ri-pê-lönt) adj repugnante, repelente
repentance (ri-pên-tönss) n arrepentimiento m
repertory (rê-pö-tö-ri) n repertorio m
repetition (rê-pö-ti-ʃön) n repetición f
replace (ri-pleiss) v reemplazar
reply (ri-plai) v responder; n respuesta f; in ~ en contestación
report (ri-poot) v relatar; informar; presentarse; n relación f, informe m
reporter (ri-poo-tö) n reportero m
represent (rê-pri-sênt) v representar
representation (rê-pri-sên-tei-ʃön) n representación f
representative (rê-pri-sên-tö-tiv) adj representativo

reprimand (rê-pri-maand) v reprender
reproach (ri-prouch) n reproche m; v reprochar
reproduce (rii-prö-dyuuss) v *reproducir
reproduction (rii-prö-dak-ʃön) n reproducción f
reptile (rêp-tail) n reptil m
republic (ri-pa-blik) n república f
republican (ri-pa-bli-kön) adj republicano
repulsive (ri-pal-ssiv) adj repulsivo
reputation (rê-pyu-tei-ʃön) n reputación f; renombre m
request (ri-kuêsst) n ruego m; demanda f; v solicitar
require (ri-kuaiö) v *requerir
requirement (ri-kuaiö-mönt) n requerimiento m
requisite (rê-kui-sit) adj necesario
rescue (rê-sskyuu) v rescatar; n rescate m
research (ri-ssööch) n investigación f
resemblance (ri-sêm-blönss) n semejanza f
resemble (ri-sêm-böl) v asemejarse
resent (ri-sênt) v *resentirse por
reservation (rê-sö-vei-ʃön) n reservación f
reserve (ri-sööv) v reservar; n reserva f
reserved (ri-ssöövd) adj reservado
reservoir (rê-sö-vuaa) n embalse m
reside (ri-said) v residir
residence (rê-si-dönss) n residencia f; ~ permit permiso de residencia
resident (rê-si-dönt) n residente m; adj residente; interno
resign (ri-sain) v resignar
resignation (rê-sigh-nei-ʃön) n resignación f
resin (rê-sin) n resina f
resist (ri-sisst) v resistir
resistance (ri-si-sstönss) n resistencia

f

resolute (*ré*-sö-luut) *adj* resuelto, decidido

respect (ri-*sspékt*) *n* respeto *m*; estimación *f*, reverencia *f*; *v* respetar

respectable (ri-*sspék*-tö-böl) *adj* respetable

respectful (ri-*sspékt*-föl) *adj* respetuoso

respective (ri-*sspék*-tiv) *adj* respectivo

respiration (rê-sspö-*rei*-ßön) *n* respiración *f*

respite (*ré*-sspait) *n* dilación *f*

responsibility (ri-sspon-ssö-*bi*-lö-ti) *n* responsabilidad *f*

responsible (ri-*sspon*-ssö-böl) *adj* responsable

rest (rêsst) *n* descanso *m*; resto *m*; *v* *hacer reposo, descansar

restaurant (*rê*-sstö-rong) *n* restaurante *m*

restful (*rêsst*-föl) *adj* reposado

rest-home (*rêsst*-houm) *n* casa de reposo

restless (*rêsst*-löss) *adj* inquieto

restrain (ri-*sstrein*) *v* *contener, *impedir

restriction (ri-*sstrik*-ßön) *n* restricción *f*

result (ri-*salt*) *n* resultado *m*; consecuencia *f*; *v* resultar

resume (ri-*syuum*) *v* reemprender

résumé (*rê*-syu-mei) *n* resumen *m*

retail (*rii*-teil) *v* vender al detalle; ~ **trade** comercio al por menor

retailer (*rii*-tei-lö) *n* comerciante al por menor, minorista *m*; revendedor *m*

retina (*rê*-ti-nö) *n* retina *f*

retired (ri-*taió*d) *adj* jubilado

return (ri-*töön*) *v* *volver; *n* regreso *m*; ~ **flight** vuelo de regreso; ~ **journey** vuelta *f*, viaje de regreso

reunite (rii-yuu-*nait*) *v* reunir

reveal (ri-*viil*) *v* *manifestar, revelar

revelation (rê-vö-*lei*-ßön) *n* revelación *f*

revenge (ri-*vêndz*) *n* venganza *f*

revenue (*rê*-vö-nyuu) *n* ingresos *mpl*, renta *f*

reverse (ri-*vööss*) *n* contrario *m*; reverso *m*; marcha atrás; revés *m*; *adj* inverso; *v* *dar marcha atrás

review (ri-*vyuu*) *n* reseña *f*; revista *f*

revise (ri-*vais*) *v* revisar

revision (ri-*vi*-zön) *n* revisión *f*

revival (ri-*vai*-völ) *n* recuperación *f*

revolt (ri-*voult*) *v* sublevarse; *n* rebelión *f*, revuelta *f*

revolting (ri-*voul*-ting) *adj* repugnante, chocante, repelente

revolution (rê-vö-*luu*-ßön) *n* revolución *f*

revolutionary (rê-vö-*luu*-ßö-nö-ri) *adj* revolucionario

revolver (ri-*vol*-vö) *n* revólver *m*

revue (ri-*vyuu*) *n* revista *f*

reward (ri-ᵘ*ood*) *n* recompensa *f*; *v* recompensar

rheumatism (*ruu*-mö-ti-söm) *n* reumatismo *m*

rhinoceros (rai-*no*-ssö-röss) *n* (pl ~, ~es) rinoceronte *m*

rhubarb (*ruu*-baab) *n* ruibarbo *m*

rhyme (raim) *n* rima *f*

rhythm (*ri*-ðöm) *n* ritmo *m*

rib (rib) *n* costilla *f*

ribbon (*ri*-bön) *n* cinta *f*

rice (raiss) *n* arroz *m*

rich (rich) *adj* rico

riches (*ri*-chis) *pl* riqueza *f*

riddle (*ri*-döl) *n* adivinanza *f*

ride (raid) *n* paseo *m*

***ride** (raid) *v* *ir en coche; montar

rider (*rai*-dö) *n* jinete *m*

ridge (ridz) *n* cresta *f*

ridicule (*ri*-di-kyuul) *v* ridiculizar

ridiculous (ri-*di*-kyu-löss) *adj* ridículo

riding (*rai*-ding) *n* equitación *f*

riding-school (*rai*-ding-sskuul) *n* picadero *m*

rifle (*rai*-föl) *v* rifle *m*

right (rait) *n* derecho *m*; *adj* correcto; derecho; justo; **all right!** ¡de acuerdo!; * **be** ~ *tener razón; ~ of way prioridad de paso

righteous (*rai*-chöss) *adj* justo

right-hand (*rait*-hænd) *adj* derecho

rightly (*rait*-li) *adv* justamente

rim (rim) *n* llanta *f*; borde *m*

ring (ring) *n* anillo *m*; círculo *m*; pista *f*

* **ring** (ring) *v* *sonar; ~ up llamar por teléfono

rinse (rinss) *v* enjuagar; *n* enjuague *m*

riot (*rai*-öt) *n* motín *m*

rip (rip) *v* rasgar

ripe (raip) *adj* maduro

rise (rais) *n* aumento de sueldo, aumento *m*; levantamiento *m*; subida *f*; nacimiento *m*

* **rise** (rais) *v* levantarse; subir

rising (*rai*-sing) *n* levantamiento *m*

risk (rissk) *n* riesgo *m*; peligro *m*; *v* arriesgar

risky (*ri*-sski) *adj* arriesgado

rival (*rai*-völ) *n* rival *m*; competidor *m*; *v* rivalizar

rivalry (*rai*-völ-ri) *n* rivalidad *f*; competencia *f*

river (*ri*-vö) *n* río *m*; ~ bank ribera *f*

riverside (*ri*-vö-ssaid) *n* ribera *f*

roach (rouch) *n* (pl ~) escarcho *m*

road (roud) *n* calle *f*, camino *m*; ~ fork *n* bifurcación *f*; ~ map mapa de carreteras; ~ system red de carreteras; ~ up camino en obras

roadhouse (*roud*-hauss) *n* parador *m*

roadside (*roud*-ssaid) *n* borde del camino

roam (roum) *v* vagabundear

roar (roo) *v* mugir, rugir; *n* rugido *m*, retumbo *m*

roast (rousst) *v* asar, asar en parrilla

rob (rob) *v* robar

robber (*ro*-bö) *n* ladrón *m*

robbery (*ro*-bö-ri) *n* robo *m*

robe (roub) *n* traje largo

robin (*ro*-bin) *n* petirrojo *m*

robust (rou-*basst*) *adj* robusto

rock (rok) *n* roca *f*; *v* mecer

rocket (*ro*-kit) *n* cohete *m*

rocky (*ro*-ki) *adj* rocoso

rod (rod) *n* barra *f*

roe (rou) *n* huevos de los peces, hueva *f*

roll (roul) *v* *rodar; *n* rollo *m*; panecillo *m*

roller-skating (*rou*-lö-sskei-ting) *n* patinaje de ruedas

Roman Catholic (*rou*-mön *kæ*-zö-lik) católico

romance (rö-*mænss*) *n* amorío *m*

romantic (rö-*mæn*-tik) *adj* romántico

roof (ruuf) *n* techo *m*; **thatched** ~ techo de paja

room (ruum) *n* habitación *f*; espacio *m*, sitio *m*; ~ and board pensión completa; ~ service servicio de habitación; ~ temperature temperatura ambiente

roomy (*ruu*-mi) *adj* espacioso

root (ruut) *n* raíz *f*

rope (roup) *n* soga *f*

rosary (*rou*-sö-ri) *n* rosario *m*

rose (rous) *n* rosa *f*; *adj* rosa

rotten (*ro*-tön) *adj* podrido

rouge (ruuჳ) *n* colorete *m*

rough (raf) *adj* áspero

roulette (ruu-*lêt*) *n* ruleta *f*

round (raund) *adj* redondo; *prep* alrededor de, en torno de; *n* vuelta *f*; ~ **trip** *Am* ida y vuelta

roundabout (*raun*-dö-baut) *n* glorieta *f*

rounded (*raun*-did) *adj* redondeado
route (ruut) *n* ruta *f*
routine (ruu-*tiin*) *n* rutina *f*
row¹ (rou) *n* fila *f*; *v* remar
row² (rau) *n* bronca *f*
rowdy (*rau*-di) *adj* alborotador
rowing-boat (*rou*-ing-bout) *n* bote *m*
royal (*roi*-öl) *adj* real
rub (rab) *v* frotar
rubber (*ra*-bö) *n* caucho *m*; goma de borrar; hule *mMe*; **~ band** elástico *m*
rubbish (*ra*-biʃ) *n* basura *f*; habladuría *f*, tontería *f*; **talk ~** *decir tonterías
rubbish-bin (*ra*-biʃ-bin) *n* cubo de la basura
ruby (*ruu*-bi) *n* rubí *m*
rucksack (*rak*-ssæk) *n* mochila *f*
rudder (*ra*-dö) *n* timón *m*
rude (ruud) *adj* grosero
rug (ragh) *n* alfombrilla *f*
ruin (*ruu*-in) *v* arruinar; *n* ruina *f*
ruination (ruu-i-*nei*-ʃön) *n* hundimiento *m*
rule (ruul) *n* regla *f*; régimen *m*, gobierno *m*, dominio *m*; *v* *gobernar, *regir; **as a ~** generalmente, por regla general
ruler (*ruu*-lö) *n* monarca *m*, gobernante *m*; regla *f*
Rumania (ruu-*mei*-ni-ö) Rumania *f*
Rumanian (ruu-*mei*-ni-ön) *adj* rumano
rumour (*ruu*-mö) *n* rumor *m*
*****run** (ran) *v* correr; **~ into** *encontrarse con
runaway (*ra*-nö-ᵘei) *n* fugitivo *m*
rung (ran) *v* (pp ring)
runway (*ran*-ᵘei) *n* pista de aterrizaje
rural (*ruᵒ*-röl) *adj* rural
ruse (ruus) *n* astucia *f*
rush (raʃ) *v* precipitarse; *n* junco *m*
rush-hour (*raʃ*-auᵒ) *n* hora de afluencia

Russia (*ra*-ʃö) Rusia *f*
Russian (*ra*-ʃön) *adj* ruso
rust (rasst) *n* herrumbre *f*
rustic (*ra*-sstik) *adj* rústico
rusty (*ra*-ssti) *adj* oxidado

S

saccharin (*ssæ*-kö-rin) *n* sacarina *f*
sack (ssæk) *n* saco *m*
sacred (*ssei*-krid) *adj* sagrado
sacrifice (*ssæ*-kri-faiss) *n* sacrificio *m*; *v* sacrificar
sacrilege (*ssæ*-kri-lidʒ) *n* sacrilegio *m*
sad (ssæd) *adj* triste; afligido, melancólico
saddle (*ssæ*-döl) *n* silla *f*
sadness (*ssæd*-nöss) *n* tristeza *f*
safe (sseif) *adj* seguro; *n* caja fuerte, caja de caudales
safety (*sseif*-ti) *n* seguridad *f*
safety-belt (*sseif*-ti-bêlt) *n* cinturón de seguridad
safety-pin (*sseif*-ti-pin) *n* imperdible *m*
safety-razor (*sseif*-ti-rei-sö) *n* máquina de afeitar
sail (sseil) *v* navegar; *n* vela *f*
sailing-boat (*ssei*-ling-bout) *n* buque velero
sailor (*ssei*-lö) *n* marinero *m*
saint (sseint) *n* santo *m*
salad (*ssæ*-löd) *n* ensalada *f*
salad-oil (*ssæ*-löd-oil) *n* aceite de mesa
salary (*ssæ*-lö-ri) *n* sueldo *m*
sale (sseil) *n* venta *f*; **clearance ~** liquidación *f*; **for ~** de venta; **sales** rebajas *fpl*
saleable (*ssei*-lö-böl) *adj* vendible
salesgirl (*sseils*-ghööl) *n* vendedora *f*
salesman (*sseils*-mön) *n* (pl -men)

vendedor *m*

salmon (*ssæ*-mön) *n* (pl ~) salmón *m*

salon (*ssæ*-long) *n* salón *m*

saloon (ssö-*luun*) *n* bar *m*; cantina *f* Me

salt (ssoolt) *n* sal *f*

salt-cellar (*ssoolt*-ssê-lö) *n* salero *m*

salty (*ssool*-ti) *adj* salado

salute (ssö-*luut*) *v* saludar

salve (ssaav) *n* ungüento *m*

same (sseim) *adj* mismo

sample (*ssaam*-pöl) *n* muestra *f*

sanatorium (ssæ-nö-*too*-ri-öm) *n* (pl ~s, -ria) sanatorio *m*

sand (ssænd) *n* arena *f*

sandal (*ssæn*-döl) *n* sandalia *f*

sandpaper (*ssænd*-pei-pö) *n* papel de lija

sandwich (*ssæn*-ᵘidʒ) *n* bocadillo *m*; emparedado *m*

sandy (*ssæn*-di) *adj* arenoso

sanitary (*ssæ*-ni-tö-ri) *adj* sanitario; ~ towel paño higiénico

sapphire (*ssæ*-faiᵒ) *n* zafiro *m*

sardine (ssaa-*diin*) *n* sardina *f*

satchel (*ssæ*-chöl) *n* cartera *f*

satellite (*ssæ*-tö-lait) *n* satélite *m*

satin (*ssæ*-tin) *n* raso *m*

satisfaction (ssæ-tiss-*fæk*-Jön) *n* satisfacción *f*

satisfy (*ssæ*-tiss-fai) *v* *satisfacer

Saturday (*ssæ*-tö-di) *sábado m*

sauce (ssooss) *n* salsa *f*

saucepan (*ssooss*-pön) *n* cacerola *f*

saucer (*ssoo*-ssö) *n* platillo *m*

Saudi Arabia (ssau-di-ö-*rei*-bi-ö) Arabia Saudí

Saudi Arabian (ssau-di-ö-*rei*-bi-ön) *adj* saudí

sauna (*ssoo*-nö) *n* sauna *f*

sausage (*sso*-ssidʒ) *n* salchicha *f*

savage (*ssæ*-vidʒ) *adj* salvaje

save (sseiv) *v* salvar; ahorrar

savings (*ssei*-vings) *pl* ahorros *mpl*;

~ **bank** caja de ahorros

saviour (*ssei*-vyö) *n* salvador *m*

savoury (*ssei*-vö-ri) *adj* sabroso; picante

saw¹ (ssoo) *v* (p see)

saw² (ssoo) *n* sierra *f*

sawdust (*ssoo*-dasst) *n* serrín *m*

saw-mill (*ssoo*-mil) *n* serrería de maderas

* say (ssei) *v* *decir

scaffolding (*sskæ*-föl-ding) *n* andamio *m*

scale (sskeil) *n* escala *f*; escala musical; escama *f*; **scales** *pl* balanza *f*

scandal (*sskæn*-döl) *n* escándalo *m*

Scandinavia (sskæn-di-*nei*-vi-ö) Escandinavia *f*

Scandinavian (sskæn-di-*nei*-vi-ön) *adj* escandinavo

scapegoat (*sskeip*-ghout) *n* cabeza de turco

scar (sskaa) *n* cicatriz *f*

scarce (sskêᵒss) *adj* escaso

scarcely (*sskêᵒ*-ssli) *adv* apenas

scarcity (*sskêᵒ*-ssö-ti) *n* escasez *f*

scare (sskêᵒ) *v* asustar; *n* susto *m*

scarf (sskaaf) *n* (pl ~s, scarves) bufanda *f*

scarlet (*sskaa*-löt) *adj* escarlata

scary (*sskêᵒ*-ri) *adj* alarmante

scatter (*sskæ*-tö) *v* esparcir

scene (ssiin) *n* escena *f*

scenery (*ssii*-nö-ri) *n* paisaje *m*

scenic (*ssii*-nik) *adj* pintoresco

scent (ssênt) *n* perfume *m*

schedule (*Jê*-dyuul) *n* horario *m*

scheme (sskiim) *n* esquema *m*; proyecto *m*

scholar (*ssko*-lö) *n* erudito *m*; alumno *m*

scholarship (*ssko*-lö-Jip) *n* beca *f*

school (sskuul) *n* escuela *f*

schoolboy (*sskuul*-boi) *n* alumno *m*

schoolgirl (*sskuul*-ghööl) *n* alumna *f*

schoolmaster (*sskuul*-maa-sstö) *n* maestro *m*

schoolteacher (*sskuul*-tii-chö) *n* maestro *m*

science (*ssai*-önss) *n* ciencia *f*

scientific (ssai-ön-*ti*-fik) *adj* científico

scientist (*ssai*-ön-tisst) *n* científico *m*

scissors (*ssi*-sös) *pl* tijeras *fpl*

scold (sskould) *v* reprender; insultar

scooter (*sskuu*-tö) *n* motoneta *f*; patín *m*

score (sskoo) *n* tanteo *m*; *v* marcar

scorn (sskoon) *n* escarnio *m*, desprecio *m*; *v* despreciar

Scot (sskot) *n* escocés *m*

Scotch (sskoch) *adj* escocés; scotch tape cinta adhesiva

Scotland (*sskot*-lönd) Escocia *f*

Scottish (*ssko*-tiʃ) *adj* escocés

scout (sskaut) *n* explorador *m*

scrap (sskræp) *n* pedazo *m*

scrap-book (*sskræp*-buk) *n* álbum *m*

scrape (sskreip) *v* raspar

scrap-iron (*sskræ*-pai⁰n) *n* chatarra *f*

scratch (sskræch) *v* *hacer raeduras, rascar; *n* raedura *f*, rasguño *m*

scream (sskriim) *v* gritar, chillar; *n* grito *m*, chillido *m*

screen (sskriin) *n* mampara *f*; pantalla *f*

screw (sskruu) *n* tornillo *m*; *v* atornillar

screw-driver (*sskruu*-drai-vö) *n* destornillador *m*

scrub (sskrab) *v* *fregar; *n* matorral *m*

sculptor (*sskalp*-tö) *n* escultor *m*

sculpture (*sskalp*-chö) *n* escultura *f*

sea (ssii) *n* mar *m*

sea-bird (*ssii*-bööd) *n* ave marina

sea-coast (*ssii*-kousst) *n* litoral *m*

seagull (*ssii*-ghal) *n* gaviota *f*

seal (ssiil) *n* sello *m*; foca *f*

seam (ssiim) *n* costura *f*

seaman (*ssii*-mön) *n* (pl -men) marino *m*

seamless (*ssiim*-löss) *adj* sin costura

seaport (*ssii*-poot) *n* puerto de mar

search (ssööch) *v* buscar; cachear; *n* búsqueda *f*

searchlight (*ssööch*-lait) *n* reflector *m*

seascape (*ssii*-sskeip) *n* marina *f*

sea-shell (*ssii*-fêl) *n* concha *f*

seashore (*ssii*-ʃoo) *n* orilla del mar

seasick (*ssii*-ssik) *adj* mareado

seasickness (*ssii*-ssik-nöss) *n* mareo *m*

seaside (*ssii*-ssaid) *n* orilla del mar; ~ resort playa de veraneo

season (*ssii*-sön) *n* temporada *f*, estación *f*; high ~ apogeo de la temporada; low ~ temporada baja; off ~ fuera de temporada

season-ticket (*ssii*-sön-ti-kit) *n* tarjeta de temporada

seat (ssiit) *n* asiento *m*; sitio *m*, localidad *f*; sede *f*

seat-belt (*ssiit*-bêlt) *n* cinturón de seguridad

sea-urchin (*ssii*-öö-chin) *n* erizo de mar

sea-water (*ssii*-ᵁoo-tö) *n* agua de mar

second (*ssê*-könd) *num* segundo; *n* segundo *m*; instante *m*

secondary (*ssê*-kön-dö-ri) *adj* secundario; ~ school escuela secundaria

second-hand (ssê-könd-*hænd*) *adj* de segunda mano

secret (*ssii*-kröt) *n* secreto *m*; *adj* secreto

secretary (*ssê*-krö-tri) *n* secretaria *f*; secretario *m*

section (*ssêk*-ʃön) *n* sección *f*; división *f*, departamento *m*

secure (ssi-*kyuᵒ*) *adj* firme; *v* lograr

security (ssi-*kyuᵒ*-rö-ti) *n* seguridad *f*; fianza *f*

sedate (ssi-*deit*) *adj* sosegado

sedative (ssê-dö-tiv) *n* calmante *m*
seduce (ssi-*dyuuss*) *v* *seducir
***see** (ssii) *v* *ver; comprender, *darse cuenta; ~ **to** *atender a
seed (ssiid) *n* semilla *f*
***seek** (ssiik) *v* buscar
seem (ssiim) *v* *parecer
seen (ssiin) *v* (pp see)
seesaw (ssii-ssoo) *n* columpio *m*
seize (ssiis) *v* agarrar
seldom (ssêl-döm) *adv* pocas veces
select (ssi-*lêkt*) *v* seleccionar, *elegir; *adj* seleccionado, selecto
selection (ssi-*lêk*-ʃön) *n* elección *f*, selección *f*
self-centred (ssêlf-*ssên*-töd) *adj* egocéntrico
self-employed (ssêl-fim-*ploid*) *adj* independiente
self-evident (ssêl-*fê*-vi-dönt) *adj* evidente
self-government (ssêlf-*gha*-vö-mönt) *n* autonomía *f*
selfish (ssêl-fiʃ) *adj* egoísta
selfishness (ssêl-fiʃ-nöss) *n* egoísmo *m*
self-service (ssêlf-*ssöö*-viss) *n* autoservicio *m*
***sell** (ssêl) *v* vender
semblance (ssêm-blönss) *n* apariencia *f*
semi- (ssê-mi) semi-
semicircle (ssê-mi-ssöö-köl) *n* semicírculo *m*
semi-colon (ssê-mi-*kou*-lön) *n* punto y coma
senate (ssê-nöt) *n* senado *m*
senator (ssê-nö-tö) *n* senador *m*
***send** (ssênd) *v* enviar, mandar; ~ **back** *devolver; ~ **for** mandar a buscar; ~ **off** despachar
senile (ssii-nail) *adj* senil
sensation (ssên-*ssei*-ʃön) *n* sensación *f*

sensational (ssên-*ssei*-ʃö-nöl) *adj* sensacional
sense (ssênss) *n* sentido *m*; juicio *m*, razón *f*; *v* *sentir; ~ **of honour** sentido del honor
senseless (ssênss-löss) *adj* insensato
sensible (ssên-ssö-böl) *adj* sensato
sensitive (ssên-ssi-tiv) *adj* sensitivo
sentence (ssên-tönss) *n* frase *f*; sentencia *f*; *v* sentenciar
sentimental (ssên-ti-*mên*-töl) *adj* sentimental
separate[1] (ssê-pö-reit) *v* separar
separate[2] (ssê-pö-röt) *adj* separado
separately (ssê-pö-röt-li) *adv* por separado
September (ssêp-*têm*-bö) septiembre
septic (ssêp-tik) *adj* séptico; ***become** ~ infectarse
sequel (ssii-kᵘöl) *n* continuación *f*
sequence (ssii-kᵘönss) *n* sucesión *f*; serie *f*
serene (ssö-*riin*) *adj* sereno; claro
serial (ssiⁱö-ri-öl) *n* novela por entregas
series (ssiⁱö-riis) *n* (pl ~) serie *f*
serious (ssiⁱö-ri-öss) *adj* serio
seriousness (ssiⁱö-ri-öss-nöss) *n* seriedad *f*
sermon (ssöö-mön) *n* sermón *m*
serum (ssiⁱö-röm) *n* suero *m*
servant (ssöö-vönt) *n* criado *m*
serve (ssööv) *v* *servir
service (ssöö-viss) *n* servicio *m*; ~ **charge** servicio *m*; ~ **station** puesto de gasolina
serviette (ssöö-vi-*êt*) *n* servilleta *f*
session (ssê-ʃön) *n* sesión *f*
set (ssêt) *n* juego *m*, grupo *m*
***set** (ssêt) *v* *poner; ~ **menu** cubierto a precio fijo; ~ **out** partir
setting (ssê-ting) *n* escena *f*; ~ **lotion** fijador *m*
settle (ssê-töl) *v* arreglar; ~ **down**

arraigarse

settlement (ssê-töl-mönt) n acuerdo m, arreglo m, convenio m

seven (ssê-vön) num siete

seventeen (ssê-vön-tiin) num diecisiete

seventeenth (ssê-vön-tiinz) num decimoséptimo

seventh (ssê-vönz) num séptimo

seventy (ssê-vön-ti) num setenta

several (ssê-vö-röl) adj varios

severe (ssi-vi⁰) adj violento, rigoroso, severo

sew (ssou) v coser; ~ **up** *hacer una sutura

sewer (ssuu-ö) n desagüe m

sewing-machine (ssou-ing-mö-ʃiin) n máquina de coser

sex (ssêkss) n sexo m; sexualidad f

sexton (ssêk-sstön) n sacristán m

sexual (ssêk-ʃu-öl) adj sexual

sexuality (ssêk-ʃu-æ-lö-ti) n sexualidad f

shade (ʃeid) n sombra f; tono m

shadow (ʃæ-dou) n sombra f

shady (ʃei-di) adj sombreado

*****shake** (ʃeik) v sacudir

shaky (ʃei-ki) adj vacilante

*****shall** (ʃæl) v *tener que

shallow (ʃæ-lou) adj poco profundo

shame (ʃeim) n vergüenza f; deshonra f; **shame!** ¡qué vergüenza!

shampoo (ʃæm-puu) n champú m

shamrock (ʃæm-rok) n trébol m

shape (ʃeip) n forma f; v formar

share (ʃê⁰) v compartir; n parte f; acción f

shark (ʃaak) n tiburón m

sharp (ʃaap) adj afilado

sharpen (ʃaa-pön) v afilar

shave (ʃeiv) v rasurarse, afeitarse

shaver (ʃei-vö) n máquina de afeitar

shaving-brush (ʃei-ving-braʃ) n brocha de afeitar

shaving-cream (ʃei-ving-kriim) n crema de afeitar

shaving-soap (ʃei-ving-ssoup) n jabón de afeitar

shawl (ʃool) n chal m

she (ʃii) pron ella

shed (ʃêd) n cobertizo m

*****shed** (ʃêd) v derramar; esparcir

sheep (ʃiip) n (pl ~) oveja f

sheer (ʃi⁰) adj absoluto, puro; fino, traslúcido

sheet (ʃiit) n sábana f; hoja f; chapa f

shelf (ʃêlf) n (pl shelves) estante m

shell (ʃêl) n concha f; cáscara f

shellfish (ʃêl-fiʃ) n marisco m

shelter (ʃêl-tö) n refugio m; v abrigar

shepherd (ʃê-pöd) n pastor m

shift (ʃift) n turno m

*****shine** (ʃain) v *relucir; brillar, *resplandecer

ship (ʃip) n buque m; v transportar; **shipping line** línea de navegación

shipowner (ʃi-pou-nö) n armador m

shipyard (ʃip-yaad) n astillero m

shirt (ʃööt) n camisa f

shiver (ʃi-vö) v *temblar, tiritar; n escalofrío m

shivery (ʃi-vö-ri) adj estremecido

shock (ʃok) n choque m; v chocar; ~ **absorber** amortiguador m

shocking (ʃo-king) adj chocante

shoe (ʃuu) n zapato m; **gym shoes** sandalias de gimnasia; ~ **polish** betún m; grasa fMe

shoe-lace (ʃuu-leiss) n cordón m

shoemaker (ʃuu-mei-kö) n zapatero m

shoe-shop (ʃuu-ʃop) n zapatería f

shook (ʃuk) v (p shake)

*****shoot** (ʃuut) v tirar

shop (ʃop) n tienda f; v *ir de compras; ~ **assistant** dependiente m; **shopping bag** saco de compras; **shopping centre** centro comercial

shopkeeper (/ʃop-kii-pö) n tendero m
shop-window (/ʃop-ᵘin-dou) n escaparate m
shore (/ʃoo) n ribera f, orilla f
short (/ʃoot) adj corto; bajo; ~ circuit cortocircuito m
shortage (/ʃoo-tidʒ) n carencia f, escasez f
shortcoming (/ʃoot-ka-ming) n deficiencia f
shorten (/ʃoo-tön) v acortar
shorthand (/ʃoot-hænd) n taquigrafía f
shortly (/ʃoot-li) adv pronto, próximamente
shorts (/ʃootss) pl pantalones cortos; plAm calzoncillos mpl
short-sighted (/ʃoot-ssai-tid) adj miope
shot (/ʃot) n disparo m; inyección f; secuencia f
*should (/ʃud) v *tener que
shoulder (/ʃoul-dö) n hombro m
shout (/ʃaut) v gritar; n grito m
shovel (/ʃa-völ) n pala f
show (/ʃou) n representación f, espectáculo m; exposición f
*show (/ʃou) v *mostrar; enseñar; *demostrar
show-case (/ʃou-keiss) n vitrina f
shower (/ʃauᵒ) n ducha f; aguacero m
showroom (/ʃou-ruum) n salón de demostraciones
shriek (/ʃriik) v chillar; n chillido m
shrimp (/ʃrimp) n camarón m
shrine (/ʃrain) n santuario m
*shrink (/ʃringk) v encogerse
shrinkproof (/ʃringk-pruuf) adj no encoge
shrub (/ʃrab) n arbusto m
shudder (/ʃa-dö) n estremecimiento m
shuffle (/ʃa-föl) v barajar
*shut (/ʃat) v *cerrar; ~ in *encerrar
shutter (/ʃa-tö) n persiana f
shy (/ʃai) adj esquivo, tímido
shyness (/ʃai-nöss) n timidez f

Siam (ssai-æm) Siam m
Siamese (ssai-ö-miis) adj siamés
sick (ssik) adj enfermo; que tiene náuseas
sickness (ssik-nöss) n enfermedad f; náusea f
side (ssaid) n lado m; partido m; one-sided adj unilateral
sideburns (ssaid-bööns) pl patillas fpl
sidelight (ssaid-lait) n luz lateral
side-street (ssaid-sstriit) n calle lateral
sidewalk (ssaid-ᵘook) nAm acera f
sideways (ssaid-ᵘeis) adv lateralmente
siege (ssiidʒ) n sitio m
sieve (ssiv) n tamiz m; v tamizar
sift (ssift) v tamizar
sight (ssait) n vista f; aspecto m; curiosidad f
sign (ssain) n signo m, señal f; gesto m, seña f; v suscribir, firmar
signal (ssigh-nöl) n señal f; v *hacer señales
signature (ssigh-nö-chö) n firma f
significant (ssigh-ni-fi-könt) adj significativo
signpost (ssain-poust) n poste de indicador
silence (ssai-lönss) n silencio m; v acallar
silencer (ssai-lön-ssö) n silenciador m
silent (ssai-lönt) adj callado; *be ~ callarse
silk (ssilk) n seda f
silken (ssil-kön) adj sedoso
silly (ssi-li) adj necio, bobo
silver (ssil-vö) n plata f; de plata
silversmith (ssil-vö-ssmiz) n platero m
silverware (ssil-vö-ᵘêô) n plata labrada
similar (ssi-mi-lö) adj similar
similarity (ssi-mi-læ-rö-ti) n semejanza f
simple (ssim-pöl) adj ingenuo, sim-

ple; ordinario

simply (*ssim*-pli) *adv* simplemente

simulate (*ssi*-myu-leit) *v* simular

simultaneous (ssi-möl-*tei*-ni-öss) *adj* simultáneo

sin (ssin) *n* pecado *m*

since (ssinss) *prep* desde; *adv* desde entonces; *conj* desde que; puesto que

sincere (ssin-*ssi*ö) *adj* sincero

sinew (*ssi*-nyuu) *n* tendón *m*

*****sing** (ssing) *v* cantar

singer (*ssing*-ö) *n* cantante *m*; cantadora *f*

single (*ssing*-ghöl) *adj* solo; soltero

singular (*ssing*-ghyu-lö) *n* singular *m*; *adj* singular

sinister (*ssi*-ni-sstö) *adj* siniestro

sink (ssingk) *n* pileta *f*

*****sink** (ssingk) *v* hundirse

sip (ssip) *n* sorbo *m*

siphon (*ssai*-fön) *n* sifón *m*

sir (ssöö) *n* señor *m*

siren (*ssai*ö-rön) *n* sirena *f*

sister (*ssi*-sstö) *n* hermana *f*

sister-in-law (*ssi*-sstö-rin-loo) *n* (pl sisters-) cuñada *f*

*****sit** (ssit) *v* *estar sentado; ~ **down** *sentarse

site (ssait) *n* sitio *m*

sitting-room (*ssi*-ting-ruum) *n* sala de estar

situated (*ssi*-chu-ei-tid) *adj* situado

situation (ssi-chu-*ei*-fön) *n* situación *f*; ubicación *f*

six (ssiks) *num* seis

sixteen (ssiks-*tiin*) *num* dieciséis

sixteenth (ssikss-*tiinz*) *num* decimosexto

sixth (ssikssz) *num* sexto

sixty (*ssikss*-ti) *num* sesenta

size (ssais) *n* tamaño *m*, número *m*; dimensión *f*; formato *m*

skate (sskeit) *v* patinar; *n* patín *m*

skating (*sskei*-ting) *n* patinaje *m*

skating-rink (*sskei*-ting-ringk) *n* pista de patinaje

skeleton (*sskê*-li-tön) *n* esqueleto *m*

sketch (sskêch) *n* dibujo *m*, bosquejo *m*; *v* dibujar, bosquejar

sketch-book (*sskêch*-buk) *n* cuaderno de diseño

ski[1] (sskii) *v* esquiar

ski[2] (sskii) *n* (pl ~, ~s) esquí *m*; ~ **boots** botas de esquí; ~ **pants** pantalones de esquí; ~ **sticks** bastones de esquí

skid (sskid) *v* patinar

skier (*sskii*-ö) *n* esquiador *m*

skiing (*sskii*-ing) *n* esquí *m*

ski-jump (*sskii*-dʒamp) *n* salto de esquí

skilful (*sskil*-föl) *adj* hábil, diestro

ski-lift (*sskii*-lift) *n* telesilla *m*

skill (sskil) *n* habilidad *f*

skilled (sskild) *adj* hábil; especializado

skin (sskin) *n* piel *f*; cáscara *f*; ~ **cream** crema para la piel

skip (sskip) *v* saltar; brincar

skirt (sskööt) *n* falda *f*

skull (sskal) *n* cráneo *m*

sky (sskai) *n* cielo *m*; aire *m*

skyscraper (*sskai*-sskrei-pö) *n* rascacielos *m*

slack (sslæk) *adj* lento

slacks (sslækss) *pl* pantalones *mpl*

slam (sslæm) *v* *dar un portazo

slander (*sslaan*-dö) *n* calumnia *f*

slant (sslaant) *v* inclinarse

slanting (*sslaan*-ting) *adj* oblicuo, pendiente, inclinado

slap (sslæp) *v* pegar; *n* bofetada *f*

slate (ssleit) *n* pizarra *f*

slave (ssleiv) *n* esclavo *m*

sledge (sslêdʒ) *n* trineo *m*

sleep (ssliip) *n* sueño *m*

*****sleep** (ssliip) *v* *dormir

sleeping-bag (*sslii*-ping-bægh) *n* saco de dormir

sleeping-car (*sslii*-ping-kaa) *n* coche cama

sleeping-pill (*sslii*-ping-pil) *n* somnífero *m*

sleepless (*ssliip*-löss) *adj* desvelado

sleepy (*sslii*-pi) *adj* soñoliento

sleeve (*ssliiv*) *n* manga *f*; funda *f*

sleigh (*sslei*) *n* trineo *m*

slender (*sslên*-dö) *adj* esbelto

slice (*sslaiss*) *n* tajada *f*

slide (*sslaid*) *n* desliz *m*; tobogán *m*; diapositiva *f*

***slide** (*sslaid*) *v* deslizarse

slight (*sslait*) *adj* ligero; leve

slim (*sslim*) *adj* esbelto; *v* adelgazar

slip (*sslip*) *v* deslizarse, resbalar; *n* desliz *m*; combinación *f*; fondo *mMe*

slipper (*ssli*-pö) *n* zapatilla *f*

slippery (*ssli*-pö-ri) *adj* resbaladizo

slogan (*sslou*-ghön) *n* lema *m*, slogan *m*

slope (*ssloup*) *n* pendiente *f*; *v* inclinarse

sloping (*sslou*-ping) *adj* inclinado

sloppy (*sslo*-pi) *adj* chapucero

slot (*sslot*) *n* ranura *f*

slot-machine (*sslot*-mö-ʃiin) *n* máquina tragamonedas

slovenly (*ssla*-vön-li) *adj* descuidado

slow (*sslou*) *adj* lerdo, lento; ~ **down** desacelerar, *ir más despacio; frenar

sluice (*ssluuss*) *n* compuerta *f*

slum (*sslam*) *n* barrio bajo

slump (*sslamp*) *n* baja *f*

slush (*sslaʃ*) *n* aguanieve *f*

sly (*sslai*) *adj* astuto

smack (*ssmæk*) *v* pegar; *n* bofetada *f*

small (*ssmool*) *adj* pequeño; menudo

smallpox (*ssmool*-pokss) *n* viruelas *fpl*

smart (*ssmaat*) *adj* elegante; inteli-

gente, listo

smell (*ssmêl*) *n* olor *m*

***smell** (*ssmêl*) *v* *oler; *heder

smelly (*ssmê*-li) *adj* hediondo

smile (*ssmail*) *v* sonreír; *n* sonrisa *f*

smith (*ssmiz*) *n* herrero *m*

smoke (*ssmouk*) *v* fumar; *n* humo *m*; **no smoking** prohibido fumar

smoker (*ssmou*-kö) *n* fumador *m*; compartimento para fumadores

smoking-compartment (*ssmou*-king-köm-paat-mönt) *n* compartimento para fumadores

smoking-room (*ssmou*-king-ruum) *n* sala para fumar

smooth (*ssmuuð*) *adj* llano, liso; dulce

smuggle (*ssma*-ghöl) *v* contrabandear

snack (*ssnæk*) *n* tentempié *m*

snack-bar (*ssnæk*-baa) *n* cafetería *f*

snail (*ssneil*) *n* caracol *m*

snake (*ssneik*) *n* culebra *f*

snapshot (*ssnæp*-ʃot) *n* instantánea *f*

sneakers (*ssnii*-kös) *plAm* zapatos de gimnasia

sneeze (*ssniis*) *v* estornudar

sniper (*ssnai*-pö) *n* francotirador *m*

snooty (*ssnuu*-ti) *adj* arrogante

snore (*ssnoo*) *v* roncar

snorkel (*ssnoo*-köl) *n* esnórquel *m*

snout (*ssnaut*) *n* hocico *m*

snow (*ssnou*) *n* nieve *f*; *v* *nevar

snowstorm (*ssnou*-sstoom) *n* nevasca *f*

snowy (*ssnou*-i) *adj* nevoso

so (*ssou*) *conj* por tanto; *adv* así; a tal grado, tan; **and ~ on** etcétera; ~ **far** hasta ahora; ~ **that** así que, a fin de

soak (*ssouk*) *v* empapar, remojar

soap (*ssoup*) *n* jabón *m*; ~ **powder** jabón en polvo

sober (*ssou*-bö) *adj* sobrio; ponderado

so-called (ssou-*koold*) *adj* así llamado

soccer (*sso*-kö) *n* fútbol *m*; ~ **team** equipo *m*

social (*ssou*-ſöl) *adj* social

socialism (*ssou*-ſö-li-söm) *n* socialismo *m*

socialist (*ssou*-ſö-lisst) *adj* socialista; *n* socialista *m*

society (ssö-*ssai*-ö-ti) *n* sociedad *f*; asociación *f*; compañía *f*

sock (ssok) *n* calcetín *m*

socket (*sso*-kit) *n* casquillo *m*; sóquet *mMe*

soda-water (*ssou*-dö-ᵁoo-tö) *n* agua de soda, soda *f*

sofa (*ssou*-fö) *n* sofá *m*

soft (ssoft) *adj* blando; ~ **drink** bebida no alcohólica

soften (*sso*-fön) *v* ablandar

soil (ssoil) *n* suelo *m*; tierra *f*

soiled (ssoild) *adj* manchado

sold (ssould) *v* (p, pp sell); ~ **out** agotado

solder (*ssol*-dö) *v* *soldar

soldering-iron (*ssol*-dö-ring-ai°n) *n* soldador *m*

soldier (*ssoul*-dʒö) *n* militar *m*, soldado *m*

sole¹ (ssoul) *adj* único

sole² (ssoul) *n* suela *f*; lenguado *m*

solely (*ssoul*-li) *adv* exclusivamente

solemn (*sso*-löm) *adj* solemne

solicitor (ssö-*li*-ssi-tö) *n* procurador *m*, abogado *m*

solid (*sso*-lid) *adj* robusto, sólido; macizo; *n* sólido *m*

soluble (*sso*-lyu-böl) *adj* soluble

solution (ssö-*luu*-ſön) *n* solución *f*

solve (ssolv) *v* *resolver

sombre (*ssom*-bö) *adj* sombrío

some (ssam) *adj* algunos, unos; *pron* algunos, unɔs; un poco; ~ **day** uno u otro día; ~ **more** algo más; ~ **time** alguna vez

somebody (*ssam*-bö-di) *pron* alguien

somehow (*ssam*-hau) *adv* de un modo u otro

someone (*ssam*-ᵁan) *pron* alguien

something (*ssam*-zing) *pron* algo

sometimes (*ssam*-taims) *adv* a veces

somewhat (*ssam*-ᵁot) *adv* algo

somewhere (*ssam*-ᵁêô) *adv* en alguna parte

son (ssan) *n* hijo *m*

song (ssong) *n* canción *f*

son-in-law (*ssa*-nin-loo) *n* (pl sons-) yerno *m*

soon (ssuun) *adv* rápidamente, pronto, en breve; **as** ~ **as** tan pronto como

sooner (*ssuu*-nö) *adv* más bien

sore (ssoo) *adj* doloroso; *n* llaga *f*; úlcera *f*; ~ **throat** dolor de garganta

sorrow (*sso*-rou) *n* tristeza *f*, sufrimiento *m*, pena *f*

sorry (*sso*-ri) *adj* apenado; **sorry!** ¡dispense usted!, ¡disculpe!, ¡perdón!

sort (ssoot) *v* clasificar, *disponer; *n* clase *f*; **all sorts of** toda clase de

soul (ssoul) *n* alma *f*

sound (ssaund) *n* sonido *m*; *v* *sonar, *resonar; *adj* bueno

soundproof (*ssaund*-pruuf) *adj* insonorizado

soup (ssuup) *n* sopa *f*

soup-plate (*ssuup*-pleit) *n* plato para sopa

soup-spoon (*ssuup*-sspuun) *n* cuchara *f*

sour (ssauᵒ) *adj* agrio

source (ssooss) *n* fuente *f*

south (ssaus) *n* sur *m*; **South Pole** polo sur

South Africa (ssaus æ-fri-kö) África del Sur

south-east (ssaus-*iisst*) *n* sudeste *m*

southerly (*ssa*-ðö-li) *adj* meridional
southern (*ssa*-ðön) *adj* meridional
south-west (ssauz-ᵘêsst) *n* sudoeste *m*
souvenir (*ssuu*-vö-niᵒ) *n* recuerdo *m*
sovereign (*ssov*-rin) *n* soberano *m*
*sow (ssou) *v* *sembrar
soy (ssoi) *n* soja *f*
spa (sspaa) *n* balneario *m*
space (sspeiss) *n* espacio *m*; distancia *f*; *v* espaciar
spacious (*sspei*-föss) *adj* espacioso
spade (sspeid) *n* azada *f*, pala *f*
Spain (sspein) España *f*
Spaniard (*sspæ*-nyöd) *n* español *m*
Spanish (*sspæ*-nif) *adj* español
spanking (*sspæng*-king) *n* zurra *f*
spanner (*sspæ*-nö) *n* llave inglesa
spare (sspêᵒ) *adj* de reserva, disponible; *v* pasarse sin; **~ part** pieza de repuesto; **~ room** cuarto para huéspedes; **~ time** tiempo libre; **~ tyre** neumático de repuesto; **~ wheel** rueda de repuesto
sparing (*sspêᵒ*-ing) *adj* escaso; económico
spark (sspaak) *n* chispa *f*
sparking-plug (*sspaa*-king-plagh) *n* bujía *f*
sparkling (*sspaa*-kling) *adj* centelleante; espumante
sparrow (*sspæ*-rou) *n* gorrión *m*
*speak (sspiik) *v* hablar
spear (sspiᵒ) *n* lanza *f*
special (*sspê*-föl) *adj* especial; **~ delivery** por expreso
specialist (*sspê*-fö-lisst) *n* especialista *m*
speciality (sspê-fi-æ-lö-ti) *n* especialidad *f*
specialize (*sspê*-fö-lais) *v* especializarse
specially (*sspê*-fö-li) *adv* en particular
species (*sspii*-fiis) *n* (pl ~) especie *f*

specific (sspö-*ssi*-fik) *adj* específico
specimen (*sspê*-ssi-mön) *n* espécimen *m*
speck (sspêk) *n* mancha *f*
spectacle (*sspêk̬*-tö-köl) *n* espectáculo *m*; **spectacles** anteojos *mpl*
spectator (sspêk-*tei*-tö) *n* espectador *m*
speculate (*sspê*-kyu-leit) *v* especular
speech (sspiich) *n* habla *f*; discurso *m*; lenguaje *m*
speechless (*sspiich*-löss) *adj* atónito
speed (sspiid) *n* velocidad *f*; rapidez *f*, prisa *f*; **cruising ~** velocidad de cruce; **~ limit** límite de velocidad
*speed (sspiid) *v* *dar prisa; correr demasiado
speeding (*sspii*-ding) *n* exceso de velocidad
speedometer (sspii-*do*-mi-tö) *n* velocímetro *m*
spell (sspêl) *n* encanto *m*
*spell (sspêl) *v* deletrear
spelling (*sspê*-ling) *n* deletreo *m*
*spend (sspênd) *v* gastar; pasar
sphere (ssfiᵒ) *n* esfera *f*
spice (sspaiss) *n* especia *f*
spiced (sspaisst) *adj* condimentado
spicy (*sspai*-ssi) *adj* picante
spider (*sspai*-dö) *n* araña *f*; **spider's web** telaraña *f*
*spill (sspil) *v* *verter
*spin (sspin) *v* hilar; *hacer girar
spinach (*sspi*-nidʒ) *n* espinacas *fpl*
spine (sspain) *n* espinazo *m*
spinster (*sspin*-sstö) *n* solterona *f*
spire (sspaiᵒ) *n* aguja *f*
spirit (*sspi*-rit) *n* espíritu *m*; humor *m*; **spirits** bebidas espirituosas; moral *f*; **~ stove** calentador de alcohol
spiritual (*sspi*-ri-chu-öl) *adj* espiritual
spit (sspit) *n* esputo *m*, saliva *f*; espetón *m*

* **spit** (sspit) *v* escupir
in spite of (in sspait ov) a pesar de
spiteful (*sspait*-föl) *adj* malévolo
splash (ssplæʃ) *v* salpicar
splendid (*ssplên*-did) *adj* magnífico, espléndido
splendour (*ssplên*-dö) *n* esplendor *m*
splint (ssplint) *n* tablilla *f*
splinter (*ssplin*-tö) *n* astilla *f*
* **split** (ssplit) *v* *hender
* **spoil** (sspoil) *v* echar a perder; mimar
spoke[1] (sspouk) *v* (p speak)
spoke[2] (sspouk) *n* radio *m*
sponge (sspandʒ) *n* esponja *f*
spook (sspuuk) *n* fantasma *m*
spool (sspuul) *n* bobina *f*
spoon (sspuun) *n* cuchara *f*
spoonful (*sspuun*-ful) *n* cucharada *f*
sport (sspoot) *n* deporte *m*
sports-car (*sspootss*-kaa) *n* coche de carreras
sports-jacket (*sspootss*-dʒæ-kit) *n* chaqueta de deporte
sportsman (*sspootss*-mön) *n* (pl -men) deportista *m*
sportswear (*sspootss*-u̯êᵒ) *n* conjunto de deporte
spot (sspot) *n* mancha *f*; lugar *m*, puesto *m*
spotless (*sspot*-löss) *adj* inmaculado
spotlight (*sspot*-lait) *n* proyector *m*
spotted (*sspo*-tid) *adj* moteado
spout (sspaut) *n* chorro *m*
sprain (ssprein) *v* *torcerse; *n* torcedura *f*
* **spread** (ssprêd) *v* *extender
spring (sspring) *n* primavera *f*; muelle *m*; manantial *m*
springtime (*sspring*-taim) *n* primavera *f*
sprouts (ssprautss) *pl* col de Bruselas
spy (sspai) *n* espía *m*
squadron (*ssku̯o*-drön) *n* escuadrilla *f*

square (ssku̯êᵒ) *adj* cuadrado; *n* cuadrado *m*; plaza *f*
squash (ssku̯oʃ) *n* zumo *m*
squirrel (*ssku̯i*-röl) *n* ardilla *f*
squirt (ssku̯ööt) *n* chisguete *m*
stable (*sstei*-böl) *adj* estable; *n* establo *m*
stack (sstæk) *n* montón *m*
stadium (*sstei*-di-öm) *n* estadio *m*
staff (sstaaf) *n* personal *m*
stage (ssteidʒ) *n* escenario *m*; fase *f*; etapa *f*
stain (sstein) *v* manchar; *n* mancha *f*; **stained glass** vidrio de color; ~ **remover** quitamanchas *m*
stainless (*sstein*-löss) *adj* inmaculado; ~ **steel** acero inoxidable
staircase (*sstêᵒ*-keiss) *n* escalera *f*
stairs (sstêᵒs) *pl* escalera *f*
stale (ssteil) *adj* viejo
stall (sstool) *n* puesto *m*; butaca *f*
stamina (*sstæ*-mi-nö) *n* vigor *m*
stamp (sstæmp) *n* sello *m*; *v* sellar; patear; *n* estampilla *fMe*; ~ **machine** máquina expendedora de sellos
stand (sstænd) *n* puesto *m*; tribuna *f*
* **stand** (sstænd) *v* *estar de pie
standard (*sstæn*-död) *n* norma *f*; normal; ~ **of living** nivel de vida
stanza (*sstæn*-sö) *n* estrofa *f*
staple (*sstei*-pöl) *n* grapa *f*
star (sstaa) *n* estrella *f*
starboard (*sstaa*-böd) *n* estribor *m*
starch (sstaach) *n* almidón *m*; *v* almidonar
stare (sstêᵒ) *v* mirar
starling (*sstaa*-ling) *n* estornino *m*
start (sstaat) *v* *empezar; *n* comienzo *m*; **starter motor** arranque *m*
starting-point (*sstaa*-ting-point) *n* punto de partida
state (ssteit) *n* Estado *m*; estado *m*; *v* declarar; **the States** Estados Uni-

dos

statement (*ssteit*-mönt) *n* declaración
f

statesman (*ssteitss*-mön) *n* (pl -men)
estadista *m*

station (*sstei*-ʃön) *n* estación *f*; puesto *m*

stationary (*sstei*-ʃö-nö-ri) *adj* estacionario

stationer's (*sstei*-ʃö-nös) *n* papelería f

stationery (*sstei*-ʃö-nö-ri) *n* papelería
f

station-master (*sstei*-ʃön-maa-sstö) *n*
jefe de estación

statistics (sstö-*ti*-sstikss) *pl* estadística
f

statue (*sstæ*-chuu) *n* estatua f

stay (sstei) *v* quedarse; hospedarse;
n estancia f

steadfast (*sstèd*-faasst) *adj* constante

steady (*sstè*-di) *adj* firme

steak (ssteik) *n* biftec *m*

*steal (sstiil) *v* hurtar

steam (sstiim) *n* vapor *m*

steamer (*sstii*-mö) *n* vapor *m*

steel (sstiil) *n* acero *m*

steep (sstiip) *adj* abrupto

steeple (*sstii*-pöl) *n* campanario *m*

steering-column (*ssti*ö-ring-ko-löm) *n*
columna del volante

steering-wheel (*ssti*ö-ring-ᵘiil) *n* volante *m*

steersman (*ssti*ös-mön) *n* (pl -men) timonel *m*

stem (sstèm) *n* tallo *m*

stenographer (sstê-*no*-ghrö-fö) *n* taquígrafo *m*

step (sstèp) *n* paso *m*; peldaño *m*; *v*
pisar

stepchild (*sstêp*-chaild) *n* (pl
-children) hijastro *m*

stepfather (*sstêp*-faa-ðö) *n* padrastro
m

stepmother (*sstêp*-ma-ðö) *n* madras-

tra f

sterile (*sstê*-rail) *adj* estéril

sterilize (*sstê*-ri-lais) *v* esterilizar

steward (*sstyuu*-öd) *n* camarero *m*

stewardess (*sstyuu*-ö-dêss) *n* azafata
f

stick (sstik) *n* palo *m*

*stick (sstik) *v* pegar

sticky (*ssti*-ki) *adj* pegajoso

stiff (sstif) *adj* tieso

still (sstil) *adv* todavía; sin embargo;
adj quieto

stillness (*sstil*-nöss) *n* silencio *m*

stimulant (*ssti*-myu-lönt) *n* estimulante *m*

stimulate (*ssti*-myu-leit) *v* estimular

sting (ssting) *n* picadura f

*sting (ssting) *v* picar

stingy (*sstin*-dʒi) *adj* mezquino

*stink (sstingk) *v* apestar

stipulate (*ssti*-pyu-leit) *v* estipular

stipulation (ssti-pyu-*lei*-ʃön) *n* estipulación f

stir (sstöö) *v* *mover; *revolver

stirrup (*ssti*-röp) *n* estribo *m*

stitch (sstich) *n* punto *m*, punzada f;
sutura f

stock (sstok) *n* existencias *fpl*; *v* *tener en existencia; ~ **exchange** bol-
sa de valores, bolsa f; ~ **market**
bolsa f; **stocks and shares** acciones *fpl*

stocking (*ssto*-king) *n* media f

stole[1] (sstoul) *v* (p steal)

stole[2] (sstoul) *n* estola f

stomach (*ssta*-mök) *n* estómago *m*

stomach-ache (*ssta*-mö-keik) *n* dolor
de estómago

stone (sstoun) *n* piedra f; piedra preciosa; hueso *m*; de piedra; **pumice**
~ piedra pómez

stood (sstud) *v* (p, pp stand)

stop (sstop) *v* cesar; dejar de; *n* parada f; **stop!** ¡alto!

stopper (*ssto*-pö) *n* tapón *m*
storage (*sstoo*-ridʒ) *n* almacenaje *m*
store (sstoo) *n* repuesto *m*; almacén *m*; *v* almacenar
store-house (*sstoo*-hauss) *n* almacén *m*
storey (*sstoo*-ri) *n* piso *m*
stork (sstook) *n* cigüeña *f*
storm (sstoom) *n* tormenta *f*
stormy (*sstoo*-mi) *adj* tempestuoso
story (*sstoo*-ri) *n* cuento *m*
stout (sstaut) *adj* gordo, corpulento
stove (sstouv) *n* estufa *f*; cocina *f*
straight (sstreit) *adj* derecho; honesto; *adv* directamente; ~ **ahead** todo seguido; ~ **away** directamente, en seguida; ~ **on** todo seguido
strain (sstrein) *n* esfuerzo *m*; tensión *f*; *v* *forzar; filtrar
strainer (*sstrei*-nö) *n* escurridor *m*
strange (sstreindʒ) *adj* extraño; raro
stranger (*sstrein*-dʒö) *n* extranjero *m*; forastero *m*
strangle (*sstræng*-ghol) *v* estrangular
strap (sstræp) *n* correa *f*
straw (sstroo) *n* paja *f*
strawberry (*sstroo*-bö-ri) *n* fresa *f*
stream (sstriim) *n* arroyo *m*; corriente *f*; *v* *fluir
street (sstriit) *n* calle *f*
streetcar (*sstriit*-kaa) *nAm* tranvía *m*
street-organ (*sstrii*-too-ghön) *n* organillo *m*
strength (sstrêngz) *n* fuerza *f*, vigor *m*
stress (sstrêss) *n* esfuerzo *m*; énfasis *m*; *v* acentuar
stretch (sstrêch) *v* estirar; *n* trecho *m*
strict (sstrikt) *adj* estricto; severo
strife (sstraif) *n* lucha *f*
strike (sstraik) *n* huelga *f*
*strike (sstraik) *v* golpear; atacar; impresionar; *estar en huelga; arriar

striking (*sstrai*-king) *adj* impresionante, notable, vistoso
string (sstring) *n* cordel *m*; cuerda *f*
strip (sstrip) *n* faja *f*
stripe (sstraip) *n* raya *f*
striped (sstraipt) *adj* rayado
stroke (sstrouk) *n* ataque *m*
stroll (sstroul) *v* pasear; *n* paseo *m*
strong (sstrong) *adj* fuerte
stronghold (*sstrong*-hould) *n* plaza fuerte
structure (*sstrak*-chö) *n* estructura *f*
struggle (*sstra*-ghöl) *n* combate *m*, lucha *f*; *v* luchar
stub (sstab) *n* talón *m*
stubborn (*ssta*-bön) *adj* testarudo
student (*sstyuu*-dönt) *n* estudiante *m*; estudiante *f*
study (*ssta*-di) *v* estudiar; *n* estudio *m*; despacho *m*
stuff (sstaf) *n* substancia *f*; cachivache *m*
stuffed (sstaft) *adj* rellenado
stuffing (*ssta*-fing) *n* relleno *m*
stuffy (*ssta*-fi) *adj* sofocante
stumble (*sstam*-böl) *v* *tropezarse
stung (sstang) *v* (p, pp sting)
stupid (*sstyuu*-pid) *adj* estúpido
style (sstail) *n* estilo *m*
subject[1] (*ssab*-dʒikt) *n* sujeto *m*; súbdito *m*; ~ **to** sujeto a
subject[2] (ssöb-*dʒêkt*) *v* someter
submit (ssöb-*mit*) *v* someterse
subordinate (ssö-*boo*-di-nöt) *adj* subalterno; subordinado
subscriber (ssöb-*sskrai*-bö) *n* abonado *m*
subscription (ssöb-*sskrip*-ʃön) *n* suscripción *f*
subsequent (*ssab*-ssi-kʷönt) *adj* posterior
subsidy (*ssab*-ssi-di) *n* subsidio *m*
substance (*ssab*-sstönss) *n* sustancia *f*
substantial (ssöb-*sstæn*-ʃöl) *adj* mate-

rial; real; sustancial

substitute (*ssab*-ssti-tyuut) *v* *substituir; *n* sustituto *m*

subtitle (*ssab*-tai-töl) *n* subtítulo *m*

subtle (*ssa*-töl) *adj* sutil

subtract (ssöb-*trækt*) *v* restar

suburb (*ssa*-bööb) *n* suburbio *m*

suburban (ssö-*böö*-bön) *adj* suburbano

subway (*ssab*-ᵘei) *nAm* metro *m*

succeed (ssök-*ssiid*) *v* *tener éxito; suceder

success (ssök-*ssêss*) *n* éxito *m*

successful (ssök-*ssêss*-föl) *adj* de éxito

succumb (ssö-*kam*) *v* sucumbir

such (ssach) *adj* tal; *adv* tan; ~ **as** tal como

suck (ssak) *v* chupar

sudden (*ssa*-dön) *adj* súbito

suddenly (*ssa*-dön-li) *adv* repentinamente

suede (ssᵘeid) *n* gamuza *f*

suffer (*ssa*-fö) *v* sufrir

suffering (*ssa*-fö-ring) *n* sufrimiento *m*

suffice (ssö-*faiss*) *v* bastar

sufficient (ssö-*fi*-jönt) *adj* suficiente, bastante

suffrage (*ssa*-fridʒ) *n* derecho electoral, sufragio *m*

sugar (*ʃu*-ghö) *n* azúcar *m/f*

suggest (ssö-*dʒêsst*) *v* *sugerir

suggestion (ssö-*dʒêss*-chön) *n* sugestión *f*

suicide (*ssuu*-i-ssaid) *n* suicidio *m*

suit (ssuut) *v* *convenir; adaptar; *ir bien; *n* traje *m*

suitable (*ssuu*-tö-böl) *adj* apropiado, apto

suitcase (*ssuut*-keiss) *n* maleta *f*

suite (ssᵘiit) *n* apartamento *m*

sum (ssam) *n* suma *f*

summary (*ssa*-mö-ri) *n* resumen *m*, sumario *m*

summer (*ssa*-mö) *n* verano *m*; ~ **time** horario de verano

summit (*ssa*-mit) *n* cima *f*

summons (*ssa*-möns) *n* (pl ~es) citación *f*

sun (ssan) *n* sol *m*

sunbathe (*ssan*-beið) *v* tomar el sol

sunburn (*ssan*-böön) *n* quemadura del sol

Sunday (*ssan*-di) *n* domingo *m*

sun-glasses (*ssan*-ghlaa-ssis) *pl* gafas de sol

sunlight (*ssan*-lait) *n* luz del sol

sunny (*ssa*-ni) *adj* soleado

sunrise (*ssan*-rais) *n* amanecer *m*

sunset (*ssan*-ssêt) *n* ocaso *m*

sunshade (*ssan*-ʃeid) *n* quitasol *m*

sunshine (*ssan*-ʃain) *n* sol *m*

sunstroke (*ssan*-sstrouk) *n* insolación *f*

suntan oil (*ssan*-tæn-oil) aceite bronceador

superb (ssu-*pööb*) *adj* grandioso, soberbio

superficial (ssuu-pö-*fi*-jöl) *adj* superficial

superfluous (ssu-*pöö*-flu-öss) *adj* superfluo

superior (ssu-*piô*-ri-ö) *adj* mejor, mayor, superior

superlative (ssu-*pöö*-lö-tiv) *adj* superlativo; *n* superlativo *m*

supermarket (*ssuu*-pö-maa-kit) *n* supermercado *m*

superstition (ssuu-pö-*ssti*-jön) *n* superstición *f*

supervise (*ssuu*-pö-vais) *v* supervisar

supervision (ssuu-pö-*vi*-ʒön) *n* supervisión *f*

supervisor (*ssuu*-pö-vai-sö) *n* supervisor *m*

supper (*ssa*-pö) *n* cena *f*

supple (*ssa*-pöl) *adj* flexible, ágil

supplement (*ssa*-pli-mönt) *n* suplemento *m*

supply (ssö-*plai*) *n* abastecimiento *m*, suministro *m*; existencias *fpl*; oferta *f*; *v* suministrar

support (ssö-*poot*) *v* apoyar, *sostener, soportar; *n* apoyo *m*; ~ **hose** medias elásticas

supporter (ssö-*poo*-tö) *n* aficionado *m*

suppose (ssö-*pous*) *v* *suponer; **supposing that** dado que

suppository (ssö-*po*-si-tö-ri) *n* supositorio *m*

suppress (ssö-*prêss*) *v* reprimir

surcharge (*ssöö*-chaadʒ) *n* sobretasa *f*

sure (ʃuᵒ) *adj* seguro

surely (ʃuᵒ-li) *adv* seguramente

surface (*ssöö*-fiss) *n* superficie *f*

surf-board (*ssööf*-bood) *n* tabla para surf

surgeon (*ssöö*-dʒön) *n* cirujano *m*; **veterinary** ~ veterinario *m*

surgery (*ssöö*-dʒö-ri) *n* operación *f*; consultorio *m*

surname (*ssöö*-neim) *n* apellido *m*

surplus (*ssöö*-plöss) *n* sobra *f*

surprise (ssö-*prais*) *n* sorpresa *f*; *v* sorprender; extrañar

surrender (ssö-*rên*-dö) *v* *rendirse; *n* rendición *f*

surround (ssö-*raund*) *v* rodear, cercar

surrounding (ssö-*raun*-ding) *adj* circundante

surroundings (ssö-*raun*-dings) *pl* alrededores *mpl*

survey (*ssöö*-vei) *n* resumen *m*

survival (ssö-*vai*-völ) *n* supervivencia *f*

survive (ssö-*vaiv*) *v* sobrevivir

suspect[1] (ssö-*sspêkt*) *v* sospechar

suspect[2] (ssa-sspêkt) *n* persona sospechosa

suspend (ssö-*sspênd*) *v* suspender

suspenders (ssö-*sspên*-dös) *plAm* tirantes *mpl*; **suspender belt** portaligas *m*

suspension (ssö-*sspên*-ʃön) *n* suspensión *f*; ~ **bridge** puente colgante

suspicion (ssö-*sspi*-ʃön) *n* sospecha *f*; suspicacia *f*, desconfianza *f*

suspicious (ssö-*sspi*-ʃöss) *adj* sospechoso; suspicaz, desconfiado

sustain (ssö-*sstein*) *v* soportar

Swahili (ssᵘö-*hii*-li) *n* suahili *m*

swallow (ssᵘo-lou) *v* tragar; *n* golondrina *f*

swam (ssᵘæm) *v* (p swim)

swamp (ssᵘomp) *n* marisma *f*

swan (ssᵘon) *n* cisne *m*

swap (ssᵘop) *v* *trocar

swear (ssᵘêö) *v* jurar

sweat (ssᵘêt) *n* sudor *m*; *v* sudar

sweater (ssᵘê-tö) *n* suéter *m*

Swede (ssᵘiid) *n* sueco *m*

Sweden (ssᵘii-dön) Suecia *f*

Swedish (ssᵘii-diʃ) *adj* sueco

sweep (ssᵘiip) *v* barrer

sweet (ssᵘiit) *adj* dulce; lindo; *n* caramelo *m*; dulce *m*

sweeten (ssᵘii-tön) *v* endulzar

sweetheart (ssᵘiit-haat) *n* amor *m*, querida *f*

sweetshop (ssᵘiit-ʃop) *n* confitería *f*

swell (ssᵘêl) *adj* magnífico

swell (ssᵘêl) *v* hincharse

swelling (ssᵘê-ling) *n* hinchazón *f*

swift (ssᵘift) *adj* veloz

swim (ssᵘim) *v* nadar

swimmer (ssᵘi-mö) *n* nadador *m*

swimming (ssᵘi-ming) *n* natación *f*; ~ **pool** piscina *f*

swimming-trunks (ssᵘi-ming-trangkss) *n* calzón de baño

swim-suit (ssᵘim-ssuut) *n* traje de baño

swindle (ssᵘin-döl) *v* estafar; *n* estafa *f*

swindler (ssᵘin-dlö) *n* estafador *m*

swing (ssᵘing) *n* columpio *m*

*swing (ssᵘing) *v* oscilar; columpiarse

Swiss (ssᵘiss) *adj* suizo

switch (ssᵘich) *n* interruptor *m*; *v* cambiar; ~ **off** apagar; ~ **on** **encender

switchboard (ssᵘich-bood) *n* cuadro de distribución

Switzerland (ssᵘit-ssö-lönd) Suiza *f*

sword (ssood) *n* espada *f*

swum (ssᵘam) *v* (pp swim)

syllable (ssi-lö-böl) *n* sílaba *f*

symbol (ssim-böl) *n* símbolo *m*

sympathetic (ssim-pö-zê-tik) *adj* cordial, compasivo

sympathy (ssim-pö-zi) *n* simpatía *f*; compasión *f*

symphony (ssim-fö-ni) *n* sinfonía *f*

symptom (ssim-töm) *n* síntoma *m*

synagogue (ssi-nö-ghogh) *n* sinagoga *f*

synonym (ssi-nö-nim) *n* sinónimo *m*

synthetic (ssin-zê-tik) *adj* sintético

syphon (ssai-fön) *n* sifón *m*

Syria (ssi-ri-ö) Siria *f*

Syrian (ssi-ri-ön) *adj* sirio

syringe (ssi-rind3) *n* jeringa *f*

syrup (ssi-röp) *n* jarabe *m*

system (ssi-sstöm) *n* sistema *m*; **decimal** ~ sistema decimal

systematic (ssi-sstö-mæ-tik) *adj* sistemático

T

table (tei-böl) *n* mesa *f*; tabla *f*; ~ **of contents** índice *m*; ~ **tennis** tenis de mesa

table-cloth (tei-böl-kloz) *n* mantel *m*

tablespoon (tei-böl-sspuun) *n* cuchara *f*

tablet (tæ-blit) *n* pastilla *f*

taboo (tö-buu) *n* tabú *m*

tactics (tæk-tikss) *pl* táctica *f*

tag (tægh) *n* etiqueta *f*

tail (teil) *n* cola *f*

tail-light (teil-lait) *n* farol trasero

tailor (tei-lö) *n* sastre *m*

tailor-made (tei-lö-meid) *adj* hecho a la medida

*take (teik) *v* coger; tomar; llevar; comprender, **entender; ~ **away** quitar; llevarse; ~ **off** despegar; ~ **out** sacar; ~ **over** encargarse de; ~ **place** **tener lugar; ~ **up** ocupar

take-off (tei-kof) *n* despegue *m*

tale (teil) *n* cuento *m*

talent (tæ-lönt) *n* talento *m*

talented (tæ-lön-tid) *adj* dotado

talk (took) *v* hablar; *n* conversación *f*

talkative (too-kö-tiv) *adj* locuaz

tall (tool) *adj* alto

tame (teim) *adj* manso, domesticado; *v* domesticar

tampon (tæm-pön) *n* tapón *m*

tangerine (tæn-d3ö-riin) *n* mandarina *f*

tangible (tæn-d3i-böl) *adj* tangible

tank (tængk) *n* tanque *m*

tanker (tæng-kö) *n* buque cisterna *m*

tanned (tænd) *adj* tostado

tap (tæp) *n* grifo *m*; golpecito *m*; *v* golpear

tape (teip) *n* cinta *f*; **adhesive** ~ cinta adhesiva; esparadrapo *m*

tape-measure (teip-mê-3ö) *n* centímetro *m*, cinta métrica

tape-recorder (teip-ri-koo-dö) *n* magnetófono *m*

tapestry (tæ-pi-sstri) *n* tapiz *m*

tar (taa) *n* brea *f*

target (taa-ghit) *n* objetivo *m*, blanco *m*

tariff (tæ-rif) *n* arancel *m*

tarpaulin (taa-poo-lin) *n* lona impermeable

task (taassk) *n* tarea *f*

taste (teisst) *n* gusto *m*; *v* *saber a; *probar

tasteless (*teisst*-löss) *adj* insípido

tasty (*tei*-ssti) *adj* rico, sabroso

taught (toot) *v* (p, pp teach)

tavern (*tæ*-vön) *n* taberna *f*

tax (tækss) *n* impuesto *m*; *v* *imponer contribuciones

taxation (tæk-*ssei*-jön) *n* impuesto *m*

tax-free (*tækss*-frii) *adj* libre de impuestos

taxi (*tæk*-ssi) *n* taxi *m*; ~ **rank** parada de taxis; ~ **stand** *Am* parada de taxis

taxi-driver (*tæk*-ssi-drai-vö) *n* taxista *m*

taxi-meter (*tæk*-ssi-mii-tö) *n* taxímetro *m*

tea (tii) *n* té *m*; merienda *f*

***teach** (tiich) *v* enseñar

teacher (*tii*-chö) *n* profesor *m*, maestro *m*; profesora *f*; institutor *m*

teachings (*tii*-chings) *pl* enseñanza *f*

tea-cloth (*tii*-kloz) *n* trapo de cocina

teacup (*tii*-kap) *n* taza de té

team (tiim) *n* equipo *m*

teapot (*tii*-pot) *n* tetera *f*

tear[1] (tiö) *n* lágrima *f*

tear[2] (téö) *n* rasgón *m*; ***tear** *v* desgarrar

tear-jerker (*tiö*-dʒöö-kö) *n* cuplé lacrimoso

tease (tiis) *v* tomar el pelo

tea-set (*tii*-ssét) *n* juego de té

tea-shop (*tii*-ʃop) *n* salón de té

teaspoon (*tii*-sspuun) *n* cucharilla *f*

teaspoonful (*tii*-sspuun-ful) *n* cucharadita *f*

technical (*têk*-ni-köl) *adj* técnico

technician (têk-*ni*-jön) *n* técnico *m*

technique (têk-*niik*) *n* técnica *f*

technology (têk-*no*-lö-dʒi) *n* tecnolo-

gía *f*

teenager (*tii*-nei-dʒö) *n* jovencito *m*

teetotaller (tii-*tou*-tö-lö) *n* abstemio *m*

telepathy (ti-*lê*-pö-zi) *n* telepatía *f*

telephone (*tê*-li-foun) *n* teléfono *m*; ~ **book** *Am* listín telefónico, guía telefónica; ~ **booth** cabina telefónica; ~ **call** llamada telefónica; ~ **directory** guía telefónica, listín telefónico; directorio telefónico *Me*; ~ **exchange** central telefónica; ~ **operator** telefonista *f*

telephonist (ti-*lê*-fö-nisst) *n* telefonista *f*

television (*tê*-li-vi-ʒön) *n* televisión *f*; ~ **set** televisor *m*; **cable** ~ televisión por cable; **satellite** ~ televisión por satélite

telex (*tê*-lêkss) *n* télex *m*

***tell** (têl) *v* *decir; *contar

temper (*têm*-pö) *n* cólera *f*

temperature (*tôm* prö-chö) *n* tcmperatura *f*

tempest (*têm*-pisst) *n* tempestad *f*

temple (*têm*-pöl) *n* templo *m*; sien *f*

temporary (*têm*-pö-rö-ri) *adj* provisional, temporal

tempt (têmpt) *v* *tentar

temptation (têmp-*tei*-jön) *n* tentación *f*

ten (tên) *num* diez

tenant (*tê*-nönt) *n* inquilino *m*

tend (tênd) *v* *tender a; cuidar de; ~ **to** *tender a

tendency (*tên*-dön-ssi) *n* inclinación *f*, tendencia *f*

tender (*tên*-dö) *adj* tierno, delicado

tendon (*tên*-dön) *n* tendón *m*

tennis (*tê*-niss) *n* tenis *m*; ~ **shoes** zapatos de tenis

tennis-court (*tê*-niss-koot) *n* campo de tenis, cancha *f*

tense (tênss) *adj* tenso

tension (*tên-ʃön*) *n* tensión *m*

tent (tênt) *n* tienda *f*

tenth (tênz) *num* décimo

tepid (*tê-pid*) *adj* tibio

term (tööm) *n* término *m*; período *m*, plazo *m*; condición *f*

terminal (*töö-mi-nöl*) *n* estación terminal

terrace (*tê-röss*) *n* terraza *f*

terrain (tê-*rein*) *n* terreno *m*

terrible (*tê-ri-böl*) *adj* tremendo, terrible, pésimo

terrific (tö-*ri*-fik) *adj* tremendo

terrify (*tê-ri-fai*) *v* aterrorizar; **terrifying** aterrador

territory (*tê-ri-tö-ri*) *n* territorio *m*

terror (*tê-rö*) *n* terror *m*

terrorism (*tê-rö-ri-söm*) *n* terrorismo *m*, terror *m*

terrorist (*tê-rö-risst*) *n* terrorista *m*

terylene (*tê-rö-liin*) *n* terilene *m*

test (têsst) *n* prueba *f*, ensayo *m*; *v* *probar, ensayar

testify (*tê-ssti-fai*) *v* testimoniar

text (têksst) *n* texto *m*

textbook (*têkss-buk*) *n* libro de texto

textile (*têk-sstail*) *n* textil *m*

texture (*têkss-chö*) *n* textura *f*

Thai (tai) *adj* tailandés

Thailand (*tai-*lænd) Tailandia *f*

than (ðæn) *conj* que

thank (zængk) *v* *agradecer; ~ **you** gracias

thankful (*zængk-*föl) *adj* agradecido

that (ðæt) *adj* aquel, ese; *pron* aquél, eso; que; *conj* que

thaw (zoo) *v* descongelarse; *n* deshielo *m*

the (ðö,ði) *art* el *art*; **the ... the** cuanto más ... más

theatre (*zi°*-tö) *n* teatro *m*

theft (zêft) *n* robo *m*

their (ðê°) *adj* su

them (ðêm) *pron* les

theme (ziim) *n* tema *m*, sujeto *m*

themselves (ðöm-*ssêlvs*) *pron* se; ellos mismos

then (ðên) *adv* entonces; después; en tal caso

theology (zi-*o*-lö-dʒi) *n* teología *f*

theoretical (zi°-*rê*-ti-köl) *adj* teórico

theory (*zi°*-ri) *n* teoría *f*

therapy (*zê-*rö-pi) *n* terapia *f*

there (ðê°) *adv* allí; hacia allá

therefore (*ðê°-*foo) *conj* por lo tanto

thermometer (zö-*mo*-mi-tö) *n* termómetro *m*

thermostat (*zöö-*mö-sstæt) *n* termostato *m*

these (ðiis) *adj* éstos

thesis (*zii*-ssiss) *n* (pl theses) tesis *f*

they (ðei) *pron* ellos

thick (zik) *adj* espeso; denso

thicken (*zi*-kön) *v* espesar

thickness (*zik*-nöss) *n* espesor *m*

thief (ziif) *n* (pl thieves) ladrón *m*

thigh (zai) *n* muslo *m*

thimble (*zim*-böl) *n* dedal *f*

thin (zin) *adj* delgado; flaco

thing (zing) *n* cosa *f*

think (zingk) *v* *pensar; reflexionar; ~ **of** *pensar en; *recordar; ~ **over** considerar

thinker (*zing*-kö) *n* pensador *m*

third (zööd) *num* tercero

thirst (zöösst) *n* sed *f*

thirsty (*zöö*-ssti) *adj* sediento

thirteen (zöö-*tiin*) *num* trece

thirteenth (zöö-*tiinz*) *num* treceno

thirtieth (*zöö-*ti-öz) *num* treintavo

thirty (*zöö*-ti) *num* treinta

this (ðiss) *adj* este, esto; *pron* éste

thistle (*zi*-ssöl) *n* cardo *m*

thorn (zoon) *n* espina *f*

thorough (*za*-rö) *adj* minucioso

thoroughbred (*za*-rö-brêd) *adj* pura-sangre

thoroughfare (*za*-rö-fê°) *n* ruta principal, arteria principal

those (ðous) *adj* aquellos; *pron* aquéllos

though (ðou) *conj* si bien, aunque;
adv sin embargo

thought[1] (zoot) *v* (p, pp think)

thought[2] (zoot) *n* pensamiento *m*

thoughtful (*zoot*-fól) *adj* pensativo;
atento

thousand (*zau*-sönd) *num* mil

thread (zrêd) *n* hilo *m*; *v* enhebrar

threadbare (*zrêd*-bê⁶) *adj* gastado

threat (zrêt) *n* amenaza *f*

threaten (*zrê*-tön) *v* amenazar;
threatening amenazador

three (zrii) *num* tres

three-quarter (zrii-kᵘoo-tö) *adj* tres
cuartos

threshold (*zrê*-ʃould) *n* umbral *m*

threw (zruu) *v* (p throw)

thrifty (*zrif*-ti) *adj* económico

throat (zrout) *n* garganta *f*

throne (zroun) *n* trono *m*

through (zruu) *prep* a través de

throughout (zruu-*aut*) *adv* por todas
partes

throw (zrou) *n* lanzamiento *m*

***throw** (zrou) *v* tirar, arrojar

thrush (zraʃ) *n* tordo *m*

thumb (zam) *n* pulgar *m*

thumbtack (*zam*-tæk) *nAm* chinche *f*

thump (zamp) *v* golpear

thunder (*zan*-dö) *n* trueno *m*; *v* *tronar

thunderstorm (*zan*-dö-sstoom) *n* tronada *f*

thundery (*zan*-dö-ri) *adj* tormentoso

Thursday (*zöös*-di) jueves *m*

thus (ðass) *adv* así

thyme (taim) *n* tomillo *m*

tick (tik) *n* señal *f*; ~ **off** señalar

ticket (*ti*-kit) *n* billete *m*; multa *f*;
boleto *mMe*; ~ **collector** revisor
m; ~ **machine** máquina de billetes

tickle (*ti*-köl) *v* cosquillear

tide (taid) *n* marea *f*; **high** ~ pleamar
f; **low** ~ bajamar *f*

tidings (*tai*-dings) *pl* noticias *fpl*

tidy (*tai*-di) *adj* aseado; ~ **up** arreglar

tie (tai) *v* anudar, atar; *n* corbata *f*

tiger (*tai*-ghö) *n* tigre *m*

tight (tait) *adj* estrecho; angosto,
apretado; *adv* fuertemente

tighten (*tai*-tön) *v* estrechar, *apretar; estrecharse

tights (taitss) *pl* traje de malla

tile (tail) *n* azulejo *m*; teja *f*

till (til) *prep* hasta; *conj* hasta que

timber (*tim*-bö) *n* madera de construcción

time (taim) *n* tiempo *m*; vez *f*; **all
the** ~ continuamente; **in** ~ a tiempo; ~ **of arrival** hora de llegada; ~
of departure hora de salida

time-saving (*taim*-ssei-ving) *adj* que
economiza tiempo

timetable (*taim*-tei-böl) *n* horario *m*

timid (*ti*-mid) *adj* tímido

timidity (ti-*mi*-dö-ti) *n* timidez *f*

tin (tin) *n* estaño *m*; lata *f*; **tinned
food** conservas *fpl*

tinfoil (*tin*-foil) *n* papel de estaño

tin-opener (*ti*-nou-pö-nö) *n* abrelatas
m

tiny (*tai*-ni) *adj* menudo

tip (tip) *n* punta *f*; propina *f*

tire[1] (tai⁶) *n* neumático *m*; llanta
fMe

tire[2] (tai⁶) *v* cansar

tired (tai⁶d) *adj* cansado; ~ **of** harto
de

tissue (*ti*-ʃuu) *n* tejido *m*; pañuelo de
papel

title (*tai*-töl) *n* título *m*

to (tuu) *prep* hasta; a, para, en, hacia

toad (toud) *n* sapo *m*

toadstool (*toud*-sstuul) *n* hongo *m*

toast (tousst) *n* pan tostado; brindis

m

tobacco (tö-*bæ*-kou) *n* (pl ~s) tabaco *m*; ~ **pouch** petaca *f*

tobacconist (tö-*bæ*-kö-nisst) *n* estanquero *m*; **tobacconist's** estanco *m*

today (tö-*dei*) *adv* hoy

toddler (*tod*-lö) *n* párvulo *m*

toe (tou) *n* dedo del pie

toffee (*to*-fi) *n* caramelo *m*

together (tö-*ghê*-ðö) *adv* juntos

toilet (*toi*-löt) *n* retrete *m*; ~ **case** neceser *m*

toilet-paper (*toi*-löt-pei-pö) *n* papel higiénico

toiletry (*toi*-lö-tri) *n* artículos de tocador

token (*tou*-kön) *n* señal *f*; prueba *f*; ficha *f*

told (tould) *v* (p, pp tell)

tolerable (*to*-lö-rö-böl) *adj* tolerable

toll (toul) *n* peaje *m*

tomato (tö-*maa*-tou) *n* (pl ~es) tomate *m*; jitomate *mMe*

tomb (tuum) *n* tumba *f*

tombstone (*tuum*-sstoun) *n* lápida *f*

tomorrow (tö-*mo*-rou) *adv* mañana

ton (tan) *n* tonelada *f*

tone (toun) *n* tono *m*; timbre *m*

tongs (tongs) *pl* tenazas *f*

tongue (tang) *n* lengua *f*

tonic (*to*-nik) *n* tónico *m*

tonight (tö-*nait*) *adv* esta noche

tonsilitis (ton-ssö-*lai*-tiss) *n* amigdalitis *f*

tonsils (*ton*-ssöls) *pl* amígdalas *fpl*

too (tuu) *adv* demasiado; también

took (tuk) *v* (p take)

tool (tuul) *n* herramienta *f*; ~ **kit** bolsa de herramientas

tooth (tuuz) *n* (pl teeth) diente *m*

toothache (*tuu*-zeik) *n* dolor de muelas

toothbrush (*tuuz*-braʃ) *n* cepillo de dientes

toothpaste (*tuuz*-peisst) *n* pasta dentífrica

toothpick (*tuuz*-pik) *n* palillo *m*

toothpowder (*tuuz*-pau-dö) *n* polvo para los dientes

top (top) *n* cima *f*; parte superior; tapa *f*; superior; **on** ~ **of** encima de; ~ **side** parte superior

topcoat (*top*-kout) *n* sobretodo *m*

topic (*to*-pik) *n* asunto *m*

topical (*to*-pi-köl) *adj* actual

torch (tooch) *n* antorcha *f*; linterna *f*

torment¹ (too-*mênt*) *v* atormentar

torment² (*too*-mênt) *n* tormento *m*

torture (*too*-chö) *n* tortura *f*; *v* torturar

toss (toss) *v* echar

tot (tot) *n* niño pequeño

total (*tou*-töl) *adj* total; completo, absoluto; *n* total *m*

totalitarian (tou-tæ-li-*tê*ö-ri-ön) *adj* totalitario

totalizator (*tou*-tö-lai-sei-tö) *n* totalizador *m*

touch (tach) *v* tocar; *concernir; *n* contacto *m*, toque *m*; tacto *m*

touching (*ta*-ching) *adj* conmovedor

tough (taf) *adj* duro

tour (tuᵒ) *n* vuelta *f*

tourism (*tu*ᵒ-ri-söm) *n* turismo *m*

tourist (*tu*ᵒ-risst) *n* turista *m*; ~ **class** clase turista; ~ **office** oficina para turistas

tournament (*tu*ᵒ-nö-mönt) *n* torneo *m*

tow (tou) *v* remolcar

towards (tö-ᵘ*oods*) *prep* hacia; para con

towel (tauᵒl) *n* toalla *f*

towelling (*tau*ᵒ-ling) *n* tela para toallas

tower (tauᵒ) *n* torre *f*

town (taun) *n* ciudad *f*; ~ **centre** centro de la ciudad; ~ **hall** ayunta-

miento *m*
townspeople (*tauns*-pii-pöl) *pl* ciudadanos *mpl*
toxic (*tok*-ssik) *adj* tóxico
toy (toi) *n* juguete *m*
toyshop (*toi*-ʃop) *n* juguetería *f*
trace (treiss) *n* huella *f*; *v* rastrear
track (træk) *n* vía *f*; pista *f*
tractor (*træk*-tö) *n* tractor *m*
trade (treid) *n* comercio *m*; oficio *m*; *v* comerciar
trademark (*treid*-maak) *n* marca de fábrica
trader (*trei*-dö) *n* comerciante *m*
tradesman (*treids*-mön) *n* (pl -men) tendero *m*
trade-union (treid-*yuu*-nyön) *n* sindicato *m*
tradition (trö-*di*-ʃön) *n* tradición *f*
traditional (trö-*di*-ʃö-nöl) *adj* tradicional
traffic (*træ*-fik) *n* tránsito *m*; ~ **jam** embotellamiento *m*; ~ **light** semáforo *m*
trafficator (*træ*-fi-kei-tö) *n* indicador *m*
tragedy (*træ*-dʒö-di) *n* tragedia *f*
tragic (*træ*-dʒik) *adj* trágico
trail (treil) *n* rastro *m*, sendero *m*
trailer (*trei*-lö) *n* remolque *m*; *nAm* caravana *f*
train (trein) *n* tren *m*; *v* amaestrar, entrenar; **stopping** ~ tren de cercanías; **through** ~ tren directo; ~ **ferry** transbordador de trenes
training (*trei*-ning) *n* entrenamiento *m*
trait (treit) *n* rasgo *m*
traitor (*trei*-tö) *n* traidor *m*
tram (træm) *n* tranvía *m*
tramp (træmp) *n* vagabundo *m*; *v* vagabundear
tranquil (*træng*-kᵘil) *adj* tranquilo
tranquillizer (*træng*-kᵘi-lai-sö) *n* cal-

mante *m*
transaction (træn-*sæk*-ʃön) *n* transacción *f*
transatlantic (træn-söt-*læn*-tik) *adj* transatlántico
transfer (trænss-*föö*) *v* *transferir
transform (trænss-*foom*) *v* transformar
transformer (trænss-*foo*-mö) *n* transformador *m*
transition (træn-*ssi*-ʃön) *n* transición *f*
translate (trænss-*leit*) *v* *traducir
translation (trænss-*lei*-ʃön) *n* traducción *f*
translator (trænss-*lei*-tö) *n* traductor *m*
transmission (træns-*mi*-ʃön) *n* transmisión *f*
transmit (træns-*mit*) *v* transmitir
transmitter (træns-*mi*-tö) *n* emisor *m*
transparent (træn-*sspêᵒ*-rönt) *adj* transparente
transport[1] (*træn*-sspoot) *n* transporte *m*
transport[2] (træn-*sspoot*) *v* transportar
transportation (træn-sspoo-*tei*-ʃön) *n* transporte *m*
trap (træp) *n* trampa *f*
trash (træʃ) *n* basura *f*
travel (*træ*-völ) *v* viajar; ~ **agency** agencia de viajes; ~ **agent** agente de viajes; ~ **insurance** seguro de viaje; **travelling expenses** gastos de viaje
traveller (*træ*-vö-lö) *n* viajero *m*; **traveller's cheque** cheque de viajero
tray (trei) *n* bandeja *f*; charola *fMe*
treason (*trii*-sön) *n* traición *f*
treasure (*trê*-ʒö) *n* tesoro *m*
treasurer (*trê*-ʒö-rö) *n* tesorero *m*
treasury (*trê*-ʒö-ri) *n* Tesorería *f*
treat (triit) *v* tratar
treatment (*triit*-mönt) *n* tratamiento

m

treaty (*trii*-ti) *n* tratado *m*

tree (trii) *n* árbol *m*

tremble (*trêm*-böl) *v* *temblar; vibrar

tremendous (tri-*mên*-döss) *adj* tremendo

trespass (*trêss*-pöss) *v* infringir

trespasser (*trêss*-pö-ssö) *n* intruso *m*

trial (trai⁰l) *n* proceso *m*; prueba *f*

triangle (*trai*-æng-ghöl) *n* triángulo *m*

triangular (trai-*æng*-ghyu-lö) *adj* triangular

tribe (traib) *n* tribu *m*

tributary (*tri*-byu-tö-ri) *n* afluente *m*

tribute (*tri*-byuut) *n* homenaje *m*

trick (trik) *n* truco *m*

trigger (*tri*-ghö) *n* gatillo *m*

trim (trim) *v* recortar

trip (trip) *n* excursión *f*, viaje *m*

triumph (*trai*-ömf) *n* triunfo *m*; *v* triunfar

triumphant (trai-*am*-fönt) *adj* triunfante

trolley-bus (*tro*-li-bass) *n* trolebús *m*

troops (truupss) *pl* tropas *fpl*

tropical (*tro*-pi-köl) *adj* tropical

tropics (*tro*-pikss) *pl* trópicos *mpl*

trouble (*tra*-böl) *n* preocupación *f*, molestia *f*; *v* molestar

troublesome (*tra*-böl-ssöm) *adj* molesto

trousers (*trau*-sös) *pl* pantalones *mpl*

trout (traut) *n* (pl ~) trucha *f*

truck (trak) *nAm* camión *m*

true (truu) *adj* verdadero; real, auténtico; leal, fiel

trumpet (*tram*-pit) *n* trompeta *f*

trunk (trangk) *n* baúl *m*; tronco *m*; *nAm* portaequipajes *m*; **trunks** *pl* pantalones de gimnasia

trunk-call (*trangk*-kool) *n* conferencia interurbana

trust (trasst) *v* confiar en; *n* confianza *f*

trustworthy (*trasst*-ᵘöö-ði) *adj* confiable

truth (truuz) *n* verdad *f*

truthful (*truuz*-föl) *adj* verídico

try (trai) *v* intentar; *esforzarse; *n* tentativa *f*; ~ **on** *probarse

tube (tyuub) *n* tubo *m*

tuberculosis (tyuu-böö-kyu-*lou*-ssiss) *n* tuberculosis *f*

Tuesday (*tyuus*-di) martes *m*

tug (tagh) *v* remolcar; *n* remolcador *m*; estirón *f*

tuition (tyuu-*i*-Jön) *n* enseñanza *f*

tulip (*tyuu*-lip) *n* tulipán *m*

tumbler (*tam*-blö) *n* vaso *m*

tumour (*tyuu*-mö) *n* tumor *m*

tuna (*tyuu*-nö) *n* (pl ~, ~s) atún *m*

tune (tyuun) *n* tonada *f*; ~ **in** sintonizar

tuneful (*tyuun*-föl) *adj* melodioso

tunic (*tyuu*-nik) *n* túnica *f*

Tunisia (tyuu-*ni*-si-ö) Túnez *m*

Tunisian (tyuu-*ni*-si-ön) *adj* tunecino

tunnel (*ta*-nöl) *n* túnel *m*

turbine (*töö*-bain) *n* turbina *f*

turbojet (töö-bou-*dʒêt*) *n* avión turborreactor

Turk (töök) *n* turco *m*

Turkey (*töö*-ki) Turquía *f*

turkey (*töö*-ki) *n* pavo *m*

Turkish (*töö*-kiʃ) *adj* turco; ~ **bath** baño turco

turn (töön) *v* girar; *volver; *n* cambio *m*, vuelta *f*; curva *f*; turno *m*; ~ **back** *volver; ~ **down** rechazar; ~ **into** *convertirse en; ~ **off** *cerrar; ~ **on** *encender; abrir; ~ **over** *volver; ~ **round** *volver; *volverse

turning (*töö*-ning) *n* vuelta *f*

turning-point (*töö*-ning-point) *n* punto decisivo

turnover (*töö*-nou-vö) *n* volumen de transacciones; ~ **tax** impuesto sobre la venta

turnpike (*töön*-paík) *nAm* autopista de peaje

turpentine (*töö*-pön-tain) *n* trementina *f*

turtle (*töö*-töl) *n* tortuga *f*

tutor (*tyuu*-tö) *n* maestro particular; tutor *m*

tuxedo (tak-*ssii*-dou) *nAm* (pl ~s, ~es) smoking *m*

tweed (t*u*iid) *n* lana tweed

tweezers (t*u*ii-sös) *pl* pinzas *fpl*

twelfth (t*u*êlfz) *num* duodécimo

twelve (t*u*êlv) *num* doce

twentieth (t*u*ên-ti-öz) *num* vigésimo

twenty (t*u*ên-ti) *num* veinte

twice (t*u*aiss) *adv* dos veces

twig (t*u*igh) *n* ramita *f*

twilight (t*u*ai-lait) *n* crepúsculo *m*

twine (t*u*ain) *n* trenza *f*

twins (t*u*ins) *pl* gemelos *mpl*; **twin beds** camas gemelas

twist (t*u*isst) *v* *torcer; *n* torsión *f*

two (tuu) *num* dos

two-piece (tuu-*piiss*) *adj* de dos piezas

type (taip) *v* escribir a máquina, mecanografiar; *n* tipo *m*

typewriter (*taip*-rai-tö) *n* máquina de escribir

typewritten (*taip*-ri-tön) mecanografiado

typhoid (*tai*-foid) *n* tifus *m*

typical (*ti*-pi-köl) *adj* característico, típico

typist (*tai*-pisst) *n* dactilógrafa *f*

tyrant (*tai*⁰-rönt) *n* tirano *m*

tyre (tai⁰) *n* neumático *m*; ~ **pressure** presión del neumático

U

ugly (*a*-ghli) *adj* feo

ulcer (*al*-ssö) *n* úlcera *f*

ultimate (*al*-ti-möt) *adj* último

ultraviolet (al-trö-*vai*⁰-löt) *adj* ultravioleta

umbrella (am-*brê*-lö) *n* paraguas *m*

umpire (*am*-pai⁰) *n* árbitro *m*

unable (a-*nei*-böl) *adj* incapaz

unacceptable (a-nök-*ssêp*-tö-böl) *adj* inaceptable

unaccountable (a-nö-*kaun*-tö-böl) *adj* inexplicable

unaccustomed (a-nö-*ka*-sstömd) *adj* desacostumbrado

unanimous (yuu-*næ*-ni-möss) *adj* unánime

unanswered (a-*naan*-ssöd) *adj* sin contestación

unauthorized (a-*noo*-zö-raisd) *adj* desautorizado

unavoidable (a-nö-*voi*-dö-böl) *adj* inevitable

unaware (a-nö-*u*ê⁰) *adj* inconsciente

unbearable (an-*bê*⁰-rö-böl) *adj* insufrible

unbreakable (an-*brei*-kö-böl) *adj* irrompible

unbroken (an-*brou*-kön) *adj* intacto

unbutton (an-*ba*-tön) *v* desabotonar

uncertain (an-*ssöö*-tön) *adj* incierto

uncle (*ang*-köl) *n* tío *m*

unclean (an-*kliin*) *adj* sucio

uncomfortable (an-*kam*-fö-tö-böl) *adj* incómodo

uncommon (an-*ko*-mön) *adj* insólito, raro

unconditional (an-kön-*di*-ʃö-nöl) *adj* incondicional

unconscious (an-*kon*-ʃöss) *adj* inconsciente

uncork (an-*kook*) v descorchar

uncover (an-*ka*-vö) v destapar

uncultivated (an-*kal*-ti-vei-tid) *adj* inculto

under (*an*-dö) *prep* debajo de, bajo

undercurrent (*an*-dö-ka-rönt) *n* resaca *f*

underestimate (an-dö-*rê*-ssti-meit) v subestimar

underground (*an*-dö-ghraund) *adj* subterráneo; *n* metro *m*

underline (an-dö-*lain*) v subrayar

underneath (an-dö-*niiz*) *adv* debajo

undershirt (*an*-dö-ʃööt) *n* camiseta *f*

undersigned (*an*-dö-ssaind) *n* suscrito *m*

*understand (an-dö-*sstænd*) v comprender

understanding (an-dö-*sstæn*-ding) *n* comprensión *m*

*undertake (an-dö-*teik*) v emprender

undertaking (an-dö-*tei*-king) *n* empresa *f*

underwater (*an*-dö-ᵘoo-tö) *adj* subacuático

underwear (*an*-dö-ᵘêᵒ) *n* ropa interior

undesirable (an-di-*saiᵒ*-rö-böl) *adj* indeseable

*undo (an-*duu*) v desatar

undoubtedly (an-*dau*-tid-li) *adv* sin duda

undress (an-*drêss*) v desnudarse

undulating (*an*-dyu-lei-ting) *adj* ondulante

unearned (a-*nöönd*) *adj* inmerecido

uneasy (a-*nii*-si) *adj* inquieto

uneducated (a-*nê*-dyu-kei-tid) *adj* inculto

unemployed (a-nim-*ploid*) *adj* desocupado

unemployment (a-nim-*ploi*-mönt) *n* desempleo *m*

unequal (a-*nii*-kᵘöl) *adj* desigual

uneven (a-*nii*-vön) *adj* desigual; irregular

unexpected (a-nik-*sspêk*-tid) *adj* imprevisto, inesperado

unfair (an-*fêᵒ*) *adj* improbo, injusto

unfaithful (an-*feiz*-föl) *adj* infiel

unfamiliar (an-fö-*mil*-yö) *adj* desconocido

unfasten (an-*faa*-ssön) v desatar

unfavourable (an-*fei*-vö-rö-böl) *adj* desfavorable

unfit (an-*fit*) *adj* inadecuado

unfold (an-*fould*) v *desplegar

unfortunate (an-*foo*-chö-nöt) *adj* desafortunado

unfortunately (an-*foo*-chö-nöt-li) *adv* por desgracia, desgraciadamente

unfriendly (an-*frênd*-li) *adj* poco amistoso

unfurnished (an-*föö*-niʃt) *adj* desamueblado

ungrateful (an-*ghreit*-föl) *adj* ingrato

unhappy (an-*hæ*-pi) *adj* desdichado

unhealthy (an-*hêl*-zi) *adj* insalubre

unhurt (an-*hööt*) *adj* ileso

uniform (*yuu*-ni-foom) *n* uniforme *m*; *adj* uniforme

unimportant (a-nim-*poo*-tönt) *adj* insignificante

uninhabitable (a-nin-*hæ*-bi-tö-böl) *adj* inhabitable

uninhabited (a-nin-*hæ*-bi-tid) *adj* inhabitado

unintentional (a-nin-*tên*-ʃö-nöl) *adj* no intencional

union (*yuu*-nyön) *n* unión *f*; liga *f*, confederación *f*

unique (yuu-*niik*) *adj* único

unit (*yuu*-nit) *n* unidad *f*

unite (yuu-*nait*) v unir

United States (yuu-*nai*-tid ssteitss) Estados Unidos

unity (*yuu*-nö-ti) *n* unidad *f*

universal (yuu-ni-*vöö*-ssöl) *adj* gene-

ral, universal
universe (*yuu*-ni-vööss) *n* universo *m*
university (yuu-ni-*vöö*-ssö-ti) *n* universidad *f*
unjust (an-*dʒasst*) *adj* injusto
unkind (an-*kaind*) *adj* desagradable, arisco
unknown (an-*noun*) *adj* desconocido
unlawful (an-*loo*-föl) *adj* ilegal
unlearn (an-*löön*) *v* desacostumbrar
unless (ön-*léss*) *conj* a menos que
unlike (an-*laik*) *adj* diferente
unlikely (an-*lai*-kli) *adj* improbable
unlimited (an-*li*-mi-tid) *adj* ilimitado
unload (an-*loud*) *v* descargar
unlock (an-*lok*) *v* abrir
unlucky (an-*la*-ki) *adj* desafortunado
unnecessary (an-*né*-ssö-ssö-ri) *adj* innecesario
unoccupied (a-*no*-kyu-paid) *adj* desocupado
unofficial (a-nö-*fi*-föl) *adj* extraoficial
unpack (an-*pæk*) *v* desempaquetar
unpleasant (an-*plé*-sönt) *adj* desagradable; antipático
unpopular (an-*po*-pyu-lö) *adj* impopular
unprotected (an-prö-*têk*-tid) *adj* indefenso
unqualified (an-*kᵘo*-li-faid) *adj* incompetente
unreal (an-*riᵒl*) *adj* irreal
unreasonable (an-*rii*-sö-nö-böl) *adj* irrazonable
unreliable (an-ri-*lai*-ö-böl) *adj* no confiable
unrest (an-*rêsst*) *n* desasosiego *m*; inquietud *f*
unsafe (an-*sseif*) *adj* inseguro
unsatisfactory (an-ssæ-tiss-*fæk*-tö-ri) *adj* poco satisfactorio
unscrew (an-*sskruu*) *v* destornillar
unselfish (an-*ssêl*-fiʃ) *adj* desinteresado

unskilled (an-*sskild*) *adj* no especializado
unsound (an-*ssaund*) *adj* enfermizo
unstable (an-*sstei*-böl) *adj* inestable
unsteady (an-*ssté*-di) *adj* vacilante, inestable
unsuccessful (an-ssök-*ssêss*-föl) *adj* fracasado
unsuitable (an-*ssuu*-tö-böl) *adj* inadecuado
unsurpassed (an-ssö-*paasst*) *adj* sin igual
untidy (an-*tai*-di) *adj* desaliñado
untie (an-*tai*) *v* desatar
until (ön-*til*) *prep* hasta
untrue (an-*truu*) *adj* falso
untrustworthy (an-*trasst*-ᵘöö-ði) *adj* indigno de confianza
unusual (an-*yuu*-ʒu-öl) *adj* inusitado, insólito
unwell (an-ᵘêl) *adj* indispuesto
unwilling (an-ᵘi-ling) *adj* desinclinado
unwise (an-ᵘais) *adj* imprudente
unwrap (an-*ræp*) *v* *desenvolver
up (ap) *adv* hacia arriba, arriba
upholster (ap-*houl*-sstö) *v* tapizar
upkeep (*ap*-kiip) *n* manutención *f*
uplands (*ap*-lönds) *pl* altiplano *m*
upon (ö-*pon*) *prep* sobre
upper (*a*-pö) *adj* superior
upright (*ap*-rait) *adj* derecho; *adv* de pie
upset (ap-*ssêt*) *v* trastornar; *adj* trastornado
upside-down (ap-ssaid-*daun*) *adv* al revés
upstairs (ap-*sstêᵒs*) *adv* arriba
upstream (ap-*sstriim*) *adv* río arriba
upwards (*ap*-ᵘöds) *adv* hacia arriba
urban (*öö*-bön) *adj* urbano
urge (öödʒ) *v* estimular; *n* impulso *m*
urgency (*öö*-dʒön-ssi) *n* urgencia *f*
urgent (*öö*-dʒönt) *adj* urgente

urine (*yuᵒ*-rin) *n* orina *f*
Uruguay (*yuᵒ*-rö-gh^uai) Uruguay *m*
Uruguayan (yu^ᵒ-rö-*gh^uai*-ön) *adj* uruguayo
us (ass) *pron* nosotros
usable (*yuu*-sö-böl) *adj* utilizable
usage (*yuu*-sidʒ) *n* uso *m*
use[1] (yuus) *v* usar; *be used to *estar acostumbrado a; ~ **up** consumir
use[2] (yuuss) *n* uso *m*; utilidad *f*; *be of ~ *servir
useful (*yuuss*-föl) *adj* útil
useless (*yuuss*-löss) *adj* inútil
user (*yuu*-sö) *n* usuario *m*
usher (*a*-ʃö) *n* acomodador *m*
usherette (a-ʃö-*rêt*) *n* acomodadora *f*
usual (*yuu*-ʒu-öl) *adj* usual
usually (*yuu*-ʒu-ö-li) *adv* habitualmente
utensil (yuu-*tên*-ssöl) *n* herramienta *f*, utensilio *m*
utility (yuu-*ti*-lö-ti) *n* utilidad *f*
utilize (*yuu*-ti-lais) *v* utilizar
utmost (*at*-mousst) *adj* extremo
utter (*a*-tö) *adj* completo, total; *v* emitir

V

vacancy (*vei*-kön-ssi) *n* vacante *f*
vacant (*vei*-könt) *adj* vacante
vacate (vö-*keit*) *v* vaciar
vacation (vö-*kei*-ʃön) *n* vacaciones *fpl*
vaccinate (*væk*-ssi-neit) *v* vacunar
vaccination (væk-ssi-*nei*-ʃön) *n* vacunación *f*
vacuum (*væ*-kyu-öm) *n* vacío *m*; ~ **cleaner** aspirador *m*; ~ **flask** termo *m*
vagrancy (*vei*-ghrön-ssi) *n* vagancia *f*
vague (veigh) *adj* vago
vain (vein) *adj* vanidoso; vano; **in** ~

inútilmente, en vano
valet (*væ*-lit) *n* ayuda de cámara
valid (*væ*-lid) *adj* vigente
valley (*væ*-li) *n* valle *m*
valuable (*væ*-lyu-böl) *adj* valioso; **valuables** *pl* objetos de valor
value (*væ*-lyuu) *n* valor *m*; *v* valuar
valve (vælv) *n* válvula *f*
van (væn) *n* camioneta *f*
vanilla (vö-*ni*-lö) *n* vainilla *f*
vanish (*væ*-niʃ) *v* *desaparecer
vapour (*vei*-pö) *n* vapor *m*
variable (*vêᵒ*-ri-ö-böl) *adj* variable
variation (vê^ᵒ-ri-*ei*-ʃön) *n* variación *f*; cambio *m*
varied (*vêᵒ*-rid) *adj* variado
variety (vö-*rai*-ö-ti) *n* variedad *f*; ~ **show** espectáculo de variedades; ~ **theatre** teatro de variedades
various (*vêᵒ*-ri-öss) *adj* varios
varnish (*vaa*-niʃ) *n* barniz *m*; *v* barnizar
vary (*vêᵒ*-ri) *v* variar; cambiar; *diferir
vase (vaas) *n* vaso *m*
vaseline (*væ*-ssö-liin) *n* vaselina *f*
vast (vaasst) *adj* vasto
vault (voolt) *n* bóveda *f*; caja de caudales
veal (viil) *n* carne de ternera
vegetable (*vê*-dʒö-tö-böl) *n* legumbre *f*
vegetarian (vê-dʒi-*têᵒ*-ri-ön) *n* vegetariano *m*
vegetation (vê-dʒi-*tei*-ʃön) *n* vegetación *f*
vehicle (*vii*-ö-köl) *n* vehículo *m*
veil (veil) *n* velo *m*
vein (vein) *n* vena *f*; **varicose** ~ varice *f*
velvet (*vêl*-vit) *n* terciopelo *m*
velveteen (vêl-vi-*tiin*) *n* pana *f*
venerable (*vê*-nö-rö-böl) *adj* venerable

venereal disease (vi-*ni⁰*-ri-öl di-*siis*) enfermedad venérea

Venezuela (vê-ni-*sᵘei*-lö) Venezuela *f*

Venezuelan (vê-ni-*sᵘei*-lön) *adj* venezolano

ventilate (*vên*-ti-leit) *v* ventilar; airear

ventilation (vên-ti-*lei*-ſön) *n* ventilación *f*; aireo *m*

ventilator (*vên*-ti-lei-tö) *n* ventilador *m*

venture (*vên*-chö) *v* arriesgar

veranda (vö-*ræn*-dö) *n* veranda *f*

verb (vööb) *n* verbo *m*

verbal (*vöö*-böl) *adj* verbal

verdict (*vöö*-dikt) *n* sentencia *f*, veredicto *m*

verge (vöödʒ) *n* borde *m*

verify (*vê*-ri-fai) *v* verificar

verse (vööss) *n* verso *m*

version (*vöö*-ſön) *n* versión *f*

versus (*vöö*-ssöss) *prep* contra

vertical (*vöö*-ti-köl) *adj* vertical

vertigo (*vöö*-ti-ghou) *n* vértigo *m*

very (*vê*-ri) *adv* mucho, muy; *adj* preciso, verdadero; extremo

vessel (*vê*-ssöl) *n* embarcación *f*, buque *m*; vasija *f*

vest (vêsst) *n* camiseta *f*; *nAm* chaleco *m*

veterinary surgeon (vê-tri-nö-ri ssöö-dʒön) veterinario *m*

via (vai⁰) *prep* por

viaduct (*vai⁰*-dakt) *n* viaducto *m*

vibrate (vai-*breit*) *v* vibrar

vibration (vai-*brei*-ſön) *n* vibración *f*

vicar (*vi*-kö) *n* vicario *m*

vicarage (*vi*-kö-ridʒ) *n* casa del párroco

vice-president (vaiss-*prê*-si-dönt) *n* vicepresidente *m*

vicinity (vi-*ssi*-nö-ti) *n* vecindad *f*

vicious (*vi*-ſöss) *adj* vicioso

victim (*vik*-tim) *n* víctima *f*

victory (*vik*-tö-ri) *n* victoria *f*

video (*vi*-di-ou) *n* vídeo *m*; ~ **camera** videocámara; ~ **cassette** videocasete; ~ **recorder** videograbadora

view (vyuu) *n* vista *f*; parecer *m*, opinión *f*; *v* mirar

vigilant (*vi*-dʒi-lönt) *adj* despierto

villa (*vi*-lö) *n* villa *f*

village (*vi*-lidʒ) *n* pueblo *m*

villain (*vi*-lön) *n* villano *m*

vinegar (*vi*-ni-ghö) *n* vinagre *m*

vineyard (*vin*-yöd) *n* viña *f*

vintage (*vin*-tidʒ) *n* vendimia *f*

violation (vai⁰-*lei*-ſön) *n* violación *f*

violence (*vai⁰*-lönss) *n* violencia *f*

violent (*vai⁰*-lönt) *adj* violento; impetuoso

violet (*vai⁰*-löt) *n* violeta *f*; *adj* morado

violin (vai⁰-*lin*) *n* violín *m*

virgin (*vöö*-dʒin) *n* virgen *f*

virtue (*vöö*-chuu) *n* virtud *f*

visa (*vii*-sö) *n* visado *m*

visibility (vi ʒö-*bi*-lö-tl) *n* visibilidad *f*

visible (*vi*-sö-böl) *adj* visible

vision (*vi*-ʒön) *n* visión *f*

visit (*vi*-sit) *v* visitar; *n* visita *f*; **visiting hours** horas de visita

visitor (*vi*-si-tö) *n* visitante *m*

vital (*vai*-töl) *adj* esencial

vitamin (*vi*-tö-min) *n* vitamina *f*

vivid (*vi*-vid) *adj* vivo

vocabulary (vö-*kæ*-byu-lö-ri) *n* vocabulario *m*; glosario *m*

vocal (*vou*-köl) *adj* vocal

vocalist (*vou*-kö-lisst) *n* vocalista *m*

voice (voiss) *n* voz *f*

void (void) *adj* nulo

volcano (vol-*kei*-nou) *n* (pl ~es, ~s) volcán *m*

volt (voult) *n* voltio *m*

voltage (*voul*-tidʒ) *n* voltaje *m*

volume (*vo*-lyum) *n* volumen *m*; tomo *m*

voluntary (*vo*-lön-tö-ri) *adj* voluntario

volunteer (vo-lön-*ti°*) *n* voluntario *m*

vomit (*vo*-mit) *v* vomitar

vote (vout) *v* votar; *n* voto *m*; votación *f*

voucher (*vau*-chö) *n* recibo *m*, comprobante *m*

vow (vau) *n* voto *m*, juramento *m*; *v* prestar juramento

vowel (vau°l) *n* vocal *f*

voyage (*voi*-idʒ) *n* viaje *m*

vulgar (*val*-ghö) *adj* vulgar; popular, ordinario

vulnerable (*val*-nö-rö-böl) *adj* vulnerable

vulture (*val*-chö) *n* buitre *m*

W

wade (ᵘeid) *v* vadear

wafer (ᵘ*ei*-fö) *n* oblea *f*

waffle (ᵘo-föl) *n* barquillo *m*

wages (ᵘ*ei*-dʒis) *pl* paga *f*

waggon (ᵘ*æ*-ghön) *n* vagón *m*

waist (ᵘeisst) *n* cintura *f*

waistcoat (ᵘ*eiss*-kout) *n* chaleco *m*

wait (ᵘeit) *v* esperar; ~ **on** *servir

waiter (ᵘ*ei*-tö) *n* camarero *m*; mesero *mMe*

waiting *n* espera *f*

waiting-list (ᵘ*ei*-ting-lisst) *n* lista de espera

waiting-room (ᵘ*ei*-ting-ruum) *n* sala de espera

waitress (ᵘ*ei*-triss) *n* camarera *f*; mesera *fMe*

***wake** (ᵘeik) *v* *despertar; ~ **up** *despertarse

walk (ᵘook) *v* *andar; pasear; *n* caminata *f*; andadura *f*; **walking** a pie

walker (ᵘ*oo*-kö) *n* paseante *m*

walking-stick (ᵘ*oo*-king-sstik) *n* bastón *m*

wall (ᵘool) *n* muro *m*; pared *f*

wallet (ᵘ*o*-lit) *n* cartera *f*

wallpaper (ᵘ*ool*-pei-pö) *n* papel pintado

walnut (ᵘ*ool*-nat) *n* nogal *m*

waltz (ᵘoolss) *n* vals *m*

wander (ᵘ*on*-dö) *v* vagar, *errar

want (ᵘont) *v* *querer; desear; *n* necesidad *f*; carencia *f*, falta *f*

war (ᵘoo) *n* guerra *f*

warden (ᵘ*oo*-dön) *n* guardián *m*

wardrobe (ᵘ*oo*-droub) *n* guardarropa *m*, vestuario *m*

warehouse (ᵘ*ê°*-hauss) *n* almacén *m*

wares (ᵘê°s) *pl* mercancías *fpl*

warm (ᵘoom) *adj* caliente; *v* *calentar

warmth (ᵘoomz) *n* calor *m*

warn (ᵘoon) *v* *advertir

warning (ᵘ*oo*-ning) *n* advertencia *f*

wary (ᵘ*ê°*-ri) *adj* prudente

was (ᵘos) *v* (p be)

wash (ᵘoʃ) *v* lavar; ~ **and wear** no precisa plancha; ~ **up** *fregar

washable (ᵘ*o*-ʃö-böl) *adj* lavable

wash-basin (ᵘ*oʃ*-bei-ssön) *n* palangana *f*

washing (ᵘ*o*-ʃing) *n* lavado *m*; ropa sucia

washing-machine (ᵘ*o*-ʃing-mö-ʃiin) *n* máquina de lavar

washing-powder (ᵘ*o*-ʃing-pau-dö) *n* jabón en polvo

washroom (ᵘ*oʃ*-ruum) *nAm* cuarto de aseo

wash-stand (ᵘ*oʃ*-sstænd) *n* lavabo *m*

wasp (ᵘossp) *n* avispa *f*

waste (ᵘeisst) *v* *perder; *n* desperdicio *m*; *adj* baldío

wasteful (ᵘ*eisst*-föl) *adj* derrochador

wastepaper-basket (ᵘeisst-*pei*-pö-baasskit) *n* cesto para papeles

watch (ᵘoch) v mirar, observar; vigilar; n reloj m; ~ **for** acechar; ~ **out** *tener cuidado

watch-maker (ᵘoch-mei-kö) n relojero m

watch-strap (ᵘoch-sstræp) n correa de reloj

water (ᵘoo-tö) n agua f; **iced** ~ agua helada; **running** ~ agua corriente; ~ **pump** bomba de agua; ~ **ski** esquí acuático

water-colour (ᵘoo-tö-ka-lö) n color de aguada; acuarela f

watercress (ᵘoo-tö-krêss) n berro m

waterfall (ᵘoo-tö-fool) n cascada f

watermelon (ᵘoo-tö-mê-lön) n sandía f

waterproof (ᵘoo-tö-pruuf) adj impermeable

water-softener (ᵘoo-tö-ssof-nö) n ablandador m

waterway (ᵘoo-tö-ᵘei) n vía navegable

watt (ᵘot) n vatio m

wave (ᵘeiv) n ondulación f, ola f; v *hacer señales

wave-length (ᵘeiv-lêngz) n longitud de onda

wavy (ᵘei-vi) adj ondulado

wax (ᵘækss) n cera f

waxworks (ᵘækss-ᵘöökss) pl museo de figuras de cera

way (ᵘei) n manera f; camino m; lado m, dirección f; distancia f; **any** ~ de todos modos; **by the** ~ a propósito; **one-way traffic** dirección única; **out of the** ~ apartado; **the other** ~ **round** al revés; ~ **back** vuelta f; ~ **in** entrada f; ~ **out** salida f

wayside (ᵘei-ssaid) n borde del camino

we (ᵘii) pron nosotros

weak (ᵘiik) adj débil; flojo

weakness (ᵘiik-nöss) n debilidad f

wealth (ᵘêlz) n riqueza f

wealthy (ᵘêl-zi) adj rico

weapon (ᵘê-pön) n arma f

*wear (ᵘêᵒ) v llevar; ~ **out** gastar

weary (ᵘiᵒ-ri) adj cansado

weather (ᵘê-ðö) n tiempo m; ~ **forecast** boletín meteorológico

*weave (ᵘiiv) v tejer

weaver (ᵘii-vö) n tejedor m

wedding (ᵘê-ding) n matrimonio m, boda f

wedding-ring (ᵘê-ding ring) n anillo de boda

wedge (ᵘêdʒ) n cuña f

Wednesday (ᵘêns-di) miércoles m

weed (ᵘiid) n mala hierba

week (ᵘiik) n semana f

weekday (ᵘiik-dei) n día laborable

weekend (ᵘii-kênd) n fin de semana

weekly (ᵘii-kli) adj semanal

*weep (ᵘiip) v llorar

weigh (ᵘei) v pesar

weighing-machine (ᵘei-ing-mö-ʃiin) n báscula f

weight (ᵘeit) n peso m

welcome (ᵘêl-köm) adj bienvenido; n bienvenida f; v *dar la bienvenida

weld (ᵘêld) v *soldar

welfare (ᵘêl-fêᵒ) n bienestar m

well[1] (ᵘêl) adv bien; adj sano; **as** ~ también; **as** ~ **as** así como; **well!** ¡bueno!

well[2] (ᵘêl) n pozo m

well-founded (ᵘêl-faun-did) adj fundamentado

well-known (ᵘêl-noun) adj notorio

well-to-do (ᵘêl-tö-duu) adj acomodado

went (ᵘênt) v (p go)

were (ᵘöö) v (p be)

west (ᵘêsst) n occidente m, oeste m

westerly (ᵘê-sstö-li) adj occidental

western (ᵘê-sstön) adj occidental

wet (ᵁêt) *adj* mojado ; húmedo

whale (ᵁeil) *n* ballena *f*

wharf (ᵁoof) *n* (pl ~s, wharves) muelle *m*

what (ᵁot) *pron* qué ; lo que ; ~ **for** para que

whatever (ᵁo-tê-vö) *pron* cualquier cosa que

wheat (ᵁiit) *n* trigo *m*

wheel (ᵁiil) *n* rueda *f*

wheelbarrow (ᵁiil-bæ-rou) *n* carretilla *f*

wheelchair (ᵁiil-chêô) *n* silla de ruedas

when (ᵁên) *adv* cuándo ; *conj* cuando

whenever (ᵁê-nê-vö) *conj* cuando quiera que

where (ᵁêô) *adv* dónde ; *conj* donde

wherever (ᵁêô-rê-vö) *conj* dondequiera que

whether (ᵁê-ðö) *conj* si ; **whether ... or** si ... o

which (ᵁich) *pron* cuál ; que

whichever (ᵁi-chê-vö) *adj* cualquiera

while (ᵁail) *conj* mientras ; *n* rato *m*

whilst (ᵁailsst) *conj* mientras

whim (ᵁim) *n* antojo *m*, capricho *m*

whip (ᵁip) *n* azote *m* ; *v* batir

whiskers (ᵁi-sskös) *pl* patillas *fpl*

whisper (ᵁi-sspö) *v* susurrar ; *n* susurro *m*

whistle (ᵁi-ssöl) *v* silbar ; *n* silbato *m*

white (ᵁait) *adj* blanco

whitebait (ᵁait-beit) *n* boquerón *m*

whiting (ᵁai-ting) *n* (pl ~) merluza *f*

Whitsun (ᵁit-ssön) Pentecostés *m*

who (huu) *pron* quien ; que

whoever (huu-ê-vö) *pron* quienquiera

whole (houl) *adj* completo, entero ; intacto ; *n* total *m*

wholesale (houl-sseil) *n* venta al por mayor ; ~ **dealer** mayorista *m*

wholesome (houl-ssöm) *adj* saludable

wholly (houl-li) *adv* totalmente

whom (huum) *pron* a quien

whore (hoo) *n* puta *f*

whose (huus) *pron* cuyo ; de quien

why (ᵁai) *adv* por qué

wicked (ᵁi-kid) *adj* malvado

wide (ᵁaid) *adj* vasto, ancho

widen (ᵁai-dön) *v* ensanchar

widow (ᵁi-dou) *n* viuda *f*

widower (ᵁi-dou-ö) *n* viudo *m*

width (ᵁidz) *n* anchura *f*

wife (ᵁaif) *n* (pl wives) esposa *f*, mujer *f*

wig (ᵁigh) *n* peluca *f*

wild (ᵁaild) *adj* salvaje ; feroz

will (ᵁil) *n* voluntad *f* ; testamento *m*

*will (ᵁil) *v* *querer

willing (ᵁi-ling) *adj* dispuesto

willingly (ᵁi-ling-li) *adv* gustosamente

will-power (ᵁil-pauô) *n* fuerza de voluntad

*win (ᵁin) *v* vencer

wind (ᵁind) *n* viento *m*

*wind (ᵁaind) *v* serpentear ; *dar cuerda, enrollar

winding (ᵁain-ding) *adj* tortuoso

windmill (ᵁind-mil) *n* molino de viento

window (ᵁin-dou) *n* ventana *f*

window-sill (ᵁin-dou-ssil) *n* antepecho *m*

windscreen (ᵁind-sskriin) *n* parabrisas *m* ; ~ **wiper** limpiaparabrisas *m*

windshield (ᵁind-ʃiild) *nAm* parabrisas *m*

windy (ᵁin-di) *adj* ventoso

wine (ᵁain) *n* vino *m*

wine-cellar (ᵁain-ssê-lö) *n* cueva *f*

wine-list (ᵁain-lisst) *n* carta de vinos

wine-merchant (ᵁain-möö-chönt) *n* vinatero *m*

wine-waiter (ᵁain-ᵁei-tö) *n* camarero *m*

wing (ᵁing) *n* ala *f*

winkle (ᵁing-köl) *n* caracol marino

winner (ᵘi-nö) n vencedor m

winning (ᵘi-ning) adj ganador; **winnings** pl ganancias fpl

winter (ᵘin-tö) n invierno m; ~ **sports** deportes de invierno

wipe (ᵘaip) v enjugar

wire (ᵘaiö) n alambre m

wireless (ᵘaiö-löss) n radio f

wisdom (ᵘis-döm) n sabiduría f

wise (ᵘais) adj sabio

wish (ᵘiʃ) v desear; n deseo m

witch (ᵘich) n bruja f

with (ᵘið) prep con; de

***withdraw** (ᵘið-droo) v retirar

within (ᵘi-ðin) prep dentro de; adv de dentro

without (ᵘi-ðaut) prep sin

witness (ᵘit-nöss) n testigo m

wits (ᵘitss) pl razón f

witty (ᵘi-ti) adj chistoso

wolf (ᵘulf) n (pl wolves) lobo m

woman (ᵘu-mön) n (pl women) mujer f

womb (ᵘuum) n matriz f

won (ᵘan) v (p, pp win)

wonder (ᵘan-dö) n milagro m; asombro m; v preguntarse

wonderful (ᵘan-dö-föl) adj estupendo, maravilloso; delicioso

wood (ᵘud) n madera f; bosque m

wood-carving (ᵘud-kaa-ving) n talla f

wooded (ᵘu-did) adj selvoso

wooden (ᵘu-dön) adj de madera; ~ **shoe** zueco m

woodland (ᵘud-lönd) n arbolado m

wool (ᵘul) n lana f; **darning** ~ hilo de zurcir

woollen (ᵘu-lön) adj de lana

word (ᵘööd) n palabra f

wore (ᵘoo) v (p wear)

work (ᵘöök) n obra f; trabajo m; v trabajar; funcionar; **working day** día de trabajo; ~ **of art** obra de arte; ~ **permit** permiso de trabajo

worker (ᵘöö-kö) n obrero m

working (ᵘöö-king) n funcionamiento m

workman (ᵘöök-mön) n (pl -men) obrero m

works (ᵘöökss) pl fábrica f

workshop (ᵘöök-ʃop) n taller m

world (ᵘööld) n mundo m; ~ **war** guerra mundial

world-famous (ᵘööld-fei-möss) adj de fama mundial

world-wide (ᵘööld-ᵘaid) adj mundial

worm (ᵘööm) n gusano m

worn (ᵘoon) adj (pp wear) gastado

worn-out (ᵘoon-aut) adj gastado

worried (ᵘa-rid) adj inquieto

worry (ᵘa-ri) v inquietarse; n preocupación f, inquietud f

worse (ᵘööss) adj peor; adv peor

worship (ᵘöö-ʃip) v venerar; n culto m

worst (ᵘöösst) adj pésimo; adv peor

worsted (ᵘu-sstid) n estambre m/f

worth (ᵘööz) n valor m; *be ~ *valer; *be worth-while *valer la pena

worthless (ᵘööz-löss) adj sin valor

worthy of (ᵘööz-ði öv) digno de

would (ᵘud) v (p will) *soler

wound[1] (ᵘuund) n herida f; v ofender, *herir

wound[2] (ᵘaund) v (p, pp wind)

wrap (ræp) v *envolver

wreck (rêk) n pecio m; v *destruir

wrench (rênch) n llave f; tirón m; v dislocar

wrinkle (ring-köl) n arruga f

wrist (risst) n muñeca f

wrist-watch (risst-ᵘoch) n reloj de pulsera

***write** (rait) v escribir; **in writing** por escrito; ~ **down** anotar

writer (rai-tö) n escritor m

writing-pad (rai-ting-pæd) n bloque m; bloc mMe

writing-paper (*rai*-ting-pei-pö) *n* papel de escribir

written (*ri*-tön) *adj* (pp write) por escrito

wrong (rong) *adj* impropio, erróneo; *n* mal *m*; *v* agraviar; **be* ~ no **tener razón

wrote (rout) *v* (p write)

X

Xmas (*kriss*-möss) Navidad *f*
X-ray (*êkss*-rei) *n* radiografía *f*; *v* radiografiar

Y

yacht (yot) *n* yate *m*
yacht-club (*yot*-klab) *n* club de yates
yachting (*yo*-ting) *n* deporte de vela
yard (yaad) *n* corral *m*
yarn (yaan) *n* hilo *m*
yawn (yoon) *v* bostezar
year (yi⁰) *n* año *m*
yearly (*yi⁰*-li) *adj* anual
yeast (yiisst) *n* levadura *f*
yell (yêl) *v* gritar; *n* grito *m*
yellow (*yê*-lou) *adj* amarillo
yes (yêss) sí
yesterday (*yê*-sstö-di) *adv* ayer
yet (yêt) *adv* aun; *conj* pero, sin embargo
yield (yiild) *v* producir; ceder

yoke (youk) *n* yugo *m*
yolk (youk) *n* yema *f*
you (yuu) *pron* tú; a ti; usted; a usted; vosotros; os; ustedes
young (yang) *adj* joven
your (yoo) *adj* de usted; tu; vuestro, tuyos
yourself (yoo-*ssêlf*) *pron* te; tú mismo; usted mismo
yourselves (yoo-*ssêlvs*) *pron* se; vosotros mismos; ustedes mismos
youth (yuuz) *n* juventud *f*; ~ **hostel** albergue para jóvenes

Z

zeal (siil) *n* celo *m*
zealous (*sê*-löss) *adj* celoso
zebra (*sii*-brö) *n* cebra *f*
zenith (*sê*-niz) *n* cenit *m*; apogeo *m*
zero (*si⁰*-rou) *n* (pl ~s) cero *m*
zest (sêsst) *n* energía *f*
zinc (singk) *n* cinc *m*
zip (sip) *n* cremallera *f*; ~ **code** *Am* código postal
zipper (*si*-pö) *n* cierre relámpago
zodiac (*sou*-di-æk) *n* zodíaco *m*
zone (soun) *n* zona *f*; región *f*
zoo (suu) *n* (pl ~s) jardín zoológico
zoology (sou-*o*-lö-dʒi) *n* zoología *f*

Léxico gastronómico

Comidas

almond almendra

anchovy anchoa

angel food cake pastel confeccionado con clara de huevo

angels on horseback ostras envueltas en tocino, asadas y servidas en pan tostado

appetizer entremés

apple manzana
~ **charlotte** pastel de compota de manzanas y pan rallado
~ **dumpling** pastel de manzanas
~ **sauce** puré de manzanas

apricot albaricoque

Arbroath smoky róbalo ahumado

artichoke alcachofa

asparagus espárrago
~ **tip** punta de espárrago

aspic (en) gelatina

assorted variado

aubergine berenjena

avocado (pear) aguacate

bacon tocino
~ **and eggs** huevos con tocino

bagel panecillo en forma de corona

baked al horno
~ **Alaska** helado cubierto con merengue, dorado en el horno;

se sirve flameado como postre
~ **beans** judías blancas en salsa de tomates
~ **potato** patata sin pelar cocida al horno

Bakewell tart pastel de almendras con mermelada de frambuesas

baloney especie de mortadela

banana plátano
~ **split** dos mitades de plátano servidas con helado y nueces, rociadas con almíbar o crema de chocolate

barbecue 1) carne picada de ternera en una salsa a base de tomates, servida en un panecillo 2) comida al aire libre
~ **sauce** salsa de tomates muy picante

barbecued asado a la parrilla con carbón de leña

basil albahaca

bass lubina (pescado)

bean judía, haba, fríjol

beef carne de ternera
~ **olive** rollo de carne de ternera

beefburger bistec de carne picada, asado y a veces servido en un panecillo

beet, beetroot remolacha
bilberry arándano
bill cuenta
  ∼ **of fare** lista de platos
biscuit 1) galleta (GB) 2) panecillo (US)
black pudding morcilla
blackberry zarzamora
blackcurrant grosella negra
bloater arenque salado, ahumado
blood sausage morcilla
blueberry arándano
boiled hervido
Bologna (sausage) especie de mortadela
bone hueso
boned deshuesado
Boston baked beans judías blancas con tocino y melaza
Boston cream pie torta rellena de nata en capas superpuestas, cubierta de chocolate
brains sesos
braised asado
bramble pudding pudín de zarzamoras (a menudo con manzanas)
braunschweiger salchichón de hígado ahumado
bread pan
breaded empanado
breakfast desayuno
bream brema (pescado)
breast pecho, pechuga
brisket pecho
broad bean haba
broth caldo
brown Betty especie de compota de manzanas, con especias y cubierta de pan rallado
brunch comida que reemplaza el desayuno y el almuerzo
brussels sprout col de Bruselas
bubble and squeak patatas y coles picadas que se fríen, mezcladas a veces con trozos de carne de ternera (especie de tortilla)
bun 1) panecillo dulce confeccionado con frutas secas 2) especie de panecillo (US)
butter mantequilla
buttered con mantequilla
cabbage col, repollo
Caesar salad ensalada verde con ajo, anchoas, cuscurro y queso rallado
cake pastel, torta
cakes galletas, pastelillos
calf ternera
Canadian bacon lomo de cerdo ahumado que se corta en lonchas finas
cantaloupe melón
caper alcaparra
capercaillie, capercailzie urogallo grande
caramel caramelo
carp carpa
carrot zanahoria
cashew anacardo
casserole cacerola
catfish siluro (pescado)
catsup salsa de tomate
cauliflower coliflor
celery apio
cereal cereal
  hot ∼ gachas
chateaubriand solomillo de ternera
check cuenta
Cheddar (cheese) queso de textura firme y de sabor ligeramente ácido
cheese queso
  ∼ **board** bandeja de quesos
  ∼ **cake** pastel de queso doble crema, ligeramente azucarado
cheeseburger bistec de carne pica-

da, asado con una loncha de queso, servido en un panecillo

chef's salad ensalada de jamón, pollo, huevos cocidos, tomates, lechuga y queso

cherry cereza

chestnut castaña

chicken pollo

chicory 1) endibia (GB) 2) escarola, achicoria (US)

chili pepper chile, ají

chips 1) patatas fritas (GB) 2) chips (US)

chitt(er)lings tripas de cerdo

chive cebolleta

choice elección, surtido

chop costilla

~ **suey** plato hecho con carne picada de cerdo o de pollo, arroz y legumbres

chopped picado

chowder sopa espesa a base de mariscos

Christmas pudding pudín inglés hecho con frutas secas, a veces flameado, muy nutritivo y que se sirve en Navidad

chutney condimento indio muy sazonado, con sabor agridulce

cinnamon canela

clam almeja

club sandwich bocadillo doble con tocino, pollo, tomates, lechuga y mayonesa

cobbler compota de frutas cubierta con una capa de pasta

cock-a-leekie soup sopa de pollo y puerros

coconut coco

cod bacalao

Colchester oyster ostra inglesa muy afamada

cold cuts/meat fiambres

coleslaw ensalada de col

compote compota

condiment condimento

cooked cocido

cookie galleta

corn 1) trigo (GB) 2) maíz (US)

~ **on the cob** mazorca de maíz

cornflakes copos de maíz

corned beef carne de ternera sazonada

cottage cheese requesón

cottage pie carne picada que se cuece con cebollas y se cubre con puré de patatas

course plato

cover charge precio del cubierto

crab cangrejo de mar

cracker galletita salada

cranberry arándano agrio

~ **sauce** mermelada de arándanos agrios

crawfish, crayfish 1) cangrejo de río 2) langosta (GB) 3) langostino (US)

cream 1) nata 2) crema (sopa) 3) crema (postre)

~ **cheese** queso doble crema

~ **puff** pastelillo con nata

creamed potatoes patatas cortadas en forma de dados en salsa blanca

creole plato muy condimentado con tomates, pimientos y cebollas; suele servirse con arroz blanco

cress berro

crisps patatas a la inglesa, chips

croquette croqueta

crumpet especie de panecillo redondo, asado y untado de mantequilla

cucumber pepino

Cumberland ham jamón ahumado, muy conocido

Cumberland sauce jalea de grosellas sazonada de vino, jugo de naranja y especias

cupcake pastelillo, hojaldre
cured salado y ahumado
currant 1) pasa de Corinto 2) grosella
curried con curry
custard 1) crema 2) flan
cutlet 1) chuleta 2) escalope 3) fina lonja de carne
dab lenguado
Danish pastry pastelillos hojaldrados
date dátil
Derby cheese queso blando picante, de color amarillo claro
dessert postre
devilled con aliño muy fuerte
devil's food cake torta de chocolate muy nutritiva
devils on horseback ciruelas pasas cocidas en vino tinto, rellenas de almendras y anchoas, envueltas en tocino, asadas y servidas en una tostada
Devonshire cream crema doble muy espesa
diced cortado en daditos
diet food alimento dietético
dill eneldo
dinner cena
dish plato
donut, doughnut buñuelo en forma de anillo, rosquilla
double cream doble crema, nata
Dover sole lenguado de Dover, muy afamado
dressing 1) salsa para ensalada 2) relleno para aves (US)
Dublin Bay prawn langostino
duck pato
duckling anadón
dumpling albóndiga de pasta
Dutch apple pie tarta de manza-

nas, cubierta con una capa de azúcar negra y mantequilla
éclair pastelillo relleno de crema de chocolate o de café
eel anguila
egg huevo
  boiled ~ pasado por agua
  fried ~ frito
  hard-boiled ~ duro
  poached ~ escalfado
  scrambled ~ revuelto
  soft-boiled ~ poco pasado por agua
eggplant berenjena
endive 1) escarola, achicoria (GB) 2) endibia (US)
entrecôte solomo de ternera
entrée 1) entrada (GB) 2) plato principal (US)
fennel hinojo
fig higo
filet mignon solomillo
fillet filete de carne o de pescado
finnan haddock róbalo ahumado
fish pescado
  ~ **and chips** filetes de pescado y patatas fritas
  ~ **cake** albóndigas, galleta de pescado y patatas
flan tarta de frutas
flapjack hojuela espesa
flounder fleso (pescado)
forcemeat relleno, picadillo
fowl ave
frankfurter salchicha de Francfort
French bean judía verde
French bread pan francés
French dressing 1) vinagreta (GB) 2) salsa cremosa de ensalada con salsa de tomates (US)
french fries patatas fritas
French toast rebanada de pan, mojada en huevos batidos, frita en una sartén y servida con

mermelada o azúcar
fresh fresco
fried frito, asado
fritter buñuelo
frogs' legs ancas de rana
frosting capa de azúcar garrapiñado
fruit fruta
fry fritura
galantine trozos de carne y picadillo cocidos en gelatina
game caza
gammon jamón ahumado
garfish anguila de mar
garlic ajo
garnish aderezo
gherkin pepinillo
giblets menudillos de ave
ginger jengibre
goose ganso
~**berry** grosella espinosa
grape uva
~**fruit** pomelo, toronja
grated rallado
gravy jugo de carne, salsa
grayling pescado de la familia del salmón
green bean judía verde
green pepper pimiento verde
green salad ensalada verde
greens verduras
grilled asado a la parrilla
grilse salmón joven
grouse urogallo
gumbo 1) legumbre de origen africano 2) plato criollo a base de *okra*, con carne o pescado y tomates
haddock róbalo
haggis panza de cordero rellena de copos de avena
hake merluza
half mitad, semi
ham jamón

~ **and eggs** huevos con jamón
hamburger hamburguesa
hare liebre
haricot bean alubia blanca
hash 1) carne picada 2) picadillo de carne y ternera cubierto con patatas y legumbres
hazelnut avellana
heart corazón
herb hierba aromática
herring arenque
home-made de confección casera
hominy grits crema espesa de harina de maíz, especie de polenta
honey miel
~**dew melon** tipo de melón cuya carne es de color verde amarillento
hors-d'œuvre entremeses
horse-radish rábano picante
hot 1) caliente 2) con especias
~ **cross bun** bollito con pasas (que se come durante la Cuaresma)
~ **dog** salchicha caliente en un panecillo
huckleberry especie de arándano
hush puppy buñuelo a base de harina de maíz
ice-cream helado
iced helado
icing capa de azúcar garrapiñado
Idaho baked potato patata sin pelar cocida al horno
Irish stew guisado de cordero con cebollas y patatas
Italian dressing vinagreta
jam confitura
jellied en gelatina
Jell-O postre a la gelatina
jelly gelatina o jalea de frutas
Jerusalem artichoke aguaturma
John Dory especie de dorada
jugged hare estofado de liebre

juice jugo, zumo
juniper berry baya de enebro
junket leche cuajada azucarada
kale col rizada
kedgeree migajas de pescado aderezadas con arroz, huevos y mantequilla
ketchup salsa de tomates
kidney riñón
kipper arenque ahumado
lamb cordero
Lancashire hot pot guisado de chuletas y riñones de cordero, con patatas y cebollas
larded mechado
lean magro
leek puerro
leg pierna, muslo, corvejón
lemon limón
   ~ **sole** especie de platija
lentil lenteja
lettuce lechuga, ensalada verde
lima bean haba grande
lime lima (limón verde)
liver hígado
loaf pan, hogaza
lobster bogavante
loin lomo
Long Island duck pato de Long Island, muy afamado
low-calorie pobre en calorías
lox salmón ahumado
lunch almuerzo
macaroni macarrones
macaroon macarrón (almendrado)
mackerel caballa
maize maíz
mandarin mandarina
maple syrup jarabe de arce
marinade escabeche
marinated en escabeche
marjoram mejorana
marmalade mermelada de naranja

u otros sabores
marrow tuétano
   ~ **bone** hueso con tuétano
marshmallow dulce de malvavisco
marzipan mazapán
mashed potatoes puré de patatas
mayonnaise mayonesa
meal comida
meat carne
   ~**ball** albóndiga de carne
   ~ **loaf** carne picada preparada en forma de un pan y que se cuece al horno
medium (done) a punto
melted derretido
Melton Mowbray pie especie de empanada de carne
menu lista de platos
meringue merengue
milk leche
mince picadillo
   ~ **pie** tarta de frutas confitadas cortadas en daditos, con manzanas y especias (con o sin carne)
minced picado
   ~ **meat** carne picada
mint menta
mixed mezclado, surtido
   ~ **grill** brocheta de carne
molasses melaza
morel morilla
mousse postre de nata aromatizada
mulberry mora
mullet mújol (pescado)
mulligatawny soup sopa de pollo muy picante de origen indio
mushroom champiñón
muskmelon tipo de melón
mussel mejillón
mustard mostaza
mutton carnero
noodle tallarín
nut nuez

oatmeal (porrdige) gachas de avena

oil aceite

okra fruto del *gumbo* utilizado generalmente para espesar las sopas y guisados

olive aceituna

omelet tortilla

onion cebolla

orange naranja

ox tongue lengua de buey

oxtail cola de buey (sopa)

oyster ostra

pancake hojuela espesa, torta de sartén

paprika pimiento

Parmesan (cheese) queso parmesano

parsley perejil

parsnip chirivía

partridge perdiz

pastry pastel, pastelillo

pasty empanadilla de carne

pea guisante

peach melocotón

peanut cacahuete, maní

~ **butter** manteca de cacahuete

pear pera

pearl barley cebada perlada

pepper pimienta

peppermint menta

perch perca

persimmon caqui

pheasant faisán

pickerel lucio pequeño (pescado)

pickle 1) legumbre o fruta en vinagre 2) pepinillo (US)

pickled conservado en salmuera o vinagre

pie torta a menudo cubierta con una capa de pasta, rellena de carne, legumbres, frutas o crema inglesa

pig cerdo

pigeon pichón

pike lucio

pineapple piña

plaice platija, acedía

plain natural

plate plato

plum ciruela, ciruela pasa

~ **pudding** pudín inglés hecho con frutas secas, a veces flameado, muy nutritivo y que se sirve en Navidad

poached escalfado

popcorn palomitas de maíz

popover panecillo esponjoso cocido en el horno

pork cerdo

porridge gachas

porterhouse steak lonja espesa de solomillo de res

pot roast carne de ternera asada y legumbres

potato patata, papa

~ **chips** 1) patatas fritas (GB) 2) chips (US)

~ **in its jacket** patata sin pelar

potted shrimps mantequilla sazonada, derretida y enfriada, servida con camarones

poultry ave de corral

prawn camarón grande

prune ciruela seca

ptarmigan perdiz blanca

pudding pudín blando o consistente hecho con harina, relleno de carne, pescado, legumbres o frutas

pumpernickel pan hecho con harina gruesa de centeno

pumpkin calabaza

quail codorniz

quince membrillo

rabbit conejo

radish rábano

rainbow trout trucha arco iris

ıisin pasa
rare poco hecho
raspberry frambuesa
raw crudo
red mullet salmonete
red (sweet) pepper pimiento morrón
redcurrant grosella roja
relish condimento hecho con trocitos de legumbres y vinagre
rhubarb ruibarbo
rib (of beef) costilla (de ternera)
rib-eye steak solomillo
rice arroz
rissole croqueta de pescado o carne
river trout trucha de río
roast(ed) asado
Rock Cornish hen pollo tomatero
roe huevos de pescado
roll panecillo
rollmop herring filete de arenque escabechado con vino blanco, enrollado con un pepinillo en medio
round steak filete de pierna de ternera
Rubens sandwich carne de ternera en pan tostado, con col fermentada, queso suizo y salsa para ensalada; se sirve caliente
rump steak filete de lomo de ternera
rusk rebanadas tostadas de pan de molde
rye bread pan de centeno
saddle cuarto trasero
saffron azafrán
sage salvia
salad ensalada
~ bar surtido de ensaladas
~ cream salsa cremosa para ensalada, ligeramente azucarada

~ dressing salsa para ensalada
salmon salmón
~ trout trucha asalmonada
salt(ed) sal(ado)
sandwich bocadillo, emparedado
sardine sardina
sauce salsa
sauerkraut col fermentada
sausage salchicha
sauté(ed) salteado
scallop 1) venera 2) escalope de ternera
scampi langostino
scone panecillo tierno hecho con harina de avena o cebada
Scotch broth caldo a base de carne de carnero o de buey y legumbres
Scotch woodcock pan tostado con huevos revueltos y crema de anchoas
sea bass róbalo, lubina
sea kale col marina
seafood mariscos y peces marinos
(in) season (en su) época (estación del año)
seasoning condimento, sazón
service servicio
~ charge importe que se paga por el servicio
~ (not) included servicio (no) incluido
set menu menú fijo
shad alosa, sábalo
shallot chalote
shellfish marisco
sherbet sorbete
shoulder espalda
shredded wheat hojuelas de trigo en croquetas (se sirven en el desayuno)
shrimp camarón, gamba
silverside (of beef) codillo (de ternera)

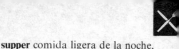

sirloin steak bistec del solomillo

skewer brocheta

slice loncha, rodaja

sliced cortado en lonchas

sloppy Joe carne picada de ternera con una salsa picante de tomates, se sirve en un panecillo

smelt eperlano

smoked ahumado

snack comida ligera

sole lenguado

soup sopa, crema

sour agrio

soused herring arenque conservado en vinagre y especias

spaghetti espaguetis

spare rib costilla de cerdo casi descarnada

spice especia

spinach espinaca

spiny lobster langosta

(on a) spit (en un) espetón

sponge cake bizcocho ligero y esponjoso

sprat arenque pequeño, sardineta

squash calabaza

starter entrada

steak and kidney pie empanada de carne de ternera y riñones

steamed cocido al vapor

stew guisado

Stilton (cheese) queso inglés afamado (blanco o con mohos azules)

strawberry fresa

string bean judía verde

stuffed relleno

stuffing (el) relleno

suck(l)ing pig lechón

sugar azúcar

sugarless sin azúcar

sundae copa de helado con frutas, nueces, nata batida y a veces jarabe

supper comida ligera de la noche, cena

swede naba de Suecia

sweet 1) dulce 2) postre

~ **corn** maíz blanco

~ **potato** patata dulce

sweetbread lechecillas

Swiss cheese queso suizo (Emmenthal)

Swiss roll bizcocho enrollado y relleno de mermelada

Swiss steak lonja de ternera asada con legumbres y especias

T-bone steak bistec y filete de ternera separados por un hueso en forma de T

table d'hôte menú fijo

tangerine especie de mandarina

tarragon estragón

tart tarta de frutas

tenderloin filete de carne

Thousand Island dressing salsa para ensalada, sazonada, hecha de mayonesa y pimientos

thyme tomillo

toad-in-the-hole carne de ternera (o salchicha) cubierta de pasta y cocida al horno

toast pan tostado, tostada

toasted tostado

~ **cheese** pan tostado con queso derretido

tomato tomate

tongue lengua

tournedos bistec espeso del filete (ternera)

treacle melaza

trifle pastel con jerez o aguardiente, hecho con almendras, mermelada y crema batida o natillas y crema de vainilla

tripe tripas, callos

trout trucha

truffle trufa

tuna, tunny atún
turbot rodaballo, rombo
turkey pavo
turnip nabo
turnover pastelillo relleno de compota o mermelada
turtle tortuga
underdone poco hecho
vanilla vainilla
veal ternera
~ bird pulpeta de ternera
vegetable legumbre
~ marrow calabacín
venison caza, corzo
vichyssoise sopa fría preparada con puerros, patatas y crema
vinegar vinagre
Virginia baked ham jamón cocido al horno, adornado con clavos de especia, rebanadas de piña y cerezas; se le baña con el jugo de las frutas
vol-au-vent pastel de hojaldre relleno de salsa con crema, trozos de carne y champiñones
wafer barquillo
waffle especie de barquillo caliente

walnut nuez
water ice sorbete
watercress berro de agua
watermelon sandía
well-done bastante hecho
Welsh rabbit/rarebit queso derretido sobre una tostada
whelk buccino (molusco)
whipped cream nata batida
whitebait boquerón
Wiener schnitzel escalope de ternera empanado
wine list lista de vinos
woodcock becada
Worcestershire sauce condimento líquido picante a base de vinagre, soja y ajo
yoghurt yogur
York ham jamón de York (ahumado)
Yorkshire pudding especie de pasta de hojuelas que se sirve con el rosbif
zucchini calabacín
zwieback rebanadas tostadas de pan de molde

Bebidas

ale cerveza negra, ligeramente azucarada, fermentada a elevada temperatura
bitter ~ negra, amarga y más bien pesada
brown ~ negra de botella, ligeramente azucarada
light ~ dorada de botella

mild ~ negra de barril, bastante fuerte
pale ~ dorada de botella
angostura esencia aromática amarga que se añade a los cócteles
applejack aguardiente de manzanas

Athol Brose bebida escocesa hecha con whisky, miel, agua y a veces copos de avena

Bacardi cocktail cóctel de ron con ginebra, jarabe de granadina y jugo de limón

barley water bebida refrescante a base de cebada y aromatizada con limón

barley wine cerveza negra muy alcoholizada

beer cerveza
bottled ~ de botella
draft, draught ~ de barril

bitters aperitivos y digestivos a base de raíces, corteza o hierbas

black velvet champán mezclado con *stout* (acompaña con frecuencia las ostras)

bloody Mary vodka, jugo de tomate y especias

bourbon whisky americano, a base de maíz

brandy 1) denominación genérica de los aguardientes de uvas y otras frutas 2) coñac
~ **Alexander** mezcla de aguardiente, crema de cacao y nata

British wines vino fermentado en Gran Bretaña, fabricado a base de uvas o jugo de uvas importados

cherry brandy licor de cerezas

cider sidra
~ **cup** mezcla de sidra, especias, azúcar y hielo

claret vino tinto de Burdeos

cobbler *long drink* helado a base de frutas, al que se añade vino o licor

coffee café
~ **with cream** con nata
black ~ solo
caffeine-free ~ descafeinado

white ~ con leche, cortado

cordial licor estimulante y digestivo

cream nata

cup bebida refrescante a base de vino helado, sifón, un espirituoso y adornada con una raja de naranja, de limón o de pepino

daiquiri cóctel de ron con jugo de limón y de piña

double doble porción

Drambuie licor a base de whisky y miel

dry martini 1) vermú seco (GB) 2) cóctel de ginebra con algo de vermú seco (US)

egg-nog bebida de ron u otro licor fuerte con yemas de huevos batidas y azúcar

gin ginebra

gin and it mezcla de ginebra y vermú italiano

gin-fizz mezcla de ginebra, jugo de limón, sifón y azúcar

ginger ale bebida sin alcohol, perfumada con extracto de jengibre

ginger beer bebida ligeramente alcohólica, a base de jengibre y azúcar

grasshopper mezcla de crema de menta, crema de cacao y nata

Guinness (stout) cerveza negra, con gusto muy pronunciado y algo dulce, con mucha malta y lúpulo

half pint aproximadamente 3 decilitros

highball whisky o aguardiente diluido con agua, soda o *ginger ale*

iced helado

Irish coffee café con azúcar y whisky irlandés, cubierto con nata batida (Chantilly)

Irish Mist licor irlandés a base de whisky y miel

Irish whiskey whisky irlandés menos áspero que el whisky escocés *(scotch);* además de cebada contiene centeno, avena y trigo

juice jugo, zumo

lager cerveza dorada ligera

lemon squash zumo de limón

lemonade limonada

lime juice zumo de lima (limón verde)

liqueur licor, poscafé

liquor aguardiente

long drink licor diluido en agua o tónica y servido con cubitos de hielo

madeira vino de Madera

Manhattan whisky americano, vermú y *angostura*

milk leche

∼ **shake** batido

mineral water agua mineral

mulled wine vino caliente con especias

neat bebida pura, sola, sin hielo y sin agua

old-fashioned whisky, *angostura,* cerezas con marrasquino y azúcar

on the rocks con cubitos de hielo

Ovaltine Ovomaltina

Pimm's cup(s) bebida alcohólica compuesta por alguno de los siguientes licores; se mezcla con zumo de fruta y algunas veces con agua de Seltz

∼ **No. 1** a base de ginebra

∼ **No. 2** a base de whisky

∼ **No. 3** a base de ron

∼ **No. 4** a base de aguardiente

pink champagne champán rosado

pink lady mezcla de clara de huevo, Calvados, zumo de limón, jarabe de granadina y ginebra

pint aproximadamente 6 decilitros

port (wine) (vino de) Oporto

porter cerveza negra y amarga

punch ponche

quart 1,14 litro (US 0,95 litro)

root beer bebida edulcorada efervescente, aromatizada con hierbas y raíces

rum ron

rye (whiskey) whisky de centeno, más pesado y más áspero que el *bourbon*

scotch (whisky) whisky escocés, mezcla de whisky de trigo y de whisky de cebada

screwdriver vodka y zumo de naranja

shandy *bitter ale* mezclada con zumo de limón o con una *ginger beer*

sherry jerez

short drink todo licor no diluido, puro

shot dosis de cualquier licor espirituoso

sloe gin-fizz licor de endrina con sifón y zumo de limón

soda water agua gaseosa

soft drink bebida sin alcohol

spirits aguardientes

stinger coñac y crema de menta

stout cerveza negra con mucho lúpulo y alcohol

straight alcohol que se bebe seco, sin mezcla

tea té

toddy ponche hecho de ron, agua, limón y azúcar

Tom Collins ginebra, zumo de limón, sifón y azúcar

tonic (water) (agua) tónica, agua gaseosa, a base de quinina

vermouth vermú
water agua
whisky sour whisky, zumo de
  limón, azúcar y sifón
wine vino
  dessert ~ de postre

dry ~ seco
red ~ tinto
rosé ~ clarete, rosado
sparkling ~ espumoso
sweet ~ dulce (de postre)
white ~ blanco

Mini-gramática

El artículo

El artículo determinado (el, la, los, las) tiene una sola forma: *the*.

the room, the rooms	el cuarto, los cuartos
the end of the month	el fin del mes

El artículo indeterminado (un, una, unos, unas) tiene dos formas: *a* se usa cuando precede a sonidos consonantes; *an* antes de sonidos vocales.

a coat un abrigo   **an umbrella** un paraguas   **an hour** una hora

Plurales

El plural de la mayor parte de los nombres se forma añadiendo *-(e)s* al singular. Según el sonido final del singular, el plural se pronuncia *-ss* o *-s* o *-is* (que forma una sílaba extra).

cup — cups (taza — tazas)   **dress — dresses** (vestido — vestidos)

Los plurales siguientes son irregulares:

man — men (hombre/s)	**foot — feet** (pie/s)
woman — women (mujer/es)	**tooth — teeth** (diente/s)
child — children (niño/s)	**mouse — mice** (ratones/es)

El posesivo

1. Si el poseedor es una persona: los nombres en singular y los plurales que no terminan en *-s* añaden *'s*.

the boy's room	el cuarto del muchacho
the children's clothes	los vestidos de los niños

Los nombres terminados en *-s* (incluyendo la mayoría de los plurales), añaden solamente el apóstrofe (').

the boys' room   el cuarto de los muchachos

2. Si el poseedor no es una persona: se emplea la preposición *of*.

the key of the door   la llave de la puerta

Adjetivos

Los adjetivos preceden normalmente al nombre.

a large brown suitcase   una maleta marrón grande

El comparativo y el superlativo de los adjetivos se pueden formar de dos maneras:

1. Los adjetivos monosílabos y muchos adjetivos bisílabos añaden *-(e)r* y *-(e)st*.

small (pequeño) **— smaller — smallest**
busy (ocupado) **— busier — busiest**

2. Los adjetivos de tres sílabas o más y algunos adjetivos de dos sílabas (los que terminan en *-ful* o *-less*, por ejemplo) no sufren inflexión y forman los comparativos y superlativos con las palabras *more* y *most*.

expensive (caro) **— more expensive — most expensive**
careful (cuidadoso) **— more careful — most careful**

Nótense los siguientes comparativos irregulares:

good (bueno) — **better** — **best**
bad (malo) — **worse** — **worst**
little (poco) — **less** — **least**
much/many (mucho) — **more** — **most**

Pronombres

	Sujeto	Objeto (dir./indir.)	Posesivo 1	2
Singular				
1ª persona	I	me	my	mine
2ª persona	you	you	your	yours
3ª persona (m)	he	him	his	his
(f)	she	her	her	hers
(n)	it	it	its	—
Plural				
1ª persona	we	us	our	ours
2ª persona	you	you	your	yours
3ª persona	they	they	their	theirs

Nota: en inglés you es tanto singular como plural. No existe la distinción como en español entre «tú» y «usted».

El caso acusativo se usa también para el complemento indirecto y antes de las preposiciones.

Give it to me.	Dámelo.
He came with us.	Él vino con nosotros.

La forma 1 del posesivo se usa antes del nombre, la forma 2 se usa sola.

Where's my key?	¿Dónde está mi llave?
That's not mine.	Ésa no es mía.

Verbos

La misma forma que el infinitivo para todas las personas excepto la 3ª persona del singular, ésta se forma añadiendo -(e)s al infinitivo.

	to love amar	to come venir	to go ir
I	love	come	go
you	love	come	go
he/she	loves	comes	goes
we	love	come	go
they	love	come	go

Los negativos se forman empleando el verbo auxiliar *do/does* + *not* + infinitivo.

We do not (don't) like this hotel.	No nos gusta este hotel.
She does not (doesn't) smoke.	Ella no fuma.

Los interrogativos se forman empleando el verbo auxiliar *do* + pronombre + infinitivo.

Do you like it?	¿Te gusta?
Does he live here?	¿Vive aquí?

Verbos irregulares

En la siguiente lista damos los verbos irregulares ingleses. Los verbos compuestos o los que llevan un prefijo se conjugan como los verbos simples, por ej.: *mistake* y *overdrive* se conjugan como *take* y *drive*.

Infinitivo	*Pret. indefinido*	*Participio pasado*	
arise	arose	arisen	*levantarse*
awake	awoke	awoken	*despertarse*
be	was	been	*ser, estar*
bear	bore	borne	*soportar*
beat	beat	beaten	*batir*
become	became	become	*llegar a ser*
begin	began	begun	*comenzar*
bend	bent	bent	*doblar*
bet	bet	bet	*apostar*
bid	bade/bid	bidden/bid	*pedir*
bind	bound	bound	*atar*
bite	bit	bitten	*morder*
bleed	bled	bled	*sangrar*
blow	blew	blown	*soplar*
break	broke	broken	*romper*
breed	bred	bred	*criar*
bring	brought	brought	*traer*
build	built	built	*construir*
burn	burnt/burned	burnt/burned	*quemar*
burst	burst	burst	*reventar*
buy	bought	bought	*comprar*
can*	could	—	*poder*
cast	cast	cast	*arrojar*
catch	caught	caught	*coger*
choose	chose	chosen	*escoger*
cling	clung	clung	*adherirse*
clothe	clothed/clad	clothed/clad	*vestir*
come	came	come	*venir*
cost	cost	cost	*costar*
creep	crept	crept	*arrastrar*
cut	cut	cut	*cortar*
deal	dealt	dealt	*distribuir*
dig	dug	dug	*cavar*
do (he does)	did	done	*hacer*
draw	drew	drawn	*dibujar*
dream	dreamt/dreamed	dreamt/dreamed	*soñar*
drink	drank	drunk	*beber*
drive	drove	driven	*conducir*
dwell	dwelt	dwelt	*habitar*
eat	ate	eaten	*comer*
fall	fell	fallen	*caer*

* presente de indicativo

feed	fed	fed	*alimentar*
feel	felt	felt	*sentir*
fight	fought	fought	*luchar*
find	found	found	*encontrar*
flee	fled	fled	*huir*
fling	flung	flung	*lanzar*
fly	flew	flown	*volar*
forsake	forsook	forsaken	*renunciar*
freeze	froze	frozen	*helar*
get	got	got	*obtener*
give	gave	given	*dar*
go	went	gone	*ir*
grind	ground	ground	*moler*
grow	grew	grown	*crecer*
hang	hung	hung	*colgar*
have	had	had	*tener*
hear	heard	heard	*oír*
hew	hewed	hewed/hewn	*cortar*
hide	hid	hidden	*esconder*
hit	hit	hit	*golpear*
hold	held	held	*sostener*
hurt	hurt	hurt	*herir*
keep	kept	kept	*guardar*
kneel	knelt	knelt	*arrodillarse*
knit	knitted/knit	knitted/knit	*juntar*
know	knew	known	*saber*
lay	laid	laid	*acostar*
lead	led	led	*dirigir*
lean	leant/leaned	leant/leaned	*apoyarse*
leap	leapt/leaped	leapt/leaped	*saltar*
learn	learnt/learned	learnt/learned	*aprender*
leave	left	left	*marcharse*
lend	lent	lent	*prestar*
let	let	let	*permitir*
lie	lay	lain	*acostarse*
light	lit/lighted	lit/lighted	*encender*
lose	lost	lost	*perder*
make	made	made	*hacer*
may*	might	—	*poder*
mean	meant	meant	*significar*
meet	met	met	*encontrar (personas)*
mow*	mowed	mowed/mown	*segar*
must*	—	—	*tener que*
ought (to)*	—	—	*deber*
pay	paid	paid	*pagar*
put	put	put	*poner*
read	read	read	*leer*
rid	rid	rid	*desembarazar*
ride	rode	ridden	*cabalgar*

* presente de indicativo

ring	rang	rung	*sonar*
rise	rose	risen	*ascender*
run	ran	run	*correr*
saw	sawed	sawn	*aserrar*
say	said	said	*decir*
see	saw	seen	*ver*
seek	sought	sought	*buscar*
sell	sold	sold	*vender*
send	sent	sent	*enviar*
set	set	set	*poner*
sew	sewed	sewed/sewn	*coser*
shake	shook	shaken	*agitar*
shall*	should	—	*deber*
shed	shed	shed	*desprenderse*
shine	shone	shone	*brillar*
shoot	shot	shot	*tirar*
show	showed	shown	*mostrar*
shrink	shrank	shrunk	*encogerse*
shut	shut	shut	*cerrar*
sing	sang	sung	*cantar*
sink	sank	sunk	*hundir*
sit	sat	sat	*sentarse*
sleep	slept	slept	*dormir*
slide	slid	slid	*resbalar*
sling	slung	slung	*lanzar*
slink	slunk	slunk	*escabullirse*
slit	slit	slit	*rajar*
smell	smelled/smelt	smelled/smelt	*oler*
sow	sowed	sown/sowed	*sembrar*
speak	spoke	spoken	*hablar*
speed	sped/speeded	sped/speeded	*apresurarse*
spell	spelt/spelled	spelt/spelled	*deletrear*
spend	spent	spent	*gastar*
spill	spilt/spilled	spilt/spilled	*derramar*
spin	spun	spun	*girar*
spit	spat	spat	*escupir*
split	split	split	*rajar*
spoil	spoilt/spoiled	spoilt/spoiled	*estropear*
spread	spread	spread	*extender*
spring	sprang	sprung	*saltar*
stand	stood	stood	*estar de pie*
steal	stole	stolen	*robar*
stick	stuck	stuck	*hundir*
sting	stung	stung	*picar*
stink	stank/stunk	stunk	*apestar*
strew	strewed	strewed/strewn	*esparcir*
stride	strode	stridden	*andar a pasos largos*
strike	struck	struck/stricken	*golpear*
string	strung	strung	*atar*

* presente de indicativo

strive	strove	striven	*esforzarse*
swear	swore	sworn	*jurar*
sweep	swept	swept	*barrer*
swell	swelled	swollen	*hinchar*
swim	swam	swum	*nadar*
swing	swung	swung	*balancearse*
take	took	taken	*tomar*
teach	taught	taught	*enseñar*
tear	tore	torn	*desgarrar*
tell	told	told	*decir*
think	thought	thought	*pensar*
throw	threw	thrown	*arrojar*
thrust	thrust	thrust	*impeler*
tread	trod	trodden	*pisotear*
wake	woke/waked	woken/waked	*despertar*
wear	wore	worn	*llevar puesto*
weave	wove	woven	*tejer*
weep	wept	wept	*llorar*
will*	would	—	*querer*
win	won	won	*ganar*
wind	wound	wound	*enrollar*
wring	wrung	wrung	*torcer*
write	wrote	written	*escribir*

---

* presente de indicativo

Abreviaturas inglesas

AA	*Automobile Association*	Asociación Automovilística
AAA	*American Automobile Association*	Asociación Automovilística de los Estados Unidos
ABC	*American Broadcasting Company*	Sociedad Privada de Radiodifusión y Televisión (EE.UU.)
A.D.	*anno Domini*	año de Cristo
Am.	*America; American*	América; americano
a.m.	*ante meridiem (before noon)*	de la mañana (de 00.00 a 12.00 h.)
Amtrak	*American railroad corporation*	Sociedad Privada de Compañías de Ferrocarriles Americanos
AT & T	*American Telephone and Telegraph Company*	Compañía Americana de Teléfonos y Telégrafos
Ave.	*avenue*	avenida
BBC	*British Broadcasting Corporation*	Sociedad Británica de Radiodifusión y Televisión
B.C.	*before Christ*	antes de Cristo
bldg.	*building*	edificio
Blvd.	*boulevard*	bulevar
B.R.	*British Rail*	Ferrocarriles Británicos
Brit.	*Britain; British*	Gran Bretaña; británico
Bros.	*brothers*	hermanos
¢	*cent*	1/100 de dólar
Can.	*Canada; Canadian*	Canadá; canadiense
CBS	*Columbia Broadcasting System*	Sociedad Privada de Radiodifusión y Televisión (EE.UU.)
CID	*Criminal Investigation Department*	Oficina de Investigación Criminal
CNR	*Canadian National Railway*	Ferrocarriles Canadienses
c/o	*(in) care of*	al cuidado de
Co.	*company*	compañía
Corp.	*corporation*	compañía
CPR	*Canadian Pacific Railways*	Compañía Privada de Ferrocarriles Canadienses
D.C.	*District of Columbia*	Distrito de Columbia (Washington, D.C.)
DDS	*Doctor of Dental Science*	Dentista

dept.	*department*	departamento, división administrativa
EEC	*European Economic Community*	Comunidad Económica Europea
e.g.	*for instance*	por ejemplo, verbigracia
Eng.	*England ; English*	Inglaterra ; inglés
excl.	*excluding ; exclusive*	no incluido
ft.	*foot/feet*	pie/pies (medida: 30,5 cm.)
GB	*Great Britain*	Gran Bretaña
H.E.	*His/Her Excellency ; His Eminence*	Su Excelencia ; Su Eminencia
H.H.	*His Holiness*	Su Santidad
H.M.	*His/Her Majesty*	Su Majestad
H.M.S.	*Her Majesty's ship*	navío de guerra británico
hp	*horsepower*	caballos de vapor
Hwy	*highway*	carretera principal
i.e.	*that is to say*	a saber, es decir
in.	*inch*	pulgada (medida: 2,54 cm.)
Inc.	*incorporated*	Sociedad Anónima
incl.	*including, inclusive*	incluido
£	*pound sterling*	libra esterlina
L.A.	*Los Angeles*	Los Angeles
Ltd.	*limited*	Sociedad Anónima
M.D.	*Doctor of Medicine*	médico
M.P.	*Member of Parliament*	Miembro del Parlamento
mph	*miles per hour*	millas por hora
Mr.	*Mister*	Señor
Mrs.	*Missis*	Señora
Ms.	*Missis/Miss*	Señora/Señorita
nat.	*national*	nacional
NBC	*National Broadcasting Company*	Sociedad Privada de Radiodifusión y Televisión (EE.UU.)
No.	*number*	número
N.Y.C.	*New York City*	Ciudad de Nueva York
O.B.E.	*Officer (of the Order) of the British Empire*	Caballero de la Orden del Imperio Británico
p.	*page ; penny/pence*	página ; 1/100 de libra
p.a.	*per annum*	por año
Ph.D.	*Doctor of Philosophy*	Doctor en Filosofía
p.m.	*post meridiem (after noon)*	de la tarde/noche (de 12.00 a 24.00 h.)
PO	*Post Office*	Oficina de Correos
POO	*post office order*	giro postal

pop.	*population*	población
P.T.O.	*please turn over*	vuelva la página, por favor
RAC	*Royal Automobile Club*	Real Club Autómovil (Gran Bretaña)
RCMP	*Royal Canadian Mounted Police*	Policía Montada de Canadá
Rd.	*road*	carretera
ref.	*reference*	referencia
Rev.	*reverend*	Reverendo (pastor de la Iglesia Anglicana)
RFD	*rural free delivery*	distribución del correo en el campo
RR	*railroad*	ferrocarril
RSVP	*please reply*	se ruega contestación
$	*dollar*	dólar
Soc.	*society*	sociedad
St.	*saint ; street*	santo(a); calle
STD	*Subscriber Trunk Dialling*	teléfono automático
UN	*United Nations*	Organización de las Naciones Unidas
UPS	*United Parcel Service*	Compañía Privada de Expedición de Paquetes (EE.UU.)
US	*United States*	Estados Unidos de América
USS	*United States Ship*	navío de guerra (EE.UU.)
VAT	*value added tax*	tasa al valor añadido
VIP	*very important person*	persona importante que beneficia de ventajas particulares
Xmas	*Christmas*	Navidad
yd.	*yard*	yarda (medida : 91,44 cm.)
YMCA	*Young Men's Christian Association*	Asociación Cristiana de Muchachos
YWCA	*Young Women's Christian Association*	Asociación Cristiana de Muchachas
ZIP	*ZIP code*	número de distrito postal

Numerales

Cardinales		Ordinales	
0	zero	1st	first
1	one	2nd	second
2	two	3rd	third
3	three	4th	fourth
4	four	5th	fifth
5	five	6th	sixth
6	six	7th	seventh
7	seven	8th	eighth
8	eight	9th	ninth
9	nine	10th	tenth
10	ten	11th	eleventh
11	eleven	12th	twelfth
12	twelve	13th	thirteenth
13	thirteen	14th	fourteenth
14	fourteen	15th	fifteenth
15	fifteen	16th	sixteenth
16	sixteen	17th	seventeenth
17	seventeen	18th	eighteenth
18	eighteen	19th	nineteenth
19	nineteen	20th	twentieth
20	twenty	21st	twenty-first
21	twenty-one	22nd	twenty-second
22	twenty-two	23rd	twenty-third
23	twenty-three	24th	twenty-fourth
24	twenty-four	25th	twenty-fifth
25	twenty-five	26th	twenty-sixth
30	thirty	27th	twenty-seventh
40	forty	28th	twenty-eighth
50	fifty	29th	twenty-ninth
60	sixty	30th	thirtieth
70	seventy	40th	fortieth
80	eighty	50th	fiftieth
90	ninety	60th	sixtieth
100	a/one hundred	70th	seventieth
230	two hundred and thirty	80th	eightieth
		90th	ninetieth
1,000	a/one thousand	100th	hundredth
10,000	ten thousand	230th	two hundred and thirtieth
100,000	a/one hundred thousand		
1,000,000	a/one million	1,000th	thousandth

La hora

Los británicos y los americanos utilizan el sistema de 12 horas. La abreviatura *a.m. (ante meridiem)* designa las horas anteriores al mediodía, *p.m. (post meridiem)* las de la tarde o de la noche. Sin embargo, en Gran Bretaña existe la tendencia, cada vez más acentuada, a indicar los horarios como en el continente.

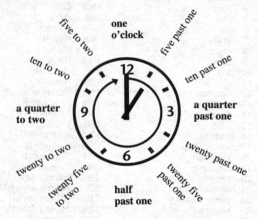

I'll come at seven a.m.   Vendré a las 7 de la mañana.
I'll come at two p.m.   Vendré a las 2 de la tarde.
I'll come at eight p.m.   Vendré a las 8 de la noche.

Los días de la semana

Sunday	domingo	*Thursday*	jueves
Monday	lunes	*Friday*	viernes
Tuesday	martes	*Saturday*	sábado
Wednesday	miércoles		